Agent Technology

Theory and Application

T0135521

Band 7

Agent Technology

Theory and Application

Band 7

Daniel Moldt (Ed.)

Nicolas Denz

Process-Oriented Analysis and Validation of Multi-Agent-Based Simulations

Logos Verlag Berlin

λογος

Agent Technology. Theory and Application

Daniel Moldt (Ed.)

Universität Hamburg
Fachbereich für Informatik
Vogt-Kölln-Str. 30
D-22527 Hamburg

moldt@informatik.uni-hamburg.de

Bildquelle: Modifiziert nach L. Cabac, N. Knaak, D. Moldt, and H. Rlke: Analysis of Multi-Agent Interactions with Process Mining Techniques, S. 17. In: Proceedings of the 4th German Conference on Multiagent System Technology (MATES 2006 in Erfurt), S. 12-23, Springer, September 2006.

Bibliografische Information der Deutschen Nationalbibliothek

Die Deutsche Nationalbibliothek verzeichnet diese Publikation in der Deutschen Nationalbibliografie; detaillierte bibliografische Daten sind im Internet über http://dnb.d-nb.de abrufbar.

ISBN 978-3-8325-3874-3
ISSN 1614-676X

Logos Verlag Berlin GmbH
Comeniushof, Gubener Str. 47,
10243 Berlin

Tel.:   +49 (0)30 / 42 85 10 90
Fax: +49 (0)30 / 42 85 10 92
http://www.logos-verlag.de

Process-Oriented Analysis and Validation of Multi-Agent-Based Simulations

Concepts and Case Studies

Dissertation

zur Erlangung des akademischen Grades
Dr. rer. nat.

an der
Fakultät für Mathematik,
Informatik und Naturwissenschaften
der Universität Hamburg

eingereicht beim
Fach-Promotionsausschuss Informatik
von

Nicolas Denz

aus Hamburg

Einreichung: 03.12.2012
Disputation: 11.06.2013

Gutachter

Prof. Dr.-Ing. Bernd Page (Erstgutachter)
Modellbildung und Simulation
Fachbereich Informatik
MIN-Fakultät
Universität Hamburg (Deutschland)

Dr. Daniel Moldt
Theoretische Grundlagen der Informatik
Fachbereich Informatik
MIN-Fakultät
Universität Hamburg (Deutschland)

Abstract

In multi-agent-based simulation (MABS) the behavior of individual actors is modelled in large detail. The analysis and validation of such models is rated as difficult in the literature and requires support by innovative methods, techniques, and tools. Problems include the complexity of the models, the amount and often qualitative representation of the simulation results, and the typical dichotomy between microscopic modeling and macroscopic observation perspectives.

In recent years, the application of data mining techniques has been increasingly propagated in this context. Data mining might, to some degree, bear the potential to integrate aspects of automated, formal validation on the one hand and explorative, qualitative analysis on the other hand. A promising approach is found in the field of process mining. Due to its rooting in business process analysis, process mining shares several process- and organization-oriented analysis perspectives and use cases with agent-based modeling.

On the basis of detailed literature research and practical experiences from case studies, this thesis proposes a conceptual framework for the systematic application of process mining to the analysis and validation of MABS. As a foundation, agent-oriented analysis perspectives and simulation-specific use cases are identified and embellished with methods, techniques, and further results from the literature.

Additionally, a partial formalization of the identified analysis perspectives is sketched by utilizing the concept of process dimensions by Rembert and Ellis as well as the MAS architecture MULAN by Rölke. With a view to future tool support the use cases are broadly related to concepts of scientific workflow and data flow modeling. Furthermore, simulation-specific requirements and limitations for the application of process mining techniques are identified as guidelines.

Beyond the conceptual work, process mining is practically applied in two case studies related to different modeling and simulation approaches. The first case study integrates process mining into the model-driven approach of Petri net-based agent-oriented software engineering (PAOSE). On the one hand, process mining techniques are practically applied to the analysis of agent interactions. On the other hand, more general implications of combining process mining with reference net-based agent modeling are sketched.

The second case study starts from a more code-centric MABS for the quantitative analysis of different logistic strategies for city courier services. In this context, the practical utility and applicability of different process mining techniques within a large simulation study is evaluated. Focus is put on exploratory validation and the reconstruction of modularized agent behavior.

Kurzfassung

In der agentenbasierten Simulation wird das Verhalten individueller Akteure detailliert im Modell abgebildet. Die Analyse und Validierung dieser Modelle gilt in der Literatur als schwierig und bedarf der Unterstützung durch innovative Methoden, Techniken und Werkzeuge. Probleme liegen in der Komplexität der Modelle, im Umfang und der oft qualitativen Darstellungsform der Ergebnisse sowie in der typischen Dichotomie zwischen mikroskopischer Modellierungs- und makroskopischer Beobachtungssicht begründet.

In den letzten Jahren wurde in diesem Zusammenhang zunehmend der Einsatz von Techniken aus dem Data Mining propagiert. Diese bergen in gewisser Weise das Potenzial, Aspekte der automatisierten, formalen Validierung mit denen der explorativen, qualitativen Analyse zu vereinen. Einen vielversprechenden Ansatz bietet das sogenannte Process Mining, welches aufgrund seiner Nähe zur Geschäftsprozessmodellierung mit der agentenbasierten Modellierung vergleichbare prozess- und organisationsorientierte Modellsichten (Perspektiven) und Anwendungsfälle aufweist.

Ziel der vorliegenden Arbeit ist es, auf Basis umfangreicher Literaturrecherche und in Fallstudien gesammelter Erfahrungen ein konzeptionelles Rahmenwerk für den systematischen Einsatz von Process Mining zur Analyse und Validierung agentenbasierter Simulationsmodelle vorzuschlagen. Als Grundlage werden agentenspezifische Analyseperspektiven und simulationsspezifische Anwendungsfälle identifiziert und durch Methoden, Techniken und weitere Ergebnisse aus der Literatur ausgestaltet.

Darüber hinaus wird ansatzweise eine Teilformalisierung der Analyseperspektiven unter Verwendung des Prozessdimensionen-Konzepts nach Rembert und Ellis sowie der auf Referenznetzen basierenden Architektur MULAN nach Rölke angestrebt. Die Anwendungsfälle werden mit Blick auf eine mögliche Werkzeugunterstützung mit Konzepten der wissenschaftlichen Workflow- und Datenflussmodellierung in Beziehung gesetzt und durch die Identifikation simulationsspezifischer Anwendungsrichtlinien für das Process Mining ergänzt.

Neben der konzeptionellen Arbeit wird der Einsatz von Process Mining praktisch in unterschiedlichen Modellierungs- und Simulationsansätzen erprobt. Die erste Fallstudie integriert Process Mining konzeptionell und technisch in den modellgetriebenen Ansatz der Petrinetz-basierten agentenorientierten Softwareentwicklung (PAOSE). Dabei wird einerseits der praktische Einsatz von Process Mining-Techniken zur Interaktionsanalyse von Agenten beschrieben. Andererseits zeigt die Studie generelle Implikationen der Kombination von Process Mining und Referenznetz-basierter Agentenmodellierung auf.

Ausgangspunkt der zweiten Fallstudie ist eine eher Code-zentrierte agentenbasierte Simulation zur quantitativen Analyse verschiedener Logistikstrategien für Stadtkurierdienste. Im Rahmen dieser Fallstudie werden Process Mining-Techniken im Hinblick auf Anwendbarkeit und Nutzen für eine große Simulationsstudie untersucht. Dabei steht die explorative Validierung und die Rekonstruktion modularisierten Agentenverhaltens im Vordergrund.

Acknowledgement

I would like to thank my supervisors Prof. Dr.-Ing. Bernd Page and Dr. Daniel Moldt for their support, patience, and inspiration during the long years of work on this thesis. I appreciate the close cooperation with a number of colleagues and (former) students including Dr. Ralf Bachmann, Dr. Lawrence Cabac, Rainer Czogalla, Nils Erik Flick, Dr. Björn Gehlsen, Johannes Haan, Dr. Frank Heitmann, Sven Kruse, Ruth Meyer, Florian Plähn, Thomas Sandu, and Felix Simmendinger, who all made valuable contributions to the presented work.

Further thanks go to my former colleagues at the University of Hamburg's Department of Informatics including (but not limited to) Dr. Marcel Christ, Prof. Dr. Andreas Fleischer, Dr. Johannes Göbel, Dr. Philip Joschko, Arne Koors, Dr. Matthias Mayer, Prof. Dr.-Ing. Matthias Riebisch, Prof. Dr. Volker Wohlgemuth, and Dr. Claudia Wyrwoll. I would also like to thank my co-workers at ifu Hamburg GmbH for their patience with my 'second job' and especially Dr. Dorli Harms for proofreading parts of this thesis.

Finally I want to thank my family for their love, support, patience, and belief in me. You know who you are. Love to Kim and Simon, you are my soulmates.

Contents

1. Introduction

Multi-agent systems (MAS) are a promising theoretical concept to approach practical challenges related to the flexibility, adaptivity, and distribution of computer systems. The agent metaphor combines an object-oriented encapsulation of program state and control flow with ideas on the "mechanics of [...] decision making" (Davis et al., 1989) rooted in artificial intelligence, sociology, and economics.[1] One common example of MAS are teams of real or simulated robots competing in the robot soccer league *Robo Cup*[2] (see e.g. Nair et al., 2004).

Accordingly, agent-based abstractions are used in "several subfields of computer science; e.g. software engineering, distributed systems, and robotics." (Page and Kreutzer, 2005, pp. 339). Independent from the application context, a major problem is posed by the need to analyze and understand the behavior of agent-based systems, and in particular to assess their validity. This term, which will be defined precisely later, means in short that a system fulfills its intended functions in an appropriate way.

An agent-based simulation model should, for instance, represent the microscopic agent-level as well as the macroscopic system-level of the corresponding original system in detail to allow for reliable conclusions about reality. The increasing application of agent technology in domains with high safety or real-time requirements (e.g. manufacturing control) calls for particularly powerful validation techniques. The call for appropriate methods and tools to support the analysis and validation of agent-based systems has been uttered in early publications on agent-based software engineering already (e.g. Gasser and Huhns, 1989) and apparently not been answered sufficiently (see e.g. Guessoum et al., 2004, pp. 440). Therefore, the aim of this thesis is to shed light on innovative techniques to validate agent-based models.

1.1. Motivation

For a number of reasons, the analysis and validation of MAS poses severe problems that are inherent to the approach. "The distributed system state and high sensitivity of ABS [agent-based simulations] often results in an unmanageable and unpredictable global behaviour." (Knaak, 2007, p. 29, see also Klügl, 2008, Sec. 2.2). Minor deviations in the system's initial conditions might give rise to strong deviations in behavioral trajectories (Rand et al., 2003, p. 2)[3]. "Due to the microscopic modelling perspective, global [system] properties are not influenced directly" (Knaak, 2007, pp. 29-30), but only by specifying the behavior of individual agents. Since relations between microscopic causes and macroscopic effects are generally hard to determine in distributed

---

[1] A paragraph with similar content also forms the introduction to our pre-publication (Cabac et al., 2006c).

[2] http://robocup.org, last visit 2012-11-17

[3] page numbers relate to the version of the article downloadable at http://masi.cscs.lsa.umich.edu/sluce/publications/sluce-abs.pdf (last visit 2012-10-06)

systems, this situation often complicates tasks like calibration and optimization (Klügl, 2000, p. 205).

Certain uses of the agent metaphor even prohibit an a-priori specification of the system's behavior as in traditional software engineering: Innovative fields such as social simulation, swarm intelligence (Kennedy, 2001) or the engineering of self-organizing systems (Potgieter, 2004) explicitly strive to investigate or benefit from self-organizing or *emergent* effects observed in certain MAS (David et al., 2002, p. 91). For the analysis and validation of MAS several approaches reaching from formal to simulation-based techniques have been proposed.

Formal verification is based on representations using formalisms such as Petri nets or modal logic. Due to their conciseness, formal methods are increasingly applied in agent-oriented software-engineering. However, as noted in (Cabac et al., 2006b, Sec. 1) only "simple and often practically irrelevant classes of MAS (Edmonds and Bryson, 2004)" can be analyzed with formal methods alone.

The simulation-based approach relies on the empirical observation of operational MAS and an a-posteriori analysis of the observed behavior. The empirical analysis of MAS and agent behavior is an important means for validation, often outperforming the application of formal methods (see e.g. Cohen, 1995 and Guessoum et al., 2004). According to Uhrmacher (2000, p. 39) "the development of software agents is [...] mainly an experimental process"[4]. However, as cited in (Cabac et al., 2006b, Sec. 1) "the observation of even simple multi-agent systems might produce large and complex amounts of data (Sanchez and Lucas, 2002)", the interpretation of which requires complex, computer-supported analysis techniques.

The literature provides complementary approaches for analyzing and validating MAS based on empirical observations: While confirmatory techniques such as statistical hypothesis tests or model-based trace-analysis (e.g. Howard et al., 2003) allow for the falsification of a-priori specifications or hypotheses, exploratory techniques serve to investigate and better understand previously unknown aspects of MAS behavior (e.g. Botía et al., 2004).

Due to the experimental character of MAS development (Uhrmacher, 2000, p. 39), exploratory analysis techniques seem well-suited to foster analysis and validation tasks. Several MAS development tools support exploratory analysis by means of powerful visualization techniques (e.g. Ndumu and Nwana, 1999). To overcome inherent drawbacks of visualization (e.g. in handling large amounts of high-dimensional data) the additional use of *data mining* (DM) in MAS analysis and validation has increasingly been proposed in the last years (e.g. Remondino and Correndo, 2005).[5]

The notion of data mining will be introduced later in detail. For the moment it is used as an umbrella term for computer supported methods from machine learning and exploratory statistics that automatically generate models from large amounts of data. In MAS analysis, data mining is in particular suited to find implicit interaction patterns and relations between processes at multiple levels of a system. Such patterns can serve as meaningful high-level system descriptions supporting data-intensive analysis tasks such as validation (see also Remondino and Correndo, 2005). This has some tradition in simulation analysis where simulation output is aggregated to more abstract meta models used in result interpretation, validation, and optimization (e.g. Barton and Szczerbicka, 2000).

---

[4]All literal citations from German sources were translated by the author of this thesis.
[5]see also Cabac et al. (2006b, Sec. 1)

"Since *processes* are an important aspect and event logs an important data source in ABS, a class of highly appropriate techniques is found in a DM subfield called *process mining* (PM) (Aalst and Weijters, 2004). These techniques are typically applied in workflow management and serve to reconstruct process models from workflow execution logs.

Similar to ABS, PM research considers multiple *system views* with a focus on concurrent control flow and organisational models. Despite these similarities, relations between both fields have not been considered in the literature often. There are only few explicit entries (e.g. Hiel, 2005) and [...] recent [...] case example[s] ([e.g.] Dongen et al., 2006b)." (Knaak, 2007, p. 30)

However, process mining has been applied in 'MAS-like' domains, such as inter-organizational workflows (e.g. Aalst, 2004), computer-supported cooperative work (Aalst, 2005a), or web services (e.g. Gombotz et al., 2005). Related techniques such as grammar inference have been applied to the analysis of MAS as well (e.g. Mounier et al., 2003).

Summarizing – as will be substantiated later – the 'research landscape' in this field has evolved rapidly within the last years on the one hand (see also Dongen et al., 2006b). On the other hand, the approaches appear heterogeneous and sometimes far from being applicable to real world scenarios in MAS and simulations.

1.2. Objectives and Contributions of the Thesis

Though the spectrum of topics and applications discussed in this thesis is quite broad, the presented work is positioned in the field of multi-agent-based simulation (MABS). More specific, the main objective is to *evaluate and methodologically enhance the applicability of process mining and related techniques to the analysis and validation of MABS.*

This restriction seems sensible for several reasons: Firstly, the motivation for this work originates from the lack of appropriate validation techniques in agent-based simulation that became apparent to the author during a research project on courier service logistics (Bachmann et al., 2004; Deecke et al., 2004; Knaak et al., 2003). Secondly, analyzing and validating simulation output is a restricted problem characterized by good data quality and a need for semi- (instead of fully) automated techniques. Considering the current state of process mining techniques, this problem seems manageable, and developments from this context can be extended in the future towards more complex tasks such as autonomous learning. Thirdly, the presented approach can straightforwardly be transfered to the more general but closely related field of agent-oriented software engineering (AOSE).

1.2.1. Research Questions

To refine the general objective stated above, the following research questions will be discussed in the thesis:

1. *Q1 - State-of-the-art*: In which way have process mining and related techniques already been applied to MABS and similar domains? What aspects of the systems have been analyzed and which analysis tasks (such as validation or calibration) have been supported?

2. *Q2 - Conceptual foundations*: What is an appropriate conceptual foundation for the integration of process mining, simulation, and MAS? What are the general possibilities and limitations of this integration and in what way does it contribute to the respective fields?

3. *Q3 - Techniques for interaction mining*: How can process mining algorithms and related techniques be combined and extended to foster the complex task of analyzing and validating simulated agents' interactions?

4. *Q4 - Tool integration*: How can process mining techniques and tools be embedded into software environments for simulation studies?

5. *Q5 - Practical benefit*: What is the practical value of process mining in model-driven and code-centric simulation approaches?

6. *Q6 - Level-encompassing validation*: How can process mining be combined with advanced techniques from simulation (e.g. simulation-based optimization) in order to support the task of analyzing and validating processes at multiple levels of a (simulated) MAS?[6]

Note that the scope of the research questions *Q2* to *Q4* covers most constituents of an *approach* (i.e. "tools, applications, techniques, and methods", Cabac, 2010, p. 23) according to the definition by Moldt (1996, p. 30, cited in Cabac, 2010, p. 23).

1.2.2. Conceptual Framework

The first question is tackled by means of a literature review, where the objective is to evaluate the current state-of-the-art in analysis and validation of MA(B)S[7]. Due to the broad applicability of the agent metaphor, this review has to take into account several neighboring fields such as distributed systems, software reverse engineering, and social network analysis.

In order to answer the second question, a conceptual framework for the integration of process mining and MABS will be derived from the literature review. The framework includes complementary dimensions of *analysis perspectives* (i.e. what aspects of MAS can be analyzed), *use cases* (i.e. when and how automated analysis techniques can be applied in the different phases of a simulation study), *techniques* (i.e. what mining, representation, and support techniques can be applied, and how they can be combined), as well as *simulation-specific requirements and limitations*.

Despite the large body of case examples, there are only few general attempts to integrate automated analysis techniques into AOSE or MABS (e.g. Arroyo et al., 2010; Köster, 2002; Ndumu and Nwana, 1999; Remondino and Correndo, 2005) that the presented framework combines and extends. The contribution is therefore twofold: On the one hand, it allows to classify the heterogeneous work found in the literature in a coherent way and point out directions for further research. On the other hand, it serves as a guideline for the practical application of process mining techniques during a simulation study.

---

[6]Note that the thesis by Chen (2009), which was published in parallel to the work on the thesis at hand, is solely dedicated to this question. This work will be cited and related to the presented approach in many places in the following (e.g. Sections 5.2.2.4 and 6.2.6).

[7]This notation is used when both multi-agent systems (MAS) and multi-agent-based simulation (MABS) are addressed.

"A novel aspect [of the framework] is the use of the Petri net-based MULAN model (MULti Agent Nets, Rölke, 2004) as a formal foundation" (Knaak, 2007, p. 30) for integrating process mining into MA(B)S. MULAN is a Petri net-based MAS architecture that builds upon the Reference net formalism by Kummer (2002). Petri nets are a common means for result representation in process mining. MULAN provides further structure by distinguishing multiple Petri net-based views of a MAS. Thereby, it might help to formalize the framework's analysis perspectives in order to perform more MAS-specific analyses. Reference nets can also be used to formalize the use cases in the style of scientific workflows.

1.2.3. Techniques, Tools, and Case Studies

After defining the conceptual frame, the scope of the discussion is narrowed down to the application and extension of specific process mining techniques and tools for MABS analysis (and thereby refer to research questions 3, 4, and 5). From the various perspectives discussed before, the focus is put on agent behavior and interactions. Two complementary modeling and simulation approaches developed at the University of Hamburg will be chosen as case examples for an integration of process mining. These will be explained in the following.

1.2.3.1. Process Mining in the PAOSE Approach

The first is the model-driven Petri net-based AOSE (PAOSE, see e.g. Cabac, 2010) approach developed at the University of Hamburg's theoretical foundations group (TGI). In PAOSE, simulation is mainly used to validate the developed applications. Since process mining appears as a promising support technique due to its strong relation to the Petri net formalism, an integration is attempted in cooperation with members of this group (mainly Dr. Lawrence Cabac and Dr. Daniel Moldt).

At the conceptual level, it will be shown that the MULAN model (Rölke, 2004) with its related development process and tools (Cabac, 2010) is an appropriate basis for realizing the analysis and validation tasks described in the framework. This is mainly due to the fact, that a common executable formalism is available to represent the conceptual and computer model, the meta-models extracted from observed data, and the experimentation and analysis processes themselves.

At the technical level, an approach towards the reconstruction of agent interaction protocols from message logs observed during simulation is presented. *Agent interaction mining* is a complex task that requires to combine and extend several existing process mining techniques. While the interaction mining approach is closely related to parallel work from the web service context (e.g. Gaaloul, 2005; Gombotz et al., 2005), it contains some novel aspects indicated in the following.

A processing chain will be presented as an extension of work by Schütt (2003) that allows to reconstruct models of basic interactions between pairs of agents. One central part is a simple algorithm to mine process models with non-unique activity labels from event-based message logs. Schütt (2003) proposes a hybrid algorithm consisting of a subsequent grammar inference and concurrency detection stage. The grammar inference is, however, restricted to cycle-free models and the concurrency detection is only described conceptually.

The grammar inference is therefore extended towards cyclic models by using the well-known *k-RI* algorithm (Angluin, 1982), the concurrency detection is operationalized, and the algorithm is compared to related approaches based on log preprocessing (e.g. Gu et al., 2008) and the theory of regions (e.g. Rubin et al., 2006). Furthermore, a preceding log segmentation and role mining stage is integrated (based on work from, among others, Dustdar and Gombotz, 2006; Greco et al., 2004; Schütt, 2003; Srinivasa and Spiliopoulou, 2000; Vanderfeesten, 2006) that clusters similar courses of interaction in the absence of unique conversation and protocol identifiers.

The basic interaction mining chain is conceptually expanded towards the reconstruction of hierarchical and multicast protocols. Multicast protocols are special hierarchical protocols closely related to the *multiple instantiation* workflow pattern, where a variable number of instances of the same activity (or message) are executed (or sent) in parallel (see e.g. Guabtni and Charoy, 2004).

While several workflow patterns can be detected by process mining algorithms (see e.g. Gaaloul et al., 2004), first (and partly rather preliminary) approaches to reconstruct control flow models containing multiple instantiation constructs have only been presented recently (e.g. Canbaz, 2011; Kikas, 2011; Kumar et al., 2010; Lou et al., 2010b). In this thesis, an algorithm for reconstructing multicast protocols and detecting synchronizations between the participating agents will be sketched and compared to the related approaches.

At the tool level, the plugin-based architecture of the Petri net simulator RENEW (Kummer et al., 2006) and the lightweight component mechanism of *net components* (Cabac, 2002) are employed to model analysis and validation processes (called *mining chains* here) as hierarchical scientific workflows (see e.g. Guan et al., 2006). At a small example it is shown how validation and roundtrip engineering can be supported.

1.2.3.2. Process Mining in a Discrete Event Simulation Study

The second case study is conducted on the basis of a research project on the simulation of sustainable logistics strategies for large city courier services (Deecke et al., 2004). The author of this thesis started to work on this project during his diploma thesis (Knaak, 2002) and developed parts of the employed software framework. As a domain for process mining, the courier service study complements the PAOSE approach in several respects: (1) The software development is mainly code-centric, based on the discrete event simulation framework DESMO-J (Lechler and Page, 1999) and its extension FAMOS for agent-based simulation (Knaak, 2002; Meyer, 2008). (2) The study employs discrete event simulation to perform a quantitative analysis of a target system. (3) The number of agents in the model is relatively high, and large amounts of log data are produced.

The applicability of process mining to this example is investigated in an affiliated bachelor thesis by Haan (2009). Beyond the results gained from this study, the author of this thesis presents a first, strongly simplified implementation of the complex interaction mining procedure mentioned above and discusses ways to further continue the integration of MABS with process mining techniques and tools.

In particular, it is sketched how process mining-based analysis workflows can be integrated into a generic simulation environment (Czogalla et al., 2006) that helps users to perform experiments with (in principle) arbitrary simulators based on the programming language *Java* (e.g. Arnold et al., 2000). The environment is conceptually rooted in experimentation and analysis tools developed earlier at the University of Hamburg's simulation group (MBS) such as *DISMO* (Gehlsen, 2004), *CoSim* (Bachmann, 2003), and *MOBILE* (Hilty et al., 1998). The tool is implemented in the form of plugins for the well-known *Eclipse* platform[8].

A prototypical integration of process mining algorithms implemented in the tool *ProM* (Dongen et al., 2005) is tackled with the aid of the scientific workflow system *KNIME* (Chair for Bioinformatics and Information Mining at Konstanz University, 2007) and might in the future employ RENEW as an alternative, possibly more flexible, workflow engine (Simmendinger, 2007; Simmendinger et al., 2007). Beyond that, it will be discussed how the environment relates to recent similar efforts like the framework *WorMS* (Workflows for Modeling and Simulation) by Rybacki et al. (2011).

1.3. Outline of the Thesis

Due to the relatively broad scope of the thesis, the presentation is grouped into two parts: (1) foundations and state of the art, (2) concepts and case studies. An overview of the structure of the thesis is shown in Figure 1.1.[9] The first part starts with an introduction of concepts from modeling and simulation in Chapter 2. This chapter introduces basic modeling techniques from the domains of discrete event simulation (DES), Petri net theory, and workflow modeling. A particular way of using the UML 2 notation (e.g. Jeckle et al., 2002) for simulation modeling is introduced and related to the DES world views[10] and the reference net formalism. Beyond that, the chapter reviews "the later stages of the modeling process" (Edmonds, 2000, p. 23) including experimentation, analysis, and validation as the main focus of this thesis.

Chapter 3 reviews basic concepts from multi-agent systems and agent-based simulation, covers modeling and implementation techniques from MABS and AOSE, and finally focuses on the problem of analysis and validation (i.e. ultimately *understanding*) of agent-based models. With respect to the techniques used in the thesis, the focus is put on UML 2 and the reference net-based MULAN architecture. Besides providing the reader with the thesis' conceptual foundations, a main objective of the chapter is to motivate the need for advanced analysis and validation techniques.

Chapter 4 completes the foundations by presenting data mining and especially process mining as promising candidate methods. After introducing foundations concerning the validation of agent-based simulations in general, Chapter 5 brings together both fields by presenting an extensive review of related work on MABS analysis and validation with the aid of data mining, process mining, or similar techniques.

The second part of the thesis elaborates on the author's contributions described in Section 1.2. Based on the literature review, Chapter 6 presents the conceptual framework for integrating process mining and MABS. It closes by classifying (small parts of) the previously reviewed

---

[8]`http://www.eclipse.org`, last visit 2012-11-17

[9]It is no surprise that several theses on topics related to modeling use precedence graphs to display dependencies between chapters (e.g. Klügl, 2000, p. 5; Medeiros, 2006, p. 12). This thesis is no exception.

[10]based on pre-publications like Page and Kreutzer (2005, Sec. 4) and Knaak (2006)

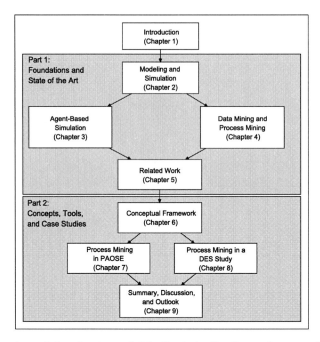

Figure 1.1.: Overview of the chapters of this thesis in the form of a precedence graph. A directed edge in the graph indicates that a chapter largely builds upon the results of a previous chapter.

work along the framework's dimensions in order to present a coherent view on the 'research landscape' and identify promising directions for the development of new techniques.

Chapter 7 reports the first case study in the PAOSE approach with a focus on agent interaction mining techniques as well as architectural integration into MULAN. Chapter 8 reviews the procedure and results of the second case study in the DESMO-J context with a focus on evaluating the practical value of process mining in a large simulation project. Chapter 9 concludes the thesis by deriving implications from the two case studies, critically discussing their results and pointing out directions for further research.

As a final remark it should be emphasized that the work presented in this thesis (like most similar projects) was neither developed 'in isolation', nor written down 'in one go'. Therefore, several parts were developed in cooperation with colleagues, and some of the texts were previously published as part of conference and journal papers as well as a textbook on simulation. Though these pre-publications were partly written together with other authors, this monograph naturally focuses on those parts that the author of this thesis contributed to most.

In particular, parts of the Chapters 2 and 3 are based on Chapters 4 (UML modeling), 8 (model validation) and 11 (multi-agent-based simulation) of the *Java Simulation Handbook* (Page and Kreutzer, 2005), as well as on articles about simulation modeling with UML 2 by (Knaak and Page, 2005, 2006). The practical application of UML 2 to discrete event simulation modeling was investigated together with Thomas Sandu.

As already mentioned, much of the research presented in Chapters 6 and 7 was conducted together with Dr. Daniel Moldt and Dr. Lawrence Cabac from the Department of Informatics' theoretical foundations group (TGI). The monitoring tool presented in Chapter 7 was implemented by Frank Heitmann and Florian Plähn. Intermediate results were pre-published as conference papers and technical reports (Cabac et al., 2006a,b,c, 2008a; Knaak, 2006, 2007).

Several parts of the second case study from Chapter 8 were conducted as part of the bachelor thesis by Johannes Haan (2009) and the study project by Sven Kruse (2005). The simulation system described in the latter Sections of this chapter was developed together with Rainer Czogalla and several (former) students including Felix Simmendinger and Philip Joschko. Intermediate results were pre-published in conference papers by Czogalla et al. (2006), Simmendinger et al. (2007), and the diploma thesis by Simmendinger (2007).

To emphasize this embedding of an individual dissertation project into a larger community (including you as a reader), the first person plural narrative mode[11] ('we') will often be preferred in the following.[12]

---

[11]http://en.wikipedia.org/wiki/First-person_narrative, last visit 2012-11-17
[12]for a similar discussion see Eagleman (2011, p. 266)

Part I.

Foundations and State of the Art

2. Modeling and Simulation

This chapter reviews relevant foundations from system theory and simulation and brings out their connotations in the context of this thesis. After an introduction to fundamental terms, we focus "on the later stages of the modelling process" (Edmonds, 2000, p. 23) including experimentation, output analysis, and validation, as the thesis' main topics. The presentation is largely based on the simulation handbook by Page and Kreutzer (2005, Chs. 1, 2, 4, 5, 7, 8, and 9). Chapters 4 and 8 of that book were co-written by the author of this thesis.

2.1. Basic System Theory

According to Page and Kreutzer (2005, p. 4) a *system* is "a subset of reality which we study to answer a question; i.e. its *boundary* to the environment in which it is embedded will be determined by the question we wish to ask." Important points of this definition are that (a) the term is generic, i.e. anything can be regarded as a system, and that (b) system identification is a constructive act, since systems are always considered in relation to an observer and an observation goal.

Further following Page and Kreutzer (2005, p. 5), "a system must have a number of distinct and clearly identifiable *components* which may themselves be considered as systems at a "lower" level." Systems are decomposed hierarchically to perform a complexity reduction (Kouvastos, 1976, p. 1081). We distinguish between elementary components with basic *properties* (such as position or velocity, see also Page and Kreutzer, 2005, p. 25) and non-elementary sub-systems whose properties emerge from the interplay of their components. The set of all properties observed at a certain instant is called *system state* (Page and Kreutzer, 2005, p. 5).

The system theoretical stance is characterized by a "duality of structure and behaviour" (London, 2004, p. 166). *Structure* refers to the statical aspects of a system, i.e. the network of relations between the existing elements and their roles within this network (see e.g. Wikipedia, 2007). System behavior is described in terms of one or more *processes*, where a process is understood as a chronological sequence of state variable vectors (Page and Kreutzer, 2005, p. 5).

System structure and behavior are closely linked and mutually dependent (Wikipedia, 2007). Whereas the system structure sets up boundary conditions for the processes running within it, the processes can modify the structure, thus giving rise to new boundary conditions for future behavior. Due to such complicated interrelations, system behavior often appears "counter intuitive and hard to predict" (Page and Kreutzer, 2005, p. 5).

2.1.1. Complexity and Emergence

Auyang (1998, p. 13) notes that "there is no precise definition of complexity and degree of complexity in the natural sciences", and continues by identifying two different meanings of the term.

On the one hand, it is applied in an *intuitive* way "to describe self-organized systems that have many components and many characteristic aspects, exhibit many structures in various scales, undergo many processes in various rates, and have the capability to change abruptly and adapt to external environments" (Auyang, 1998, p. 13). In the same manner, Page and Kreutzer (2005, p. 5) state that "system complexity depends on the number of state variables (properties) and the density of their connections."

On the other hand, *formal* approaches from computer science define the term more concisely. A well-known measure is the *computational complexity* of a problem, i.e. the number of steps (*computation time complexity*) and the amount of memory (*computation space complexity*) needed to algorithmically solve the problem in relation to the size of its encoding (see e.g. Auyang, 1998, p. 13 or Gruska, 1997, Ch. 5).

Another formal measure is the *information content complexity*[1] of a character sequence defined as "the length in bits of the smallest program capable of specifying it completely to a computer" (Auyang, 1998, p. 13). This measure assigns the lowest complexity to very regular sequences, and the highest complexity to purely random sequences without any patterns (Auyang, 1998, p. 13). While the former seems plausible, the latter might appear counter-intuitive, since complexity is not commonly understood as a complete lack of structure.

Formal definitions of complexity seem less useful in the context of this thesis due to their limited scope: Computational complexity is a different concept than complexity in system theory. Information content complexity might be interpreted to that effect that a more complex system (program) is able to generate more variable patterns of behavior (character sequences). A purely random sequence contains so many variations that it cannot be described more compactly than by stating the sequence itself (Auyang, 1998, p. 13). In system theory, we are often interested in phenomena with a *medium* information content complexity, i.e. systems that exhibit behavioral variety, but still allow for the recognition of patterns.[2] The possibility to aggregate system behavior to a more compact description is of great importance for the applicability of data mining techniques described below.

A related quality of complex systems is *emergence*. This concept is based on the observation that systems include multiple levels with at least a macroscopic level of the system as a whole and a microscopic level of the basic components. According to Jones (2003, p. 418), "the term is applied to the appearance of novel, coherent objects [at the macroscopic level] that are not predictable from the system's [microscopic] parts."

The notion of emergence is used quite ambiguously, since for some authors, it denotes "an invocation of something mystical" (Jones, 2003, p. 418), while others use it as a "shorthand explanation" for multi-level phenomena within a reductionist world view (Jones, 2003, p. 421). Cariani (1991, p. 771)[3], for instance, subsumes the fact that "complex global forms can arise from local computations" under the notion of *computational emergence*. This includes deterministic phenomena like swarm formation in artificial life simulations or the appearance of identifiable shapes in cellular automata.

In this thesis, we use the term *complexity* in the *intuitive* way for systems that

---

[1]which is also called *Kolmogorov complexity*, see e.g. Gruska (1997, p. 398)

[2]See also the discussion on "pattern-formation" by Gribbin (2005, p. 135), who uses the term "edge of chaos".

[3]cited in Jones (2003, p. 418)

- consist of a large number of components, where each component itself exhibits a certain behavioral variability and flexibility (i.e. complex micro-level processes),

- contain a large number of relations and interactions between the components (including feedback) and possibly a variable structure (i.e. complex macro-level structures and processes),

- can be viewed at multiple levels, where relations between the levels are often obscured due to distributed and sensitive cause-effect dependencies (i.e. complex inter-level relations).

We will avoid using the term *emergence* due to its non-scientific connotations. However, we will regard multi-agent systems that exhibit computational emergence where macroscopic patterns emerge from microscopic interactions through deterministic computations. Data mining will be applied to expose such patterns and the rules that generated them from observed data.

2.1.2. Models

The term *model* describes a simplified image of a system. As a main benefit, a model allows to conduct controlled experiments that might be inconvenient or impossible with the real system (see Niemeyer, 1977, p. 57 cited in Page and Kreutzer, 2005, p. 5).

The complexity of the system under analysis is reduced by considering only the most relevant parts in the model and by putting them in a simplified form (see e.g. Heinrich, 2002, p. 1046). This "*abstraction* and *idealization*" (Page and Kreutzer, 2005, p. 6) needs to preserve structural similarity between the model and the real system (Heinrich, 2002, p. 1046) with regard to a "certain purpose or set of questions [... the model] can answer" (Page and Kreutzer, 2005, p. 5). Given this similarity, the model is considered as *valid* and its analysis allows to draw conclusions on the real system.

The notion of models is also central to statistics and data mining. In this context, Hand et al. (2001, p. 9) define a model (structure) as "a global summary of a data set". According to Han and Kamber (2000, p. 24), one main purpose of data mining is "finding *models* [...] that describe and distinguish data classes or concepts [...] The derived model is based on the analysis of a set of *training data* [...]".

Large data sets are thus algorithmically aggregated to abstract models that describe the data more compactly. This is somehow similar to modeling in simulation with the exception that the abstraction is performed automatically. One important property of models in statistics and machine learning is *generalization*. To be useful for prediction and classification tasks (see Han and Kamber, 2000, p. 24), a model should not only describe the specific training data set that it has been derived from, but a possibly large range of data that the underlying system might be able to generate. We will continue this discussion in Section 4.1.2.

2.2. Computer Simulation

To understand complex systems we analyze abstract models and draw conclusions on the original. The analysis of formal models can be performed either with *analytical* methods that allow to compute a closed-form solution 'in one go', or by using *simulation*, where the model state is advanced step by step in order to emulate the temporal development of the real system (Page and Kreutzer, 2005, p. 10).

Simulation can thus be defined as "the process of describing a real system and using this model for experimentation with the goal of understanding the system's behaviour or to explore alternative strategies for its operation" (Shannon, 1975, cited in Page and Kreutzer, 2005, p. 9). This general definition fits many activities in computer science such as the stepwise execution of a computer program for the purpose of debugging or the token-game in Petri nets (see Section 2.3.2.1).

Though this general meaning is sometimes referred to here, we mostly draw to the more specific definition of Page and Kreutzer (2005, p. 9), who use the term to denote the field of *computer simulation* as well as the execution of a *computer simulation study*. In this context, "the *model building process* is explicitly mentioned", and simulation is characterized as "the modelling of dynamic processes in real systems, based on real data and seeking predictions for a real system's behaviour [. . . where] *models* are represented by (simulation) programs, and simulation experiments ("runs") are performed by a models's execution for a specific data set." (Page and Kreutzer, 2005, p. 9)

This definition emphasizes the embedding of the actual 'simulations' into a scientific or industrial research study, where activities like data acquisition, model validation, experimentation, result analysis, and presentation are of equal importance than the modeling and simulation itself.

2.2.1. Classification of Simulation Models

Typical dimensions for the classification of models in simulation, which may also apply to other fields, are shown in Figure 2.1 (e.g. form of analysis, purpose, etc.). From these dimensions, Page and Kreutzer (2005, pp. 6) emphasize the purpose, the representation medium, and the type of state changes occurring in the model.[4]

2.2.1.1. Purpose of Models

Models are used to better *explain* and understand the represented system, to *predict* its future behavior, to support the *design* of a planned system or to optimize the operation of an existing one (Page and Kreutzer, 2005, p. 7): The purpose of a model strongly influences its properties. Explanatory models should represent the system's structure *and* behavior in an appropriate and interpretable way to allow for an understanding of the observed phenomena. For predictive models it might be sufficient to mimic the system's behavior closely enough for successful predictions, even if the model's behavior is generated by unrealistic or not explicitly understandable structures. We will take up this point in Section 4.1.2.

2.2.1.2. Representation Forms

Models are represented in different forms ranging from *physical* and *verbal* models to *graphical* and *mathematical* models (Page and Kreutzer, 2005, p. 6). One might additionally consider the explicitness and conciseness of model representation (Page and Kreutzer, 2005, p. 6): *Mental*

---

[4]Brade (2003, Sec. 1.2) focuses on the latter two dimensions as well.

models only exist in the modeller's mind while *external* models are represented in some other medium for means of communication. *Formal* models are described in a language with a concise formal semantics which permits their operationalization. In this thesis we further differentiate between *explicit* formal models represented in a modeling language such as UML or Petri nets, and *implicit* formal models 'hidden' in programming language code. While this criterion is somewhat fuzzy, explicit models are deemed more understandable and verifiable than implicit models.

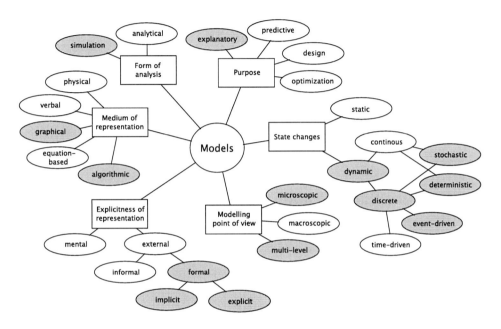

Figure 2.1.: Common dimensions for the classification of models. Compiled with modifications from Brade (2003); Klügl (2001); Lechler and Page (1999); Page and Kreutzer (2005). Model types treated in this thesis are shaded in grey.

2.2.1.3. Types of State Changes

An important criterion to characterize dynamic simulation models is the type of state changes, which might occur continuously or instantaneously at discrete points in time. The next model state can be determined by its predecessor in a deterministic or stochastic fashion (Page, 1991, p. 6). Concerning discrete simulation models we distinguish two kinds of simulation time advance (Page et al., 2000, p. 6): In *time-driven* models, the clock proceeds in equidistant intervals and the model state is permanently re-computed. In *event-driven models*, time advance is triggered by a sequence of events that occur in arbitrary intervals. Since the model state is only updated 'when something has happened', event-driven models often exhibit a lower computational complexity (Page et al., 2000, p. 6).

2.2.1.4. Modeling Point of View

A complementary dimension for simulation model classification is the *modeling point of view*. According to Klügl (2000, p. 42) a *macroscopic model* "represents the whole system as a single object, describes its state by means of variables and relates them to each other with respect to certain parameters", while a *microscopic model* consists of multiple components whose interactions generate the model's overall behavior. A *multi-level model* is composed of "multiple micro models at different levels of aggregation" (Klügl, 2000, p. 44).

While macroscopic models are mostly formulated in terms of differential equations (Klügl, 2000, p. 42), microscopic modeling styles are more diverse, ranging from cellular automata to discrete event as well as individual- and agent-based models.[5] By comparison, microscopic modeling allows for a more detailed and straightforward representation of real systems consisting of multiple components, and is better suited for the explanation of their behavior (Klügl, 2000, p. 72). Problems are the models' high computational complexity and the difficulty to find an appropriate level of detail (Klügl, 2000, pp. 73).[6]

This thesis is, on the one hand, concerned with agent-based simulation models, i.e. microscopic discrete event models whose overall behavior is encoded by an (often implicit) algorithmic description of the components. On the other hand, explicit formal and graphical models at different levels are reconstructed from observations of the models' behavior to aid analysis and validation.

2.2.2. World Views of Discrete Event Simulation

The traditional world views in discrete event simulation (DES) are event-, process-, activity-, and transaction-orientation (see e.g. Page and Kreutzer, 2005, Ch. 5). These are characterized by different, but closely akin concepts for relating model state and simulation time (Page and Kreutzer, 2005, pp. 24) depicted in Figure 2.2.

The basic unit in discrete modeling is the *event*. Events describe instantaneous system state changes at discrete but arbitrary points in (simulation) time. At the next level of aggregation, we consider time-consuming *activities*, where each activity consists of a start and end event. Multiple related activities can be aggregated to a *process* describing an entity's life-cycle.

Each concept builds the foundation for one or more modeling styles. In *event-orientation* (see e.g. Page and Kreutzer, 2005, Ch. 5.2.2), we identify relevant entities and events of the system. In the model, each event is represented by an event class with an event routine that algorithmically describes the caused state changes. This modeling style often (but not necessarily) takes in a top-down view in that each event describes "the set of *all* transformations of *all* relevant entities at specified points in time" (Page and Kreutzer, 2005, p. 108).

In contrast, the *process-oriented* world view takes in a bottom-up view where all state changes concerning an entity are aggregated into a single algorithmic description, i.e. the entities *lifecycle* executed as a *simulation process* (Page and Kreutzer, 2005, p. 98). During simulation, a

---

[5]For an overview see e.g. Klügl (2000, Ch. 3.2)

[6]In fact, this author discusses agent-based versus macroscopic models, but many arguments apply to microscopic models in general.

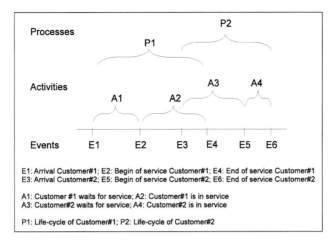

Figure 2.2.: Relations between events, activities, and processes with a possible interpretation in a DES model (adopted with modifications from Page, 1991, p. 27).

process undergoes alternating phases of computational activity and passiveness. Active phases correspond to events where the process instantaneously modifies its own or other entities' states. Simulation time only passes during the passive phases. These either represent conceptually active states, where the process executes an activity after which it re-activates itself, or passive states, where the process waits for re-activation by another process (Page and Kreutzer, 2005, p. 100). Process interaction is often limited to untyped activation signals, but might also include typed signals to represent interrupt conditions (Page and Kreutzer, 2005, p. 105).

Activity-oriented models (Page and Kreutzer, 2005, pp. 131) are described in terms of time consuming activities together with preconditions for their invocation (see the level 'activities' in Figure 2.2). Their execution somehow resembles rule-based systems: A scheduler chooses the next activity whose preconditions hold and executes it by advancing the simulation clock to its end time and performing the assigned state changes. *Transaction-oriented* models consist of a net of permanent resources (blocks) that transient entities (transactions) flow through (Page and Kreutzer, 2005, p. 129). Page and Kreutzer (2005, p. 129 and p. 132) show how both modeling styles can be mapped to process-oriented models.

2.3. Modeling Techniques

Executable simulation models are often stated implicitly in the form of program code while conceptual models are specified using explicit graphical notations. To narrow this semantic gap (see e.g. Klügl, 2000, p. 76) several formal and semi-formal notations are applied. In the following, we introduce the Unified Modeling Language (UML) and reference nets as notations used to explicitly represent simulation models in this thesis.

2.3.1. UML 2

As noted in (Knaak and Page, 2006, p. 33), UML is quite commonly used as a simulation modeling language today. Several applications (see e.g. De Wet and Kritzinger, 2004) and extensions (see e.g. Oechslein et al., 2001) are reported in the literature (Knaak and Page, 2006, p. 33). Page and Kreutzer (2005, Ch. 4) as well as Knaak and Page (2006) present our way of applying and extending UML 2 for discrete event simulation that is briefly reviewed below.

2.3.1.1. The Unified Modeling Language

In (Page and Kreutzer, 2005, p. 60)[7] we have introduced the Unified Modeling Language by determining

> "what UML is and – of equal importance – what it is not. According to the *UML reference manual*, it is "a general-purpose visual modeling language that is used to specify, visualise, construct, and document the artifacts of a software system". As Jeckle et al. (2002, p. 10) point out, UML is *not* "complete, not a programming language, not a formal language, not specialized to an application area and [...] first of all not a method or software process"."

Further following the shorter presentation in (Knaak and Page, 2006, pp. 34-35):

> "UML 2.0 contains a total of 13 diagram types to visualise different aspects of object-oriented modelling (Jeckle et al., 2002, p. 15). According to Jeckle et al. (2002, p. 16) these diagrams can be broadly divided into three classes [mirroring the dualism of structure and behavior mentioned in Section 2.1]:
>
> - *Structural diagrams* model the static structure of a system. Among them are *class diagrams, object diagrams, package diagrams, component diagrams, composition structure diagrams* and *deployment diagrams.*
>
> - *Behaviour diagrams* serve to display the [...] behaviour of objects or components at different levels of detail. This [...] includes *use case diagrams, activity diagrams, statechart diagrams* and several *interaction diagram* types.
>
> - *Interaction diagrams* are special behaviour diagrams that focus on the interactions going on between [...] objects in a system. [... They] can be divided into *sequence diagrams* and *timing diagrams* that emphasise the temporal order of interaction events on the one hand and *communication diagrams* that highlight the general structure of the cooperation between partners in an interaction on the other hand (Jeckle et al., 2002, p. 391). [...] *interaction overview* [...] diagrams represent a mixture between activity diagrams and interaction diagrams showing the causal and temporal interplay among different interaction scenarios (Jeckle et al., 2002, p. 419).

> [...] the concepts and notations of the UML are [...] defined in [a so-called *meta*] model that is [itself] expressed in terms of the UML (Born et al., 2004, p. 12). This object-oriented language definition makes extensions of the UML quite easy. [...] Such extensions are either stated as extensions of the metamodel itself, or by using a lightweight extension mechanism called *stereotyping* (Born et al., 2004, p. 245). According to Jeckle et al. (2002, p. 95) a

---

[7]and similarly in (Knaak and Page, 2006)

stereotype is a "a class in the metamodel that is able to further specify other classes [...] by extension".

[... As an example, we might] represent entity types in DES models [by extending] the meta class `Class` [...] with a stereotype `<entity>`. [...] Now entity types in class diagrams are marked by attaching the term `<entity>` in angle brackets to the respective model elements."

2.3.1.2. UML in Simulation

A main feature that makes UML suitable "for the DES domain [... is] the event-based communication model underlying all behaviour diagrams (see Jeckle et al., 2002, pp. 172)" (Knaak and Page, 2006, p. 36). Similar to DES, an event in UML is a "relevant occurrence" such as sending a message or invoking an operation (Jeckle et al., 2002, p. 173). Different from DES, a UML event has a lifecycle consisting of creation, distribution and consumption, and its occurrence in a real system might consume time (Jeckle et al., 2002, p. 173). We can, however, abstract from these aspects and regard UML events in DES models as instantaneous.

Simulation practitioners "benefit from UML diagrams as a common and simulation-software independent basis for documenting, visualizing and understanding the model structure (Richter and März, 2000, p. 2). The different UML diagrams provide multiple views focusing on [... complementary] *aspects* of the model." (Knaak and Page, 2006, p. 36)

In an industrial or non-computer-science context, the diagrams might be understood more easily than more abstract formal languages like Petri nets (see Section 2.3.2.1). Nevertheless, "the quite concise semi-formal semantics of UML 2 behaviour diagrams [...] provide support for the task of model validation and verification" as well as code generation (Knaak and Page, 2006, p. 36). Current approaches towards *model driven software development* apply transformation rules that map UML models to executable code.[8]

In the following, we briefly introduce UML activity and interaction diagrams for modeling the dynamics of discrete simulations. The presentation is based on Page and Kreutzer (2005, Ch. 4) and Knaak and Page (2006). Basic concepts of object orientation (such as inheritance) and their representation in class, object and package diagrams are taken for granted (for an overview see e.g. Jeckle et al., 2002, Chs. 3, 4, 5).

2.3.1.3. Activity Diagrams

In (Page and Kreutzer, 2005, pp. 77), we introduced activity diagrams with a focus on DES:

"According to Jeckle et al. (2002, p. 199) *activity diagrams* are [an appropriate] notation [...] for modelling [...] operations, use cases, and business processes. [... Consequently, they] are particularly well suited for modelling lifecycles of simulation processes in [... DES]. Since they provide features such as concurrency, object flow[,] and message passing they are convenient for showing the synchronization of two or more processes. [...] In UML 2.0, the statechart-like event-handling semantics of [UML 1.x ...] has been replaced by a Petri net-like token semantics [see also Section 2.3.2.1]."

---

[8]On the application of model driven software development in the simulation context see Sandu (2007).

In (Knaak and Page, 2005, p. 404) we observed that the synchronization operations of the process-oriented world view (see Section 2.2.2)

"map quite obviously to *send- and receive-signal actions* [...] (Jeckle et al., 2002, p. 214). [...] Generally any time consumption is modelled using receive-signal actions, whereas normal action nodes correspond to active process phases without passing of simulation time.

Figure 2.3 shows [an example of] two process classes [...] that synchronize via sending and reception of activation signals."

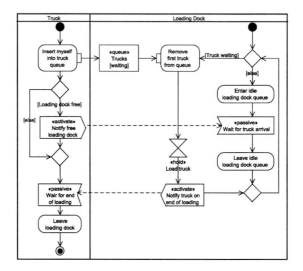

Figure 2.3.: "Synchronisation of [... simulation processes in an imaginary] "Gravel Pit" model via sending and reception of signals." Figure and caption adopted from Knaak and Page (2006, p. 38).

The separation by *activity regions* (Jeckle et al., 2002, pp. 245) makes it possible to display multiple interacting processes in a single diagram. As carried out in (Knaak and Page, 2006, p. 38) we denote process activations

"by a send-signal action (Jeckle et al., 2002, p. 214) with the stereotype «activate». [...] The passive state is indicated by a receive-signal action (Jeckle et al., 2002, p. 214) with the stereotype «passive». [...]

[In compliance with ...] Jeckle et al. (2002, p. 215) [... the hold operation is] modelled using a *time signal reception node* depicted by an hour glass symbol [...] with the additional stereotype «hold» [... that] delays incoming tokens for a specified duration."

Further following Knaak and Page (2006, p. 39), data flow is displayed with the aid of

"*object nodes* depicted by rectangles (Jeckle et al., 2002, pp. 218). When the outgoing edge of an action node is connected to an object node, execution of the action produces a so called *data token* that contains the result object of the execution. The data token is stored in the object node and might serve as input to another action [... Object nodes can be] used as synchronisation constructs in [... process- and transaction-oriented] models [see Figure 2.3]. We use the stereotype **‹queue›** to indicate that an object node has a queue semantic."

A mapping of UML activity diagrams to further DES-specific constructs (e.g. interrupts) and modeling styles (e.g. transaction orientation) is presented by Knaak and Page (2006) and Page and Kreutzer (2005, Ch. 4 and 5).

2.3.1.4. Interaction Diagrams

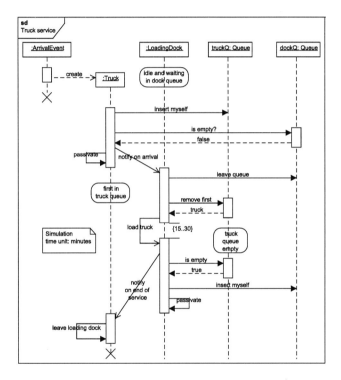

Figure 2.4.: An example of using basic sequence diagrams in DES (adopted from Page and Kreutzer, 2005, p. 89)

In (Page and Kreutzer, 2005, pp. 87-91) we described UML interaction diagrams as follows:

"[While] the main purpose of [... activity] diagrams is the description of individual [...] behaviour [...] *interaction diagrams* are often better suited to model the interplay between multiple entities.

[...] basic [...] *sequence diagrams* display timely ordered message sequences describing an interaction scenario [...] Figure 2.4 shows an [...] example [...that] can be regarded as a possible [refined] execution sequence of the activity diagrams shown in Figure 2.3.

[...] the different [...] roles [...] taking part in an interaction are plotted along the horizontal axis, while the vertical axis represents time (Jeckle et al., 2002, p. 327). The main diagram elements are the *lifelines* of the interaction partners and what *messages* pass between them.

[...] UML distinguishes several communication modes, each of which is symbolized by a different arrow-head (Jeckle et al., 2002, p. 346). A filled black arrowhead indicates a *synchronous* message, where the sender waits [...] until the message has been processed by the receiver. The receiver answers by sending a *response message*, represented by a dashed arrow with filled arrowhead. [...]

Asynchronous messages are symbolized by an open arrowhead. [... Here] the sender continues its lifecycle *without* waiting for the message to be processed by the receiver. [We model method calls as synchronous messages and process interactions including passivation as asynchronous messages.]

[...] Conditions ensuring the correctness of a scenario [...] can be expressed by [...] *state invariants* (Jeckle et al., 2002, p. 356) [...] symbolized by using rounded rectangles [...]

[...] Time constraints can be inserted at any place in the diagram where they are meaningful (Jeckle et al., 2002, p. 352).

[...] in UML 2 it is also possible to represent alternative, optional, parallel, and repeated sequences of interaction [using block-structured *interaction fragments*]. Furthermore, diagrams might contain references to other sequence diagrams that contain a refined description of particular interaction steps. Due to their derivation from [...] *High Level Message Sequence Charts* (Jeckle et al., 2002, p. 332), we will refer to this notation as "high level sequence diagrams".

Like activity diagrams [...], high level sequence diagrams do not display a single scenario but rather a class of possible interaction sequences. A drawback of the extended notation is that such diagrams can become [...] difficult to understand." (Page and Kreutzer, 2005, pp. 87-91)

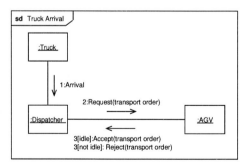

Figure 2.5.: A communication diagram displaying an interaction at an imaginary container terminal.

A more detailed description of UML 2 sequence diagrams including a comparison with the similar AgentUML interaction diagrams is provided in Section 3.3.2.1. An alternative view upon communicating entities is provided by *communication diagrams* as shown in Figure 2.5 (see also Jeckle et al., 2002, pp. 391). The example shows a possible interaction taking place at a container terminal.[9] On the arrival of a truck, the order dispatcher generates a transport order to fetch a certain container and dispatches it to an automatic guided vehicle (AGV) that might accept or reject the order depending on its state.

Note that communication diagrams do not focus on control flow (Jeckle et al., 2002, p. 392) but display relations between communication partners similar to a *social network* Aalst and Song (see e.g. 2004b). Nevertheless it is possible to indicate the order of messages by consecutive numbering. While alternatives are expressed using the UML guard notation, other interaction fragments (e.g. loops) are not supported (Jeckle et al., 2002, pp. 400).

2.3.2. Petri Nets

Despite several attempts to formalize and execute UML models, the UML remains a semi-formal language without an explicit operational semantic. In contrast, Petri nets (PN) are formal models to represent concurrent processes. In the following, we will focus on the reference net formalism by Kummer (2002) and its relations to simulation and UML.

2.3.2.1. Petri Nets

Rölke (2004, p. 251) informally introduces a PN as "a directed graph with two different node types: *places* and *transitions*. A place [drawn as a circle] is a passive element corresponding to a storage [...] while a transition [drawn as a rectangle] represents an action or processing step. *Arcs* can only connect a place with a transition or vice versa."

The PN formalism was proposed by Petri (1962) to model distributed system states and concurrency (Rölke, 2004, p. 253). A set of events or actions are concurrent if they are not causally interrelated and might therefore be executed in an arbitrary order or even simultaneously (Rölke, 2004, p. 253). The state of a PN is indicated by a *marking* of its places with *tokens* (Rölke, 2004, p. 251), where each place can contain a number of tokens up to a certain (possibly unlimited) *capacity*.

The behavior of a PN is realized by the firing of transitions. A transition's ability to fire depends on its *local environment*, i.e. the *input places* connected via incoming arcs and the *output places* connected via outgoing arcs (Rölke, 2004, pp. 251). The transition is *activated* if all input places contain enough tokens (with respect to the incoming arcs' *weights*) and the firing of the transition does not exceed any output place's capacity (with respect to the outgoing arcs' weights) (Jessen and Valk, 1987, p. 39). The firing removes tokens from the input places and puts tokens into the output places (Rölke, 2004, p. 252).

Figure 2.6 exemplifies a PN representing a 'gravel pit' model with two loading docks.[10] Since places and arcs do not contain numerical inscriptions, each place capacity is unlimited and each arc weight is 1 by default.

In the following, we review further aspects of PNs that will be relevant later in this thesis. As usual (see e.g. Baumgarten, 1996 or Bause and Kritzinger, 1996) we distinguish between structural and dynamic properties.

---

[9]On the simulation of container terminal logistics, see e.g. the diploma thesis by Planeth and Willig (2004)

[10]The 'gravel pit' example is adopted from Page and Kreutzer (2005, p. 32).

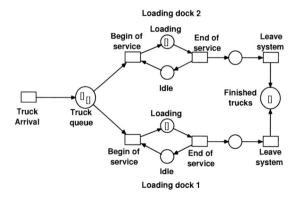

Figure 2.6.: A very abstract PN model of a 'gravel pit' with two loading docks. Note that this model neglects simulation time consumption and queueing strategies.

2.3.2.2. Structural Patterns and Properties

Structural properties are based on the *net graph* $N = (P, T, F)$, where P is the set of places, T the set of transitions and F the set of arcs or *flow relation*. To handle the potential complexity of general net graphs, we can identify common structural patterns (see e.g. Rölke, 2004, pp. 254) on the one hand and consider simplified net classes on the other hand.

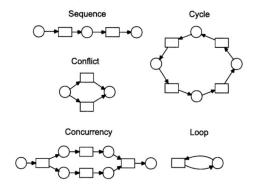

Figure 2.7.: Basic structural patterns commonly found in Petri nets (adopted with modifications from Rölke, 2004, p. 255 and Baumgarten, 1996, p. 53, 72)

Common structural patterns are displayed in Figure 2.7. The definition of sequences and cycles (Baumgarten, 1996, p. 72) is straightforward. Cycles of length 1 are called *loops* (Baumgarten, 1996, p. 53). A *conflict* corresponds to a decision node in an activity diagram (see Section 2.3.1.3. The *concurrent* pattern splits and re-joins the control flow into parallel threads similar to fork and join nodes in activity diagrams.

Restricted sub classes of net graphs considered in this thesis are workflow, free-choice, and causal nets. According to Aalst and Hee (2002, p. 271) a *workflow-net* (WF net) serves to model the control flow of workflow instances (*cases*).[11] Its transitions are interpreted as the basic activities (*tasks*) occurring in the workflow, while arcs and places represent the causal relations and states of the workflow (Aalst and Hee, 2002, p. 271).

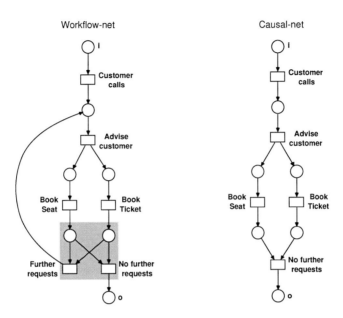

Figure 2.8.: Left: A WF net representing a simple ticket reservation workflow. The grey section mixes an alternative split and a parallel join but nevertheless has the free-choice property. Right: A causal net representing a single ticket reservation case without cycles and conflicts. Example model adopted with modifications from Page (1991, pp. 46).

A WF net comprises a single input place *i* (i.e. a place without input transitions) and a single output place *o* (i.e. a place without output transitions) to indicate a well-defined begin and end of the represented workflow (Aalst and Hee, 2002, p. 272). As a further condition, all places and transitions of a WF net must be on a path from the input to the output place to prevent the modeling of unused tasks and states (Aalst and Hee, 2002, p. 272). An example is shown in Figure 2.8.

A WF net strongly resembles an activity diagram with an initial and final node. However, Aalst and Hee (2002, p. 277) note that most control flow notations (including activity diagrams) do not model conditions as explicit places but as an implicit part of the decision nodes. Therefore, it is not possible to include a routing construct like the grey area of Figure 2.8. It is nevertheless possible to build an equivalent structure composed from decision and fork/join nodes.

---

[11]on workflow modeling see Dumas et al. (2005) and Section 2.3.3

A net composed from elementary parallel and decision blocks has the *free-choice* property (Aalst and Hee, 2002, p. 277) characterized by the fact that "output transitions of places branched in forward direction are not branched in backward direction" (Baumgarten, 1996, p. 74). In workflow modeling, free choice nets are preferred due to their compatibility with common modeling languages and their better understandability and analyzability (Aalst and Hee, 2002, p. 279). Furthermore non-free-choice nets might exhibit a behavior where the decision of conflicts depends on the order of previously executed tasks (Aalst and Hee, 2002, p. 278).

Further net classes with structural restrictions are (generalized) state machines, (generalized) synchronisation graphs, and causal nets (Baumgarten, 1996, p. 72): In a *(generalized) state machine*, every transition has exactly (or at most in the generalized form) one input and one output place (i.e. no concurrency). In a *(generalized) synchronisation graph*, each place has exactly (or at most in the generalized form) one input and one output transition, i.e. there are no conflicts. Cycle-free generalized synchronisation graphs are called *causal nets* (see Figure 2.8). These are used for the formal definition of processes on Place/Transition-nets.

2.3.2.3. Representing the Dynamics of Place/Transition Nets

Place/Transition-nets (P/T-nets) are used to model the dynamics of processes. They consist of a net graph $N = (P, T, F)$, an initial marking M_0, a capacity function C for the places, and a weighting function W for the arcs (see e.g. Baumgarten, 1996, p. 79).

Starting from the initial marking, the behavior of a P/T-net develops according to the firing rule described informally above. This behavior can be illustrated by different representations that depend on the purpose of the analysis. A state-based representation is the *reachability graph*, which nodes represent reachable markings of the PN; connected according to the possible firing of transitions (Bause and Kritzinger, 1996, pp. 110).

A *firing sequence* is an event-based representation of a certain process running on a PN. It consists of an ordered 'recording' of firing transitions' names (see e.g. Bause and Kritzinger, 1996, p. 103). The set of all possible firing sequences of a PN N represents a formal language L_N. This language can be further restricted, e.g. by considering only those firing sequences leading to a certain *goal marking* or those leading to a *deadlock* (Baumgarten, 1996, p. 154).

Baumgarten (1996, p. 108) notes that in a firing sequence all conflicts and concurrencies of the underlying net are resolved, which corresponds to the *interleaving semantics* of PNs. An alternative representation that resolves conflicts but preserves concurrency is the *net process* corresponding to the *partial order semantics* of PNs (Baumgarten, 1996, p. 110). A net process is an unfolding of the original net into a causal net (Baumgarten, 1996, pp. 108). A constructive definition of net processes is stated in (Jessen and Valk, 1987, p. 46). The re-construction of the original net from the net process can be considered as a *folding*, i.e. a mapping of nodes with the same type onto a single node (Baumgarten, 1996, p. 67).

2.3.2.4. Extended Net Classes

This section reviews common extensions to the basic PN formalism considered in simulation and process mining.

Labelled Petri Nets In practical modeling tasks we can label PN elements in order to provide them with a domain-specific meaning. A *labelled P/T-net* is a P/T-net extended by a labeling function h that assigns a label from an arbitrary alphabet to every transition (Baumgarten, 1996, p. 152). Similar to the 'firing sequence language' described above a 'label language' is defined by mapping each firing sequence to a label sequence according to the homomorphism generated by h (Baumgarten, 1996, p. 153).

Baumgarten (1996, p. 153, 341) shows that while every firing sequence language is also a label language, the opposite is not true. Broadly speaking, this is due to the fact that labelled nets allow for a more 'flexible' naming of transitions. Normally, each transition is implicitly identified by a unique name. In a labelled net, however, multiple transitions can be mapped to the same label (also called *duplicate tasks*, see e.g. Li et al., 2007) and transitions can be assigned the empty label λ (also called *hidden tasks*). Both possibilities can occasionally ease modeling but complicate formal analyses and process mining (Aalst and Weijters, 2004).

Timed Augmented Petri Nets An important requirement for PNs in DES is the introduction of time. According to Bause and Kritzinger (1996, p. 161) temporal information can either be assigned to places (timed places PN or TPPN) or to transitions (timed transitions PN or TTPN): *TPPN* define a token *sojourn time* for each place. A token that enters a place becomes available to output transitions only after this time has passed (Bause and Kritzinger, 1996, p. 161). In *TTPN* each transition is assigned a *firing delay*. When the transition becomes activated, it does not fire immediately but with the specified delay.

Time information can either be deterministic (timed PN or TPN) or stochastic (stochastic PN or SPN) (Bause and Kritzinger, 1996, p. 162). To allow for formal analyses, SPN often pose strong restrictions on the applicable random distributions. A common class are continous-time stochastic PN (also called SPN) where each transition t_i is assigned a transition rate λ_i that specifies an exponentially distributed firing delay (Bause and Kritzinger, 1996, p. 163). An SPN thus represents a Markov process whose Markov chain is the reachability graph of the related P/T-net with the assigned transition rates (Bause and Kritzinger, 1996, p. 165). Since the focus of this thesis is not on the formal analysis of time-augmented PNs we refer to Bause and Kritzinger (1996, Part III) and the summary by Strümpel (2003) for further details.

Colored Petri Nets Another important extension to model real world systems is the introduction of typed, distinguishable tokens that are historically called *colored tokens* (see Rölke, 2004, p.251). A *colored petri net* (CPN) is defined by extending the net graph $N = (P, T, F)$ as follows (Valk, 2006, p. 82,86): A set $\mathcal{C}$ of color sets is introduced, where each color set is a token type and each color is a value. A *color domain mapping cd* assigns a type from $\mathcal{C}$ to each place of the net and the adjacent arcs. Furthermore, a set of *variables* with the token types as domains is introduced, and each transition is assigned a *guard* predicate over these variables.

Markings, arc weights, and firing are re-defined with respect to these extensions (see Valk, 2006, pp. 86): A *marking* of a CPN is a vector of bags[12] of appropriate token colors. *Arc weights* are stated as bags of token colors and variables. A transition is *activated* if all input places contain appropriate tokens that fit the incoming arcs' weights and the guard condition holds

---

[12]Different from a set, a bag or multiset can contain multiple instances of an element.

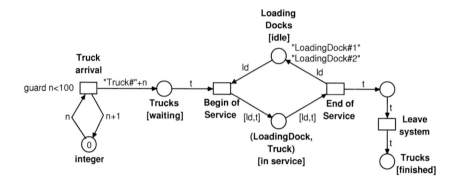

Figure 2.9.: A slightly more detailed variant of the gravel pit model from Figure 2.6 represented as a colored PN.

with respect to a possible binding of the contained variables. It can then *fire* by putting tokens into the output places according to the outgoing arcs' weights and the current variable binding.

Figure 2.9 shows that the above simulation example can be modelled more compactly as a CPN. Tokens are identified as distinct simulation entities. Duplicate net elements from the previous example are folded onto a common structure. Note that arc weights and guards in this example are stated as programming language expressions, which is a common extension of CPNs (see e.g. Bause and Kritzinger, 1996, p. 152).

2.3.2.5. Reference Nets

Reference nets (Kummer, 2002) are a CPN variant that combines many properties of previous formalisms. This includes object oriented concepts, the idea of using nets as tokens in other nets, the synchronisation of transitions via synchronous channels, a time concept, and some additional arc types (see e.g. Rölke, 2004, pp. 254). Figures 2.10 and 2.11 show simple, yet typical 'customer' and 'server' processes from discrete simulation modeled as reference nets (example inspired by Page, 1991).[13] The level of detail is comparable to typical process-oriented simulations.

Different from 'flat' PNs, the example exhibits an object oriented structure. Following Strümpel (2003), the model consists of multiple 'process nets' representing the relevant entities with their life-cycles. Simulation-specific Java classes for queues, random number generation, etc. are re-used from the simulation framework DESMO-J (see Lechler and Page, 1999 and Section 3.4.4) via a static (singleton) *facade* (Gamma et al., 1995, p. 193).

As in object orientation *net classes* are templates to create *net instances* (Valk, 2006, p. 108). Each net instance has an identity and encapsulates an individual state described by its marking (Rölke, 2004, p. 257). Net instances can reside as tokens on places of superordinate nets, which

---

[13]An example of a simple discrete event simulation in RENEW is also found in the RENEW User Guide (Kummer et al., 2006).

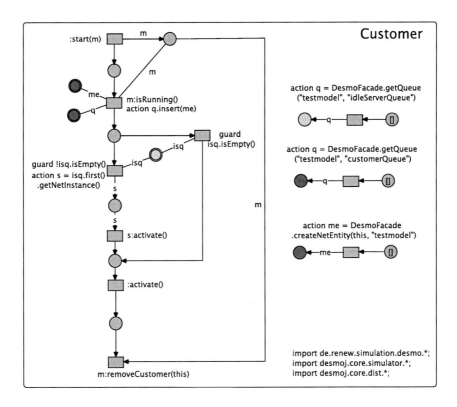

Figure 2.10.: A simple 'customer' process modeled as a reference net. The example includes simulation-specific Java classes from the framework DESMO-J for queueing (including statistical data collection) and random number generation via net inscriptions.

allows to model locality and mobility. This *token refinement* has a *reference semantic*: A net instance can be assigned to multiple tokens at the same time, since the tokens only hold *references* to it (Valk, 2006, p. 108). A transition inscribed with the expression n: `new net` creates a new instance of the class `net` bound to the variable n (Rölke, 2004, p. 258).

Net instances communicate via *synchronous channels* that synchronize the pairwise firing of transitions (Rölke, 2004, p. 257). A synchronous channel consists of two end-points called *uplink* and *downlink*. The downlink is a transition inscription of the form `net:channel(parameters)`, where `net` is a reference to a net instance, `channel` is the channel's name, and `parameters` is a parameter list (Rölke, 2004, p. 258). The downlink transition can only fire if it is activated in its local environment *and* if a transition providing a compatible[14] *uplink* of the form `:channel(parameters)` is activated in the net instance referenced by `net` (Rölke, 2004, p. 257). Then both transitions fire synchronously and the parameters are passed between them. Using

---

[14]i.e. identical channel name and fitting parameter list

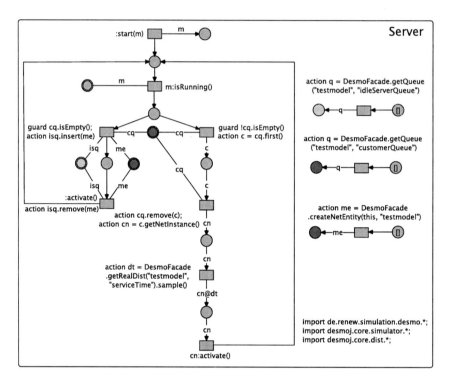

Figure 2.11.: A simple 'server' process modeled as a reference net with Java inscriptions calling DESMO-J.

the keyword `this` in the downlink allows to synchronize transitions of the same net (Valk, 2006, p. 106).

Firing delays of transitions can be specified as inscriptions `n@dt` of their outgoing arcs, where `n` is a token produced by the transition and `dt` is a fixed or dynamically computed relative delay specified in real-valued units of simulation time (Strümpel, 2003, p. 57). The simulation semantic of timed reference nets is event-driven (Strümpel, 2003, pp. 57).

Reference nets provide further elements shown in Figure 2.12 (Rölke, 2004, pp. 255): A *virtual place* is used as a link to a place in order to enhance the visual presentation of a net. A *reserve arc* is a shortcut notation for two arcs of a loop. A *test arc* is similar with the exception that a token on a place can be *tested* concurrently by multiple transitions connected via test arcs. A *flexible arc* allows to transport a variable number of tokens. The number and type of tokens is specified by an inscription with a variable of an array type. An *inhibitor arc* activates the connected transition if the connected place contains *no* appropriate tokens (Kummer et al., 2006, p. 55), and a *clear arc* removes *all* tokens from the assigned place (Kummer et al., 2006, p. 54).[15]

---

[15]Due to an unclear concurrency semantics related to the problem of *zero tests*, inhibitor arcs and clear arcs are only available in the sequential mode of the RENEW simulator.

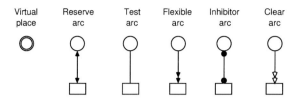

Figure 2.12.: Additional elements of reference nets (adopted with modifications from Rölke, 2004, p. 255,257).

The Java-based RENEW[16] (Reference Net Workshop, see Kummer et al., 2006) toolset provides a modeling environment and simulator for reference nets. The net inscription language is also Java combined with elements of functional programming languages such as pattern matching and a notation for tuples (square brackets) and lists (curly braces). This combination of reference nets with custom Java classes ensures a good practical applicability. The simulator runs in several modes including a *concurrent* mode supporting true concurrency and a *sequential* mode for timed nets.

2.3.2.6. Petri Nets and Reference Nets in Simulation

Though PNs have often been applied to DES (see e.g. Kämper, 1990), their suitability to this domain is not without controversy. The notation is sometimes deemed too abstract and general for modeling real-world problems. However, this does not depend as much on the formalism itself as on the availability of additional structuring mechanisms and appropriate tools for building and executing large PN models.

Kämper (1990, p. 82) summarizes advantages of PNs as a 'simulation language': PNs are at the same time an intuitive graphical notation and an executable formal language. Structural and behavioral aspects of the model are described with a small number of symbols. The *token game* (e.g. Badouel et al., 2007) helps to understand and validate the model's dynamics. Formal methods can be applied to the verification of (at least simplified variants of) the model. Causality, concurrency, and synchronization are naturally displayed. More domain-specific graphical notations can straightforwardly be mapped to PNs as an operational semantics.

The generality and compactness of the PN language is also a drawback for simulation modeling (Kämper, 1990, p. 83). It results in a low aggregation level without simulation-specific constructs. This is problematic for two reasons: Firstly, domain experts are accustomed to their specific concepts and symbols (like machines or stores) even if the semantics conform to places or transitions. Secondly, many PN-based tools do not sufficiently support simulation tasks like data collection or random number generation.

These drawbacks are to a certain extent compensated by advanced structuring mechanisms and modeling tools. Kämper (1990), for instance, uses hierarchical modeling and provides

---

[16]http://www.renew.de, last visit 2013-11-03

simulation-specific constructs in the form of sub nets. Aarhus University's CPN simulator *CP-NTools*[17] provides relatively mature support for data collection and random number generation.

Strümpel (2001) rates the ease of modeling with reference nets superior to programming language-based simulation frameworks due to the straightforward graphical notation. Flexibility and extensibility are similar thanks to the integration with Java. On this basis, Strümpel (2003) extends RENEW with classes for data collection and random distributions.

Another drawback is that reference nets with many Java inscriptions partly loose their conceptual clarity and formal verifiability. The complex simulator's performance is naturally inferior to a simple DES scheduler. Important simulation-specific functionality (such as e.g. queues of unlimited size) is still missing in RENEW. The author has prototypically integrated classes from the simulation framework DESMO-J (see Figures 2.10 and 2.11), to re-use queueing strategies, repeatable random number generation, and reporting. The RENEW simulator in sequential mode serves as simulation scheduler. However, this rudimentary integration still suffers from conceptual and technical drawbacks (e.g. a means to stop all nets of a simulation at a certain point in simulation time).

Compared to domain-specific graphical simulation tools, RENEW's flexibility is obviously higher, while the reference net language might be harder to understand for domain experts. The *Socionics* project has shown that reference nets can be taught to non-computer scientists (in this case sociologists) as a means to build domain-specific models (von Lüde et al., 2003). Based on experiences with reference nets in large simulation studies (see e.g. Bessey, 2004), Szczerbicka (2006) mentions the formalism's complex firing semantics as the main criticism.

To improve the customizability of RENEW, Strümpel (2003, p. 127) proposes to replace places, transitions, tokens, or subnets with domain-specific graphical symbols.[18] As an intermediate step – reminiscent of Kämper (1990) – the *net components* tool is used to integrate simulation constructs into RENEW's graphical user interface (Strümpel, 2003, p. 122).

Net components (Cabac et al., 2003) are re-usable sub nets that roughly correspond to programming language idioms or patterns. Each sub net can be assigned to a button in a custom tool palette of RENEW. The mechanism is rather light-weight, since net components merely provide a graphical grouping of net elements that can be inserted and modified in RENEW. Additional tool support to parameterize net components (as proposed by Kämper, 1990) or to 'collapse' the assigned elements into an abstract symbol is currently not available.

2.3.3. Workflow Modeling and Patterns

The modeling of business processes or *workflows* (e.g. Dumas et al., 2005) is a domain that is closely related to simulation and multi-agent systems with respect to the need to explicitly represent complex control flow. According to Dumas et al. (2005, p. 22):

> "Workflow is usually regarded as "the computerized facilitation or automation of a business process, in whole or in part" (Hollingworth, 1995). It consists of a coordinated set of activities that are executed to achieve a predefined goal. Workflow management aims at

---

[17]http://cpntools.org, last visit 2013-11-03

[18]The current version of RENEW already supports custom images for tokens and the addition of custom figures without functionality to a net drawing.

supporting the routing of activities (i.e. the flow of work) in an organization such that the work is efficiently done at the right time by the right person with the right software tool."

Similar to software development, simulation, and multi-agent systems, business process modeling (BPM) attempts to reduce the complexity of the modeled workflows by considering different *perspectives* (Aalst et al., 2003b, p. 6). Aalst et al. (2003b, p. 6) state the examples of the *control flow perspective* (control flow of a business process), the *data perspective* (data items and documents considered in a workflow), and *resource perspective* (organizational and technical resources required in a business process).

A contribution of workflow modeling that is also valuable beyond the domain of business process management consists in the identification of a large set of so-called *workflow patterns*, as presented by Aalst et al. (2003b). Similar in spirit to (object-oriented) design patterns, workflow patterns abstractly describe routing structures that re-appear in many BPM languages and tools (Aalst et al., 2003b, p. 7). In doing so, different languages and tools can be compared and modeling requirements are stated in a general form (Aalst et al., 2003b, p. 5).

According to Aalst et al. (2003b, p. 8), "the [...] patterns range from fairly simple constructs present in any workflow language to complex routing primitives not supported by today's [...] systems". Among the simple patterns, we find basic control flow constructs like *sequence* (*P*1 in Aalst et al., 2003b, p. 10), *parallel split* (*P*2 in Aalst et al., 2003b, p. 10-11), or *exclusive choice* (*P*4 in Aalst et al., 2003b, p. 11) already mentioned above. More complex patterns include structures like *multi-choice* (also called *or split*, see *P*6 in Aalst et al., 2003b, p. 13) and *cancel activity* (*P*19 in Aalst et al., 2003b, p. 38).

A class of workflow patterns that are closely related to interactions in multi-agent systems (see e.g. Section 3.3.2.1) are "patterns involving multiple instances" (Aalst et al., 2003b). These patterns will be reconsidered later in the context of auction and mediation protocols where a central agent (e.g. an auctioneer) engages in similar conversations with multiple other agents (e.g. bidders) in parallel. In the context of workflow management, Aalst et al. (2003b, Sec. 2.4) distinguish the following variants of multiple instantiation patterns:

- *Multiple instances without synchronization* (*P*12 in Aalst et al., 2003b, p. 23): Several similar threads are run concurrently without further synchronized interaction among each others or with the main process.

- *Multiple instances with a-priori design time knowledge* (*P*13 in Aalst et al., 2003b, p. 24): A workflow runs a previously *fixed* number of similar activities or sub-processes in parallel and waits until all have terminated.

- *Multiple instances with a-priori runtime time knowledge* (*P*14 in Aalst et al., 2003b, p. 25-26): Different from the previous pattern, the number of concurrent activities is not fixed in the workflow model, but remains constant once the processing of the workflow case has started. This variant might be most common in agent interaction protocols such as e.g. *contract net* (Smith, 1980; see also Section 3.3.2.3).

- *Multiple instances without a-priori runtime time knowledge* (*P*15 in Aalst et al., 2003b, p. 27): Here the number of concurrent threads might even change *after* the processing has started

In this thesis, we will not further focus on BPM itself, but only on the closely related analysis technique of *process mining* that mirrors many BPM concepts like workflow perspectives and patterns (see Section 4). For relations of BPM to further topics considered in this thesis, we refer to the literature on *workflow simulation* (e.g. Rozinat et al., 2009c) and *agent-oriented workflow management systems* (e.g. Reese, 2009).

2.4. Experimentation, Analysis, and Validation

After introducing different modeling techniques, we will turn to result analysis, and validation, as the main focus of the thesis. Though modeling might itself provide important insights into a system, the main purpose of a simulation study is to conduct experiments with a model, to analyse the observed behavior, and to draw conclusions from the results of the analysis (see also Kelton and Barton, 2003, p. 59). While simulation modeling and implementation can be understood as a special 'software development project', the character of experimentation, analysis, and validation is closer to an empirical scientific study (Wittmann, 1993, p. 47).[19]

2.4.1. Experimentation

In (Czogalla et al., 2006, Sec. 2), we have described the experimentation phase based on the terminology used by Wittmann:

> "An *experiment* is "a number of [simulation] runs that we execute with different models in order to answer a certain question" (literal interpretation of Wittmann, 1993, p. 57). This definition mirrors the separation of models and experiments [postulated by Zeigler, see e.g. Zeigler et al., 2000]: Different experiments can be conducted with the same model if the attended questions lie within the model's validity range, and an experiment can include different models (e.g. for the purpose of model comparison).

> Wittmann refines the notion of models by distinguishing a *model* from a *model class*. As in object orientation, a model class is a template that is defined by "a set of model elements [i.e. constants, parameters, state variables, and derived elements] and a description of their dynamics" (Wittmann, 1993, p. 55). A model is an instance of a model class with concrete values assigned to these elements.

> [In this context ...], it seems reasonable to neglect internal model structure and behaviour and consider a model class as a *black-box* with a well-defined input-output interface. Following Bachmann (2003, pp. 77), a model class is defined by a set of *access points*, i.e. typed *model and experiment parameters* as inputs and observable *results* and *runtime variables* as output. Thus, an experiment might be reused with any model realizing the same model class.

> An experiment is described by means of an *experiment specification* and an *experimental setup* that jointly constitute a kind of *experimental frame* (see e.g. Zeigler et al., 2000). The experiment specification states which model classes to use and how to vary their parameter values. Parameter variations are either specified in terms of *iterations* (e.g. similar to "for/to/next" loops) or through higher-level specifications of experiment objectives. We refer to the former as *manual experimental design* and call the latter *automated experimental design*.

---

[19]also reviewed in (Czogalla et al., 2006, Sec. 2)

Following the often-cited idea of a "virtual laboratory", the experimental setup describes the control and observation apparatus applied in an experiment. This includes settings of experiment control parameters (e.g. simulation duration) on the one hand, and the setup of observers and analyses on the other hand. The execution of an experiment specification within an experimental setup leads to a series of *simulation runs* (see also Wittmann, 1993, p. 56)."

2.4.1.1. Experimental Design

The main goal of experimental design is to evaluate a preferably wide range of simulation model behavior by simulating a possibly small number of parameter configurations, also called *scenarios* (Page and Kreutzer, 2005, p. 190). In *manual experimental design* this goal is achieved through systematic parameter variations. A common approach is the 2^k *factorial design* (Page and Kreutzer, 2005, p. 190). In this design, we identify a characteristic *high* and *low* value for each of the model's k parameters.[20] We then perform a simulation run for each combination of parameter values leading to a total of 2^k runs. More advanced techniques for experimental design are e.g. presented by Law and Kelton (2000, Ch. 12).

The main technique for automated experimental design is *simulation-based optimization* (see e.g. Page and Kreutzer, 2005, pp. 190 and Ch. 13) which is used to automatically optimize scenarios that are too complex for analytical optimisation. Simulation and optimization techniques are integrated as follows (Page and Kreutzer, 2005, Sec. 13.2): Given a model class, an initial parameter configuration is chosen, and a simulation of this scenario is run. The results of the simulation are then evaluated by means of an *objective function*. Based on this evaluation, an optimization algorithm tries to compute a 'better' configuration that is again evaluated in a simulation run. This iterative process usually continues until the objective value converges. Note that simulation-based optimization is not guaranteed to find an optimal configuration due to the use of (stochastic) simulation and often heuristic optimization techniques (e.g. genetic algorithms, see Gehlsen, 2004).

2.4.2. Output Analysis

Law and Kelton (2000, pp. 496) note that the proper output analysis of (stochastic) simulations is an often neglected aspect in practical studies. In contrast, many textbooks largely emphasize techniques for statistical analysis (examples include Law and Kelton, 2000, Ch. 9-11; Banks et al., 1999, Ch. 12-13). However, the diversity of analysis techniques applied in simulation exceeds mere statistics since informal as well as formal techniques from several fields can be applied. The classification scheme in Figure 2.13 shows one possibility to structure the different analysis techniques applied in simulation.

The well-known distinction of statistical analysis techniques into the exploratory and the confirmatory *approach* is also relevant in simulation (see e.g. Köster, 2002). "*Exploratory* techniques are applied to gather knowledge about a model's structural or behavioural features, while *confirmatory*

---

[20]The 2^k factorial design is thus related to software engineering's equivalence partitioning and extreme input testing (see e.g. Balci, 1998, pp. 370).

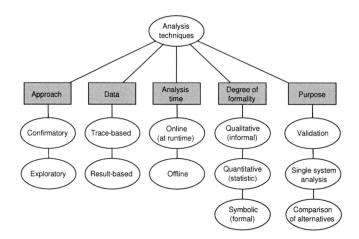

Figure 2.13.: A classification scheme for analysis techniques. The scheme was derived from several sources in the literature and from our classification of validation techniques presented in (Page and Kreutzer, 2005, p. 211; see also Figure 2.16).

techniques serve to test [...] pre-established hypotheses" (Page and Kreutzer, 2005, p. 210) that represent expectations on a scenario (in model comparisons) or knowledge about the real system (in validation).

Following Ritzschke and Wiedemann (1998, Sec. 1), output analyses are either based on raw event *traces* observed during simulation or on preprocessed results (*simulation reports*) produced by specific data collectors in the experimental setup (e.g. average queue waiting times): In *trace-based analysis* all available information are logged and subsequently filtered and aggregated. This allows for detailed and temporally fine-grained analyses. Furthermore, the trace can be analysed from different view angles without modifications of the experimental setup and rerun of the simulation (Ritzschke and Wiedemann, 1998, Sec. 1). A drawback of trace-based analyses is the high computational effort necessary to process large trace files, and the reduced convenience compared to *result-based analyses* with specific data collectors connected to the model components (Ritzschke and Wiedemann, 1998, Sec. 1).

Analyses can either be performed after the simulation, taking into account the whole observed data set (*offline analysis*) or during the simulation, taking into account the currently available data (*online analysis*).[21] Apart from *animations* (Page and Kreutzer, 2005, Sec. 9.6), online analyses only appear reasonable if a feedback of results into the running simulation is required. A typical example is the reset of statistical counters after detecting the end of a simulated process' transient phase (Page and Kreutzer, 2005, pp. 174). Generally, online analyses are algorithmically more demanding than offline analyses due to the need to incrementally update the results when more data becomes available.

Another typical criterion to classify analysis techiques is the *degree of formality*, which is subdivided into qualitative, quantitative, and symbolic techniques in (Page and Kreutzer, 2005,

---

[21]see e.g. Page and Kreutzer (2005, p. 242)

p. 210): *Qualitative techniques* are mostly based on *visualization*. Quantitative methods are often rooted in statistics. In this thesis we will also consider symbolic techniques from fields like data mining or formal verification (Page and Kreutzer, 2005, p. 210; see also Brade, 2003, p. 56).

Common *purposes* for the application of data analysis techniques in simulation include the *analysis of real system data during model building*, the *analysis of a single simulation run*, the *comparison of multiple scenarios* (see e.g. Law and Kelton, 2000, Ch. 9,10), and *operational validation* as a comparison between simulation and real system data (see Section 2.4.3).

2.4.3. Validation

When simulation models are used as a basis for decision making, it is vital to ensure that the analysis of the model leads to similar decisions as an analysis of the represented system (Page, 1991, p. 147), i.e. the model is *valid* (Page and Kreutzer, 2005, pp 195). In (Page and Kreutzer, 2005, p. 196), we emphasized the attention paid to validation in the simulation literature:

> "Following Page (1991, pp. 146) we should ideally accept model validity as one of the most important criteria for judging model quality. [...] the wide range of literature on this topic reflects its importance. There are numerous papers and textbooks, which emphasise different aspects, such as practical techniques (e.g. Balci, 1998), statistical methodology (e.g. Kleijnen, 1999), or [...] similarities between [... simulation] validation and [...] the philosophy of science (e.g. Naylor and Finger, 1967).

> Other disciplines, such as software engineering, theoretical computer science, or statistics have developed approaches [...] which are also relevant for simulation. Kleindorfer and Ganeshan (1993, p. 50) emphasize the "eclectic" character of validation in this regard [...]"

2.4.3.1. Basic Terms

The following list adopted from (Page and Kreutzer, 2005, p. 196) reviews relevant terms in simulation validation based on definitions by Brade (2003, Ch. 1.5):[22]

- *Model validation* serves to ensure that a simulation model is a "suitable representation of the real system with respect to an intended purpose of the model's application" (Brade, 2003, p. 16 cited with minor modifications in Page and Kreutzer, 2005, p. 198). Furthermore, "the term *validation* is also [...] used as an umbrella term for all quality assurance activities (i.e. [...] model validation, verification, and testing)" (Page and Kreutzer, 2005, p. 198).

- *Model verification in the wide sense* serves to ensure that "a model is correctly represented and was correctly transformed from one representation into another" (Brade, 2003, p. 14 cited with minor modifications in Page and Kreutzer, 2005, p. 198). *Model verification in the narrow sense* denotes the application of formal methods to "prov[e ...] the correctness of model representations and their transformations" (Page and Kreutzer, 2005, pp. 198).

---

[22] Actually, the definitions by Brade (2003) include the terms validation and verification. The distinction between verification in the wider and narrower sense and the notion of testing are added. A detailed discussion of different forms and 'degrees' of verification is led by Fetzer (2001), who uses the term "verification in the broad sense" (Fetzer, 2001, p. 243). A similar definition for testing from the software engineering domain is found in Whittaker (2000, p. 77).

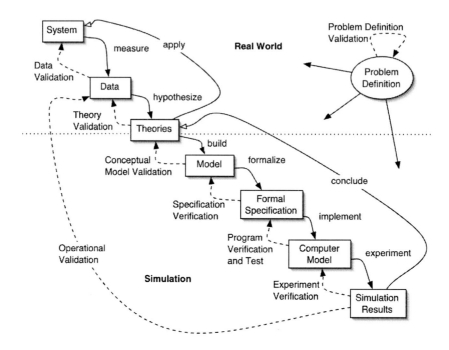

Figure 2.14.: A refined validation process based on Balci (1998, p. 337) and Sargent (2001, p. 109). Adoped from Page and Kreutzer (2005, p. 200).

- *Model testing* denotes the execution of "a computerized simulation model in order to corroborate that it correctly implements its corresponding conceptual model. [...] testing is regarded as an important technique for model verification in the wide[...] sense." (Page and Kreutzer, 2005, p. 199)

2.4.3.2. Validation in the Model Building Cycle

In (Page and Kreutzer, 2005, pp. 199-200) we contrasted different variants of the process followed to conduct a simulation study:

"Many authors, e.g. Page (1991) and Sargent (2001), differentiate between three main validation phases [in the model building cycle]:

1. *Conceptual model validation* is performed during the conceptual modelling phase. It aims to ensure that the model is a plausible representation of the real system; i.e. suitable to answer all questions raised by the problem definition.

2. *Model verification* (in the wide sense) is performed during the implementation phase and seeks to establish that the computerized model implements the conceptual model correctly.

3. *Operational model validation* is conducted before and during simulation experiments. It aims to determine how closely a model's behaviour resembles the real system's behaviour. [...] To achieve this, data collected during model execution is compared with corresponding data gathered during the real system's operation."

The more complex variant of this basic process shown in Figure 2.14 "has been strongly influenced by Sargent (2001, p. 109), Balci (1998, p. 3), and the "V&V triangle" (standing for validation and verification) presented in Brade (2003, p. 62)" (Page and Kreutzer, 2005, p. 200). We will only clarify some basic principles by means of this figure. A more detailed description is provided in (Page and Kreutzer, 2005, pp. 200).

Firstly, as noted in (Page and Kreutzer, 2005, p. 200), the placement of the *problem definition* above the whole process indicates that "a simulation model is built with respect to the study objectives and its credibility is judged with respect to those objectives" (Balci, 1998, p. 346 cited in Page and Kreutzer, 2005, pp. 200-201). "Validation [...] can never guarantee "absolute" model validity [... but] only improve models' credibility for answering certain questions [...] by means of certain simulation experiments. Zeigler et al. (2000, p. 369) refer to this endeavour as an "experimental frame"." (Page and Kreutzer, 2005, p. 201)

Secondly, as also cited in (Page and Kreutzer, 2005, p. 201), "validation should be conducted throughout the whole model building process." (Page, 1991, p. 148). "Every phase [of the model building cycle] must be complemented by an associated validation activity" (Page and Kreutzer, 2005, p. 201) ensuring the validity of the artifacts produced in that phase. "Although the process shown in Figure 2.14 is reminiscent of [. . . a] classical waterfall model, it must be stressed that model building is a strongly iterative activity" (Page and Kreutzer, 2005, p. 202).

2.4.3.3. Validation and the Philosophy of Science

To put the validation of simulation models into a broader context, many authors (e.g. Naylor and Finger, 1967; Birta and Özmizrak, 1996, p. 79) cite its relation to problems considered in the philosophy of science. In (Page and Kreutzer, 2005, p. 203) we summarized these relations as well:

"As Cantú-Paz et al. (2004, p. 1) point out, "computer simulations are increasingly being seen as the third mode of science, complementing theory and experiments". If we regard simulation models as "miniature scientific theories" (Kleindorfer and Ganeshan, 1993, p. 50), it becomes obvious that there is a close correspondence between validation of simulation models and the more general problem of validating a scientific theory (see Troitzsch, 2004, p. 5 cited in Küppers and Lenhard, 2004, p. 2). The latter problem traditionally belongs to the domain of the *philosophy of science* and has been studied extensively.

[... According to Popper's *critical rationalism*], the main characteristic of the so-called "scientific method" [is the permanent] effort to *falsify* [...] preliminary theories. [...] falsification is superior to verification [...], since inductions from facts [...] to theories can never be justified on logical grounds alone [...] (Popper, 1982, p. 198). We can, however, use empirical observations to falsify a theory. A single wrong prediction suffices. [...]

[A more ...] practical viewpoint, proposed by Naylor and Finger (1967, pp. B-95), takes a "utilitarian" view of validation, with a mixture of rationalist, empiricist and pragmatist aspects [...]:

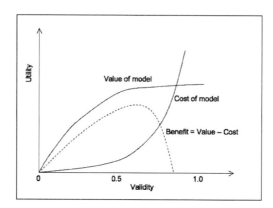

Figure 2.15.: "Estimation of cost, value, and benefit in model validation (adopted with modifications from Shannon, 1975, p. 209)". Figure and caption cited from Page and Kreutzer (2005, p. 207).

1. *Rationalist step*: assessment of intuitive plausibility of model structure. By following the rationalist approach, i.e. criticising a model based on well-founded a-priori knowledge, this step seeks to eliminate obviously erroneous assumptions.

2. *Empiricist step*: detailed empirical validation of those assumptions that have "survived" the first step.

3. *Pragmatist step*: validation of model behaviour by comparing model output to corresponding output obtained from the target system (if available). In this step the model's ability to predict the real system's behaviour is tested. [...]

Using the terminology introduced [... above], the steps 1 and 2 are concerned with conceptual model validation. Step 3 views the model as a "black box" and corresponds to [...] operational validation [...]."

2.4.3.4. General Guidelines

Due to the large number and variety of available validation approaches, it can be useful to have a list of guidelines at hand when performing practical model validation. In (Page and Kreutzer, 2005, pp. 205), we cited the following guidelines derived from similar treatments by Page (1991, Ch. 5.2) and Balci (1998, Ch. 10.3):

- "*Degrees of Model Validity*: [...] rationalists and empiricists are interested in models that explain the behaviour of systems in terms of their structure. In contrast to this, pragmatists simply view systems as black boxes and rate model quality solely on the basis of a model's predictive power. In the simulation domain these two perspectives have led to the definition of different degrees of model validity, which Bossel (1989, p. 14) summarizes as [...] (cited from Martelli, 1999, pp. 88): *structural validity* [...,] *behavioural validity* [...,] *empirical validity* [..., and] *application validity*" (Page and Kreutzer, 2005, p. 206).

- "*Scope and Effort of Model Validation*: [...] the impossibility of empirical theory verification strongly suggests that the establishment of "absolute" model validity is also a logical impossibility.

This belief is confirmed by many other results [...] including the limits of formalization explored by Goedel and Turing (see e.g. Gruska, 1997, Ch. 6). [...] Shannon (1975, pp. 208) [... therefore] stresses the need for an "economic" approach to validation activities. The pseudo-quantitative estimation in Figure 2.15 shows that value and cost of a model do not increase in a linear fashion with [...] validity. [...] In several cases simple but suitably accurate models are better than extremely detailed ones, whose complexity and data requirements quickly become intractable. This is another example of the principle of "Occam's Razor", which [...] claims that a simpler theory with fewer parameters should be preferred [...], based on its easier testability (Popper, 2004, p. 188)." (Page and Kreutzer, 2005, pp. 206-207)

- *Value of Human Insight*: "In critical domains such as model validation, people often call for increased formality, automation, and tool-support [...]. However, according to Page (1991, p. 147), "the application of mathematical and statistical methods in model validation is limited" and such methods typically impose strong restrictions on model representation and complexity [... Furthermore they] only cover a narrow aspect of model validity. Brade (2003, p. 90) concludes that "although automated computer-based validation techniques are more objective, more efficient, more likely to be repeatable, and even more reliable than human review, the human reviewer plays an extremely important role for the V&V of models and simulation results". [...] In recognition of this, proponents of formal and automated techniques [like those discussed in this thesis] should seek to develop tools whose primary focus is the support and augmentation of human modelling and validation activities." (Page and Kreutzer, 2005, p. 208)

2.4.3.5. Classification of Validation Techniques

As recognized in (Page and Kreutzer, 2005, p. 210):

"The simulation literature offers more (e.g. Balci, 1998) or less (e.g. Garrido, 2001) exhaustive listings of model validation techniques [... that] originate in different fields [of ...] computer science. To bring some structure into this "chaos", many authors propose their own schemes for classifying validation techniques; [... including] Balci (1998, p. 27) [...,] Garrido (2001, p. 216) [...,] Page (1991, p. 16) [..., and] Brade (2003, p. 56) [...]

To integrate these different schemes into a coherent classification, we [...] arrange validation techniques along the following dimensions [based on proposals by the above authors[23]]:

- *Approach*: [As in output analysis] we separate exploratory from confirmatory validation techniques. [...]

- *Phase in model building cycle*: This dimension describes whether a validation technique is mainly used for conceptual model validation, model verification, or operational validation; or one of the phases attached to a more sophisticated validation process.

- *Degree of formality*: Along this dimension we differentiate between qualitative informal, [statistical, and exhaustive ...] validation methods. [...]

- *System view*: This dimension refers to the perspective which characterizes a validation technique. [...]"

---

[23]For a detailed review of these sources see Page and Kreutzer (2005, p. 210). Since validation is closely related to analysis, the scheme shown in Figure 2.16 strongly resembles the classification of analysis techniques in Section 2.4.2.

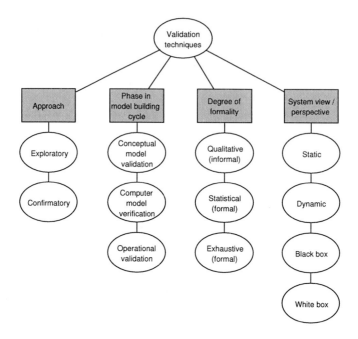

Figure 2.16.: A classification scheme for validation techniques in simulation (adopted with modifications from Page and Kreutzer, 2005, p. 211)

Note that in (Page and Kreutzer, 2005, p. 211), we originally stated the same 'degrees of formality' as in the classification of analysis techniques presented in Section 2.4.2. However, in the context of this thesis, a distinction between statistical and exhaustive techniques seems more appropriate to cover the range of validation techniques treated. Besides statistical techniques for log and output analysis, we can also apply exhaustive formal verification techniques to simplified versions of a simulation model. In either case, both symbolic and numeric analysis techniques might be used.

3. Agent-Based Simulation

This chapter provides an introduction to concepts, modeling techniques, and tools for multi-agent systems (MAS) and multi-agent-based simulation (MABS). The structure and content of the presentation is largely based on Klügl (2000, Chs. 2,3,4). Several sections were adopted from Page and Kreutzer (2005, Ch. 11), co-written by and partly based on the diploma thesis (Knaak, 2002) of the author.

3.1. Agents and Multi-Agent Systems

According to Page and Kreutzer (2005, p. 340) "multi-agent systems have become an important metaphor" in system analysis and modeling (see also Klügl, 2000, p. 9). In the following, we explain the meaning of the term 'agent' in the context of this thesis. Subsequently, we review common agent architectures and discuss dimensions that influence their complexity with respect to analysis and validation. The focus is then turned to MAS for the same purpose.

3.1.1. Agents

Concerning definitions of the term 'agent' we noted in (Page and Kreutzer, 2005, pp. 340-341):

> "Unfortunately, no agreement on exact definitions [...] and what distinguishes agency from related concepts (e.g. *objects*) has so far been reached [see e.g. Klügl, 2001, p. 10]. As a result, ambiguous usage of terms remains a concern for MAS research. To address this concern and retain enough flexibility to capture all the diversity of the subject, some authors resort to very general and abstract definitions. An often cited example [e.g. in Klügl, 2000, p. 10] for this is the following characterization [...] by Franklin and Graesser (1997, p. 25): *"An autonomous agent is a system situated within and a part of an environment that senses that environment and acts on it, over time, in pursuit of its own agenda and so as to effect what it senses in the future."* [...] Another prominent and [...] more concrete approach is the definition of agents by means of a set of properties, all or some of which a prospective agent must possess (see e.g. Klügl, 2000, pp. 10, Ferber, 1995, p. 10, [... Gilbert and Troitzsch, 1999, and Wooldridge and Jennings, 1995, pp. 116-118]):
>
> - *Autonomy*: An agent is able to fulfil its tasks without or with only minor interventions by other entities.
>
> - *Situatedness*: An agent inhabits some environment that it can sense and act upon.
>
> - *Reactivity*: An agent is able to respond to changes in its environment in a timely fashion.
>
> - *Goal-orientation*: An agent does not merely react to environmental stimuli, but can act pro-actively – according to a set of persistent goals. To meet these goals, it is able to execute plans over time.

- *Sociality*: In order to reach its goals an agent communicates and interacts with other agents in a cooperative or competitive manner.

- *Adaptivity*: An agent can adapt its future behaviour based on past experiences; i.e. it can learn.

- *Mobility*: An agent is able to change its location within a physical or virtual environment (e.g. a computer network)." (Page and Kreutzer, 2005, pp. 340-341)

While these properties are listed in many textbooks, their appropriateness is a subject of continuing discussions. One common objection says that the conceptual framework of agents might not provide significant advantages, because computer science has dealt with systems exhibiting similar properties before; e.g. in *active objects* or *expert systems* which can be regarded as predecessors of agents (Wooldridge, 2003, pp. 26). A second popular objection says that talking about computer systems hardly justifies the use of philosophically or sociologically biased terms like autonomy.

In the following, we will discuss the benefits and limitations of the agent metaphor and compare it with related concepts. The presentation is based on Klügl (2000), Wooldridge (2003), Ferber (1995), and Padgham and Winikoff (2004).

3.1.1.1. Benefits and Limitations of the Agent Metaphor

As criticized in the first objection, MAS are indeed nothing 'new', but a mixture of concepts from object-orientation, distributed systems, artificial intelligence, and sociology. Their main purpose is to provide a "natural abstraction and decomposition of complex [...] systems" (Padgham and Winikoff, 2004, p. 5). In this context, sociological and economic terms are used as a metaphor. Though MAS research has gained relevant results at the *technological* level, the provision of a new[1] *conceptual* framework might be regarded as the main contribution.

The unreflected adoption of sociological and economic terms, however, leads to the second objection. Therefore it is important to narrow down the scope of biased notions like autonomy in the context of MAS. In this thesis (as often in agent-based simulation) the terms are on the one hand used to conceptually describe actors from a real system. On the other hand, several notions can be given a technical interpretation that helps to distinguish agents from related concepts.

Situatedness, for instance, is a characteristic property because it delimits agents from earlier AI artifacts like expert systems (Wooldridge, 2003, p. 27). According to Ferber (1995, p. 53), classical AI programs are abstract "thinkers" that can at the utmost *advise* users how to act on the basis of presented data. In contrast agents percieve and change their environment directly. They can only percieve, act, and move within a certain local radius (Klügl, 2000, p. 59), which fits the modeling of real-world actors in simulation well (see also Klügl, 2000, p. 6).

Autonomy, even in a restricted sense, distinguishes agents from the object-oriented world view (Wooldridge, 2003, p. 25). This is summarized in the often-cited sentence that "objects do it for free [while] agents do it because they want to" (Wooldridge, 2003, p. 26). Some authors concretize the term by identifying different degrees of autonomy. According to Klügl (2000, p. 11) *autonomy of control* means that an agent can perform its tasks without extensive interventions

---

[1]but nevertheless historically grown, as indicated above

of users. This is a rather unspecific property in the simulation context, since entities in many simulation models exhibit autonomy of control without being regarded as agents. *Autonomy of behavior* denotes learning agents that autonomously modify their behavior based on past experiences.

Though autonomous control and behavior can be implemented in an object-oriented language, autonomy is not an inherent concept of this world view, which is dominated by the principle of *design by contract* (see e.g. Meyer, 1997).

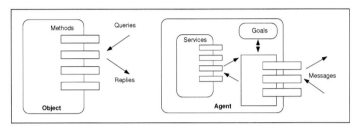

Figure 3.1.: "Conceptual distinction between objects and agents (adopted [with modifications] from Ferber, 1995, p. 58)." (Caption and figure cited from Page and Kreutzer, 2005, pp. 353)

In (Page and Kreutzer, 2005, p. 352), we reviewed the discussion by Ferber (1995) on this subject:

> "Objects are defined through their interfaces; i.e. the services they can perform on demand. Their implementation must therefore ensure that all methods are correctly implemented and that expected results are returned (Ferber, 1995, p. 57). This viewpoint clashes with the requirement for agent autonomy, which leaves agents free to pursue their own goals. Agents can, for example, refuse a request if it would cause conflict or if some information is currently unavailable (Ferber, 1995, p. 58).
>
> The important point of distinction is that such decisions are based on the perceived state of an environment, as well as the state of the agent's internal knowledge base. The same request can therefore lead to different reactions at different times. In a typical implementation this results in an additional *filtering* level, which mediates between service requests and internal agent processes (see Figure 3.1). In this way agents themselves retain tight control over their own behaviour."

An agent's actions can fail in certain situations (Wooldridge, 2003, p. 24) or it might select between different possibilities to satisfy its clients' needs based on their respective preferences (Garion and van der Torre, 2006, p. 175; see also Knaak, 2002, p. 7). This leads to higher demands on the agent's 'intelligence' where the term denotes behavioral flexibility. Agents with flexible behavior provide increased robustness "in situations in which the environment is challenging" (Padgham and Winikoff, 2004, pp. 4–5).

The presented benefits of the agent metaphor must be contrasted by a number of problems:

1. The slightly 'esoteric' terminology of MAS might lead to an over-expectation. As discussed above, this can be avoided by clearly distinguishing between conceptual and technical implications of the metaphor. According to Padgham and Winikoff (2004, p. 4), "agents are not magic [but ...] simply an approach to structuring and developing software".

2. The very general agent metaphor might be overused in situations where other concepts appear more appropriate. An example is the modeling of a spatial environment as a specific 'agent' in simulation (Klügl, 2000, p. 104). Moss (2000, p. 2) notes that MA(B)S research often seems to exhibit an overstated focus on its abstract concepts instead of practical applications.

3. Complex agent systems tend to be hard to analyze and validate (Klügl, 2000, p. 190). While this problem can be partly reduced by finding an appropriate level of modeling detail (Klügl, 2000, p. 74) and applying proven software engineering methods, it is also inherent to the modeling style.

3.1.2. Agent Architectures[2]

According to Klügl (2000, p. 14) an agent's *architecture* determines its internal information processing, i.e. how perceptions are mapped to actions. Many agent architectures have been proposed, ranging from intentionally simple designs to complex reasoning systems (Klügl, 2000, p. 15).

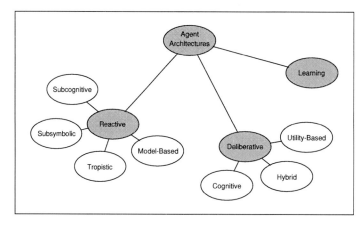

Figure 3.2.: Classification of agent architectures based on Ferber (1995); Klügl (2000); Müller (1996); Russel and Norvig (2003).

In view of this variety, the literature distinguishes several classes of agent architectures. Different classification schemes are reviewed and integrated by Klügl (2000, Sec. 2.2.1), who regards the *complexity of the internal representation* as the main classification criterion (Klügl, 2000, p. 14). Figure 3.2 displays a structured overview of the architectural types mentioned in this summary. Most authors distinguish between reactive and deliberative agents as the two main classes.

The behaviour of *reactive agents* is constituted by more or less direct reactions to stimuli. Their design is often inspired by the idea of a collective "intelligence without reason" (Brooks, 1999) emerging from basic interactions (Klügl, 2000, p. 20). Klügl (2000, p. 20) criticizes that the

---

[2]This Section is based on (Page and Kreutzer, 2005, Ch. 11.2.3), which contains a more detailed presentation of exemplary agent architectures based on the diploma thesis of the author (Knaak, 2002, Sec. 2.4).

term 'reactive' is misleading since deliberative agents can also react to external stimuli.[3] Instead she identifies two classes of 'non-deliberative' architectures: *Subsymbolic architectures* use non-symbolic internal representations such as neural networks (Klügl, 2000, p. 18). *Subcognitive architectures* apply symbolic information processing, often based on rule-based production systems or finite automata (Klügl, 2000, pp. 19).

Russel and Norvig (2003, Ch. 2.4) take the presence of an internal memory as a further criterion to classify reactive agents:[4] A *simple reflex agent*[5] is 'memory-less' without an internal model of its environment. A *model-based reflex agent*, in contrast, has an internal state that additionally influences its action selection.

Deliberative agents hold internal representations of goals and are able to generate and execute plans for their achievement (Klügl, 2000, pp. 20). Again, several sub-classes can be identified. Russel and Norvig (2003, Sec. 2.4) distinguish between *plan-based* agents capable of dynamic planning, and *utility-based* agents that can additionally evaluate the utility of alternative plans with respect to their current goals.[6] Müller (1996, cited in Klügl, 2000, p. 15) adds the class of *hybrid* architectures that consist of at least one deliberative and one reactive layer.

Klügl (2000, pp. 22) introduces the class of *cognitive* architectures, i.e. deliberative agents the design of which is explicitly based on theories from cognitive science. As examples, she names the *BDI (Belief, Desire, Intention)* architecture (e.g. Rao and Georgeff, 1995) based on a theory of rational action by Bratman (1987) and the *PECS (Physics, Emotion, Cognition, Status)* architecture by Urban (1997) that strives to include non-rational aspects related to physics and emotions into agent design (Klügl, 2000, pp. 22-23).

Learning agents (also called *adaptive agents* by some authors) can autonomously acquire new or adapt existing abilities from the observation of their environment (Russel and Norvig, 2003, Sec. 2.4).

3.1.3. Multi-Agent Systems

As reviewed by Page and Kreutzer (2005, p. 341):

> "A straightforward definition of *multi-agent systems* (MAS) views them as systems in Section [... 2.1]'s sense. MAS' defining property is that its components are sets of agents, located and cooperating in a shared environment (Wooldridge, 2003, pp. 105)."

A formal definition mirroring this explanation is e.g. stated by Ferber (1995). Thereby, a MAS might also contain further passive components (objects or resources) that are not understood as agents.

The analysis of MAS is often focused on how structures and processes at the macroscopic level emerge from interactions of agents at the microscopic level without or with only few influence of a central control instance (Jennings et al., 1998, cited in Klügl, 2000, p. 13). The MAS metaphor is thus closely connected to questions of distributed problem solving based on local

---

[3]cited in (Page and Kreutzer, 2005, p. 343)
[4]also cited by Klügl (2000, pp. 16)
[5]called a *tropistic agent* by Ferber (1995, p. 192; see also Klügl, 2000, p. 15)
[6]see also Klügl (2000, p. 16-17)

information (Jennings et al., 1998, cited in Klügl, 2001, p. 13), computational emergence (see Section 2.1.1), and (self-)organisation (e.g. Holland, 1998); see also the brief discussion in (Page and Kreutzer, 2005, p. 342).

3.2. The Agent-Based Simulation World View

Meyer (2008) regards multi-agent-based simulation (MABS) as a distinct world view that complements the typical modeling styles from discrete simulation (see Section 2.2.2). This section introduces MABS in the context of other simulation world views as well as other relations between simulation and agent technology. The former allows to identify specific requirements on analysis and validation. The latter helps to position the subject of this thesis in the broader context of simulation and MAS.

3.2.1. Relations between Agents and Simulation

In (Page and Kreutzer, 2005, Sec. 11.3) we reviewed the different relations between the fields of MAS and simulation:

> "The relationship between agent technology and simulation can be viewed and exploited in a number of different ways (Uhrmacher, 2000, p. 16) [see also Ören (2000, p. 1758) using the umbrella term of *agent-directed simulation*]:
>
> 1. Due to the complexity of agents' internal processes and interactions, software systems based on an agent metaphor are often hard to validate and test. While formal verification methods are only of limited use, simulation provides an important tool for the operational validation of MAS (Moss, 2004, p. 2). Simulated environments for testing software or hardware agents are often called *agent testbeds*. Ören (2000, p. 1758) refers to this application of simulation to agent technology as *agent simulation*.
>
> 2. The MAS metaphor brings an additional modelling perspective to simulation. MAS theory offers a framework for improving both understanding and modeling of systems consisting of multiple, autonomous, and goal-oriented actors. This agent-based modeling perspective has been referred to as *multi-agent-based simulation (MABS)* and is most frequently used to simulate social, biological, and economic systems. However, in MABS, agent concepts are often employed exclusively at the conceptual modeling level, while the corresponding computer models are implemented in a more or less conventional object-oriented style (Drogoul et al., 2002, p. 11).
>
> 3. Simulation software can be designed and implemented using agent technology. According to Uhrmacher (2000, p. 16), such agent-based simulation tools can enhance distribution and interoperability [...] Software agents employing AI techniques, such as data mining, can offer support for experimentation in knowledge-intensive domains; e.g. simulation data analysis, validation, parameter calibration, or experiment planning. Ören (2000, p. 1758) calls this application of agent technology to simulation *agent-supported simulation*.
>
> Note that all three views of agent-oriented simulation are closely related. Agent simulation and MABS only differ in that software agents populating a software engineering model are usually destined to function in a "real" environment later, whereas simulated agents

in MABS models do not exist outside the model [see also the discussion by Klügl (2000, pp. 62)].

Finally, due to the inherent complexity of data analysis in agent-based models (Sanchez and Lucas, 2002, p. 117), simulation tools built on the agent metaphor may occasionally even be helpful during an agent-based model's design and analysis (Drogoul et al., 2002, pp. 10)."

This thesis is focused on the process-oriented analysis and validation of *MABS*, but the presented concepts and techniques might also be applied in agent simulation. The main distinction is the *analysis objective* with a scientific focus in MABS and a software-technical focus in agent simulation. The integration of the presented analysis techniques into automated assistants might as well be regarded as agent-supported simulation.

3.2.2. Components of Agent-Based Models

A MABS is a MAS in a simulated (spatial and temporal) environment that serves to represent a real system (Klügl, 2000, p. 60). Thus the main components of a MABS include (see Klügl, 2000, p. 60 and the review in Page and Kreutzer, 2005, pp. 353):

- a simulation scheduler,

- a set of simulated agents,

- an infrastructure for communication and organization,

- a (possibly spatial) environment.

These components are briefly described below with one exception: It seems not sensible to elaborate on specific properties of simulated agents since these do not significantly differ from other types of software agents described in Section 3.1. The main difference is that simulated agents exist in simulated time and space (Meyer, 2008), which normally allows to keep their sensors and effectors simple (Klügl, 2000, p. 64). The following description is based on Klügl (2000, pp. 63) and our review in (Page and Kreutzer, 2005, pp. 354).

3.2.2.1. Scheduling in MABS

As reviewed in (Page and Kreutzer, 2005, p. 354):

> "Scheduling in MABS can be both time- or event-driven. For models with few complex agents, which communicate via messages, event-driven scheduling is often the better choice. Conversely, time-driven control may be preferable where models consist of large numbers of agents with similar behaviour, and where every agent is activated in every simulation cycle and similar actions are executed in a regular[...] fashion.
>
> Execution order of agents is an important aspect in time-driven, and to a lesser extent in event-driven scheduling strategies. While conceptually agents will act in parallel, the serialization of actions required to execute on a single processor may

introduce so-called "artifacts" into the model.[7] The execution order of agents in time-driven models is therefore often randomized at each simulation step (Klügl, 2001, p. 157)."

Davidsson (2000, p. 100) argues that event-driven scheduling contradicts the autonomy of agents, because the scheduler imposes a central control by ordering the individual actions on a global event list. Meyer (2008) rightly disagrees with this in two respects: On the one hand, a time-driven simulation scheduler must also impose a global execution order to ensure repeatable simulation results. On the other hand, MABS deals with autonomy mainly on the conceptual level and not in (distributed) implementations (see also Section 3.1.1.1).

As indicated in Section 2.2.1, the event-driven approach is more general because time-driven scheduling can be emulated and integrated by means of equidistant clock pulse events. Similarly, the analysis of event-driven models might be regarded as more general, since non-equidistant inter-event durations must be coped with (e.g. in time-weighted statistics over event-traces). This thesis is concerned with trace-based analysis techniques for event-driven models, which are straightforwardly applied to time-driven models as well.

3.2.2.2. Communication and Organization

Two different modes of communication are found in MABS: Agents either communicate explicitly via messages or implicitly by placing objects in a common environment (Ferber, 1995, p. 13).[8] An appropriate communication model should be chosen with respect to the represented system, e.g. implicit communication via 'pheromones' in anthill simulations (Ferber, 1995, pp. 389). Message-based communication requires a communication infrastructure that might exhibit an own dynamic, e.g. to simulate delayed or unreliable forwarding of messages (Page and Kreutzer, 2005, p. 355).

The analysis of models with explicit communication seems less demanding than the implicit case, because message passing events can be clearly identified in the simulation trace. Therefore, we will focus on the analysis of MABS with explicit (message-based) communication in this thesis.

An important objective in MABS is to investigate the mutual influences between individual behaviour and organizational structures, which requires an appropriate representation of these structures in the model. In some cases, organizational structures are represented implicitly in terms of the spatial model, where spatial proximity of two agents might e.g. be interpreted as 'sharing a similar culture' (e.g. Axelrod, 1995).

Agent-Group-Role Model A well-known framework for the explicit representation of organizational structures is the *agent-group-role* (AGR) model by Ferber and Gutknecht (1998). It describes an infrastructure that allows agents to dynamically found, disband, join, and leave groups in a virtual environment. Within groups, agents can play roles that represent their organizational positions, specific abilities, or responsibilities. As an example, several agents

---

[7]In particular such "model-artifacts" are artificial causal dependencies due to the serialization of originally concurrent actions.

[8]see also Page and Kreutzer (2005, p. 354)

might enact the role 'professor' in the group 'University of Hamburg'. Groups and roles allow agents to reference others in an indirect or "deictic" (Klügl, 2000, p. 64) way, e.g. 'the professor who teaches my computer science course at the University of Hamburg'. Extensions of the AGR model towards spatial constructs (places, locations, and paths) are described by Rupert et al. (2007).

FIPA Standard   Another common (but more technical) model is the communication and platform infrastructure defined in the *FIPA*[9] standard. Following our review in (Page and Kreutzer, 2005, p. 360):

> "This standard defines an agent communication language (ACL), as well as a platform architecture consisting of an agent communication channel (ACC) and two special agents called AMS (Agent Management System) and DF (Directory Facilitator) (see e.g. Rölke, 2004, pp. 87). By registering and de-registering agents with a unique identifier, the AMS provides so-called "white page services". The DF manages the agents' service descriptions [which are roughly comparable to roles in the AGR model] ("yellow page services"). The internal agent architecture is not part of the FIPA standard."

The ACL is a standardized message format for agent communication specified in (FIPA, 2002b): A FIPA ACL message contains a number of attributes including message type (*performative*), sender, receiver, and content. The performative indicates the intention pursued by sending the message. It can be chosen from a set of standardized *communicative acts* such as `request` or `propose` (FIPA, 2002a).[10]   The content can be specified in an arbitrary format, but the FIPA advocates the use of certain knowledge representation languages including SL (semantic language), RDF (resource description framework), and KIF (knowledge interchange format, see FIPA, 2005).

An ACL message can include further optional attributes for self-description and communication control (FIPA, 2002b): The former comprises information on the `language` (e.g. SL) and `ontology` (i.e. the domain-specific terminology) of the content. The latter includes the attributes `reply-with` and `in-reply-to` to identify threads of related messages that were sent in reply to each other as well as `conversation-id` and `protocol-id` to identify the conversation and the protocol that a message belongs to. The FIPA specifies a number of standardized protocols for common interaction types (mainly auctions or negotiations, see FIPA, 2005). Due to their representation in AgentUML, a detailed description is deferred to Section 3.3.2.1.

Implicit versus Explicit Organization   Organizational structures (e.g. groups and roles) and processes (e.g. interaction protocols) in MABS are either pre-defined by the modeler or emerge from local interactions during the simulation (see Ferber, 1995, p. 114 cited in Page and Kreutzer, 2005, p. 355). As in reality, a combination of both approaches is found most often: We might e.g. pre-define a set of basic interaction protocol classes. However, the agents' actual execution and combination of these protocols into cooperative tasks might not be predictable from the (static) specification but can only be observed at runtime.

---

[9]Foundation for Physical Intelligent Agents (FIPA, 2005)

[10]The idea of communicative acts is based on the *speech act theory* by Searle (1974), in which communication is understood as a specific form of action.

The analysis of implicit organizational patterns is challenging because (a) the patterns are often hidden in the data observed during simulation, and (b) an automated analysis is complicated by the fact that many organizational concepts cannot be straightforwardly reduced to simple quantitative measures. This topic is further discussed in Section 3.5.

3.2.2.3. Spatial Environment

A spatial environment is a central component of many MABS. In most cases, it represents a 'real' spatial topology, e.g. a landscape in an ecological model or a traffic network in logistic simulation. As mentioned above, some social simulations also visualize more abstract concepts like group formation by means of the agents' spatial distribution. The presentation in this section is in particular influenced by the view on spatial modeling described by Meyer, 2008 and implemented in our MABS framework *FAMOS* (Knaak, 2002; Knaak et al., 2002; Meyer, 2008; see also Section 3.4.4).

Spatial Structures Several spatial models are employed in MABS (e.g. Gilbert and Troitzsch, 1999; Meyer, 2008): A common representation is a two-dimensional grid consisting of rectangular cells. Other regular (e.g. hexagons) and irregular cell shapes (e.g. Voronoi tesselations), or higher dimensional grids are less frequently used. Grid-based models include a *neighborhood relation* that determines which neighboring cells an agent can reach from a certain position. As in cellular automata, this relation is often defined homogeneously on the whole grid.

A more flexible alternative are graph-based models that consist of nodes representing locations and edges representing (un)directed connections between locations (Meyer, 2001). Graphs are well suited to model heterogeneous topologies in logistics (road networks, see Page and Kreutzer, 2005, p. 357 and Meyer, 2001), telecommunications (communication networks), and abstract sociological models (social networks). Arbitrary grid-based models can be mapped to graphs by associating nodes with centers of grid cells and edges with (possibly heterogeneous) neighborhood relations (Meyer, 2001).

A less common alternative are continuous spatial models, that are e.g. used in pedestrian simulation. An example is the simulation of aircraft boarding and deplaning processes described by Matzen and Czogalla (2003).

Dynamics of the Environment The most obvious environmental dynamics result from the agents' movements. Depending on the modeled domain, different movement strategies are employed (see Meyer, 2008; Page and Kreutzer, 2005, p. 357): The most common are *random walk* as a simple exploration strategy, *following gradient fields* (e.g. simulated pheromone trails in ant foraging), and movement along previously planned *routes*.

Agents must be able to sense and modify other agents or objects in the environment. This is often constrained by an (individual) perception and action range to represent behavioral locality. Depending on the model's purpose, restrictions on spatial resources (e.g. the number of agents that 'fit' on a grid cell) are considered as well. The environment can exhibit an additional dynamic that is caused by environmental processes modeled in a more abstract fashion (e.g. as cellular automata). An example stated in (Page and Kreutzer, 2005, p. 357) is the re-growth of 'sugar' resources in the well-known *Sugar Scape* model by Epstein and Axtell (1996)

As indicated in Section 3.1.1.1 interactions between an agent and its environment are often modeled similar to interactions between agents (e.g. using message passing). This leads to a view on the environment as a particular agent (Klügl, 2000, pp. 103), which is a common 'workaround' if agents are the only available modeling construct. It should, however, be avoided in favour of more specific means to model objects and environments (Page and Kreutzer, 2005, p. 355).

3.2.3. Comparison with other Simulation World Views

To complete the introduction to MABS, we briefly compare it to related simulation world views. The structure and content of this Section is largely adopted from (Page and Kreutzer, 2005, Ch. 11.4.4) co-written by and based on the diploma thesis (Knaak, 2002, Sec. 3.2.1) of the author. The presentation complements the treatment in (Klügl, 2001, pp. 27,45,61,84) with a stronger focus on discrete event simulation.

3.2.3.1. Event-Oriented Simulation versus MABS

The event-oriented world view mirrors the implementation of event-driven scheduling. Though this is an appropriate technical basis for MABS (see Section 3.2.2.1), the concepts of event-oriented modeling as described in Section 2.2.2 contradict the agent metaphor in two respects (see Page and Kreutzer, 2005, p. 351 and Knaak, 2002, p. 29): Firstly, events are often defined on a level above individual agents, which contradicts the microscopic modeling perspective. Secondly, entities are regarded as passive elements which state is modified by events 'from the outside'. This obviously contradicts the concept of autonomy.

However, Page and Kreutzer (2005, p. 351) note that:[11]

> "Some authors like Spaniol and Hoff (1995) [...] view event-orientation differently, and attach no event routines to events. Instead, events are processed by *active entities*, which contain the event's relevant actions. Each entity groups state changing actions for all events in which it participates and performs these on demand; i.e. whenever relevant events occur. This viewpoint matches agent-based modeling frameworks much better. It offers an efficient base for controlling a set of simulated agents' behaviour and is instantiated in some software systems, such as [the well-known MABS framework] *Swarm* [Minar et al., 1996 ...] It should be noted that in this context agents act only if an external event occurs, or if a relevant event has been triggered by the agent itself. Between events the agents' states remain constant."

3.2.3.2. Process-Oriented Simulation versus MABS

Further following Page and Kreutzer (2005, p. 352)[12], we find that

---

[11]based on (Knaak, 2002, p. 29)
[12]again based on (Knaak, 2002, pp. 29)

"A simulation *process* is an active and persistent entity, whose behaviour is described from a local perspective [...] Although the agent concept is somewhat more general, it fits a process-based simulation's world view quite well (Klügl, 2001, p. 94). Inter-process communications occur either through direct or indirect synchronizations; i.e. processes are delayed in their lifecycles and must wait until reactivated, or they must queue for a resource. Patterns of communication in agent-based models can be richer. Some MABS models may even require negotiations according to complex protocols.

The behavioural flexibility of simulation processes, in whose lifecyles a linear sequence of actions unfolds in a synchronous fashion, also falls short of some MABS models' requirements. Agents may be placed in highly dynamic environments and must react quickly to asynchronous events. Different from the process interaction world view, spatial location often also plays an important role in MABS. Simulation processes should therefore be viewed as particularly simple, pro-active agents, with limited capabilities for communication and movement."

On two occasions, the author was pointed to the fact that the original process-oriented simulation language *Simula* with its extension library *DEMOS* (Birtwistle, 1979) can be regarded as a predecessor of MABS due to its innovative concepts of co-routines and object-orientation.[13]

3.2.3.3. Individual-Based Simulation versus MABS

This umbrella term subsumes simulation world views that take up the microscopic modeling perspective of individual entities.[14] According to Klügl (2000, Sec. 3.2) this includes some process- and object-oriented models as well as cellular automata and so-called microanalytical models[15]. Though most agent-based models can be regarded as indvidual-based, the following differences must be mentioned as summarized by Klügl (2000, pp. 61):

- Agent-based modeling is more general in that the agent metaphor is not restricted to individuals (Klügl, 2000, p. 61). Depending on the modeling level, groups or organizations can be modeled as agents as well (Klügl, 2000, p. 61).

- Agent-based models are often more complex and heterogeneous than individual-based models with respect to behavioral and spatial modeling (Klügl, 2000, p. 62). AI methods for learning and planning are usually not found in individual-based models either.

Nevertheless the distinction between individual and agent-based models is not clear-cut, and both modeling styles apply to similar domains, such as sociology and biology.

3.2.3.4. Activity- and Transaction-Oriented Simulation versus MABS

As mentioned in Section 2.2.2 an activity-oriented model is stated as a set of rules that describe pre- and post-conditions of time-consuming activities, which is also common in MABS. Klügl

---

[13]This relation was pointed out by Prof. Dr. Horst Oberquelle at the University of Hamburg as well as a reviewer of the author's contribution (Knaak, 2004) to the Fujaba Days 2004.

[14]A comparison of agent- and individual-based modeling is also found in (Klügl, 2000; Knaak, 2002; Meyer, 2008).

[15]This model type will not be treated here. For a summary see Klügl (2000, pp. 45)

(2000, pp. 112-113) explicitly relates her (time-driven) activity-based MABS modeling approach to activity-oriented modeling. Besides the different scheduling approach (Klügl, 2000, p. 113), a main distinction between both world views is that rules in activity-based models are specified at the system level, while rules in MABS are assigned to specific agents. This provides an additional object-oriented structure to the rule set (Klügl, 2000, p. 109).

A comparison of MABS and transaction-oriented models is not reasonable in the first place. Both world views differ strongly with respect to the modeling perspective and target systems. However, some application domains imply a combination of both approaches. A prominent example are so-called 'holonic factories', i.e. production systems without central control, where each machine (or even workpiece) is regarded as an autonomous agent responsible for its own processing (see e.g. Giret and Botti, 2009). In this scenario, the factory layout and the processing of workpieces can be modeled in a transaction-oriented fashion, while a controller agent is assigned to each machine. The transaction-oriented model can thus be regarded as part of the MABS's environment.

3.3. Modeling Techniques for Agent-Based Simulation

Appropriate modeling techniques are an important means to handle the complexity of MA(B)S. While declarative modeling might still be the most common paradigm, descriptions based on UML or Petri nets provide better means to represent the processes running in a MABS. In the following, these modeling techniques are introduced and compared with respect to their ability to handle the complexity of agent-based models.

3.3.1. Declarative Modeling

Declarative (rule-based) models are a traditional logic-based representation in AI. We briefly introduce the foundations of this paradigm and review its advantages and disadvantages for MABS. The presentation follows Luger (2002), Klügl (2000), and our summary in (Page and Kreutzer, 2005, Sec. 11.4.4.1 based on Knaak, 2002, Sec. 4.1).

3.3.1.1. Rule-Based Production Systems

A rule-based system (also called *production system*) consists of a rule-base containing rules and a knowledge-base containing facts (Ferber, 1995, p. 134). Each rule has a condition and an action part (Klügl, 2000, p. 53): The condition is checked with respect to the facts in the knowledge-base. If it holds, the rule becomes *activated* and the action can be executed. This causes modifications of the knowledge-base as well as possible side-effects if the production system is embedded into an environment.

Rules are specified in several formal languages (Ferber, 1995, p. 134) ranging from simple programmatic if-then clauses to declarative languages based on propositional or predicate logic (e.g. *Prolog*, Bratko, 1990). Subsymbolic descriptions are employed in adaptive rule-based *classifier systems* (see e.g. Holland et al., 2000; Ferber, 1995, p. 135). The execution of rules is guided by a rule interpreter (sometimes called *reasoning engine*) that defines an execution order for the subsequent or parallel activation of multiple rules (Luger, 2002, cited in Klügl, 2000, p. 53).[16]

The reasoning process can be either data-driven (forward chaining) or goal-driven (backward chaining); see (Klügl, 2000, p. 55). Clearly, forward chaining is an appropriate strategy for reactive agents while backward chaining is a basis for planning (Klügl, 2000, p. 55).

3.3.1.2. Advantages and Drawbacks of Declarative Modeling

According to Klügl (2000, p. 52), a main advantage of declarative modeling is the separation of the model specification from the execution logic encapsulated in the rule interpreter. The high abstraction level is further ensured by the fact that many rule-based languages provide powerful programming constructs including unification and pattern matching (Klügl, 2000, p. 54). Another advantage of rule-based models is their inherent modularization at the rule-level (Klügl, 2000, p. 56): Since rules can only invoke each other indirectly through modifications of the knowledge base, easy changeability and extensibility is ensured.

However, according to Klügl (2000, p. 57), these properties also lead to drawbacks. Due to the indirect coupling of rules it is not straightforward to model sequences of actions (Klügl, 2000, p. 57). If the modeling and execution environment provides no structuring concepts above rules, larger models become hard to understand (Klügl, 2000, p. 57). Furthermore, the performance of execution might suffer from the need to check a large rule set in every execution cycle when no additional structure of the rule base is available (Klügl, 2000, p. 57).

3.3.1.3. Agent-Based Structuring of Rule-Based Models

Klügl (2000, Sec. 5.3.1) presents different approaches to partition a rule set in MABS. A basic distinction is drawn between horizontal and vertical partitioning (Klügl, 2000, p. 110): Horizontal partitioning is oriented towards "functional categories", i.e. rules related to the same task, role, target object, etc. (Klügl, 2000, p. 110). Vertical partitioning bundles rules that belong to the same phase of the rule interpreter's execution cycle, e.g. 'sense, reason, and act' in case of an agent (Klügl, 2000, p. 110).

Activity Automata The agent-based world view suggests an obvious structure by partitioning the overall rule set into different subsets for each (type of) agent (Klügl, 2000, p. 109). However, since the rule set of an agent can become rather large, additional structuring means are proposed. The approach by Klügl (2000, pp. 114) partitions rules by *similar preconditions*. This leads to (possibly hierarchical) automata-like structures – called *activity automata* in (Klügl, 2000, p. 115) – where each state represents a set of common pre-conditions for all assigned rules.

---

[16]Klügl (2000, p. 53) actually cites a previous edition of (Luger, 2002).

Agent Architectures Many agent architectures provide additional means to partition an agent's rule and knowledge base.[17] One example is the *subsumption architecture* by Brooks (1999) shown in Figure 3.3. In this reactive architecture the agent's behaviour is modularized into a number of distinct tasks, where each module is described by a set of stimulus-response rules or an automaton. The modules are ordered hierarchically according to their priority. When a rule of a lower level module becomes activated, it immediately inhibits all rules of higher level modules until the agent's survival has been ensured.

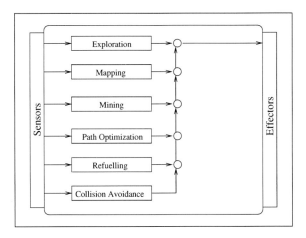

Figure 3.3.: "Schematic representation of a subsumption architecture for controlling an ore mining robot (adopted with modifications from Ferber, 1995, pp. 132)". Figure and caption cited from (Page and Kreutzer, 2005, p. 345), also found in (Knaak, 2002).

A partitioning for the knowledge base is accomplished by the well-known deliberative *Belief-Desire-Intention (BDI) architecture* (e.g. reviewed in Klügl, 2000, pp. 22; Wooldridge, 2003, pp. 82; Wooldridge, 1999; Page and Kreutzer, 2005, pp. 345 based on Knaak, 2002): As the name indicates, the set of facts is divided into three categories called beliefs, desires, and intentions. Beliefs represent the agent's (individual and possibly erroneous) knowledge about the current state of the environment (Klügl, 2000, p. 22). Desires represent future states that the agent strives to achieve in general (Klügl, 2000, p. 101). As in reality, an agent's different desires can, to a certain degree, contradict each other, which is finally resolved by the rule interpreter (see Wooldridge, 1999, cited in Page and Kreutzer, 2005, p. 346). In every execution cycle, the BDI interpreter refines a set of non-contradictory desires into actual intentions, whose assertion into the knowledge base triggers the execution of a related plan for their achievement (see Wooldridge, 1999, cited in Page and Kreutzer, 2005, p. 346).

---

[17]The subsumption and BDI architectures presented in the following might be two of the most typical agent architectures. Therefore they are often selected as examples in the literature (e.g. in Braubach, 2007 and Page and Kreutzer, 2005, pp. 344).

3.3.2. UML-Based Modeling

Though declarative formalisms can be used to describe several structural and behavioural aspects of agent-based models, the rule-based representation is strongly tailored towards one *modeling perspective*, i.e. behaviour descriptions of entities like simulated agents or other active model components. UML diagrams, in contrast, provide more specific means to represent and visualize multiple model aspects, including structure, individual behaviour, and interactions (see Section 2.3.1).

Due to the close relation between agents and objects (see Section 3.1.1.1) the idea to establish the mature and wide-spread UML as a standard modeling technique for agent-based simulations seems plausible (see e.g. Oechslein et al., 2001; Page and Kreutzer, 2005, p. 359). Nevertheless, extensions are necessary for those agent-specific concepts not covered in object-orientation. The following sections review relevant attempts towards this endeavor.

3.3.2.1. AgentUML

AgentUML (or AUML, Odell et al., 2000) is an early and well-accepted attempt to extend a subset of UML 1.x diagrams for agent modeling. It was adopted by the FIPA to model standardized interaction protocol templates (see Section 3.2.2.2). However, since many of the proposed extensions are nowadays covered by the standard UML (especially version 2.x), the further development of AUML has been discontinued recently (AgentUML, 2007).

The extensions provided by AUML focus on protocol modeling and (to a lesser extent) structural modeling with extended class diagrams (AgentUML, 2007). Odell et al. (2000) present a layered approach towards modeling interaction protocols with sequence, statechart, and activity diagrams. The main intention is to provide a means to visualize parameterizable interaction protocol patterns that can be re-used for and adapted to different domains.

At the highest specification level, AUML introduces protocol packages that contain extended UML sequence diagrams for the modeled interactions (Odell et al., 2000, p. 4).[18] These are re-usable templates that can be parameterized with domain-specific interaction roles, message types, and deadlines using the standard UML template syntax (Odell et al., 2000, p. 5).

The second layer covers the actual agent interactions. It includes extended UML 1.x sequence diagrams to model roles as well as "concurrent threads of interaction" (Odell et al., 2000, p. 6). These diagrams form the most prominent part of AUML.

The first extension enables *n:m*-relations between agents and roles, i.e. an agent (type) can change its role during a communication and a role can be covered by multiple (types of) agents. Different from standard UML, lifelines are identified by a term *agentName/role : agentType* where name and role are optional (Odell et al., 2000, p. 6). Role changes can be depicted in several different forms shown in (Odell et al., 2000, pp. 11).

The second major extension is the addition of control-flow constructs including 'and', 'or', and 'exclusive or' split and join nodes (Odell et al., 2000, p. 6). Different from UML sequence

---

[18]page numbers relate to the version of the article downloadable at http://www.jamesodell.com/ ExtendingUML.pdf (last visit 2012-09-15)

diagrams, the AUML variant can not only display exemplary courses of interaction, but also depict protocol templates with branches, multiple threads (concurrency), and cycles.

According to Odell et al. (2000, pp. 6), control flow nodes can be inserted along the lifeline of an agent to indicate conditional or concurrent processing. Furthermore, it is possible to connect message arrows with these nodes to display conditional or concurrent sending and reception of messages. It is not necessary to re-join multiple concurrent or conditional messages on the receiver's lifeline. Horizontally or vertically stacked activation bars can be used instead. Cabac et al. (2003, p. 114) notes that some of these possibilities prohibit to provide the diagrams with a concise formal semantics (for details see Section 3.3.3.3). Figure 3.4 shows an example AUML sequence diagram.

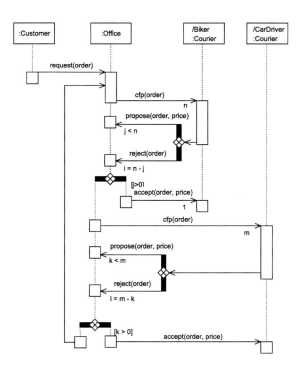

Figure 3.4.: An example AUML interaction diagram showing a simplified version of the 'contract net'-like order mediation protocol used in our agent-based simulations of city courier services described in Chapter 8. The diagram was drawn with the Agent Interaction Protocol Diagram editor of the CAPA agent platform (see Section 3.4.5).

As a further extension, *cardinalities* and related constraints can be added to the message arrows of the diagram in order to display multicast communication. Cardinality constraints are stated as arbitrary terms over message cardinalities. The example in Figure 3.4 e.g. states that the *office* agent broadcasts n call-for-proposal messages to the registered *courier* agents. These either reply by proposing an abstract price or by refusing the call. The number of propose and refuse messages adds up to n, i.e. *courier* agents *always* answer in this protocol variant.[19] In addition, deadlines can be added to the diagram using the UML note symbol (Odell et al., 2000, p. 3). They often serve to indicate when an agent will stop waiting for answers to its last message and pro-actively continue its processing.

The third layer of AUML represents the internal processing of agents, i.e. the refinement of the sequence diagrams' activation bars into state chart or activity diagrams (Odell et al., 2000, Sec. 6). The only extension proposed in this context is a proprietary notation for sending and receiving messages in activity diagrams (Odell et al., 2000, p. 9). Odell et al. (2000, pp. 8) show that both diagram types can also be employed to model interaction protocols on level 2. However, the authors prefer the agent-centric view of sequence diagrams over the state-centric view of statecharts for protocol modeling (Odell et al., 2000, p. 9). Statecharts are understood as an additional "constraint mechanism" to ensure that the overall protocol performs correct state transition (Odell et al., 2000, p. 9).

A very preliminary specification by the FIPA (2003) proposes additional AUML extensions for class diagrams. An *agent class diagram* is introduced as a UML class diagram with several extended classifiers. The stereotype «agent» indicates an agent class with compartments for roles (the agent can play), organisations (the agent is part of), and protocols (the agent can execute) (FIPA, 2003, p. 3).

An agent class can be associated further stereotyped classifiers that represent agent concepts. A *capability* describes "what an agent is able to do under what circumstances" (FIPA, 2003, p. 4). A *service description* defines a provided service in terms of the related protocols, ontology, communication language, and context language (FIPA, 2003, pp. 5).

3.3.2.2. SeSAm UML

Oechslein et al. (2001) propose extensions of UML 1.x for MABS. The main focus lies on extended activity diagrams, called *activity graphs*, that are partly inspired by features of activity automata (see Section 3.3.1.3) proposed by Klügl (2000). Since activity graphs can be designed and executed in the SeSAm simulation system (see Section 3.4.3), the UML dialect is called *SeSAm UML* (Oechslein, 2004).

SeSAm UML builds upon UML 1.3, where activity diagrams already include send and receive signal as well as object nodes. The proposed extensions focus on means to model different patterns of agent interaction including *exchange of resources, agent creation, modification of shared state variables*, and *direct communication via messages* (Oechslein, 2004, p. 86).

The activity graph notation supported by the SeSAm tool provides further extensions. This includes (1) a proprietary *time symbol* indicating that an activity consumes a certain amount of simulation time, (2) an *emergency node* with associated *emergency rules*, the activation of which causes the agent to terminate its current activity and enter an exception handling procedure, and (3) an *activity graph node* that contains a subgraph to support hierarchical modeling (Oechslein, 2004, p. 129).

Beyond activity graphs, SeSAm UML also includes minor extensions to UML class diagrams. These are mainly stereotypes to tag the different components of a MABS (see Section 3.2.2)

---

[19]different from the actual courier service model described in Chapter 8

such as «agent», «world», or «resource» (Oechslein, 2004, p. 78). An agent class includes compartments to display state variables, behaviours, and assertions (i.e. invariants, pre-, and post conditions) stated in OCL (Oechslein, 2004, p. 79).

SeSAm UML contains many of the features of UML 2 that are rated as useful for (discrete event) simulation by Knaak and Page (2006). Different from the standard, SeSAm UML has a *time-driven* execution semantics specified in a formal language named *SeSAm-Impl*. Due to its partial deviations from the current UML standard and its extension mechanisms, SeSAm UML is at the moment exclusively supported by the SeSAm tool and cannot extend other CASE tools as a UML profile.

3.3.2.3. Application and Extension of UML 2

While Agent UML is based on UML 1.x, Bauer and Odell (2005) discuss applications of the follower version UML 2 to the modeling of agents and MAS. The authors also identify a need to extend UML 2 with better support for agent-specific concepts. This includes "constructs to express: goals, agents, groups, multicasting, generative functions, such as cloning, birthing, reproduction, parasitism and symbiosis, emergent phenomena, and many other nature-based constructs ..." (Bauer and Odell, 2005, p. 19).[20] In the following we provide a brief overview of their applications and extensions of UML 2 for agent-based modeling. Similar to the original the presentation mirrors the UML-inherent classification into structure, behavior, and interaction diagrams.

Structure diagrams: As reviewed in (Page and Kreutzer, 2005, p. 359), "*class diagrams* can be employed to model agent organizations and ontologies; i.e. the domain-dependent parts of an agent communication language (Bauer and Odell, 2005, p. 5)." *Stereotypes* tag specific constructs such as agents or groups (Bauer and Odell, 2005, p. 8). Using the inheritance arrow, hierarchies of concepts like goals, tasks, or roles can be depicted. Object diagrams serve to display the state of agents or communicative acts at runtime (Bauer and Odell, 2005, p. 6).

Further focus is put on *composite structure diagrams*, a new diagran type to display "organizations and dependencies among components" (Bauer and Odell, 2005, p. 7). It is shown how these diagrams can be used to display collaborations between and within groups, roles, and workflows of an organization (Bauer and Odell, 2005, p. 7). However, the possibilities do not seem to differ substantially from former use case and collaboration diagrams.

Behavior diagrams: In OOSE, *use case diagrams* serve to display requirements on a software system in terms of intended use cases, (sub-)system boundaries and external actors (Bauer and Odell, 2005, p. 10–11). Plain, undirected associations describe relations between use cases and actors. For the application of these diagrams in agent-based modeling, Bauer and Odell (2005, p. 11) propose some extensions and a redefinition: Firstly, associations between external actors and use cases can be directed and inscribed with event types, names of providing (internal) agents, and multiplicities. Secondly, the actor symbol is not only used for external entities interacting with the system but also for agents as parts of the modeled MAS. This redefinition

---

[20]page numbers relate to the version of the article downloadable at `http://www.jamesodell.com/` `EAAI-Bauer-Odell.pdf` (last visit 2012-09-15)

of the original UML semantic is due to the generality of the agent concept. It is also implicitly stated in the context of discrete event simulation by Knaak and Page (2006, p. 36).

As mentioned in (Page and Kreutzer, 2005, p. 360):

> "*Statecharts*: [...] can be used to model reactive agents' state-dependent responses to message or signal reception. They are also used occasionally to represent protocols or agents' reactive plans (Bauer and Odell, 2005, p. 14). [...] Since they focus on how agents react to asynchronous events, statecharts might be better suited for modelling reactive agents than activity diagrams.

> *Activity diagrams* [...] model an agent's tasks; i.e. its plans or protocols (Bauer and Odell, 2005, p. 13). Patterns of synchronization between concurrent tasks performed by different agents, or within the same agent, can be modelled using synchronization bars or send and receive signal actions."

Interaction Diagrams: According to Bauer and Odell (2005, p. 15), *sequence diagrams* are the most prominent interaction diagram type in agent-based modeling. The authors mainly focus on the differences between the UML 2 notation for (high level) sequence diagrams and the UML 1.x-based AgentUML interaction diagrams. To their conclusion, the UML 2 notation includes all control flow patterns from AgentUML and adds advanced constructs such as critical fragments (Bauer and Odell, 2005, p. 15). Note that UML 2 sequence diagrams are strictly block-structured, while AgentUML allows to connect elements more freely. As described in Section 3.3.2.1 the latter can lead to unclear semantics.

To compensate the drawback that roles, multicast communication, and constraints on message cardinalities remain unsupported in UML 2, the authors – broadly speaking – propose to transfer the respective AgentUML extensions to the new notation (Bauer and Odell, 2005, p. 15). The different appearance of UML 2 and AgentUML is visualized by the example of the FIPA contract net protocol which is cited in Figure 3.5. The block-structured UML 2 notation might appear less readable due to visually overlapping message arrows and interaction fragments (Bauer and Odell, 2005, p. 17; see also the review in Page and Kreutzer, 2005, p. 360).

Communication diagrams are rated less useful for agent based modeling due to their limited control flow constructs (Bauer and Odell, 2005, p. 16). The authors propose to apply the aforementioned extensions for roles and multicast communication to this diagram type as well. In this case, each node in a communication diagram corresponds to a role and role changes are indicated by connecting nodes with a stereotyped dashed arrow.

A more powerful diagram type for agent-based modeling are interaction overview diagrams, i.e. activity diagrams with sequence diagrams embedded in the activity nodes (Bauer and Odell, 2005, p. 17). The authors emphasize the improved visual clearness compared to UML 2 interaction diagrams when it comes to displaying protocols with complex control flow (Bauer and Odell, 2005, p. 17). Note that these diagrams are especially suitable to display hierarchical protocols where a number of basic interaction patterns (displayed in the activity nodes) are embedded into a larger (multi-agent) workflow.

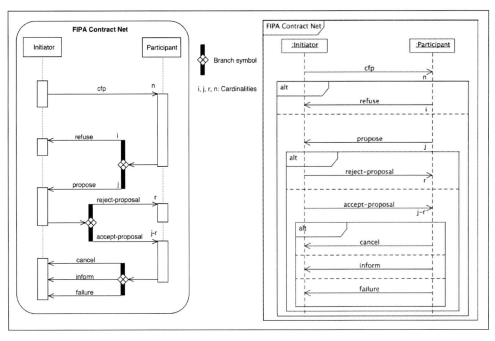

Figure 3.5.: "An example for modelling agent interaction protocols with AUML (left) and UML 2 (right). Both diagrams show the popular *Contract Net* protocol for distributed task allocation (adopted with modifications from Bauer and Odell, 2005, p. 16)." Figure and caption adopted from Page and Kreutzer (2005, p. 359).

3.3.3. Petri Nets and Mulan

Beyond the application of UML as a visual modeling technique for MA(B)S, Petri net-based approaches strive to provide a concise semantic for agent-based models which, among other advantages, leads to executable models. Rölke (2004, Ch. 5) presents an overview of several approaches to model (parts of) MAS by means of Petri nets. He furthermore introduces the MULAN architecture that also builds a formal basis for the integration of MABS and process mining in this thesis.

In the following the MULAN architecture and its aplications to AOSE as well as its suitability for MABS are reviewed. It is also compared to a recent approach by Stuit et al. (2007b) that has been mentioned in the context of process mining in the literature.

3.3.3.1. MULti Agent Nets

The MULAN architecture was developed in the dissertation by Heiko Rölke (2004) at the University of Hamburg's Department of Informatics. The main intention is to employ reference nets to model agents and multi agent systems. Especially the concept of nets-within-nets is used to "describe the natural hierarchies in an agent system" (Duvigneau et al., 2003, p. 62).

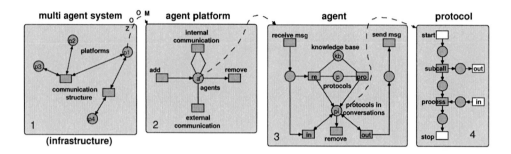

Figure 3.6.: Overview of the MULAN architecture (adopted from Rölke, 2004, as cited in Cabac et al., 2006c, p. 14).

As indicated in Figure 3.6, the MULAN architecture consists of four levels, i.e. protocol, agent, platform, and multi-agent system. Entities on all levels are modeled as nets with Java inscriptions and connected through token refinement (see Section 2.3.2.5). This means that entities of a higher level (e.g. platforms) contain entities of the next lower level (e.g. agents) as tokens.

Agent Level   According to Cabac et al. (2008a, p. 39), a MULAN agent consists of a main *agent net* and several sub-components: *protocols, decision components*, a *knowledge base*, and a *protocol factory*. The agent net represents the agent's interface to the environment. Since all agent interaction in MULAN is message-based (Duvigneau et al., 2003, p. 62), the net contains two transitions with synchronous channels :send() and :receive() that are employed to exchange messages with other agents via the platform.

For the sake of adaptivity, the behaviour of an agent is not modeled statically in the agent net but by means of distinct *protocols* which can be dynamically created and removed (Rölke, 2004, pp. 112). Each protocol is a workflow-like net (template) that describes a task or plan the agent can execute. Protocol nets are instantiated either as a reaction to messages or proactively triggered by agent-internal events. Active protocol instances reside on a certain place of the agent net from which they are removed when the protocol terminates.

Protocol instantiation is executed by the knowledge base and the protocol factory: The knowledge base contains facts that map message types to handler protocols. When the agent receives a new message, it first checks if this message belongs to a conversation lead by an already active protocol instance.[21] If the message does not belong to an active protocol, the knowledge base is queried for a protocol matching the type of the new message. The corresponding net token is added to the place for active protocols and the protocol is started.

Besides mappings between trigger messages and protocols, the knowledge base can contain further facts reresenting the knowledge of an agent. This includes pro-active triggers for protocol instantiation as well as further knowledge used by active protocols. Note that besides the basic net structure and the synchronous channels used for communication, MULAN poses no

---

[21]The FIPA-ACL tag in-reply-to is used to store this information. The tag conversation-id is currently not used in MULAN.

restrictions on the particular design of agent net, knowledge base, and protocol factory, which allows for implementations with different complexity (for the knowledge base see e.g. Rölke, 2004, pp. 150).

Protocols and Decision Components Protocols model the behaviour of agents. Different from a common use of the term to describe the course of an *interaction*, a MULAN protocol represents the behaviour of a *single* agent (role) during an interaction (Cabac et al., 2008a, p. 39). Different types of protocols and supportive constructs are distinguished (see Rölke, 2004, Sec. 6.3; Cabac et al., 2008a, pp. 39):

- (elementary) protocol nets,

- subnets and decision components,

- higher order protocols,

- meta-protocols.

A *protocol net* describes a plan to perform a task (e.g. Cabac, 2010, pp. 58): Protocols can be arbitrary reference nets that respect the channel names of the agent net for communication and knowledge base access. There must be a single start point in the form of a transition with an uplink :start() and it is generally recommended to use a workflow net-like structure with a single end point and without 'dead' transitions.

To improve readability and convenience of modeling, Cabac et al. (2003) introduced a set of standardized net components (see Section 2.3.2.6) for protocols. These include common constructs to model control flow and interactions quite similar to AgentUML sequence or UML 2 activity diagrams. As shown in Figure 3.7, each component is given a concise semantic by the contained net elements. To ease the understandability of the resulting models, data flow-related aspects are not covered by the components. Rölke (2004, p. 152) recommends to store only local data within protocol nets, while data between different protocols must be exchanged via message passing or the agent's knowledge base.

For this reason it is not advisable to model all aspects of an agent's behaviour as protocols. Supportive sub-routines can be modeled as arbitrary *subnets* that exchange data with the calling protocol net directly via synchronous channels (Rölke, 2004, p. 136). A net component *SubCall* standardizes the communication between protocols and subnets (Rölke, 2004, pp. 135). Specific subroutines that encapsulate algorithms for decision making are called *decision components* (DCs, Cabac et al., 2008a, p. 40). These also serve as interfaces to "external tools or legacy code as well as a graphical user interface" (Cabac et al., 2008a, p. 40). There is a set of net components to model DCs and their communication with protocol nets.

Elementary protocol nets are re-usable behavior modules that can be composed to larger workflows by *higher order protocols*. These are nets that take other protocols as parameters and link their control flow in a certain way, e.g. by sequential, concurrent, conditional, or iterated execution (Rölke, 2004, p. 137). While elementary protocols are identified in the knowledge base by the name of the protocol net, higher order protocols are denoted by a parameterized protocol descriptor. As an example, XOR(p1,p2) might describe a higher-order protocol XOR for the exclusive-or execution of two protocols p1 and p2 (Rölke, 2004, p. 142).

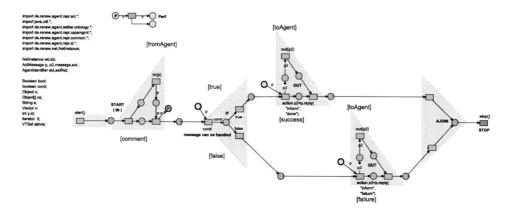

Figure 3.7.: A simple protocol net with components for protocol start, message sending, message reception, exclusive-or split, and merge. The net only serves for demonstration and was therefore not refined into an implementation.

Specific higher order protocols that ease the modeling of adaptivity are called *meta protocols* (Rölke, 2004, p. 142). While higher order protocols normally just impose a certain order on the execution of multiple elementary protocols, meta protocols can additionally "influence the [internal] control flow of the passed (complex) protocols" (Rölke, 2004, p. 142). As an example, Rölke (2004, p. 143) shows a protocol that adopts a new protocol sent in a message into the knowledge base if the corresponding descriptor is not already known to the agent.

Platform Level As indicated in Figure 3.6 a MULAN platform hosts references to a number of agents on a dedicated place (Rölke, 2004, p. 158). Its main purpose is to provide the inhabiting agents with an infrastructure for communication. This includes internal message passing between agents on one platform as well as external communication with agents on other connected platforms (Rölke, 2004, p. 164). Further responsibilities of the platform are lifecycle management (especially creation and deletion of agents), mediation of services, and support for agent migration (Rölke, 2004, p. 159,161).

Rölke (2004, p. 197) notes that "MULAN was modelled 'in the spirit of' the FIPA specifications. This means that MULAN nets are not sufficient to be completely compatible to the specification. However, no specification is violated either." Therefore, agent management and service mediation on a MULAN platform are carried out by two dedicated agents *AMS* and *DF*. Both are standard MULAN agents that possess specific protocols to perform their tasks like the registration of a new agent (AMS) or the resolution of a service description (DF) (Rölke, 2004, pp. 175).

An important concept in MULAN is the analogy between platforms and agents (Rölke, 2004, pp. 181): The behavior of an agent is constituted by its active protocols, and the behavior of a platform is realized by its inhabiting agents (see also Cabac et al., 2006b, Sec. 2.2). This leads to a hierarchical view of agents as platforms that host a number of (simpler) agents as 'protocols'. On the other hand, platforms are agents that communicate via message passing with other platforms within a multi agent system. This analogy allows for arbitrary hierarchies of nested agent systems.

Rölke (2004, pp. 183) claims that using the concept of an agent as the *only* abstraction offers several advantages. However, he admits that the four-level hierarchy of the MULAN architecture has proven to be easier understandable than the more abstract concept that "everything is an agent" (Rölke, 2004, p. 181). In the fully FIPA-compliant MULAN implementation CAPA (see Section 3.4.5), the platform is nevertheless realized as an agent. This simplifies the (message-based) communication between platform and AMS agent and allows for a hierarchical embedding of platforms (Rölke, 2004, p. 201).

MAS Level A MULAN MAS is a net that represents a domain-specific infrastructure for agent communication and mobility between multiple platforms (Rölke, 2004, p. 158). This system net "consists of places that contain platform nets and transitions that build the infrastructure of the agent system" (Rölke, 2004, p. 158). As an example, Rölke (2004, p. 222) shows a system net that represents different rooms of a one-family house inhabited by a simulated housekeeping robot.

Though Rölke (2004) does not cover the MAS level in detail, the aspect of mobility receives attention due to its close relation to the nets-within-nets formalism. Köhler et al. (2003, p. 125) identify four classes of mobility of an object net within a system net that depend on the net(s) that exercise control over the migration. Rölke (2004, p. 191) also shows agent protocols for migration from a source to a destination platform.

3.3.3.2. Petri Net-Based Agent-Oriented Software Engineering

The good practical applicability of the MULAN architecture in combination with the Petri net development environment RENEW (for examples see Rölke, 2004, Ch. 9) allowed to establish the software engineering approach PAOSE (Petri net-based Agent Oriented Software Engineering) (Cabac et al., 2007). This approach strives to tackle the problems of complexity, concurrency, and distribution in software development by using concepts of reference nets and MAS. PAOSE can be considered *model-driven* since it stipulates the stepwise transformation of reference nets and UML-based models (see Section 3.3.3.3) from specification to implementation. It therefore relies on a set of additional tools reviewed in Section 3.4.5.

Different from other AOSE approaches, PAOSE targets the developed software artifacts *and* the software development process with similar agent-based concepts. In particular, the MAS metaphor is applied as a "guiding metaphor" to the development team and process ("multi-agent system of developers", see Cabac, 2007, p. 8). This allows for a unified view upon technical and organizational aspects of software development and emphasizes properties commonly associated with the (technical) MAS metaphor such as flexibility, self-responsibility, and self-organization in the development team (Cabac, 2007, pp. 8).

The basic process model of PAOSE is shown in Figure 3.8 (left): After an initial analysis of requirements, the phases of design, implementation, and integration are executed repeatedly to produce several incremental software milestones. A regular re-consideration and refinement of requirements is also included. The implementation of agents, interactions, and ontology

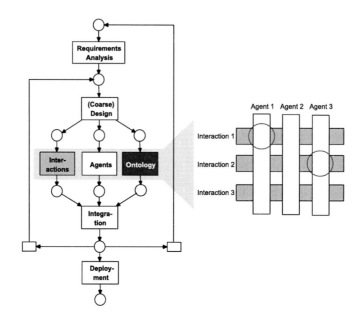

Figure 3.8.: Principles of PAOSE: Basic process model (left) and matrix organization with well-defined intersection points (right). Adopted with modifications from (Cabac, 2007, pp. 6,7).

proceeds in a "concurrent and higly interactive" manner supported by the development tools described in Section 3.4.5 (Cabac, 2007, p. 7). This partitioning of the system under development into three orthogonal perspectives of "structure, behaviour, and terminology" allows for a *matrix organization* (see Figure 3.8, right) with well-defined intersection points between the different development tasks (Cabac, 2007, p. 6).

3.3.3.3. Mulan and UML

Besides reference nets, several UML-like diagram types are applied in PAOSE. For practical modeling tasks these diagrams provide a more specialized and compact model representation that can be automatically transformed into implementations in the form of reference nets with Java inscriptions. The diagram types used in PAOSE are use case diagrams, agent interaction protocol (AIP) diagrams, role-dependency (RD) diagrams, and ontology diagrams (Cabac et al., 2007, Sec. 3).

Use case diagrams are applied during the coarse design phase to provide an overview of agent roles (displayed as actors) and their interactions (displayed as use cases); see Cabac et al. (2007, p. 42). From these diagrams the matrix shown in Figure 3.8 (right) can be derived. Intersection points in the matrix are represented as connections between use cases and actors in the use case diagram (Cabac et al., 2007, p. 42).

AIP diagrams are basically AgentUML sequence diagrams (see Section 3.3.2.1) with restrictions that allow to provide a precise formal semantics in terms of reference nets (Cabac et al., 2003). The main restriction is that message split elements are not used due to their unclear semantics. In particular a message split violates the chronological order of tasks on the receiver's lifeline. In AIP diagrams, only control flow split elements on the lifeline of the sender are allowed (Cabac et al., 2003, p. 114). Message join elements are used to express the situation when a receiver expects exactly one of several alternative replies (Cabac et al., 2003, p. 114). With these restrictions it is straightforward to transform the elements of AIP diagrams to MULAN net components (Cabac et al., 2003, pp. 114–115). Thus (a template for) an executable protcol net can be constructed for every lifeline in the AIP diagram.

The remaining two diagram types are variants of UML class diagrams that are used to model the structure and the terminology of the MAS under development. *R/D diagrams* are a mixture of class and component diagrams (Cabac et al., 2007, p. 42). To describe the system structure, different types of entities (service interfaces, agent roles) and dependencies (specializes, uses, requires) are used (see e.g. Cabac et al., 2007, p. 42).

Service interfaces are drawn as rectangles tagged with the stereotype «Interface» that include one compartment with the name of a single service description. *Role* entities describe all relevant aspects of a certain agent role. They are also displayed as rectangles with the stereotype «AgentRole». Four different types of members can be declared (see e.g. Cabac et al., 2007, p. 42):

- *incoming messages* that the role can handle,
- *protocols* executed by the role in response to certain trigger messages,
- *state descriptions* including factual knowledge and pro-active protocol triggers,
- *required services* of the role.

Connections in a R/D diagram describe the relations between roles and services (Cabac et al., 2007, p. 42): The relations *provides* and *requires* indicate that a certain service is provided or required by a role. The relation *specializes* is drawn as an inheritance arrow from the specialized to the general role. Abstract (base) roles are also possible. Note that the member types of agent roles correspond to the elements of a MULAN agent introduced in Section 3.3.3.1. Thus, one or more agent roles describe a certain MULAN agent class.

To model the terminology of a MULAN MAS, common ontology notations can be used. One easily understandable notation are *concept diagrams*, i.e. class diagrams that use inheritance and associations as the only relations (Cabac et al., 2007, p. 43). Due to these restrictions, concept diagrams can be mapped to a PN formalism called *feature structure nets* which is tailored towards data modeling (Wienberg et al., 2006). This formalism and the concept diagram notation is directly supported by RENEW (Cabac et al., 2007, p. 43).

3.3.3.4. Mulan as a MABS Framework

As already discussed in Section 2.3.2.6 the suitability of MULAN for simulation is not as much a question of general modeling power as of appropriate tool support. Several case studies (see e.g.

Rölke, 2004, Ch. 9) show that the architecture can be used to structure even large agent-based models.

The simulation scheduler functionality of RENEW in the sequential mode is also available for MULAN. As noted in (Page and Kreutzer, 2005, p. 362): "further built-in simulation support, e.g. for experimental planning, data collection, or data analysis, is currently not offered. However, [as discussed above] prototypical data analysis tools, which help in using RENEW for discrete and agent-based simulations, have been developed Strümpel, 2003."

The inherent concepts of locality and mobility allow to employ MULAN for spatially explicit simulations as well. A discrete spatial model can be represented by a system net with locations modeled as places and pathways modeled as connected arrows and transitions; or an arbitrary spatial model implemented in Java can be connected to the MULAN MAS (see Rölke, 2004).

While the former approach provides a formal representation of (spatial) mobility in terms of Petri nets (Köhler et al., 2003), the latter might offer an improved performance and the possibility to integrate grid-based and continuous spatial models as well. An overhead of the PN-based spatial model is that each place (location) must in principle contain a full MULAN platform that allows the agent to communicate with the local environment.

3.3.3.5. Other Petri-Net Based Approaches

Though there is a relevant number of alternative approaches towards agent-based modeling with Petri nets, we will only review one more here. This approach was developed at Groningen University's 'The Agent Lab' (TAL) and shows some parallels to PAOSE. Most important for this thesis, it has been extended with machine learning techniques and an integration of process mining has been proposed (Stuit et al., 2007b, Sec. 7). The objective of the TAL approach is to support the modeling and implementation of inter-organizational business processes with agent concepts. Its cornerstones are the visual modeling language TALL (The Agent Lab Language) and the simulation environment AGE (Agent Growing Environment). The following presentation is based on a paper by (Stuit et al., 2007b) and a related poster (Stuit et al., 2007a).

Similar to PAOSE, TALL combines UML-like elements with an extension of Petri nets called *Behavior Nets*. The TALL diagrams comprise two modeling levels:

- On the high level, interactions are described using *Interaction Structure* diagrams (Stuit and Wortmann, 2012, pp. 144): As shown in Figure 3.9 (top), these diagrams display interactions with the participating roles and agents bound to these roles.

- On the low level, the behavior of interacting agents is described by means of Behavior Nets (see Figure 3.9, bottom) (Stuit et al., 2007b, Sec. 3): These are basically workflow nets with input and output places depicted similar to initial and final nodes of activity diagrams. Behavior Nets of multiple interaction roles can be combined into a sequence diagram-like structure using message places (marked with a 'letter' symbol) and swimlanes. As indicated by Stuit et al. (2007b, Sec. 3) Behavior Nets are thus rather similar to protocol nets in MULAN.

A concept in TALL that goes beyond standard interaction protocols are so-called *interaction beliefs* (IBs, see Stuit et al., 2007b, Sec. 3). IBs are part of an agent's knowledge base, where each IB represents an agent's assumptions about a certain interaction between itself and a

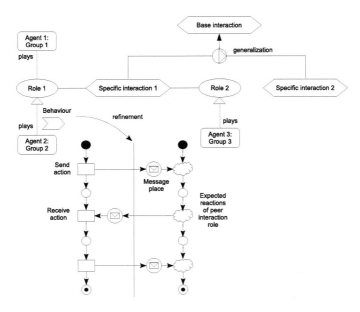

Figure 3.9.: Overview of the TALL notation. Adopted with modifications from (Stuit et al., 2007a).

number of other roles. An IB consists of multiple Behavior Nets separated by swim lanes. One dedicated swim lane is tagged with the keyword me, and represents the behavior associated with the agent's own interaction role. All other swimlanes, in contrast, represent the way that the agent *expects* other interaction roles to behave during the conversation (Stuit et al., 2007b, Sec. 3).

The actual behavior of other agents in an interaction might differ from these expectations depending on their own interaction beliefs. To visualize this uncertainty, transitions of 'foreign' Behavior Nets are depicted by a cloud symbol (Stuit et al., 2007b, Sec. 3). When an agent's actual communication partner behaves other than expected, further following the predefined protocol might lead to failure. The agent can thus either autonomously *align* its behavior to the new situation or enter a so-called *escape mode* to expect an *intervention* by another agent or user (Stuit et al., 2007b, Sec. 5).

Interaction beliefs, escape mode, and interventions are central to the TAL modeling approach because they allow to model and simulate stakeholders' different views upon a decentralized business process with a focus on strategies to resolve conflicts resulting from different expectations (Stuit et al., 2007a, Sec. 3). The involvement of stakeholders into the modeling process is supported by AGE, a visual development and simulation environment for TALL models. AGE allows participatory simulations called 'gaming sessions' (Stuit et al., 2007a, Sec. 4) in which human domain experts incrementally provide training to simulated agents that entered escape mode due to conflicting expectations. The agents should then learn how to resolve the conflict by observing the user. The actual and planned application of machine learning techniques in this context is detailed in Section 5.3.4.5.

3.3.3.6. Summary

In the previous sections we have reviewed different modeling techniques for MABS. In this thesis, all presented modeling styles will be considered due to their specific advantages and drawbacks. Code-centric and rule-based modeling provides high flexibility and productiveness for simulation practitioners with programming skills and is found in many real-world settings. The use of UML and reference nets eases modeling and validation due to the explicit graphical notation.

Current approaches towards roundtrip engineering and model driven development provide transformations between the different representations. This thesis focuses on the 'inverse' direction of reconstructing reference net and UML-like models from simulation traces by means of process mining. While the benefit of such trace abstraction is obvious in code-centric and rule-based simulation, we will also consider specific advantages of process mining in connection with reference nets and UML. Furthermore, we apply reference nets as a means to model workflows for experimentation, result analysis, and validation.

3.4. Implementation of Agent-Based Models

For the implementation of MABS a large number of tools exist that can be characterized as follows (see Oechslein et al., 2001, Sec. 3; Klügl, 2001, Sec. 4.4):

- simulation-specific extensions of agent frameworks and platforms

- agent-specific extensions of object-oriented simulation frameworks and systems

- frameworks and simulation systems originally developed for MABS

According to (Page and Kreutzer, 2005, pp. 263) a *simulation framework* is a software framework that adds simulation-specific functionality to an underlying programming language via a customizable object-oriented class library. The framework can be extended at certain 'hot spots' by means of inheritance (white box framework) and composition (black box framework); see Page and Kreutzer (2005, p. 264). While simulation frameworks mainly support model building and implementation, a *simulation system* is a tool that supports all phases of a simulation study (Page and Kreutzer, 2005, pp. 245).

Following Page and Kreutzer (2005, p. 360):

> "An agent platform is "a software environment agents live in"; i.e. a runtime environment for agent-based software (Rölke, 2004, p. 159). Most available platforms are based on Java and follow the *FIPA* (Foundation for Intelligent Physical Agents) standard [see Section 3.2.2.2]. [...]
>
> Agent platforms can be employed to build MABS as well. This offers a number of advantages:
>
> - Agent platforms often come with powerful frameworks for modelling complex agents (e.g. those of the BDI architecture [...]), which are rarely available in pure simulation environments.

- Since agent platforms are usually designed as distributed systems, the distributed execution of complex models is supported in a natural way. Platform interoperabilty is ensured by the FIPA standard.

- Agents interacting with a simulated environment on an agent platform can be easily deployed in their "real" environment after the testing phase.

Since simulation is not an application domain most agent platforms were originally designed for, there are also disadvantages to their use:

- Often there is no simulation scheduler for managing simulation time, and for synchronizing agents with simulated environments.

- Typical simulation tasks like stochastic modelling, planning experiments, data collection, and statistical data analysis are usually not directly supported.

- Agents running on typical agent platforms are often quite "heavy-weight" objects, with one or more concurrent threads of control. This might cause performance problems in models with many such agents.

There are, however, a number of agent platforms which make simulation support available as an integral part of their architecture or as an add-on."

In the following, we briefly review some common agent platforms and MABS frameworks as well as the simulation framework FAMOS and the agent platform CAPA used in this thesis.

3.4.1. JADE Agent Platform

As described in (Page and Kreutzer, 2005, p. 361):

> "The *Java Agent DEvelopment Framework* [...] (Bellifemine et al., 2001) is a widely used open source agent platform, which follows [...] the FIPA standard. JADE offers a distributed agent runtime environment, an extensible framework for behaviour modelling, and some graphical agent management and debugging tools; e.g. a so-called "sniffer agent" which constructs simple UML sequence diagrams tracing agent communications. An agent's [...] behaviour is composed of so-called *behaviour objects*, each of which represents a single agent task. Since these tasks can be added to and removed from an agent dynamically at runtime, the architecture offers a powerful base for defining complex behaviour. There are extension packages for behaviour modelling with hierarchical UML statecharts (Griss et al., 2002) or the Jadex BDI architecture (Pokahr et al., 2003). Some graphical modelling tools are also available.
>
> JADE has not been specifically designed to support MABS, but a so-called *time service*, i.e. a process-oriented simulation scheduler encapsulated in a JADE agent, has been developed as an add-on package by Braubach et al. (2003). [... Furthermore], it provides some interesting tools for analysing agent behaviour based on ACL message traces. In addition to the above mentioned "sniffer agent", a tool called *ACLAnalyser* (Botía et al., 2004) can be used to aggregate message traces into social networks at different levels of detail. JADE has occasionally been applied in MABS; e.g. for the agent-based simulation of supply chains (Ahn and Park, 2004)."[22]

Simulation-specific extensions have been realized by Gildhoff (2007) and Koppehel (2007) in the context of the Jadex project.

---

[22]JADE is available at `http://jade.tilab.com`, last visit 2014-02-16.

3.4.2. MadKit Agent Platform and Simulation Framework

MadKit (Ferber et al., 2012) is at the same time a Java-based framework and platform for agent development and a library for time-driven agent-based simulation reminiscent of the 'classic' MABS framework *Swarm* (Minar et al., 1996). Simulations are executed in a so-called *synchronous engine* that builds upon the agent platform. The modeling and execution of simulated agents slightly differs from agents developed for the 'real' platform.

The common organizational concept used in both 'modes' (i.e. agent platform and synchronous engine) is the AGR model described in Section 3.2.2.2. The reviewed version 4 of MadKit extends the basic AGR model with a construct for (network) communities.

Agents on the MadKit platform run in an own thread and define an own life cycle. They can be assigned an exchangeable behavior module (*controller*) and communicate via messages quite similar to JADE. MadKit supports several languages and tools for behavior description including Java, the JESS[23] rule engine, and a graphical modeling tool for different formalisms including extended Petri nets. Different from JADE, a MadKit agent can only run one controller module at a time. The execution policy is event-driven, which leads to a strong similarity of the the Java-based MadKit agent with a simulation process running in real-time.

In agent-based simulations with the synchronous engine, agents do not have an own life cycle and normally do not use an own controller. Instead, a so-called *Activator* is defined that implements a time-driven schedule for a group of agents. A scheduler agent running in a thread on the MadKit platform merges and synchronizes the schedules of all activators. A more abstract simulation framework named *Turtle Kit* builds upon the synchronous engine and allows to implement simple models comparable to the *Star Logo* system.

For simulation observation, MadKit adopts the *probe* construct from Swarm (Minar et al., 1996). Probes provide well-defined programmatic interfaces to observe properties and collect data about agents from a certain group and role. Basic statistic measures like minimum, maximum, and average of the observed values can be computed. The MadKit platform comprises further visualization tools such as a *group viewer* and a message traffic observer named *spy agent*, quite similar to the JADE *Sniffer*.

3.4.3. SeSAm Simulation System

SeSAm (*ShEll for Simulated Agent SysteMs*)[24] is a simulation system for MABS that was developed at the University of Würzburg. The initial version of SeSAm was designed by Klügl (2000) as part of her dissertation and implemented in the object-oriented LISP variant CLOS. As a simulation system (Page and Kreutzer, 2005, p. 245), SeSAm supports all phases of a simulation study with visual tools. The CLOS version in particular contains a graphical editor to model the behavior of agents by means of activity automata (see Section 3.3.1.3). A summary of this version's functionality is also given by Page and Kreutzer (2005, pp. 364).

The current version of SeSAm is a re-implementation of the original CLOS-based system in Java. It was mainly designed and implemented as part of the dissertation by Oechslein (2004),

---

[23]http://herzberg.ca.sandia.gov, last visit 2012-09-17

[24]http://www.simsesam.de, last visit 2012-01-12

on which the following description is based. A main difference to the initial version is the use of the UML dialect *SeSAm UML* (see Section 3.3.2.2) for agent modeling instead of the proprietary activity automata notation. The SeSAm editor supports all elements of activity graphs described in Section 3.3.2.2.

Besides activity graphs, SeSAm provides a visual editor to design grid-based environments. Sensors and effectors of agents can be specified by means of pre-defined as well as custom primitives via graphical dialogs. Experimental designs can be set up in an experiment specification language based on the formal language *SeSAm Impl* mentioned in Section 3.3.2.2. The language supports manual as well as automated experimental design (see Section 2.4.1) and can be extended with custom Java code.

Furthermore, online- and offline analyses might be registered with a model for result analysis based on simulation traces. The SeSAm simulator also runs in a client/server mode that allows to distribute parallel simulation runs (e.g. for simulation-based optimization) in a computer network. The SeSAm system can be extended using a plugin mechanism.

3.4.4. FAMOS and DESMO-J

FAMOS (Framework for Agent-based MOdeling and Simulation) is a framework for agent-based discrete event simulation. It was developed at the University of Hamburg's Department for Informatics as an extension of the discrete event simulator DESMO-J (Discrete Event Simulation and MOdeling in Java). FAMOS integrates common features of frameworks for agent development with the world views of discrete event simulation (Knaak, 2002; Knaak et al., 2002). Furthermore it offers powerful and extensible constructs for spatial modeling (Meyer, 2001, 2008).

3.4.4.1. DESMO-J

The discrete event simulator DESMO-J (see e.g. Page et al., 2000, Ch. 10) is a strongly extended and re-designed object-oriented Java implementation of the Simula library DEMOS (Birtwistle, 1979). It offers support for event scheduling, process interaction, and combined models. Transaction- and activity-oriented models are mapped to process interaction models with specific synchronization constructs such as resources. DESMO-J furthermore offers constructs for queues, statistical data-collectors, a configurable reporting system, and a simulation infrastructure based on the conceptual separation of models and experiments (see Section 2.4.1). A simple Desktop- and Web-based graphical user interface to configure, run, and observe experiments is also included (Kiesel, 2004).

3.4.4.2. Agents in FAMOS

Though MABS is often understood as an extension of process interaction, agents in DESMO-J are technically based on event-oriented constructs. The reasons for this design decision are performance (since every simulation process employs an own Java thread) and better suitability for asynchronous event handling (Page and Kreutzer, 2005, p. 363).

Figure 3.10 shows the structure of a FAMOS agent (see also Knaak, 2002, Sec. 5.2.1): As an extended entity, it actively handles so-called signals. These are either received from other agents (external signals) or self-scheduled as future intentions (internal signals). Pending signals are stored chronologically on an 'inner' schedule, which is encapsulated from the environment as opposed to the global event list of DESMO-J (Page and Kreutzer, 2005, p. 363).

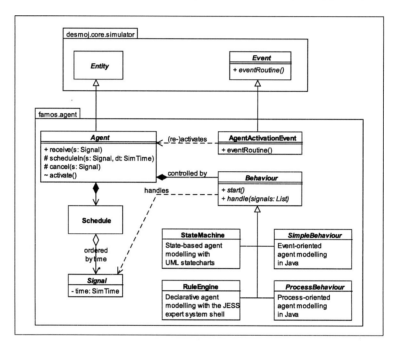

Figure 3.10.: "Integration of FAMOS agents into the framework *DESMO-J* (adopted with modifications from Knaak et al., 2002)". Figure and caption cited from (Page and Kreutzer, 2005, p. 365).

When the agent receives a signal, it dequeues and handles all signals that are scheduled for the current simulation time. This can cause the execution of actions (encapsulated in methods) and the addition of new signals (i.e. intentions) to the schedule. Finally, an external agent activation event is scheduled on DESMO-J's global event list for the time point of the first (earliest) signal on the internal schedule.

To allow for flexible behavior modeling, the actual handling of signals is delegated to a behavior module that is derived from an abstract base class `Behaviour`. As indicated above, this design is rather common in agent modeling. Similar to MadKit or JADE, different techniques for behavior modeling are supported by sub-classes of `Behaviour`. FAMOS currently includes the following modules (Knaak et al., 2002):

- A *simple event-oriented behavior* merely declares two abstract methods to implement reactions to signals and pro-active initial actions.

- A *process-oriented behavior* runs in a thread and provides methods for process synchronisation (such as `hold`) and signal handling. This module is rather similar to the standard agent behaviour in MadKit (see Section 3.4.2).

- The state machine encapsulates an interpreter for hierarchical and concurrent UML state charts. It is basically a modified version of the state chart framework from the open source CASE tool *Fujaba*[25] (Köhler, 1999). Implementation details and a comparison with Fujaba are provided in (Knaak, 2004). The domain-specific part of the state chart code is generated from XML scripts built with an included graphical editor.

- The rule engine encapsulates the JESS forward chaining rule interpreter for declarative modeling, quite similar to the integration of JESS into MadKit (see Section 3.4.2).

Different from behavior architectures in some agent platforms, the internal scheduler of a FAMOS agent does not run in an own thread. While this improves the performance of models with many agents, it complicates the implementation of dynamic deliberative architectures. As in MadKit, a FAMOS agent is equipped with one fixed behavior module. The architecture could be extended to a dynamic plan execution environment by using the composite pattern (Gamma et al., 1995) similar to JADE. A possible design is sketched by Knaak (2002, Sec. 5.3.4). Czogalla and Matzen (2003) implemented a simple deliberative architecture to simulate the goal-directed behavior of passengers boarding an airplane.

3.4.4.3. Agent-Based Models in FAMOS

The main component of a FAMOS model is the environment that serves as a container for all agents. Furthermore it provides access to a communication infrastructure, a group-based organizational structure, and an optional spatial model.[26]

The standard communication infrastructure is rather simple: transfer of signals is assumed to be instantanious and error-free. It could, however, be exchanged with a more complex implementation that e.g. simulates transfer durations and failure probabilities according to random distributions (Knaak, 2002, p. 87).

The organizational structure is based on the AGR model as implemented in MadKit. Different from the standard version, FAMOS supports the hierarchical embedding of groups reminiscent of the seminal MABS framework *Swarm* (Minar et al., 1996). In fact, this makes the role concept dispensable at the implementation level because roles contained in a group can be mapped to sub-groups. For compatibility, a subclass `RoleGroup` that supports roles is also included. Groups can receive signals that they broadcast to all contained agents. They furthermore provide means for the functional referencing of contained agents similar to SeSAm (see Section 3.4.3).

As a main focus, FAMOS provides an extensible framework to model spatial structures and dynamics (i.e. agent movement and environmental processes). Spatial structures are represented in terms of abstract positions and connecting links. This abstract representation is realized by different topologies. FAMOS currently includes graph-based models and different kinds of

---

[25]`http://www.fujaba.de`, last visit 2012-09-17
[26]The following description is based on (Knaak, 2002, Secs. 5.2.3, 5.5).

regular and irregular grids (Meyer, 2008). Czogalla and Matzen (2003) implemented a 'vector-based' continuous model to represent cabin layouts of airplanes.

The movement of agents is realized by different *movement strategies*. These strategies determine how and when an agent moves between different positions of the spatial topology. Available movement strategies include random walk, gradient following, and movement along previously planned routes (Page and Kreutzer, 2005, p. 364). Due to the abstract spatial representation, movement strategies can in principle be re-used with different spatial topologies.

Besides agents, arbitrary objects implementing a certain interface can be located in the spatial environment. For each agent, the environment manages an individual horizon of perception and action, and the agent can query the environment for observable objects. The environment can also manage groups that agents automatically enter and leave when they reach certain spatial positions. Dynamics of environmental properties can be represented by macroscopic modeling constructs from DESMO-J such as events.

For the observation of agents, a variant of the probe concept from Swarm is used. DESMO-J provides so-called *access points*[27] that provide a uniform interface to arbitrary object properties (Page and Kreutzer, 2005, p. 364). FAMOS includes a statistical observer (class `Individual-Observer`) that observes the access points of a set of agents. The results are displayed by the DESMO-J reporting system as tables, and common statistical quantities are computed over numerical properties.

3.4.5. Capa Agent Platform

CAPA (Duvigneau, 2003) is an "agent platform built on top of the Java-based Petri net simulator RENEW" (Page and Kreutzer, 2005, p. 361) described in Section 2.3.2.5. It is a fully FIPA-compliant re-implementation of the MULAN architecture (Section 3.3.3.1) realized with reference nets and Java code. This "provides an explicit and easily understandable architecture for both platform and agent models" (Page and Kreutzer, 2005, p. 362). The FIPA compatibility allows CAPA to interact with other FIPA platforms such as JADE (Section 3.4.1).

CAPA includes a number of additional visual development tools that support the different phases of the PAOSE approach:

- Net components for protocol nets and decision components are provided as additional toolbars in the RENEW IDE.

- An editor for use case diagrams is embedded into RENEW to document the results of the coarse design phase. From these diagrams a generator can build a new development project skeleton including folder structure and diagram templates (Cabac et al., 2007, p. 41).

- Another RENEW plugin allows to draw AIP diagrams of agent interactions. These are automatically mapped to protocol net templates for every participant of the communication. To implement an executable agent, the user fills these templates with Java code for elementary agent actions (Cabac et al., 2007, pp. 44).

---

[27]the term was adopted from the work by Bachmann (2003)

- R/D-diagrams are drawn with a RENEW plugin called *knowledge base editor*. From the diagrams the tool generates so called *role descriptions* that can be integrated into knowledge bases of agents. Functionality to manage and start multi-agent applications is offered as well (Cabac et al., 2007, p. 43).

- Ontology diagrams are either created with the external tool *Protege*[28] or by using the feature structure (FS) plugin of RENEW. Both tools also offer (at least experimental in the latter case) Java code generators (Cabac et al., 2007, p. 43).

The main tool to debug applications developed with CAPA is the MULAN *Viewer* (Cabac et al., 2008b, Sec. 3). It provides a tree-structured view on the state of the platform according to the four levels of the MULAN architecture (Cabac et al., 2008b, p. 403). Starting from this view, it is possible to inspect the markings of all involved nets. A hierarchical inspection of net tokens and a UML-like display of data tokens is also possible (Cabac et al., 2008b, p. 404). Furthermore the MULAN Viewer provides basic functionality to control agents and log ACL messages (Cabac et al., 2008b, p. 404). A dedicated message monitoring tool named MULAN *Sniffer* was developed in the context of this thesis and is described in Section 7.4.1.

3.5. The Problem of Analysis and Validation

In the previous sections, it has become clear that agent-based models tend to be complex and allow for a high degree of modeling freedom. This Section briefly reviews the problems that this inherent complexity poses on their analysis and validation. On this basis, properties of appropriate validation techniques are discussed with respect to the classification scheme presented in Section 2.4.3.5. Concrete validation techniques for MABS will be reviewed in Section 5.1.

In (Knaak, 2006), we divided the difficulties to analyze and validate a MABS into three main categories based on the literature (mainly Klügl, 2001; Edmonds, 2000):

> "The possibility to simulate complex micro-macro relations is at the same time an opportunity and a drawback of MABS. Understanding and controlling the behaviour of the models remains a challenging task. [...] the first [difficulty, ...] we call the *problem of model complexity*: MABS contain numerous agents running complex internal processes and external interactions. The agent-based modelling style itself poses few restrictions on model complexity (Edmonds, 2000). During simulation of even simple MABS, large amounts of data (such as event logs of the agents' interactions) are observed, whose analysis requires advanced techniques (Sanchez and Lucas, 2002).
>
> The second difficulty is the *problem of result representation and interpretation*: MABS usually produce complex, qualitative results, such as spatial or organisational patterns, that cannot be reduced to simple statistical measures. The models' explanatory function prohibits to regard MABS as black boxes and analyse global simulation outputs only. The model must in principle be analysed at multiple levels (Edmonds, 2000). Furthermore, the sensitivity of many MABS to initial conditions (see below) often leads to strongly divergent simulation trajectories (Rand et al., 2003) that complicate the application of standard statistical aggregation techniques. Instead temporally fine-grained analyses are required that take into consideration intermediate simulation states (Edmonds, 2000).

---

[28]`protege.stanford.edu`, last visit 2012-09-17

The validation, optimisation, and calibration of MABS is complicated by the [... *problem of distributed system state*[29]]. Many MABS contain sensitive free parameters at the agent-level that strongly influence the overall behavior. Due to the typical causal spread appearing in distributed systems, it is often hard to tell how certain microscopic parameters influence macroscopic properties of the overall system (Fehler et al., 2004; Klügl, 2001). Therefore, fitting microscopic parameters to produce certain macro-level phenomena might lead to a tedious process of trial and error (Klügl, 2001, p. 83). The calibration of MABS suffers from further problems: Due to the models' high level of detail, lack of real-world data is a major concern, and parameters of agents' 'mental' processes can often not be measured sufficiently (Horne and Meyer, 2005; Oechslein et al., 1999)." (Knaak, 2006)

Note that Klügl (2008, Sec. 2.2) settles for quite analogical problem categories when discussing the problems of analysis and validation of MABS. This related approach is reviewed in Section 5.1.1.2.

In (Knaak, 2006), we further observed that

"Due to these difficulties, it is especially hard to determine if a MABS model is a sufficient representation of reality. Many techniques for model validation (for an overview see e.g. Page and Kreutzer, 2005, Ch. 8) are of limited use: Static validation techniques fail because the structure of MABS is often variable and incompletely specified in advance. The applicability of formal verification techniques is limited due to large state spaces and often non-explicit computational model representations (Moss, 2004). Generally, confirmative techniques contradict the explorative character of many MABS studies where the focus is put on experimental investigations of cause-effect relations in decentralized systems (see e.g. Uhrmacher, 2000).

Taking into account the qualitative character of MABS results, *informal techniques* [...] seem appropriate for analysing and validating MABS. However, important patterns might go unrecognised within the large amounts of observed data."

In the next chapter, we introduce data mining and process mining as potential techniques to tackle this problem.

---

[29]In (Knaak, 2006) we named this issue the "problem of sensitivity and causal spread" (adopting the term "causal spread" from Edmonds, 2000, p. 22). Recapitulating, however, distributed system state seems to be the more pristine cause for the described difficulties.

4. Data Mining and Process Mining

This chapter introduces foundations of data mining and the more specialized subfield of process mining. The presentation of data mining concepts and techniques mainly follows Dunham (2003) and Cios et al. (2007). For process mining as the main topic of this thesis a large number of sources are reviewed. A summary of the current state-of-the art in process mining and its applications (mainly) to the domain of business process management is also provided in the book by Aalst (2011a).

4.1. Data Mining

Following Page and Kreutzer (2005, p. 228):

> "*Data mining* [DM] is "the automated analysis of large or complex data sets in order to discover significant patterns or trends that would otherwise go unrecognised" (Woods and Kyral, 1997, p. 6, cited in Köster, 2002, p. 54).
>
> The goals of data mining are quite similar to those of traditional exploratory statistics, but the technique focuses more strongly on algorithms that automatically abstract complex hypotheses (i.e. models) from large sets of data [see also Köster, 2002]."

DM is often considered as part of the larger process of Knowledge Discovery in Databases (KDD) where DM is the crucial step of automated hypothesis generation. Chamoni (2009, cited in Haan, 2009, p. 40) relates to this point of view as "data mining in the narrower sense", whereas "data mining in the wider sense" includes the whole KDD process.

For the purpose of DM, a large number of interpolation and machine learning techniques are applied, rooted in different fields like *soft computing* (e.g. neural networks and genetic algorithms), symbolic machine learning (e.g. inductive logic programming), and statistical data analysis (e.g. regression). Specific *process mining* techniques for the reconstruction and analysis of process models (see e.g. Aalst and Weijters, 2004 and Section 4.2) are in the focus of this thesis due to their close relation to the perspectives of agent-based modeling.

An often-cited example application of data mining is market basket analysis (see e.g. Dunham, 2003, p. 5), which serves to detect typical patterns in the shopping behavior of customers. Simply speaking, the goal is to automatically detect *association rules* that describe correlated products (e.g. "customers who buy product A and product B are likely to buy product C as well").

Note, however, that most algorithms and models used in data mining are application-independent. Hence, association rules can be applied to describe the navigation behavior of web site visitors as well as decision strategies of agents in a MABS.

4.1.1. The KDD Process

Data mining activities are usually embedded into a broader knowledge acquisition process called 'Knowledge Discovery in Databases' (KDD). Most variants of this process contain five phases originally proposed by Fayyad et al. (1996). The following description is based on Dunham (2003, p. 10):

1. *Selection*: Data is selected from one or more, possibly heterogeneous, sources like files, databases, or non-electronic sources.

2. *Preprocessing*: The raw data is prepared to meet the requirements of the applied mining algorithms. This includes the elimination of outliers and errors as well as the addition of missing data based on estimations.

3. *Transformation*: The original, often heterogeneous, data formats are transformed into a common format that serves as input to the mining algorithms. Many algorithms work on vector-based data, i.e. *feature vectors* encoding relevant attributes.

4. *Data Mining*: Patterns are extracted from the transformed data using a DM algorithm. The extracted patterns should be 'useful' for the problem under study. In the context of the KDD process, data mining is often understood in a rather broad sense that covers simple *SQL* queries or methods from explorative statistics as well as complex machine learning techniques.

5. *Interpretation of Results*: The mined patterns are interpreted by a person to gain insight into the analyzed data. Appropriate visualization techniques are crucial in this step to understand and rate the quality of the discovered patterns (Dunham, 2003, p. 14).

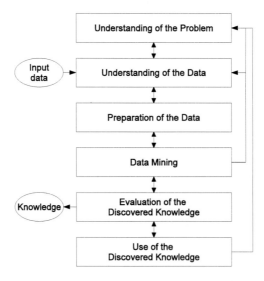

Figure 4.1.: The KDP model of Knowledge Discovery in Databases (adopted with modifications from Cios et al., 2007, p. 15).

Extensions of the basic process have been stated in scientific and industrial contexts. The six-step KDP model (Cios et al., 2007, pp. 14) based on the industrial CRISP-DM[1] process is shown in Figure 4.1. This variant puts a specific focus on validation and iterative refinement.

The KDP model starts with two steps related to the clear definition and understanding of the problem and the collected data. Furthermore, every step allows to return to previous phases due to detected inconsistencies and errors. The fifth step includes a thorough assessment of the discovered knowledge including "understanding [of] the results, checking whether the discovered knowledge is novel and interesting, interpretation of the results by domain experts, and checking the impact of the discovered knowledge. [...] A list of errors made in the process is prepared" (Cios et al., 2007, p. 16).

The KDP model is rather akin to the simulation model building cycle as presented in Section 2.4.3.2. While the core methods for system analysis differ (i.e. data mining on the one hand and modeling and simulation on the other hand) the overall procedures are very similar.

4.1.2. Classification of Data Mining Techniques

This section presents a number of properties that can be used to structure the variety of existing data mining techniques.

4.1.2.1. Data Mining Tasks

Data mining algorithms are often classified by the task accomplished. Though there are minor differences, the identification of these tasks is rather homogeneous in the literature. Basically, DM is applied (a) to describe the analyzed data in a generalized form (*descriptive data mining*) and (b) to make predictions about missing or future data from the same domain (*predictive data mining*) (Dunham, 2003, p. 5). This classification mirrors the distinction between explanatory and predictive simulation models in Section 2.2.1.

The basic DM tasks can be refined into several subtasks. Dunham (2003, pp. 7) identifies the following descriptive tasks:

- *Clustering* (Dunham, 2003, pp. 7-8): The input data set is algorithmically partitioned into disjoint classes of 'similar' items. Elements from different classes should be 'different' with respect to their features. Similarity is defined by a formal *similarity measure* calculated over the feature vectors. Clustering is also referred to as *segmentation* and closely related to *unsupervised learning* (see Section 4.1.2.3).

- *Summarization* (Dunham, 2003, p. 8): The information contained in a dataset is condensed into an aggregate form that makes key aspects easier accessible. The calculation of aggregate statistics or performance indicators is a typical example.

- *Association rules* (Dunham, 2003, pp. 8-9): Relations between data items are extracted from input data in the form of rules. These describe common correlations in the data and should not be mistaken for causal relations.

---

[1]CRoss-Industry Standard Process for Data Mining, see e.g. Cios et al. (2007, pp. 32).

- *Sequence discovery* (Dunham, 2003, p. 9): In this special form of association rule learning, frequent temporal (or ordering) relations of time-stamped data items are sought. An example is the reconstruction of common browsing patterns from web server logs to analyse and improve web navigation. Note that several process mining algorithms fall into this category as well.

Among the predictive data mining tasks, Dunham (2003, pp. 5) mentions:

- *Classification* (Dunham, 2003, p. 5): From a set of input data items with previously known classes, a mapping function (*classifier*) is learned. The classifier is used to determine the class of new data items based on their features (*pattern recognition*). Classification is related to *supervised learning* (see Section 4.1.2.3).

- *Regression* (Dunham, 2003, p. 6): A real-valued function of a previously known type (e.g. linear) is learned from the input data. It can be used to extrapolate missing or future values.

- *Time series analysis* (Dunham, 2003, p. 6): The variations of a feature are examined over time with the purpose to automatically classify or compare time series based on similar behavior, or to predict future development based on historical data.

- *Prediction*: (Dunham, 2003, p. 7): This term is used to describe classification, regression, or time series analysis with the purpose to predict future values based on past observations.

4.1.2.2. Interpretability of models

Another important aspect to classify data mining techniques is the *interpretability* of the models that represent the generated hypotheses. Generally we can identify two classes of models that mirror the distinction between predictive and descriptive data mining tasks described above (see e.g. Diaz et al., 2005, pp. 32,36):

- *Interpretable models* represent hypotheses with the aid of *symbols* that convey a meaning to the user. Therefore these models can be used for a compact and readable description of the observed patterns and aid in their explanation.

- *Non-interpretable models*, in contrast, are an abstraction of the analyzed data in terms of non-symbolic units such as bit strings in classifiers (Holland et al., 2000) or weighted connections in artificial neural networks (Haykin, 1999). The structure of such models can not straightforwardly be 'read' by a human. However, these models can be rather efficient in classification or prediction tasks.

Note that the two classes of models correspond to the classification of agent architectures by Klügl (2000) into subsymbolic and symbolic architectures. It is straightforward to see that an adaptive agent can (in principle) use data mining techniques to learn an internal representation of its environment (including other agents' behavior) by applying data mining algorithms to observations from the environment.

In this case, symbolic models better allow the user to understand and validate the models learned by the agent. They might also enable the agent to 'reflect' upon the learned models itself using pre-implemented algorithms. Generally, interpretable models are of greater utility with respect to the analysis and validation of agent-based systems, since an interpretation of the information conveyed by the mined models is crucial in these tasks.

4.1.2.3. Types of Learning Algorithms

At the core, many data mining techniques are machine learning algorithms that adapt a model to properties of the input data. These can be divided into four classes (Cios et al., 2007, pp. 49):

1. *Supervised learning* (Cios et al., 2007, pp. 52-53): These algorithms are provided with a set of input data samples together with the desired outputs. During the training phase, the algorithm learns an input-output mapping representing the sample data to solve classification or regression problems.

2. *Unsupervised learning* (Cios et al., 2007, pp. 49-52): In unsupervised learning, the desired output (e.g. classes) is not known beforehand. Often the learning algorithm structures the data into clusters of similar items using a distance measure. Thus, the algorithm does not only generate a mapping of the training data to a predefined classification scheme, but it generates the classification scheme itself.

3. *Reinforcement learning* (Cios et al., 2007, p. 53): This variant lies in between supervised and unsupervised learning. Different from unsupervised learning, the algorithm is provided with an external feedback on the quality of the learned model, but in a less detailed form than in supervised learning. After processing the sample data, the learner receives an abstract reward based on a domain-specific performance measure. Since this learning mechanism resembles 'natural' learning situations, it is well suited to model learning in MA(B)S (Kruse, 2008).

4. *Semi-supervised learning* (Cios et al., 2007, p. 54): In a basically unsupervised setting, domain-specific knowledge is applied to influence the clustering process. For example, the similarity of selected data items from a larger set is rated by a domain expert as a guidance for clustering.

Another technical distinction covers the way that the learned model is updated during the training phase (Cios et al., 2007, p. 383): *Batch* or non-incremental learning algorithms process the whole training data set at once and produce a single output model. If the data set is changed or extended, the procedure must be repeated. *Online* or incremental learning algorithms start from an initial (often random) model and update it step by step while processing sample data. The training thus results in a series of models that represent the problem domain with (preferably) increasing precision.

Incremental algorithms are superior in real time learning situations where sample data is not completely available beforehand, or the problem domain might change over time (Cios et al., 2007, p. 40). Furthermore, incremental algorithms usually exhibit a lower computation space complexity: In every step, the algorithm must only keep a single data item and the learned model in memory (see e.g. Dongen et al., 2007). In contrast, offline learning algorithms are often simpler and more precise.

4.1.3. Model Validity in Data Mining

A hypothesis generated by a DM algorithm is a model of the problem domain in the form of a function that maps input variables (data items) to output variables (Cios et al., 2007, p. 470), such as predicted values or classes. The model is estimated from sample data by means of an algorithm. Like any model, it can be invalid, such that the system under analysis is not appropriately represented. The following discussion of validity and validation in DM is based on Cios et al. (2007, pp. 470) and Dunham (2003, pp. 14).

4.1.3.1. Quality and Availability of Data

Like computer simulation, KDD often suffers from a *lack of available sample data*. This typically leads to models that do not provide a statistically valid description of the target system, but an overly specialized representation of the sample data set.

Other problems related to data quality are *missing data and noise* (Dunham, 2003, p. 15): Errors introduced during measurement, sampling, or preprocessing of input data can lead to missing or invalid data items. As in signal processing, such *noise* will be reflected more or less heavily in the mined models and interfere with or superimpose onto the actual reference data.

Even complete and error-free data sets are difficult to handle when the number of considered data attributes (features) is large. The term *curse of dimensionality* (see e.g. Geenens, 2011, p. 30) subsumes the fact that the algorithmic complexity as well as the number of required samples to gain valid results increases largely with the dimension of the feature vectors. Therefore, input data should be reduced to those features that are most relevant for the considered problem, which is not always straightforward to see. Cios et al. (2007, pp. 208) discuss criteria and algorithms for *feature selection*.

4.1.3.2. Quality of Mined Models

To be useful, data mining algorithms must generalize from input data during the training phase. However, it is not straightforward to find an appropriate level of generalization (Cios et al., 2007, p. 470): *Under-fitting* (or over-generalization) means that the mined model is too simple and represents a too unspecific superset of data generated by the target system. *Over-fitting* makes the mined model unnecessarily complex and specific to the training data set.

In statistics, the complexity of a model is quantified by its *degrees of freedom*, i.e. the "number of independent pieces of information required for estimating the model" like mean or variance, which typically equal the number of model parameters (Cios et al., 2007, p. 470).

The performance of a mined model is described by two measures (Cios et al., 2007, p. 470): *Goodness of fit* describes the ability to correctly represent the training data set in terms of a low deviation between actual and predicted data values. *Goodness of prediction* measures the ability to predict values beyond the training data set.

These concepts are quantified in error calculation. From a statistical viewpoint, a mined model is an *estimator* for the underlying distribution of data. In the following, we restrict the presentation to *point estimation* of a single parameter p by an estimator $\hat{p}$ (see Dunham, 2003, p. 47).

The *bias* $B(\hat{p})$ describes the systematic error of $\hat{p}$ induced by the sampling procedure or the learning algorithm, which "cannot be reduced by increasing the sample size" (Cios et al., 2007, p. 471). It is calculated as difference between the expectation of the estimator $\hat{p}$ and the actual value of the parameter p (Cios et al., 2007, p. 471):

$$B(\hat{p}) = E[\hat{p}] - p \qquad (4.1)$$

The influence of the algorithm and its parameterization is sometimes called *inductive bias* (Aalst and Weijters, 2004, Sec. 5.1): Strong inductive bias means that a "strong tendency [...] towards certain solutions" (Luykx, 2009, p. 2) is built into an algorithm. Data mining users might be unaware of this and mistakenly consider models as 'pure' representations of data-intrinsic properties.

The *variance* $S^2(\hat{p})$ is the mean square deviation of estimations by $\hat{p}$ from actual values of p in N independent experiments (Cios et al., 2007, p. 471):

$$S^2(\hat{p}) = \frac{\sum_{i=1}^{N} (\hat{p}_i - p_i)^2}{N - 1} \qquad (4.2)$$

Variance and squared bias constitute the mean square error (MSE) as one of the most common error measures in data mining (Cios et al., 2007, p. 471):

$$MSE(\hat{p}) = E[\hat{p} - p]^2 = S^2(\hat{p}) + B^2(\hat{p}) \qquad (4.3)$$

The decomposition of error into bias and variance leads to the notion of the *bias/variance dilemma* (Geman et al., 1992) that describes an inevitable tradeoff in inductive learning: Simple data mining algorithms with few parameters and regarded features usually have a strong bias (Cios et al., 2007, p. 209). Such estimators tend to be stable but more likely to be stuck in local optima (Luykx, 2009, p. 2). When the bias is reduced by making algorithm and feature set more complex, the variance increases (Cios et al., 2007, p. 209), which tends to make the estimator unstable (Luykx, 2009, p. 2).

In general, an appropriate balance between bias and variance must be reached (AiAccess, 2010). Apart from that, Aalst and Weijters (2004, Sec. 5.1) advocate the use of biased algorithms when few data but good background knowledge about the searched models is available: When flexibility is not an issue, biased algorithm require less data, are more robust to noise, and computationally less complex.

4.1.3.3. Common Approaches to Validation

According to Cios et al. (2007, p. 469), model validation in data mining – similar to computer simulation – largely depends on ratings by domain experts. Nevertheless, several approaches have been developed that help to improve the quality of mined models independent from or additional to expert reviews (Cios et al., 2007, p. 469).

First of all, different types of learning algorithms require different validation approaches (Cios et al., 2007, p. 471): In supervised learning, the quality of a model is measured based on the number of correctly classified training data items. Validation is more difficult in unsupervised learning (Cios et al., 2007, p. 471): On the one hand, we can calculate the conformance of a cluster partition to the underlying data distribution as average distance between cluster centroids and sample data items. On the other hand, the appropriateness and consistence of the partitioning itself must be validated using measures for cluster validity (Cios et al., 2007, Ch. 9).

Cios et al. (2007, p. 471) subdivide validation techniques into data-reuse (resampling) methods, heuristic methods, analytical methods, and interestingness criteria. These are briefly reviewed in the following.

Data Reuse Methods are, broadly speaking, concerned with the question how to gain the best model quality from a limited sample data set. Simply re-using identical data for training and validation is clearly not a good choice.

Therefore, the available data is split into training and test parts, where the training part should consist of about 1/2 or 2/3 of the overall data items chosen by random (Cios et al., 2007, p. 473). Since this *simple split* typically leads to high bias and low variance, a more elaborate *k-fold cross validation* might be performed (Cios et al., 2007, p. 473): The data set is randomly partitioned into k equal parts with $k-1$ parts for training and 1 part for validation. The MSE is then calculated from k repetitions of the procedure (Cios et al., 2007, p. 473).

Heuristic Methods for model validation are informal but rather common due to their simplicity (Cios et al., 2007, p. 471). As a simple heuristic for model selection, a variant of *Occam's Razor* (see also Section 2.4.3.4) can e.g. be applied by preferring, from a number of models with similar performance, the most 'simple' one like the model with the fewest degrees of freedom (Cios et al., 2007, p. 470, p. 474). However, Cios et al. (2007, p. 475) note that this is not always a good heuristic in practice: Firstly, similar heuristics are part of many data mining algorithms already and might therefore not be appropriate for the validation of their results. Secondly, a simple model might not be appropriate to describe a very complex system.

Analytical Methods are applied to formally measure model validity (Cios et al., 2007, p. 475). Some of these methods assume knowledge about the optimal mapping from input to output data with respect to the training set, while others do not require such knowledge (Cios et al., 2007, p. 477).

In the first category, we find several measurements based on the *confusion matrix* that describes the performance of a classifier (Dunham, 2003, p. 79). In the style of Dunham (2003, p. 79), we assume a classifier $\hat{c}$ that accepts or rejects data items $s \in S$ according to their assumed membership to a class C. The confusion matrix contains four entries (adopted with modifications Dunham, 2003, p. 79):

- TP (true positive): $\hat{c}$ accepts s and $s \in C$,

- FP (false positive): $\hat{c}$ accepts s though $s \notin C$,

- TN (true negative): $\hat{c}$ rejects s and $s \notin C$,

- FN (false negative): $\hat{c}$ rejects s though $s \in C$.

From this matrix, several performance measures for classifiers can be calculated including recall, specifity, accuracy, and precision (Cios et al., 2007, p. 478). *Recall* and *specifity* express the classifier's ability to correctly identify elements belonging (or not belonging) to C (adopted with modifications from Cios et al., 2007, p. 478):

$$Recall(\hat{c}) = \frac{TP}{TP + FN} \tag{4.4}$$

$$Specifity(\hat{c}) = \frac{TN}{TN + FP} \tag{4.5}$$

Precision originates from text mining and describes the ability of a classifier (e.g. a web search engine) to retrieve *relevant* documents (adopted with modifications from (Cios et al., 2007, p. 478)):

$$Precision(\hat{c}) = \frac{TP}{TP + FP} \tag{4.6}$$

Accuracy captures the general ability of a classifier to perform correct predictions on the sample set S and is a rather weak measure compared to specifity and recall (adopted with modifications from Cios et al., 2007, p. 478):

$$Accuracy(\hat{c}) = \frac{TP + TN}{|S|} \tag{4.7}$$

The above measures can only be applied in supervised learning settings where *a-priori* knowledge about class membership is available. Other analytical methods (e.g. for hypothesis testing) pose additional restrictions on the data distribution (e.g. normal) often not met in practice (Cios et al., 2007, p. 475).

When none of these assumptions hold, *information content complexity* (see Section 2.1.1) can be applied for model assessment (Cios et al., 2007, p. 475). From an information-theoretical viewpoint, learning a model as an input/output mapping from a set of sample data can be regarded as a *compression* of the data set (Cios et al., 2007, p. 475). According to the well-known *minimum description length* (MDL) principle, the worst-case complexity of a model is the size of the represented data set (Cios et al., 2007, p. 475), which corresponds to maximal overfitting in the bias-variance dilemma (Cios et al., 2007, p. 476).

According to Cios et al. (2007, p. 476) "the MDL principle can be seen as a formalization of the Occam's Razor heuristic". Let $|M|$ denote the length of the (shortest) binary encoding of a model M, and let $|M(S)|$ denote the size of the sample dataset S compressed with M, then following the MDL principle, we prefer the model with the minimal sum

$$|M| + |M(S)| \rightarrow Min! \tag{4.8}$$

as the best compromise between over- and under-fitting (adopted with modifications from Cios et al., 2007, p. 475).

Interestingness criteria, finally, are an attempt to formalize the relevance of discovered rules to users based on domain-specific and general interestingness measures. A brief summary of this approach can be found in (Cios et al., 2007, pp. 484).

4.1.4. Exemplary Data Mining Techniques

To provide the reader with an impression how data mining is actually performed, exemplary DM algorithms will be reviewed in the following. Focus is put on techniques also relevant in the context of process mining.

4.1.4.1. Decision Tree Learning

A decision tree is a classifier generated by supervised learning. Dunham (2003, p. 59) illustrates the concept as

> "a tree where the root node and each internal node are labelled with a question. The arcs emanating from each node represent each possible answer to the associated question. Each leaf node represents a prediction of a solution to the problem under consideration."

Decision trees are interpretable classification models, the application of which can be roughly compared to the "20 questions game" played by children (Dunham, 2003, pp. 58): Trying to guess a person by asking yes/no-questions only, an experienced player will choose questions that presumably divide the search space into partitions of equal size (such as 'Is the person male or female?'). The same principle underlies decision tree learning.

Though several algorithms for decision tree learning exist, a common basic structure can be identified that is sketched by Dunham (2003, p. 94). Given a sample dataset $S = s_1, s_2, \ldots, s_n$ of feature vectors $s_i \in A_1 \times A_2 \cdots \times A_k$ with k categorical attributes, a decision tree T can be obtained with the following procedure (adopted with modifications from Dunham, 2003, p. 94):

1. Set $T := \emptyset$.

2. Find the 'best' attribute A_i to split the sample data set S.

3. Add a (root) node n to T and label it with A_i.

4. For each attribute value $a \in A_i/S$ appearing in S, add an outgoing edge e_a to n and label it with a.

5. For each edge e_a:

   a) Let $S_a \subseteq S$ be the subset of data items containing attribute value a.

   b) If a stopping criterion is met, then append a leaf node to e_a and label it with the associated class.

   c) Otherwise apply the above procedure recursively to the subset S_a and append the resulting subtree T_a to e_a.

This "simplistic [...] algorithm" (Dunham, 2003, p. 94) contains several placeholders including the choice of a splitting criterion, the number of splits taken, the preferred tree structure (e.g. deep vs. flat), an appropriate stopping criterion, and the pruning strategy to reduce tree size (Dunham, 2003, p. 94-95). Effectiveness and efficiency of real-world decision tree learners depend on how these placeholders are filled.

Dunham (2003, p. 94) stresses that the performance of decision tree learning is mainly influenced by the number of processed data items and by the selection of a splitting criterion. One viable approach is the use of entropy in the well-known algorithm *ID3* (Dunham, 2003, p. 97). Entropy is applied in information theory to quantify "the amount of [...] surprise or randomness in a data set" (Dunham, 2003, p. 97).

The entropy of a data set S is minimal when all contained items are members of the same class (Dunham, 2003, p. 97). Since the objective of decision tree mining is to partition the input data by class membership, the problem can be reduced to a minimization of the overall partition entropy (Dunham, 2003, p. 98).

Formally[2], we assume that the items $s \in S$ can be divided into n disjoint classes $\{C_1, C_2, \ldots, C_k\}$. Let $p_i = P(s \in C_i)$ denote the probability that an item s is member of C_i. Then the entropy of S is expressed by (Dunham, 2003, p. 98):

$$H(S) = H(p_1, p_2, \ldots, p_n) = \sum_{i=1}^{n} p_i \cdot \log(1/p_i). \tag{4.9}$$

To find the best splitting criterion for a given input S, the ID3 algorithm evaluates the entropy gained by the particular split (Dunham, 2003, p. 98). Let $\pi_A(S) = \{S_1, S_2, \ldots, S_k\}$ be a partition of S into k disjoint subsets by a splitting attribute A. The *entropy gain* of the split is expressed by (Dunham, 2003, p. 98):

$$Gain(\pi_A(S)) = H(S) - \sum_{i=1}^{k} P(S_i) \cdot H(S_i). \tag{4.10}$$

By choosing the splitting criterion with maximum gain, the ID3 algorithm strives to achieve a division of the input data into possibly equal-sized partitions in every step, roughly comparable to the presented "20 questions game" heuristics (Dunham, 2003, p. 97).

On the downside, the algorithm must occasionally assign the same splitting attribute to multiple nodes of the generated tree and "favors attributes with many divisions" (Dunham, 2003, p. 100). The widely-used *C*4.5 algorithm extends ID3 in several aspects including "missing data [...], continuous data [...], pruning strategies [...]" (Dunham, 2003, p. 100), and an improved splitting criterion that reduces the number of divisions in the resulting tree (Dunham, 2003, p. 101).

4.1.4.2. Clustering

In clustering (Dunham, 2003, pp. 125), an input data set S is segmented into clusters of similar items, where each cluster represents a different class. Since the number of classes and

---

[2]The formalizations in this and the following paragraphs are adopted with modifications from Dunham (2003, p. 98) using partition notation in the style of Angluin (1982).

their membership functions are unknown in advance, unsupervised learning is applied. Several clustering algorithms exists that differ in the used clustering strategies and in the applied similarity measures.

Clustering Strategies Concerning clustering strategies, Dunham (2003, p. 128) distinguishes hierarchical, partitional, categorical, and large database approaches and characterizes them as follows:

Hierarchical algorithms compute an increasingly (or decreasingly) refined hierarchy of clusterings. In the coarsest partition, all data items are in the same cluster, while in the finest partition each item belongs to an own cluster (Dunham, 2003, p. 128). *Agglomerative* (bottom-up) strategies start from the finest partition and proceed to an appropriate clustering by cluster merging (Dunham, 2003, p. 132). *Divisive* (top-down) strategies begin with the coarsest partition and proceed by splitting inappropriate clusters (Dunham, 2003, p. 138). In any case, the user can choose the most appropriate clustering from the hierarchy which is often output in the form of a *dendrogram*, i.e. a tree of increasingly refined clusters (Dunham, 2003, p. 131).

Partitional algorithms only provide a single clustering as an output (Dunham, 2003, p. 138). The main problem is therefore to find an appropriate number of clusters, which can be either predefined by the user as an input parameter (Dunham, 2003, p. 138) or determined by the algorithm at runtime using an error threshold (Dunham, 2003, p. 142).

Categorical algorithms are dedicated to the problem of clustering categorical (i.e. non-continuous) data (Dunham, 2003, p. 157). *Large database approaches* focus on the clustering of large real-world databases where the input data set does not fit into working memory at once (Dunham, 2003, p. 149).

Distance Measures (or *similarity measures* as the 'inverse' term) are used by cluster algorithms to determine the distance (or similarity) between data items and clusters. Generally, the distance between neighboring items belonging to the same cluster should be less than the distance between those from different clusters (Dunham, 2003, p. 129).

The distance between two data items is measured depending on the domain of the data attributes. For data encoded by numerical feature vectors over a metric vector space, measures like the Euclidian distance are applied (Dunham, 2003, p. 59):

$$dist(\mathbf{x}, \mathbf{y}) = \sqrt{\sum_{i=1}^{d}(x_i - y_i)^2} \qquad (4.11)$$

where $\mathbf{x}, \mathbf{y}$ denote vectors of dimension d and x_i, y_i their components. As indicated above, different measures must be used for categorical data. One example is the *Jaccard coefficient*

$$sim(\mathbf{x}, \mathbf{y}) = \frac{\mathbf{x} \cap \mathbf{y}}{\mathbf{x} \cup \mathbf{y}} \qquad (4.12)$$

that determines the similarity of two data tuples $\mathbf{x}, \mathbf{y}$ by dividing the number of common components by the number of overall components in both tuples (Dunham, 2003, p. 158).

Example: Nearest Neighbour Algorithm   Though numerous clustering algorithms exist, we will only review one example here, that will also be applied in the process mining study reported in Chapter 7. The *Nearest Neighbor algorithm* is a simple partitional algorithm based on shortest cluster distance (Dunham, 2003, p. 142).

Let $S = s_1, s_2, \ldots, s_n$ be a list of input data items, $dist : S \times S \rightarrow [0, 1]$ a distance measure and $t \in [0, 1]$ a predefined threshold value. Then a set $C = C_1, C_2, \ldots, C_k$ of clusters can be computed as follows (adopted with modifications from Dunham (2003, p. 142)):

1. Set $C := \emptyset$.

2. Dequeue the first item s_0 from the list S and set $C := \{\{s_0\}\}$ as the initial cluster.

3. While $|S| > 0$:

   a) Dequeue the next item s from the list.

   b) Find the cluster $C_i \in C$ that contains the item $s' \in C_i$ with the minimum distance $dist(s, s')$ of all items clustered so far.

      i. If $dist(s, s') < t$ set $C_i := C_i \cup \{s\}$.

      ii. Otherwise set $C := C \cup \{\{s\}\}$.

4. Output the resulting cluster set C.

Different from other partitional algorithms, the number of output clusters is not stated explicitly, but depends on the threshold t (Dunham, 2003, p. 142). The time complexity of the algorithm is $O(n^2)$ since all pairs of input data items are compared (Dunham, 2003, p. 142). An overview of further clustering algorithms is e.g. found in Dunham (2003, Ch. 5) and Cios et al. (2007, Ch. 9)

4.1.4.3. Inductive Logic Programming

Inductive Logic Programming (ILP) is closely related to knowledge representation in predicate logic and programming languages like *Prolog* (Bratko, 1990). According to Muggleton et al. (1995, p. 243), the deduction process of inference engines (see Section 3.3.1.1) is *inverted* in ILP: From an example knowledge base containing positive and negative facts, a set of predicate logic rules (theory) is learned (induced) that abstractly describes the represented knowledge.

Nienhuys-Cheng and de Wolf (1997, pp. 166) formalize the basic ILP setting like this: A theory is a finite set of clauses $\Sigma = \{C_1, C_2, \ldots, C_n\}$. E^+ and E^- denote possibly infinite sets of positive and negative example clauses (typically ground literals), and B denotes a finite, possibly empty, set of clauses representing available *background knowledge*.

Further following Nienhuys-Cheng and de Wolf (1997, p. 166), a theory Σ is *correct* with respect to E^+ and E^- if it is consistent with E^- and complete with respect to E^+. Completeness means that every clause $e \in E^+$ can be derived from Σ (denoted as $\Sigma \models E^+$). Consistency means that no assignment of boolean values to predicates can be found that satisfies $\Sigma \cup \overline{E^-}$ where $\overline{E^-} = \{\neg e_i | e_i \in E^-\}$.

On this foundation a basic induction procedure is stated (adopted with modifications from Nienhuys-Cheng and de Wolf, 1997, p.168): Let E^+, E^-, B be defined as above, such that B is correct with respect to E^+ and E^-. Then Σ is induced as follows:

1. Set Σ to an initial value (e.g. $\Sigma := \emptyset$).

2. If $\Sigma \cup B$ is correct with respect to E^+ and E^- then terminate and output Σ.

3. If $\exists e \in E^+ : \Sigma \cup B \not\models e$ ($\Sigma \cup B$ is too weak) then generalize Σ and return to the second step.

4. If $\exists e \in E^- : \Sigma \cup B \models e$ ($\Sigma \cup B$ is too strong) then specialize Σ and return to the second step.

ILP implementations refine this basic scheme in several dimensions, e.g. reviewed by Nienhuys-Cheng and de Wolf (1997, pp. 169). Important criteria include the predefined *language bias* related to the available logical language (e.g. Horn clauses) and the rules to modify, create, and delete predicates of Σ (Nienhuys-Cheng and de Wolf, 1997, pp. 171).

4.1.4.4. Bayesian Networks

Bayesian networks are acyclic graph models that display dependencies between multiple random variables in order to "represent knowledge about an uncertain domain" (Ben-Gal, 2007, p. 1). The name relates to Bayes' well-known theorem to calculate conditional probabilities (e.g. Kjaerulff and Madsen, 2005, p. 45).

According to Ben-Gal (2007, p. 1), "nodes [... in the graph] represent random variables [... and] edges represent [their] direct dependencies". Every node is furthermore inscribed with the conditional probability distribution of the respective variable depending on its predecessors in the graph (Ben-Gal, 2007, p. 1), (Chen, 2009, p. 121).

From an existing Bayesian network, new knowledge can be inferred in the form of *predictive* and *diagnostic support* (Ben-Gal, 2007, p. 3): In the former case, the joint probability of a child note ('effect') is calculated from the estimated probabilities of its predecessors ('causes') (Ben-Gal, 2007, p. 3).[3] In the latter case, the probabilities of causes are calculated from the observation of an effect (Ben-Gal, 2007, p. 3).

Besides deductive reasoning, Bayesian networks can also be induced from observations (i.e. data mining) with algorithms like *maximum likelihood estimation* and *expectation minimization* (Ben-Gal, 2007, pp. 3-4). We will encounter Bayesian networks in the review of approaches towards the identification of cause-effect relations in MABS (e.g. Chen, 2009) in Section 5.

4.1.4.5. Techniques from Soft Computing

The term *Soft Computing* describes a range of algorithms and data representations inspired by natural or social phenomena. Soft computing techniques include (Maimon and Rokach, 2008, p. 1):

---

[3]The use of the terms 'cause' and 'effect' in this context is adopted from authors like Kjaerulff and Madsen (2005, p. 2).

- *artificial neural networks*: models and algorithms inspired by brain functions found in animals and humans.

- *evolutionary algorithms*: optimization algorithms inspired by natural evolution.

- *fuzzy logic*: data representation and deduction rules based on 'soft', possibly overlapping categories instead of boolean logic.

- *swarm intelligence*: optimization algorithms that simulate self organization and division of labor found in natural swarming phenomena and colonies of insects.

In the following, we briefly review neural networks, and evolutionary algorithms, that will be referred to later in the context of process mining. Fuzzy logic is e.g. treated by Lämmel and Cleve (2008, Sec. 2.4), swarm intelligence by Kennedy (2001).

Artificial Neural Networks: From the large body of neural network models and algorithms, we present feed-forward networks and self-organizing maps as two common examples that support different data mining tasks.

A feedforward neural network consists of formal neurons as shown in Figure 4.2. In rough analogy to natural neurons, these are basically threshold elements that compute a weighted sum of their input signals. From this sum, an output is generated using a threshold (or activation) function like a sigmoid or step function (see e.g. Ferber, 1995, p. 137).

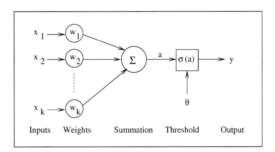

Figure 4.2.: "Functionality of a formal neuron (from Haykin, 1999, p. 11)". Figure and caption adopted from Page and Kreutzer (2005, p. 343; also in Knaak, 2002, p. 11).

A single neuron can solve simple classification problems: When the components of a (numerical) feature vector are assigned to the neuron's inputs, the output signal indicates class membership (Dunham, 2003, p. 103). To learn a classification function over an input vector space S, the input weights of a neuron are adapted by supervised learning using the *delta rule*; e.g. described by Lämmel and Cleve (2008, p. 185).

The classification ability of single neuron layers is restricted to *linearly separable functions* (Lämmel and Cleve, 2008, p. 187). This limitation is overcome by networks of multiple interconnected layers. To train a multi-layer network, the simple delta rule cannot be applied directly but error information must be fed back through the network using *back propagation* (see e.g. Lämmel and Cleve, 2008, pp. 191; Ferber, 1995, p. 138).

A class of neural networks tailored towards clustering with unsupervised learning is called *self organizing maps* (see e.g. Lämmel and Cleve, 2008, p. 261). A self-organizing map consists of an input layer $N_I = \{m_1, m_2, \ldots m_n\}$ and a map layer $N_M = \{n_1, n_2, \ldots n_k\}$ of neurons m_i, n_j (see e.g. Lämmel and Cleve (2008, p. 261)). The number of input neurons equals the dimension n of the input vector space S, while the number k of map neurons is a fixed parameter.

Each input neuron m_i is connected to all map neurons n_j via weighted arcs w_{ij} (Lämmel and Cleve, 2008, p. 262), i.e. each n_j is assigned a vector $\mathbf{w}_j = (w_{1j}, w_{2j}, \ldots, w_{kj})$ (Lämmel and Cleve, 2008, p. 265). This vector can be interpreted as the position of n_j in S and used for visualization in low-dimensional cases (Lämmel and Cleve, 2008, p. 268). In a training process called *competitive learning*, the neurons are moved towards the centers of (preferably distinct) clusters of input vectors (see e.g. Lämmel and Cleve, 2008, pp. 260, 265, 267).

Evolutionary Algorithms are heuristic optimization algorithms that simulate natural evolution. Data mining can be viewed as an optimization problem where the task is to find the most appropriate model for the given input data (Dunham, 2003, p. 67).

Two common classes of evolutionary algorithms are *genetic algorithms* (GA) and *genetic programming* (GP); see Burke and Kendall (2005, p. 14). Both approaches work with *populations* of *individuals*: Like a DNA encodes features of an organism, each individual represents a solution to the given problem in a well-defined encoding (Dunham, 2003, p. 67).

In every iteration of the algorithm (*generation*), only the 'fittest' individuals with respect to an objective function 'survive'. The next generation is set up by *selection*, splitting and combination (*crossover*), and random modifications (*mutation*) of these individuals (Dunham, 2003, p. 67; Medeiros et al., 2004b, p. 5). The process is repeated until a stopping criterion, like a maximum number of iterations or a desired goodness of the fitness function, is met (e.g. Medeiros et al., 2004b, p. 13).

GA and GP mainly differ in the encodings of individuals. GA are domain-independent since very general encodings like bit strings are used. The main challenge is to encode problem instances in this general form, and to define appropriate crossover and mutation operations[4]. In GP, individuals represent expressions of a programming language (e.g. LISP) in the form similar to parsing trees (Poli et al., 2008, p. 9). Crossover and mutation are defined with respect to the syntax of the underlying programming language, i.e. branches of the operator trees are exchanged or modified (Poli et al., 2008, pp. 15).

Due to large numbers of generations and individuals, the computational complexity of evolutionary algorithm tends to be rather high. However, the inherent parallelism of the approach allows for a straightforward execution in distributed environments (see e.g. Gehlsen, 2004).

4.1.5. Tools for Data Mining

In rough analogy to Page's (1991, Sec. 6.1) classification scheme for simulation software, we can distinguish the following types of software systems for data mining:

1. General programming languages and data mining APIs[5],

---

[4] see Medeiros et al. (2004b, pp. 8) reviewed in Section 4.2.3.4 for an example from process mining

[5] Application Programming Interface

2. data mining-specific programming languages and databases,

3. knowledge discovery and scientific workflow systems

4.1.5.1. Programming Languages and APIs

Obviously, data mining algorithms can be implemented in any general programming language. C and C++ are often preferred for performance reasons, while Java is especially common in the academic field. One important aspect is database access, which many current programming languages support in the form of libraries for database access via SQL (e.g. *JDBC*[6] for Java) and object/relational mappers (e.g. *Hibernate*[7]).

To promote re-usability and standardization, several object-oriented frameworks and APIs for data mining have been developed in industry and education. A common academic example is the Java-based open source framework *WEKA* from Waikato University (New Zealand) (Hall et al., 2009). This framework provides common interfaces and base classes for different data mining tasks as well as implementations of several data mining algorithms.

4.1.5.2. Data Mining-Specific Languages

These are often extensions of database query languages like SQL (Structured Query Language; see e.g. Cannan, 1993). One example is DMQL (Data Mining Query Language) that extends SQL with data mining-specific constructs to state background knowledge in the form of ontologies, rules for data mining, threshold values, etc. (Dunham, 2003, p. 18).

The development of data mining-specific query languages must be accompanied by extensions of database management systems (DBMS) towards data mining, as well as extensions of data mining algorithms towards the handling of real-world databases (Dunham, 2003, p. 17). However, Dunham (2003, p. 17) notes that the state of the art in data mining systems is roughly comparable to the state of DBMS "in the early 1960s".

4.1.5.3. Knowledge Discovery Systems

Analogous to the classification scheme by Page (1991, Sec. 6.1), Ahonen (1998) defines a *knowledge discovery system* (KDS) as a software tool that supports a relevant number of phases in the knowledge discovery process (see Section 4.1.1).

Dunham (2003, p. 18) uses the related term "knowledge and data discovery management system (KDDMS)" to describe (next generation) data mining systems

> "that include not only data mining tools but also techniques to manage the underlying data, ensure its consistency, and provide concurrency and recovery features. A KDDMS will provide access via ad hoc data mining queries that have been optimized for efficient access."

---

[6]see http://www.oracle.com/technetwork/java/overview-141217.html, last visit 2012-09-18
[7]http://www.hibernate.org, last visit 2012-09-18

The definition of KDS includes KDDMS but also applies to systems with a less distinct DBMS focus. Ahonen (1998) states that "a lot of generic single-task tools [are] available" in data mining and regards the intuitive integration of such tools, the related "concepts and vocabulary", and available domain-specific knowledge as main challenges in the development of KDS.

Today, an increasing number of systems dedicated or at least applicable to knowledge discovery can be found. These are rooted in fields like statistics (e.g. the commercial *SPSS* suite[8]) and scientific computing (e.g. *MATLAB*[9]). The open source tool WEKA (see above) can also be regarded as a knowledge discovery system since it includes three graphical user interfaces *Explorer, Experimenter*, and *Knowledge Flow* that support the interactive and automated execution of knowledge discovery processes (Hall et al., 2009, pp. 10).

In the following paragraphs, a common technique to model knowledge discovery processes in KDS is described. The choice of content and literature references is largely based on the diploma thesis by Simmendinger (2007, Ch. 3).

4.1.5.4. Data Flow Modeling

Different from control flow modeling, *data flow modeling* is focused on multi-step transformations from input to output data (Shields, 2007, cited in Simmendinger, 2007, p. 32). A – possibly concurrent – execution order of the transformations is defined by dependencies between producers and consumers of the exchanged data elements (Simmendinger, 2007, p. 32).

Data flow diagrams (DFDs) from structured system analysis are one popular notation to model data flow at the conceptual level using four symbols shown in Figure 4.3 (see e.g. Lee and Tan, 1992, pp. 4-5). These symbols are sufficient to display the fundamental data flow between processes of a system, while omitting details of control flow (see e.g. Bruza and van der Weide, 1993, p. 1).

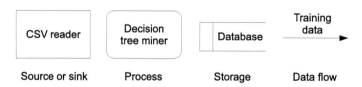

Figure 4.3.: Elements of data flow diagrams with example instantiations from the data mining domain (adopted with modifications from Lee and Tan, 1992, p. 5).

Since the informal notation of DFDs lacks a concise operational semantics (Bruza and van der Weide, 1993, p. 2), extensions and mappings to formal languages like path expressions and Petri nets (see Section 2.3.2.1) have been proposed (e.g. Bruza and van der Weide, 1993, pp. 4-9). Mapping data flow notations to executable formalisms leads to the challenge to represent data and control flow in the same model while retaining understandability and maintainability (Bowers et al., 2006, p. 2) as well as support for concurrency and stream processing (Bowers et al., 2006, p. 1, cited in Simmendinger, 2007, p. 33).

---

[8]http://www.spss.com, last visit 2010-12-01.
[9]http://www.mathworks.com, last visit 2010-12-01.

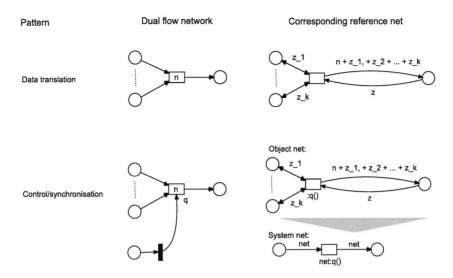

Figure 4.4.: Two of four mappings of DFN patterns to reference nets shown by Farwer and Varea (2005, p. 8).

This problem is caused by the fact that control flow constructs are, to a certain extent, also required in data flow applications, e.g. to realize fault-tolerance, adaptivity, and access to complex data structures (Bowers et al., 2006, p. 2). However, the modeling of control flow with mere data flow constructs often results in unnecessarily complicated workflows that mix low level control flow constructs with high level components (Bowers et al., 2006, p. 2). In the following we briefly review a theoretical and a practice-oriented approach to tackle this problem.

Dual Flow Nets and Object Petri Nets Farwer and Varea (2005) propose to disentangle data and control flow with the aid of an object-based nets-within-nets formalism (see Section 2.3.2.5). The proposal is based on *Dual Flow Nets* (DFNs), a variant of P/T nets with 3 node types including places as storage elements, transitions as control flow elements, and *hulls* as transformational elements for arithmetic operations on data (Farwer and Varea, 2005, p. 2). DFNs are an earlier attempt to solve the problem of combined data and control flow by means of a modified execution semantics (Farwer and Varea, 2005, p. 1).

A marking of a place p is a tuple (n, z), where n is the number of control flow tokens and z an integer data element residing at p (Farwer and Varea, 2005, p. 3). The synchronization of data- and control flow proceeds in two directions: A transition can be inscribed with a guard function from the set $G = \{=, \neq, <, >, \leq, \geq\}$ as an additional firing condition evaluated over the data tokens on incoming places (Farwer and Varea, 2005, p. 2). Hulls are triggered by the firing of incoming transitions to perform a summation of data elements from incoming places (Farwer and Varea, 2005, pp. 4,8).

4. Data Mining and Process Mining

Farwer and Varea (2005) transform DFNs to a subset of reference nets to receive a more 'Petri net-like' firing semantics. Basically, the control flow of the DFN is extracted into a system net. The arithmetic operations by the hulls are realized in an object net flowing through the system net, where the triggering of hulls by transitions is mapped to synchronous channels. Farwer and Varea (2005, p. 8) map four main patterns of DFNs to reference nets (see Figure 4.4) and present a net for the computation of the Fibonacci series as an example (Farwer and Varea, 2005, p. 11).

Structured Composition of Data and Control Flow Bowers et al. (2006) present a more practical approach to combine data and control flow modeling implemented in the scientific workflow system *Kepler*. As summarized by Simmendinger (2007, p. 44), the approach utilizes a combination of *Dataflow Process Networks*, a common notation for data flow modeling, and finite state machines to model control flow. Furthermore, Bowers et al. (2006, p. 4) distinguish between *actor* components as implementations of concrete processing algorithms and *frames* as abstract specifications of functionality by signatures (i.e. input and output ports).

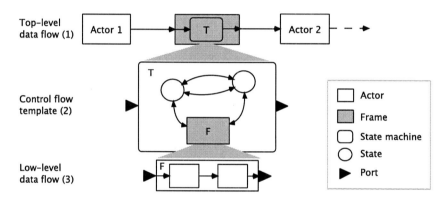

Figure 4.5.: Structured modeling of scientific workflows with alternating data and control flow layers. Adopted with modifications from Bowers et al. (2006, p. 6, cited in Simmendinger, 2007, p. 45).

These concepts are recursively embedded in a three-level hierarchy shown in Figure 4.5 and reviewed by Simmendinger (2007, p. 44) as follows: (1) On the top level, data flow components for specific tasks are composed into a data flow network. (2) A top level frame is implemented by one or more alternative state machines representing the local control flow of the respective task. (3) Each state of the automaton is again a frame that can be implemented by a data flow network for the actual data processing performed in that state.

By keeping control flow local to the state machines, implementations of data processing algorithms remain largely stateless and easy to re-use as part of different workflows (Simmendinger, 2007, p. 44). Simmendinger (2007, p. 44) gives the example of a workflow in a web service-based system: Communication-related aspects like load-balancing and authentication can be modelled in the state machine and thereby kept out of the data flow model that performs the actual processing when an appropriate state is reached.

Despite the different underlying intentions (i.e. theoretical verifiability vs. practical applicability), the approach by Bowers et al. (2006) also shares a few common ideas with the reference net-based model by Farwer and Varea (2005):

1. Layers 2 (control flow) and 3 (low level data flow) in the model by Bowers et al. (2006) roughly correspond to the separation of system and object nets in the model by Farwer and Varea (2005). However, the low-level data flow models in the former approach do not 'move' through the superordinate control flow model but are assigned to fixed states.

2. The combination of multiple task-specific notations (i.e. data flow networks and state machines) slightly resembles the possibility to use different *formalisms* in RENEW (Simmendinger, 2007, p. 44).

4.1.5.5. Scientific Workflow Systems

Data flow modeling in scientific applications has recently received recurring interest under the notion of *scientific workflows*. The basic idea is to apply and adapt concepts and tools from business processes modeling for the scientific domain. Based on the literature, Simmendinger (2007) summarizes the following characteristics of scientific workflows as compared to business workflows (described in Section 2.3.3):

- increased importance of data flow (Simmendinger, 2007, p. 27),

- integration of several heterogeneous tools and data formats into a common workflow (Simmendinger, 2007, pp. 27, 44),

- appropriate user interaction and guidance in complex tasks (Simmendinger, 2007, pp. 29, 44),

- support for ressource-intensive, long running calculations in distributed environments (Simmendinger, 2007, p. 29).

The aspect of distribution has received specific attention in the context of recent distribution concepts like *Grid* (e.g. Guan et al., 2006) or *Cloud Computing* (e.g. Hoffa et al., 2008). It is, however, not a defining property of scientific workflow systems. Especially in data mining, several workflow-based systems mainly focus on data flow modeling, method and tool integration, and user assistance.

Authors like Rice and Boisvert (1996) use the term 'Problem Solving Environment' (PSE) for systems that combine domain specific libraries with a user interface, a knowledge base of common patterns, and methods for tool integration (cited in Simmendinger, 2007, p. 28). Simmendinger (2007, p. 29) notes that the guiding patterns from the knowledge base can be well realized in the form of workflows.

Two common examples of PSEs reviewed by Simmendinger (2007, Sec. 3.4) are *Keppler/Ptolemy*[10] and *KNIME*[11]. Keppler is a Java-based scientific computing system that utilizes the structured modeling approach by Bowers et al. (2006) described above. *KNIME* (Knowledge Information Miner) is a workflow-based, extendable knowledge discovery system that builds

---

[10]http://www.kepler-project.org, last visit 2010-12-15.

[11]http://www.knime.org, last visit 2010-12-15.

upon the Eclipse platform and integrates several third-party libraries (e.g. *WEKA*) in the form
of components. Section 8.4.3 presents our application of *KNIME* for a prototypical integration
of process mining techniques into an Eclipse-based simulation system.

4.2. Process Mining

In this section, process mining is introduced as a specific form of data mining guided by perspectives of (business) process and organizational modeling. After reviewing general definitions
and classifications, process mining techniques with relevance for this thesis are presented. A
brief summary of applications is finally followed by an introduction of the process mining tool
ProM. This tool forms a de-facto standard in process mining and the basis for the algorithms
implemented in this work.

4.2.1. Definitions

In (Cabac et al., 2006b, Sec. 3.1) we cited an early definition by Maruster et al. (2002, p. 1)
that describes process mining as "method for distilling a structured process description from a set of
real executions". Thus, the objective is to reconstruct a previously unknown process model from
log data produced by example executions, and to present the results in a structured modeling
language like e.g. Petri nets or UML diagrams.

Since the field has undergone large progress during the last decade, the above definition seems
too narrow to capture the diversity of current research activities in process mining (Dongen
et al., 2006b, p. 145). According to Aalst (2010a, p. 29), "The idea of process mining is to discover,
monitor and improve real processes (i.e. not assumed processes) by extracting knowledge from event
logs." Similarly, a call for workshop papers states that "the area of process mining is concerned
with the analysis of business processes in general, where the basis of this analysis is formed by the
recorded behavior of an information system in the form of an event log."[12] These descriptions imply
that process mining is not limited to 'mining' (i.e. process discovery) in the narrow sense, but
includes further tasks like conformance checking and extension of process models as well (Aalst,
2010a, p. 29).

Authors like Aalst (2010a, p. 28) emphasize the proximity of process mining to (business)
process modeling and analysis, which is mirrored in the alias term 'workflow mining'. Business
process analysis is the most prominent application of process mining. A major contribution of
business process modeling (BPM) consists in a set of 'process mining perspectives' derived from
BPM methodologies and notations. These perspectives represent different views that guide the
analysis of process logs.

With this broad definition in mind, a clear distinction between process mining and data mining
is not easy. Based on the literature, different aspects can be identified:

- *Type of input data*: Process mining is normally performed on process execution logs, i.e.
  lists of time stamped or at least chronologically ordered event or activity traces (Aalst

---

[12]http://www.mail-archive.com/petrinet@informatik.uni-hamburg.de/msg00770.html, last visit 2010-12-
28.

et al., 2012, p. 174). However, log data is not the only input for process mining algorithms: *Attributional data* embedded into process logs is considered to reconstruct decision models (Rozinat and Aalst, 2006) or ontologies (Medeiros et al., 2007). The *extension* of *input models* into improved output models is also regarded as process mining (Aalst, 2010a, p. 29).

- *Type of output models:* Process mining typically deals with graph-structured models related to process modeling notations (Aalst and Weijters, 2004, p. 239) like Petri nets, event-driven process chains (EPCs) or communication diagrams ('social networks'). In contrast, data mining is often concerned with models that "are not process-centric" (Aalst et al., 2012, p. 176), like rule-based and numerical models. However, this distinction appears rather weak since process mining has increasingly adopted algorithms and models from data mining (e.g. decision trees in Rozinat and Aalst, 2006), and data mining considers sequence, automata, and network models as well.

- *Application domain:* Most work in process mining is rooted in the field of business process analysis. Other application fields like e.g. software engineering (Rubin et al., 2007) have been considered as well.

- *Guiding perspectives:* One of the most characteristic properties of process mining is its guidance by perspectives from BPM (Aalst et al., 2012, p. 176). While multi-perspective approaches are also a topic of data mining research (see e.g. Furtado, 1999), the closest tie of mining techniques to multi-perspective modeling might be observed in process mining.

In the following chapters, we argue that the relation of process mining to multi-perspective modeling approaches makes these techniques especially well-suited for the analysis of multi-agent systems and simulations. For the moment, we can summarize the above observations from the literature as follows: Process mining is a sub-discipline of data mining concerned with computer-aided techniques for the acquisition, analysis, validation, improvement, and transformation of (business) process and organizational models on the basis of event- or activity-oriented logs of process executions. The development and application of process mining techniques is guided by process modeling languages and methodologies covering multiple perspectives.

4.2.2. Classification of Process Mining Techniques

Due to the broad scope of process mining, several attempts have been made to structure the field by classification of the available techniques. As one result of a workshop on "Process Mining and Monitoring of Services and Processes", Aalst (2006, p. 3-4) proposes the following (mostly orthogonal) dimensions for classification:[13]

1. Three different 'types' of process mining are distinguished by the *presence of an a-priori model*: In *process discovery*, no model exists beforehand, but a model is discovered from an execution log. In *conformance checking* and *extension*, an existing model is validated or modified respectively.

2. Several *perspectives* can be identified as different functional and non-functional views upon the analyzed system. The functional perspectives include aspects of control flow,

---

[13]The reduction of the original number of 6 dimensions to 5 by integrating the dimensions *perspectives* and *functional vs. non-functional* follows the summary by Weber and Wittenberger (2007, p. 12).

organization, work cases, resources, or data. The non-functional perspectives include measures of process performance and quality.

3. The considered *number of process instances* might range from a single case over multiple cases to all cases observed in a process log.

4. The examined *time period* can take into account *historic* data to discover characteristic process behavior or *real time* data to analyze the present situation.

5. Different *result types* are distinguished by their purpose, i.e. if the result merely *informs* about properties of the reconstructed process, or if an *action* is taken on this basis.

Actual classifications are often limited to process mining types and perspectives (e.g. Weber and Wittenberger, 2007, Sec. 2.1–2.2), additionally taking into account certain data- and algorithm-related properties that are considered as challenging (e.g. Weber and Wittenberger, 2007, p. 14). In the following, we inspect these most relevant dimensions in detail.

4.2.2.1. Process Mining Perspectives

The introduction of different perspectives into process mining was mainly promoted by the research group at Eindhoven University (the Netherlands; see e.g. Aalst and Song, 2004a) and a group of authors around Professor Clarence Ellis from the University of Colorado-Boulder (USA; see Rembert and Ellis, 2009). While the former researchers identify process mining perspectives in an ad-hoc fashion (Rembert and Ellis, 2009, p. 35), the latter provide a formalization based on the *Information Control Net* (ICN) meta-model for BPM (Rembert and Ellis, 2009, p. 37). Both approaches are contrasted in the following.

Eindhoven Approach   As criticized by Rembert and Ellis (2009), the Eindhoven research group mainly *enumerates* relevant perspectives driven by the development and application of algorithms. Nevertheless, this proceeding helped to identify a number of important perspectives. There is some agreement in the literature that the most relevant perspectives – with respect to the number of available algorithms and applications – are the *control flow perspective* and, to a lesser extent, the *organizational perspective* (e.g. Aalst, 2010a, p. 30; see also Figure 4.6).

Though publications differ in the identification of further relevant perspectives, the following list can be compiled from the literature:

1. *Control flow perspective*: The control flow of the considered process is reconstructed or analyzed based on log data (Aalst, 2010a, p. 30). The analysis might include basic control flow constructs like "sequences, branches, loops, and concurrency" (Cabac et al., 2006b, Sec. 3.1.1), as well as complex *workflow patterns* such as transactions. Aalst and Weijters (2004, p. 235) note that the focus on concurrency distinguishes process mining from earlier approaches for *grammar inference* (see Section 4.2.3.3).

2. *Organizational perspective*: This perspective "focuses on the "structure and the population" of the organization in which the processes are observed [..., including] "relations between roles [...] groups [...] and other artifacts" (Aalst and Weijters, 2004, p. 10)" (Cabac et al., 2006b, Sec. 3.1.1). It is alternatively called *resource perspective* (Aalst, 2006, p. 4).

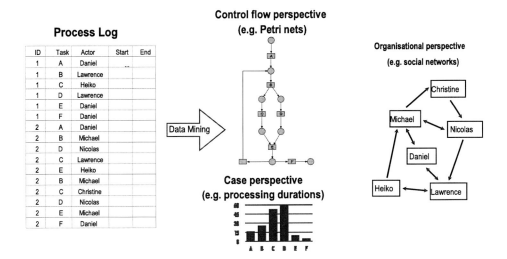

Figure 4.6.: A visualization of example process mining perspectives identified by the Eindhoven research group. Adopted with modifications from Dumas et al. (2005, p. 239).

3. *Information perspective*: This perspective is concerned with properties of "control and production data" processed in a workflow (Aalst and Weijters, 2004, p. 237), and is also called *data perspective* (Aalst, 2006, p. 4). One example is the reconstruction of branching decisions of a control flow model from attributes of the processed data (decision mining; see e.g. Rozinat and Aalst, 2006).

4. *Application perspective*: According to Aalst and Weijters (2004, p. 237), the view is on software applications used during the processing of a workflow. Though the authors do not name particular examples, work on *web service mining* (Dustdar and Gombotz, 2006) might be assigned to this perspective.

5. *Case perspective*: This perspective concentrates on work case-related properties like the particular path taken in the workflow, the actors involved, or values of certain data attributes in a workflow instance (Aalst, 2010a, p. 30).

6. *Performance perspective*: This non-functional perspective deals with quantitative "key performance indicators such as flow time, utilization, service level, etc." (Aalst, 2006, p. 4). Due to the focus on temporal measures, *time perspective* is an alternative name (Aalst, 2006, p. 4).

7. *Quality perspective*: Another non-functional perspective concerned with "quality measures, e.g. the number of failures, near-failures, customer satisfaction, etc." (Aalst, 2006, p. 4).

8. *Semantic perspective*: In a position paper on semantic process mining (Medeiros et al., 2007, p. 1253), this perspective is characterized by a focus on semantic concepts and relations (i.e. *ontologies*) that underly a process definition. On the one hand, logs can be enriched with semantic information to improve the capabilities of mining algorithms; on

the other hand, (parts of) ontologies might be reconstructed from process logs (Medeiros et al., 2007, p. 1253).

Two further research directions in the Eindhoven group with a focus on specific log types are *activity mining* and *change mining*. Both are not explicitly introduced as perspectives but might be understood this way. *Activity mining* is concerned with the reconstruction of well-defined task descriptions (such as 'submit order') from logs containing low-level operations like access to certain database attributes (see e.g. Günther et al., 2010). *Change mining* attempts to detect changes of a workflow schema (e.g. addition or removal of tasks) over time from logged *change operations* (see e.g. Günther et al., 2006).

Researchers have repeatedly stressed the need for algorithms that take into account perspectives other than control flow (see e.g. Aalst and Weijters, 2004, p. 237). Aalst and Weijters (2004, p. 237) especially emphasize the relevance of links between different perspectives. Nevertheless, a strong focus on the control flow perspective can still be observed, followed by significantly fewer work on organizational and data perspectives. Further perspectives are more or less limited to individual researchers and publications.

Information Control Net Approach   Rembert and Ellis (2009, p. 35) argue that an ad-hoc approach complicates the definition of new perspectives and algorithms as well as the comparison of existing algorithms for the same perspective (Rembert and Ellis, 2009, p. 36). These authors even hold this shortcoming responsible for the lack of work on perspectives beyond control flow (Rembert and Ellis, 2009, p. 35). As a solution, they propose a formalization of process perspectives based on the concept of process dimensions from the *Information Control Net* (ICN) meta-model (Rembert and Ellis, 2009, p. 36):

> "A *process dimension* is any measurable characteristic of a business process, such as the activities that compose it, the agents that collaboratively execute it, and the artifacts it uses and produces. [...]
>
> A *process perspective* is a pair of sets (D, M) where D is a set of process dimensions and M is a set of dimensional mappings over and between those process dimensions in D."

The entities and relations of a certain process perspective are explicitly represented by either a process model or a process pattern (Rembert and Ellis, 2009, p. 37). Both terms are distinguished as follows:

> "A *process entity* is any abstract, concrete, active, or functional resource that is used during the execution of a process instance. A process entity can be decomposed into an arbitrary number of (sub)process entities. [...]" (Rembert and Ellis, 2009, p. 36)
>
> "A *process model* [...] describes the appropriate mappings between all of the process entities in the process dimensions used in a particular process perspective. [...]
>
> A *process pattern* [...] describes the relationships of only a portion of the process entities in one or all of the process dimensions used." (Rembert and Ellis, 2009, p. 37)

An example of a process model is a global control flow model that relates *all* activities (process entities in the process dimension *activities*) of a process based on their precedences (Rembert and Ellis, 2009, p. 37). An example of a process pattern is a mapping in the *decision perspective*[14] that relates *some* activities (namely the decision activities) of a process model to decision rules (Rembert and Ellis, 2009, p. 37).

Practical benefit of the presented definitions is established by relating it to logs used in process mining and by stating a procedure for the systematic development of mining algorithms for arbitrary perspectives. The relation between process perspectives and logs is straightforward: A log can be regarded as a matrix where each column represents a process dimension (e.g. process instance, activity name, executing agent, and time stamp) and each row represents a logged event with certains values bound to each dimension (Rembert and Ellis, 2009, p. 37).

The proposed approach towards mining arbitrary process perspectives is a rather sketchy, general procedure that consists of four steps (Rembert and Ellis, 2009, p. 38):

1. The relevant dimensions D and the process entities that constitue their domains[15] are identified for the given perspective.

2. The relevant dimensional mappings M are identified.

3. An appropriate process model or pattern to represent the given perspective is chosen or designed.

4. A mining algorithm is chosen or developed that reconstructs the values and mappings for the considered dimensions from the log.

Rembert and Ellis (2009, Secs. 4.1, 4.2) apply this procedure to the *behavioral* (or control flow) perspective by reconstructing ICN *Activity Precedence Graphs*, and to the role assignment perspective (i.e. information about which role executes which activities) by discovering ICN *Role Assignment Graphs* from event logs. The authors also name several examples of further process perspectives, such as data flow (Rembert and Ellis, 2009, p. 40), and dimensions, such as spatial locations, money, or goals (Rembert and Ellis, 2009, p. 37).

By the example of role assignment mining, Rembert and Ellis (2009, p. 40) show that the complexity of the reconstruction step might differ depending on the domains of the process dimensions: If the domain *roles* consists of *atomic* process entities (e.g. represented by role names like 'customer' or 'insurance agent'[16]), the relation between roles and activities can be reconstructed by simple selection of values from the log. If the log only contains agent names without explicit role information, the reconstruction is more difficult. Roles must be inferred from the relation between agents and activities as composite process entities, e.g. by means of clustering (Rembert and Ellis, 2009, p. 40).

In Section 6.2, we will follow the approach by Rembert and Ellis (2009) to identify perspectives for process mining in MA(B)S.

4.2.2.2. Process Mining Tasks and Use Cases

The distinction between different process mining "types" depending on the existence of an a-priori model is another common dimension for classification (see e.g. Aalst, 2010a, p. 29). In

---

[14]also called information or data perspective above

[15]Rembert and Ellis (2009, p. 36) call the domain of a process dimension the *dimensional type*.

[16]examples inspired by Rembert and Ellis (2009, p. 36)

accordance with researchers like Goedertier et al. (2008, p. 47), we refer to this dimension as *process mining tasks* for better compliance with the data mining literature (see Section 4.1.2.1). In the following, we briefly review the main process mining tasks and relate them to the predictive and descriptive data mining tasks listed in Section 4.1.2.1.

Classification by the Eindhoven Research Group   The main process mining tasks identified by the Eindhoven research group include (see Aalst, 2006, p. 3, cited in Weber and Wittenberger, 2007, p. 12):

- *Process discovery*: Process mining in the narrower sense, i.e. reconstruction of process and organizational models from execution logs.

- *Conformance checking*: Techniques for the assessment of conformance between process models and logs. This includes algorithms and distance measures to analyze the similarity between different process models (*delta analysis*) as well as techniques to check the compliance of execution logs against a process model.

- *Extension*: An existing process model is extended, enriched, or improved. Extension algorithms take a process model and an execution log as input and return a new process model that is extended by information mined from the log.

Ailenei et al. (2012) refine these basic process mining tasks by identifying and validating a set of 18 more detailed *use cases* for process mining in an empirical study. The use cases capture common requirements on process mining techniques and tools, such as determining the "most frequent path in the process" (in process discovery) or "exceptions from the normal path" (in conformance checking); see Ailenei et al. (2012, p. 79).

In the context of business process mining and simulation, Aalst (2010b, pp. 6) distinguishes 10 different "activities" performed to improve business processes on the basis of simulation models and event logs: discovery, enhancement, diagnosis, detection (of deviations), (conformance) checking, comparison, promotion (of actual model features into reference models), exploration, prediction, and recommendation. The activities are subsumed under the metaphors of "*cartography, auditing*, and *navigation*" (Aalst, 2010b, p. 7)

Section 6.3 will present use cases for the application of process mining to MA(B)S. Concerning their granularity, these might be positioned in between the general process mining tasks from (Aalst, 2006) and the fine-grained use cases from (Ailenei et al., 2012). They also exhibit close relations to the "activities" (e.g. use case 'exploration') identified by Aalst (2010b).

Relations to Data Mining Tasks   In Section 4.1.2.1 we have cited the most common data mining tasks. We will now discuss their meaning for process mining and their relation to the three process mining tasks.

Classification is on the one hand related to conformance checking, which can be regarded as a (binary) classification problem, whether or not a given log complies to a process model. On the other hand, supervised algorithms to learn classification models can be applied to process discovery. This includes decision trees in the data (Rozinat and Aalst, 2006) and role assignment perspectives (Ly et al., 2006) as well as ILP in the control flow perspective (Goedertier et al., 2008).

Predicting the future course of a running process based on historical log data is important for process analysis. One approach towards flow prediction based on process mining is found in (Schütt, 2003).

Regression analysis has been used for process mining in the control flow perspective (Maruster et al., 2002) and for the analysis of resource behavior (Nakatumba and Aalst, 2009). *Time series analysis* has, to our knowledge, not been applied in the process mining context yet.

Clustering is an important supplementary task in process mining. It is applied when relevant composite process entities (e.g. activities, roles, or process instances) are not explicitly logged (see Rembert and Ellis, 2009, p. 40; reviewed in Section 4.2.2.1). If, for example, a log contains execution instances stemming from different process models, an overall model mined from the log might be unclear and adulterant. Clustering can appropriately partition the log prior to process discovery (see e.g. Medeiros et al., 2008b).

Summarization: Besides the reconstruction of process models, simple summarizations of process logs (e.g. which event types and executing agents appear) are also relevant for process mining and supported by software tools like *ProM* (see Section 4.2.6.1).

Association rule mining is well-applicable to the data perspective. According to Günther et al. (2008, p. 75), association rules can e.g. display correlations between process model changes and values of certain data attributes as hints why the model was changed.

Though *sequence discovery* is closely related to process discovery, there is one important difference: The goal is not to reconstruct a full process model, but a set of frequent process patterns (according to the above definitions from Rembert and Ellis, 2009) that display common temporal relations between activities.

4.2.2.3. Properties of Data and Algorithms

Besides perspectives and tasks (or use cases), a number of algorithm- and data-related properties are commonly used to classify process mining techniques. This includes:

1. properties of the input data (logs) that an algorithm operates on,

2. characteristics of the algorithm itself,

3. ability of an algorithm to cope with certain constructs in the process model that generated a log, and

4. properties of the output model representation.

Properties of Log Data Process logs can be event- or activity-based[17] (see e.g. Sun et al., 2011, p. 296), where both terms are used analogous to Section 2.2.2: Event-based logs consist of entries that represent momentary, possibly time-stamped, events listed in chronological ordered (Sun et al., 2011, p. 296). Activity-based logs contain related start and end events of time-consuming activities (Sun et al., 2011, p. 296). In terms of Petri nets, an event-based log

---

[17]Authors like Medeiros (2006, p. 16) also refer to these as logs of atomic (i.e. event-based) and non-atomic (i.e. activity-based) task.

corresponds to a sequence and an activity-based log to a causal net (Section 2.3.2.3; see also Dongen and Aalst, 2004, p. 366; Dongen et al., 2006a).

Since temporal overlaps between activities provide hints towards concurrency, activity-based logging eases the detection of concurrent tasks (Medeiros, 2006, p. 16). Log entries might contain further data values of arbitrary process dimensions as additional information for process mining.

Incomplete or noisy logs, in contrast, impede process discovery in general: *Completeness* refers to the fact that any data mining algorithm requires an appropriate number of samples to reliably infer properties of the underlying model (Aalst, 2010a, p. 37). In control flow discovery, different degrees of log completeness are considered (Aalst, 2010a, p. 37): The strong notion of completeness requires *every* execution path through a process model to be present in the log, which is practically impossible for cyclic models. Local completeness only requires every possible *direct succession* of activities to be traced.

Characteristics of Mining Algorithms   Based on the work by Medeiros (2006, Sec. 2.1), Lang (2008, p. 55) summarizes a number of dimensions to classify control flow mining techniques by algorithm-related properties. Among others, this includes:

- *Single-phase vs. multi-phase*: Some algorithms reconstruct the resulting model 'in one go', while others execute a chain of steps with intermediate model representations (Medeiros, 2006, p 16).

- *Mining strategy*: Aalst and Weijters (2004, p. 240) refer to this as the "local/global dimension". *Locally-optimizing techniques* stepwise reconstruct a model from elementary local information (e.g. the successor relation), while *globally-optimizing techniques* search for a model that describes the whole input data set at once (Lang, 2008, p. 56). *Hybrid approaches* integrate local and global search (Lang, 2008, p. 56).

- *Causality metrics*: Lang (2008, pp. 56) mainly distinguishes *neighborhood-based metrics* from *successor-based metrics*: The former only regard for direct succession, while the latter also take indirect succession into account.

- *Mined modeling constructs*: This dimension will be discussed in more detail in the next paragraph.

Besides the above dimensions, Medeiros (2006, p. 16) considers the fact if a *whole model* or a *partial model* is mined. In a comprehensive review of current process mining research, Tiwari et al. (2008, pp. 7) use the *origin of the applied technique* as another dimension. According to their review, existing techniques are based on genetic algorithms, event driven process chains, Markov chains, cluster analysis, neural networks, Petri nets, data mining, and other algorithmic approaches. The majority of reviewed algorithms is based on Petri nets (> 20), data mining techniques (> 5), and other approaches (> 25); see Tiwari et al. (2008, p. 10).

Properties of Generating Models   A number of control flow constructs have been identified as difficult to be reconstructed from process logs (e.g. Aalst and Song, 2004a). An early approach by Herbst (2001, pp. 61) classifies process models by the presence or absence of *concurrency* and *duplicate tasks* (see Section 2.3.2.4), where process models with both constructs are regarded as the most demanding.

In their research agenda, Aalst and Weijters (2004) present a more exhaustive list of challenging constructs including hidden tasks, duplicate tasks, (short) loops, and non-free-choice constructs (see Section 2.3.2.4). Medeiros (2006, pp. 54) identifies relations between these constructs and substantiates the difficulty of their reconstruction, among others, by the fact that "the same set of ordering relations [...] can be inferred when the original net contains one of these constructs." Naively speaking, we can e.g. infer from the repeated occurrence of an activity a in the trace of a process instance that either a is part of a cycle or that a is a non-unique label.

In recent years, several algorithms have been developed that target these constructs as well as more complex workflow patterns, such as transactions (see e.g. Gaaloul et al., 2004). A quantitative overview of existing techniques for the most relevant control flow constructs is found in (Tiwari et al., 2008, p. 15).

Properties of Output Model Representations The choice of an appropriate representation for reconstructed models depends on the domain context of process mining, i.e. which modeling language is common there. Internally, many algorithms for control flow discovery use rather abstract representations which are transformed into more readable notations for display. In this regard, Schütt (2003, p. 34) distinguishes algorithms based on *dependency graphs* (or matrices) and algorithms based on *grammars* (or automata). The former are tailored towards the detection of concurrency, while the latter are better suited to detect alternatives (Schütt, 2003, p. 34), cycles, and duplicate tasks.

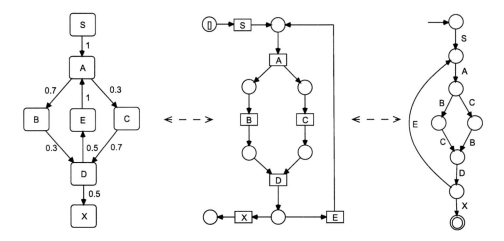

Figure 4.7.: Different model representations in process mining: Dependency graphs, Petri nets, and finite automata (from left to right).

Figure 4.7 shows different model representations used in process mining. The precedence graph displays the precedence relation of activities. In the example, edges are annotated with probabilities that activities directly follow each other in the analyzed log.[18] While all models show similar precedences, the relation between activities B and C is interpreted as concurrency in the Petri net and as alternatives in the automaton. Techniques to reconstruct and convert between these model representations are reviewed in Section 4.2.3.

Output model representations for control flow discovery include, among others, EPCs (Dongen et al., 2005), (UML) sequence diagrams (Lassen et al., 2007), and block structured languages like *ADONIS* (Herbst, 2001). Aalst and Weijters (2004, pp. 239) note that the *generality* of a modeling language is 'inversely proportional' to the *inductive bias* that it imposes on a mining algorithm. The assumption that the target model is block-structured e.g. constrains the search space stronger than the assumption that the analysed log might be generated by an arbitrary Petri net (Aalst and Weijters, 2004, p. 239).

4.2.3. Control Flow Mining

In the following, we review a number of algorithms for control flow discovery that appear suitable for control flow mining in the context of MA(B)S. The requirements in this domain, which will be substantiated in Chapters 6 and 7, include

- ability to handle concurrency, alternatives, arbitrary cycles, and duplicate tasks,
- reliable process discovery from noise-free, event-based logs,
- relatively straightforward understandability and usability,
- possibility to extend (enrich) the reconstructed control flow models with information mined from other perspectives.

More general overviews of techniques for the control flow perspective are e.g. found in (Lang, 2008; Medeiros, 2006).

4.2.3.1. Alpha Algorithm

The Alpha (α) algorithm was one of the first techniques to discover concurrent processes (Aalst, 2010a, p. 34). It is driven by Petri net theory and the question, which process models can be inferred from the direct successor relation of activities in a log (Aalst et al., 2003a, p. 249). The basic algorithm has a strong academic and demonstrative focus: It is very simple and elegant but fails under many practically relevant conditions (Aalst, 2010a, p. 34).

The original α algorithm can provably rediscover a sound, structured workflow net without hidden elements, duplicate tasks, and short cycles of length 1 or 2 from a noise-free, locally complete event-based log (Medeiros et al., 2004a, p. 7).[19] Aalst (2010a, p. 37-38) shows that the reliance on local completeness provides the algorithm with a strong bias towards imputing concurrency: To identify 10 different activities as concurrent, $10! = 3628800$ different traces (i.e. every potential interleaving) are required under the strong notion of completeness, while the α algorithm gets along with 90 variations at best (Aalst, 2010a, p. 38).

---

[18]The figure is leaned on the result representation of the *Heuristics Miner* algorithm by Weijters et al. (2006).
[19]Recall the description of Petri net properties from Section 2.3.2.1.

The basic procedure consists of two steps: Firstly, four different ordering relations are reconstructed from the log. Secondly, a workflow net is generated from these relations. The following formalization is adopted with modifications from (Aalst, 2010a, pp. 34): Let A be a set of activities. A bag of strings over A is called an *event log* $L \in Bag(A^*)$. A string $\sigma \in L$ is called a *trace*. For pairs of activities $a, b \in A$, the following ordering relations can be defined over L (Aalst, 2010a, p. 34):

1. $a >_L b \equiv \exists \sigma \in L$: b directly follows a in σ,

2. $a \rightarrow_L b \equiv (a >_L b) \wedge \neg(b >_L a)$

3. $a\|_L b \equiv (a >_L b) \wedge (b >_L a)$,

4. $a\#_L b \equiv \neg(a >_L b) \wedge \neg(b >_L a)$.

The semantics of these relations is explained as follows (Medeiros et al., 2004a, p. 8): $>_L$ contains pairs of direct *followers*. $a \rightarrow_L b$ provides a hint towards *causality* based on the observation that a is directly followed by b, but not vice versa. The relation $\|_L$ marks potentially *parallel* activities, while $\#_L$ contains pairs of *unrelated* activities. Together, both relations "are used to differentiate between parallelism and choice" (Aalst et al., 2003a, p. 250) in the reconstructed net.

From the four relations, a workflow net $N = \alpha(L) = (P_L, T_L, F_L)$ is built by means of the following rules (Aalst, 2010a, p. 35):

1. Transitions are created for all activities in the log. 'Input' ('output') transitions correspond to the first (last) elements of a trace:

   - $T_L = \{t_a | \exists \sigma \in L : a \in \sigma\}$
   - $T_I = \{t_i | \exists \sigma \in L : first(\sigma) = i\}$
   - $T_O = \{t_o | \exists \sigma \in L : last(\sigma) = o\}$

2. Places are introduced to connect maximal sets of mutually unrelated transitions according to the causal relation $\rightarrow_L$. Additionally, there is a single input and output place:

   - $X_L = \{(A, B) | A, B \subseteq T_L \wedge (\forall a \in A, b \in B : a \rightarrow_L b) \wedge (\forall a_1, a_2 \in A : a_1 \#_L a_2) \wedge (\forall b_1, b_2 \in B : b_1 \#_L b_2)\}$
   - $Y_L = \{(A, B) \in X_L | \forall A', B' \in X_L : (A \subseteq A' \wedge B \subseteq B') \implies (A, B) = (A', B')\}$,
   - $P_L = \{p_{(A,B)} | (A, B) \in Y_L\} \cup \{p_i, p_o\}$

3. Arcs connect places with their related transitions:

   - $F_L = \{(a, p_{(A,B)}) | (A, B) \in Y_L \wedge a \in A\} \cup \{(p_{(A,B)}, b)) | (A, B) \in Y_L \wedge b \in B\} \cup \{(t, p_o) | t \in T_O\} \cup \{(p_i, t) | t \in T_I\}$

Medeiros et al. (2004a) extend the basic algorithm with the ability to correctly discover short cycles of length 1 (loops) and 2. Loops are detected during pre-processing from the observation that an activity is directly followed by itself in some trace (Medeiros et al., 2004a, p. 16). The detection of length 2-cycles requires to distinguish patterns like *aba*, that indicate a short cycle, from patterns that indicate parallelism (i.e. $\|_L$) (Medeiros et al., 2004a, p. 11); as well as a redefinition of local completeness (Medeiros et al., 2004a, p. 10).

Medeiros et al. (2004a, Sec. 5) and Wen et al. (2006) present further extensions to discover an extended class of sound structured workflow nets that are allowed to contain certain non-free-choice constructs. The latter authors note that the time complexity of this 'α^{++} algorithm' is "linear in the size of the log [... and] exponential in the number of tasks" (Wen et al., 2006, p. 21). Wen et al. (2004) present a variant of the α algorithm for activity-based logs.

4.2.3.2. Mining Duplicate Tasks

Duplicate tasks are a means to improve the understandability and to enforce certain formal properties of control flow models (see e.g. Medeiros, 2006, Sec. 3.3). Figure 4.8 (left) shows an example adopted from Medeiros (2006, p. 40). It models the ordered execution of two activities A and B, where one activity is optional, but not both. The net on the right hand side of this figure exhibits the same label language without duplicate tasks. However, this is at the expense of two hidden tasks and an additional place for the condition that 'only one of the activities might be skipped'.

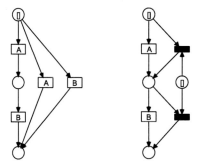

Figure 4.8.: Two different Petri nets with the label language $L = \{A, B, AB\}$. The net on the left was adopted from Medeiros (2006, p. 40) and contains duplicate tasks, while the net on the right contains hidden tasks.

The identification of duplicate tasks from an execution log is difficult when no *a-priori* information on the structure of the generating model, such as the number of transitions with the same label, is available (Herbst, 2001, p. 62). The reviews by Medeiros (2006, Sec. 2), Lang (2008, Sec. 3), and Tiwari et al. (2008, Sec. 3) show that only few control flow discovery algorithms are able to reconstruct process models that contain duplicate tasks, concurrency, and loops at the same time. Most existing approaches are based on one of the following ideas:

1. global search through a space of labeling functions (Herbst, 2001; Medeiros, 2006),

2. clustering of activity occurrences based on the local succession relation during log preprocessing (e.g. Gu et al., 2008; Schimm, 2004),

3. two-step approaches that combine (regular) grammar inference with the subsequent synthesis of a concurrent model (Rubin et al., 2006; Schütt, 2003).

Example algorithms of the classes 1 and 2 are briefly reviewed below. The third class incorporates the control flow mining technique applied and extended in this thesis (see Section 7.2) and is therefore described more detailed in Section 4.2.3.3.

Approaches based on global search In his dissertation, Herbst (2001) presents the *SplitPar* algorithm as the first technique to reconstruct models containing concurrent and duplicate activities. The following description is based on summaries by Lang (2008, pp. 65), Medeiros (2006, p. 23), and Aalst et al. (2003a, pp. 256).

Similar to the α algorithm, *SplitPar* is a two-step procedure that uses different model representations for internal processing and presentation. The first step (*induction*) consists of a search procedure with embedded graph generation (Aalst et al., 2003a, p. 256). From the *indirect follower* relation defined on the log (Aalst et al., 2003a, p. 257), a *stochastic activity graph* (SAG) is induced, that describes the relative frequency of succession for each pair of activities (Lang, 2008, pp. 65).[20]

Different from the α algorithm, *SplitPar* does not induce ordering relations on a fixed set of activities, but a whole *lattice* of mappings between log events and graph nodes, which are partially ordered by increasing specialization (Aalst et al., 2003a, p. 256). The *most general* SAG contains a single node for each activity name, i.e. there are no duplicate tasks, while in the *most specific* SAG, every log event is assigned an own node (Medeiros, 2006, p. 23; Aalst et al., 2003a, p. 256).

A search procedure is run on the lattice to identify an optimal mapping between log events and activities with respect to duplicate tasks. The objective is to maximize a likelihood function that describes the conformance of a SAG to the log traces (see Aalst et al., 2003a, p. 257; Lang, 2008, p. 66). To improve this measure during search, a mapping can be specialized by splitting selected activities (Aalst et al., 2003a, p. 256) into duplicate tasks.

After termination of the search, the 'best' SAG is *transformed* into an output model in the block-structured *ADONIS* language (Aalst et al., 2003a, p. 257). The main challenge of the transformation consists in the identification of alternative and concurrent routing constructs which are not explicitly distinguished in the SAG (Aalst et al., 2003a, p. 258).

Medeiros (2006, Sec. 5) describes an alternative approach to discover duplicate tasks employing global search with genetic algorithms. Her algorithm is shown to successfully reconstruct (among others) examples from Herbst's dissertation (2001), but "the models tend to have more duplicates than necessary" (Medeiros, 2006, p. 121). A brief review of genetic process mining is given in Section 4.2.3.4.

Approaches based on local preprocessing: The dissertation by Schimm (2004) presents an approach to reconstruct block-structured process models from activity-based logs using concepts from grammar inference, process algebra, and term rewriting (Medeiros, 2006, p. 24). Though the approach does not focus on duplicate tasks, it is proposed to detect these from local successor relations during pre-processing of the log (Medeiros, 2006, p. 24).

---

[20]similar to the leftmost model in Figure 4.7

This idea is operationalized in two akin approaches by Li et al. (2007) and Gu et al. (2008), who extend the α algorithm with log preprocessing to handle duplicate tasks. Both approaches search for local patterns, somewhat similar to the 'length-1 loop' extension of the α algorithm described above.

Li et al. (2007, pp. 403) state 3 simple heuristic rules based on the observation that duplicate tasks typically have different successors and predecessors in log traces. Their rules also regard for the fact that a distinct neighborhood might be merely caused by different interleaving of concurrent tasks (called "cross-equivalence"; Li et al., 2007, p. 399). In Section 7.2.4, a related technique will be applied, also together with the α algorithm, on *automata* to implement the concurrency detection approach by Schütt (2003).

Li et al. (2007, p. 404) developed a preprocessing stage for the α algorithm that compares all events in a log by the above conditions and marks duplicate tasks with different indices. The algorithm was evaluated against 8 logs from different process models including "sequential processes, concurrent processes[,] and loops" (Li et al., 2007, p. 406) as well as variable numbers of duplicate tasks ranging from 1 to 3 (Li et al., 2007, p. 405). While these examples are successfully identified from logs containing 1000 traces, the simple heuristics can fail under more realistic conditions like globally incomplete logs (Li et al., 2007, p. 406).

Gu et al. (2008, p. 362) criticize that the above approach does not "take account of both cyclic constructs and duplicate tasks synchronously". These authors present an extended preprocessing stage with a larger number of pattern detection rules that also regard for short cycles. The rules are formally proven to detect duplicate tasks in a number of routing constructs of sound SWF nets and applied to several examples (Gu et al., 2008, pp. 363-368). However, this rather theoretical approach might pose a number of challenges on a practical implementation: The algorithm might e.g. only be able to handle locally complete logs when it takes advantage of the fact that the pattern detection is performed on sub-strings of arbitrary length.[21]

Wang et al. (2009) present another related approach to "discover duplicate tasks based on directed diagram[s]" where the handling of "multistep loop[s]" is named as future work (Wang et al., 2009, p. 262).

4.2.3.3. Grammatical Inference and Two-Step Approaches

In the following we review a set of well-investigated techniques from theoretical informatics that have recently received increased interest in process mining, i.e. *grammatical inference* and the *theory of regions*. In combination, these allow for the detection of duplicate tasks and a number of other important control flow constructs from process execution logs.

Grammatical Inference (GI) is closely related to the theory of formal languages (Higuera, 2005, p. 1332). The objective is to induce a generating grammar or an accepting automaton from a set of example words (Higuera, 2005, p. 1332). Since many GI techniques have been developed during the 1970s and 80s, Aalst (2010a, p. 33–34) regards GI as a predecessor of process discovery without focus on concurrency and high level process modeling languages.

---

[21]Only limited by the size of the considered trace $\sigma \in L$.

Nevertheless, an important lesson that process mining can learn from GI lies in the rigorous formal analysis of grammar induction problems (Aalst and Weijters, 2004, p. 237). Researchers like Gold (1967) and Angluin and Smith (1983) have thoroughly investigated the general possibilities and algorithmic complexity of formal language induction from examples. The following review of results is based on the article by Angluin and Smith (1983) and the brief summary by Vidal (1994).

Two basic concepts for inductive inference are identification in the limit and identification by enumeration (Gold, 1967, cited in Angluin and Smith, 1983, Sec. 1.2). *Identification in the limit* means that inference procedures generate a (possibly infinite) sequence of models, increasingly refined with the number of presented data items (Angluin and Smith, 1983, p. 240). An inference algorithm A correctly identifies a model M in the limit if it produces a sequence of estimations $m_1, m_2, \ldots$ with $m_k = m_{k+1} = m_{k+2} = \ldots$ for some integer k where m_k is an appropriate estimation of M (Angluin and Smith, 1983, p. 240); i.e. A *converges* towards a suitable solution.

Identification by enumeration describes an inference strategy that is "very general and powerful but also rather impractical because [of] the size of the space that must be searched [...]" (Angluin and Smith, 1983, p. 241). Let S^+ be a set of positive examples (words generated by the target grammar G) and S^- be a set of negative examples (words not generated by G). If the search space of possible target grammars is recursively enumerable, G can be identified in the limit by enumerating all possible grammars and checking, for each candidate, if it generates S^+ and not S^- (Angluin and Smith, 1983, p. 241).

Feasibility and Complexity   Based on these concepts, a number of important feasibility and complexity results have been obtained, as summarized by Vidal (1994, p. 1–3). Feasibility and complexity of language identification mainly depend on the expressiveness of the target language class and on the presence of negative examples.

While "any enumerable class of recursive languages (context-free and below) can be identified in the limit from complete presentation (both positive and negative data) [....,] no superfinite class of languages can be identified in the limit from only positive presentation. A superfinite class of languages is one that contains all finite languages and at least one infinite language" (Vidal, 1994, p. 1). These results directly follow from the concept of identification by enumeration where negative examples serve as constraints to avoid over-generalization (Vidal, 1994, p. 1).

Several subclasses (Vidal, 1994, p. 2) but only few superclasses of the regular languages can be identified in the limit from positive examples only (Vidal, 1994, p. 3). The question, if a certain class of languages can be identified in the absence of negative examples is already undecidable for the context-free languages (Vidal, 1994, p. 3).

Though possible in general, the problem to discover the smallest regular grammar or deterministic finite automaton (DFA) from positive and negative examples is NP-hard (Gold, 1978, cited in Vidal, 1994, p. 1). However, by either (a) dropping the minimality or exactness constraints, (b) resorting to less expressive language subclasses, or (c) applying stochastic and heuristic techniques, polynomial algorithms for both complete and positive presentation could be developed (Vidal, 1994, p. 2).

These results make immediately plausible why process mining often resorts to limited net classes and heuristic methods. In general, though suggested by authors like Aalst (2010a, p. 33), theoretical results from grammar inference might not have received sufficient attention in process mining so far. The framework of *Petri net languages*, as studied by Jantzen (1979), could e.g. provide an appropriate foundation for a transfer.

Positive and Negative Examples   Vidal (1994, p. 1) and Aalst (2010a, p. 34) accordingly state that GI and process mining often focus on positive presentation for reasons of lower algorithmic complexity and practical lack of negative examples. Nevertheless, several GI algorithms have been developed for complete presentation as well. In process mining, a first approach to make use of negative examples is presented by Goedertier et al. (2008) in an ILP context.

The lack of negative examples is due to the fact that real logs normally contain positive examples of executed process instances only (Goedertier et al., 2008, p. 42). Goedertier et al. (2008, p. 47) extend logs with artificial *negative events* expressing "that a state transition [in the process model] could not take place". Since most workflow engines do not expose information about inhibited transitions, Goedertier et al. (2008, p. 47) derive negative events from (positive) logged examples. Though this approach does not add 'new' information to the log, it enables the use of supervised classification learners in process mining (Goedertier et al., 2008, p. 47).

When regarding only positive examples, the subclasses of regular languages that can be identified in the limit in polynomial time include (see Rey, 2003 and Yokomori, 1995):

- *k-reversible languages*: According to the informal characterization by Pilato and Berwick (1985, p. 71), a regular language L is k-reversible if, "whenever two prefixes [of two words in L] whose k last [... symbols] match have a tail in common, then the prefixes have all tails in common".

- *subclasses of the k-testable languages* (see e.g. Yu, 1997), such as "k-testable languages in the strict sense (k-TLSS) [...] Informally speaking, [... these are] defined by a finite set of substrings of length k that are allowed to appear in the strings of the language." (Garcia and Vidal, 1990, p. 921). The k-TLSS are a subclass of the k-reversible languages that can be inferred using specific, more performant algorithms (Garcia and Vidal, 1990, p. 923).

- *languages identified by strictly deterministic automata*: These are deterministic finite automata (DFA, see definition below) where each transition label starts with a different character from the underlying alphabet (Yokomori, 1995, p. 154). In the case of single letter labels, they might be described as 'DFA without duplicate tasks'.

In the following, we review a well-investigated algorithm for the identification of the rather general class of k-reversible languages. This algorithm will be applied as part of a procedure to discover agent interaction protocols in Section 7.2.

Inference Algorithm k-RI   The k-*RI* algorithm by Angluin (1982) learns a minimal k-reversible DFA ($k \geq 0$) in the limit from positive examples (Angluin, 1982, p. 759). It is based on a definition of k-reversibility in terms of automata. Let $A = (Q, I, F, \delta)$ be an automaton with sets Q, I, F of states, initial states, and final states, and a transition relation $\delta \subseteq Q \times U \times Q$ over an alphabet U (Angluin, 1982, p. 745).

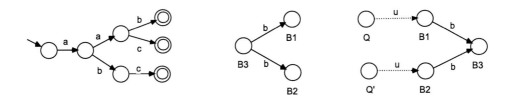

Figure 4.9.: Illustrations of the k-RI algorithm. Left: A PTA for the regular language $L = \{aab, aac, abc\}$. Middle: States B_1 and B_2 are merged to enforce determinism according to condition 1 below. Right: States B_1 and B_2 are merged to enforce k-reversibility according to condition 2 below.

In case of $k = 0$, the definition of reversibility is rather simple: An automaton A is deterministic if $|I| = 1$ and $\delta : Q \times U \to Q$ is a function (Angluin, 1982, p. 745). Let A^r be the *reverse automaton* of A obtained by 'inverting' the transition relation δ. A is 0-reversible if and only if its reverse A^r is deterministic (Angluin, 1982, p. 745).

For $k > 0$ a weaker notion of determinism is introduced: A string $u \in U^*$ of length k is called a k-*leader* of a state $q \in Q$ if q can be reached from some state $q' \in Q$ by input of u, and k-*follower* of q if some q' can be reached from q by input of u (Angluin, 1982, p. 749). Let $q_1, q_2 \in Q$ be either initial states, or both states can be reached from a state q_3 by input of the same $a \in U$. An automaton A is *deterministic with lookahead* k if it contains no such states q_1, q_2 that share a common k-follower $u \in U^*$ (Angluin, 1982, p. 749). A DFA A is k-reversible whenever its reverse acceptor A^r is deterministic with lookahead k (Angluin, 1982, p. 749).

The algorithm k-*RI* starts by constructing a *prefix tree acceptor* (PTA) from an example log of traces over U (Angluin, 1982, p. 759). This DFA represents every log trace by a transition sequence from the initial state to a final state, such that traces with a common prefix share common states and transitions (see Figure 4.9).

The state space of the PTA is reduced by *merging* appropriate pairs of similar states. Broadly speaking, two states are considered as similar if both represent the same set of "possible future strings that can stem from it" (Walkinshaw et al., 2008, p. 274).[22] Then both states are replaced by a single new state, whose incoming and outgoing transitions are the unions of the respective sets from the original states.

The k-*RI* algorithm first merges all final states of the PTA into one. This is a precondition to make the reverse acceptor deterministic. Then the algorithm repeatedly merges pairs of states that violate the conditions of determinism or k-reversibility in A, thus producing a sequence of automata $A_0, A_1, \ldots, A_L$ with decreasing size of the state space. The procedure is repeated until no further state merging is possible and the resulting automaton A_L is returned.

The conditions for state merging are formalized as follows and illustrated in Figure 4.9:[23]

---

[22]Walkinshaw et al. (2008, p. 274) actually relate to grammar inference in general.

[23]The synonymous use of the terms 'state' and 'block' and the notion of "enforc[ing ...] determinism" in the following definitions are derived from Pilato and Berwick (1985, p. 72).

1. *Enforce determinism*: Let U be an alphabet and $b \in U$ an input character. If there exist states $B_1, B_2, B_3 \in Q$ such that $\delta(B_3, b) = B_1$ and $\delta(B_3, b) = B_2$, then B_1 and B_2 are merged (Angluin, 1982, p. 759).

2. *Enforce k-reversibility*: If there exist states "B_1 and B_2 [that] have a common k-leader [...] and either B_1 and B_2 are both final states [...] or there exists a [... state] B_3 [...] and a symbol $b \in U$ such that B_3 is a b-successor of both B_1 and B_2" (Angluin, 1982, p. 759), then B_1 and B_2 are merged.

Angluin (1982, p. 760) proves that this algorithm identifies the smallest k-reversible language in the limit that contains the examples from the log. The identification is correct with respect to a given k-reversible language L whenever the log contains a so-called *characteristic sample* $S \subseteq L$. This subset is well-defined and can be algorithmically derived from an automaton accepting L (Angluin, 1982, pp. 750).

Angluin (1982, p. 760) shows that "the algorithm k-*RI* may be implemented to run in time $O(kn^3)$, where n is one more than the sum of the lengths of the input strings". The simplified algorithm ZR ('zero-reversible') for the special case $k = 0$ "may be implemented to run in time $O(n\alpha(n))$ where n [is defined as above ...] and α is a very slowly growing function" (Angluin, 1982, p. 758). To obtain a minimal k-reversible DFA, the output A_L of the k-RI algorithm is minimized (Angluin, 1982, p. 761) in time $O(m^2)$ where m is the number of states in A_L (Hopcroft et al., 2003, p. 153).

Two-Step Approaches Though GI typically neglects concurrency, well-known GI algorithms can be applied to the mining of concurrent processes as follows (Herbst, 2001):

1. Grammar inference techniques are extended to generate concurrent models instead of sequential automata. This is e.g. done by Herbst (2001) and Schimm (2004).

2. A standard GI algorithm is employed to induce a sequential automaton from a process log. The automaton is subsequently converted into a (possibly) concurrent model. Such procedures are proposed by Herbst (2001), Schütt (2003), and Kindler et al. (2006).

Though Herbst (2001) expresses his preference towards the first approach, procedures of the second type have recently received attention under the name of *two-step process mining* (e.g. Rubin et al., 2006).[24] An important building block of these procedures is an appropriate technique to convert a finite automaton into a concurrent model. For this purpose, the following techniques might be applied:

- The *theory of regions* serves to synthesize a Petri net from an automaton, such that the automaton is bi-similar to the Petri net's reachability graph (Badouel and Darondeau, 1998, p. 529). Herbst (2001) was probably the first to propose a combination of GI and region theory in process mining. Related algorithms and case studies are reported (among others) by Kindler et al. (2006), Rubin et al. (2006), Carmona et al. (2008), and Bergenthum et al. (2007).

---

[24]Rubin et al. (2006) only apply this term to their combination of automata inference and the theory of regions. In the opinion of the author of this thesis, the term also fits other approaches that combine automata inference with the synthesis of a concurrent model.

- Graph rewriting can be used to identify patterns of concurrency in an automaton and transform it to a higher-level modeling language. This approach is e.g. taken by Schütt (2003).

- From the precedence relation defined by an automaton's labelled transitions, a dependency graph can be generated and transformed into a concurrent model. The process mining tool ProM (Section 4.2.6.1) e.g. offers the possibility to run the standard α algorithm (Section 4.2.3.1) on an automaton instead of a log.

Theory of Regions The theory of regions (see e.g. Badouel and Darondeau, 1998) provides means to synthesize Petri nets from finite automata, often called *transition systems* in this context. One goal of Petri net synthesis is to reduce the size of the model (see e.g. Aalst et al., 2010, p. 101 and Verbeek et al., 2008, p. 153): Automata for concurrent processes tend to be large since every interleaving of concurrent tasks is represented by an own path. This *state explosion* (Verbeek et al., 2008, p. 153) can be avoided by transformation to concurrent models like Petri nets (Aalst et al., 2010, p. 89).

An important feature of region-based synthesis is *bi-similarity*, i.e. the synthesized net *exactly* mimics the behavior of the automaton, which can be interpreted as the net's *reachability graph* (see Section 2.3.2.3) (Carmona et al., 2008, p. 364). In process mining, bi-similarity might be unwanted because an abstraction from the observed process executions is required (Carmona et al., 2008, p. 358).

We briefly review the basic formalism of region theory and an extension towards process mining, both following Carmona et al. (2008): Let $TS = (S, E, A, s_{in})$ be a transition system with a set of states S, transitions A, transition labels (events) E, and an initial state s_{in} (Carmona et al., 2008, p. 360). On TS, the following relations can be defined that relate an event $e \in E$ to a subset of states $S' \subseteq S$ (Carmona et al., 2008, p. 361):

- $enter(e, S')$: At least one transition $a \in A$ labelled with e enters a state $s \in S'$, emanating from a state $s' \notin S'$.

- $exit(e, S')$: At least one transition $a \in A$ labelled with e leaves a state $s \in S'$, targeting a state $s' \notin S'$.

- $nocross(e, S')$: At least one transition $a \in A$ labelled with e connects two states s, s' that are either both inside or both outside of S'.

A subset $r \subseteq S$ is called a *region* of TS if exactly one of the relations $enter(e, r)$, $exit(e, r)$, or $nocross(e, r)$ holds for all events in E (Carmona et al., 2008, p. 361). The region can be understood as a place in a Petri net with well-defined pre- and post-sets of transitions, where each state $s \in r$ corresponds to a different marking (Carmona et al., 2008, p. 361). The set of regions that an event $e \in E$ enters (exits) are called its *pre-regions* (*post-regions*) (Carmona et al., 2008, p. 362). The *excitation region* of an event e is the set of states that e is enabled in (Carmona et al., 2008, p. 363).

A Petri net can be synthesized by building places from the regions of a transition system, transition from its events, and arcs according to the events' pre- and post-regions (Carmona et al., 2008, p. 363). To avoid place redundancy, only *minimal regions* are considered. A region r is called minimal if no subset $S' \subset r$ is a region (Carmona et al., 2008, p. 362).

Bi-similarity between the original transition system TS and the reachability graph of the synthesized net is only reached if TS is *excitation closed* (for a definition see Carmona et al., 2008, p. 364). This property can be achieved for an arbitrary transition system by means of *label-splitting*, i.e. dividing single transitions into multiple copies with the same label but emanating from different states (Carmona et al., 2008, p. 364). Carmona et al. (2008, Sec. 3.1) drop this requirement to better fit region-based synthesis to the needs of process mining, since the reachability graph of a Petri net synthesized from a non-excitation closed transition system can be shown to be an *over-approximation* (generalization) of the original transition system.

The theory of regions allows to synthesize several subclasses of P/T nets: Structural properties like free-choice (Section 2.3.2.2) can be enforced by means of label splitting and different strategies for place generation (Aalst et al., 2010, p. 103). While algorithms to synthesize k-bounded nets were developed by Badouel et al. (1995, cited in Carmona et al., 2009b, p. 327), higher level classes like colored or object-oriented nets have not been considered so far (see also Flick et al., 2010).

A main problem of region-based Petri net synthesis is its high algorithmic complexity. Though even the synthesis of k-bounded nets is possible in polynomial time (Badouel et al., 1995, cited in Carmona et al., 2009b, p. 327), the algorithms might become practically intractable on large transition systems (Verbeek et al., 2008, p. 166) and log sizes considered in process mining (Carmona et al., 2009b, p. 327). Iterative (Dongen et al., 2007) as well as divide-and-conquer strategies (Carmona et al., 2009a) have been proposed to reduce complexity, but the problem of efficient, practically applicable, Petri net synthesis remains challenging (see e.g. Verbeek et al., 2008, p. 166).

Approach by Kindler, Rubin, and van Dongen Kindler et al. (2006) were the first to practically apply a combination of automata inference and region-based net synthesis to process mining. This so-called "two-step approach", continued in the work by Rubin et al. (2006)[25], consists of an automata inference stage followed by Petri net synthesis (Rubin et al., 2006, p. 3) using the tool *Petrify* (Cortadella et al., 1997). Interestingly, no existing grammar inference algorithms are employed for automata inference, but an own framework to reconstruct finite automata from event logs is developed. This 'reinvention' leads to certain advantages and drawbacks discussed in the following.

Similar to grammar inference, the basic idea of Rubin et al. (2006, p. 14) is to reconstruct explicit state information from an event-based log, resulting in a possible generating transition system. Basically, states are identified from the events that occurred before or after a certain position in a log trace. The authors propose to implement this simple strategy by applying variations along three dimensions, which leads to an overall of 36 strategies for state identification (Rubin et al., 2006, p. 17):

1. *Filtering*: are all events from the log or only events from a certain subset taken into account (Rubin et al., 2006, p. 16)?

2. *Horizon*: are the events before (past), after (future) or both considered to identify a state? How long are the considered pre- or postfixes (Rubin et al., 2006, pp. 14)?

---

[25]and also reported in (Aalst et al., 2010)

3. *Order*: Is the order and number of event occurrences before or after a certain position in the log relevant, i.e. are states defined by sequences, sets, or multisets of events (Rubin et al., 2006, p. 15)?

Rubin et al. (2006, p. 32) emphasize that an advantage of their approach is the large number of possible strategies: These allow to fine-tune transition system identification to reach an appropriate balance between specialization and generalization. A disadvantage of their rather practical approach is that, different from classical grammar inference, it is not related to formal language theory. Therefore it is not clearly stated which classes of languages can be identified from which sets of example words.

It might, however, be straightforward to establish this relation in several cases. In terms of the above strategies, the k-RI algorithm e.g. applies no filtering, an infinite 'past' horizon, and the 'sequence' semantics (i.e. event order is considered) during the generation of the PTA. When merging the states of the PTA, a 'past' horizon of k and a 'future' horizon of 1 are applied together with the 'sequence' semantics. Though this comparison is rather preliminary, further attempts to relate formal grammar inference to the practical framework of Rubin et al. (2006) might be useful.

Before performing region-based synthesis, Rubin et al. (2006) apply certain modifications to the reconstructed transition system in order to improve the quality of the synthesized net. The following strategies are implemented using the basic operations of arc addition, arc removal, and state merging (Rubin et al., 2006, p. 20):

- "Kill loops" (Rubin et al., 2006, p. 20): Loops are removed to either create an acyclic transition system or to avoid self-loops. The latter are produced as artifacts by the 'set' semantics of state representation when an event occurs more than once.

- "Extend" (Rubin et al., 2006, p. 21): Arcs are added to the transitions system to amend traces with a certain interleaving of presumably concurrent events[26] not observed in the log.

- "Merge by output" (Rubin et al., 2006, p. 22): States with the same output events are merged under certain conditions.

For the second step, Petri net synthesis, the existing tool *Petrify* is applied without modifications. The authors note that a wealth of different net classes can be generated using different parameter settings (Rubin et al., 2006, p. 22). Though the large number of possible strategies for automata inference and net synthesis leads to high versatility (Rubin et al., 2006, p. 32), the related degrees of freedom might also make the overall algorithm hard to understand for users without a strong theoretical background.

Approach by Schütt   Prior to Rubin et al. (2006), Schütt (2003) proposed an alternative 'two-step approach' consisting of automata inference and transformation into a concurrent model as part of his Diploma thesis. Unlike the former authors, Schütt (2003) (a) explicitly relates his automata inference stage to grammar inference (e.g. Schütt, 2003, p. 35) and (b) does not apply region-based synthesis but a pattern-based technique for "concurrency detection" (Schütt, 2003, pp. 58).

---

[26]called "state diamonds" by Rubin et al. (2006, p. 21)

The automata inference stage is inspired by the work of Schimm (2004), who uses grammar inference-like techniques to mine block-structured models containing concurrent and alternative routing as well as loops from activity-based logs (see Schütt, 2003, pp. 11,35). Schütt (2003) only applies grammar inference as an intermediate step to reconstruct a sequential, non-cyclic model with choices as the only routing construct.

Algorithmically, this is achieved by performing so-called "prefix tree induction" and "postfix optimization" on the observed traces (Schütt, 2003, pp. 55). First a prefix tree automaton (PTA) is built from the log (Schütt, 2003, pp. 55). Next, the PTA is postfix-optimized by merging different, but identically labelled (partial) paths starting from the final state (Schütt, 2003, pp. 57). The procedure bears strong resemblance with the k-RI algorithm except that no cycles are introduced.

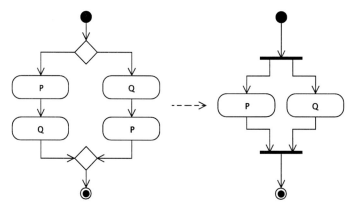

Figure 4.10.: Simple pattern-based concurrency detection: Assuming interleaving semantics, the left activity diagram with a choice can be simplified into the right diagram with concurrent fork and join. Adopted with modifications from (Schütt, 2003, p. 59).

Concurrency detection is applied in the second step to further reduce the size of the reconstructed model in case of concurrent control flow. Basically, the algorithm searches the sequential model for "state diamonds" (already mentioned in Rubin's approach) as a hint towards different interleavings of concurrent tasks. Figure 4.10 reviews an example by Schütt (2003, p. 59): Two alternative paths labelled PQ and QP with the same source and target are merged into a concurrent routing construct.

Note that the behavior of the two diagrams in Figure 4.10 is bi-similar only if interleaving semantics (see Section 2.3.2.3) is assumed. Under partial order semantics, the right diagram allows for a temporally overlapped execution of the tasks P and Q while the left diagram does not. This restriction also holds for the approach by Rubin et al. (2006).

Schütt (2003, pp. 59) further proposes to optimize potentially concurrent models by detecting causal dependencies of larger subgraphs called "atomic blocks". Figure 4.11 shows an example where an atomic block $(A \oplus B)$ is identified to be concurrent to a task sequence (CD). Imitating the notation from (Schütt, 2003, pp. 59), the Petri net on the right of this figure displays the intended execution semantics.

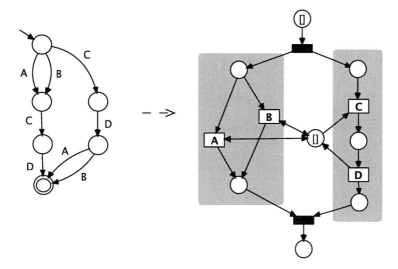

Figure 4.11.: Using the concept of atomic blocks proposed by Schütt (2003, pp. 59), the automaton on the left might be simplified into the Petri net on the right. The identified concurrent atomic blocks $(A \oplus B)$ and (CD) are shaded grey. Figure inspired by (Schütt, 2003, p. 60).

Since concurrency detection is described as an optional, conceptual extension of the sequential control flow mining approach (see Schütt, 2003, pp. 61), there are only few hints towards its implementation, computational complexity, and proof of correctness. In Section 7.2 we discuss our implementation of parts of the concurrency detection in order to optimize cyclic automata reconstructed by the *k-RI* algorithm.

4.2.3.4. Heuristic Algorithms

The mining algorithms described so far neglect the frequency with which patterns, like e.g. direct succession of activities, are found in the log. This means that rare patterns affect the reconstructed model as much as very frequent patterns. A major drawback of these approaches is their low robustness against noise (see Section 4.1.3.1) because occasional errors in the log strongly influence the mining results.

Heuristics Miner To cope with noisy logs, heuristic algorithms have been developed that take pattern frequencies into account. A common example is the *Heuristics Miner* algorithm by Weijters et al. (2006). This algorithm calculates log relations quite similar to the α algorithm, where each relation element (e.g. $a \to b$) is assigned a plausibility value based on pattern frequencies. From these relations, a dependency graph is constructed employing a number of parametrizable heuristics.

The basic precedence relation of the Heuristics Miner is expressed by (Weijters et al., 2006, p. 7):

$$a \Rightarrow_L b = \frac{|a >_W b| - |b >_W a|}{|a >_W b| + |b >_W a| + 1} \qquad (4.13)$$

with $>_L$ defined similar to the α algorithm (see Section 4.2.3.1). Different from the relation $\rightarrow_L$ used by the α algorithm, the domain of $\Rightarrow_L$ is the interval $]-1, 1[$ (Weijters et al., 2006, p. 7). "A high $A \Rightarrow_L B$ value strongly suggests that there is a dependency relation between activity A and B" (Weijters et al., 2006, p. 7). The interval borders are not reached due to the additional summand 1 in the denominator of equation 4.13, which emphasizes the 'heuristic' character of the algorithm (Haan, 2009, p. 49).

The Heuristics Miner starts by calculating a dependency matrix that contains the $\Rightarrow_L$ values for all pairs of activities occurring in the log L (Weijters et al., 2006, p. 8). To build a dependency graph from the matrix without a fixed dependency threshold, the so-called *all-activities-connected* heuristics is applied (Weijters et al., 2006, p. 8):

1. *Initial activities* of the graph are identified by the fact that their assigned matrix column contains no positive value.

2. *Final activities* are those whose assigned column does not contain a negative value.

3. Starting from the initial activities, every activity a is connected to its most likely successor b with the maximum value of $a \Rightarrow_L b$ among all activities $b' \in A$ (with ($b' \neq a$).

4. If necessary, every activity a is additionally connected to its most likely predecessor b with the highest $b \Rightarrow_L a$ value among all $b' \in A$ (with $b' \neq a$).

The restriction to the most likely successor and predecessor of every activity results in a dependency graph that only mirrors the *most common behavior* of the observed process. To fine-tune the level of detail of the reconstructed process model (Weijters et al., 2006, p. 9), several threshold parameters are introduced (Weijters et al., 2006, p. 8):

- *dependency threshold*: minimum required $\Rightarrow_L$ value of a dependency to occur in the dependency graph,

- *positive observation threshold*: minimum required number of observations of a dependency to occur in the graph,

- *relative-to-best-threshold*: maximum allowed difference between the value of an assumed dependency $a \Rightarrow b$ and the highest $\Rightarrow_L$ value in the dependency matrix.

Besides the basic dependency relation $\Rightarrow_L$ the Heuristics Miner considers further relations that represent the presence of self-loops ($a \Rightarrow_L a$), length-two-cycles ($a \Rightarrow_L^2 b$), and concurrent splits ($a \Rightarrow_L b \wedge c$). The values of the relations concerned with short cycles increase with the number of patterns found that indicate the respective cycle, i.e. aa for self-loops and $[aba, bab]$ for length-two-cycles (Weijters et al., 2006, p. 9). The 'concurrency' relation is based on the idea that for a concurrent split $a \rightarrow b \wedge c$, direct successions of b and c (in arbitrary order) are frequently found in the log, while for an alternative split $a \rightarrow b \oplus c$ they are impossible (Weijters et al., 2006, p. 9).

Weijters et al. (2006, p. 12) further explain how the Heuristics Miner identifies long distance dependencies where the path taken in a process depends on a choice of activities several steps before: This is achieved by determining tasks that often appear together in the same trace, and by establishing an additional precedence between these tasks if necessary.

Due to its convincing performance on both error-free and noisy data (see e.g. the experimental results presented by Weijters et al., 2006, Sec. 3), the Heuristics Miner is one of the most widely used process mining algorithms in practice. It has been applied, analyzed, and compared to other mining algorithms in several studies (e.g. Rozinat et al., 2009a; Weber, 2009). The main drawbacks of the Heuristics Miner are its inability to handle duplicate tasks and the large number of parameters that must be calibrated to the given data.

The former issue might be compensated by applying preprocessing or embedding the Heuristics Miner into a two-step approach as described above. To tackle the latter issue, Burattin and Sperduti (2010) present a procedure to automatically calibrate the parameters of a Heuristics Miner variant for activity based logs (HM^{++}). Weijters and Ribeiro (2011) developed an extended algorithm *Flexible Heuristics Miner* with an improved representation of concurrent and alternative routing constructs in *augmented C-nets*.

Evolutionary Algorithms The most algorithms presented so far are locally-optimizing (see Section 4.2.2.3) approaches where the mined model is reconstructed stepwise from relations between elementary activities. De Medeiros (see e.g. Medeiros, 2006; Medeiros et al., 2004b) proposes a process mining approach based on genetic algorithms (GA, see Section 4.1.4.5) as a heuristic, globally optimizing technique that can also handle noise. We will not discuss this approach in detail but only provide a brief overview of its advantages and drawbacks.

In general, the application of evolutionary algorithms to process mining, requires solutions to the following problems (Medeiros et al., 2004b, p. 10):

- mapping of process models to individuals encoded for processing by genetic operators like mutation and crossover,

- generation of an initial population,

- choice of an objective function to rate the fitness of the generated process models with respect to the analyzed log, and

- identification of appropriate genetic operators and a stopping criterion.

Medeiros et al. (2004b, pp. 5) employ an encoding based on binary dependency matrices (causal matrices), from which Petri nets can be generated. The initial population of individuals is built from random variations of the heuristic relations $a \Rightarrow_L b$, $a \Rightarrow_L a$, and $a \Rightarrow_L^2 b$ (see above) on the analyzed log (Medeiros et al., 2004b, pp. 8). As an objective function, different measures for the conformance of the generated process models to the log are applied (Medeiros et al., 2004b, pp. 11).[27]

The procedure finishes if either a maximum number n of iterations, an 'optimal' process model with the highest possible fitness value of 1, or a 'plateau' in the search space without relevant changes of the best individual during $n/2$ iterations has been reached (Medeiros et al., 2004b,

---

[27]see also Section 4.2.5.4 on conformance checking

p. 13). Otherwise, a new population is generated by applying genetic operators described in (Medeiros et al., 2004b, Sec. 3.4).

Medeiros (2006, Chs. 4,5,8) shows by experiments that genetic process mining can reconstruct complex process models including non-free-choice constructs, invisible, and duplicate tasks also in the presence of noise. Drawbacks include the algorithms' high computational complexity (Medeiros, 2006, p. 230) and the large number of parameters to be set by the user.

To compensate the former drawback, Bratosin (2011) presents a distributed genetic process mining algorithm that works on a Grid architecture. Turner et al. (2008) propose an alternative evolutionary process mining approach based on a genetic programming technique called *Graph Based Program Evolution* that works on graph structures directly instead of a causal matrix. The authors claim that this representation can be manipulated more flexibly and straightforwardly by genetic operators and that fitness evaluation is more efficient (Turner et al., 2008, pp. 1307).

4.2.3.5. Mining Complex Workflow Patterns

Recalling the workflow patterns introduced in Section 2.3.3, control flow mining might go beyond basic routing constructs as well. However, only few process mining approaches deal with more complex patterns like transactions or multiple instantiations in parallel. Due to the relevance of such patterns in MAS, we review two approaches towards their reconstruction in the following.

Workflow Patterns Mining Gaaloul et al. (2005) present an algorithm that identifies the control flow patterns *sequence, xor-split/join, and-split/join, or-split,* and *m-out-of-n-join* from statistical properties of event-based logs. In (Gaaloul and Godart, 2005) the approach is extended towards mining transactional properties of workflows.

Similar to the *Heuristics Miner* (Section 4.2.3.4) the algorithms are based on a matrix of direct follower relations named *initial statistical dependency table* (SDT, Gaaloul et al., 2005, p. 27). An entry at matrix position (i, j) represents the relative frequency $P(A_i/A_j) \in [0, 1]$ by which activity A_i directly follows A_j in the observed log (Gaaloul et al., 2005, p. 26). The absolute frequency of each task A_i is counted as $\#A_i$ (Gaaloul et al., 2005, p. 26).

To mark potentially concurrent tasks, a second matrix (*final SDT*) is set up (Gaaloul et al., 2005, p. 27): It contains an entry of -1 for each pair of tasks with $P(A_i/A_j) \neq 0 \wedge P(A_j/A_i) \neq 0$, i.e. A_i and A_j are 'causally' independent. An entry of 1 indicates $P(A_i/A_j) \neq 0 \wedge P(A_i/A_j) = 0$, meaning that A_j 'causally' depends on A_i.

To discover indirect dependencies, every activity is assigned a value called *activity concurrent window* (ACW, Gaaloul et al., 2005, p. 27). Since interleaving of concurrent activities masks the direct follower relation in the log, the ACW counts how often an activity or one of its predecessors are concurrent to other tasks (Gaaloul et al., 2005, pp. 27). On this basis, further dependencies might be added to the final SDT (Gaaloul et al., 2005, p. 28).

Gaaloul et al. (2005, Sec. 3.2) show that several control flow patterns can be identified from the activity count and the final SDT. A *sequence* $A \rightarrow B$ is e.g. characterized by the rule (Gaaloul et al., 2005, p. 30):

$$\#A = \#B \wedge P(A/B) = 1. \tag{4.14}$$

A non-exclusive *or-split* between an activity A and a set of activities B_i $(0 \leq i \leq n)$, which is neglected by most process mining algorithms, can be identified using a more complex set of rules (Gaaloul et al., 2005, p. 30):

$$
\begin{aligned}
(\#A \leq \sum_{i=0}^{n} \#B_i) \wedge (\forall 0 \leq i \leq n : \#B_i \leq \#A) \\
(\forall 0 \leq i \leq n : P(B_i/A) = 1) \wedge (\exists 0 \leq i, j \leq n : P(B_i/B_j) = -1)
\end{aligned}
\tag{4.15}
$$

Based on the identified patterns, an overall control flow graph could be reconstructed from a complete log (Gaaloul et al., 2005, p. 29). However, the authors stress that "local discovery" is a particularly useful ability of their approach, e.g. when "only fractions of workflow log[s]" are available (Gaaloul et al., 2005, p. 29).

Gaaloul and Godart (2005) extend the algorithm towards mining transactional properties of activities (*activity transactional properties*) and workflows (*transactional flow*) (Gaaloul and Godart, 2005, pp. 177). These properties characterize how a workflow behaves in order to recover a consistent state after failures.

Transactional properties are defined under the assumption of a set of observable activity states including *completed, aborted,* and *failed* (Gaaloul and Godart, 2005, p. 178). Depending on the set of possible transitions between these states, an activity A is said to be *re-triable* (A is repeated after failure until completion), *pivot* (the effect of A persists and cannot be undone after its completion), or both (Gaaloul and Godart, 2005, p. 178).

Transactional flow relates to the control flow of recovery procedures that a workflow or an external entity executes to ensure a consistent state after an activity has failed (Gaaloul and Godart, 2005, pp. 179,180). In this context, Gaaloul and Godart (2005, p. 180) focus on *alternative dependencies* (which activities B_i are executed for recovery after a certain activity A has failed) and *abortion dependencies* (which activities B_i must be aborted after A's failure).

To mine transaction-related properties from workflow logs, Gaaloul and Godart (2005, p. 179) build two SDTs that only contain dependencies observed after an activity has failed. From these SDTs, transactional properties such as 're-triable' are reconstructed using simple rules quite similar to those for workflow pattern mining.

The work by Wen et al. (2010) is dedicated to another complex workflow pattern, i.e. the mining of *batch processing features*. Batch processing means that certain steps of multiple instances of a process are executed in a synchronized fashion, such as common rides of multiple travelers with the same destination in workflows of a car-sharing agency (Wen et al., 2010, p. 393). Wen et al. (2010, pp. 395) present an algorithm to identify *batch processing areas* (Wen et al., 2010, p. 393) on the basis of event logs. Using this algorithm, logs of "batch processing processes" can be preprocessed such that conventional control flow mining techniques are applicable for their analysis (Wen et al., 2010, p. 393).

Mining Traces of Interleaved Threads   All above algorithms work under the assumption that each case in the analyzed log corresponds to a single instantiation of the underlying workflow model. Therefore, task repetitions are either interpreted as cycles or duplicates. However, this assumption does not hold in the presence of *multiple instantiation* patterns as described in Section 2.3.3.

Lou et al. (2010b,c) present the first algorithm to reconstruct workflow models from traces generated by multiple interleaved threads. Their approach is targeted towards dynamic software reverse engineering of multi-threaded programs. Based on practical experience, the authors assume that the analyzed log does not necessarily contain an explicit mapping of events to threads (Lou et al., 2010c, p. 613). Thus, threading information must be reconstructed by means of process mining.

The algorithm's ability to handle multiple instantiations of the same sub-workflow is enabled by considering *indirect* dependency relations that also hold true in presence of interleaved threads (Lou et al., 2010c, p. 613). From these relations, a simple initial workflow model without loops, shortcuts, and multiple instantiation is first reconstructed and subsequently refined by applying heuristics based on replay of log traces (Lou et al., 2010b, p. 613).

The procedure does not rely on the 'direct follower' relation but on four indirect dependency relations observed over a log L (Lou et al., 2010c, pp. 615):

- *Forward dependency*: $A \rightarrow_f B$ if in every trace $s \in L$ containing A, there is at least one B after the occurrence of A.

- *Backward dependency*: $A \rightarrow_b B$ if in every trace $s \in L$ containing A, there is at least one A before the occurrence of B.

- *Strict forward dependency*: $A \rightarrow_{sf} B$ if in every trace $s \in L$, every occurrence of A is (directly or indirectly) followed by at least one related occurrence of B.

- *Strict backward dependency*: $A \rightarrow_{sb} B$ if in every trace $s \in L$, every occurrence of B is (directly or indirectly) preceded by at least one related occurrence of A.

- *Unrelated*: $A\|B$ if A and B stand in none of the above relations.

The authors note that the strict dependency relations imply their non-strict counterpart and that any relation (except for $\|$) implies a path from activity A to activity B in the generating workflow model (Lou et al., 2010c, p. 616). Based on these observations, an initial model is reconstructed from estimates of the dependency relations and expressed in terms of the automata-based modeling language shown in Figure 4.12.

Lou et al. (2010c, p. 615) apply the terms *fork* and *join* to states (diamond shape) where multiple threads running the same sub-workflow are instantiated and re-synchronized. The authors compare this situation to a workflow net that contains multiple tokens in the initial place (Lou et al., 2010c, p. 614) of the fork construct.[28] In contrast, 'static' concurrent flow known from standard workflow nets, is expressed by *split* and *merge* states with a rectangular shape (Lou et al., 2010c, p. 615).

---

[28]This comparison only applies to the fork node, since it neglects the synchronisation necessary at the join node.

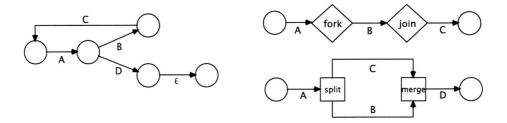

Figure 4.12.: Elements of the automata-based formalism used by Lou et al. (2010b). Left: sequential automaton with decision node, loop, and shortcut transition labelled with the empty event ϵ. Bottom right: concurrent split and merge nodes. Top right: fork and join nodes spawning multiple threads. Adopted with modifications from (Lou et al., 2010c, p. 615).

The initial workflow model is constructed from the mined dependencies by applying the following steps (see Lou et al., 2010c, pp. 617):

1. *Eliminate bidirectional dependencies* (Lou et al., 2010c, p. 617): For the cycle shown in Figure 4.12 (left), both $B \to_b C$ and $C \to_f B$ hold, which makes the dependency pruning of step 3 run into an infinite loop. Bidirectional dependencies are therefore eliminated by introducing a cloned event B' and replacing the forward dependency $C \to_f B$ with $C \to_f B'$.

2. *Identify successors and predecessors* (Lou et al., 2010c, p. 617): For each event X, a predecessor list $prec(X)$ and a successor list $succ(X)$ are constructed: If $(A \to_f B) \vee (A \to_b B)$ then $succ(A) := succ(A) \cup \{B\}$ and $prec(B) := prec(B) \cup \{A\}$.

3. *Prune indirect dependencies* (Lou et al., 2010c, p. 617): If $A \in prec(C) \wedge A \in prec(B) \wedge B \in prec(C)$, then A is removed from $prec(C)$. Equally, if $C \in succ(A) \wedge B \in succ(A) \wedge C \in succ(B)$, then C is removed from $succ(A)$. After pruning, cloned events introduced in step 1 are replaced with their originals again.

4. *Introduce initial and final states* based on the observation which events start and finish traces in the log with a support of at least 5% to compensate for noise (Lou et al., 2010c, pp. 617-618).

5. *Identify control flow patterns* (Lou et al., 2010c, p. 618): Alternative and concurrent split and merge states are identified in the model based on rules quite similar to the workflow patterns mining approach by Gaaloul et al. (2005). One example given by the authors is the relation $\#A = \#B$ for a concurrent split state with two outgoing transitions labelled A and B.

To detect cycles, fork/join nodes, and shortcut transitions, Lou et al. (2010c, pp. 618) refine the initial workflow model based on statistical properties observed during replay of the analyzed traces. The authors describe the procedure for loop identification as follows (Lou et al., 2010c, pp. 618;Lou et al., 2010b, pp. 11-12):

For each log trace $s \in L$, a new instance (thread) m_0 of the simple workflow model M_0 is started in the initial state s_0. As long as w_0 can interpret the events of s, the current state of w_0 is updated according to the transition function of M_0. If w_0 cannot interpret an event of s, a new instance (thread) w_1 of M_0 is tentatively started from its initial state.

If the trace s can be interpreted as an interleaving of w_0 and w_1, the procedure is repeated, optionally starting further instances of M_0. However, if the current event E of s does not fit any interleaving of multiple instances, the initial workflow model M_0 must be refined by introducing a shortcut transition looping back to a previous state. The target state of this transition is unambiguous when the model contains no duplicate tasks. The source state, however, could be the current state of an arbitrary active thread. Lou et al. (2010c, p. 618) therefore determine the state q of M_0 for which the probability that event E cannot be interpreted is maximal over all traces $s \in L$. This state is assumed to be the shortcut transition's source state.

Since "fork/join states do not expose any unique statistical properties" and "event traces that can be interpreted by a workflow W_1 with loop structures can also be interpreted by a workflow W_2 [...] with fork/join structures, [...] but not vice versa" (Lou et al., 2010c, p. 618), the authors apply a complexity-based heuristics to decide between cycles and fork/join patterns. This heuristics prefers the construct that leads to a lower overall number of transitions and sub-workflow types in the resulting model (Lou et al., 2010c, p. 618). If both variants have the same complexity, cycles are preferred (Lou et al., 2010c, p. 618). Detailed algorithms for all steps of the procedure are found in the appendices of (Lou et al., 2010c) and (Lou et al., 2010b).

Lou et al. (2010c, Sec. 6) show by experiments that their algorithm is effective and efficient on simulated as well as real-world examples from the domain of program comprehension. Though the computational complexity of the refinement procedure is not considered formally, search appears to be expensive especially in case of multiple interleaved threads. Further drawbacks are the inability to handle duplicate tasks and a tendency for over-generalization in presence of long-distance dependencies (Lou et al., 2010c, p. 21).

To improve this, the authors plan to include further "domain or existing knowledge about a program" into their approach in the future (Lou et al., 2010c, p. 21). In Section 7.3, we present a procedure to reconstruct multicast protocols that is less general than the approach by Lou et al. (2010c) but already makes use of additional information (e.g. thread identifiers) available in logs of multi-agent simulations.

4.2.4. Organizational Perspective

Complementary to the control flow perspective, the organizational perspective focuses on deriving information about actors and organizational entities from process execution logs (Song and Aalst, 2008, p. 5).[29] The temporal dimension, which is central to control flow mining, is often neglected. Following Song and Aalst (2008, p. 3), relevant problems in organizational mining include:

1. *Social Network Analysis* (SNA): Networks of organizational actors and their relations are reconstructed and formally analyzed.

---

[29] page numbers relate to the pre-print of the article downloadable at `http://wwwis.win.tue.nl/~wvdaalst/publications/p484.pdf` (last visit 2012-09-28)

2. *Organizational model mining*: A model of an organizational structure (i.e. teams, roles, or staff assignment rules) is mined from log data. The role mining approach by Rembert and Ellis (2009, Sec. 4.2) was already presented in Section 4.2.2.1.

3. *Information flow mining*: The information flow between organizational entities (e.g. roles) is analyzed by means of SNA and control flow mining techniques.

As a fourth category, the reconstruction and analysis of frequent *interaction patterns* (e.g. Dustdar and Hoffmann, 2007) might be added. In the following, we review relevant approaches for SNA, organizational model mining, and interaction pattern analysis. Mutual benefits of combining organizational process mining with MAS are treated in Sections 5.3.4 and 6.2.3.

4.2.4.1. Social Network Mining and Analysis

In Social Network Analysis (SNA) social positions and relations are mapped to a graph structure $G = (V, E)$ called *sociogram* (Aalst and Song, 2004b, p. 9).[30] Vertices $v \in V$ represent individual or abstract actors, while (un)directed and possibly weighted edges $e \in E$ model their relations (Aalst and Song, 2004b, p. 9) based on quantitative measures like frequency of e-mail communication (Aalst and Song, 2004b, p. 2).

After building a sociogram from observations, its properties like node degree and distance are calculated and related to properties of the analyzed society, such as the status of certain actors or the efficiency of communication (Aalst and Song, 2004b, p. 10). Though this analysis is rather abstract and neglects informal social interaction (Aalst and Song, 2004b, p. 38), SNA has been applied to diverse areas ranging from education to defense against terrorism (Aalst and Song, 2004b, p. 1,9).[31]

Social Network Mining on Workflow Logs Aalst and Song (2004b, p. 2) argue that workflow logs are a highly appropriate data source for SNA due to the amount and quality of logged data. To reconstruct a sociogram from workflow logs, the authors define the following metrics (presentation based on the summary by Dustdar and Hoffmann, 2007, Sec. 4):

1. *Follower relations of events*: Aalst and Song (2004b, pp. 12) distinguish between *handover of work* and *subcontracting* metrics: For handover of work, a link from an actor A to an actor B is added to the sociogram if A performs a task on a workflow case directly before B. For subcontracting, a link from A to B is added, if B works on a case in between two tasks performed by A. Both metrics can be further refined, e.g. by measuring the *degree of causality*, i.e. how many other actors work on the task in between A and B (Dustdar and Hoffmann, 2007, p. 148).

2. *Joint cases*: A weighted edge between two actors A and B indicates the relative number of cases on which these actors worked together (Dustdar and Hoffmann, 2007, p. 148; Aalst and Song, 2004b, p. 17).

---

[30] page numbers relate to the version of the article available at `http://wwwis.win.tue.nl/~wvdaalst/publications/p233.pdf` (last visit 2012-09-28)

[31] For further details on sociographic metrics, tools, applications, and literature see e.g. the brief summary by Aalst and Song (2004b).

3. *Joint activities* (Dustdar and Hoffmann, 2007, p. 149): A matrix $\mathbf{C}$ is set up with actors as columns and observed activities as rows. A matrix element c_{ij} counts how often actor i performed activity j. By applying a vector distance to the columns of $\mathbf{C}$, the similarity of actors can be rated in terms of performed activities.

4. *Special event types*: One example of this metric is the use of the special event type *delegation* to identify hierarchical relations in an organization (Dustdar and Hoffmann, 2007, p. 149).

The above metrics for social network mining were implemented as part of a tool named *MiSoN* (Aalst and Song, 2004b, Sec. 5) and integrated into the process mining system *ProM* (Song and Aalst, 2008, Sec. 6.1). Aalst and Song (2004b, pp. 23) present a large case study from the "Dutch national public works department", in which social networks are mined with *MiSoN* and subsequently analysed using the SNA tool *AGNA*[32].

Social Network Dynamics Fewer SNA approaches attempt to mine models of *structural dynamics* in social networks. One example is the work by Lahiri and Berger-Wolf (2008), who tackle the problem of "[frequent] periodic subgraph mining for dynamic networks" (Lahiri and Berger-Wolf, 2008, p. 373). The task is to identify, from a time series of network graphs $\mathbf{G} = \{G_1, G_2, \ldots, G_n\}$ (called a *dynamic network*), those subgraphs F that re-occur with a fixed period (Lahiri and Berger-Wolf, 2008, p. 373).

Lahiri and Berger-Wolf (2008, pp. 374-378) present a polynomial time algorithm to mine subgraphs that are *frequent, maximal, periodic*, and *pure*[33] from a dynamic network with unique node labels. Different from Aalst and Song (2004b), the analyzed dynamic networks are not constructed from workflow logs but from more diverse and less formalized data sources. Examples presented in (Lahiri and Berger-Wolf, 2008, Sec. 6) include a business e-mail archive, movement profiles of Plains Zebra, and an image database of Hollywood celebrities. By the latter example, Lahiri and Berger-Wolf (2008, pp. 380) show that their algorithm is able to detect periodic events like award shows or weekly television series from the joint occurrence of celebrities on pictures in the image database.

4.2.4.2. Mining Organizational Models

The 'joint activities' metrics described above can be applied to cluster actors by similar "profiles" (Aalst and Song, 2004b, p. 17) of performed activities. Since these profiles provide hints towards the organizational *role* of a performer, they are an appropriate basis for *role mining*, i.e. identifying which roles exist in an organization and which actors are assigned (Song and Aalst, 2008, p. 11).

Song and Aalst (2008, pp. 11) apply hierarchical agglomerative clustering (see Section 4.1.4.2) based on the joint activities metrics to reconstruct a hierarchical role model from a workflow log. Hierarchical clustering seems appropriate since organizational models are often structured hierarchically (Song and Aalst, 2008, p. 11), e.g. in a hospital there might be a role 'nurse' with

---

[32]http://www.oocities.org/imbenta/agna (last visit 2011-11-13)

[33]This means that the non-periodic support of a subgraph is small compared to its periodic support (*purity measure*; Lahiri and Berger-Wolf, 2008, p. 376).

the specialization 'lead nurse' (Ly et al., 2006, p. 178): Both basically perform the same set of activities, but the lead nurse has additional responsibilities such as creating a service schedule.

Song and Aalst (2008, Sec. 6) show that their approach is able to reconstruct plausible organizational models from workflow logs of a large Dutch municipality. By using the 'joint cases' metric instead of 'joint activities' the algorithm can be tuned towards the mining of *teams*, i.e. people with different roles working together on the same cases, rather than roles (Song and Aalst, 2008, p. 12). The organizational mining algorithm, a graphical notation, and an XML-based format (OMML) to display and persist hierarchical organizational models were implemented as part of *ProM* (Song and Aalst, 2008, pp. 8, 16).

As a drawback, the current organizational mining approach can only assign a single role to each performer. Song and Aalst (2008, p. 21) propose to "apply non-disjoint clustering methods ro reflect an organization in which originators play multiple roles" in the future. Due to the use of unsupervised learning, it is necessary that a 'meaning' is assigned to the detected roles by an analyst based on the underlying performers and activity profiles after mining. Furthermore, process dimensions beyond task and originator names are not taken into account.

The latter two issues are adressed in a *staff assignment* mining approach by Ly et al. (2006). Different from Song and Aalst (2008), these authors assume that an organizational model is known *a-priori*, whereby supervised learning becomes possible (Ly et al., 2006, p. 183). Organizational modeling is based on a meta-model that comprises the concepts of agents, roles, abilities, organizational positions, and organizational units (Ly et al., 2006, p. 181).

Given a workflow log and an organizational model, Ly et al. (2006) apply the $C4.5$ algorithm to mine decision trees (see Section 4.1.4.1) that represent staff assignment rules, i.e. which roles and abilities are necessary to perform a certain task. Negative examples, stating which activities are *not* performed by actors with certain roles and abilities in the analyzed log, are also taken into account (Ly et al., 2006, pp. 183).

Song and Aalst (2008, p. 20) emphasize the similarity between organizational model mining and role mining in the context of *role-based access control* for resource management (e.g. computer network administration). Molloy et al. (2009) e.g. provide a summary and evaluation of role mining algorithms from this domain. Zhao et al. (2012) present an alternative approach where roles and their interactions, as displayed in so-called *role-activity diagrams* (Zhao et al., 2012, p. 404), are reconstructed based on the "diversity degree[s]" of their activities and interactions using genetic algorithms (Zhao et al., 2012, p. 402).

4.2.4.3. Detection of Interaction Patterns

Dustdar and Hoffmann (2007) use social networks reconstructed from workflow logs as a basis to detect specific interaction patterns found in an organization. Their approach is not 'mining' in the narrower sense of hypothesis generation, but the objective is to recognize a set of pre-defined patterns related to (object-oriented) software engineering (Dustdar and Hoffmann, 2007, pp. 140):

- *Proxy*: provides services on behalf of another actor. The proxy receives requests of a fixed type from several clients, pre-processes the requests, forwards them to another actor, and returns the answer to the client after performing some post-processing (Dustdar and Hoffmann, 2007, pp. 140,143).

- *Broker*: receives different kinds of requests and propagates them to a fixed server per request type (Dustdar and Hoffmann, 2007, pp. 140,145).

- *Master/slave*: A master receives requests of a fixed type, splits the requested task into subtasks, forwards the subtasks to a set of slaves, and collects the (partial) results returned (Dustdar and Hoffmann, 2007, pp. 140,143).

Based on these specifications, the authors implemented 3 rules as *Java* classes that work on a social network represented in terms of an object model (Dustdar and Hoffmann, 2007, pp. 141,145). For pattern detection, the rules check properties of the social network for conformance with the above specifications. To detect proxies, tests are e.g. performed if a candidate node in the social network communicates with a minimum of two peers, if all received requests are of a common type, etc. (Dustdar and Hoffmann, 2007, pp. 142).

This intrinsically simple pattern detection is complicated by a number of difficulties (Dustdar and Hoffmann, 2007, p. 141):

1. Actors might appear in different roles like e.g. proxies for different task types.

2. To handle a log containing multiple communications, it must be possible to trace back reactive tasks to an initial client request.

3. Specific task types (like pre-processing, post-processing or decomposition) must be identified to distinguish the different patterns.

Dustdar and Hoffmann (2007, p. 141) solve these issues by explicitly enriching the log with the necessary data including "causal information, [...] task-subtask relation[s ..., and] the kind of request". Taking into account these enrichments, a "pattern finding algorithm" reconstructs social networks from the log that represent the contained "single communication tie[s]" (Dustdar and Hoffmann, 2007, p. 146).

The effectivity of the pattern detection is demonstrated by analyzing example logs recorded with the workflow management system *Caramba*, which is tailored towards keeping *ad-hoc* processes (Dustdar and Hoffmann, 2007, Sec. 5). For future work, the authors suggest to lead their approach back to the software engineering field and apply pattern detection to the analysis of web service interactions (Dustdar and Hoffmann, 2007, p. 154).

Data mining in a more traditional sense is applied to interaction pattern detection in the approach by Yu et al. (2010). These authors use frequent subtree mining to identify common interaction patterns emerging in discussions between multiple persons at meetings. For data collection, different meeting situations are filmed and subsequently interpreted by assigning performative-like tags to the observations, including the communicative acts "*propose, comment, acknowledgement, requestInfo, askOpinion, pos[itive]Opinion and neg[ative]Opinion*" (Yu et al., 2010, p. 2).

In the resulting communication logs, the contained discussion threads (*sessions*) are identified together with the initiating pro-active events (Yu et al., 2010, p. 3). The reactions of other participants to these events are recursively aggregated into an *interaction flow* represented by a multicast tree-like data structure displayed in Figure 4.13. The identified interaction flows are encoded in a normalized form that takes account of isomorphic subtrees and stored in a database (Yu et al., 2010, Sec. 4.1).

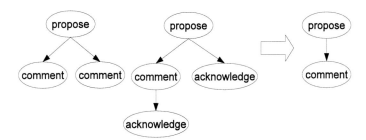

Figure 4.13.: Two interaction flows (left) an a derived subtree representing the common interaction pattern *propose* → *comment* (right). Adopted with modifications from (Yu et al., 2010, p. 4).

On the database, a frequent pattern mining algorithm is applied, that returns a set of subtrees for the most common interaction patterns (Yu et al., 2010, Sec. 4.2). The algorithm was evaluated in exemplary real world discussions on subjects including "PC purchase [,...] trip-planning [,...] soccer preparation [...], and [...] job selection" (Yu et al., 2010, p. 7).

A drawback of the procedure is its current inability to handle indirect causal dependencies, which the authors plan to compensate by using so-called *embedded subtrees* for representation (Yu et al., 2010, p. 10). Furthermore, the algorithm seems to be unable to abstract from multiple similar reactions to an event: Thus, 3 subtrees representing 1, 2, and 3 comments to the same proposal are identified as different patterns. Yu et al. (2011) present an alternative, graph-based pattern mining approach that only regards for the number of interacting persons and the order, direction, and frequency of their interactions.

4.2.5. Further Perspectives and Tasks

So far we have treated the main mining perspectives of control flow and organizational structure and the main task of discovery. However, a large number of further process mining perspectives and tasks have been identified, on which fewer work exists. Relevant examples with ties to MABS (as explained later) are presented in the following.

4.2.5.1. Log Clustering

In Section 4.2.4.2, we explained how unsupervised clustering is applied to the reconstruction of organizational models. Clustering algorithms can also be used to provide additional structure to logs and mined process models in the absence of explicit structuring information. From the literature, 4 main applications can be identified:

1. Some logs are not composed of events representing high-level activities but contain low-level data like transactional database change sets (Ellis et al., 2006, p. 56). The clustering of similar sets of low-level operations into aggregated high-level activities is called *activity mining* by Günther et al. (2010, cited from the brief summary in Lang, 2008, p. 83). A rather similar approach is presented by Ellis et al. (2006, Sec. 3.2)

2. Though a log contains high-level events, these are not explicitly assigned to a certain process instance (i.e. missing case identifier). In this situation clustering allows to group related events into distinct traces for each process instance (see e.g. Schütt, 2003, pp. 47). Aalst et al. (2005, p. 21) refer to this as "chained correlation".

3. When cases can be identified, but were generated by multiple different process models or variants, clustering can be applied to group traces into sub-logs for each model (Song et al., 2008, p. 110). A set of smaller models reconstructed from each sub-log is often more understandable than a large model mined from the overall log, which might soon become unmanageable (e.g. Song et al., 2008, p. 110). Algorithms for trace clustering are (among others) presented by Greco et al. (2004) and Song et al. (2008).

4. Clustering of similar sub-structures found in a process log or model is the basis for mining *hierarchical models* that represent control flow at multiple levels of abstraction. Approaches by Medeiros et al. (2008b) and Bose et al. (2011b) are reviewed in the next section.

The former three types of log clustering are rather similar except that the grouping of entities is performed at different levels of abstraction: (1) *activity mining* = assignment of low-level events to high-level activities, (2) *chaining* = assignment of activities to traces, (3) *trace clustering* = assignment of traces to process models. Günther et al. (2010, p. 129) also emphasize the applicability of their log segmentation approach to both activity mining and "trace discovery", i.e. a combination of (2) and (3).

Existing approaches differ in the used clustering algorithms, the encoding of entities, and the applied distance measures. The main challenge lies in choosing an appropriate encoding to represent log entities by characteristic feature vectors (Greco et al., 2004, pp. 57). Given this representation, standard algorithms like k-means (Greco et al., 2004, p. 56; Song et al., 2008, p. 115), Agglomerative Hierarchical (Jung and Bae, 2006, p. 385; Song et al., 2008, p. 115), or Nearest Neighbour-like clustering (Ellis et al., 2006, pp. 57) and distance measures like Euclidian, Hamming, or Jaccard distance (Song et al., 2008, p. 115) can be applied.

A number of encodings of log traces as feature vectors are summarized by Song et al. (2008, pp. 113):

- *Activity profiles*: The elements of the feature vector represent the different activity types found in the log. In a vector $\mathbf{s}$ representing trace $s \in L$, an element s_i is set to the number of times activity A_i appears in s.

- *Transition profiles*: Every vector component represents a direct follower relation found in the log. It is set to the number of times the represented trace contains the respective transition.

- *Originator profiles*: The vector components stand for the different activity performers involved in the represented case.

- *Attribute profiles*: Cases are represented by vectors containing values or counts of certain data attributes assigned to the case or its events.

- *Performance profiles*: Cases are represented by performance measures like trace length or duration.

These basic encodings are refined and domain-specifically adapted in several articles on workflow clustering. Jung and Bae (2006, pp. 382) and Kastner et al. (2009, Sec. 3) cluster workflow instances by activity and transition similarity taking into account control flow constructs beyond direct follower relations. Dustdar and Gombotz (2006, p. 263) present encodings to rate session (i.e. case) similarity in the context of web service interaction mining that are detailed in Section 5.3.3.1.

4.2.5.2. Mining Hierarchical Models

Hierarchical models are an important means to display complex control flow in a readable form. In the following, two approaches are reviewed where the first combines control flow mining with clustering while the second is based on pattern recognition and log abstraction. In Section 7.3 we present a concept for mining hierarchical agent interaction protocols which is akin to the reviewed approaches but also accounts for the detection of multicast communication.

Mining Hierarchies of Workflow Schemas Based on their clustering approach mentioned above, Greco et al. (2006) developed a technique to reconstruct a hierarchy of increasingly refined workflow models from an event log. The algorithm is improved, generalized, and adopted into the ProM framework by Medeiros et al. (2008b). According to these authors, "the goal [...] is to allow for the mining of processes with very diverse cases [...] while avoiding over-generalization" (Medeiros et al., 2008b, p. 21). The basic procedure works as follows (Medeiros et al., 2008b, pp. 22):

1. An initial process model is reconstructed from the overall log by means of a control flow mining algorithm.

2. The model's quality and compliance to the represented log is determined with a conformance measure.

3. If the quality of the model is insufficient, the related traces from the log are partitioned into disjoint clusters. For each cluster, the above procedure is repeated starting from step 1. If multiple clusters exist, the cluster belonging to the model with the worst quality is considered for splitting first.

4. If the quality of all discovered models suffices,the resulting hierarchy of disjoint models (with their assigned traces) is output as a result.

Medeiros et al. (2008b, p. 23) emphasize that their approach should be understood as a template in which concrete mining algorithms can be plugged in to support the different steps. For control flow mining the *Heuristics Miner* (Section 4.2.3.4) is chosen due to its robustness (Medeiros et al., 2008b, p. 24). Following the original proposal by Greco et al. (2004, 2006), the k-means algorithm is applied for clustering (Medeiros et al., 2008b, p. 24).

As a distance measure for clustering and quality assessment Medeiros et al. (2008b, p. 23) use a feature identification scheme adopted from (Greco et al., 2004, 2006): "A relevant feature is a sequence [...] $t_1, \ldots, t_n$ together with a task [...] t_{n+1} such that [...] (i) $t_1, \ldots, t_n$ is *frequent*, [...] (ii) t_n, t_{n+1} is also frequent [...], but, (iii) the whole sequence $t_1, \ldots, t_n, t_{n+1}$ is *not* frequent" (Medeiros et al., 2008b, pp. 23) in the analysed log.

After identifying features with relevant support, all traces are mapped to vectors over the feature space, which serve as input to the k-means algorithm (Medeiros et al., 2008b, p. 24). To assess the quality of a reconstructed model Medeiros et al. (2008b, p. 23) propose to check for over-generalization in terms of the number of patterns that are implied by the model but not found in the log. Greco et al. (2006, p. 1017) suggest to refine the model with the lowest *soundness*[34] or – for the sake of efficiency – the model with the highest number of alternative splits.

Greco et al. (2008, p. 79) further extend the algorithm by restructuring the resulting model tree into a *taxonomy* of workflow models, where each 'non-leaf' model can be composed from its (disjoint) sub models. They also present an application of the hierarchical mining approach to real world log data from the domain of container terminal logistics (Greco et al., 2008, Sec. 6.3).

Process Maps   Li et al. (2010) approach the problem of hierarchical model reconstruction with a two-step procedure of pattern-based log abstraction and subsequent control flow mining on the abstracted log (Li et al., 2010, p.110). In the first step, (combinations of) events from the original log are mapped to a more abstract alphabet. One example is the aggregation of frequent sub-processes into higher-level activities.

In the second step, a control flow mining algorithm is applied (1) to the abstracted traces to reconstruct the overall model structure, and (2) to the sub-traces belonging to each abstraction to mine the hierarchical refinements (Li et al., 2010, p. 117). Like the approach by Medeiros et al. (2008b), the work by Li et al. (2010, p. 110) is also intended as a template to plug in different algorithms for log abstraction and control flow mining.

The pattern detection procedure used in (Li et al., 2010, p. 112) searches for *maximal repeats* of event sequences in the log:[35] Basically, if a sequence like $p_0 = [a, b, c, d]$ appears frequently in the analyzed log, it is identified as a sub-process and each occurrence is replaced by a symbol from an abstracted alphabet, e.g. x (Li et al., 2010, p. 111).

The implemented procedure is more complex since it also regards for variations (e.g. $p_1 = [a, c, b, d]$ might be a variation of p_0 due to concurrency of b and c; see Li et al., 2010, p. 113) and hierarchical embeddings (e.g. $p_2 = [a, b]$ and $p_3 = [c, d]$ might be sub-processes of p_0; see Li et al., 2010, p. 114) of patterns.[36] Nevertheless, pattern detection can be performed "in *linear* time and space with respect to the length of the traces" (Bose et al., 2011b, p. 35).

For control flow mining, Li et al. (2010, p. 117) apply the *Fuzzy Miner* algorithm by Günther and Aalst (2007) with a modification that allows to "zoom" into the abstracted sub-processes by aggregating the related pattern variations. The overall procedure is validated at the example of log data from a Dutch house rental agency (Li et al., 2010, p. 118). Bose et al. (2011b) describe an implementation in the form of multiple *ProM* plugins including an additional pattern abstraction stage for loop constructs. A semi-automated, interactive definition of pattern abstractions is also supported (Bose et al., 2011b, p. 37).

In comparison to other techniques for hierarchical mining like (Medeiros et al., 2008b), the authors emphasize the domain-specific adaptability of their approach by defining context-

---

[34]Here, soundness is characterized by a low relative number of possible process model executions that do not fit an actual trace from the log (see Greco et al., 2006, p. 1011 and Greco et al., 2004, p. 55).

[35]as one of several patterns defined by the authors

[36]All adopted examples were modified by the author.

dependent abstractions, and the practical suitability of "[log] abstraction from a functionality/subprocess point of view" (Li et al., 2010, p. 120).

4.2.5.3. Mining Non-Stationary Processes

Most process mining techniques presuppose a *stationary* process, i.e. the model that generated the analyzed log has not *changed* over time (Bose et al., 2011a, pp. 391). However, this assumption is too restrictive for many real-world and simulated processes (Bose et al., 2011a, p. 392), which exhibit *second-order dynamics* (Bose et al., 2011a, pp. 391). Applying a conventional control flow mining algorithm like α^{++} (Section 4.2.3.1) to the log of a non-stationary process will at best yield a result that represents the 'sum' of all behavior variants observed over time.

In the following we review two of the few approaches dedicated to the mining of control flow models from non-stationary processes. While the work by Günther et al. (2006) implies that changes to the process model (e.g. insertion of a new transition) are explicitly logged, the approach by Bose et al. (2011a) tackles the problem of deriving information on such changes from implicit data. In Section 6.2.5 we identify second order dynamics as an important characteristic of MABS and discuss possible applications and extensions of the reviewed 'change mining' techniques in this context.

Change Mining   The change mining approach by Günther et al. (2006, p. 310) is rooted in *adaptive process management systems* (PMS). Here, modifications of a workflow model can be performed during execution and are explicitly logged. The adaptive PMS thus generates, besides the conventional execution (or enactment) log, an additional *change log* (Günther et al., 2006, p. 312) where process model changes including insertion, deletion, and movement of model elements (Günther et al., 2006, p. 315) are listed.

The straightforward idea of change mining consists in the application of standard control flow mining algorithms to change logs in order to "provide an aggregated overview of all changes that happened" (Günther et al., 2006, p. 309) to the analyzed model. Furthermore, data from the change log and the execution log can be correlated to identify possible reasons for process model changes (integrated analysis); see Günther et al. (2006, pp. 312).

To practically solve the problem of change mining, Günther et al. (2006) proceed as follows:

1. The XML-based log data format of the framework *ProM* (Section 4.2.6.1) is extended with fields to store change information including the change operation, the affected activity, and its context in the model graph (i.e. preceding and following activities); see Günther et al. (2006, p. 317). Change logs are imported from the adaptive PMS *ADEPT* (Günther et al., 2006, pp. 322).

2. Exemplary control flow mining algorithms implemented in *ProM* are applied to the imported change logs. In (Günther et al., 2006, p. 321) the *Multi Phase Mining* algorithm by Dongen and Aalst (2004) is chosen due to its "robust[ness] in handling fuzzy branching conditions".

3. The idea of *commutativity* of change operations is employed to reduce the size of the mined model representing the change process (Günther et al., 2006, p. 320): Two change

operations are commutative if their application leads to the same result regardless of execution order. Causal dependencies between commutative operations can therefore be omitted from the reconstructed model of the change process.

4. A concept is developed for integrated analysis (Günther et al., 2006, pp. 312): Frequent patterns found in the change log are related to data attributes of corresponding traces from the enactment log. Decision tree learning might be applied to the combined data, to unveil possible causes for the observed changes.

Günther et al. (2008) report an experimental analysis of further existing control flow mining algorithms for change mining at the example of clinical pathways. A main drawback of this approach is the low availability of process-aware information systems logging change information in practice (Bose et al., 2011a, p. 393).

Detection of Concept Drift   Due to this drawback Bose et al. (2011a, p. 392) focus on the detection and characterization of change points in standard execution logs. These authors consult time-series analysis and data mining and adopt the term *concept drift* to characterize second order dynamics that change a process model at runtime (Bose et al., 2011a, pp. 391). A transfer of existing techniques to handle concept drift is not straightforward, because most are tailored towards models that only consist of a few simple variables (Bose et al., 2011a, p. 392).

Due to the initiating character of their work, Bose et al. (2011a) start by identifying relevant problems and perspectives related to concept drift in process mining:

- Three major problems are stated including "change (point) detection [...,] change localization and characterization [..., and] unravel[ling of] process evolution" (Bose et al., 2011a, p. 392): The first problem refers to the identification of change points in the log. The second problem consists in the detection and description of which model parts actually changed. The third problem is related to the derivation of a change process from the detected changes, somehow similar to the work by Günther et al. (2006).

- Bose et al. (2011a, p. 393) observe that second order dynamics can affect a model at different process perspectives (see Section 4.2.2.1). Typical change operations are identified for three main perspectives. While the control flow perspective is treated similar to (Günther et al., 2006), some examples for the data and resource (i.e. organizational) perspectives are added (Bose et al., 2011a, Sec. 3).

- Finally, the authors pinpoint 4 different types of concept drift (Bose et al., 2011a, pp. 394): *Sudden drift* means that a process model M is suddenly replaced by a changed model M'. In *recurring drift* the old and new models keep re-occurring with a certain (ir)regular period.[37] *Gradual drift* says that the old model does not disappear immediately but keeps existing together with the new model for a certain duration. *Incremental drift* relates to the situation where the observed changes do not happen to the model all at once, but stepwise during an extended period of time.

In their practical work, Bose et al. (2011a, p. 395) address the detection and characterization of change points for sudden drift in the control flow perspective. Their approach is basically

---

[37]similar to the dynamic (social) network mining technique by Lahiri and Berger-Wolf (2008) reviewed in Section 4.2.4.1

similar to log clustering (Section 4.2.5.1): One (local features) or more (global features) traces are mapped to feature vectors, and change points are detected by measuring deviations between these features over time (Bose et al., 2011a, pp. 396). The similarity between log clustering and concept drift detection is put forward in the approach by Luengo and Sepulveda (2012) detailed below.

Bose et al. (2011a, p. 396) propose four control flow-related feature mappings rooted in data and process mining. To detect change points in execution logs, Bose et al. (2011a, p. 397) proceed similar to statistical time series analysis: The log is segmented into multiple (non-)overlapping windows and the traces from each sub-log are encoded into feature vectors using one of the above measures. By applying statistical hypothesis tests to the different vector subsets, it is assessed if the statistical properties of the encoded features differ over time, thus revealing possible changes in the underlying process model (Bose et al., 2011a, p. 397).

After their identification, change points are characterized by further analyzing the features of the related sub-logs (Bose et al., 2011a, p. 402). As a simple example, one might observe that the relation 'b *follows* a' frequently occurs in a sub-log L spanning the time period $[t_0, t_1[$, but not in the following sub-log L' starting at t_1. This could lead to the conclusion that the transition $a \rightarrow b$ was removed from the process model around change point t_1.[38]

Bose et al. (2011a, Sec. 5) successfully evaluate their approach at the example of artificial logs reflecting four local changes to an insurance claim workflow. Despite this initial success, the authors identify several challenges for future work including (1) definition of more specific features, (2) reduction of the currently high-dimensional feature space (see also Section 4.1.3.1), (3) inclusion of further mining perspectives, (4) application of change detection techniques beyond hypothesis tests, and (5) analysis of the minimum sample size needed to detect certain changes (Bose et al., 2011a, p. 404).

A slightly different approach towards concept drift detection by Luengo and Sepulveda (2012, p. 154) explicitly "include[s] the temporal dimension" as an attribute into the feature vectors presented to a mining algorithm. Hickey and Black (2001, p. 23) refer to this technique as "TSAR (Time Stamp Attribute Relevance)". These authors propose 3 different possibilities to tag feature vectors with time stamps in batch learning of decision trees: (1) simple distinction between "current" or "new" batches of feature vectors (Hickey and Black, 2001, p. 23), (2) feature vectors tagged with explicit "batch identifiers" (Hickey and Black, 2001, p. 24), (3) "continuous time stamping [of ...] training example[s ...] without regard to batch[es]" (Hickey and Black, 2001, p. 25).

In a similar way, Luengo and Sepulveda (2012, pp. 154) detect concept drift in process mining by including time stamps into feature vectors that encode process instances by maximal repeat (MR) patterns according to the approach by Li et al. (2010); see Section 4.2.5.2. They experimentally evaluate possibilities to weight the temporal and MR pattern-related features in a distance measure (Luengo and Sepulveda, 2012, p. 155). Comparing their approach to the work by Bose et al. (2011a), Luengo and Sepulveda (2012, p. 154) stress the linear time complexity and the ability to handle "sudden, recurring, gradual, and incremental changes".

---

[38]More realistic examples are provided by Bose et al. (2011a, pp. 401-403).

4.2.5.4. Conformance Checking

So far we have reviewed techniques related to the task of *process discovery*. In the next two Sections we will discuss the additional tasks of conformance checking and process model extension.

Following Rozinat and Aalst (2008, p. 1)[39], "Conformance checking, also referred to as conformance analysis, aims at the detection of inconsistencies between a process model and its corresponding execution log and their quantification by the formation of metrics". In general, four main approaches for conformance analysis can be identified: (1) comparison of high-level features using distance measures, (2) model and trace checking against specifications in (temporal) logic, (3) analyses based on log replay, and (4) detection of pre-defined patterns related to control flow and other perspectives in the log. These are briefly characterized in the following.

Feature-Based Approaches   Feature abstraction, as reviewed in the previous sections, forms one possible basis for conformance analysis: Two traces, logs, or models are abstracted to common high-level features and the conformance between the feature values of both instances is assessed by means of a distance measure (see Section 4.2.5.1). This analogy between conformance checking and clustering-related techniques is e.g. noted by Medeiros et al. (2008b, Sec. 5) in the context of their hierarchical process mining approach (Section 4.2.5.2).

Compared to the symbolic techniques presented further below, conformance checking based on high-level features exhibits some characteristic advantages and drawbacks. On the positive side, it allows for an equal comparison of logs and models when both can be abstracted into similar features. Abstract representations like *causal footprints*[40] even permit to compare models represented in different modeling languages, possibly lacking exact execution semantics (Dongen et al., 2006c, p. 127). Medeiros et al. (2008b, p. 28) see a specific advantage of their metrics-based approach in the detection and characterization of over-generalizations.

A disadvantage of feature-based conformance checking is the lack of exactness when heuristics are used to encode and compare the features. However, the use of heuristics and high-level abstractions might reduce the computational complexity of conformance analysis compared with exact techniques like model checking.

Model and Trace Checking   In (Page and Kreutzer, 2005, Ch. 8), we have described model checking in the context of discrete simulation. Since the typical complexity of models in this context is rather similar to those treated in process mining, we briefly repeat the presentation here (Page and Kreutzer, 2005, pp. 214):

> "Finite state machines offer a suitable base for *model checking*, a formal verification technique that has gained [...] relevance in several applications; e.g. protocol analysis (Holzmann, 1991, Ch. 11). The core idea of model checking is to give a specification of expected

---

[39]page numbers relate to the version of the article downloadable at http://www.processmining.org/_media/publications/rozinat_conformancechecking.pdf (last visit 2012-09-30)

[40]In fact, causal footprints are not feature vectors, but graph-based "description[s] of what can and cannot be done" in a control flow model (Dongen et al., 2006c, p. 127). However, due to their high level of abstraction, an equivalent treatment might be admissible.

model behaviour in a logical language, and then apply a "model checker" tool to verify if the finite state model's behaviour conforms to this specification.

Since we are interested in [...] model behaviour, a *temporal logic* is chosen as specification language. Temporal logics are extensions of propositional or predicate logic with temporal operators, such as 'until' and 'next' [... which] allow [...] to specify properties for feasible state sequences of a FSM. [...]

An important advantage of model checking [...] is that it provides *exhaustive* verification: This means that it can verify that a specification holds *for all possible state sequences*. This advantage is a consequence of the finite state property of the input model."

The state spaces of models or programs considered in practice are, however, often infinite or at least too large to allow for exhaustive verification. One possible solution is the application of model checking only to sample traces (i.e. a log) generated during the execution of a model. As discussed in Section 4.2.3.3 a log of traces corresponds to a finite state machine, e.g. in the form of a prefix tree automaton. Further following our discussion in (Page and Kreutzer, 2005, p. 221):

"*Model-based trace checking* [...] (e.g. Howard et al., 2003) applies the concept of model checking to log-file analysis. As in "traditional" model checking the expected [...] behaviour is described in terms of a temporal logic. However, instead of a finite state model, a trace of a single [...] run is checked for correspondence with its specification."

The *ProM* framework contains a plugin named *LTL Checker* that supports model-based trace checking in linear temporal logic (e.g. Dongen et al., 2006b, Sec. 1.4.4), the simplest extension of propositional logic with temporal operators (Page and Kreutzer, 2005, p. 214). An application of this plugin to our MABS of courier service logistics is reported in Section 8.3.1.1. Dongen et al. (2006b, Sec. 1.4.4) report an application to another MABS reviewed in Section 5.3.4.2.

Conformance Checking by Log Replay   is related to the idea of formal language acceptors. Given a log and a process model, it is checked in how far the model *accepts* the traces from the log and to which degree the model exhibits behavior *beyond* what is observed in the log (Rozinat and Aalst, 2008, p. 69). In combination, both metrics provide a characterization of conformance between model and log (Rozinat and Aalst, 2008, p. 69).

Rozinat and Aalst (2008, Sec. 3) operationalize this idea by means of a fitness and several appropriateness metrics. *Fitness* describes the model's ability to accept (parts of) the logged traces (Rozinat and Aalst, 2008, p. 69). Given a workflow net $N = (S, T, F, m_0)$, fitness is measured by replaying every distinct log trace $s_i \in \{s_1, \ldots, s_k\}$, from the initial marking m_0 while updating statistical counters including (Rozinat and Aalst, 2008, p. 70):

- n_i: number of traces in the log that are equal to s_i

- m_i: number of artificial tokens that must be added externally during log replay to make N 'accept' s_i

- r_i: number of tokens that remain in N after replay of s_i

- c_i: overall count of tokens consumed while replaying s_i

- p_i: overall count of tokens produced while replaying s_i

From these statistics, Rozinat and Aalst (2008, p. 70) calculate a fitness measure $f \in [0; 1]$ that decreases with an increasing number of tokens missing and remaining in the net in relation to the tokens consumed and produced overall:[41]

$$f = \frac{1}{2} \left(2 - \frac{\sum_{i=1}^{k} n_i \cdot m_i}{\sum_{i=1}^{k} n_i \cdot c_i} - \frac{\sum_{i=1}^{k} n_i \cdot r_i}{\sum_{i=1}^{k} n_i \cdot p_i} \right) \tag{4.16}$$

Log replay might be complicated by missing tokens, enablement of invisible tasks, and non-deterministic enablement of multiple duplicate tasks at the same time (Rozinat and Aalst, 2008, p. 72). Missing tokens to enable the next logged transition for replay are inserted on demand and noted in the statistics (Rozinat and Aalst, 2008, p. 70). In case of invisible tasks and non-determinism, the replay engine must perform a look-ahead search in the state space of N (Rozinat and Aalst, 2008, p. 72, Sec. 7.2).

Measuring *appropriateness* is less straightforward due to its rather subjective characterization as "the degree of accuracy in which the process model describes the observed behaviour, combined with the degree of clarity in which it is represented" (Rozinat and Aalst, 2008, p. 69). To capture these requirements, Rozinat and Aalst (2008, Sec. 5) define metrics for behavioral and structural appropriateness in a simple and advanced form.

The conformance checking techniques are implemented as *ProM* plugins, also including a visualization of detected mismatches (Rozinat and Aalst, 2008, Sec. 7.2). Section 7.3 of this thesis presents a prototypical implementation of a simple conformance checker in terms of reference nets. In this context, future requirements on the RENEW simulator towards an improved support for log replay-based analysis will also be discussed briefly.

Pattern-Based Compliance Checking   Instead of replaying logs in global control flow models, Ramezani et al. (2012) apply Petri net-based conformance checking to evaluate the compliance of a log to one or more *patterns* related to the control flow, data (flow), and organizational perspectives (Ramezani et al., 2012, Sec. 4.1). Their approach is thus closely related to trace-based model checking with the exception that the patterns are not defined using temporal logic but in terms of Petri nets (Ramezani et al., 2012, Sec. 4.2).

Ramezani et al. (2012) present a large "collection of compliance rules" (Ramezani et al., 2012, Sec. 4.2) ranging from simple rules like "Direct Precedence of a Task" to more complex situations like "Bounded Existence of [a] Sequence of Tasks" (Ramezani et al., 2012, Sec. 4.3) . For every rule, a "parametrized Petri net pattern" (Ramezani et al., 2012, Sec. 4.2) is defined that can be checked against a log using an alignment technique developed by Adriansyah et al. (2011)[42]. An advantage of this technique is that it can exactly identify deviations of 'almost' fitting log instances from the predefined patterns (Ramezani et al., 2012, Sec. 3).

The organizational and data perspectives are analyzed by simply 'unfolding' the related data elements (e.g. originators of actions) into multiple labelled transitions of the Petri net pattern (Ramezani et al., 2012, Sec. 5.1). Ramezani et al. (2012, Sec. 5.2) state the example of two transition labels $[A, R]$ and $[A, \neg R]$: The first indicates that action A was executed by originator R, while the second says that A was executed by another user.

---

[41]adopted with minor modifications
[42]see Ramezani et al. (2012, Sec. 3)

This proceeding can clearly lead to a 'state explosion' in the represented patterns when many different data types and values must be considered. An extension of the conformance checker towards a higher level representation mechanism (such as *colored Petri nets*) is identified as a topic for future work (Ramezani et al., 2012, Sec. 7). In Sections 6.2.6.2 and 7.1.3.1 of this thesis we will relate the work by Ramezani et al. (2012) to a somewhat similar approach from the MABS domain (Chen, 2009; Chen et al., 2008, 2010) and sketch how reference nets can be applied to model compliance rules comprising multiple perspectives.

4.2.5.5. Model Extension

As described in Section 4.2.2.2, the process mining task of *extension* deals with the improvement of existing process models based on information mined from a log (e.g. Aalst, 2006, p. 3). In the following, we review techniques for the enrichment of control flow models with branching conditions and performance data. Like conformance checking (Section 4.2.5.4) some of these techniques are based on log-replay. The additional information are collected while replaying traces annotated with data attributes of the respective process dimensions (e.g. time stamps).

Decision Mining The assignment of branching conditions to decision nodes (e.g. in UML activity diagrams, see Section 2.3.1.3) is an obvious extension for control-flow related models. Herbst (2001) and Rozinat and Aalst (2006) employ decision tree mining, Schütt (2003) uses fuzzy rule mining techniques for this endeavor.

We exemplarily review the "decision point analysis" by Rozinat and Aalst (2006, p. 421), which will be experimentally applied to our courier service simulations in Section 8.3.3 due to its availability in the *ProM* framework. As input, the decision point analysis takes a Petri net and a log in which cases or events are enriched with data attributes (Rozinat and Aalst, 2006, p. 421). An example[43] is the assignment of a boolean attribute *isUrgentOrder* to an event *orderReceived*.

At first, "place[s] with multiple outgoing arcs" (Rozinat and Aalst, 2006, p. 421) in the Petri net are tagged as decision points. Then every decision point is assigned a set of data attributes belonging to events or cases that triggered the related transitions (Rozinat and Aalst, 2006, p. 422). Mapping this data to the triggered transition at the decision point forms a classification problem that can be solved by decision tree learning (Rozinat and Aalst, 2006, p. 422).

The decision point analysis implemented by Rozinat and Aalst (2006, p. 423) uses the Data Mining system *WEKA* (Section 4.1.5.1) to perform the actual decision tree mining with the $C4.5$ algorithm (Section 4.1.4.1). The decision trees returned by *WEKA* are assigned to the respective decision nodes in the Petri net and can be visualized in *ProM* (Rozinat and Aalst, 2006, p. 424).

Similar to log replay-based conformance checking, decision point analysis is complicated by constructs like loops or duplicate and invisible tasks, where the determination of the route through a decision point is not straightforward (Rozinat and Aalst, 2006, p. 422).

---

[43]inspired by our courier service simulations described in Chapter 8

Performance Analysis The enrichment of process models with timing- and performance-related data is an important requirement on process mining in the context of discrete simulation (see Section 6.4). While many other techniques exist to collect, display, and analyze performance data, process mining offers the advantage of automatically relating this data to appropriate parts of the process model.

Hornix (2007) implemented techniques to add performance data to process models displayed in the form of Petri nets and UML-like sequence diagrams (see Section 2.3.1.4). The *Petri Net Performance Analysis* (PAPN) is based on log-replay and relies on the existence of a (mined or modelled) Petri net with a compatible log containing time stamps (Hornix, 2007, p. 24).

The log replay engine collects timing data from which key performance indicators (KPIs), including throughput times of cases, sojourn times of tokens at places, and durations between the firing of transitions, are derived (Hornix, 2007, pp. 26). For the KPIs, typical statistical measures like mean, standard deviation, minimum, and maximum are calculated (Hornix, 2007, p. 26). The user interface of the performance analysis component in the *ProM* framework can visualize the performance data directly in the underlying Petri net, including a color-coding of performance bottlenecks (Hornix, 2007, p. 31).

The *performance sequence diagram analysis* (PSDA) does not require an *a-priori* model but mines all relevant information from the time-stamped log (Hornix, 2007, p. 23). Basically, the user can choose from a number of process dimensions, including activities and performers (Hornix, 2007, p. 32). A sequence diagram for a case is drawn by taking the first entity from the respective trace and measuring how long this entity remains active (Hornix, 2007, pp. 32). This information is encoded by the length of the assigned task node in the sequence diagram (Hornix, 2007, p. 35).

When another entity (e.g. performer) becomes active in the logged case, an arrow is drawn between the task nodes of the previous and the new entity and the procedure repeats (Hornix, 2007, p. 34). This arrow is assigned the duration passed between the activation of both entities (Hornix, 2007, p. 35). To abstract from different interleaving of concurrent tasks, a control flow mining algorithm (multi-phase miner, see Dongen and Aalst, 2004) converts the traces into causal nets (see Section 2.3.2.2) prior to performance analysis (Hornix, 2007, p. 32).

To improve the readability of sequence diagrams derived from large logs, similar sequences can be aggregated into patterns (Hornix, 2007, Sec. 4.3.2) based on two different equivalence metrics (strict and flexible equivalence, see Hornix, 2007, p. 38). In this case, the implementation of the sequence diagram-based performance analysis in *ProM* can calculate aggregated performance measures for each pattern (Hornix, 2007, p. 40) and display the resulting patterns sorted by frequency (Hornix, 2007, p. 39).

4.2.6. Tools and Applications

After reviewing a number of process mining concepts and techniques with relevance for the analysis and validation of MABS we will provide a brief overview of practical aspects covering software tools and applications.

4.2.6.1. Process Mining Tools

Tool support in process mining is nowadays dominated by the Java-based open source framework *ProM*[44], developed and maintained at Eindhoven University. This toolset has become a de-facto standard in (scientific) process mining. Therefore our application and extension of process mining techniques for MABS analysis will also be based on this software framework.

ProM 4 and 5   In Cabac et al. (2006b, Sec. 3.1.3) we have summarized the functionality of the *ProM* framework with respect to its former version 4:

> "Aalst et al. present the *ProM* process mining tool that is extensible through a plugin mechanism (Dongen et al., 2005). The basic application framework can be extended by mining, import, export, and analysis plugins. *ProM* relies on a general [XML-based] log data format [MXML, short for 'Mining XML'], where each trace entry contains information on event name, event type, process instance, process type, originator, [data attributes,] and time stamp. In ProM, process mining is seen as the core tool functionality, while functions such as data acquisition, simulation, formal analysis of mining results, etc. are regarded as extensions. To generate data for testing process mining algorithms, Medeiros and Günther (2005) integrated the CPN-Tools Petri net simulator as a *ProM* plugin."

In addition, *ProM* contains several visualization plugins that support techniques like dotted chart plots or process log inspection to provide a quick overview of an analyzed log. Up to version 5, however, complex non-interactive batch analyses composed from several steps formed a weakness of the system that we mentioned in (Cabac and Denz, 2008, p. 89):

> "Interoperability is ensured by a large number of supported input and output formats. Though the plugin architecture of ProM resembles the idea of a processing chain with data acquisition, mining, conversion, analysis, and visualization steps, the current user interface is merely tailored towards an interactive application."

This drawback becomes manifest in the user interface as well as in the architecture that suffers from a lack of separation between functional and presentation layers (Verbeek et al., 2011, p. 70). As an example, a 'mining result' object is in the first place described by its graphical representation in a desktop *frame*. In Sections 7.4.2.1 and 8.4 we present our approach to overcome this drawback by integrating wrapped *ProM* plugins into simulation tools using data flow modeling.

ProM 6   The Eindhoven research group developed *ProM* further into a similar direction with the current version 6. In this context, the system underwent an architectural re-design including a better separation of program logic and user interface (Verbeek et al., 2011, p. 70). Further improvements are summarized by Verbeek et al. (2011, pp. 70):

- The four different plugin types mentioned above were merged into a single general plugin interface, which eases plugin composition.

---

[44]short for 'PROcess Mining', `http://www.processmining.org/prom/start` (last visit 2011-13-12)

- Input and output data of algorithms is stored in a common object pool that is accessible to all plugins.

- A software assistant-like user interface supports the chaining of plugins into complex analysis procedures: Starting from input data in the object pool, the user is offered a pre-selection of all plugins that can handle the contained objects. After selecting a plugin, the output type of this plugin is displayed and the user can select a further plugin that takes this type of data as input.

- Plugin variants can be defined that offer the same functionality on different data types.

- Besides MXML, *ProM* 6 supports the more generic log data format XES (eXtensible Event Stream).

Different from MXML, the XES schema contains only few predefined concepts including *log*, *trace*, *event*, and *attribute* (Verbeek et al., 2011, p. 63). Specific domain entities like activity names, timestamps, and originators are consistently added as attributes in the form of typed key-value pairs, where attribute hierarchies are also supported (Verbeek et al., 2011, p. 63). A support tool named *XESame* allows to define import mappings from other data formats without having to implement *Java* code (Verbeek et al., 2011, p. 67).

Despite these advantages, the implementations and experiments presented in this thesis will not be based on *ProM* 6 due to its late availability in relation to the accomplishment of (large parts of) the reported practical work.

Further Process Mining Tools   Most process mining tools developed in parallel or prior to the *ProM* framework only support a single mining algorithm. Examples include *Emit* (α algorithm) and *MiSoN* (social network mining) from the Eindhoven research group (Aalst, 2005a, p. 452) as well as *Involve* (algorithm by Herbst, 2001), and *Workflow Miner* (approach by Schimm, 2004).

As indicated above, *ProM* delegates specific process mining subtasks like decision tree mining, log data generation, or Petri net synthesis to external tools including *WEKA* (see Section 4.1.5), *CPN Tools*[45], and *Petrify* (see Section 4.2.3.3). A more advanced command line tool for Petri net synthesis that also offers process mining functionality is *Genet* by Carmona et al. (2009a). The process mining approach by Lou et al. (2010b) reviewed in Section 4.2.3.5 was also implemented as a command line tool with an integrated process simulator using a simple text-base format to describe models and logs.

Further process mining systems akin to the data flow-based tool integration presented in this thesis will be reviewed in Section 5.4.1.

4.2.6.2. Application and Evaluation of Process Mining Algorithms

Process mining research is largely driven by practical applications, where the most prominent domains are workflow management (e.g. Aalst et al., 2007) and software engineering (e.g. Rubin et al., 2007). In this section, we review an exemplary case study in which process mining

---

[45]`http://www.cpntools.org` (last vist 2012-10-03)

algorithms are applied to and evaluated in a real-world problem. We choose the study by Lang (2008) due to its comprehensiveness and methodological clearness. Further case studies with a closer relation to the subject of this thesis will be reviewed in Section 5.3.4.

The dissertation by Lang (2008) provides an exhaustive evaluation of control flow mining algorithms and log clustering metrics in the domain of medical image processing. The author implements a knowledge discovery process to extract log data generated by radiological diagnostic workflows from databases of a large hospital, preprocess and cluster the data, and import it into the MXML format.

Several control flow mining techniques including the α algorithm, the Heuristics miner, the DWS miner, etc. are applied to these logs and evaluated with respect to 6 requirements. The requirements include (1) faithfulness of the reconstructed models, (2) ability to handle noise, (3) detection of sequences, alternative branches, and concurrency, (4) ability to detect loops, (5) handling of duplicate tasks and sub-processes, and (6) ability to cope with non-unique start and end points of processes (Lang, 2008, Sec. 4.3.2).

As one result of the study, Lang (2008, p. 219) finds that control flow mining algorithms based on direct succession metrics only (e.g. the α algorithm) perform worse in the presence of noise than techniques that also regard for indirect succession. Consequently, Lang (2008, Sec. 7.2.5) proposes a concept to improve the differentiation between loops and multiple task instances that slightly resembles the approach by Lou et al. (2010b).

The case study on process mining in MABS performed by Haan (2009) and presented in Chapter 8 of this thesis is orientated on the methodology by Lang (2008) but puts focus on different requirements and research questions. Several further case and evaluation studies covering multiple process mining perspectives can be found in the literature, including the work by Aalst et al. (2007, analysis of invoice handling in a Dutch government agency) and Rozinat et al. (2009a, analysis of test processes in wafer production).

5. Related Work

The introductions to MABS and process mining in the previous chapters provided a first impression why process mining might be useful to tackle the problem of MABS analysis and validation. In this chapter, we review existing research related to this topic in particular. Due to the broad scope of both MAS and process mining, an appreciation of related work must cover several interconnected research fields some of which are displayed in Figure 5.1.

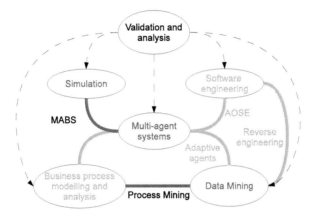

Figure 5.1.: Research fields related to the thesis at hand. The darker a circle or connection is drawn, the closer it is related to the subject of this thesis.

5.1. Analysis and Validation of MABS

One field of related work concerns methodologies and techniques for the validation of MA(B)S. While most validation approaches do not explicitly refer to data or process mining, related ideas and starting points for an integration can be identified.

5.1.1. Methodologies for MABS Validation

In recent years, a number of validation methodologies with a focus on MA(B)S have been developed. These range from theoretical concepts rooted in social science to tool-centric approaches from software engineering. We also find modifications and extensions of 'classical' simulation model building cycles. In the following, selected examples from each category are described. For a more exhaustive overview, we refer to the list by Ören and Yilmaz (2010, p. 206).

5.1.1.1. Approaches to Validate MABS

After an initial[1] focus on modeling under the multi-agent paradigm, the MABS research community identified a need to spend more "effort on the later stages of the modeling process (analysis, interpretation, and application)" to increase their models' utility (Edmonds, 2000, p. 23).

Edmonds et al. In his position paper postulating this focal change, Edmonds (2000) does not present a validation methodology, but discusses a number of properties of agent-based models with respect to validation. One claim concerns the need for detailed validation due to the lack of constraints posed by the methodology:

> "Strengthening validation means checking the output of the simulation in as many ways as possible by comparison with the system goals or actual target behaviour." (Edmonds, 2000, p. 23)

> "We should seek to verify and validate our models on as many levels of detail as possible [and ...] at a finer temporal level. [...] the intermediate stages of the resulting processes in the simulation should be checked [...]" (Edmonds, 2000, p. 29).

> "The increased descriptive realism [of MABS means ...] that the simulation has imported more of the [... real] system's behaviour including its unpredictability and complexity [...] The practical import of this is that the analysis and interpretation stages [...] require much more attention than in simple deterministic or stochastic mathematical models." (Edmonds, 2000, p. 22)

Illustrated by an 'agent-based' variant of the halting problem, Edmonds and Bryson (2004, p. 937) stress the unsuitability of deductive formal methods to tackle realistic MABS in favor of experimentalism and *a-posteriori* analysis. As an example, Edmonds et al. (2006) present an approach to characterize the whole scope of trajectories of a stochastic simulation (with respect to a numerical variable) by its upper and lower bounds. Due to the use of *constraint logic programming* (CLP) for model representation, these bounds can be explored by queries without the need to simulate many scenarios (Edmonds et al., 2006, p. 6).

David et al. (2002) reason about the requirements that self-organizing MABS of artificial or real societies pose on software engineering and validation. An important characteristic is that 'surprising' effects due to self-organisation are, to a certain degree, wanted and should not be suppressed by rigid *a-priori* specification (David et al., 2002, p. 91).

David et al. (2002, p. 90) claim that the distinction between dynamic verification and validation therefore becomes blurred in MABS: It is not always clear if an unexpected macroscopic behavior emerging at runtime is inherent to the conceptual model or caused by faulty implementation. Proposed techniques to tackle this problem include model alignment and specific software metrics (David et al., 2002, Sec. 4.1) as well as hierarchical model specifications ("hyperstructures") that include multiple layers of aggregate ("emergent") entities (David et al., 2002, Sec. 2.3).

---

[1] partly rather theoretical, see also Moss (2000)

Drogoul et al. (2002) sketch a model building cycle for MABS in modification of previous work from discrete and social simulation. One characteristic of this methodology is the explicit introduction of three roles, i.e. *thematician* (domain expert), *modeler*, and *computer scientist* (Drogoul et al., 2002, Sec. 3), that we have adopted with minor modifications in (Page and Kreutzer, 2005, Ch. 8.2.2). Another peculiarity is the explicit distinction between domain knowledge at the microscopic and macroscopic levels: "Micro knowledge" builds the basis for modeling while "macro knowledge" guides validation, experimentation, and analysis (Drogoul et al., 2002, p. 9).

Within the role model Drogoul et al. (2002, p. 10) observe that agent concepts are frequently used by domain experts and modelers. However, as already cited in Section 3.2.1, implementations of MABS mostly employ object-oriented or rule-based techniques lacking the properties of agents postulated in distributed AI (DAI); see Drogoul et al. (2002, p. 10). The authors claim that especially MABS experimentation and validation can profit from DAI techniques (Drogoul et al., 2002, Sec. 4), thereby arguing for *agent supported simulation*:[2]

1. *Participatory simulation* is performed by letting domain experts play the role of agents in a simulation. Computational agents with the ability to learn could observe users and derive behavioral models from their actions (Drogoul et al., 2002, p. 11).

2. *Agent-aided interpretation* means that the simulation contains observer agents that perform intelligent data analysis on a local portion of the simulation results (Drogoul et al., 2002, p. 11). On the one hand, this supports result interpretation. On the other hand, the detection of certain 'emergent' patterns might give rise to "macro agents" that explicitly represent macroscopic phenomena in the simulation (Drogoul et al., 2002, p. 12). As an example, Drogoul et al. (2002, p. 12) cite hydrological multi-level simulations conducted by Servat et al. (1998).

3. *System-level adaptation* is related to the implementation of flexible distributed simulations with the aid of mobile computational agents (Drogoul et al., 2002, p. 12).

4. *Agent-aided calibration* might be performed by distributed problem solving and local optimization (Drogoul et al., 2002, p. 13).

While the presented concepts remain rather abstract in (Drogoul et al., 2002), later work by the same research group focuses on participatory simulation (e.g. using decision tree mining in Chu et al., 2009) and distributed simulation (Scerri et al., 2010). In Section 6.3, we discuss how process mining can add to agent-supported simulation as envisioned in the work by Drogoul et al. (2002).

Kennedy et al. (2006) evaluate the utility of validation techniques from the catalog by Balci (1998) for MABS. For this purpose, a selection of validation techniques is applied to an agent-based and an equation-based model of the evolution of *natural organic matter* (NOM), roughly following the validation process by Sargent (see e.g. 2001, p. 108).

The authors choose validation techniques from the discrete event simulation domain because the "discrete event modelling approach is the most closely [related] approach [... to] agent-based modelling [...]" (Xiang et al., 2005, p. 54). In addition, a comparison of different model implementations

---

[2]as to use the term by Ören (2000) cited in Section 3.2.1

Validation techniques	MABS	Equation-based
Face validation	very good	very good
Turing test of real and simulated output	very good	good
Sensitivity against random seed	very good	n/a
Tracing	fair	excellent
Black-box input/output testing	good	good
Model alignment	very good	very good
Comparison with historical data	very good	very good
Sensitivity analysis	good	good
Prediction of new data	good	fair

Table 5.1.: A rating of the utility of validation techniques for MABS and equation-based modeling. The applied scale comprises the levels *fair*, *good*, *very good*, and *excellent*. Adopted with slight modifications from (Kennedy et al., 2006, p. 102).

(model alignment, see Section 5.1.2.3) is performed to identify artifacts introduced during implementation (Xiang et al., 2005, p. 23).

A main result of the study by Kennedy et al. (2006, p. 102) is a rating of the utility of validation techniques on a four-level scale. This overview is cited in Table 5.1, where some validation techniques are renamed for better understandability. For additional explanations of the listed techniques see Kennedy et al. (2006)

The authors confine the validity of the results to the specific study and provide few details about reasons for their ratings. In the context of this thesis, it is especially interesting why *tracing* is rated as *excellent* for equation-based modeling but only *fair* for MABS. One reason might be the higher complexity of MABS traces, the handling of which requires powerful analysis techniques.

5.1.1.2. Validation Methodology by Klügl

Klügl (2008) presents a validation methodology for MABS based on common validation processes and techniques from computer simulation.[3] Furthermore, she identifies a set of typical problems in MABS validation (Klügl, 2008, Sec. 2.2) and proposes metrics to assess the complexity of multi-agent models (Klügl, 2007). Klügl's thoughts on validation problems are rather similar to the discussion in (Knaak, 2006) and Section 3.5. This is not surprising since our argumentation is largely based on Klügl's (2000) view upon MABS.

As a starting point, Klügl (2008, Sec. 2.2) identifies 5 typical problems in MABS validation:

1. The identification of "characteristic output descriptors" to compactly describe simulation results is difficult especially at the microscopic level (Klügl, 2008, p. 40). This problem roughly corresponds to the *problem of result representation and interpretation* mentioned in (Knaak, 2006).

---

[3] A review of the approach by Klügl (2008) with some focus on its relations to process mining is found in the bachelor thesis by Haan (2009).

2. The "focus on transient dynamics" in MABS forbids the application of conventional steady state statistics (Klügl, 2008, p. 40).

3. "Non-linearities and brittleness" in the model's behavior (mainly due to "feedback loops") and parameter space complicate calibration and validation (Klügl, 2008, p. 40). In Section 3.5, we attribute this effect to the *problem of distributed system state*.[4]

4. The "size of the validation task" is large due to the size of the model and the need for "multi-level validity", and sufficient real world data is often not available for comparison (Klügl, 2008, p. 41). In (Knaak, 2006) we subsume similar issues under the *problem of model complexity*.

5. It might be impossible to falsify (see Section 2.4.3.3) one of two competing models due to a lack of available data and overfitting in the presence of many free parameters (Klügl, 2008, p. 41).

From these observations, Klügl (2008, Sec. 3) derives a validation process drawing on common techniques. In the first step, *face validity* is established by letting experts rate animations and output of the simulation. This might be complemented by "immersive assessment" (Klügl, 2008, p. 42), i.e. participatory simulation.

Face validation is followed by *sensitivity analysis* and *calibration* of model parameters (Klügl, 2008, p. 42). In this context, Klügl (2008, p. 42-43) advocates the use of automated methods like optimization and reinforcement learning (see Section 5.1.2.2). Finally, a statistical validation of the model is performed using different input data than calibration (Klügl, 2008, p. 43); i.e. *cross validation*, see Section 4.1.3.2.

Klügl (2007) further attempts to quantify the "sources of [model] complexity" (Klügl, 2007, p. 123) that aggravate the "understandability [...] and [...] predictability of the model dynamics and output" (Klügl, 2007, p. 136) by means of software metrics. For this purpose, she identifies several system-, agent-, and interaction-level metrics (Klügl, 2007, Sec. 5).

System-level metrics include (among others) the number of agent and resource types, the minimal and maximal numbers of active agents and resources counted during simulation, as well as an "agent-resource relation" defined as the quotient of agent and resource counts in the model (Klügl, 2007, pp. 128). At the interaction-level, measures like the number of references between agents and resources or the number of agent movements are taken (Klügl, 2007, pp. 132).

An important metric at the agent-level is the "architectural complexity rank" where three increasingly complex types of agent architectures, i.e. "behavior-describing [...,], behavior-configuring [..., and] behavior-generating architectures", are identified (Klügl, 2007, p. 130). Further agent-level metrics include the size of an agent's rule base and procedural knowledge (Klügl, 2007, p. 131) as well as the "action plasticity metric" that depends on the parameter variability of the agent's actions (Klügl, 2007, pp. 130).

In relation to the thesis at hand, it is interesting that Klügl (2008, p. 40) points out the potential of data mining to validate transient dynamics: "There, the current progress in trend analysis and data mining for time series may provide methods and tools for supporting validation of transient dynamics produced by agent-based simulation. However, the application to validation of

---

[4]based on the discussions led in the dissertation by Klügl (2000)

agent-based simulation is still missing." Haan (2009, p. 55) briefly sketches how process mining might support the validation process by Klügl (2008):

> "In face validation, the two tests *animation* and *immersive assessment* could be well realized using process mining [...] Basically, these [... tests relate to] the control flow perspective [of process mining] on the one hand and to [... an] agent perspective on the other hand. The organizational perspective could be considered to additionally further validation. In *sensitivity analysis* and *calibration*, the decision point analysis plugin [of *ProM*] might be an [... appropriate] aid."

5.1.1.3. Engineering of Self-Organizing Systems

Self-organizing systems often contain a large number of rather simple agents that must accomplish coherent global behavior only by local interactions (Wolf et al., 2005, p. 139). The engineering of self-organizing systems resembles MABS in the need to understand relations between the microscopic modeling level and the macroscopic outcomes; at least enough to tune the local behavior towards the intended global results. Since self-organizing systems are increasingly deployed to the real world due to advantages like fault tolerance and efficiency of computation (Wolf et al., 2005, p. 141), validation is even more an issue (Wolf et al., 2005, p. 140).

It has often been argued that neither "traditional top-down oriented development approaches" (Sudeikat and Renz, 2009, p. 32) nor formal specification and verification are appropriate to design reliable self-organizing systems (Wolf et al., 2005, pp. 140). Instead, simulation-based analysis has become the method of choice (Sudeikat and Renz, 2009, p. 32). While MABS allows for detailed experimentation with self-organizing systems before deployment, it does not solve the problem of *understanding* system behavior due to the system complexity "imported" (Edmonds, 2000, p. 22) into the simulation.

An increasingly popular approach towards modeling, analysis, and validation of self-organizing systems employs complementary macroscopic equation-based and microscopic agent-based representations. Work in this direction has been carried out (among others) by Sierra et al. (2004), Sudeikat and Renz (2009), and Wolf et al. (2005).

SADDE Methodology The SADDE (Social Agents Design Driven by Equations) methodology (Sierra et al., 2004) applies top-down modeling to self-organizing systems engineering as shown in Figure 5.2. First an equation-based model (EBM) is created that "model[s] the desired global behaviour of the agent society [... without] references to individuals in that society" (Sierra et al., 2004, p. 197). With this specification in mind, a model of the agents' interactions (electronic institution model, EIM) is built that regulates the allowed communication in terms of interaction protocols, scenes (i.e. higher order protocols in terms of MULAN), and norms (Sierra et al., 2004, pp. 197, 204-205). From the EIM, an agent-based model (ABM) is derived with a focus on parametrizable individual decisions, and implemented as a MAS (Sierra et al., 2004, pp. 197,198).

Experiments are conducted with the MAS under different parameter settings and the results are compared to those predicted by the EBM (Sierra et al., 2004, p. 197). Deviations in

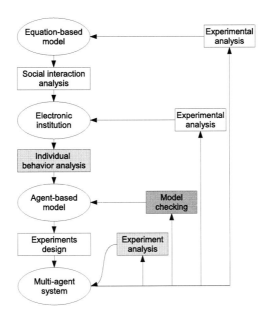

Figure 5.2.: The SADDE methodology visualized as a Petri net. Places stand for models, transitions for modeling and validation steps. The shading of transitions indicates the degree of automation, i.e. manual (white), semi-automatic (light grey), and automatic (dark grey). Adopted with modifications from the diagram by Sierra et al. (2004, p. 196).

the simulation results trigger manual or semi-automated modifications of the model and its parameters (Sierra et al., 2004, p. 198). In addition, automatic model checking of the specified norms and protocols is performed to assess the validity of the ABM (Sierra et al., 2004, p. 198).

Sierra et al. (2004, Sec. 8) calibrate the parameters of an ABM representing an electricity market to fit the dynamics of a related EBM with the aid of genetic algorithms and an objective function over multiple global variables. A sufficient adaptation could be reached after about 20 iterations of the genetic algorithm (Sierra et al., 2004, p. 214).

Other Approaches The work by Sudeikat and Renz (2009) is based on a similar idea but employs different techniques. Here, causal loop diagrams (CLDs) from System Dynamics are used for macroscopic modeling (Sudeikat and Renz, 2009, pp. 34). This simplifies the display of causal relations and feedback cycles between aggregate entities of the ABM (e.g. groups and roles); see Sudeikat and Renz (2009, pp. 35). Sudeikat and Renz (2006, Secs. 3.2,5.1) additionally show how macroscopic Markovian rate equations can be derived from goal hierarchies of BDI agents.

Time series-based correlation analysis serves to substantiate the specified causal relations in the macroscopic behavior of the MABS (Sudeikat and Renz, 2009, pp. 39). Based on the *Jadex* platform (see Section 3.4.1), the authors implemented an agent-supported simulation system that allows for manual experiment planning, distributed execution, and time series analysis by integration of a numerical computing environment (Sudeikat and Renz, 2009, pp. 39)

De Wolf and Holvoet (2007), whose work is also cited by Sudeikat and Renz (2009), show how macroscopic causal relations can be validated by following the object flow in UML 2 activity diagrams (Section 2.3.1.3) that model the behavior of interacting agents. Their example is a simulation of decentralized AGV (Automated Guided Vehicle) control in a warehouse, rather similar to the courier service model introduced in Chapter 8.1. At the same example, Wolf et al. (2005, pp. 141,143) perform an "equation-free" analysis to validate trends in the temporal development of macroscopic variables. Simulation effort is reduced by extrapolating these variables using numerical integration (Wolf et al., 2005, p. 144).

5.1.1.4. Validation of Deliberative Agents

Agent-oriented software engineering (AOSE) typically considers systems of few complex agents employing deliberative architectures like BDI (see Section 3.3.1.3). Since the agents often pursue well-defined common goals for distributed problem solving, these systems can in principle be designed with conventional top-down approaches (David et al., 2002, p. 90). Nevertheless, the validation of deliberative agents' complex internal processes and external interactions is difficult and often adressed with the aid of advanced monitoring and debugging tools.

Debugging by Corroboration In the context of the *ZEUS* agent platform, Ndumu and Nwana (1999) present a tool-supported validation methodology named *debugging by corroboration*. The core idea is to detect errors and identify their causes by observing and visualizing a MAS from several different perspectives. Clearly, this approach fulfills the requirement of multi-level validation postulated by Edmonds (2000).

Ndumu and Nwana (1999) developed 4 visualization tools based on static analysis of agent specifications and runtime observation of exchanged messages. Abstracting from the tools, Weiss and Jakob (2005, pp. 113-114) list related perspectives for MAS analysis:

1. The *society perspective* is concerned with organizational structures and message exchange (Weiss and Jakob, 2005, p. 113). It is supported by the *society tool* that derives a social network from static role relations and visualizes the actual message exchange, also supporting filter, record, and playback functionality (Ndumu and Nwana, 1999, Sec. 4.1)

2. The *task perspective* focuses on the decomposition, distribution, and execution of (collaborative) tasks over time (Weiss and Jakob, 2005, p. 113). The related *report tool* visualizes the assignment and execution states of selected tasks using *Gantt* charts (Ndumu and Nwana, 1999, Sec. 4.2).

3. The *agent perspective* is related to the knowledge base, activities, and communication of individual agents (Weiss and Jakob, 2005, p. 113). The *micro tool* allows to observe these properties while the *control tool* lets the users modify agents' states at runtime (Ndumu and Nwana, 1999, Sec. 4.3-4.4).

4. The *statistical perspective* shows global performance statistics of distributed problem solving (Weiss and Jakob, 2005, p. 114). The related *statistics tool* collects and visualizes

different indicators on the levels of individual agents and the MAS (Ndumu and Nwana, 1999, Sec. 4.5).

Ndumu and Nwana (1999, p. 333) emphasize that neither the debugging approach nor the related tools are in principle limited to the ZEUS agent platform. The authors further note that the value of their methodology does not lie in the tools as such but in their reasonable application and combination by developers (Ndumu and Nwana, 1999, pp. 331,333) for "multi-perspective" debugging (Weiss and Jakob, 2005, p. 113). In Section 6.2 we merge these and other analysis perspectives from MAS design with the perspectives from process mining to establish a conceptual framework for process mining in MABS.

Validation in Jadex Advanced validation tools are also available for the BDI framework *Jadex* by Pokahr et al. (2003); see Section 3.4.1. From the often-cited (e.g. by Sudeikat et al., 2007, p. 187) categorization of validation techniques for AI systems by Menzies and Pecheur (2005), the work by Sudeikat and Renz (2006) and Sudeikat et al. (2007) covers the categories of testing, runtime monitoring, and static analysis; as displayed in Figure 5.3.

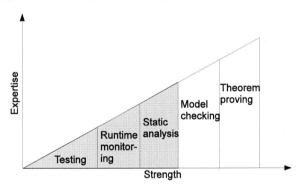

Figure 5.3.: Categorization of validation techniques for AI systems by Menzies and Pecheur (2005). Techniques applied in the *Jadex* system are shaded grey. Adopted with minor modifications from Sudeikat et al. (2007, p. 187)

For static analysis, Sudeikat et al. (2007, pp. 197-198) developed a tool that extracts message sender and receiver relations from agent specifications. Results are visualized as a social network, which allows to detect missing communication and "orphaned message events" (Sudeikat et al., 2007, p. 197). Additionally, events that do not trigger the execution of plans as expected are monitored at runtime (Sudeikat et al., 2007, p. 197).

Runtime monitoring and testing is implemented in the style of crosscutting concerns from aspect-oriented programming (AOP). AOP distinguishes *core concerns*, that represent the core functionality of a system, from *crosscutting concerns* that realize supplementary functionality re-used by multiple core concerns, like e.g. logging (Sudeikat and Renz, 2006, pp. 179). The execution environment (in this case the BDI interpreter) *weaves* the functionality of core and crosscutting concerns at well-defined *join points* during runtime (Sudeikat and Renz, 2006, p. 180).

In *Jadex*, crosscutting concerns for logging and assertion checking are realized similar to core concerns as specific agent *capabilities* (i.e. functional components), which allows for a "minimal intrusive" addition of monitoring functionality when needed (Sudeikat and Renz, 2006, p. 179). Assertions specified as *Java* code can be assigned to several BDI constructs (e.g. plans) and are automatically checked on the respective state changes (Sudeikat et al., 2007, p. 194). Logging is used as a basis for the numerical analyses described in (Sudeikat and Renz, 2006, 2009) and reviewed in Section 5.1.1.3.

5.1.2. Techniques

In the previous section, we named several validation techniques for MABS. We will now provide further details on techniques with relevance for this thesis. For this purpose, we cite parts of our reviews in (Page and Kreutzer, 2005, Ch. 8) and (Bachmann et al., 2004). To provide a representative extract of different concepts, we proceed along two dimensions related to the classification scheme for validation techniques from Section 2.4.3.5, i.e. the distinction between confirmatory and exploratory techniques and the degree of automation. An overview is shown in Figure 5.4.

	Confirmatory	Exploratory
High automation	**Knowledge-based validation of simulation results** [Birta and Özmizrak 1996] **(Trace-based) model checking** [Howard et al. 2003], [Walton 2004], [Bosse et al. 2006]	**Automated calibration** [Oechslein et al. 2001], [Sierra et al. 2004], [Fehler et al. 2004] **Meta-modelling** [Kilmer et al. 1997]
Low automation	**Pattern-based validation** [Rand et al. 2003], ... **Multi-Level Analysis** [Chen et al. 2008, 2010] **Model alignment / docking** [Axtell et al. 1996], ...	**Visual Debugging** [Ndumu et al. 1999] [Grimm 2002] **Data Visualization** [Schroeder and Noy 2001] [Sanchez and Lucas 2002]

Figure 5.4.: Overview of MABS validation techniques with exemplary publications.

5.1.2.1. Model-Based Validation and Verification

Due to the close relation between dynamic verification and operational validation in MABS (David et al., 2002, p. 90), both phases can be equally supported by automated techniques to check the conformance of simulation outputs and traces with respect to an abstract specification. In (Page and Kreutzer, 2005, p. 229), we relate these techniques to the 'test-first' approach (see e.g. Link, 2002, cited in Page and Kreutzer, 2005, p. 219) and regression testing in software engineering:

> "The core idea there is that we must write [...] specifications of expected behaviour (e.g. a unit test) *prior* to implementation. During implementation we then use a test automation tool [...] to constantly re-check all [... existing implementations] against these specifications.

Since most test tools only support functional unit tests, this approach is only of limited use to simulation [see e.g. Overstreet, 2002, cited in Page and Kreutzer, 2005, pp. 229].

However, the "test first" approach can still contribute to dynamic model verification and operational validation if we can draw on suitable tool support for automatically checking simulation results. For this the following proposals are found in the literature:

- As already mentioned, model-based trace checking can determine if a simulation trace conforms to a specification in temporal logic (see e.g. Brade, 2003, Ch. 5.3). As in regression tests, this check must be repeated whenever the model is extended or refactored.

- Birta and Özmizrak (1996) propose a knowledge-based system for automatic result validation. The user can define several kinds of numerical validity criteria, such as required causal dependencies of input and output quantities or so-called "change-in-value relationships". The latter represent statements of the type "if the value of [an ...] input parameter [...] is increased by a given amount, the value of [a related ...] output variable [...] should increase correspondingly". The system can automatically check if the output of a single simulation run or the aggregate output of several runs adhere to their specifications." (Page and Kreutzer, 2005, pp. 229)

Birta and Özmizrak (1996, Secs. 5-6) further present an automated experimental design technique that ensures a high coverage of model behavior with respect to the specified validity criteria.

Exhaustive model checking can in principle be applied to MAS as well. Walton (2004) e.g. translates simple auction protocols for web services to the language *PROMELA* of the widely used model checker *SPIN* (Holzmann, 1997). Nevertheless, resorting to traces is reasonable due to model complexity in practice. In (Page and Kreutzer, 2005, p. 221) we discuss the advantages and drawbacks of model-based trace checking in comparison with another approach to handle infinite state spaces, i.e. program abstraction:

"*Program abstraction* (Visser et al., 2003) is based on the idea that we can derive a finite state model from a program that exhibits *at least* all erroneous behaviour of the original code. The derivation of this model could be performed manually, which is in itself a complex and error-prone task. Alternatively,Visser et al. (2003) propose a tool for the automatic abstraction of Java programs, named *Java PathFinder*. However, this approach only works on a restricted subset of Java, and its practical applicability is therefore limited. [...]

Model-based trace checking is easier to perform than program abstraction and will, in principle, work for arbitrarily complex models. [...]

A drawback [...] is that it offers no exhaustive behaviour verification, but rather checks a single simulation trajectory. In order to gain reasonable levels of confidence in the correctness of stochastic simulations we must therefore consider traces for several independent simulation runs. Brade (2003, pp. 81) has developed a tool called *Violade* for assisting in model checking of simulation traces on the basis of Propositional Linear Temporal Logic (PLTL)."

Several applications of trace checking to MAS are reported in the literature. Howard et al. (2003), who introduce the term *model-based trace checking*, translate traces from a travel agency case study to *PROMELA* in order to verify them against PLTL formulae with the model checker *SPIN*.

Bosse et al. (2006) automatically compare traces of a MABS simulating unmanned aerial vehicles (UAVs) to assertions stated in the formal language TTL (Temporal Trace Language). TTL is an expressive temporal logic that allows to formulate queries like "There is an interval with length i in which target tg is visited *at least* twice (by two different [UAV] agents)" (Bosse et al., 2006, p. 728). This expressiveness is, among other things, due to the use of real valued variables (Bosse et al., 2006, p. 725). On the downside, it makes exhaustive model checking infeasible (Bosse et al., 2006, p. 726). In addition to trace checking, Bosse et al. (2006, Sec. 4) employ a trace visualization tool (see Section 5.2.4.2) to support the understanding of reasons for assertion failures.

Further applications of conformance checking to MAS with relations to process mining are reviewed in Sections 5.2.2.4, 5.3.3.3, and 5.3.4.5. In Section 6.3.3.3, we sketch how model-based result checking might be extended beyond numerical analysis (as in Birta and Özmizrak, 1996) to handle 'qualitative' patterns based on data mining.

5.1.2.2. Calibration and Meta-Modeling

In the previous sections, we have already cited several characteristics of MABS that inherently complicate the task of calibration. In (Bachmann et al., 2004, Sec. 1) we summarized the main problems when attempting to fit the macroscopic behavior of a MABS to real system behavior by adapting microscopic parameters based on the literature:[5]

> "One problem is that the complex behavior of intelligent actors is often not sufficiently understood by the modeler or that strong simplifications are required due to limitations of modeling formalisms and computing power. [...]
>
> Calibration is further aggravated by the typically large number of free parameters in [...] agent-based models (Köster, 2002) as well as the often non-linear and hardly predictable responses of the model [see also Klügl, 2008, cited in Section 5.1.1.2]. Specific problems occur when large populations of agents must be modeled on the basis of limited data (Drogoul et al., 2002, p. 12), or when parameters exhibit a large global sensitivity because they influence the local behavior models of many agents (Klügl, 2001, p. 83). A practical impediment that hinders the exploration of model behavior is the high computational complexity due to detailled modeling."

In (Bachmann et al., 2004, Sec. 2) we also cite an early proposal of MABS calibration techniques by Oechslein et al. (1999):

> "In (Oechslein et al., 1999, ...) different possibilities are described to support the calibration of agent-based models with the aid of software tools:
>
> - manual comparison of variable trajectories,
> - definition of microscopic and macroscopic constraints that can be verified during simulation,
> - separate calibration of partial models,

---

[5] A far more detailed discussion on this subject is also led in the dissertation by Fehler (2011) dedicated to the problem of MABS calibration.

- definition of microscopic meta-models that contain the parameters to calibrate but are more abstract than the original models.

The application of systems for simulation-based optimization is proposed by Klügl (2001, p. 213) but rated as difficult due to the necessary computational effort and the problem of defining an appropriate objective function."

In continuation of the work by Oechslein et al. (1999), Fehler et al. (2004, pp. 306) distinguish between black box and white box approaches for MABS calibration. *Black box calibration* is related to simulation-based optimization as e.g. employed in the SADDE methodology[6]: An objective function is defined over output variables of the simulation. A search algorithm explores different parameter scenarios guided by the objective function, where each scenario is evaluated in a simulation run. Different from this global approach, Fehler et al. (2006a) also perform calibration by local learning at the agent level.

In (Page and Kreutzer, 2005, p. 223) we discuss potential pitfalls in the definition of the objective function:[7]

> "In general terms calibration can be viewed as a multi-criteria optimization problem (Drogoul et al., 2002, p. 12), whose goal is to minimize deviations between model and system output (Klügl, 2001, p. 213) Using suitable weights, multiple criteria for model validity can be collapsed into a single objective function G (Zitzler, 1999). In an (often too) simplistic approach, G computes a weighted sum of all deviations between relevant model [outputs $F_i(\mathbf{x})$] and system outputs [y_i]:
>
> $$G(\mathbf{x}) = \min \left(\sum_{i=1}^{n} w_i \cdot |F_i(\mathbf{x}) - y_i| \right) \qquad (5.1)$$
>
> [...] A major challenge is the appropriate choice of weighting factors w_i for output quantities with different dimensions. The collapse of multiple complex validity criteria into a single number may also require invalid simplifications. These difficulties might be resolved by delegating responsibility for evaluating results to the users and feedback *their* ratings into the optimization's attempts at improving parameter settings. An example for such an approach are the interactive genetic algorithms proposed by Boschetti (1995)."

In the same discussion, we name further general problems related to calibration. This includes the danger "to misuse [... it] for "tuning" a model's performance by varying parameter values in order to cover errors in model structure" (Page and Kreutzer, 2005, p. 222). Another difficulty is "to decide if model and system output are "sufficiently similar", particularly if models contain stochastic components and the simulations' results are complex, e.g. spatial patterns in multi-agent-based simulations" (Page and Kreutzer, 2005, p. 223).

Fehler et al. (2004, pp. 306) regard the application-independence of simulation-based optimization (e.g. Gehlsen and Page, 2001) as an advantage and drawback at the same time, since it forbids to constrain the calibration process with context-specific knowledge besides restricted variation ranges of parameters. The authors therefore propose a methodology for *white box*

---

[6]which is also cited by Fehler et al. (2004, p. 307)
[7]A similar German description is also found in (Bachmann et al., 2004, pp. 116-117).

calibration (Fehler et al., 2004, Secs. 4-6). It comprises several context-aware model "decomposition and abstraction methods" (Fehler et al., 2004, p. 320), related to the proposals by Oechslein et al. (1999), to reduce the complexity of calibration (Fehler et al., 2004, p. 308).

Decomposition aims at the extraction of possibly independent model components and states that can be calibrated in isolation (Fehler et al., 2004, p. 308). Proposed dimensions include functional, goal-oriented, behavioral, and temporal decomposition (Fehler et al., 2004, Secs. 5.2-5.5). Using functional decomposition, one might e.g. calibrate the behavior of a single agent or of spatial dynamics without influences by other agents (Fehler et al., 2004, p. 309).

Abstraction means that microscopic sub-models are manually or (semi-)automatically aggregated into macroscopic models and that deterministic or irrelevant model components are simplified and eliminated (Fehler et al., 2004, p. 313). Among the techniques for automated model abstraction, Fehler et al. (2004, p. 314) name *distribution fitting* to replace a microscopic sub-model with a stochastic process and *meta-modeling*. The latter technique is explained in (Page and Kreutzer, 2005, p. 224) as follows:

> "Simply put, meta-modelling is about building a more abstract or, as Zeigler et al. (2000, p. 32) call it, "lumped" model, which exhibits similar relevant behaviour as the original. [...]
>
> A common technique used in meta-modelling is to derive mathematical approximations of input-output functions computed by the original model. [...] Parameters are [...] systematically varied within given ranges, and the corresponding results are sampled. From these samples a *reaction surface* is computed, using an interpolation technique such as polynomial fitting or neural networks (Kilmer et al., 1997).
>
> There are applications of meta-modelling in validation which go beyond explorations of the original model's response surface. For example, we can use the comparison of meta-models as a quantitative operational validation technique [...] by checking the coefficients of [... polynomial] meta-models [of the simulation and the real system] for similarity."

Fehler et al. (2004, pp. 315) additionally propose an order in which to perform the different decomposition and abstraction tasks to reduce overall calibration effort. They emphasize that decomposition can only be performed in case of sufficiently independent model components (Fehler et al., 2004, p. 308). After abstracting and calibrating appropriate sub-models, it is important to perform a final integrative calibration (Fehler et al., 2004, p. 316), possibly supported by simulation-based optimization (Fehler et al., 2004, p. 320).

Besides decomposition and abstraction, Fehler et al. (2006b, Sec. 4.5) describe a further technique for the "reverse-engineering" of environmental models such that they fit the simulated agent models in the same way that real agent behavior and real environments match. Technical details of this and the above methods are provided in the dissertation by Fehler (2011).

5.1.2.3. Pattern-Based Validation and Model Alignment

Grimm (2002, p. 25), among others, constates a "communication crisis" in the MABS community concerning the scientific value of models and the clarity of publications. This is caused by several factors related to model complexity:

- Different from mathematical models, a concise and falsifiable publication of agent-based models is impractical because one would in principle have to publish the source code of the model (Grimm, 2002, p. 24).

- Due to the few restrictions of the modeling formalism (Klügl, 2000, p. 73), it is hard to decide and validate if an appropriate level of detail is modelled (Grimm et al., 2005, p. 987).

- For similar reasons models and experiments are seldom compared, re-used, and enhanced within the community (Axtell et al., 1996, p. 124).

- In-depth analysis and validation of relations between microscopic behavior and macroscopic outcomes is seldom performed (Railsback et al., 2002, p. 84).

In the following, we review manual and semi-automated validation techniques to improve this situation. The focus in this section is on techniques to confirm (or falsify) previously stated hypotheses. The next section treats explorative techniques, mainly based on visualization.

Pattern-Based Modeling and Validation   rests upon the idea that a reasonable validity criterion for agent-based models is the ability to reproduce certain *characteristic macro-level patterns* of the real system (Railsback et al., 2002, p. 84). According to Rand et al. (2003, p. 2) a focus on macroscopic patterns is preferable since microscopic trajectories in MABS might differ strongly between different (stochastic) simulation runs due to path-dependence and sensitivity to initial conditions. Beyond that, a concentration on the macro-level furthers the generality (Rand et al., 2003, p. 2) and comparability of models, even allowing to "contrast [...] alternative theories" (Grimm et al., 2005, p. 988).

Similar to test-driven software development, target patterns at multiple levels of aggregation are defined *before* the model is implemented (Grimm et al., 2005, p. 987). Thus, the modelled entities and their levels of detail are constrained by the model's ability to reproduce the relevant patterns (Grimm et al., 2005, pp. 987-988). Another advantage is the possibility for incremental model development, ideally focusing on one pattern per iteration (Grimm et al., 2005, p. 988).

The patterns considered in actual studies largely depend on the modelled domain. In a simulation of urban development Rand et al. (2003, pp. 3) consider two patterns from the literature including (1) a power law relation between the size of population clusters and the number of similarly sized clusters and (2) a negative exponential decrease of population density with increasing distance from the city center. Grimm et al. (2005, p. 989) report on a beech forest model where one requirement consists in the reproduction of a "horizontal mosaic of developmental stages" in the spatial distribution of the (simulated) trees.

Note that the potential to automate pattern-based validation in a model-based validation system (as proposed by Birta and Özmizrak, 1996) depends on the types of patterns considered. While the numerical relations by Rand et al. (2003) are straightforwardly validated with statistical techniques, an automated detection of the 'mosaic' structure mentioned by Grimm et al. (2005) appears more demanding.

Model Alignment   or *docking* relates to comparisons of different models representing the same domain. Docking studies are mainly performed for two reasons:

1. If no sufficient data from the real system is available, a new model can be validated against an existing simulation as an initial plausibility check (Xiang et al., 2005, p. 48).

2. Relations between alternative models by different developers are evaluated. In doing so, model hierarchies (such as 'model A is a special case of model B') can be established (Axtell et al., 1996, p. 124) and results can be confirmed or falsified experimentally, somehow similar to the natural sciences (Hales et al., 2003).

A seminal study of the second type was conducted by Axtell et al. (1996, pp. 124), who compared the well-known *Sugarscape* model by Epstein and Axtell (1996) with *Axelrod's cultural transmission model* (ACM, Axelrod, 1995). Both models simulate cultural spread in societies in a very abstract form. The purpose of the study was to reproduce the results of the ACM with a modified variant of the "more general *Sugarscape* system" (Axtell et al., 1996, pp. 124). The authors successfully aligned both models (Axtell et al., 1996, p. 135) and analyzed the effect of certain properties, such as agents' ability to move, on the simulation of cultural spread (Axtell et al., 1996, p. 131).

Axtell et al. (1996, p. 135) also discuss the level at which simulation results should be compared for alignment. Similar to pattern-based validation, they propose two equivalence criteria at the global level: *Distributional equivalence*, as the strict variant, demands that "two models produce distributions of results that cannot be distinguished statistically" (Axtell et al., 1996, p. 135). *Relational equivalence* "mean[s] that the two models can be shown to produce the same internal relationship among their results", like e.g. the power law relation in the land-use model by Rand et al. (2003).

5.1.2.4. Visual Debugging and Analysis

Despite progress in formal and quantitative analysis, "visualising the simulation and observing the interactions" (Chen et al., 2008, p. 2) is still one of the main techniques to explore the behavior of MABS. In (Page and Kreutzer, 2005, pp. 224-225) we discussed the advantages and drawbacks of visualization as an explorative validation technique:

- "Often statistical methods [...] cannot be used due to overly restrictive statistical assumptions or the lack of comparable system data (Sargent, 2001, p. 110).

- Given a descriptive representation of model dynamics, human experts can often detect faults more quickly and more reliably than [...] computer-aided analysis methods.

- Visualization and animation help model developers to detect obvious errors during design and implementation. It also helps to improve communication with customers.

Unfortunately, visualizations also have a number of important disadvantages. [...] since it is only a single snapshot which might show completely untypical random behaviour, modellers must be very careful not to draw overly general conclusions from the animation of single stochastic simulation trajectories. This is a particular concern if such animations are (mis)used as the sole basis for making decisions. In addition, visual analysis of simulation results is largely subjective and must draw on expert knowledge which cannot be readily automated or objectified."

In the following, we review selected approaches to visually analyze and debug MABS. Note that some of these approaches are even supported by data mining.

Visual Debugging   In Section 5.1.1.4, we described the often-cited 'debugging by corroboration' approach of Ndumu and Nwana (1999) with its 4 perspectives and related visualization tools. The focus of these tools conforms well to the most common bug types in (message-based) multi-agent systems identified by Poutakidis et al. (2003, pp. 630): "failure to send a message [....,] uninitialised agents [....,] sending a message to the wrong recipient [....,] sending the wrong message [..., and] sending the same message multiple times".

Grimm (2002) presents a tool that is tailored towards visually debugging MABS of many (simple) agents situated in a spatial environment. He argues that due to model complexity, the debugging of MABS should not primarily be performed at the code level but in terms of high-level visualization and animation (Grimm, 2002, pp. 27). Based on these ideas, a user interface to a simulation of plant populations in South African grassland is implemented with the Java-based *GECKO* system (Grimm, 2002, p. 30).

The user interface can display the spatial model as well as all relevant local and global state variables (Grimm, 2002, p. 32) using common visualizations like time series, scatter plots, and histograms (see e.g. Sargent (2001, p. 111), cited in (Page and Kreutzer, 2005, p. 225)). Furthermore, all relevant model parameters can be modified and the simulation can be run in either single step or batch mode (Grimm, 2002, p. 28) using a 'CD player-like' control panel (Grimm, 2002, p. 32). All traces and results are also stored to files for further analysis (Grimm, 2002, p. 29).

Grimm (2002, pp. 33) emphasizes that, despite the additional coding effort (Grimm, 2002, p. 32), interactive user interfaces to observe and control all relevant state variables are crucial to provide domain experts with the possibility to explore and validate agent-based models.

Advanced Visual Data Analysis   Visualizations like simple time series are often inappropriate to display state spaces and trajectories of many interacting agents. Therefore, several proposals have been made to 'intelligently' aggregate raw simulation output prior to visualization by means of data mining. In the following, we name some visualization-related work before turning to general data mining support for MABS in Section 5.2.

Sanchez and Lucas (2002) employ (among other techniques) visualizations of regression trees, neural networks, and three-dimensional response surface plots to analyze the impact of parameter changes on the behavior of MABS in large-scale experiment series. St. Amant et al. (2001) use 3D visualization and an automated constraint-based camera assistant to 'integrate' users as closely as possible into a spatially explicit military planning simulation.

Schroeder and Noy (2001) cluster groups of related agents based on multivariate data, e.g. related to message exchange. To improve the visualization of clusters in high-dimensional feature spaces, they apply Principal Component Analysis (PCA), which allows to automatically detect those (combinations of) feature dimensions with the highest variability (Schroeder and Noy, 2001, p. 87). Gabbai et al. (2004) perform dimension reduction in MAS visualization with the aid of self-organizing maps (SOM, see Section 4.1.4.5).

5.2. Data Mining in Multi-Agent Systems and Simulations

The validation techniques presented above can be useful to improve the credibility of MABS. Nevertheless, there are several limitations that we already discussed in Section 3.5.

In recent years, data mining and, to some extent, process mining (Chapter 4) have been increasingly applied to support MABS validation with automated hypothesis generation. Figure 5.5 illustrates that data mining may provide a 'link' between confirmatory and exploratory as well as (automated) quantitative and (less automated) qualitative validation.

Data mining supports model exploration with the automated extraction of aggregate formal representations from large simulation output datasets (see e.g. Remondino and Correndo, 2006, p. 14). Since mined models like association rules or decision trees are relatively straightforward to understand, they bear larger potential to formalize 'qualitative' results of MABS than mere numerical representations (see e.g. Remondino and Correndo, 2006, Sec. 3.2).

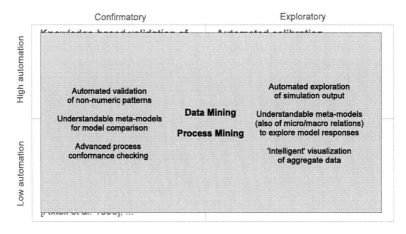

Figure 5.5.: Potential of data and process mining in the context of validation techniques reviewed in Section 5.1.2.

The following sections review methods and techniques related to data and process mining in MA(B)S. While these approaches mirror the ideas sketched in Figure 5.5, the field is still in its infancy (see also Arroyo et al., 2010, p. 418 reviewed in Section 5.2.2.3). In chapter 6, we will attempt to integrate the reviewed approaches into a coherent conceptual framework for data mining and especially process mining in MABS.

5.2.1. Relations between Data Mining and MAS

In general, 3 relevant relations between the research fields of data mining and MAS can be identified:

1. *Adaptive agents*: Agents are equipped with the ability for data mining to increase their robustness, flexibility, and autonomy (Zhang et al., 2005, p. 56). Remondino and Cor-

rendo (2005, p. 4) refer to this variant as *endogenous modeling*.[8] Applications of adaptive agents reach from information extraction on the internet to simulated persons in social simulation.

2. *Analysis of MA(B)S*: As indicated above, the behavior of complex MAS can be analyzed with the aid of data mining. Such analyses might support verification and validation in AOSE as well as MABS. Remondino and Correndo (2005, p. 4) call this application *exogenous modeling*.

3. *Agent-supported data mining*: Similar to the idea of agent-supported simulation (see Ören, 2000, reviewed in Section 3.2.1), agent technology can be utilized to develop improved (distributed) data mining algorithms and systems (Zhang et al., 2005, p. 52).

The focus of this thesis and the following literature review is on the second variant, i.e. *data mining as a support techniques for the validation and analysis of MABS*. The case of adaptive agents is covered briefly in Section 6.3.5, focusing on similarities and differences in the requirements of 'endogenous' and 'exogenous' mining.[9]

Agent-supported data mining is not explicitly treated in this thesis. The article by Zhang et al. (2005, Secs. 2,4) presents an overview of this topic and states examples including an agent-based decomposition of the WEKA library (see Section 4.1.5.1) and a plugin-based financial trading system.

Adopting this perspective, the reference net-based 'mining chains' that will be presented in Sections 7.1.3 and 7.4.2 might be understood as a basis for a future MULAN-based agent-supported data mining system with a similar objective as the examples by Zhang et al. (2005), i.e. distribution, encapsulation, and flexible plugin-based composition of data mining procedures. Though not explicitly 'agent-based', the assistant-supported, plugin-based *ProM 6* system described in Section 4.2.6.1 fits this category as well.

Further information on all variants of integrating agents and data mining is provided in the book by Cao (2009) and on the website of the special interest group on *Agent and Data Mining Interaction and Integration* (AMII).[10]

5.2.2. Data Mining in MABS

This section reviews methodologies, techniques, and tools to integrate data mining and MABS. Among the presented approaches, the work by Köster (2002) and Nair et al. (2004) might have influenced this thesis most strongly. The approach by Remondino and Correndo (2005) is parallel work guided by rather similar objectives and ideas. To simplify the comparison between different methodologies and our integrated approach in Section 6.3, respective modeling cycles will be presented in a coherent Petri net notation.[11]

---

[8]page numbers relate to the version of the article downloadable at `http://www.di.unito.it` `/~remond/Ric/Remondino_ECMS2005.pdf` (last visit 2012-10-07)

[9]as to use the terminology by Remondino and Correndo (2005)

[10]`www.agentmining.org` (last visit 2012-01-03)

[11]This approach is inspired by the comparison of agent architectures in the dissertation by Rölke (2004) and further similar work in the MULAN context (e.g. the dissertation by Fix, 2012).

5.2.2.1. Simulation Data Analysis with Knowledge Discovery in Databases

The dissertation by Köster (2002) proposes a methodology to integrate knowledge discovery in databases (KDD, see Section 4.1.1) and simulation. As shown in Figure 5.6, the former phases of his process (grey) form a conventional model building cycle, while the latter (white) are taken from the KDD process (Köster, 2002, p. 88). The iterative and exploratory character of the process is indicated by the possibility to revise all phases during validation (Köster, 2002, p. 89).

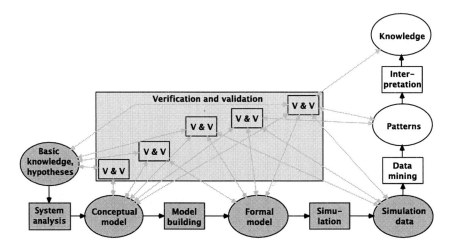

Figure 5.6.: Integrated process of simulation and KDD displayed as a Petri net. Adopted with modifications from the diagram by Köster (2002, p. 88)

Köster (2002) applies the integrated process to an individual-based epidemiological simulation and to an interactive flight training simulator, where the objectives differ in both case studies:

- In individual-based simulation, the goal is to support model exploration and validation with the automated detection of dependencies between (changes of) local parameters and global outcomes (Köster, 2002, p. 89). "Furthermore, the results of the data mining can be used to identify model components that do not significantly contribute to the (global) behavior of the model"

- "In the context of [...] interactive training simulators, two important goals are in the focus of the application: on the one hand to derive objective criteria to rate the performance of candidates; on the other hand to thoroughly identify deficiencies in the way they handle the system." (Köster, 2002, p. 91)

In both case studies, a new data mining technique is applied that combines multivariate time-series analysis with data flow modeling and evolutionary algorithms. Numerical time series of state variables, such as the simulated persons' strength of exposition to a pathogen, serve as input (Köster, 2002, p. 188). Additionally, a target variable is specified, e.g. the infection state of a person at the end of simulation (Köster, 2002, p. 188).

From this input, a supervised learning algorithm constructs classifier trees based on a pool of predefined selector, filter, and processor components for time series analysis. Using an evolutionary algorithm, it attempts to identify those combinations of nodes that best predict the target variable from (a selection of) the provided time series. From analyzing the nodes and connections in the resulting data flow networks, a deeper understanding of cause/effect-relations in the model might be gained (Köster, 2002, p. 192).

Köster (2002, Chs. 5,6.8) further presents mature implementations of a data mining tool (*EA Mole*) and an interactive individual-based simulation system (*iEpiSim*²). While not in the research focus, Köster (2002, p. 90) also briefly discusses the potential of simulation as a support technique for KDD: On the one hand, the structure provided by a conceptual simulation model might improve insight into the analyzed domain. On the other hand, valid simulation results can, to a certain degree, compensate the typical lack of data in KDD projects.

For future work, Köster (2002, pp. 226) especially suggests to apply the proposed methodology to the validation of (individual-based) simulation models. In personal communication with the author of this thesis, Köster (2004) mentioned first attempts of using EA Mole for the validation and prediction of trajectories in swarming and population simulations.

5.2.2.2. Analysis of Simulated Robot Soccer Games

Nair et al. (2004) apply data mining to the analysis of team behavior in simulated robot soccer (*Robo Cup*¹²). An interesting aspect of their work is the explicit definition of multiple analysis perspectives, related to the debugging approach by Ndumu and Nwana (1999); see Section 5.1.1.4. From a common log format, the implemented system *ISAAC* reconstructs meta-models of the observed simulations on three levels with different data mining techniques:

- The "individual agent model" is a situation-oriented decision tree that represents conditions under which certain "critical events", like e.g. a shot on the goal, fail or succeed (Nair et al., 2004, Sec. 3). Given a user-defined specification of critical events and relevant attributes, decision trees (Section 4.1.4.1) are learned from the log with the supervised $C5.0$ algorithm (Nair et al., 2004, p. 10).

- The "multiple agent model" describes action sequences that form characteristic strategies of a team in terms of stochastic automata (Nair et al., 2004, Sec. 4). Again, the user can specify a critical event (e.g. a goal) as the final state of the automaton (Nair et al., 2004, p. 17). Further parameters include a *window size* that constrains the considered pattern length and a *structural generalization* factor that influences the induction of cycles (Nair et al., 2004, p. 21).

- The "global team model" is also represented by decision trees that relate macro-level statistics (e.g. ball possession time) to overall outcomes of soccer games (Nair et al., 2004, Sec. 5).

Besides the analysis perspectives, Nair et al. (2004, p. 2) name 4 main requirements for their assistant: "Locating key aspects of team behaviour [...]; diagnosing [...], particularly, problematic behaviour; [...] suggesting alternative courses of action; and [...] presenting the relevant information

---

¹²http://www.robocup.org (last visit 2012-10-07)

to the user comprehensibly." To meet these requirements, data mining is complemented with visualization, perturbation analysis, and natural language generation.

Perturbation analysis is applied to the individual and multiple agent models to identify a minimum set of conditions that distinguish successful from ineffective (inter)actions. In the individual agent model, the conditions of a decision tree representing an unsuccessful action are inverted, one after the other, before searching for corresponding successful actions in the log (Nair et al., 2004, Sec. 3.3). In the multi agent model, the assistant "mines patterns from the behaviour traces that are very similar [to a stochastic automaton representing success], and yet end in failure" (Nair et al., 2004, p. 23).

To further compare key success factors of different teams, the assistant performs statistical tests on the distribution of the teams' frequent patterns (Nair et al., 2004, p. 23). From the global team model, newspaper-like summaries of the run of play are generated in English language (Nair et al., 2004, pp. 31).

Prior to Nair et al. (2004), Jacobs et al. (1998) used inductive logic programming (ILP, see Section 4.1.4.3) in the *Robo Cup* domain to verify[13] and validate individual agent behavior and interactions based on logs of simulated soccer games. As indicated by Nair et al. (2004, p. 46), the approach strongly depends on the availability of formalized background knowledge, which complicates a transfer to other programming paradigms.

5.2.2.3. Data Mining Applied to Agent-Based Simulation

Parallel to this thesis, Remondino and Correndo (2005) developed an attempt to conceptually integrate data mining and MABS, that we already mentioned in (Knaak, 2006, Sec. 2):[14]

> "[...] Remondino and Correndo (2005) [...] integrate DM into a basic model building process and differentiate between two main applications: [...] *endogenous DM* [... and] *exogenous DM* [... as explained in Section 5.2.1 ...]. Further applications, such as automated modelling, (automated) validation by comparison of [understandable] meta-models, and (automated) calibration of model parameters are mentioned implicitly in the context of certain mining techniques such as multiple regression, clustering, and rule inference."

The authors sketch a simple "modelling and model-revision process", depicted in Figure 5.7, in which exogenous data mining is applied to support the initial modeling phase and validation (Remondino and Correndo, 2006, p. 18). In (Remondino and Correndo, 2006, Sec. 7), they further propose to apply mining techniques to data from multiple simulation runs of different scenarios to identify previously unknown cause/effect-relations between parameters and results. However, to the understanding of the author, Remondino and Correndo (2006, Sec. 7.1) only use histograms to show that the model of their case study is able to reproduce a macroscopic pattern from the real system over a broad range of parameter settings.

In a mere conceptual study, Baqueiro et al. (2009, p. 221) extend the work of Remondino and Correndo (2006) by discussing two directions of integration, i.e. "applying DM in ABMS [Agent-Based Modeling and Simulation ... and] applying ABMS in DM". In the former direction, the

---

[13]in the wider sense

[14]misspelling in (Knaak, 2006) corrected by the author of this thesis

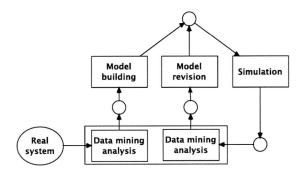

Figure 5.7.: Data mining-based model revision process by Remondino and Correndo displayed as a Petri net. Adopted with modifications from Remondino and Correndo (2006, p. 18).

authors only cite the work of Remondino and Correndo (2005, 2006) and additionally propose to abstract real and simulation data by means of rule mining, clustering, and sequence mining to aid comparisons between different simulation models and the real system (Baqueiro et al., 2009, p. 225).

In the 'inverse' direction, Baqueiro et al. (2009, pp. 226-227) propose (1) to use MABS as a testbed to train and validate data mining algorithms and (2) to compensate missing and erroneous real data with substitute simulation outputs, similar to the idea by Köster (2002). However, to generate "(a) quasi-real [...]; (b) suitable-sized [...]; (c) qualified [...]; and (d) significant" data – as claimed by Baqueiro et al. (2009, p. 226) – a high degree of model validity would be necessary.

Also citing the work of Remondino and Correndo (2006), Arroyo et al. (2010) present a more thorough integration of data mining into a model building cycle accompanied by a larger case study. As depicted in Figure 5.8, this process employs data mining on real and simulation data in the phases of model-building and validation. The authors emphasize the need for domain and data mining experts attending a simulation study to handle the large variety and complexity of mining techniques (Arroyo et al., 2010, p. 433).

Arroyo et al. (2010, p. 423) further discuss the applicability of several data mining techniques to simulation: (1) *clustering* to identify groups of related agents, (2) *PCA* to minimize the simulated agents' degrees of freedom by dimensionality reduction, (3) *time series analysis* to analyze the development of variables over time, (4) *association rules* to model and validate "hidden relationships", and (5) *graph mining* to detect frequent patterns in social networks.

In the case study, a data-intensive model of change in political and religious values during the *post-Franco era* in Spain is analyzed with the aid of clustering (Arroyo et al., 2010, Sec. 4). The authors constate that the temporal evolution of population clusters in their simulation fits clusters mined from real population data quite well regarding variables like age, religiosity, political ideology, etc. (Arroyo et al., 2010, p. 427). Thus, a successful example of data mining support for pattern-based validation (see Section 5.1.2.3) is given.

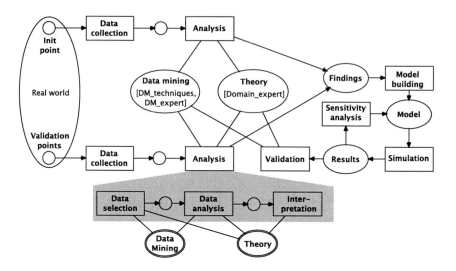

Figure 5.8.: Data mining-enhanced model building cycle displayed as a Petri net. Adopted with modifications from two figures in (Arroyo et al., 2010, pp. 421, 422)

5.2.2.4. Analysis and Discovery of Inter-Level Relations

The analysis of relations between multiple levels of aggregation is one of the most demanding tasks in MABS. It somehow mirrors the unsolved problem of micro/macro links in sociology (e.g. Malsch, 2001). Even in the restricted case of computational emergence (see Section 2.1.1) the description of non-explicitly modelled macroscopic entities and their response to local changes remains challenging, especially with regard to formalization and tool support (Chen et al., 2010, pp. 41).

Approach by Chen et al. Chen et al. (2008, 2010) present an approach to formalize computationally emergent phenomena that is rather 'process mining-like' in spirit.[15] It is based on the common observation that simulations generate events at multiple levels of abstraction. According to Chen et al. (2010, p. 45), "a simple event *se* is a state transition defined at some level of abstraction that results from the execution of a single [...] rule". Simple events are recursively aggregated into complex events denoted as *ce* (Chen et al., 2010, p. 45):

$$ce :: se|ce_1 \Diamond ce_2 \tag{5.2}$$

where $\Diamond$ is a relation with respect to time (e.g. $e_1 < e_2$), space (e.g. e_1 and e_2 occur at the same location), or data attributes (e.g. e_1 and e_2 have a different originator).[16]

---

[15]though no explicit relation to process mining techniques is drawn in (Chen et al., 2008, 2010)

[16]examples adopted with modifications from Chen et al. (2010, p. 45), also inspired by ideas from Ramezani et al. (2012)

All simple events caused by the same rule at the same abstraction level form a *simple event type SET* (Chen et al., 2010, p. 46). Accordingly, a *complex event type CET* consists of a set of simple event types and a set of relations defined over these types (Chen et al., 2010, p. 46). Chen (2009, p. 98) name 3 temporal relations (concurrency, direct succession, indirect succession), 2 spatial relations (within distance, at location), and 1 'organizational' relation (same agent) to build *CET*s.

A *CET* thus describes a pattern of interrelated events that can be visualized as a labelled (multi-)graph with simple event types as node labels and relations as edge labels (Chen et al., 2010, p. 46). *Subsystem state types SST* "represent static property descriptions" (Chen, 2009, p. 60) over multiple system components (Chen, 2009, p. 78). Based on these definitions, the authors formalize several relations that are typically stated between phenomena at different aggregation levels:

- *Scope*: An event type CET_X has a larger scope than an event type CET_A if CET_X can be *composed* from CET_A and some CET_B: $CET_X = CET_A \lozenge CET_B$ (Chen et al., 2010, p. 47).

- *Resolution*: A *supertype* CET_X has a lower resolution than a *subtype* CET_A if the observed events belonging to CET_A are a subset of those belonging to CET_X: $E(CET_A) \subseteq E(CET_X)$ (Chen et al., 2010, p. 47).

- *Level of abstraction*: An event type CET_X has a higher level of abstraction than an event type CET_Y if CET_X has a larger scope or a lower resolution than CET_Y (adopted with modifications from Chen et al., 2008, p. 5x).

- *Emergent law*: A non-simple event type CET_X and an event type CET_Y are related by an emergent law if the occurrence of an event $ce_x \in CET_X$ implies the occurrence of an event $ce_y \in CET_Y$: $CET_X \to CET_Y$ (Chen et al., 2010, p. 47).

- *Top-down constraint*: An event type CET_X exposes a top-down constraint on an event type CET_Y if $CET_X \to CET_Y$ and CET_X has a higher level of abstraction than CET_Y (adopted with modifications from Chen et al., 2010, p. 47).

Chen et al. (2010, Sec. 3) operationalize this formalism in the MABS framework of *X-machines*, a specific class of communicating automata. As an example, a simple prey-predator model of 'lions' and 'antelopes' is implemented (Chen et al., 2010, Sec. 4.1). For this model, (Chen et al., 2010, p. 49) specify exemplary *CET*s that represent the patterns "starvation" (Figure 5.9), "same lion overhunting", and "between lion overhunting",

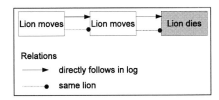

Figure 5.9.: Graph for the complex event type 'starvation': A lion dies after moving two times in succession without having the possibility to hunt (Chen et al., 2010, p. 49). Adopted with modifications from (Chen et al., 2010, p. 50).

The simulation log is matched against the specified patterns, and their occurrence is correlated with model parameters like density of population (Chen et al., 2010, pp. 49). Chen (2009, p. 107) additionally propose to employ machine learning techniques for "validating and discovering [...] models" of inter-level relations. In doing so, the following types of models are (among others) distinguished (Chen, 2009, pp. 116):

- "Associative [models ...] define a set of linear and/or non-linear relationships between a set of *CET*s and/or *SST*s" (Chen, 2009, p. 116). These models are mined by correlating occurrences of *CET*s detected in the log as shown in (Chen and Hardoon, 2010).

- "Causal [models ...] define a set of directed causal relationships between a set of *CET*s and/or *SST*s" (Chen, 2009, p. 116). Chen (2009, Sec 4.2.2) propose to use structural equation models and Bayesian networks (Section 4.1.4.4) for representation. In a Bayesian Network, nodes represent *CET*s which are connected according to their conditional occurrence probabilities estimated from log data. Potgieter (2004) and Gore (2010) also use Bayesian networks to infer inter-level relations from MA(B)S data.

- "Functional modular [models ...] define associative relations between *CET*s and/or *SST*s which can be treated as functional units" (Chen, 2009, p. 117). Under the "premise that within-module statistical association [...] is greater than between-module association for a particular function" (Chen, 2009, p. 122), it is proposed to discover modules by clustering *CET*s according to similar patterns of occurrence.

Beyond *describing* inter-level relations, Chen (2009, Sec. 4.3) also use machine learning to *predict* computationally emergent behavior modeled in terms of *CET*s. In addition, *multi-level models* that "explicitly define differences in the dependency relations between *CET*s for groups of simulations with different attributes" (Chen, 2009, p. 217) are analyzed with the aid of linear regression and hierarchical Bayesian networks (Chen, 2009, Sec. 4.4).

A future challenge of the approach lies in "implementation issues associated to the detection of *CET* occurrences" with feasible time complexity, where logic-based optimization techniques are proposed as a starting point (Chen, 2009, p. 216). In Sections 6.2 and 7.1.3.1 we discuss process mining as an alternative and relate the work by Chen (2009) to the compliance checking approach by Ramezani et al. (2012) and to reference nets.

Moncion et al. (2010), who relate themselves to the work of Chen et al. (2010)[17], present an approach towards the automated detection of emergence based on so-called *interaction signs*, i.e. arbitrary indicators for interactions observed in a MABS (Moncion et al., 2010, Sec. 3.1). Interaction signs might reach from measures like distance or direction of movement in simple flocking simulations to complex events as defined by Chen (2009) (Moncion et al., 2010, Sec. 3.1).

Based on the observation of interaction signs during a simulation, Moncion et al. (2010, Sec. 3.2) build a time-series of social networks (see also Lahiri and Berger-Wolf, 2008, reviewed in Section 4.2.4.1) where nodes represent agents and edges represent their relations with respect to an interaction sign. The time series are analyzed (a) by tracking coherent subnets over time with the aid of a clustering algorithm (Moncion et al., 2010, Sec. 4.2) and (b) by applying metrics from social network analysis in order to analyze the increase or decrease of 'order' in a simulation

---

[17]see Moncion et al. (2010, Sec. 2)

(Moncion et al., 2010, Sec. 4.1). The approach is evaluated at the example of a simple flocking simulation (Moncion et al., 2010, Sec. 5).

5.2.2.5. Data Farming

In (Knaak, 2006, Sec. 2), we briefly reviewed a methodology rooted in the military simulation domain that integrates MABS and data mining (DM):

> "Brandstein et al. (1998) propose a method called *data farming* that integrates MABS with large-scale experiment planning, distributed execution of simulation runs, visualisation, and DM. However, the current data farming research seems to focus stronger on experimentation methodology than on the integration of DM techniques. The applied DM techniques are mostly limited to the numerical analysis of factors influencing the agents' behaviour."

In the context of data farming, Sanchez and Lucas (2002) support visualization with data mining as reviewed in Section 5.1.2.4. Barry and Koehler (2004, p. 815) propose to use clustering, decision tree mining, rule mining, and Bayesian network inference on data farming results to uncover relations between simulation parameters and results over many replications. To identify relevant variables for simulation-based optimization, Brady and Yellig (2005, p. 286) use correlation analysis over keywords that reference model components in the simulation trace.

5.2.2.6. Adaptive Intelligent Model-Building for the Social Sciences (AIMSS)

As part of the AIMSS project, Kennedy et al. (2007, p. 1098) present an assistant software that supports iterative model building with data mining. At the example of a housing simulation, association rules are mined from simulation output and real data as "high level descriptions" for pattern-based validation (Kennedy et al., 2007, p. 1102).

As an example, the authors present the following rule that was mined from simulation output with maximum confidence (Kennedy et al., 2007, p. 1102):

$$incomeLevel = low \wedge moveReason = affordability \Rightarrow newHomeCost = low. \qquad (5.3)$$

This rule indicates that agents with the lowest income level, that move houses due to affordability, will always move into a house at the lowest rent level (Kennedy et al., 2007, p. 1103). The quantization of numerical data into levels is necessary since the applied association mining technique can only handle categorial data (Kennedy et al., 2007, p. 1104).

For future work, Kennedy et al. (2007, pp. 1103) plan to automate model revision on the basis of data mining results. The architecture of the assistant is already prepared for this extension due to the use of "machine readable" declarative model specifications based on XML (Kennedy et al., 2007, p. 1102).

5.2.2.7. Further Work on Data Mining in MABS

In his bachelor thesis at the University of Rostock, Enrico Seib (2008) discusses the application of data mining to (agent-based) simulation and evaluates a number of mining techniques and simulation tools (including *SeSAm* reviewed in Section 3.4.3) in this respect (Seib, 2008, p. V). As a practical example, a clustering algorithm is integrated into the MABS framework *JAMES II* and applied to a MABS of a chemical process (Seib, 2008, pp. III,V).[18]

Schmitz et al. (2010, p. 88) systematically evaluate different data mining techniques, i.e. "time series analysis, association rule mining, clustering, and social network analysis in regard to their usefulness for the[...] purpose[...]" of "validating" and "understanding" MABS of "inter-organizational networks". The applied techniques are rated with respect to different domain-specific analysis questions (Schmitz et al., 2010, p. 100). Generalization of the investigated questions and improvement of tool support are identified as topics for further work (Schmitz et al., 2010, p. 100). An interesting finding is that "at early analysis stages [...] mostly qualitative analyses are relevant [while ...] at a later point in time [...], we can expect a shift towards more quantitative analyses that better serve as input to management decisions" (Schmitz et al., 2010, pp. 100).

5.2.3. Data Mining in Other Simulation World-Views

Huber et al. (1993, p. 237) report an early application of decision tree mining to generate "a qualitative description of [... simulation] input/output behaviour [... that] can easily be interpreted by the modeller and other users because of its intuitive representation." Huber and Berthold (2000, Sec. 3.3) compare different formalisms for meta-modeling including regression analysis, neural networks, and association rules. Based on this comparison, they propose fuzzy graphs as a means to combine the straightforwardness and understandability of rule mining with the other techniques' ability to handle continuous values.

Szczerbicka and Uthmann (2000) were among the first to generally consider interactions between AI techniques and simulation: In the introduction to their anthology, the potential of AI to support the usage, modeling, optimization, and analysis of simulation models is discussed. The authors name decision tree learning and case-based reasoning as the most common data mining techniques for simulation analysis (Szczerbicka and Uthmann, 2000, Sec. 4.4).

Further articles in the anthology report on applications of different data mining techniques to validation, meta-modeling, and optimization. Barton and Szczerbicka (2000) discuss the utility of machine learning for model validation and perform simulation-based optimization with the aid of decision tree mining and a time-dependent scoring function.

Morbitzer et al. (2003) compare data mining with traditional techniques for simulation analysis. The authors emphasize the ability of data mining to (semi-) automatically generate results that are at the same time numerically quantified and visually understandable (Morbitzer et al., 2003, p. 913). This confirms the view of data mining as a 'link' between quantitative, qualitative, exploratory, and confirmatory validation mentioned in Section 5.2. However, the claim that "the method allows the analysis to be carried out by a user with a very limited understanding of the underlying numerical analysis techniques" (Morbitzer et al., 2003, p. 913) might be called into question.

Morbitzer et al. (2003, pp. 913) further discuss the appropriateness of several data mining techniques (association rules, decision trees, outlier analysis, time series analysis, and clustering)

---

[18]information extracted from the (incomplete) preview of the thesis at `books.google.de/books?` `isbn=364014547X` (last vist 2012-10-10)

to analyze a simulation of air flow in a building. Clustering is practically applied to e.g. group distributions of parameter settings, such as wind speed and ambient temperature, by the resulting temperature in the simulated building (Morbitzer et al., 2003, pp. 915).

As summarized by Czogalla (2007, p. 21), Cantú-Paz et al. (2004) use Bayesian classifiers and *k*-nearest neighbor clustering to automatically query and validate visual turbulence patterns generated by a physics simulation of a liquid.

In the context of the *AssistSim* project, Lattner et al. (2011, p. 179) use "machine learning [...] not [...] to discover knowledge from simulation results but to learn a classifier for the estimation of statistical properties". The objective is to rate the significance of simulation results and to determine the number of runs required to achieve a certain level of significance (Lattner et al., 2011, p. 177). The article also reviews further work related to data mining in simulation (Lattner et al., 2011, p. 177), mostly complementary to this thesis.

5.2.4. Data Mining in MAS

After reviewing applications of data mining to simulation, we will now present examples of data mining in MAS without specific focus on simulation. Some of these approaches already come close to the idea of 'process-oriented' analysis, which is further detailed in the next sections.

5.2.4.1. Log Analysis in the INGENIAS Methodology

INGENIAS is a tool-supported AOSE methodology that comprises multiple modeling perspectives including *agent, organization, task/goal, interaction,* and *environment* (Vigueras et al., 2008, Sec. 3). Validation is performed by *a-posteriori* analysis of message logs recorded during MAS execution. A tool named *ACLAnalyser* supports the analysis of FIPA-compliant message logs recorded on the *JADE* agent platform with visualization and data mining techniques (Botía et al., 2004).[19] Serrano et al. (2009, Sec. 4) summarize several models that are reconstructed for analysis, mostly related to the organization and interaction perspectives of *INGENIAS*.

Causality graphs display the partial order of events in a recorded conversation, where nodes represent agent states and edge labels denote messages (Serrano et al., 2009, p. 2788). To detect causal dependencies in concurrent multi-party conversations, every message is assigned a *vector clock* containing local event counters for all participating agents (Vigueras and Botia, 2008, p. 193). Figure 5.10 shows a causality graph for an example execution of the contract net protocol. Vigueras et al. (2008, Sec. 4) propose to enrich the nodes of the causality graph with detailed state information from the interaction and task/goal perspectives.

Besides causality graphs, the following further visualizations are available in the *ACL Analyser* (Serrano et al., 2009, Sec. 4.3):

- *Order graphs* are similar to causality graphs with the exception that messages are represented by graph nodes.

---

[19]see also `http://ants.dif.um.es/staff/emilioserra/ACLAnalyser` (last visit 2012-10-10) and the User's Guide (Serrano and Botia, 2011) available at this location

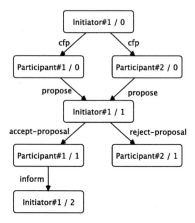

Figure 5.10.: A causality graph for an example execution of the contract net protocol. Nodes represent agent states in the form `agentName / stateId`. Edges are labelled with performatives. Adopted with modifications from (Vigueras and Botia, 2008, p. 201).

- *Abstract graphs* display the order of multiple related conversations without showing details of the conversations themselves.

- *Collaboration graphs* are social networks of communicating agents based on the send-/receive-relation of messages.

- *Sequence diagrams* of the recorded messages (Serrano and Botia, 2011, p. 17) and several conversation *statistics* (Serrano and Botia, 2011, p. 20) can be displayed as well.

Since these visualization tools are only appropriate to analyze small (cut-outs of) MAS, Serrano et al. (2009, pp. 2789) apply a knowledge discovery process including clustering and association rule mining. Clustering supports the visualization of large collaboration graphs with the possibility to zoom into and out of groups of similar agents (Botía et al., 2004, p. 305). The categorial cluster algorithm *ROCK* is employed to group agents that communicate with similar peers (Serrano et al., 2009, p. 2790). The distance-based *k*-means algorithm is used to cluster agents by frequent message exchange (Serrano et al., 2009, pp. 2791). With the aid of association rule mining, relations between performatives, senders, and receivers of messages are reconstructed (Serrano et al., 2009, p. 2790).

Though the reconstructed models somehow resemble the control-flow and organizational perspectives of process mining, it should be noted that (except for association rule mining) no generalization of the displayed dependencies is performed over multiple executions. Furthermore, background knowledge and meta-data is required: Messages must be tagged with conversation and protocol identifiers as well as vector clocks as time stamps. A state machine representing the observed protocol must be available in the *ACLAnalyser* to record conversation statistics and bindings of agents to interaction roles (Botía et al., 2004, p. 305).

5.2.4.2. Agent Software Comprehension

Similar to Vigueras and Botia (2008), Lam and Barber (2005) use causality graphs to analyze logs of MAS. Both approaches can be regarded as complementary, because the focus of Lam and Barber (2005) is on analyzing internal events of single agents (Vigueras and Botia, 2008, p. 203). As a basis, agents are instrumented with logging statements to record state changes with respect to agent-concepts like beliefs, intentions, or actions (Lam and Barber, 2005, pp. 588,589). Lam and Barber (2005, p. 589) emphasize that the concentration on the abstract level of agent concepts reduces the amount of log entries, as e.g. compared to the code level.

From the logs, a software named *Tracer Tool* extracts causal graphs to trace events back to their root causes (Lam and Barber, 2005, Sec. 3). Different from the *ACL Analyser* (see above), the partial order of causal dependencies is not reconstructed from vector clocks, but with the aid of configurable, potentially domain specific background knowledge related to the applied agents concepts (Lam and Barber, 2005, p. 589). An example for this automated log interpretation is provided by Lam and Barber (2005, p. 591):

> "if o is an action, then the algorithm searches for the last observed intention i that has some similar attribute as those of action o. If such an intention is found, a relation from intention i to action o is suggested."

Bosse et al. (2006) complement the explorative analyses of the *Tracer Tool* with confirmative trace checking with the *TTL Checker* mentioned in Section 5.1.2.1. Lam and Barber (2005, p. 593) also mention "behaviour pattern recognition" as a topic for future work.

5.2.4.3. Agent Academy

Mitkas et al. (2002) present the software framework *Agent Academy* implemented on the *JADE* agent platform. Different from the above approaches, *Agent Academy* employs data mining to improve agents' adaptivity by means of "dynamic re-training" based on data collected from previous agent behavior and from the environment.

Adaptivity is not realized by equipping individual agents with learning algorithms but by using the centralized data mining architecture depicted in Figure 5.11. This architecture makes it possible that "functionally unrelated agents within the society may benefit from each others' findings and be able to collectively exploit the shared knowledge base thereby increasing the effectiveness of the system" (Mitkas et al., 2002, p. 757).

The architecture consists of 4 main components implemented as agents that communicate via FIPA-ACL messages (Mitkas et al., 2002, p. 758): The *agent factory* creates and configures new untrained agents on demand. Based on a given ontology, the *agent use repository* stores data from multiple sources in a database. The *data mining module* extracts hypotheses from the agent use repository in the form of association rules, decision trees, and neural networks. The *agent training module* translates the models generated by the data mining module into executable behavior descriptions and transfers these to the agents.

Mitkas et al. (2002, Sec. 4) present an example system that monitors environmental data, predicts health-critical situations concerning allergies, etc. and sends alerts to registered users via different channels such as e-mail. Based on user feedback, predictions concerning alerts and

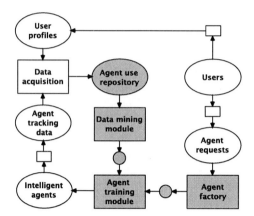

Figure 5.11.: Architecture of the *Agent Academy* framework displayed as a Petri net. Core components of the system are shaded grey. Adopted with modifications from (Mitkas et al., 2002, p. 758)

preferred distribution channels are improved by re-training. For this purpose, decision trees are mined from the agent use repository and translated into executable rules for the *Java Expert System Shell* (JESS, see Section 3.4.2) that the agents employ for decision making.

In the context of *Agent Academy*, Dimou et al. (2007) present a concept to select and apply metrics for performance evaluation of data mining agents. In Section 6.2, we will briefly discuss the modeling and validation of adaptive agents based on process mining.

5.3. Process Mining in Software Engineering and Simulation

Finally, we will focus on those approaches that are most closely akin to the thesis at hand, i.e. process mining or related techniques are applied to MAS-like systems or simulations.

5.3.1. Process Mining in Software Engineering

Interestingly, the reconstruction of software development processes was one of the first objectives for process mining (Cook and Wolf, 1998). In (Cabac and Denz, 2008, pp. 87) we reviewed previous applications of process mining to software engineering:

> "One direction of research focuses on the analysis of software development processes (which we will call *software development process mining*). The goal is to retrieve control-flow and organizational aspects of software development cycles from available data sources such as CVS [Concurrent Versions System, a common software tool for source configuration management[20]] repositories. [...] the second direction of research uses mining to analyze

---

[20]see http://www.nongnu.org/cvs (last visit 2012-10-13)

software artifacts in order to support tasks like debugging or validation (which we will call *software process mining*[21]).

Early work on software development process mining was carried out by Cook and Wolf (1998), who reconstruct models of software development processes from event-based logs and use conformance checking techniques to compare actual development activities with specified process models. They also present a tool implementing their techniques within a software development environment. Christley and Madey (2007b) apply social network mining and grammar inference to the analysis of open source projects. Rubin et al. (2007) introduce a general framework for process mining of software development processes. They consider several aspects including specific data sources, algorithms, and perspectives, and propose the ProM framework (Dongen et al., 2005) as a supporting toolset.

Software process mining is concerned with the reconstruction of abstract models of software systems from their execution traces. [...] Dallmeier et al. (2006) [e.g.] apply grammar inference to the state-based analysis of basic software objects in order to support testing."

Since the time of this review, further work on software development process mining has been reported including the dissertation by Rubin (2007) and the software framework *FRASR* (FRamework for Analyzing Software Repositories) based on *ProM* (Poncin et al., 2011). The latter allows to define so-called "event bindings" to map implicitly defined events from different sources such as code repositories and bug tracking software to MXML logs (Poncin et al., 2011, p. 6).

In the context of software process mining, Bose and Suresh (2008) apply techniques from Bioinformatics and Information Retrieval to identify root-causes for software failures. One of these techniques, i.e. *sequence alignment*, helps to identify common patterns that distinguish erroneous from successful executions.

Approaches to reconstruct understandable models from the source code and runtime observation of software systems are developed in *software reverse engineering*. One direction of work is *scenario-based synthesis* (Lassen et al., 2007, p. 13): Software systems are implemented by 'playing' example user interactions 'into' a development environment (see e.g. Harel and Marelli, 2003). These scenarios, often represented in the form of sequence diagrams, serve to (semi-)automatically generate the behavior of the system under development. The article by Lassen et al. (2007, Sec. 5) further discusses relations between process mining and scenario-based synthesis.

Gueheneuc and Ziadi (2005) propose to reconstruct UML 2 sequence diagrams (SDs, see Section 2.3.1.4) with a combination of static and dynamic analysis: Program execution traces are first transformed into basic SDs of 1 : 1 object interactions (Gueheneuc and Ziadi, 2005, p. 2).[22] Based on an additional static analysis of the source code, multiple basic SDs are then merged into a single high-level SD that represents the overall control flow (Gueheneuc and Ziadi, 2005, p. 2-3). From the high level SD, state charts of the involved interaction roles can be generated (Gueheneuc and Ziadi, 2005, p. 3). However, Gueheneuc and Ziadi (2005) do not propose any technical details on how to merge the basic SDs and identify the interaction roles.

Lassen et al. (2007) use process mining to merge multiple basic SDs into an overall control flow model: Basic SDs stored in XMI[23] are converted into a specific MXML file that contains

---

[21]In contrast, Rubin et al. (2007) use this term for the mining of development processes.

[22]page numbers relate to the version of the article downloadable at `http://citeseerx.ist.psu.edu/viewdoc/download?doi=10.1.1.83.3347&rep=rep1&type=pdf` (last visit 2014-02-23)

[23]a common XML-based format to store and exchange UML models (Lassen et al., 2007, p. 6)

case data in the form of partial orders of message send- and receive-events (Lassen et al., 2007, pp. 6). From this log, a Petri net model is reconstructed and transformed into further notations such as EPCs (Lassen et al., 2007, pp. 9). A transformation into high level SDs (e.g. in UML 2 notation) is not intended, since this diagram type is deemed less suitable "to model the full system behaviour." (Lassen et al., 2007, p. 12).

5.3.2. Mining Message Sequence Graphs

Message Sequence Graphs (MSGs) are higher level sequence diagrams quite similar to UML interaction overview diagrams (Section 2.3.1.4). Basically, a MSG is a control flow graph that contains basic message sequence charts (MSCs, quite similar to simple UML sequence diagrams) as nodes (Kumar et al., 2011, p. 93). MSGs are thus well-suited to represent complex protocols with different "phases" (Kumar et al., 2012, p. 916) of re-occurring (basic) interaction scenarios (Kumar et al., 2011, p. 94).

Kumar et al. (2011) present an approach to reconstruct MSGs from program traces consisting of send- and receive-message events. In the first step every trace is converted into a partially-ordered dependency graph that displays the 'interaction threads' of the participating objects on the basis of send- and receive-message relations (Kumar et al., 2011, pp. 93). Next, frequent subgraphs are searched in the dependency graphs in order to identify candidate scenarios (i.e. basic MSCs) that form the nodes of the reconstructed MSG (Kumar et al., 2011, pp. 94). To avoid an "exhaustive search for [matching] graph structures", a so-called *event tail* algorithm is applied that "successively merges" appropriate subgraphs starting from single events (Kumar et al., 2011, p. 95).

On the abstracted "alphabet of basic MSCs", a grammar inference algorithm (*sk-strings*) is applied to reconstruct the superordinate control flow graph of the MSG (Kumar et al., 2011, p. 96). The resulting Mealy automaton with basic MSCs as egde labels is converted into a Moore automaton with MSCs as node labels that comes closer to the MSG notation (Kumar et al., 2011, p. 96).

Besides the work by Lou et al. (2010b) reviewed in Section 4.2.3.5, the approach by Kumar et al. (2011) is among the few reverse-engineering techniques that consider multiple instantiation patterns (Section 2.3.3). Starting from the observation that "in some systems, a process may broadcast messages to multiple processes [... and] in such scenarios, the order in which messages are sent or [...] received is usually inconsequential" Kumar et al. (2011, p. 96) introduce a so-called "oracle" into the algorithm that provides additional information about message broadcast.

For an implementation of the oracle, Kumar et al. (2010, Sec. 5) propose that "the user specifies"[24] which messages and responses belong to broadcasts. Based on this information, rules are defined to construct correct dependency graphs in the presence of broadcast messages (Kumar et al., 2010, Sec. 5):

> "The first [... rule] states that there is no dependency between two send events at the same lifeline [...], if the message being sent is [... a broadcast message] and it is being sent to different lifelines. The second [... rule] states that two receive events at a lifeline have no

---

[24] Kumar et al. (2010, Sec. 5) note that "as a future extension, such exceptions can be automatically inferred [...] from statistical analysis of traces".

dependency if they arrive from different processes and are both responses to a broadcast. The third [... rule] enforces there to be no dependency between a send of a broadcast message and the receipt of [... a] response[...] from some other process."

A drawback of the approach is that it lacks a "formal notion of roles" (Kumar et al., 2011, p. 99) such that interaction patterns are identified at the level of objects rather than classes. Kumar et al. (2012) therefore present an extension towards the mining of "class level specifications". However, different from role mining techniques in process mining (Section 4.2.4.2), Kumar et al. (2012, p. 915) assume that the "analysis has prior knowledge of the classification of concrete processes [...] obtained from either the source code [...] or an input from [the] user."

Instead, the class-level mining concentrates on the reconstruction of guards for transitions between basic scenarios in the MSG (Kumar et al., 2012, Sec. III). The authors use a technique for regular expression induction to reconstruct constraints on message types, senders, receivers, and cardinalities that determine which objects enact which basic MSCs in a message sequence graph (Kumar et al., 2012, Sec. III).

Overall, the approach by Kumar et al. (Kumar et al., 2010, 2011, 2012) appears akin to the mining of (hierarchical) process maps proposed by Li et al. (2010) and the ILP-based process mining by Lamma et al. (2007b). It also exhibits several relations to our process mining-based procedure to reconstruct higher level agent interaction protocols presented in Section 7.3. A more general similarity to this thesis is the intention by Kumar et al. (2011, p. 99) to provide a "multi-view mining framework [...] which mines [...] intra-process [...] as well as [...] inter-process style specifications".

5.3.3. Web Service and Interaction Mining

Message-based communication is an important aspect of MAS. Process mining with a similar focus is applied in the context of *inter-organizational business processes*[25]. These are often implemented with the aid of *web services*, i.e. heterogeneous, self-contained, distributed components that communicate over the World Wide Web using XML-based standard formats such as SOAP (Simple Object Access Protocol) and WSDL (Web Services Description Language); see Reichert and Stoll (2004, pp. 21-22).

5.3.3.1. Approach by Dustdar and Gombotz

In (Cabac et al., 2006b, Sec. 3.1.1), we have reviewed the multi-perspective approach by Gombotz et al. (2005) towards process mining of web service behavior:

> "In the context of *web service interaction mining*, Gombotz et al. (2005, p. 3) distinguish three perspectives that integrate aspects of control flow *and* organizational structure: The *web service operation level* deals with the internal behavior of single web services. On the *web services interaction level* the focus is on "a single web service [and ...] its direct neighbors". On the *web service workflow level* "large-scale interactions and collaborations" are observed, "which together form an entire workflow" (Gombotz et al., 2005)."

---

[25]for an overview of this research field see e.g. Legner and Wende (2007)

Practical work is reported on the levels of interactions and workflows. As summarized in (Cabac et al., 2006b, Sec. 3.1.2):

> "[The] mining result[... on the interaction level] is a so-called *web service interaction graph* representing the relations of a particular web service and its neighbors. Compared to UML style interaction diagrams (see e.g. Jeckle et al., 2002), the interaction graph is closer to a *communication diagram* than to a *sequence diagram*, since it does not focus on interaction control flow."

The development of mining procedures for the workflow level is guided by the identification of 5 increasingly detailed log levels: These range from standard web server logs that record timestamps, requesting IP addresses, and requested URLs (level 1) to detailed logs that provide information on SOAP message content and workflow-related data like case and schema identifiers (level 5); see Dustdar and Gombotz (2006, Sec. 3). Dustdar and Gombotz (2006, Sec. 4) show that level 5 logs can be straightforwardly converted to MXML and mined using *ProM*.

Since level 5 logs are seldom found in practice (Dustdar and Gombotz, 2006, p. 261), a concept for process mining in the absence of workflow-related information is presented as well (Dustdar and Gombotz, 2006, Sec. 6): The main phases of the procedure are (1) reconstruction of sessions by aggregation of messages that belong to the same case, (2) similarity assessment of reconstructed sessions to validate the results of step 1 and to identify sessions belonging to the same workflow, and (3) process mining on the preprocessed logs.

To reconstruct sessions from server logs, Dustdar and Gombotz (2006, p. 263) propose to use either "temporal information" or key events like calls to a login service. Temporal session reconstruction is based on estimated parameters like minimum time between messages and maximum session duration (Dustdar and Gombotz, 2006, p. 263). For similarity assessment, Dustdar and Gombotz (2006, pp. 263-264) mention several measures including (1) session duration and size, (2) type, number, and order of consumed services, (3) initial and final services called, (4) common message parameters, and (5) frequent control flow patterns. The authors note that the latter must also account for advanced constructs like concurrency and cycles (Dustdar and Gombotz, 2006, p. 264).

5.3.3.2. Approach by Schütt

Schütt (2003) presents the software prototype *FuzFlow* for interaction mining and control flow prediction of inter-organizational workflows. Similar to Dustdar and Gombotz (2006), he assumes that the provided log contains raw messages without explicit session information. Thus, sessions must be reconstructed by data mining. Different from Dustdar and Gombotz (2006), Schütt (2003) requires that all analyzed sessions are of the same type.

The main processing pipeline is shown in Figure 5.12: The simulator creates example logs based on user-defined message types and sequence patterns (Schütt, 2003, p. 96). Message aggregation is realized by clustering messages with similar values of content attributes (Schütt, 2003, pp. 47). Process mining is performed with the (first part of the) two-step algorithm described in Section 4.2.3.3. Subsequently, the branching points of the mined process model are enriched with conditions discovered from message attributes by fuzzy rule mining. The

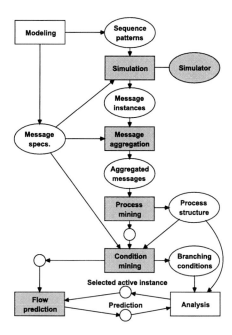

Figure 5.12.: Interaction mining procedure and architecture by Schütt (2003) displayed as a Petri net. Components mentioned in the text are shaded grey. Adopted with modifications from (Schütt, 2003, p. 99).

resulting model is considered to predict the future control flow of selected running process instances. In Section 7.2, we use the approach by Schütt (2003) as a starting point to mine agent interaction protocols.

5.3.3.3. Artifact-Centric Process Mining

Proclets are an extension of Petri nets that support an *artifact-centric* view upon workflow modeling (Fahland et al., 2011a, p. 39): This paradigm focuses on data objects (documents, orders, etc.) involved in the execution of a business process. It is strongly influenced by relational database constructs like entities, relations, and cardinalities. Extending the relational paradigm, the life cycle of each entity type is represented by an own Petri net (proclet) that interacts with other proclets over *ports* connected by *channels* (see Figure 5.13).

A proclet is formalized as a tuple $P = (N, Ports)$ where N is a labelled Petri net (Fahland et al., 2011a, p. 40). Ports $p \in Ports$ are tuples $p = (T_p, dir, card, mult)$ with the following components (Fahland et al., 2011a, pp. 40; Fahland et al., 2011b, p. 3):[26]

- The direction $dir \in \{in, out\}$ indicates an input or output port.

---

[26] page numbers from (Fahland et al., 2011b) relate to the version downloadable at `http://ceur-ws.org/Vol-705/paper1.pdf` (last visit 2012-10-13)

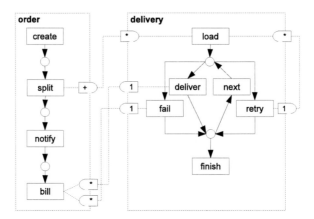

Figure 5.13.: An example proclet system modeling the delivery of orders by a transport vehicle. Adopted from Fahland et al. (2011b, p. 2). Input and output ports are only inscribed with cardinalities here.

- A set of transitions $T_p \subseteq T$ is connected to the port. In case of an output port, the firing of a transition $t_p \in T_p$ triggers p to send one or more messages. For an input port, t_p will only be enabled if p receives messages.

- The cardinality $card \in \{1, +, *\}$ determines how many messages are sent or received when port p is triggered (exactly one, at least one, or an arbitrary number).

- The multiplicity $mult \in \{1, +, *\}$ specifies how often p is triggered during the lifetime of the proclet.

Multiple proclets form a proclet system $PS = (\{P_1, \ldots, P_n\}, C)$ where C is a set of channels, each connecting an input and output port (Fahland et al., 2011a, pp. 40). Similar to reference nets and agent-based modeling, proclets are a means to reduce the complexity of workflow models by providing additional structure. This expressiveness also leads to new requirements and possibilities for process mining and conformance checking.

Conformance Checking of Proclet Systems Fahland et al. (2011a) present an approach towards conformance checking of proclet systems. Since replaying the log of a whole system at once is considered as computationally expensive, the work focuses on the sub-problems of behavioral and interaction conformance (Fahland et al., 2011a, pp. 42).

Behavioral conformance is simply assessed by splitting the log into sub-logs for each entity type and removing all ports from the corresponding proclets. Then standard log replay-based conformance checking (see Section 4.2.5.4) can be used, but all interaction-related information is lost (Fahland et al., 2011a, p. 43).

Interaction conformance is based on an "instance-aware log" (Fahland et al., 2011a, p. 46). This log contains entries $e = (a, id, SID, RID)$, where a is an action, id is the acting entity's identifier, and the sets SID and RID contain identifiers of entities that entity id sent messages to or received messages from during the execution of a (Fahland et al., 2011a, p. 46). After merging related send and receive events of communication peers into the log of the considered entity type, interaction conformance can be checked (Fahland et al., 2011a, p. 46-47).

To enable conformance checking of port cardinalities and multiplicities, a concise execution semantic for ports is defined by a mapping to *inhibitor-reset nets* (Fahland et al., 2011c, p. 26). These are Petri nets that contain inhibitor and reset arcs like e.g. reference nets (see Section 2.3.2.5). Fahland et al. (2011c, pp. 29-30) show how all combinations of port types, cardinalities, and multiplicities can be mapped to corresponding 'net components'[27] checked during log replay.

Discovery of Proclet Systems Only recently, initial effort has been made to reconstruct proclet systems from instance-aware logs. In this context, the following subtasks have been approached so far:

- A *ProM* plugin was developed for the log-based reconstruction of Entity/Relationship (E/R) diagrams as the predominant structural model of the artifact-centric view (see Popova et al., 2012, Sec. 2 and Canbaz, 2011, pp. 83,145).

- Popova and Dumas (2012, p. 1) "propose a method for translating Petri Net models into GSM [Guard-Stage-Milestone models] which gives the possibility to use the numerous existing algorithms for mining Petri Nets for discovering the life cycles of single artifacts and then generating GSM models." These represent a specific "meta-model [...] for artifact life cycles which is more declarative and supports hierarchy and parallelism within a single artifact instance." (Popova and Dumas, 2012, p. 1)

- Kikas (2011) presents an algorithm to automatically map event types found in a database to action labels of a corresponding proclet system by comparing their *behavioral profiles* of precedence relations. This is needed in the context of conformance checking, since the labels found in models and databases often differ in practice (Kikas, 2011, p. 20).

- Canbaz (2011) reconstructs the control and interaction flow of proclets as well as statistics related to cardinalities of ports from event and message logs stored in a database.

The latter two approaches are (especially in combination) very similar to our procedure to mine complex agent interaction protocols (Section 7.3) and its simple implementation to analyze our courier service model (Section 8.3.2.2). While our implementation was already influenced by the idea of instance-aware logs in (Fahland et al., 2011b), a first concept was drafted considerably earlier than process mining for proclet systems (see Knaak, 2007).

An important characteristic that both approaches share with our concept is the separate mining of inter- and intra-entity relations, where the latter are reconstructed by a pairwise comparison of logs for all entity types. Similar to one aspect of our work, Canbaz (2011, Chs. 5, 6) concentrates on collecting message statistics to reconstruct cardinalities. Similar to another aspect, Kikas (2011, Ch. 4) uses strict and interleaving order relations as proposed by Weidlich et al. (2009)[28] to reconstruct intra- and inter-entity precedences in the presence of multiply instantiated behavior threads.

---

[27]as to use the term by Cabac et al. (2003)
[28]cited in (Kikas, 2011, p. 11)

A further comparison and discussion of possibilities to merge both lines of work is given in Section 7.3. In doing so, we also broach the issue of conceptual similarities and differences between artifact-centric and agent-based modeling.

Research on artifact-centric process mining is currently continued as part of the funded EU project ACSI[29] (Artifact Centric Service Operation). According to Popova et al. (2012, p. 43), especially "the interaction aspect of the artifact model will be addressed in [the upcoming] year three of this project. This will allow to discover how artifacts and their instances relate to and communicate with each other [...]". This topic is closely related to agent-oriented process mining as discussed in this thesis.

5.3.3.4. Further Work on Web Service Mining

Early work on interaction mining in service-oriented environments was carried out by Srinivasa and Spiliopoulou (2000). These authors assume that messages in the analyzed log can simply be assigned to conversations (called interaction entities) by a unique identifier. However, since the log might contain interaction entities of different types, clustering of similarly structured entities must be performed.

For this purpose, each interaction entity "is represented by a directed graph structure, where nodes correspond to services and edges correspond to recorded transactions between services" (Srinivasa and Spiliopoulou, 2000, p. 282). The similarity between two interaction entities is expressed by the relative "overlap" of nodes and edges in their graphs $G_1 = (V_1, E_1)$ and $G_2 = (V_2, E_2)$ (Srinivasa and Spiliopoulou, 2000, p. 282):

$$overlap(G_1, G_2) = \frac{|V_1 \cap V_2| + |E_1 \cap E_2|}{|V_1 \cup V_2| + |E_1 \cup E_2|}. \tag{5.4}$$

After clustering, a state machine is reconstructed from each cluster using grammatical inference to display the generalized control flow of the corresponding interaction entity type (Srinivasa and Spiliopoulou, 2000, p. 282). Similar to the work by Vigueras and Botia (2008), message precedences are detected on the basis of logical clocks (Srinivasa and Spiliopoulou, 2000, p. 281). Srinivasa and Spiliopoulou (1999) also present a query language to retrieve "interesting" interaction entities from a database using a regular expression-like pattern syntax.

Musaraj et al. (2010) focus on message correlation and protocol mining without predefined assignment of messages to conversations. Their approach is based on a representation of protocol automata by linear equations, where each state corresponds to one equation with labels of incoming and outgoing transitions as positive and negative terms (Musaraj et al., 2010, p. 262). The equations are learned from the interaction log by linear regression (Musaraj et al., 2010, pp. 262) and converted into an automaton for display (Musaraj et al., 2010, p. 264).

Motahari-Nezhad et al. (2011) perform message correlation in web service logs based on multiple conditions. As summarized by Musaraj et al. (2010, p. 265), these authors distinguish between *key-based correlation*, where messages are aggregated by common attribute values, and *reference-based correlation*, where messages are chained by mutual references (Motahari-Nezhad et al., 2011, p. 424). Algorithms are presented to identify appropriate composite conditions

---

[29]http://www.acsi-project.eu, last visit 2012-01-17.

for message correlation and to reconstruct a hierarchical process model ("process space") on this basis (Motahari-Nezhad et al., 2011, Sec. 3).

For further literature on web service and interaction mining, the reader is e.g. referred to the reviews of related work by Musaraj et al. (2010, Sec. 6) and Motahari-Nezhad et al. (2011, Sec. 7).

5.3.4. Process Mining for Agents and Simulation

Despite the use of process mining and related techniques in many domains, applications to simulation and MAS are still not common. Before presenting a conceptual framework for this endeavor in Section 6, we review existing case studies from the literature.

5.3.4.1. Process Mining and Simulation

An early application of a process mining-like analysis to a discrete event simulation is reported by Tolujew (1999, p. 130): Traces of transaction-oriented (Section 2.2.2) queueing network simulations are aggregated into graphs that depict routes of transactions and state transitions of resources. Different from process mining, no generalization of the observed behavior is performed.

Rozinat et al. (2009d) and Wynn et al. (2010) present a 'roundtrip-engineering'-cycle for business process simulation and analysis centered around the software systems *CPNTools* and *ProM* (see Figure 5.14). As a starting point, a log and partial models from a workflow management system based on the modeling language *YAWL*[30] are imported into *ProM*. Models and mining results from the control flow, organizational, data, and performance perspectives (i.e. a Petri net, a role model, a set of branching conditions, and performance statistics) are then semi-automatically merged into an executable simulation model represented as a colored Petri net.

This net is simulated in *CPNTools* to analyze its behavior in different scenarios beyond the observed log. During the simulation, a new log is written that can again be mined with *ProM*. A conversion of the mining result back to *YAWL* allows a 're-import' into the real workflow system. Wynn et al. (2010, p. 454) emphasize that a main advantage of their approach lies in the possibility to apply the same analysis techniques (i.e. process mining) to data collected from the model and the real system.

To integrate the perspectives of control flow, data, and performance into a single executable model, Zhang et al. (2010) propose to use *event graphs* as target models in process mining. These are a common modeling formalism in event-scheduling simulation originally developed by Schruben (1983).[31] Process mining is simplified by the fact that event graphs do not contain complex control flow constructs (including concurrency) like Petri nets (Zhang et al., 2010, p. 134). The approach is experimentally evaluated at the example of a simple event-oriented manufacturing simulation (Zhang et al., 2010, Sec. 4).

---

[30]Yet Another Workflow Language, see http://www.yawlfoundation.org (also cited in Hofstede et al., 2010; last visit 2012-10-13)

[31]cited in Zhang et al. (2010, p. 132)

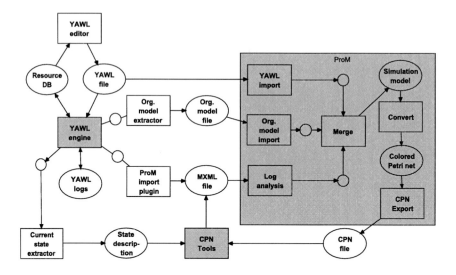

Figure 5.14.: Toolset of the 'roundtrip-engineering' approach by Wynn et al. (2010). Adopted with modifications from (Wynn et al., 2010, p. 446).

Sunindyo and Biffl (2011) use the α-algorithm in the context of simulation-based analysis of a production system. Dolean and Petrusel (2011) present an approach towards mining and conformance checking of decision processes represented in the form of *decision data models* (DDMs) based on logs of decision-support systems. DDMs are directed, acyclic graphs that depict the influence of decision variables to intermediate and final decisions, somehow similar to Bayesian networks (Dolean and Petrusel, 2011, p. 83). While the 'decision support' provided by the example software is restricted to simple 'financial' calculations, an integration of the techniques into a real decision support system, e.g. based on simulation, should be possible (Petrusel, 2012, p. 62).

5.3.4.2. Case Studies by the Eindhoven Research Group

To the knowledge of the author, the Eindhoven group has so far applied process mining (PM) and the tool *ProM* to MA(B)S in two case studies. Both examples are reviewed in the following and discussed with respect to the objectives of the thesis at hand.

Process Mining in a Multi-Agent Auctioning Simulation   Similar to our work, Dongen et al. (2006b, p. 1)[32] promote the idea of combining PM and MABS in order to (1) gain a better understanding of the complex simulations' behavior and (2) provide agents with enhanced 'intelligence' and adaptivity.

---

[32] page numbers refer to the version of the article downloadable at `http://www.win.tue.nl/`
`~hverbeek/downloads/preprints/Dongen06.pdf` (last visit 2012-10-13)

The authors use several PM techniques in order to analyze different aspects of a multi-agent auctioning simulation; namely control flow mining, decision tree mining, and LTL trace checking (Dongen et al., 2006b, Secs. 1.4.2-1.4.4). Interestingly, the latter is not used to verify properties of traces but to perform output aggregations similar to trace-based output analysis in simulation (see Section 2.4.2).

Another interesting aspect of this work is that the authors present a quite realistic case study that shows the utility of PM for MABS analysis. They use the advantage of simulation (compared to real-world MAS) that the data can be 'tailored' to fit the requirements of the mining algorithms. This becomes obvious in the insertion of data fields into the observed messages for decision mining and in an application-dependent log segmentation based on knowledge about which events start and finish a conversation (Dongen et al., 2006b, Sec. 1.4.1).

However, the analysis is restricted to properties of single agents rather than relations between multiple agents. The authors also give no hint how the auctioneer agent (that performs the process mining in the example) can technically interpret the control flow and decision models learned from the observation of other agents. In general, the article does not discuss agent- or simulation-specific requirements on process mining in detail. Though Dongen et al. (2006b, p. 2) regard MABS as a natural example to show the interplay between different PM techniques, the potential of MAS as a concept to structure the different mining perspectives and tasks is not made explicit. We will further discuss this potential in Chapter 6.

Process Mining in Robot Soccer Rozinat et al. (2009d) apply process mining to the analysis of "activity logs" (Rozinat et al., 2009d, p. 5)[33] from robot soccer games in *Robo Cup*. The objective is to improve team performance by means of "self-analysis [... and] opponent analysis", which are considered technically equivalent (Rozinat et al., 2009d, p. 2). Similar to the work by Nair et al. (2004) reviewed in Section 5.2.2.2, multiple perspectives are analyzed, i.e. individual robot behavior, team behavior, and team decisions (Rozinat et al., 2009d, Sec. 5).

The main difference of the two behavioral perspectives consists in the aggregation level of the logs imported into the MXML format (Rozinat et al., 2009d, pp. 6): In the individual perspective, activities are defined by roles that a robot adopts during its life cycle (e.g. *DefendCircle* or *PositionForPass*), and cases correspond to the behavior of a single robot during a game. In the team perspective, activities are combinations of roles that the 4 outfield players of a team adopt during a game. To reduce the huge amount of observed log data, repetitive behavior (i.e. a robot or a team adopts the same role or combination of roles in subsequent steps) is eliminated (Rozinat et al., 2009d, pp. 6).

To analyze robot and team behavior, Rozinat et al. (2009d, p. 7) reconstruct control flow models from both logs with the *Heuristics Miner* algorithm (see Section 4.2.3.4). The resulting model in the team perspective is additionally enriched with branching conditions mined from event attributes related to specific situations such as kick-offs or free kicks (Rozinat et al., 2009d, pp. 8). This analysis allows to identify and validate conditions that lead to specific team formations (Rozinat et al., 2009d, p. 9). Rozinat et al. (2009d, p. 9) further propose to support the validation of robot teams with LTL checking.

---

[33]page numbers refer to the version of the article downloadable at `http://szickler.net/index.php ?sid1=245&session=` (last visit 2012-10-13)

5.3.4.3. Experiments Using Grammar Inference

Grammar inference has occasionally been applied to the analysis of agent behavior and interaction protocols. In (Cabac et al., 2006b,c) we mentioned a few examples:

> "Mounier et al. (2003) present an approach towards *agent conversation mining* using stochastic[...] grammar inference. Mining results are represented as a stochastic automaton whose edges are labelled with message performatives. The approach neglects concurrency and interaction roles. Hiel (2005) applies extended Hidden Markov Models [... to reconstruct agent interaction protocols including dependencies between distant choice nodes]; also neglecting the aforementioned aspects. However, he suggests to improve the reconstruction of (concurrent) protocols by process mining techniques as a possible direction for future research." (Cabac et al., 2006c, p. 15)

> "Barber and Lam (2003) also propose a simple grammar inference algorithm to reconstruct models of a single agent's behaviour. However, in the continuation of this work [... see Section 5.2.4.2], they turn to more agent-specific models representing causal relations between concepts from the well-known *BDI* architecture [...]" (Cabac et al., 2006b, Sec. 3.2)

5.3.4.4. Declarative Process Mining of Agent Protocols

Lamma et al. (2007b, p. 132) use inductive logic programming (ILP, see Section 4.1.4.3) to reconstruct rule-based "integrity constraints" formulated in the temporal logic *SCIFF* from message logs of agent interaction protocols. Their examples show that different from typical control flow discovery algorithms, the approach allows to detect deadlines and precedences in protocols with multicast communication (Lamma et al., 2007b, pp. 138). The reconstructed rules can be converted into the graphical notations *DecSerFlow* and *ConDec* for declarative process modelling (Lamma et al., 2007a).

On the downside, the ILP-based algorithm requires negative examples (Lamma et al., 2007b, p. 133) and considerable predefined background knowledge about the structure of the reconstructed rules (Lamma et al., 2007b, p. 142). Different from control flow mining, the result does not display the overall course of a protocol but constraints on its execution like "the auctioneer can not answer both *win* and *loose* to the same bidder" (Lamma et al., 2007b, p. 139). Another drawback is the "high computational cost" of the algorithm (Lamma et al., 2007b, p. 143).

Further work on declarative process mining includes probabilistic (Bellodi et al., 2010) and incremental (Cattafi et al., 2010) variants of the mining algorithm as well as trace checking based of models specified in *ConDec* and *SCIFF* (Montali et al., 2008). The declarative process mining and conformance checking techniques were implemented as plugins for the *ProM* framework.

Later articles on process discovery and conformance checking by this group of authors were also published in the context of the *ACSI* project (see Section 5.3.3.3) on artifact centric modeling[34] (e.g. Maggi et al., 2012) and on the topic of agent-based simulation (Chesani et al., 2011).

---

[34]see http://www.acsi-project.eu/deliverables/ACSI-D6.3.2-V1.0.pdf (last visit 2012-10-14)

5.3.4.5. Petri Net-Based Process Mining in MAS

As advocated in this thesis, process mining fits the context of Petri net-based MAS modeling well due to the common formal foundation (Cabac et al., 2006b). Examples for the combined application of Petri nets and process mining (or related) techniques to the modeling and analysis of MAS are also found in the literature.

Multi-Agent Process Mining Based on Petri Nets Winarjo (2009) and Ou-Yang and Juan (2010) use process mining and Petri nets for the validation of MAS: First, a Petri net model of an agent interaction protocol is mined from a message log collected with the JADE platform's *Sniffer* tool (Section 3.4.1). A modified variant of the α algorithm is used, which constructs additional 'message' places to link send- and receive-events in control flow models of distinct agents. Since the algorithm does not abstract from agents to roles, every individual agent's behavior is represented by an own Petri net.

In the second step, the reconstructed Petri net is exported to *CPNTools* for simulation and formal analysis. In (Ou-Yang and Juan, 2010), the analysis focuses on the detection of potential deadlocks. Note that, given the preconditions stated in Section 4.2.3.1, the standard α algorithm always returns a *sound* WF net, which only 'deadlocks' on proper completion in the output place (Aalst, 2011a, p. 127). As shown in an example by Ou-Yang and Juan (2010, p. 144), the possibility for further deadlocks is introduced by coupling multiple agents' WF nets via message places.

Data and Process Mining in the TAL Approach In the context of the Petri net-based MABS approach developed at Groningen University's *The Agent Lab* (TAL), Meyer and Szirbik (2007) present a technique for automated behavior alignment in agent interactions. As explained in Section 3.3.3.5, agents in this model are equipped with interaction beliefs that represent the assumed course of an interaction protocol in the form of behavior nets. When the assumptions fail, an interaction cannot proceed properly and user-intervention is required.

Meyer and Szirbik (2007) assume that interventions consist in modifications of behavior nets involved in the failing interaction. To automate interventions, fixed sets of possible failure diagnoses, e.g. "an unknown message is received" (Meyer and Szirbik, 2007, p. 277), and "alignment policies" (Meyer and Szirbik, 2007, p. 278), e.g. "delete[...] an outgoing message place" (Meyer and Szirbik, 2007, p. 275), are defined. A mapping between both sets is learned by an artificial neural network (ANN, see Section 4.1.4.5).

In the training phase, failures during the execution of behavior nets are logged and resolved by a user applying appropriate alignment policies. In the productive phase, the trained ANN takes the place of the user and attempts to resolve failures automatically. If an interaction keeps failing, the user must again intervene and the ANN is retrained.

In the same line of work, Stuit and Wortmann (2012) reconstruct interaction structure (IS) diagrams from e-mail conversations spanning multiple threads. Different from most process mining techniques, no generalization is performed; hence the resulting model only represents the partial order of observed e-mail threads. To enrich the IS diagram with interaction roles (instead of particular senders and receivers), predefined organizational models are consulted; i.e. there is no 'role mining' in the sense of Section 4.2.4.2.

Further Work on Petri Nets and Process Mining in MAS   In an early approach by Poutakidis et al. (2002), interaction protocols specified in AUML are mapped to labelled P/T nets. These nets are used by a debugging agent to automatically detect protocol violations based on the observation of message traffic on a FIPA-compliant agent platform. The authors assume that the observed messages contain unique identifiers for conversations (Poutakidis et al., 2002, p. 962), but not for protocol types (Poutakidis et al., 2002, p. 964).

Therefore the debugging agent instantiates a net for *every* known protocol when a new conversation is started on the platform (Poutakidis et al., 2002, p. 964): During the conversation, transitions of all net instances matching the received messages are fired, while nonconforming nets are dropped. This procedure repeats until either a net instance completes successfully or all net instances have been dropped, thus indicating an invalid message sequence.

Mazouzi et al. (2002) present a similar approach based on a transformation of AUML interaction diagrams to colored Petri nets. As summarized by Mounier et al. (2003, p. 159), the proposed system identifies protocol types by comparing causal graphs derived from the observed messages with causal graphs of known protocol types.

Different from the work by Poutakidis et al. (2002), the system can even distinguish between protocols that only differ in the concurrent or sequential occurrence of certain events due to the use of partial order semantics (Mazouzi et al., 2002, p. 522) and tagging of messages with logical clocks (Mazouzi et al., 2002, p. 521). In contrast to grammar inference or process mining, the reconstructed causal graphs are dropped after identifying the predefined protocol (Mounier et al., 2003, p. 159). Nevertheless, Mazouzi et al. (2002, p. 525) name interaction protocol learning as a direction for future work.

In the context of *Socionics*, Martens (2002, p. 137) proposes to integrate process mining into Petri net agent platforms based on the MULAN architecture:

> "By adopting a meta-level and recording all performatives sent on a platform, process mining allows to derive novel processes, which are not realized by single agents but only emerge from a conversation of multiple agents. [...] These [processes] could be facilitated on every platform to provide foreign agents with information about behavioral norms [... In the context of Socionics ...] such information can be understood as an *organizational memory* [...]"

As a first step, Martens (2002, p. 156) shows a simple reference net-based service to collect information from messages sent on the platform. A further prototypical integration of process mining into the MULAN agent platform is realized in Section 7 of this thesis.

5.3.4.6. Organizational Process Mining in MAS

A close relation exists between agent concepts and the organizational perspective of process mining (Section 4.2.4). Though most work on organizational process mining seems to adopt a 'MAS-like' view in an *ad-hoc* manner, only few examples for an explicit integration can be found in the literature. In Section 5.3.1 we already mentioned the work by Christley and Madey (2007b) who combine static and dynamic social network analysis and MABS to analyze open source software development processes.

Beyond that, Vanderfeesten (2006) evaluates data mining and conformance validation techniques with respect to their ability to identify roles of agents in MAS. The underlying idea is similar to the organizational model mining technique by Song and Aalst (2008) (see Section 4.2.4.2): Roles are identified by considering agents' characteristic 'profiles' of actions (in this case sending and reception of message performatives) or state transitions. The approach is exemplified by role detection in the contract net protocol.

Hanachi and Khaloul (2008, p. 93) argue that agent concepts like speech acts and interaction protocols can add to the organizational perspective of process mining. The authors provide a classification of organizational structures (Hanachi and Khaloul, 2008, pp. 96) and show that background knowledge on the semantics of message performatives (e.g. *delegate*) can aid in the identification of such structures from log data (Hanachi and Khaloul, 2008, p. 100). The approach appears related to the interaction pattern detection techniques by Dustdar and Hoffmann (2007) reviewed in Section 4.2.4.3. Hanachi and Khaloul (2008, p. 99) also state an algorithm for Petri net-based protocol matching akin to the work of Poutakidis et al. (2002) and Mazouzi et al. (2002) reviewed in Section 5.3.4.5.

Abdelkafi and Bouzguenda (2010, p. 89) present a meta-model for workflow logs that includes control flow, organizational, and informational process dimensions based on MAS-related concepts like roles and performatives. A software prototype named *DiscopFlow* is developed, that allows to identify simple organizational structures like hierarchies and federations (Abdelkafi and Bouzguenda, 2010, p. 97), verify logs against predefined interaction protocols, and display the organizational position of actors in workflows in the style of the AGR model (Abdelkafi et al., 2012, p. 4). In future work, the authors intend to discover models that integrate the control flow, organizational, and informational perspectives which are currently treated separately in *DiscopFlow* (Abdelkafi et al., 2012, p. 5).

Yilmaz (2006, Sec. 5) supports the operational validation of agent-based social simulation models with automated comparisons of real and simulated event streams using metrics based on string edit distance. Though not explicitly related to process mining, the applied techniques appear rather similar.

5.3.4.7. Further Work on Integrating Process Mining and MAS

Werner-Stark and Dulai (2010) report on the combined application of (a) the results by Rozinat et al. (2009d)[35] and (b) software development process mining in the education of engineering students. This combination practically mirrors our discussion from (Cabac and Denz, 2008, p. 90) to use MAS as an integrative concept for process mining on both the software development process and the developed software.

In a later article, Werner-Stark and Dulai (2012) report on an integration of process mining techniques into a "decision agent" (Werner-Stark and Dulai, 2012, p. 430) to support the "analysis and detection of functional faults [... in the] vehicle industry" (Werner-Stark and Dulai, 2012, p. 424).

An earlier application of (Markovian) process mining techniques to "instance-based robot programming" is reported by Wen and Ping (2005). One of the first references to process mining

---

[35]i.e. analysis of robot behavior by means of process mining, see Section 5.3.4.2

in an agent context is found in the article by Furtado and Ciarlini (2001, p. 124) on the "identification of *typical plans* adopted by agents, by analysing a *Log* registering the occurrence of events".

Sperka et al. (2013, p. 515) recently applied "the analysis of agent-based simulation outputs through process mining methods and methods for analysis of agents' behavior in order to verify [...] agent-based simulations of Business Process Management" implemented in *JADE* (see Section 3.4.1).

5.4. Scientific Workflows for Simulation and Process Mining

While not in the main focus, data flow modeling and scientific workflows play an important role in the concepts and tools to integrate process mining and MABS presented in this thesis. In this Section, we briefly review related applications of scientific workflows to simulation, process mining, or both.

5.4.1. Scientific Workflow Support for Process Mining

Interestingly, the first implementation of the α algorithm by the Eindhoven research group was provided as a Petri-net based data flow model (Aalst et al., 2002, Sec. 5). The component *MiMo* (mining module) for the Petri net simulator *ExSpect*[36] implements the α algorithm as a colored Petri net annotated with programming language expressions. This net calculates the α algorithm's ordering relations from a given execution log and constructs a Petri net on this basis. Since ExSpect supports hierarchical modeling, this *workflow log analyzer* can be embedded into a transition and coupled with an (also Petri net-based) *workflow log generator* for test-data generation or with a component to import existing logs.

The implementation of a process mining algorithm in terms of a Petri net appears reasonable for instructional purposes on the one hand, and to re-use an existing Petri net simulator as an experimentation environment on the other hand. This motivation and the inherent 'self-similarity' of the approach[37] are closely akin to our idea of using net components to support roundtrip engineering with process mining in MULAN (see Cabac and Denz, 2008 and Section 7.4.2).

The Eindhoven research group resumed their efforts towards scientific workflow support for process mining only recently. Bratosin et al. (2007, p. 2)[38] propose to distribute computation-intensive process mining workflows in a grid computing environment. Grid workflows are modelled with colored Petri nets to "clarify the basic concepts" and to support their analysis, verification, and validation (Bratosin et al., 2007, p. 2). Bratosin et al. (2007, p. 18) cite our work from (Cabac and Knaak, 2007) and present two grid workflows for process mining (Bratosin et al., 2007, pp. 12) as examples.

Also citing our work from (Cabac and Denz, 2008), Westergaard (2011, p. 335) employs the interface *Access/CPN 2.0* between *CPNTools* and *Java* to compose Petri net-based process

---

[36] `http://www.exspect.com` (last visit 2012-01-27)

[37] A Petri net implementing the α algorithm generates new nets based on the analysis of logs from observed nets.

[38] page numbers relate to the version of the article downloadable at `http://wwwis.win.tue.nl/~wvdaalst/publications/p396.pdf` (last visit 2012-10-14)

mining workflows from *ProM 6* plugins. Adopting the mechanisms for plugin selection offered by *ProM 6* (see Section 4.2.6.1), the system dynamically binds transitions to appropriate mining plugins by matching names, input, and output data types.

5.4.2. Scientific Workflow Support for Simulation

Data flow modeling is commonly used to specify models, experiments, and analyses in continuous simulation. Example systems include the commercial scientific computing environment *MATLAB / Simulink*[39] as well as the open source projects *Ptolemy II*[40] and *Kepler*[41]. However, within the discrete event modeling and simulation (M&S) community, "work on supporting workflows in M&S has just started" (Rybacki et al., 2011, p. 716).

5.4.2.1. Workflows for Modeling and Simulation

The University of Rostock investigates workflow support for discrete event simulation in the research project *MoSiFlow*.[42] The utility of workflow concepts for M&S is recognized in "features like provenance, reproducibility[,] and roles support [that] are desired to overcome the "crisis of credibility" of simulation studies [...]" (Rybacki et al., 2011, p. 716). Based on traditional model building cycles, Rybacki et al. (2010, Sec. 3) identify several use cases for workflow support and state example workflows, e.g. for operational validation (Rybacki et al., 2010, Sec. 3).

The plugin-based framework *WorMS* (Workflows for Modeling and Simulation) defines a workflow architecture that can be coupled to existing simulation systems (Rybacki et al., 2011). It consists of a workflow engine and several supplemental components, the implementations of which are bound to so-called *extension points* as exchangeable plugins similar to the OSGi/Eclipse[43] platform (Rybacki et al., 2011, p. 717). Extension points are provided for the following component types (Rybacki et al., 2011, p. 719):

- *Workflow executor*: creates and executes instances of the provided workflow models.

- *Workflow repository*: stores workflow models and instances, e.g. in a database.

- *Converter*: converts workflow models into the workflow language used by the workflow executor.

- *Security management*: handles user authentication and role-based access restrictions.

- *Data store*: allows workflow tasks to store and exchange data via a common persistent medium such as a database or a file system.

- *Monitoring*: observes the execution of workflow instances and records workflow logs in the data store.

- *Analysis*: performs static and dynamic analyses of workflows based on the stored models and execution logs.

---

[39]see http://www.mathworks.com (last visit 2012-1-30)
[40]see http://ptolemy.eecs.berkeley.edu (last visit 2012-1-30)
[41]see https://kepler-project.org (last visit 2012-1-30)
[42]see http://wwwmosi.informatik.uni-rostock.de/mosi/projects/cosa/mosiflow (last visit 2012-1-30)
[43]for explanations on OSGi and Eclipse see Section 8.4

- *Administration*: Supports the administration of workflows and user accounts.

- *Plugin provider*: Provides instances of the above components implemented on a concrete plugin platform.

Rybacki et al. (2011, Sec. 3.5) present a partial implementation of the architecture in the plugin-based MABS framework *JAMES II* using WF nets (Section 2.3.2.2) as a workflow language. While *JAMES II* already provides advanced experimentation functionality and some workflow support in the form of pre-defined assistants (Rybacki et al., 2010, p. 536), the *WorMS* architecture further increases flexibility and traceability (Rybacki et al., 2011, p. 721) by breaking the hard-wired way of "orchestrating the plugins" (Rybacki et al., 2011, p. 718) in favor of extensible workflows. In addition, Rybacki et al. (2012b) present "a set of predefined [hierarchical] workflow [net] templates" for typical simulation tasks such as validation and optimization (see also Rybacki et al., 2012a, p. 102).

The ideas of simulation workflows and plugin orchestration in the work by Rybacki et al. (2011) are rather similar to our view of process-oriented validation (Section 7.1.3) and the prototypical implementations in RENEW (Section 7.4) and *Eclipse* (Section 8.4). Providing another potential link to the subject of this thesis, Rybacki et al. (2011, p. 724) mention adaptive workflows and "analysis, interpretation [...,] and report generation from information generated by the Monitoring components and [...] their visual presentation" as future challenges. While Rybacki et al. (2011, p. 723) already visualize frequent paths taken in the execution of workflow nets, process mining might provide more advanced means to analyze simulation workflows. This idea is further discussed in Section 6.3.

Görlach et al. (2011) propose an alternative *Eclipse*-based workflow system tailored towards (grid-based) simulation. In this work, *BPEL* is used as a modeling language (Görlach et al., 2011, p. 337) and the application focus seems to be put on continuous simulation (Görlach et al., 2011, Sec. 12.4).

5.4.2.2. Previous Work at the University of Hamburg

At the University of Hamburg, the textual and visual scripting language MSL (*MOBILE* Scripting Language) was developed as part of the research project *MOBILE* (Hilty et al., 1998). It served to design component-based simulation models as well as experiment and analysis workflows in the domain of traffic simulation. The *MOBILE* project also comprised an initial study on the simulation of courier services that builds the basis for the models taken as a case study in Section 8.

Kurzbach (2007, Sec. 7) realizes workflow support for simulation by integrating RENEW as a workflow engine into the *Eclipse*-based hydrodynamic simulation system *KALYPSO*. Since both systems are implemented on different plugin platforms, the whole RENEW system is wrapped into an OSGi-compliant *Eclipse* plugin (Kurzbach, 2007, p. 77). Reference nets are employed to call simulation tasks in *KALYPSO*, remote-control the user interface, and orchestrate[44] the involved *Eclipse* plugins. The overall system architecture is based on the MAS concepts of MULAN.

---

[44]as to use the term by Rybacki et al. (2011)

In Section 8.4 of this thesis, a related idea to integrate RENEW with an *Eclipse*-based simulation system is discussed, focusing on process-oriented analysis of MABS. The concept builds upon the work by Simmendinger (2007), who re-implemented parts of the RENEW plugin system using the OSGi architecture underlying *Eclipse*. As also indicated by Kurzbach (2007, p. 77), this might allow for a closer and finer-grained integration of both toolsets (see also Simmendinger, 2007, p. 3-4).

Part II.

Concepts, Tools, and Case Studies

6. Conceptual Framework

This chapter presents a conceptual framework for the process-oriented analysis and validation of MABS. It adopts, integrates, and carries on several ideas from the literature on process mining and MA(B)S reviewed above. Pre-publications of the framework in different stages of development are provided in Cabac et al. (2006b), Knaak (2006, 2007), and Cabac and Denz (2008).

The chapter is structured as follows: After motivating and introducing the conceptual framework in Section 6.1, we present analysis perspectives and use cases as its main constituents in Sections 6.2 and 6.3. In this context, we elaborate on applicable techniques for data collection, mining, and model representation. Section 6.4 points out MAS- and simulation-specific requirements and constraints on these techniques. Finally, Section 6.5 summarizes the presented work.

6.1. Motivation and Overview

To the impression gained during the literature review, existing approaches to integrate MABS with data and process mining do not yet capture the full scope of possibilities. This includes observations on 3 levels:

1. *Methodological aspects*: On the one hand, many case studies concentrate on a single mining technique (e.g. grammar inference in Mounier et al., 2003, reviewed in Section 5.3.4.3) that is thoroughly investigated under technical aspects, but less detailed from the viewpoint of MA(B)S as an application domain. Therefore, techniques are often applied *ad-hoc* without considering a systematic integration into a validation process and utilization of the gained results within this process.[1]

   On the other hand, general methodologies to integrate data mining and MABS, like the approach by Remondino and Correndo (2005, reviewed in Section 5.2.2.3), still appear preliminary. Even more elaborate work like the approach by Arroyo et al. (2010, reviewed in Section 5.2.2.3) might be improved by explicitly integrating process- and agent-oriented mining and modeling perspectives as reviewed in the previous chapters. Conceptual frameworks for process mining like the work by Rembert and Ellis (2009) are not explicitly tailored towards agent-orientation and simulation though related ideas are often contained implicitly.

2. *Technical aspects*: Most work on the integration of data mining and MABS still concentrates on numeric and rule-based techniques, though an increasing focus on process

---

[1]Mounier et al. (2003, Sec. 3) e.g. only describe the knowledge discovery process that determines how the mining itself is performed and mention automated code generation from the mined models as a future application (Mounier et al., 2003, p. 166).

and organizational perspectives can be observed (see Chapters 4 and 5). Process mining has only recently started to consider requirements that are crucial for MA(B)S, such as complex interaction protocols, non-stationary processes, and level-encompassing relations. Simulation validation often neglects the work from the process mining community though closely related techniques are applied.

3. *Tool-related aspects*: MABS still suffers from a lack of validation tools that are applicable beyond the scope of a single modeling and simulation system. The *ACLAnalyser* by Botía et al. (2004, reviewed in Section 5.2.4.1) is a notable exception but not tailored towards simulation analysis. Despite recent improvements in the usability of the process mining tool *ProM 6* (Verbeek et al., 2011, reviewed in Section 4.2.6.1), there is still few guidance for the application of mining techniques within model building cycles. The framework *WorMS* by Rybacki et al. (2011, reviewed in Section 5.4.2.1) is a first step to utilize workflows for MABS but does not (yet) focus on data mining-supported validation.[2]

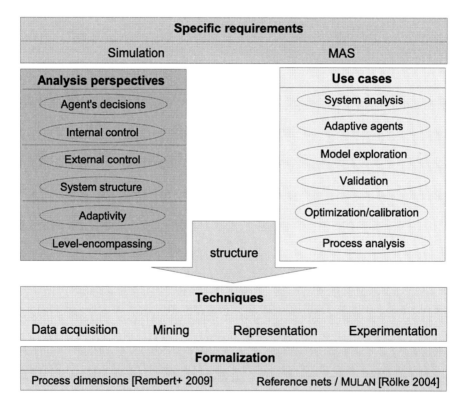

Figure 6.1.: "A Conceptual Framework for Data [and Process] Mining in MABS." Figure and caption adopted with modifications from (Knaak, 2006, Sec. 3).

---

[2]Though investigations on this subject have already been conducted within the same research group (e.g. Seib, 2008, reviewed in Section 5.2.2.7).

The literature review showed that both process mining and MABS consider modeling and analysis *perspectives* as well as *use cases* (also called tasks), either combined or in isolation, to assist the systematic application of techniques during the course of a project. By focusing on these dimensions, an integrative framework utilizes concepts that are well-understood by modeling and simulation practitioners as well as process and data mining experts.

Similar to the Eindhoven research group (see Section 4.2.2), we employ analysis perspectives and use cases to structure the available models, techniques, and data sources within an application domain. A difference lies in our main focus on MABS[3] instead of business process modeling.

Besides deviations in the identified perspectives and use cases, this difference becomes manifest in our investigation of simulation and MAS-specific requirements and constraints for the application of mining techniques within MABS analysis in Section 6.4. Since we regard data mining (especially in the form of process mining) as a valuable addition to the "eclectic" (Kleindorfer and Ganeshan, 1993, p. 50, reviewed in Section 2.4.3) portfolio of validation techniques, we must also consider its integration with existing techniques for simulation modeling, experimentation, and analysis. Note that Aalst et al. (2012, p. 190-191) regard the combination of "process mining with other types of analysis [including] operations research, [...] queueing models, [...] simulation [,...] data mining [..., and] visual analytics" as a relevant challenge for future research.

By merging the above constituents and by abstracting from the diverse perspectives, use cases, and requirements found in the literature review, we arrive at the overview diagram depicted in Figure 6.1. Though our framework is tailored towards MABS, we argue, in line with authors like Hanachi and Khaloul (2008, reviewed in Section 5.3.4.6), that an agent-oriented world view can also add to process mining in general. This is due to the close relation of process mining's main application fields, i.e. business process management and software engineering, to MAS as a modeling metaphor (see e.g. Reese, 2009).

6.2. Analysis Perspectives

There is wide consensus in the literature that perspectives (also referred to as *views*) are a common means to reduce the complexity of a target system in simulation, software engineering, and business process modeling: By observing a complex system from multiple complementary viewpoints and by applying a well-proven structure to the observations, modeling becomes tractable in the first place (see e.g. Bass et al., 2012, p. 9).

Taking into account the general advantages of data mining as a validation technique for MABS (Section 5.2), we specifically focus on process mining in this thesis for the main reason already indicated in Section 4.2.1 (see also Aalst et al., 2012, p. 176): *Different from other subfields of data mining, process mining is led by a number of explicitly defined and partly formalized analysis perspectives, closely related to those considered in agent-based modeling.*

In the literature review, we encountered the concept of perspectives in several contexts including the modeling frameworks of UML, MULAN, and TALL (Section 3.3), the process mining perspectives by Rembert and Ellis (2009), the Eindhoven research group (Section 4.2.2.1), and Dustdar and Gombotz (2006, reviewed in Section 5.3.3.1) as well as the MAS debugging approach by Ndumu and Nwana (1999, reviewed in Section 5.1.1.4) and the data mining-based

---

[3]which the Eindhoven research group only covers in few case studies, see Section 5.3.4.2

analysis assistant by Nair et al. (2004, reviewed in Section 5.2.2.2). By integrating the most frequently mentioned perspectives from process mining and MA(B)S, one might arrive at the diagram shown in Figure 6.2. Naturally, this selection of perspectives is highly subjective. However, in the following discussions and case studies we will argue why it might nevertheless be reasonable and useful.

	Perspective	Process dimensions	Mining techniques
Micro	Decisions	signals, state, actions > rules	decision tree mining
	Internal control	activities, times, internal signals, (KB state) > plans	control flow mining
Macro	External control	actions / activities, times, messages, cardinalities, roles > protocols, workflows	control flow mining, role mining, task assignment, ...
	Structure	agents, roles, groups, tasks > topologies (grids, graphs)	clustering, SOM, role / social network mining
Meta	Adaptivity	model sequences > models	change mining
	Level-encompassing	micro / macro entities > rules	association rule mining
	Domain	data > ontologies, annotations	ont. mining, extension

Figure 6.2.: Overview of analysis perspectives for MABS. Based on Ndumu and Nwana (1999), Nair et al. (2004), Aalst (e.g. 2011a), Günther et al. (2006), Dustdar and Gombotz (2006), UML (e.g. Jeckle et al., 2002), and several other sources.

The model shown in Figure 6.2 consists of six perspectives grouped into three categories. The fourth category of *domain-specific perspectives* is introduced to ensure the framework's extensibility and adaptability to different application domains. The first two categories mirror the typically opposed system views from MAS, i.e. microscopic vs. macroscopic perspectives. In the *microscopic perspectives*, we consider elementary agents as structurally indivisible entities. The analysis is therefore focused on agents' instantaneous decisions (*decision perspective*), temporally extended internal control flow (*internal control perspective*), and the relations between both (see e.g. the approach by Nair et al. (2004) reviewed in Section 5.2.2.2).

The *macroscopic perspectives* mirror the common dualism of structure and behavior (Section 2.1), as e.g. manifested in the UML meta-model (see Section 2.3.1.1). We therefore consider the perspectives of *system structure, external (i.e. interaction) control* flow, as well as their integration (e.g. "interaction flow"[4] between roles). Again, the temporal dimension is neglected in the structural perspective but central to the external control perspective.

Note that we intentionally omit structural aspects[5] at the microscopic level as well as additional 'mesoscopic' perspectives. This is due to the hierarchical view adopted from the MULAN model

---

[4]adopting the term from Yu et al. (2010)
[5]except for control flow structures composed of multiple elementary activities

(see Rölke, 2004, pp. 181 and Section 3.3.3.1) that a non-elementary agent (or mesoscopic entity) forms a MAS itself and can therefore be analyzed by taking up the macroscopic perspectives of structure and external control flow.

The *meta perspectives* are typical for MAS and often neglected in process mining (except for recent work on change mining (Günther et al., 2006) and concept drift (Bose et al., 2011a) reviewed in Section 4.2.5.3). As the name indicates, the purpose is to describe *relations between models specified in terms of the former perspectives*. In the *adaptivity perspective*, the relations span over the temporal dimension, i.e. we focus on structural and second order dynamics as typically found in adaptive agents and self-organizing MAS. In the *level-encompassing perspective* the relations span over multiple levels, i.e. we are interested in the analysis of inter-level dependencies as e.g. treated in the work by Chen et al. (2010, reviewed in Section 5.2.2.4).

Due to the generality and diversity of the agent metaphor, a general framework for the analysis of MA(B)S can (to the author's impression) not include domain-specific aspects in the first place. To nevertheless ensure its practical utility, we foresee an 'extension point'[6] of *domain specific perspectives* based on the process mining task of extension (see e.g. Aalst, 2011a, p. 10 and Section 4.2.5.5): Models mined in the 6 above perspectives can be extended or enriched to assign further domain specific meaning to their elements (e.g. performance-related extensions as in the approach by Hornix (2007) in Section 4.2.5.5).

In the following, the agent-oriented process mining perspectives are described in larger detail. While we do not provide a formalized model, we will follow the approach by Rembert and Ellis (2009, reviewed in Section 4.2.2.1) and state relevant process dimensions and some dimensional mappings to clarify the meaning and scope of several perspectives.

6.2.1. Decision Perspective

The decision perspective is frequently mentioned in work on both process mining and MAS analysis. It is also part of some multi-perspective approaches: e.g. the *single agent model* in the framework by Nair et al. (2004) and the *data perspective* in process mining (e.g. Aalst, 2006, p. 4). The term 'decision perspective' is also used by Rembert and Ellis (2009, p. 37) to describe the work by Rozinat and Aalst (2006). In (Cabac et al., 2006b, Sec. 4.2), we briefly characterized the decision perspective as follows:

> "This perspective is concerned with analyzing the rules that a single agent's decisions are based on; i.e. the question "how does the agent map observations to actions." In doing so, temporal aspects are often neglected; i.e. the agent's behavior is analyzed in a certain situation without taking into account the history leading to this situation."

6.2.1.1. Process Dimensions of the Decision Perspective

As indicated in Figure 6.2, the main process dimensions considered in the decision perspective are in accordance with rule-based agent models as e.g. described by Wooldridge (2003, pp. 50). Given an agent (type) ag and an environment e, the relevant process dimensions include:

---

[6]borrowing the software engineering term from the *Eclipse* framework

- *internal state variables* V_{ag} of the agent (type) ag,

- *external state variables* V_e of the environment observable to ag, often conveyed via a set of *signals* (or messages) S_{ag}, and

- a set of *actions* A_{ag} that the agent (type) ag can execute in reaction to its observations.

For process mining, the values of the variables are logged as preconditions together with the actions performed by the agents.[7] Note that all elements are tagged with the subscript ag above to identify the owning agent instance or type in the log of the MAS. In practice, each log entry will be tagged with an originator identifier as in MXML. The respective focus on agent instances or types depends on the purpose of the analysis, i.e. whether one is interested in a generalized decision model for a class of similar agents or in decision models of individual agents.

The dimensional mappings to be established are decision models that map (combinations of) signals and state variables to actions. As a simple example, we assume an agent type ag with a set of state variables $V_{ag} = \{v_{ag,1}, ...v_{ag,n}\}$ that processes one received signal $s \in S$ per time instant and reacts with a single action $a \in A_{ag}$. This setting is e.g. typical in discrete event simulations with our framework *FAMOS* (see Sections 3.4.4 and 8.1). The objective is to discover a *decision function* in the spirit of Wooldridge (2003, p. 50):

$$D : Dom(v_{ag,1}) \times ... \times Dom(v_{ag,n}) \times S_{ag} \to A_{ag} \tag{6.1}$$

where $Dom(v_{ag,i})$ denotes the domain of the agent's i-th state variable.

6.2.1.2. Mining Techniques for the Decision Perspective

Recall that in several approaches reviewed in the Chapters 4 and 5, decision models are discovered with supervised learning where the chosen action serves as a target variable. The reconstructed model will be biased by the assumed agent architecture (Section 3.1.2) and the applied mining technique.

The agent architecture influences the considered state variables (e.g. categorical vs. real-valued variables) and the complexity of the decision function. The simplest case is a stateless agent that directly maps observations to actions (see Section 3.1.2). In contrast, more complex architectures[8] like BDI implement a multi-step decision process that is not appropriately represented by a single decision function.

The properties of the analyzed agent architecture also influence the selection of appropriate mining techniques. In Chapters 4 and 5, we found examples of decision tree mining (the most common technique, e.g. used by Nair et al., 2004), fuzzy rule mining (Schütt, 2003), and inductive logic programming (Jacobs et al., 1998) to reconstruct rule-based decision models for a predefined set of actions.

---

[7] see e.g. the decision mining approach by Rozinat and Aalst (2006) reviewed in Section 4.2.5.5

[8] Note that even the simple logic-based example stated by Wooldridge (2003, p. 50) comprises a three-step decision process with the functions *see* (perception), *next* (update of internal state based on perception), and *action* (action selection based on the internal state).

Sometimes the objective is not the reconstruction of preconditions for a given action but the detection of the most frequent decision patterns emerging during simulation. In this case, unsupervised association rule learning can be applied as in the approach by Kennedy et al. (2007, reviewed in Section 5.2.2.6). Unsupervised statistical learning might also be used to automatically select the most relevant variables for an agent's decisions, as e.g. in the approach by Schütt (2003, reviewed in Section 5.3.3.2). Focusing on a subset of variables is crucial to reduce the dimensionality of the learning problem for agents with large state vectors (see Section 4.1.3.1).[9]

For the mining of decision processes with multiple steps, techniques to reconstruct causal chains seem more appropriate. In the literature review, we encountered causality graphs (e.g. in the work by Lam and Barber, 2005, reviewed in Section 5.2.4.2), Bayesian networks (Section 4.1.4.4), and the proprietary formalism of decision data models used by Dolean and Petrusel (2011, reviewed in Section 5.3.4.1). Within the perspectives of the conceptual framework at hand, such multi-step decision models mark the border between the decision perspective and the internal control perspective described in Section 6.2.2.

A well-known problem related to decision processes is the influence of previously executed actions on future decisions. In the simplest case, we assume a *Markovian decision process* (MDP), i.e. the chosen action only depends on the current state while neglecting the history of previous states or actions (e.g. Mahadevan, 2009, p. 419).

We will not discuss these topics in further detail here, but refer the reader to the literature on machine learning (e.g. Mahadevan, 2009; Marsland, 2009). In the following research, we will not put large focus on the decision perspective either due to the relatively large body of existing case studies and mature mining techniques. We will only report an example application of decision tree mining to the validation of the courier service model in Section 8.3.3.

6.2.2. Internal Control Perspective

The internal control perspective focuses on the control flow of agent behavior from the point of view of a single agent instance or type. Interactions and synchronization with other agents are – if at all – taken into account only from the perspective of the analyzed agent(s). This restriction, which we have not postulated with such rigor in pre-publications like (Cabac et al., 2006b, Sec. 4.2), reflects the ideas of Fahland et al. (2011a) and Kikas (2011) to enable discovery and conformance checking of proclet systems based on existing techniques for 'flat' Petri nets (see Section 5.3.3.3).

The focus on 'internal' control flow thus allows to reduce the complexity of process mining by means of a two-step procedure: Firstly, basic building blocks of single agent behavior are reconstructed. Secondly, interaction-related aspects are introduced in the context of the external control perspective (Section 6.2.4). This approach is taken in our case studies in the following chapters, but also in related work like (Winarjo, 2009, reviewed in Section 5.3.4.5) and artifact-centric process mining[10].

---

[9] on dimensionality reduction techniques for Markovian decision processes see e.g. Mahadevan (2009)

[10] e.g. Fahland et al. (2011a) and Kikas (2011) reviewed in Section 5.3.3.3

6.2.2.1. Granularity of Internal Control Flow

What to consider as 'basic building blocks' with respect to the reconstruction of understandable models of behavior depends on the complexity of the analyzed agent architecture. An architecture with a small number of fixed behavior modules, i.e. a *behavior describing* architecture in the terminology of Klügl (2007, p. 130), might be simple enough to display its overall control flow in one 'flat' model.

In a complex *behavior configuring* architecture (Klügl, 2007, p. 130) like BDI it might be more reasonable to mine elementary control flow at the level of plans and subsequently reconstruct interdependencies between different plan types. This procedure, which again mirrors the hierarchies found in MAS models like MULAN (Rölke, 2004, pp. 181), is e.g. applied by Serrano et al. (2009) to visualize agent conversations with order graphs (order within a single conversation) and abstract graphs (order of multiple conversations), as reviewed in Section 5.2.4.1.

In an adaptive *behavior generating* architecture (Klügl, 2007, p. 130) we cannot event assume stationary behavior. Therefore, valid control flow models can only be reconstructed for restricted periods of time. This problem is further discussed in the context of the adaptivity perspective in Section 6.2.5.

6.2.2.2. Process Dimensions of the Internal Control Perspective

The process dimensions for the internal control perspective are basically similar to those of the control flow perspective in process mining: As also described by Rembert and Ellis (2009, p. 38), we examine logged activities of agents with the objective to discover or validate ordering relations between them. Depending on the chosen level of aggregation, each plan execution (or agent life cycle) corresponds to a case and each type of behavior (or agent) to a process model. Mirroring the different levels of web service logs considered by Dustdar and Gombotz (2006, Sec. 3, reviewed in Section 5.3.3.1 of this thesis), identifiers of behavior instances and types can be either logged explicitly or have to be reconstructed by aggregating similar entities with cluster algorithms and distance measures.

To reconstruct a behavioral model displayed in a common notation like UML 2 activity diagrams, additional process dimensions might be taken into account. Recalling examples like our use of activity diagrams for process-oriented simulation (Section 2.3.1.3) or *SeSAm UML* (see Oechslein, 2004, reviewed in Section 3.3.2.2), the following additions can be imagined:

- Internal actions must be distinguished from message send- and receive-events in the log to identify the corresponding node types of an activity diagram.

- Log entries tagged with a simulation time stamp allow (a) for performance-related enrichments and (b) to distinguish instantaneous events from simulation time-consuming activities (displayed with the 'hourglass' symbol in UML).

- Logging the consumed or produced resources of actions enables the reconstruction of object flow. From logged resource types (e.g. access to a certain queue), object nodes and their connections to action nodes might be reconstructed.

- By integrating results from the decision perspective (Section 6.2.1), branching conditions can be added to the control flow model as shown in several process mining approaches (e.g. Rozinat and Aalst, 2006, reviewed in Section 4.2.5.5).[11]

6.2.2.3. Techniques for the Internal Control Perspective

As known from process mining, a choice of appropriate techniques for the internal control perspective mainly depends on the available control flow constructs of the target agent model (e.g. concurrency or cycles). Dongen et al. (2006b, p. 8) claims that several existing process mining algorithms are in principle suitable to reconstruct the control flow of agent behavior.

When complex control flow is composed from a small set of distinguishable events (e.g. FIPA performatives) an algorithm with the ability to detect duplicate tasks should be used to avoid over-generalization. This enables the identification of details like: 'the *accept* message received after sending a *request* is different from the *accept* received as an answer to *propose*'. Further agent- and simulation-specific requirements on control flow discovery algorithms will be discussed in Section 6.4.

6.2.3. Structural Perspective

The structural perspective is concerned with the analysis of static MAS structures while neglecting structural dynamics. Structures in agent-based models often represent either spatial or social and organizational structures of the real system. Furthermore, the reconstruction of software structures as e.g. represented in UML class or component diagrams can be relevant during computer model verification (in the wider sense).

There is a close relation between spatial and social structures in MABS: Due to agents' behavioral locality (Klügl, 2000, p. 59), the frequency of social interactions typically increases with spatial proximity (e.g. in the ACM Cultural Transmission Model by Axelrod, 1995, mentioned in Section 5.1.2.3). Social simulations like the ACM or *SugarScape* (Epstein and Axtell, 1996) even employ topological representations to model and visualize social structures.

6.2.3.1. Techniques for the Structural Perspective

Since macroscopic structures in MABS are often not specified in advance but emerge from microscopic interactions (see also Ferber, 1995, p. 114), techniques for their automated discovery and comparison are a valuable addition to validation. Structural models in MABS are commonly represented by graph or grid topologies (Gilbert and Troitzsch, 1999; Meyer, 2001). Recall from Section 3.2.2.3 that graphs can be considered as the more general representation since grid structures are straightforwardly mapped to graphs without 'quantization loss', but not vice-versa (Meyer, 2001).

---

[11]Bayraktar (2011) shows that integrating information from the organizational perspective (e.g. originators or roles) further allows to enhance reconstructed UML (or actually BPMN) activity diagrams with *swim-lanes* for different organizational units. However, in terms of our framework, this construct belongs to the external control perspective described in Section 6.2.4.

Analysis of Social Structures The analysis of graph-based social structures in MAS is closely related to the organizational perspective of process mining as described by Song and Aalst (2008, reviewed in Section 4.2.4): Authors like Botía et al. (2004, reviewed in Section 5.2.4.1) and Vanderfeesten (2006, reviewed in Section 5.3.4.6) apply similar social network analysis (SNA) and role mining techniques to MAS analysis. Hanachi and Khaloul (2008) and Abdelkafi and Bouzguenda (2010) explicitly refer to organizational process mining in the context of organizational structure detection in MAS (see Section 5.3.4.6).

The literature review showed that the most common technique to mine organizational models is unsupervised clustering. Agents are assigned to organizational entities based on similar properties with respect to a distance measure. Hierarchical clustering, as e.g. used by Song and Aalst (2008), might also allow to detect (behavioral) inheritance in object-oriented models. Dimensionality reduction techniques like self-organizing maps or PCA support the visualization of structures in high-dimensional feature spaces (for MAS-related applications see e.g. Arroyo et al., 2010; Gabbai et al., 2004; Schroeder and Noy, 2001).

Further techniques for organizational process mining include supervised decision tree learning (in the approach by Ly et al., 2006) and pattern matching for the identification of organizational structures (e.g. in the approaches by Dustdar and Hoffmann, 2007 and Hanachi and Khaloul, 2008).

Analysis of Spatial Structures As we noted in (Cabac et al., 2006b, Sec. 4.2), social network analysis might, to a certain degree, also support the analysis of spatial relations:

> "The most common metric for social network mining in MAS is the relation between message senders and receivers. However, other metrics such as relations between distributed agent platforms are considered as well; e.g. to find out which paths between distributed agent platforms were preferably taken by mobile agents moving within a network."

In this context, Flick et al. (2010, p. 4)[12] observe that spatial concepts have been widely neglected in process mining so far:[13]

> "Locations might serve as side conditions for the synchronization of agent behaviour as in rendezvous synchronisation (see e.g. Jessen and Valk, 1987). [... Nevertheless ...], locations and locality are seldom regarded in current process mining techniques. In our opinion, the focus on a nets-within-nets formalism can bring forward the handling of location-related information in process mining. On the one hand, locations and their properties might be reconstructed from a log based on hints of characteristic agent behaviour. On the other hand, available information about locations might provide heuristics to improve the reconstruction of process and organizational models."

The automated analysis of grid-based spatial models in MABS has not received much attention in the literature either (Czogalla, 2007, p. 21). At the University of Hamburg, Rainer Czogalla

---

[12]page numbers relate to the version of the article downloadable at `http://ceur-ws.org/Vol-643/` `paper09.pdf` (last visit 2012-10-20)

[13]Among the few exceptions is the work by Leotta (2012) who integrates information about locations into an approach to detect daily life habits with the aid of process mining techniques. Chai et al. (2012) also report on a recent approach for geographical process mining. The *ProM* forum contains a similar feature request at `http://www.win.tue.nl/promforum/` `discussion/28/geo-temporal-process-mining-.../p1` (last visit 2012-10-27).

(2007) developed first ideas to employ techniques from pattern recognition and image processing for this purpose. Citing our work from (Knaak, 2006), Czogalla (2007, Sec. 3) identifies 4 use cases in MABS analysis that might be supported by spatial pattern recognition:

1. *"Supporting function for interactive analysis"* (Czogalla, 2007, p. 23): Techniques for pattern recognition and image interpretation could aid the visual analysis of spatial models by automatically tagging spatial structures with high-level descriptions and pointing the analyst to 'interesting' regions. This use case resembles the idea of "agent-aided interpretation" by Drogoul et al. (2002, p. 11) and the related study by Servat et al. (1998), reviewed in Section 5.1.1.1, in that grid-based patterns are abstracted into meaningful entities (Czogalla, 2007, p. 23).

2. *"Automated comparison of simulated and empirical data"* (Czogalla, 2007, p. 24): Automated validation can be supported by extracting and comparing features of simulated and real-world spatial patterns using distance measures. Czogalla (2007, p. 24) mentions the work by Cantú-Paz et al. (2004, reviewed in Section 5.2.3) as an example. In general, feature extraction might be a promising approach to enable the automated validation of 'qualitative' patterns in MABS like the characteristic 'mosaic' structure in the beech forest model mentioned by Grimm et al. (2005, p. 989); see Section 5.1.2.3.

3. *"Identification of characteristic spatial regions"* (Czogalla, 2007, p. 24): Here, the idea is to support the simulation-based optimization of layouts (e.g. seat rows in an airplane as in the study by Matzen and Czogalla, 2003) with an automated identification of spatial regions that have an impact on the optimization goal (e.g. to minimize the duration of emergency evacuations; see Czogalla, 2007, p. 26). Czogalla (2007, p. 24) proposes to mine spatial patterns that typically appear in desired and undesired scenarios with an unsupervised learning algorithm. By correlating these patterns with potentially causative layout properties and feeding this knowledge into the optimization process, the convergence towards an advantageous configuration might be improved (Czogalla, 2007, p. 26).

4. *"Evaluation of Scenarios in Simulation-Based Optimization"* (Czogalla, 2007, p. 24): Similar to automated validation, the extraction and comparison of high level features also allows to evaluate spatial patterns in an objective function for simulation-based optimization (Czogalla, 2007, p. 24). To continue the previous example, one might attempt to (semi-)automatically calibrate the beech forest model from (Grimm et al., 2005, p. 989) towards the generation of the expected 'mosaic' pattern.

Czogalla (2007, p. 27) also mentions structural dynamics as an even more challenging setting for spatial analysis. Though his ideas provide interesting future directions for the analysis of spatially explicit simulations, an (at least partial) operationalization to confirm their utility and feasibility is still lacking (Czogalla, 2007, p. 27).

6.2.3.2. Process Dimensions of the Structural Perspective

Properties to assign agents to organizational entities can be measured along several process dimensions. Abdelkafi et al. (2012, Secs. 4,6) show that the *agent-group-role* (AGR) model by Ferber and Gutknecht (1998, reviewed in Section 3.2.2.2) is a possible target model for organizational process mining in MAS.[14] Similar models are employed in 'non-MAS-specific' process mining as well, e.g. in the work by Ly et al. (2006). Groups and roles can also be reconstructed from agent execution logs following the organizational model mining approach by Song and Aalst (2008, Sec. 5.1) reviewed in Section 4.2.4.2.

Role mining for the analysis of workflows (Song and Aalst, 2008) and MAS (Vanderfeesten, 2006) is often based on the identification of characteristic sets of actions or events. The objective is to reconstruct a *role assignment* $RA \subseteq A \times R$ between a set A of agents and a set R of roles from an event log. When analyzing logged events, such as FIPA ACL messages in (Vanderfeesten, 2006), several aspects must be taken into account.

Scope of considered events: Similar to the internal control perspective, we can vary the scope in which event "profiles"[15] are collected. Considering the whole set of actions executed during an agent's lifetime leads to the assignment of a single role per agent. As indicated by Song and Aalst (2008, p. 21), this assumption is often unrealistic. When conversation identifiers are logged, event profiles of agents can be collected *per conversation* instead. Again, the appropriate scope depends on the flexibility and complexity of the observed agent behavior.

Additional process dimensions: To avoid over-generalization in the reconstruction of roles from event profiles, further process dimensions might be taken into account. At the example of a FIPA-compliant, message-based MAS, several increasingly complex combinations of process dimensions can be considered, including:[16]

1. *Performatives*: e.g. 'agent A sent or received *req*, *cfp*, *prop*, and *acc*'.[17] Recall from Section 5.3.4.6 that according to Hanachi and Khaloul (2008), Abdelkafi and Bouzguenda (2010), and Abdelkafi et al. (2012), the relatively standardized semantics of ACL-like performatives provide valuable background knowledge for organizational process mining in general.

2. *Action / event types*: 'agent A sent *cfp* and received *prop*'. This option is e.g. taken by Vanderfeesten (2006, pp. 46).

3. *Message content*: 'agent A sent $cfp('sell - car')$ and received $prop('sell - car', 1000)$ and $prop('sell - car', 2000)$'.

4. *Communication peers*: 'agent A sent *cfp* to agents B and C and received *prop* from both agents'.

5. *Ordering relations* between events: 'agent A received *prop* immediately after sending *cfp*'.

6. In spatially explicit MABS, the *locations* visited by an agent might provide further hints towards its role.

Note that role mining with detailed event scopes and many considered process dimensions can lead to overfitting due to high vector dimensionality in combination with too few sample conversations. In the worst case, a different role is assigned to each individual agent due to

---

[14]though not many details on the applied mining techniques are provided
[15]as to use the term by Aalst and Song (2004b, p. 17)
[16]Some of the listed process dimensions are similar to those proposed by Dustdar and Gombotz (2006, pp. 263-264) for web service session reconstruction (see Section 5.3.3.1).
[17]short notation for the performatives *request, call-for-proposal, propose*, and *accept*

irrelevant, minor deviations of event profiles. Ordering relations between events might be a problematic role indicator when agents enact protocols with many possible execution paths.[18] Acquaintance relations might be more significant at the level of roles than at the level of individual agents (e.g. 'a *customer* sent a request to a *broker*' instead of 'agent A sent a request to agent B'), which might somehow lead to a 'vicious circle' with respect to role mining.

Groups in the AGR model roughly correspond to "teams" in the organizational mining approach by Song and Aalst (2008, p. 12). Thus, groups might be reconstructed based on the metric of 'joint cases' (Song and Aalst, 2008, p. 12). Alternatively (e.g. if an identification of joint cases is not straightforward) one might simply cluster agents that frequently communicate via messages.[19] In spatially explicit MABS, group assignment might also be indicated by the areas in which agents move. Section 8.1.2.1 provides the example of 'idle regions' for (simulated) city couriers.

A further dimension that is occasionally considered in the mining of structural models is the *cardinality* of communication and interaction relations. Dustdar and Hoffmann (2007), Hanachi and Khaloul (2008), and Abdelkafi and Bouzguenda (2010) use node degrees in social networks as one feature to identify organizational structures and entities (e.g. brokers). The reconstruction of class diagrams (or E/R diagrams as described by Canbaz, 2011 and Popova et al., 2012) is another example where cardinalities of relations between entity types are of interest.

6.2.4. External Control Perspective

In (Cabac et al., 2006b, Sec. 4.2), we introduced the external control perspective as follows:

> "Here we focus our interest on analyzing the dynamics of multi-agent interactions. This includes the detection of patterns on three levels: (1) Elementary conversation patterns similar to standard FIPA interaction protocols (FIPA, 2005). (2) Hierarchical models displaying dependencies between elementary agent conversations. (3) Higher-level patterns of social interaction such as those considered in the framework of *Socionics* (Malsch, 2001). The external control perspective thus unites aspects of the interaction and workflow level from web service mining [see Dustdar and Gombotz, 2006 and Section 5.3.3.1] with the organizational perspective from process mining [... see Song and Aalst, 2008 and Section 4.2.4]."

Process dimensions and mining techniques for the external control perspective thus integrate aspects of structure and behavior. An important objective is to provide additional structure to complex inter-agent control flow by (a) identifying (hierarchies of) sub-processes, as e.g. proposed in (Greco et al., 2006; Kumar et al., 2011) and (b) describing interactions at the level of abstract organizational entities instead of individual agents, as exemplified in (Song and Aalst, 2008, pp. 18, reviewed in Section 4.2.4). Note that the focus is *not* on structural changes over time, which is treated in the adaptivity perspective (Section 6.2.5) instead.

---

[18]A similar problem is noted by Dustdar and Gombotz (2006, p. 264).
[19]Note that this is related to the 'handover of work' metric proposed by Aalst and Song (2004b, pp. 12).

6.2.4.1. Process Dimensions of the External Control Perspective

The levels 1 (basic interactions) and 2 (multi-agent workflows) of external control flow mirror the constructs typically employed to model agent interactions. This is especially influenced by the distinction between basic and higher order protocols in MULAN (Rölke, 2004, p. 137); see Section 3.3.3.1.

The difference between both levels can be visualized at the example of basic UML sequence diagrams as target models for level 1 and UML interaction overview diagrams for level 2.[20] To clarify the involved process dimensions, we repeat some definitions related to interaction protocols and logs in the following. These are "based on previous approaches of interaction mining (e.g. Schütt, 2003) and on concepts from FIPA compliant multi-agent system[s]." (Cabac et al., 2006b, Sec. 5.1).

As we wrote in (Cabac et al., 2006b, Sec. 5.1), "an *interaction protocol* is a template that describes the message exchange during a cooperation between some agents." At the most general level, it is a tuple $IP = (R, M, G)$ where R is a set of *roles*[21], M is a set of *message types*, and G is a directed graph that describes the control flow of *message events* ME (see also Cabac et al., 2006b, Sec. 5.1).[22] One possible realization of G (e.g. used in out case study in Chapter 7) is a labelled Petri net $N = (S, T, F, ME)$ with message events as transition labels.

When asynchronous communication is assumed, message sending and reception must be represented by distinct send- and receive-events (see e.g. the specification mining approach by Kumar et al., 2011, p. 92): $e_s, e_r = (type, sender, message, receiver) \in \{send, receive\} \times R \times M \times R$ where e_s is precedent to e_r $(e_s < e_r)$. In synchronous communication, message sending and reception can be modelled as a single message event $e_{s,r} = (sender, message, receiver) \in R \times M \times R$. This simplification is used in the case study in Chapter 7.

Further following the terminology from (Cabac et al., 2006b, Sec. 5.1) with some formal extensions:

> "A *conversation* $[conv_{IP}]$ is an execution of an instantiated interaction protocol $[IP]$. During the conversation, communication roles are bound to agents [according to a role assignment RA, see Section 6.2.3.2] and a path through the control structure [of G] is chosen. Role bindings might be ambiguous, i.e. an agent can be bound to several roles and vice versa. A *multicast protocol* is an interaction protocol where the number of agents bound to a certain role is not fixed in the template; and might even vary during a conversation. A *conversation thread* $[thread(conv_{IP}, A_1, A_2)]$ is a part of a conversation $[conv_{IP}]$ covering the message exchange between exactly two agents $[A_1$ and $A_2]$. Note that a conversation needs not to be multicast to include multiple threads. A *conversation trace* $[trace(conv_{IP}) \in ME^*]$ describes the sequence of [...] message[... events] observed during a conversation.
>
> The [raw] message log $[ML \in ME^*]$ is the basis for [... interaction mining]. It contains an interleaving of all conversation traces observed during the analyzed execution. The message log might contain messages from several conversations $[conv_1, ..., conv_k]$ according to multiple interaction protocols $[IP_1, ..., IP_n]$."

---

[20]or message sequence charts vs. graphs, as described in the reverse engineering approach by Kumar et al. (2011)

[21]also called *lifelines* in message sequence charts, see e.g. Kumar et al. (2011, p. 93)

[22]A similar definition is e.g. stated by Quenum et al. (2006, pp. 2010).

As in web service mining (Dustdar and Gombotz, 2006, Sec. 3), the difficulty of agent interaction mining depends on whether the assignment of messages to protocol types, conversations, threads, and roles is explicitly logged. Furthermore it is relevant if a basic interaction protocol (level 1) or a multi-agent workflow (level 2) is used as the target model.

A basic interaction protocol is appropriate when every logged conversation only consists of a single conversation thread. If multiple threads exist but every role is bound to a single agent, both target model types are possible. One might either choose a (high level) sequence diagram with multiple roles or an 'interaction overview'-style model that emphasizes the 'choreography' of the conversation threads. Though AUML and UML 2 sequence diagrams allow to display multicast protocols, Section 7.3.5 argues that 'interaction overview'-like notations with support for multiple instantiation patterns might be most appropriate. This is in accordance with the claim by Lassen et al. (2007, p. 12) cited in Section 5.3.1 and the approach by Kumar et al. (2011) reviewed in Section 5.3.2.

Summarizing, a large number of process dimensions and dimensional relations are relevant for levels 1 and 2 of the external control perspective:

1. agents and their assignments to roles,

2. message events with the properties mentioned in Section 6.2.3.2,

3. assignments of messages to conversations and conversation threads,

4. assignments of conversations and conversation threads to protocol types,

5. cardinalities of messages and role bindings,

6. *internal* ordering relations of message events within conversation threads,

7. *external* ordering relations of message events between conversation threads,

8. ordering relations between conversations (as e.g. in the *abstract graph* by Serrano et al., 2009),

9. enrichments similar to the internal control perspective including branching conditions and times / deadlines (see e.g. Lamma et al., 2007b).

Level 3 of the external control perspective is concerned with the identification of high-level interaction patterns. Recalling the ideas by Czogalla (2007) cited in Section 6.2.3.2, this means that relations (or whole models) mined at the levels 1 and 2 are abstracted into high-level features which are subsequently compared to features of known interaction types (e.g. an auction). Examples towards such analyses include the work by Mazouzi et al. (2002), Dustdar and Hoffmann (2007), Hanachi and Khaloul (2008), as well as Abdelkafi and Bouzguenda (2010).

6.2.4.2. Techniques for the External Control Perspective

Due to the large number of considered process dimensions, a multitude of mining techniques are relevant to reconstruct models of external control flow:

- *Clustering* serves (1) to aggregate messages into conversation threads and conversations (e.g. Schütt, 2003), (2) to classify conversations by protocol types (e.g. Dustdar and

Gombotz, 2006; Srinivasa and Spiliopoulou, 2000), and (3) to abstract from agents to interaction roles (e.g. Song and Aalst, 2008).

- *Control flow discovery techniques* can be used to reconstruct internal and (to a certain degree) external ordering relations of message events. For the reconstruction of asynchronous communication flow, techniques based on partial order semantics are often preferred (e.g. Kumar et al., 2011; Lassen et al., 2007).

- *Frequent pattern mining techniques* aid in the detection of common sub-processes to reconstruct hierarchical control flow models (e.g. Bose et al., 2011b; Kumar et al., 2011).

- Feature- or log replay-based *conformance checking techniques* might support log abstraction for hierarchical control flow mining as well as the identification of high-level interaction patterns (level 3).

- Similar to the internal control flow perspective, *decision mining* techniques can be used to enrich interaction protocol models with branching conditions.

The literature review showed that clustering, decision mining, and conventional process mining techniques to reconstruct 'flat' control flow models have been applied to interaction mining in MAS or related systems quite frequently. In contrast, techniques that support the reconstruction of hierarchical and multicast interactions are still rare. As discussed in Chapter 5, approaches related to this endeavor, but not specialized for MAS, have only been proposed recently (Bose et al., 2011b; Canbaz, 2011; Kumar et al., 2010; Lou et al., 2010b). In Chapter 7, a partially implemented processing chain for basic interaction mining (level 1) and a concept for complex interaction mining (level 2) on the MULAN/CAPA agent platform is presented and compared to the related approaches.

6.2.5. Adaptivity Perspective

The adaptivity perspective is concerned with structural and second order dynamics. We will use the term *structural dynamics* to describe changes of *structural* models (e.g. a social network graph) over time and the term *second order dynamics* to characterize changes of *behavioral* models (e.g. a UML activity diagram).

We used the notion of a *meta-perspective* above because such dynamics can be analyzed with respect to all other perspectives in the framework. We can thus investigate how a single agent's decision or control flow models, the organizational and spatial structures and processes in a MAS, and even relations between multiple aggregation levels change over time. This view is in accordance with the claim for "holistic approaches [towards ...] change detection" in multiple process mining perspectives uttered by Bose et al. (2011a, p. 404).

Considering use cases in AOSE and MABS, the analysis of second order dynamics in the decision, internal control, and external control perspectives is closely related to the validation of learning agents (Kruse, 2008). Analyzing the dynamics of structural and level-encompassing models might add to the validation of macroscopic patterns as an "expression of self organization" (Czogalla, 2007, p. 20) in MABS. In general, the ability to tackle non-stationary structures and processes is an important requirement on process mining applied to simulation and MAS (see also Section 6.4).

The literature review in the previous chapters made obvious that research on second order dynamics in process mining is still in an early stage. As reviewed in Section 4.2.5.3, Bose et al. (2011a) only recently took first steps towards handling *concept drift*, followed by initial case studies of further authors (e.g. Luengo and Sepulveda, 2012). Aalst et al. (2012, pp. 187) name "dealing with concept drift" as a main future challenge for process mining.

Bose et al. (2011a, p. 393) observe that concept drift can occur in several process mining perspectives. Mining techniques for the adaptivity perspective are therefore basically extensions of algorithms for other perspectives towards the handling of concept drift. Since the analysis and reconstruction of non-stationary models poses a major challenge that is not in the focus of this thesis, we will only provide a rather sketchy overview of candidate mining techniques in the following.

6.2.5.1. Techniques for the Adaptivity Perspective

In the *decision perspective* changes of rule-based decision models (e.g. decision trees) must be analyzed over time. According to Lee et al. (2007, p. 639) algorithms to handle concept drift for such classification models are quite common in data mining. Techniques to reconstruct models of multi-step decision processes, like Bayesian networks, have also been extended towards non-stationary processes in recent years (e.g. Robinson and Hartemink, 2010).

In the *internal control perspective* the focus is on second order dynamics of control flow models. As reviewed in Section 4.2.5.3, two lines of work have been pursued so far: (1) *change mining* (Günther et al., 2006) as an application of 'conventional' control flow discovery techniques to *explicit* change logs, and (2) detection of *implicit* change points with statistical hypothesis tests (Bose et al., 2011a) and clustering (Luengo and Sepulveda, 2012) based on features of subsequent partial logs.

In the *structural perspective*, the analysis of dynamic grid-based structures with techniques for the processing of digital image sequences (Czogalla, 2007, p. 20), e.g. motion recognition (Fablet and Bouthemy, 2003), might be a promising direction for further research. Analyzing dynamic graph-based social (and possibly also spatial) structures is the subject of recent research in social network analysis. We mentioned exemplary approaches by Lahiri and Berger-Wolf (2008) and Christley and Madey (2007b) in Sections 4.2.4.1 and 5.3.1. Temporal changes of role assignments (Bose et al., 2011a, p. 394) are indicated by time-varying *action profiles* (Aalst and Song, 2004b, p. 17) of agents. These might be detected with similar clustering and hypothesis testing techniques as those applied to control flow models in (Bose et al., 2011a; Luengo and Sepulveda, 2012).[23]

The *external control perspective* can be regarded as an integration of the previous perspectives into (possibly hierarchical and multi-threaded) interaction models. Therefore, the techniques mentioned above should in principle suffice to analyze non-stationary interaction processes. However, recalling the discussion from Section 6.2.4, one should keep in mind that interaction mining remains challenging even for stationary processes. In particular, the need to include many different process dimensions complicates the detection of change points. Bose et al. (2011a, p. 404) reason about this aspect in the outlook section of their article:

---

[23]for a brief discussion of concept drift in the organizational perspective of process mining see also (Bose et al., 2011a, p. 394)

"[...] there could be [process] instances where more than one perspective (e.g. both control and resource [meaning the organizational perspective]) change simultaneously. Hybrid approaches considering all aspects of change holistically need to be developed. [...] Sample complexity [...] should be sensitive to the nature of changes, their influence and manifestation in traces, and the feature space and algorithms used for detecting drifts."

In terms of our framework, the claim for a holistic approach towards concept drift detection becomes especially relevant in the context of the external control perspective.

The *level-encompassing perspective* will be introduced in Section 6.2.6 below. Therefore, the discussion of techniques to analyze non-stationary inter-level relations is also deferred to this section.

6.2.5.2. Process Dimensions of the Adaptivity Perspective

To identify relevant process dimensions for the adaptivity perspective, we should first recall the distinction by Günther et al. (2006, p. 312, reviewed in Section 4.2.5.3) between change logs, enactment logs, and integrated analysis of both log types. The process dimensions recorded in a *change log* include the *change operations* performed on a (workflow) model as well as the *target model elements*[24], optional *time stamps* and *attributes* (e.g. originator) of the recorded changes (Günther et al., 2006, p. 317). Change operations describe the insertion, deletion, and modification of model elements, see e.g. Günther et al. (2006, p. 315), Li (2010, Sec. 2.2.1), and the "alignment policies" by Meyer and Szirbik (2007, p. 278) reviewed in Section 5.3.4.5.

Note that our framework on the one hand foresees the logging of change operations for any given perspective. On the other hand, the resulting change logs can also be analyzed from the point of view of every perspective. Two examples are listed in the following:

- Changes to an adaptive agent's decision model (decision perspective) are logged over time. From the change log, a control flow model (internal control perspective) is reconstructed that describes how the agent autonomously modifies its decisions. Inspecting this model might e.g. support the validation of the agent's learning process (Kruse, 2008).

- Changes to an interaction protocol (external control perspective) are logged similar to the approach by Meyer and Szirbik (2007). From the change log, a social network (structural perspective) is reconstructed that describes which agents communicated when changes occurred. This model might aid in the identification of agents with originally 'incompatible' views upon the interaction (see also Meyer and Szirbik, 2007).

The 'self-reflexivity' of the adaptivity perspective enables a wealth of possibilities to combine perspectives. In particular, an application of the adaptivity perspective to itself (i.e. 'How does a *change process* change over time?') leads to a (possibly infinite) hierarchy of models describing higher order dynamics. Moss (2000, p. 3) warns[25] that such self-reflexivity is quite popular in agent-based modeling but seldom useful in practice.

---

[24]called "subject" by Günther et al. (2006, p. 317)

[25]at the example of "infinite belief hierarchies (what I believe you believe about what I believe you believe ... about me)" (Moss, 2000, p. 2) mentioned in an article by Brainov and Sandholm (2000)

Reflecting the low availability of change logs in workflow management (Bose et al., 2011a, p. 393), only few MABS settings allow to record actual change operations. One case is the validation of learning processes where a learning algorithm performs explicit changes on an agent's behavioral model (Kruse, 2008). At the University of Hamburg, Sven Kruse (2008) develops initial concepts to adapt the change mining framework by Günther et al. (2006) to the validation of component-based reinforcement learning agents. Another case are explicitly modelled organizational structures like the AGR model (Ferber and Gutknecht, 1998), where changes to organizational entities (e.g. agents joining or leaving groups) can be logged.

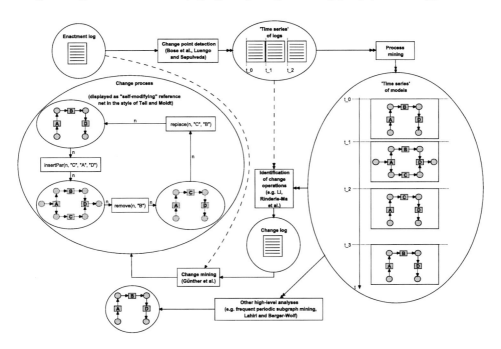

Figure 6.3.: Process mining in the adaptivity perspective. This figure integrates concepts by Günther et al. (2006, Fig. 2), Luengo and Sepulveda (2012, Fig. 1), Bose et al. (2011a), Lahiri and Berger-Wolf (2008), Rinderle-Ma et al. (2008), Li (2010), and Tell and Moldt (2005).

Explicit change operations are not available when second order or structural dynamics implicitly emerge at runtime. Instead, change points must be detected from an enactment log with the techniques reviewed above (e.g. Bose et al., 2011a; Hickey and Black, 2001; Luengo and Sepulveda, 2012). The input dimensions for change point detection include time stamps on the one hand and features of traces or log entries that indicate concept drift in the observed process on the other hand (see Luengo and Sepulveda, 2012, p. 155 and Hickey and Black, 2001, reviewed in Section 4.2.5.3). Change point detection results in a 'time series' of sub-logs as shown in Figure 6.3 and by Luengo and Sepulveda (2012, p. 156). From each sub-log, a model can be reconstructed that represents the structure of the observed process during the respective time period.

Besides manual inspection, the reconstructed series of models might serve as input to higher-level processing stages as shown in Figure 6.3. One option is the application of frequent pattern or subgraph mining algorithms to identify common (recurring) structures as in the work by Lahiri and Berger-Wolf (2008, reviewed in Section 4.2.4.1). Another possibility is the automatic identification of change operations from comparisons of subsequent models or logs from the series. Work in this direction has been carried out by Rinderle-Ma et al. (2008) and Li (2010) who target the control flow perspective in the context of adaptive workflow management.

We will not go into details on the detection of change operations here but refer the reader to the respective sources. In Section 7.1.2.4 we will only discuss extensions of reference nets by Tell and Moldt (2005) and Köhler (2006) that might serve as a basis to represent change processes in the MULAN agent model. The basic idea of a system net that changes the structure of contained object nets is already indicated in Figure 6.3.

6.2.6. Level-Encompassing Perspective

In (Cabac et al., 2006b, Sec. 4.2), we provided the following characterization of the level-encompassing perspective:[26]

> "Here we are interested in mining *relations between* the perspectives mentioned above. Thus, we focus on questions like: "How does changing a single agent's decision model affect interaction patterns observed in the MAS". The multi-level perspective is somewhat related to the general problem of *micro-macro links* mentioned in Socionics (Malsch, 2001). Not much work has been done for this perspective so far."

The latter statement still holds true in the field of process mining, where concepts of self-organization, computational emergence, and relations between multiple perspectives have not received much attention.[27] However, recent research on MABS and complex systems has started to formalize and automatically detect inter-level relations. Examples include the work by Chen (2009) and Moncion et al. (2010) reviewed in Section 5.2.2.4.[28]

Since these approaches rely on event logs, 'causal' relations, and social network analysis, an integration with process mining appears obvious. In the following, we discuss relevant process dimensions and techniques for the level-encompassing perspective and sketch possible contact points between process mining and the mentioned approaches.

6.2.6.1. Process Dimensions of the Level-Encompassing Perspective

Broadly speaking, the input dimensions for process mining in the level-encompassing perspective are models or patterns from different perspectives and levels of aggregation. The objective is to "validate[...] and/or discover[...]" (Chen, 2009, p. 104) relations between occurrences of these patterns in event logs.

---

[26]still called "multi-level perspective" in this pre-publication

[27]beyond the merging of mining results from multiple perspectives into a simulation model (e.g. Wynn et al., 2010, reviewed in Section 5.3.4.1) and the idea to detect reasons for process model changes by evaluating state attributes from the enactment log (Günther et al., 2006, reviewed in Section 4.2.5.3)

[28]though the work by Moncion et al. (2010) might also be classified under the *adaptivity perspective* of the presented framework

The most basic form of level-encompassing analysis considers dependencies between a simulation's input parameters and the corresponding (global) simulation results. Examples include the work by Barton and Szczerbicka (2000) and the ideas by Remondino and Correndo (2005).[29] The considered process dimensions are input and output variables of multiple simulation runs. The mining result describes relations between both dimensions in the form of a quantitative or qualitative meta-model; roughly corresponding to the notion of *multi-level models* by Chen (2009, Sec. 4.4).

Recent work goes beyond the detection of simple input/output mappings and attempts to include richer relations as well as arbitrary levels of aggregation. In Section 5.2.2.4 we reviewed the approach by Chen (2009), who employs the construct of *complex event types* (*CET*s), i.e. patterns of temporally, spatially, and organizationally interrelated events, for this purpose.

This viewpoint corresponds well to a definition of complex events that Gay et al. (2010, p. 3) state in the context of workflow analysis: "A complex event is an event abstraction that signifies a set of events and their relations over a time intervall". The use of multi-graphs to represent temporal, organizational, and spatial aspects of *CET*s at once (see e.g. Chen et al., 2010, p. 46) even goes beyond most process mining approaches that only form graph-based patterns for a single perspective (mostly control flow).

Similar to the perspectives of our framework, Chen (2009, p. 60) considers both "static [...] and [...] dynamic property descriptions" in inter-level modeling: *CET*s are event-based behavioral abstractions (Chen, 2009, p. 60) related to the internal and external control perspectives. Subsystem state types (*SST*s) are state-based abstractions (Chen, 2009, p. 60) related to the structural and decision perspectives. Moncion et al. (2010, Sec. 3.1) also consider arbitrary static and dynamic patterns to model their *interaction signs* and mention *CET*s as one possible realization (Moncion et al., 2010, p. 19).

We might thus generalize that the *input process dimensions* for the level-encompassing perspective are models from any of the above perspectives. A *level-encompassing model* describes relations between these abstractions over one or more simulation runs. Note that we use the term 'level-encompassing model' to subsume descriptive inter-level models, predictive inter-level models, and multi-level models from the work of Chen (2009), who himself indicates that all of these models can be integrated and combined (Chen, 2009, p. 136).

The literature review showed that level-encompassing models can take several different forms: Chen (2009) uses statistical correlation and regression models displayed as undirected graphs (associative models), directed acyclic graphs like Bayesian networks (causal models), and hierarchical Bayesian networks (multi-level models). Relations between input and output parameters over multiple simulation runs are often stated in a rule-based fashion (e.g. decision trees in Barton and Szczerbicka, 2000), which somehow corresponds to a 'macroscopic' variant of mining in the decision perspective. Moncion et al. (2010) examine time series of interaction network graphs to trace groups of related agents over time (adaptivity perspective) and use social network analysis (structural perspective) to derive global and local measures of 'order'.

Therefore, it might again be admissible to generalize that level-encompassing models can be reconstructed with a focus on *any* of the aforementioned perspectives:

---

[29]see also Cabac et al. (2006b, Sec. 4.2)

- *Decision perspective*: 'Level-encompassing decision models' show how attribute values at one aggregation level (e.g. behavioral parameters of agents) influence observations at another aggregation level (e.g. macroscopic simulation results). They are thus related to multi-level models in the work by Chen (2009).

- *Internal/external control perspective*: 'Level-encompassing control flow models' display ordering relations between complex events[30] at different aggregation levels. These are related to causal inter-level models in the work by Chen (2009, Sec. 4.2.2).

- *Structural perspective*: 'Level-encompassing structural models' relate organizational entities or spatial patterns at different aggregation levels.

- *Adaptivity perspective*: Here, one is interested in the way that level-encompassing models (from any of the above perspectives) change over time. An example is the work by Moncion et al. (2010) focusing on 'level-encompassing structural dynamics'.

Different from the base perspectives, level-encompassing models thus do not refer to elementary agents, events, or single-level abstractions (e.g. interaction roles), but to behavioral (e.g. complex events in Chen, 2009) and structural (e.g. groups of similarly behaving agents in Moncion et al., 2010) aggregations at different levels. Furthermore, they often focus on differences between these relations over multiple simulation runs with deviating initial conditions (i.e. multi-level models according to Chen, 2009).

6.2.6.2. Techniques for the Level-Encompassing Perspective

Figure 6.4 perceives the approach by Chen (2009) as a template for process mining in the level-encompassing perspective. All steps (transitions) and intermediate representations (places) are annotated with concrete realizations from the work of Chen (2009) and Moncion et al. (2010); and with possible extensions based on other data and process mining approaches reviewed in the previous chapters.

The procedure followed by Chen (2009) starts with the definition of patterns (*CET*s and *SST*s) as a basis for log abstraction. Next, relations between aggregate entities in the abstracted log (e.g. complex event occurrences) are discovered in order to gain an inter-level model (Chen, 2009, Sec. 4.3). Finally, inter-level models from multiple simulation runs are grouped or classified (e.g. by similar initial conditions) to form a multi-level model (Chen, 2009, Sec. 4.4).

Chen (2009, p. 216) himself identifies the lack of efficient techniques to detect complex event types in a log as a current weakness of his approach. Logging is based on the proprietary MABS framework of X-machines. Patterns are detected during and after simulation using *ad-hoc* mechanisms not further explained in his thesis. An integration of relatively mature process mining and modeling techniques might be a promising direction for improvement. We will only sketch some manifest possibilities in the following and leave an actual proof-of-concept to future work:

1. Log formats like MXML (Dongen et al., 2005) and XES (Verbeek et al., 2011) (see Section 4.2.6.1) might be an appropriate basis to perform level-encompassing analyses due to their

---

[30]as to use the term by Chen (2009)

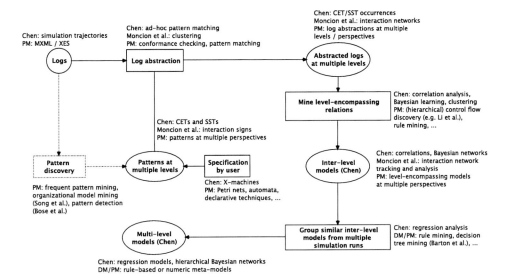

Figure 6.4.: Petri net depicting the work by Chen (2009) as a template for process mining in the level-encompassing perspective.

standardized format on the one hand and extensibility towards arbitrary event attributes (e.g. to store spatial data) on the other hand.

2. The steps of log abstraction and inter-level model discovery in the approach by Chen (2009) are closely related to hierarchical process mining (e.g. Greco et al., 2006; Li et al., 2010; reviewed in Section 4.2.5.2) and conformance checking (e.g. Ramezani et al., 2012; Rozinat and Aalst, 2008; reviewed in Section 4.2.5.4). The techniques and similarity measures proposed in such approaches might improve the modeling and detection of complex events with a focus on either expressivity or performance. Especially the pattern-based compliance checking approach by Ramezani et al. (2012) and the underlying techniques by Adriansyah et al. (2011)[31] to efficiently align logs and process models appear promising in this context. In Section 7.3 we briefly sketch how reference nets could support the modeling of *CET*s using an example by Chen (2009).

3. Complementary to the manual specification of *CET*s assumed by Chen (2009), frequent sequence and pattern mining techniques like those proposed by Bose and Aalst (2009) might support the discovery of characteristic *CET*s when less *a-priori* knowledge is available. Note that Moncion et al. (2010, p. 22) also identify the extensive background knowledge required to identify interaction signs as a drawback of their approach and name automation as a direction for further work.

4. Regarding the reconstruction of (causal) inter-level models, process mining techniques allow to discover richer control flow constructs (e.g. cycles) and organizational relations (e.g. interaction patterns like *proxy*, see Dustdar and Hoffmann, 2007) than those mentioned

---

[31]cited in (Ramezani et al., 2012)

in the work by Chen (2009). In contrast, the discovery of spatial relations between events or entities is still a weakness of most process mining approaches (see also Section 6.2.3.1).

5. The perspectives of process mining offer means to structure level-encompassing models beyond, but under integration of, the Bayesian and automata-based approach by Chen (2009) and the SNA-based approach by Moncion et al. (2010). The discussion in the previous section showed that the perspectives considered in the conceptual framework at hand offer a basis to integrate the different types of level-encompassing models described by these authors.

6.2.7. Domain-Specific Perspectives

The definition of the above perspectives is based on very general principles like the dualisms between structure and behavior and between microscopic and macroscopic observations. Though this high level of abstraction ensures general applicability, the gap towards practical modeling objectives in MABS (e.g. to reduce the emissions caused by motorized transports in our courier service model described in Section 8.1) can be rather large.

Fortunately, process mining offers the concept of *extension* (see Aalst, 2011a, p. 216 and Section 4.2.5.5) to overcome this drawback: "Through extension we add a new perspective to the process model by cross-correlating it with the log" (Aalst, 2011a, p. 216). As described in Section 4.2.5.5, this correlation is often achieved by replaying the log in the model while aggregating and assigning additional data read from the log to the elements of the model (Aalst, 2011a, p. 215).

Most approaches focus on the extension of control flow models with information gained from other perspectives like branching conditions or originator roles (Aalst, 2011a, p. 216). However, it should in principle be possible to extend models from any given perspective with domain-specific data of arbitrary type. In the following, we list some more or less common examples of possible domain specific perspectives:

- *Performance / "time perspective"* (Aalst, 2011a, p. 230): Approaches in this direction extend elements of control flow models (e.g. places and transitions of Petri nets in Hornix, 2007, Sec. 4.2) with information about "times and [path] probabilities" (Aalst, 2011a, p. 230); see also Section 4.2.5.5. However, performance-related extensions of other perspectives are also possible. One example might be average "deliberation time[s]" (Uhrmacher and Gugler, 2000, p. 102) of reconstructed decision rules (decision perspective) in testbed agent simulations (see Section 3.2.1) as e.g. reported by Uhrmacher and Gugler (2000, Sec. 5).

- *Economic perspective*: Model elements like activities in a control flow model can be annotated with related costs and revenues as a basis for economic analysis. While graph-based models are occasionally used in economic analyses (e.g. in *material flow cost accounting*, see Wagner et al., 2010), the economic perspective has not been tackled in process mining often. An approach towards "financial business process mining" is reported by Werner et al. (2012).

- *Material flow / ecologic perspective*: By considering "not only the sequence of activities but also input [...] and output materials of each activity" (Wang, 2011)[32] process mining algorithms can be extended towards the reconstruction of material flow as a basis for ecologic analyses like those conducted with the aid of *material flow networks* (Möller, 2000). Initial work pointing into this direction is reported by Wang (2011) who integrates material flow-related data into the *Heuristics Miner* algorithm (Weijters et al., 2006, reviewed in Section 4.2.3.4) to analyze carbon emissions of production processes.

- *Combined analyses* covering more than one of the above perspectives have been conducted in environmental informatics and simulation. Wohlgemuth (2005) e.g. advocates a combined analysis of ecologic and economic / performance-related measures of production processes with the aid of *material flow simulation*.

Due to the relation of domain-specific perspectives to the process mining task of extension, the relevant input process dimensions can be adopted from extension approaches like the work by Hornix (2007) in a generalized form: This includes (1) a model to be extended, (2) attributes of events or cases with relevance to the considered perspective, and (3) a mapping that assigns log elements to model elements (Hornix, 2007, p. 24). The output of the extension step is an assignment of (aggregated) attributes to model elements (Hornix, 2007, Sec. 4.2).

A challenge of model extension lies in the choice of appropriate aggregation operations for the considered attributes to derive domain-specific performance indicators. Another relevant aspect is the visual presentation of the extended models. One means to display quantitative data in graph-based models are so-called *Sankey diagrams* rooted in material and energy flow analysis (Schmidt, 2012, p. 263): A Sankey diagram is a graph in which nodes represent entities (e.g. machines in a production system) and edges represent flows between entities. Flows of different types (e.g. different materials) are visualized by different arrows colors (Schmidt, 2012, p. 266). Arrow width increases proportionally with flow quantity (Schmidt, 2012, p. 265).

Sankey diagram-like displays are occasionally used in process mining, e.g. in (Aalst, 2011a, p. 225). Hornix (2007, p. 31) uses color coding of places and transitions to indicate performance bottlenecks in Petri net-based control flow models (see Section 4.2.5.5). Aalst et al. (2012, p. 184) relate these visualization techniques to *cartography*:

> "[...] ideas from cartography can easily be incorporated in the construction of discovered process maps. For example, the size of an activity can be used to reflect its frequency or some other property indicating its significance (e.g. costs or resource use). The width of an arc can reflect the importance of the corresponding causal dependency, and the coloring of arcs can be used to highlight bottlenecks."

Figure 6.5 shows two examples of models from different mining perspectives with domain-specific annotations visualized as Sankey diagrams.[33] Note that the 'material flow' semantic of Sankey diagrams does not always match the semantic of control flow constructs in process models straightforwardly. The concurrent split in the precedence graph of Figure 6.5 (right) e.g. does *not* lead to a split or duplication of the accumulated cost depicted by the Sankey

---

[32]Cited from the English abstract. The full text of the thesis is written in Chinese language and was inaccessible to the author.

[33]The diagrams were created with the software tool *e!Sankey* (http://www.e-sankey.com, last visit 2012-11-29).

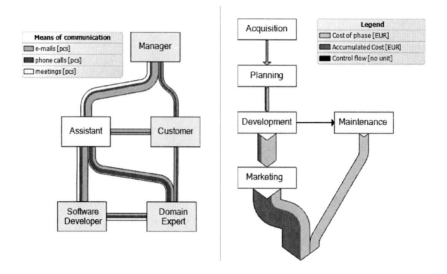

Figure 6.5.: Two examples of model extensions displayed with the aid of Sankey diagrams. Left: Social network (organizational perspective) showing frequency of communication between different roles in a fictitious software project differentiated by means of communication (adopted with extensions from Aalst, 2011a, p. 225). Right: Precedence graph showing phase successions (control flow perspective) of the same software project annotated with phase-specific and accumulated project cost (in the style of diagrams like those by Wagner et al., 2010, p. 199 and Schmidt, 2012, p. 268).

annotations. For this reason, the graph contains one mere 'control flow' edge without assigned cost flows.

6.3. Use Cases within the Model Building Cycle

In process mining, perspectives help to 'partition' analysis problems and techniques by narrowing down the *subject* of analysis to specific process dimensions and dimensional mappings (Rembert and Ellis, 2009, p. 36). Another approach (that is called an "orthogonal [...] dimension[...]" to perspectives by Song and Aalst, 2008, p. 5) to systematize process mining problems and algorithms is to focus on the *purpose* of analysis, i.e. which (general or domain-specific) tasks are to be solved. As reviewed in Section 4.2.2.2, the Eindhoven research group contributes to this dimension by identifying "three main types of process mining: discovery, conformance, and enhancement" (Aalst, 2011a, p. 9), and a set of more refined "use cases" for process mining focusing on business process analysis (Ailenei et al., 2012).

In the context of the presented framework, the objective is to specify use cases for process mining in MABS. As reviewed in Section 5.2.2, authors including Köster (2002), Remondino and Correndo (2005), Baqueiro et al. (2009), and Arroyo et al. (2010) attempted to systematize applications of data mining within (agent-based) simulation model building cycles prior and in parallel to this thesis. Integrating and extending these ideas leads to a list of 7 use cases that are also displayed in the upper right corner of Figure 6.1:[34]

1. real system analysis and (semi-)automated modeling,

2. exploratory analysis of simulation results,

3. operational validation and verification,

4. simulation-based optimization and calibration,

5. implementation of adaptive agents, and

6. analysis of the model building cycle itself.

An overview of these scenarios and their embedding into a basic model building cycle is depicted in Figure 6.6. In the following, we provide descriptions of these use cases as well as more detailed visualizations in the form of Petri nets. We also identify requirements on mining and modeling techniques posed by each use case and point out relations to the dimension of perspectives, i.e. which perspectives are most relevant in a certain use case.[35] The presentation is based on the pre-publications in (Cabac and Denz, 2008; Knaak, 2006, 2007).

6.3.1. Real System Analysis

In (Knaak, 2006, Sec. 3.3) we have described this use case as follows:

"In the system analysis phase [... of a simulation study, mining] in the decision and [internal or external] control perspectives can be employed to automatically abstract real world data into certain components of the MABS model; i.e. *automated modelling*. An example is the application of process mining techniques to reconstruct Petri net models of agents' protocols from real world process logs. On a Petri net-based simulation platform such as MULAN [see Section 3.3.3.1], these models can be executed directly as part of the simulation.

However, automated modelling of agent's decisions and processes is a complex task, and sufficient real world data is hardly available. To tackle the latter problem, Drogoul et al. (2002) propose [...] *participatory simulation* [as reviewed in Section 5.1.1.1]. This [...] enables a user to play the role of a certain agent during the simulation. The user's actions are monitored and aggregated into a decision model for a simulated agent by means of DM.

DM in the structural [, level-encompassing, and adaptivity] perspective[s] can be applied to extract typical macroscopic patterns from the real system. These serve as a reference to validate related patterns generated by the simulation model. Clustering techniques can also help to simplify the model structure by detecting similarities between certain components of the real system (Remondino and Correndo, 2005)".

---

[34]Recall that specializations of some of these use cases for spatial simulation data analysis were proposed by Czogalla (2007, pp. 23) and reviewed in Section 6.2.3.1. The use cases of exploratory analysis and validation are also contrasted by Köster (2002, p. 89).

[35]The author was pointed to the practical importance of the latter topic by a reviewer of the conference paper published as (Knaak, 2006).

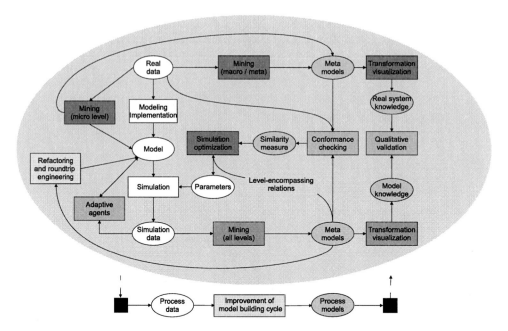

Figure 6.6.: "Embedding of use cases for data and process mining in MABS into a modified version of the model building cycle by Page and Kreutzer (2005, p. 14)". Figure and caption adopted with modifications (figure) from (Knaak, 2006, Sec. 3.3).

Data mining support for real system analysis is mentioned in the MABS methodologies by Remondino and Correndo (2005), Baqueiro et al. (2009), and especially Arroyo et al. (2010). The latter authors distinguish between different data collected for modeling and for validation (Arroyo et al., 2010, p. 419). This distinction allows to perform cross validation to avoid an over-generalization of the reconstructed models (Arroyo et al., 2010, p. 421). Data used for modeling typically stems from the microscopic level while data for validation is often observed at the macroscopic level (see Drogoul et al., 2002, p. 103, reviewed in Section 5.1.1.1).

Based on the reviewed literature, Figure 6.7 summarizes how data and process mining can support real system analysis and (semi-)automated modeling in a simulation study. The figure emphasizes that the latter will seldom be conducted in a fully automated fashion: On the one hand, process discovery can be employed to reconstruct templates for behavioral models in the internal or external control perspective (e.g. Petri nets) that are later refined into executable models by manually adding programming language annotations (e.g. Java statements in RENEW).

On the other hand, automated model extension can support the refinement and parameterization of predefined agent templates. One example is the *Agent Academy* framework by Mitkas et al. (2002), reviewed in Section 5.2.4.3, where the rule engine of an agent is extended with decision rules obtained from data mining. The simulation model mining approach by Wynn et al. (2010, reviewed in Section 5.3.4.1) automates both steps but is restricted to 'flat' workflow models instead of MABS.

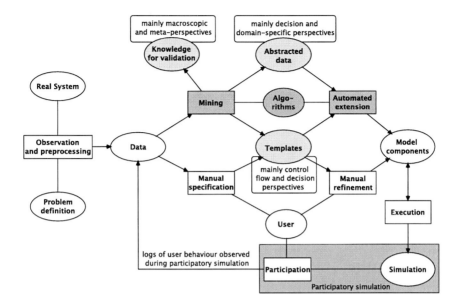

Figure 6.7.: Process mining support for real system analysis. This figure integrates aspects from the methodologies and diagrams by Arroyo et al. (2010, p. 241, reviewed in Section 5.2.2.3) and Wynn et al. (2010, p. 446, reviewed in Section 5.3.4.1).

The following list summarizes some guidelines to choose process mining techniques for the use case of real system analysis:

- Since mining is applied to data observed from a real system, there will typically be a need for data preprocessing (e.g. outlier detection) and algorithms with the ability to cope with noise.

- Techniques like the *Heuristics Miner* can be configured to focus on the main behavior of a system while neglecting infrequent special cases (Weijters et al., 2006, p. 24). This might be useful to achieve a sufficient abstraction of the generated model from the observed data.

- To support semi-automated modeling, it should be possible to export the reconstructed models into an execution environment, e.g. similar to the use of *ProM*'s *CPNTools* and *BPMN* export in the approach by Wynn et al. (2010).

- For semi-automated modeling it can in principle suffice to reconstruct a non-interpretable, executable model like e.g. a neural network (Section 4.1.4.5). However, due to the fallibility of data mining methods, interpretable models should be preferred since they provide a better basis to understand and validate the gained results.

- As usual in simulation (see e.g. Balci, 1998, p. 346, cited in Page and Kreutzer, 2005, p. 201), knowledge discovery (e.g. Cios et al., 2007, pp. 14), and process mining (Aalst et al., 2012, p. 180) the selection of input data should be guided by a concise problem definition.[36] In Section 5.2.2.3 we already cited the claim by Arroyo et al. (2010, p. 433) that both domain and data mining experts should ideally accompany a data mining-supported real system analysis to compensate the pitfalls of applying data mining techniques (e.g. unintended bias that the applied algorithm imposes on the gained results, see Arroyo et al., 2010, p. 433).

6.3.2. Exploratory Analysis of Model Behavior

The use of data mining to support the abstraction of simulation output into more understandable (meta-)models as a basis for exploratory analysis is mentioned in all methodologies reviewed in Section 5.2.2. In (Knaak, 2006, Sec. 3.3), we stated the following description of this use case:

> "In this less demanding use case [as compared to other use cases like adaptive agent design], DM techniques basically accomplish the abstraction from large amounts of data observed during simulation to interpretable meta-models representing these data in a general and understandable form. Following our above example, we can monitor the messages exchanged by agents during the simulation, and then apply process mining to reconstruct a general model of the protocol that produced the observed messages. The reconstructed protocol model can be visualised in the form of a Petri net or an AgentUML interaction diagram.
>
> Analysing the meta-model allows users to understand important features of the simulation results better than analysing the raw simulation results. In princip[le ...], all perspectives mentioned above contribute to a comprehensive understanding of the model. However, different phases of the modelling cycle emphasise different perspectives: During computer model verification we typically concentrate on the functioning of agents' internal decisions and processes as well as the adherence to certain conversation protocols (i.e. mining in the decision, internal, and external control perspective[s]). Result validation often puts a stronger focus on patterns related to global structures and processes (i.e. mining in the structural and external control perspective). During calibration, the exploratory analysis mainly concentrates on the [... level-encompassing] perspective. Obviously, the task of model exploration benefits from additional support techniques and tools for designing, executing, and managing large-scale experiments."

Based on the reviewed literature, Figure 6.8 summarizes possibilities to employ data and process mining techniques for the exploration of model behavior. The figure mirrors some of the dimensions for the classification of analysis techniques introduced in Section 2.4.2: Input data for mining can be either trace-based (logs) or result-based (reports), where the former case is characteristic for process mining. Furthermore, attributes of experiment specifications, such as parameter settings, can be fed into mining algorithms to reconstruct relations between simulation input and output data in the level-encompassing perspective (see e.g. Barton and Szczerbicka, 2000, reviewed in Section 5.2.3).

Recalling a further dimension from Section 2.4.2, the input for a mining algorithm can cover multiple simulation runs or only a single simulation run. When data from a single run is analyzed, there is clearly a high risk of gaining overly specialized and statistically invalid results.

---

[36]In their 'process mining manifesto', Aalst et al. (2012, p. 180) also formulate the principle that "log extraction should be driven by questions".

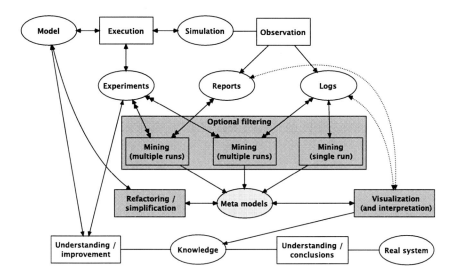

Figure 6.8.: Possibilities of process mining support for the exploration of model behavior derived from the literature. The final step of drawing conclusions from the analysis results to the real system is adopted from Page and Kreutzer (2005, p. 9), its relation to data mining (as depicted here) is discussed by Arroyo et al. (2010, p. 422).

Multiple simulation runs can serve as input for the mining algorithms for different reasons: (a) to increase the credibility and generality of the obtained results by analyzing multiple stochastically varying replications of the same simulation (see also Page and Kreutzer, 2005, pp. 173,185), and (b) to explicitly mine differences between simulation runs in dependence on varying parameter (see also Page and Kreutzer, 2005, pp. 189) settings in the level-encompassing perspective. In Section 6.4, we briefly sketch how the semantics of typical numerical simulation statistics like confidence intervals might be transferred to the output of process mining techniques.

In the description cited above, the exploratory analysis of model behavior was called a "less demanding use case" (Knaak, 2006, Sec. 3.3) for two main reasons: Firstly, since the input data for mining originates from *simulations*, noisy or incomplete data is normally not an issue. Furthermore, the logged events and attributes can be tailored to the purpose of the analysis and the requirements of the applied algorithms well. The focus of analysis towards a certain agent, class of agents, etc. can be shifted easily; either by filtering an overall log or by re-running the simulation and logging from a different perspective.

Secondly, to explore a model's behavior, a *visualization* of the mined meta-models is often sufficient, i.e. no further automated processing of these results is required in the first place. However, special cases of exploratory analysis are imaginable where a further 'post-processing' of the mining results might be required:

- As Czogalla (2007, p. 23) proposes for the analysis of spatial simulation data (see Section 6.2.3.1), mining results might be employed to aid exploratory analyses by pointing the analyst to relevant regions in simulation output. This idea can also be transferred to the process mining context: A trivial example is the marking of all events in a log that represent the support for a certain reconstructed rule or partial model; as implemented in the *Association Rule Miner* of *ProM* (see Rebuge and Ferreira, 2012, p. 102)

- Mining *executable* meta-models (or parts thereof) from simulation output can serve as a basis for *model simplification* (as e.g. mentioned in the calibration approaches by Oechslein et al., 1999 and Fehler et al., 2004, see Section 5.1.2.2) and *refactoring*. Section 8.3.2.2 will show a simple example of how an architectural improvement can be anticipated by installing a different logging perspective in a simulation model and reconstructing a behavioral model from the resulting logs.

Further use cases that employ meta-models reconstructed from simulation data beyond mere visualization are discussed in the following.

6.3.3. Validation and Verification

Besides the exploratory analysis of simulation results, data and process mining can provide support for several phases of the validation process (see Section 2.4.3.2). In Figure 6.9, this is indicated at the example of the main validation phases identified by Page (1991) and Sargent (2001), i.e. conceptual model validation, verification (in the wider and narrower sense), and operational validation (see Section 2.4.3.2). Following Page and Kreutzer (2005, pp. 221), the figure distinguishes between cases where (a) only simulation data is considered and (b) simulation data is compared to "matchable output data from the real system" (Page and Kreutzer, 2005, p. 221).

6.3.3.1. Conceptual Model Validation

Precisely speaking, process mining is not a conceptual model validation technique because it relies on logs observed from the execution of the computer model. However, by abstracting logs into understandable process models, it supports the application of typical conceptual model validation techniques such as *face validation* (see e.g. Section 5.1.1.2). For several reasons, visual mining results like Petri nets or decision trees build a good basis to let domain experts rate the plausibility of a simulation:

1. Process mining results can be presented in a 'conceptual' notation, thus abstracting from details of the computer model and low-level simulation output like traces.

2. Interpretable control flow, organizational, and decision models might nevertheless further an understanding of the mechanisms underlying a simulation beyond common high-level result statistics (see e.g. Kennedy et al., 2007, reviewed in Section 5.2.2.6).

3. Contrary to 'normal' conceptual models, process mining results are obtained from *actual simulation runs* of the computer model. Aalst et al. (2012, p. 172) emphasize the focus of process mining on *"real processes* (i.e. not assumed processes)".

4. A valid mining result that represents multiple simulation runs is more general and statistically significant than an animation of a single run.

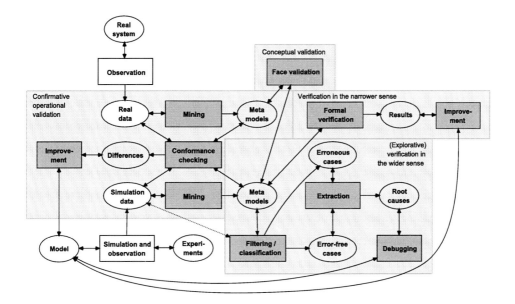

Figure 6.9.: A summary of possible data and process mining support for simulation model validation based on the literature review in Sections 4 and 5.

To benefit from these advantages, it is necessary that both simulation practitioners and domain experts are aware of the peculiarities of applying data mining or process mining algorithms: The meta-models mined for face validation should be validated themselves, e.g. using cross-validation with data from further stochastically varying simulation runs (Arroyo et al., 2010, p. 421). The statistical basis of the obtained results (e.g. number of considered cases, completeness of the analyzed log) as well as the properties and settings of the applied mining algorithms (e.g. 'hiding' of infrequent dependencies by the *Heuristics Miner* algorithm, see Section 4.2.3.4) should be made explicit as part of the experiment specification.

Displaying the behavior of a large MABS in a monolithic model can lead to overly complex processes (see e.g. the example in Section 8.3.2.2). Therefore, different mining perspectives should be applied to obtain an understandable, yet comprehensive view of the simulation results.[37]

6.3.3.2. Verification in the Wider and Narrower Sense

Process mining results can also support the verification of the computer model. A simple qualitative 'verification' (in the wider sense) is already conducted by 'manually' comparing a model mined from simulation output to the conceptual specification. Furthermore, conformance checking techniques like trace-based model checking (e.g. Howard et al., 2003, reviewed in Section 4.2.5.4) can be applied to detect constraint violations in MABS logs (see also Dongen et al.,

---

[37]as advocated in multi-perspective validation approaches like the work by Ndumu and Nwana (1999) reviewed in Section 5.1.1.4

2006b, Secs. 1.4.2-1.4.4, reviewed in Section 5.3.4.2). These might even be part of regression test suites to automatically check the output of every simulation run for inconsistencies.

When a failure in the computer model is detected (possibly on the basis of process mining results) it is crucial to trace the observed symptoms back to the causative defect in the program code (for terminology see Zeller, 2006, Sec. 1.6). As reviewed above, such root-cause analysis (e.g. Zeller, 2006, p. 4) is deemed especially demanding in MABS due to model complexity (Klügl, 2008, p. 41), unclear micro-macro relations (Klügl, 2000, p. 74), and the indefinite border between validation and verification (David et al., 2002, p. 90).

In recent years, approaches have been developed to support root-cause analysis with automated techniques including data and process mining. A thorough treatment of automated debugging techniques in software-engineering is provided in the book by Zeller (2006). In Section 5.3.1, we reviewed the work by Bose and Suresh (2008) who apply process mining for this purpose.

The basic principle of automated root cause analysis is to record multiple traces of both 'failing' and 'succeeding' program executions and then use automated techniques to identify the minimal set of states and/or events in the program that are necessary to reproduce the error (Bose and Suresh, 2008; Calderon-Ruiz and Sepulveda, 2011; Zeller, 2006). Zeller (2006, p. 305) refers to such procedures as *delta debugging* and relates them to the *scientific method* (Zeller, 2006, Ch. 6) considered in philosophy (see e.g. Popper, 1982, mentioned in Section 2.4.3.3). Characteristic states and events are described either at the level of program constructs like statements and variables (Bose and Suresh, 2008; Zeller, 2006), or – especially when process mining is used – in terms of model elements like activities.[38]

Ou-Yang and Juan (2010, reviewed in Section 5.3.4.5) show at the example of deadlock detection that process mining can also support verification in the narrower sense. Different from simulation model implementations, formal models mined from simulation logs are abstract enough to be analyzed with exhaustive verification techniques like model checking or reachability analysis. In this regard, process mining could be considered as a technique for "program abstraction".[39]

However, an important difference is that abstractions obtained via process mining are not based on the computer model's source code (as in Visser et al., 2003) but induced from example logs. Therefore the reconstructed model might be verified exhaustively indeed, but only statistical evidence can be gained that it is actually bi-similar to the original computer model.

6.3.3.3. Operational Validation

In (Knaak, 2006, Sec. 3.3), we focused on the use of data and process mining to support confirmative operational validation:

> "Though DM is in principle an explorative analysis technique, we might also employ it to support model validation in a confirmative fashion. We therefore generate meta-models of the data obtained from the real system *and* from the simulation (i.e. two models of interaction protocols in our continuing example). We then validate the simulation results by comparing properties of both meta models, thereby using the real system's meta-model

---

[38] see e.g. the failure identification approach for business processes reported by Calderon-Ruiz and Sepulveda (2011)

[39] As termed by Visser et al. (2003). Technical relations between process mining and abstract interpretation are discussed by Carmona and Cortadella (2010).

to classify the simulation results as valid or invalid [see also Remondino and Correndo (2005); Arroyo et al. (2010) reviewed in Section 5.2.2.3]. This procedure is especially valuable for structural and interaction-related patterns that are not explicitly coded in the simulation model.

Traditionally, statistical tests and non-interpretable meta-models such as neural networks (see e.g. Kilmer et al., 1997) are applied in this context. However, using more application-specific understandable meta-models such as decision trees [see e.g. Nair et al. (2004) reviewed in Section 5.2.2.2], Petri nets [see e.g. Ou-Yang and Juan (2010) reviewed in Section 5.3.4.5], or social network graphs (see e.g. Christley et al., 2004) we can support the validation of qualitative simulation results by providing the user with a better understanding of *why* results are classified as valid or invalid. Beyond that, such meta-model-based validation allows to build automated validation suites similar to the well-known *unit tests* from software engineering (see e.g. Link, 2002). A drawback of supporting automated validation with DM techniques is that the reconstructed meta models might be erroneous and require validation themselves."

This description indicates that the conformance between simulation results and real system data can be assessed with different approaches: One option is to compare high level features of meta-models reconstructed from real and simulated data. This variant especially supports the requirement to validate MABS at the macroscopic level while abstracting from microscopic trajectories (see e.g. Rand et al., 2003, p. 2, reviewed in Section 5.1.2.3). We might e.g. rate a multi-agent workflow (external control perspective) mined from simulation data as valid when (a) it exhibits similar causal precedences as a matchable model reconstructed from real data and (b) the distributions of activity durations in both models do not differ significantly.[40] The literature review indicates that feature-based comparisons of meta-models can be applied in other perspectives as well; e.g. using metrics from social network analysis in the structural perspective.

Another possibility is to evaluate the match between the meta-models reconstructed from simulation data and sample data from the real system (or vice versa). In the internal and external control perspectives, this procedure relates to log replay-based conformance checking: Traces of the real system are replayed in the process model mined from the simulation log (or vice-versa) to assess its fitness and appropriateness (see e.g. Song and Aalst, 2008, p. 6 and Section 4.2.5.4 of this thesis). For decision models used in the decision and level-encompassing perspectives we can test how well the decision rules reconstructed from the simulation succeed to classify situations observed in the real system (or vice versa). Song and Aalst (2008, p. 7) propose fitness and appropriateness measures for staff assignment rules as an example of the organizational perspective.

Again, an important precondition for purposeful meta-model-based validation is that the models reconstructed from simulation and real system data have at least passed a face validation, or better a statistical cross-validation themselves. When sufficient data from the real system is not available, the output of one or more reference models can take its place (see Xiang et al., 2005, p. 48, reviewed in Section 5.1.2.3).

---

[40]This approach is taken by Calderon-Ruiz and Sepulveda (2011).

6.3.4. Optimization and Calibration

The literature reviewed in Section 5 (e.g. the work by Remondino and Correndo, 2006, reviewed in Section 5.2.2.3, and by Barry and Koehler (2004), reviewed in Section 5.2.2.4) shows that data and process mining bear potential to support the difficult task of MABS optimization and calibration. In the pre-publication (Knaak, 2006, Sec. 3.3) the following possibilities are discussed:

> "[This ...] use case is the most demanding due to a high degree of automatisation: We can support optimisation and calibration tasks in a MABS study by combining simulation-based optimisation with DM. [...] A problem [in simulation-based optimization] is that the objective function normally returns a one-dimensional value in order to ensure the comparability of different scenarios. This is acceptable for an evaluation based on simple numerical results. However, it limits the applicability of simulation-based optimisation to MABS, whose typically complex and qualitative results cannot easily be reduced to a single value (see also Calvez and Hutzler, 2006). DM can in princip[le ...] help to tackle this problem: Again following our above example, we can integrate a process mining algorithm into the objective function that reconstructs a model of an interaction protocol from the simulation trace. Due to the explicit representation of this model, we can employ automated methods that help to judge the quality of this model (e.g. by analysing statistical properties such as delay times or formal li[v ...]eness or safety properties). From this rating we might compute an objective function value.
>
> [...] Calibrating a MABS model is often difficult, but simulation-based optimisation and DM might help to support this task [as well]. As in operational validation, we can compare properties of the real system's meta-model (usually in the external control or structural perspective) with a related meta-model extracted from the simulation's output by means of some similarity measure. The similarity measure is the objective function that we try to maximise during the simulation-based optimisation process.
>
> Another idea is to employ DM in the [level-encompassing ...][41] perspective to support the search for better parameter configurations. In simulation-based optimisation, we mostly apply blind search algorithms or application-independent heuristics (e.g. genetic algorithms). However, using DM techniques, we can try to extract an *interpretable* meta-model of *how* the varied parameters influence the results to be optimised [...]. This meta-model can either guide the search in a more application-specific way, or at least help the user to validate the course and the results of the optimisation process. For an example [...] see Barton and Szczerbicka (2000) [reviewed in Section 5.2.3].
>
> [...] An important question is to what exten[t ...] the application of automated techniques is tractable and sensible in [... simulation-based optimisation]. An alternative approach are techniques such as interactive genetic algorithms (Boschetti, 1995) that leave the rating of scenarios to the user [see Gehlsen, 2004, p. 67]. In this context DM techniques can also be employed to provide the user with meaningful and understandable representations of complex simulation results."

Figure 6.10 illustrates these and further possibilities to support simulation-based optimization with data and process mining. While 3 variants (i.e. manual result evaluation, automated model-based result evaluation, and optimization with the aid of interpretable multi-level models) have been discussed in (Knaak, 2006) as cited above, 3 further use cases can be added based on the additional literature reviewed in Section 5. These will be explained in the following.

---

[41] In (Knaak, 2006) we used the term "multi-level perspective".

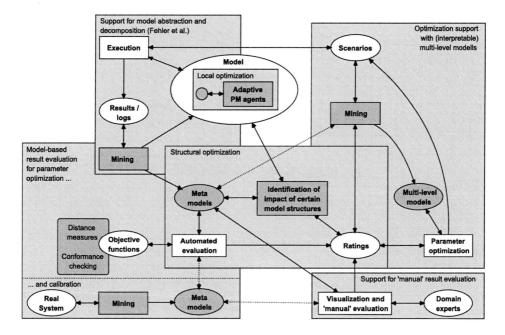

Figure 6.10.: An overview of possible integrations of data and process mining with simulation-based optimization based on the literature. The diagram also reflects the main components of simulation-based optimization systems like *DISMO* presented by Gehlsen and Page (2001, p. 513).

6.3.4.1. Structural optimization

Simulation-based optimization is commonly used to fine-tune model parameters towards an optimal solution for a given problem (Hagendorf, 2009, p. 7). Beyond that, some authors (e.g. Hagendorf, 2009, Sec. 6) also apply simulation-based optimization to the *structure* of (partial) models. Due to the possibility to obtain mining results at the conceptual modeling level, process mining techniques might provide valuable support for the optimization of the model structure. One might e.g. find that a certain precedence in a behavioral model (internal control perspective) or a cooperation between certain roles (structural perspective) leads to particularly high or low values of the objective function.

Automation could be enabled by combining optimization and process mining with an automated root-cause analysis (Zeller, 2006) as described in Section 6.3.3. While process mining has occasionally been combined with (automated) structure optimization in the context of business process analysis (see Hongtao et al., 2006) case studies in the MABS domain are still rare. The behavior alignment techniques by Meyer and Szirbik (2007, reviewed in Section 5.3.4.5) might be considered as an example.

6.3.4.2. Model Abstraction and Decomposition

In Section 5.1.2.2, we reviewed the *white box* calibration approach by Fehler et al. (2004), who apply model abstraction and decomposition to reduce the complexity of MABS calibration when *a-priori* knowledge of the model structure is available (as opposed to *black box* calibration). While Fehler et al. (2004) propose to employ distribution fitting and conventional (non-interpretable) meta-models for model abstraction, process mining techniques might be an interesting alternative due to the closer relation of the mining results to conceptual models in MABS.

By applying process mining to logs recorded at a mesoscopic level (e.g. groups of agents) one might even be able to reconstruct a "microscopic meta-model" as a basis for calibration, as proposed by Oechslein et al. (1999, reviewed in Section 5.1.2.2). Nevertheless, the semantic transfer of microscopic parameters under calibration to a higher level of aggregation remains challenging. Mining results from the level-encompassing perspective could possibly provide hints about relations between agent and group behavior.

Besides abstraction, process mining results might also support model decomposition. Fehler et al. (2004, p. 308) emphasize that a separate calibration of model components is only admissible if the components are sufficiently independent. Process mining results in the control flow and organizational perspectives can provide an overview whether dependencies between model components (e.g. 'causal' dependencies between plans or interactions of certain agent types) exist that forbid a functional or behavioral decomposition. Change point detection, as e.g. proposed by Bose et al. (2011a, reviewed in Section 4.2.5.3), can additionally help to identify phases of similar agent behavior as a basis for temporal decomposition.

6.3.4.3. Local optimization

As e.g. shown by Fehler et al. (2006a, cited in Section 5.1.2.2), an alternative possibility to perform simulation-based optimization is the equipment of individual agents with learning algorithms. This enables the modeled society of agents to learn an optimal solution (or an approximation thereof) of the given problem by means of local optimization. In the following section we will briefly discuss how process discovery and extension algorithms can support the implementation of adaptive agents.

6.3.5. Design of Adaptive Agents

The last two use cases discussed in this chapter fall out of the scope of simulation analysis and validation as the main subjects of this thesis. An integration of process mining and MABS might also add to further tasks within agent-based modeling, like the design of adaptive agents (discussed in this section) and the analysis of the model building process itself (discussed in Section 6.3.6).

In the pre-publication (Knaak, 2006, Sec. 3.3), the former of these use cases is characterized as follows:

> "The validity of many MABS models (e.g. sociological models simulating the effect of *downward causation*) can be enhanced by the integration of agents that are able to observe

and reflect on the structure and global behaviour of their environment, i.e. perform DM in the external control, structural, or even [level-encompassing[42] ...] perspective. [This case is somewhat related to the idea of "agent-aided interpretation" described by Drogoul et al. (2002, p. 11), see Section 5.1.1.1]

Agents might also acquire or adapt their internal decision and control flow models during the simulation by imitating other agents' behaviour. Following our previous example, an agent might be equipped with the ability to observe messages exchanged by its acquaintances and learn models of their protocols using process and decision mining techniques ([see also] Dongen et al., 2006b [...]). In our MULAN architecture [see Section 3.3.3.1], such protocols can be added dynamically to the agent's range of behaviour[...], which allows to simulate the ability to learn certain norms or interaction rules from observation. However, the task seems challenging, since the agent must learn *online* in a completely autonomous fashion."

Though envisioned by authors like Remondino and Correndo (2005, p. 4) and Dongen et al. (2006b, p. 1), reviewed in Sections 5.2.1 and 5.3.4.2, the development of agents that autonomously perform process mining as part of a running simulation still poses several challenges. These are related to the *fully automated* execution of mining algorithms (without letting a user select data, calibrate parameters, validate results, etc.) on the one hand and to the reconstruction of immediately *executable* models (without the need to 'manually' add programming language statements, etc.) on the other hand.

To the knowledge of the author, no fully automated process mining system or agent has been presented in the literature so far.[43] This might be due to the high modeling level and complexity of process mining results as compared to other models used in autonomous learning like neural networks. Compared to such low-level models, a learning agent built upon process mining algorithms would offer the advantage that the learned model representations (e.g. decision, control flow, and organizational models) are closer to the conceptual modeling level and therefore easier to validate by domain experts. This tradeoff between effectiveness of learning algorithms and interpretability of model representations is typical in machine learning (see e.g. Papadimitriou and Terzidis, 2005, p. 528).

Despite the limited effort and success in building autonomous process mining agents, the literature reviewed in Chapters 4 and 5 provides some starting points: The 'simulation model mining' approach by Wynn et al. (2010, reviewed in Section 5.3.4.1) shows that executable workflow simulations can be generated by merging process mining results from different perspectives with a high degree of automation. The *AgentAcademy* system by Mitkas et al. (2002) (Section 5.2.4.3) indicates that agents with a simple, standardized architecture (in this case decision rules formulated in *JESS*) can be (re-)trained with the aid of data mining techniques. The *behavior alignment* approach by Meyer and Szirbik (2007, reviewed in Section 5.3.4.5) depicts further options to adapt the behavior of Petri net-based agents without having to learn communication protocols 'from scratch'.

In the current state of research, a concentration on less automated applications of process mining, such as simulation analysis and validation, appears reasonable. Metaphorically speaking[44], the requirements of a simulation analyst and a simulated agent performing process mining

---

[42]Again, the original formulation used the term 'multi-level perspective'.
[43]One approach towards this direction is discussed by Jaroucheh et al. (2011).
[44]Of course we do not attribute any actual self-motivation to a simulated agent.

largely overlap with regard to the observed data, the considered mining perspectives, the chosen result representations, and the underlying analysis objectives (i.e. understanding, predicting, and improving the observed behavior). Therefore, concepts and techniques for simulation analysis and validation can provide a valuable basis for later extensions towards the development of autonomously learning agents.

In line with authors like Wynn et al. (2010) and Meyer and Szirbik (2007), we further argue that Petri net-based MA(B)S architectures are a particularly appropriate starting point to build adaptive process mining agents due to the similarity of model representations (see also Cabac et al., 2006b). Section 7.1.2.4 will briefly sketch an integration of process mining techniques into learning Petri net agents on the platform MULAN/CAPA. For the reasons stated above, the integration will only be considered from a software engineering point of view without discussing necessary extensions of process mining algorithms.

We continue this section with a discussion of dimensions that must be regarded when attempting to build learning agents based on process mining techniques.

6.3.5.1. Discovery vs. Extension

Agents can either learn new or adapt existing behavior models on the basis of observations. This distinction mirrors the process mining tasks of *discovery* and *enhancement*, where the latter term is used by Aalst (2011a, p. 10) to subsume the tasks of model *improvement* and *extension* (Aalst, 2006, p. 3), as reviewed in Section 4.2.2.2. For learning agents, model enhancement might be preferred for several reasons.[45]

From a *technical* point of view, coherent agent behavior might be easier to obtain when large parts have already been pre-defined by the modeler. From a *modeling* point of view, it appears plausible that an agent comes with some initial knowledge about the simulated domain (i.e. 'the world it dwells in'), which is then gradually improved during simulation. In accordance with the above characterization from (Aalst, 2011a, p. 10), process mining-based model enhancement might be applied in learning agents either as an improvement (e.g. the model structure is modified to better fit the simulated domain) or as an extension (e.g. the agent annotates its behavioral model with new information like time constraints) of the internal models.

Note that in the *TAL* approach, Stuit et al. (2007b, p. 247) initially proposed the use of process discovery to realize adaptive agents, but then settled on the implementation of an enhancement technique in the form of behavior alignment (Meyer and Szirbik, 2007); see Sections 3.3.3.5 and 5.3.4.5.

6.3.5.2. Centralized vs. Individual Mining Support

From a software engineering point of view, process mining can be added to a MA(B)S either by equipping individual agents with this functionality or by adding a distinct, singleton[46] 'process mining service' to the platform. Both variants have characteristic advantages and drawbacks.

---

[45]The following discussion is partly based on ideas by Kruse (e.g. 2008) on learning in MABS in general.

[46]roughly in the sense of the well-known design pattern described by Gamma et al. (1995, pp. 127)

Technically, it appears reasonable and resource-efficient to encapsulate complex process mining functionality offered by systems like *ProM* (see Section 4.2.6.1) in a dedicated agent that provides these services to other agents on the platform. This agent might even be "omniscient"[47] in the sense that it has access to all data logged in the current simulation and possibly to additional data from past simulations.

Conceptually, it might often be more plausible to implement process mining abilities in individual agents due to the lack of realism induced into the model by "omniscient" agents (Moreno et al., 1999, p. 210). In doing so, we can straightforwardly restrict the available training data to the local perception radius of an agent (see Klügl, 2000, p. 59, reviewed in Section 3.1.1.1). Furthermore, agents can be equipped with different mining algorithms or parameter settings to model variations in learning strategies and abilities.[48]

A combination of both approaches is also possible: An agent might simply pass its local log data and parameter settings to the (singleton) component that encapsulates the process mining system. A similar strategy is e.g. followed in (Knaak, 2002) to reduce the memory consumption of the rule engine *JESS* in MABS with the framework *FAMOS*. Note that Mitkas et al. (2002) propose a centralized mining architecture in their *AgentAcademy* system (see Section 5.2.4.3), whereas Meyer and Szirbik (2007, pp. 279) and Dongen et al. (2006b, p. 15), at least on the conceptual level, seem to assume individual process mining support for adaptive agents.

6.3.5.3. Re-Training of Simulated Agents

A further question, that shall not be discussed in detail here, is how to determine states and events that cause a re-training of learning agents in simulations. In the context of reinforcement learning, Kruse (2008) notes that most machine learning approaches assume a time-driven adaptation of the agents' internal models in regular intervals. In this regard, event-driven simulations are more demanding since the irregular time intervals between events at least require a time-weighted assessment of an agent's recent performance when determining the need to re-learn (Kruse, 2008). We refer to Kruse (2008) for a further discussion of the embedding of machine learning techniques into event-driven agent-based simulations.

6.3.6. Analysis of the Model Building Cycle

The final use case is only loosely related to the analysis and validation of simulation models as the main subject of this thesis. Here, the analysis targets are not simulation models and matchable real systems, but activities performed by persons involved in a simulation study. In Section 5.3.1, we learned that the analysis of software development processes is one of process mining's foremost applications (see e.g. Cook and Wolf, 1998; Poncin et al., 2011; Rubin et al., 2007). Simulation studies share several phases (at least real system analysis, conceptual modeling, implementation, and parts of validation) with process models for software development (see also Brade, 2003, p. 20). It therefore seems plausible that process mining can also support the analysis and improvement of simulation model building cycles.

---

[47]as to use the term by Moreno et al. (1999, p. 210) in a slightly different context
[48]see the discussion on heterogeneity of multi-agent models led by Klügl (2000, p. 62)

To transfer software development process mining (e.g. Rubin, 2007; Rubin et al., 2007) to the simulation domain, several extensions are required. This is due to the fact that the mining of "software repositories" (Rubin et al., 2007, pp. 172) typically focuses on the phases of software design (modeling), implementation, testing, and review. However, a simulation study usually comprises additional phases of operational validation, experimentation, result analysis, and transfer of knowledge to the real system (Page and Kreutzer, 2005, p. 14), which are not (or only in a rather different form) considered in a conventional software development project (see also Brade, 2003, p. 20).

Based on a diagram by Rubin et al. (2007, p. 172), Figure 6.11 sketches possible extensions of software development process mining towards the analysis of simulation studies. White diagram elements display repositories, roles, and activities of software (development) process mining adopted from (Rubin et al., 2007, p. 172). These authors consider data from bug tracking and revision management systems as well as several web- and E-mail-based sources to analyze models of software development processes.

Diagram elements shaded in grey represent additional data sources, roles, and mining approaches that are more specific for the analysis of simulation studies. Data collected from requirements tracking systems (e.g. O'Brien, 1996), analysis documents, and usage logs of modeling tools might be considered to gain a better overview of activities performed by modelers, domain experts, and managers during analysis and modeling.

While such data is also relevant for software development in general, it is particularly relevant in model-driven approaches like PAOSE (Section 3.3.3.2). From the log of the Petri net IDE RENEW (Section 2.3.2.5), one might e.g. strive to gather knowledge about relations between properties of the modelled net (such as its size, number of contained object nets, or code inscriptions) and the need to re-simulate and correct it during a modeling session.

The lower half of Figure 6.11 focuses on the experimentation-related phases that distinguish simulation studies from general software development projects. Relevant data sources for these phases include validation reports, experiment and result databases, logs of knowledge discovery processes conducted during result analysis, usage data of simulation tools, and documentations of decisions derived from simulation results. While much of this data will be hard to obtain in a form that is suitable for process mining, a few approaches from the literature might serve as starting points.

In Section 5.3.4.1 we reviewed the 'decision process mining' approach by Dolean and Petrusel (2011) and its relations to the simulation domain. However, the simple decision processes that these authors analyze on the basis of logs from decision support systems are still far from the complexity of real-world decisions based on simulation models.

The machine learning and KDD community has coined the term *meta learning* or *meta mining* for the 'self-application' of data mining techniques to the analysis of knowledge discovery processes (Hilario et al., 2011, p. 273). Hilario et al. (2011, pp. 302) e.g. apply data ming to a database of mining experiments (Hilario et al., 2011, p. 281) to relate properties of algorithms and workflows to their mining performance. *ProM* also provides a usage log in *MXML* as a source to analyze process mining sessions with the tool itself.

Due to the similarities between KDD and simulation analysis (Köster, 2002), meta mining might prove useful in the simulation domain as well. This especially holds true when a data

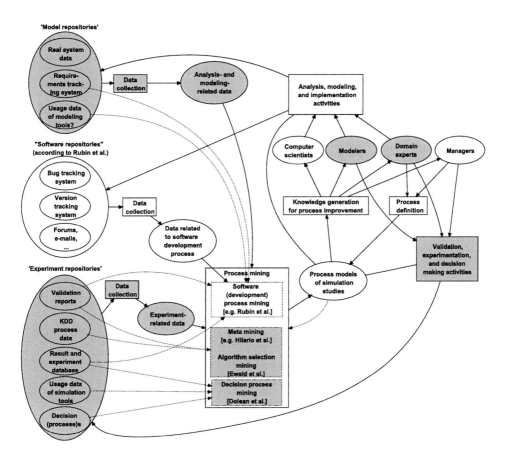

Figure 6.11.: 'Model building cycle mining' as an extension of software (development) process mining. White diagram elements are adopted with modifications from the "process mining framework for software processes" by Rubin et al. (2007, p. 172). Further cited approaches are explained in the text.

mining-based analysis process is assumed. One example of meta learning from simulation data is the work by Ewald et al. (2009): These authors apply data mining to support the selection of appropriate simulation algorithms (e.g. random number generators) for certain model types based on simulation performance data (Ewald et al., 2009, p. 14:1). As reviewed in Section 5.4.2.1, the process-aware simulation framework *WorMS* from the same research group (Rybacki et al., 2011) also foresees components to analyze the enacted workflows, but without explicit regard to process mining.

Clearly, the mining of model building cycles is not restricted to MABS in the first place. Following the argumentation by Cabac (2007), a community of model or software developers might be considered as a MAS itself. Therefore, an agent-oriented process mining framework, as advocated in this thesis, might form a suitable basis for 'model building cycle mining' in general. In doing so, the practical problems to be solved are partly similar, but also go beyond software development process mining, including:

- *Data availability*: Data from many different sources must be collected and integrated (Poncin et al., 2011, p. 5). A workflow-based simulation system like *WorMS* (Rybacki et al., 2011) and a data mapping framework like *FRASR* (Poncin et al., 2011), developed for process mining in software engineering, might be an appropriate technical basis.

- *Privacy concerns*: Process mining is not applied to simulated agents but to *real persons* involved in a simulation study. Therefore, ethical aspects of the performed analyses require specific attention (see also Aalst et al., 2012, p. 190).

- *Appropriate target studies*: Strictly structured process models like the *V-model* are typically applied in large organisations and safety-critical simulations (see e.g. Brade, 2003, pp. 30). Such processes might provide the best data quality for analysis due to formalized and well-documented workflows. However, in agile processes like PAOSE, *post-hoc* analyses with process mining could potentially deliver more interesting and relevant results.

6.4. Simulation-specific Requirements

In the preceding sections, we have punctually stated requirements that the domains of MAS and simulation pose on the application of process mining algorithms. We will now summarize and extend this discussion with a specific focus on requirements related to the analysis of different types of logs handled in simulation studies and logs collected from *multiple replications* of simulated processes.

Summarizing the findings by Remondino and Correndo (2006) as well as Cabac and Denz (2008), we can identify 3 types of logs encountered during the course of a simulation study:[49]

1. Logs observed from *real systems* are considered during real system analysis and validation.

---

[49]The author was pointed to the idea that different forms of process mining (in particular software process mining vs. software development process mining as described in Section 5.3.1) can be characterized according to the analyzed log types by a reviewer of the article published as (Cabac and Denz, 2008). This reviewer also indicated that the same approach is followed by Günther et al. (2006) to distinguish change mining from 'conventional' process mining (see Section 4.2.5.3).

2. Logs generated by *simulation models* build the basis for model exploration, validation, optimization (calibration), and the training of adaptive simulated agents. These logs can be either *program-centric* focusing on programming language constructs like methods, or *model-centric* focusing on high level activities.

3. Logs of activities performed by model developers and simulation users (called *simulation study logs* in the following) are needed for the analysis of the model building cycle.

Each type of logs poses specific requirements on the process mining algorithms applied to their analysis. In general, "multi-agent activity logs" (Rozinat et al., 2009d) can be event- or activity-based. Communication logs of message-based MAS typically contain instantaneous events. Their analysis therefore requires mining algorithms that do not depend on information about activity durations (e.g. the α algorithm, see Section 4.2.3.1).

Recalling the properties of process mining techniques summarized in Section 4.2.2.3 (based on sources like Medeiros, 2006), a number of general guidelines can be identified, that are described in the following.

6.4.1. Robustness and Degree of Generalization

Due to the potentially 'perfect' data quality of simulation logs, coping with noise and incompleteness is mainly an issue for the mining of real system and simulation study logs. An exception are testbed simulations for adaptive agents where noise is explicitly generated to challenge the robustness of the examined learning algorithms. The typical lack of data in real system analysis might suggest the use of mining algorithms with lower requirements on log completeness, such as local completeness in the α algorithm (see Aalst, 2010a, pp. 37-38, reviewed in Section 4.2.3.1).

In most MABS, events are scheduled in a purely sequential fashion to ensure the repeatability of experiments. However, in truly concurrent environments like RENEW[50] or in optimistically synchronized distributed simulations (see e.g. Page and Kreutzer, 2005, p. 376), logging mechanisms must be able to compensate causality errors of events generated by independent simulation components. We encountered this problem in the case study reported in Chapter 7. As mentioned in Section 5.2.4.1, *vector clocks* are a mechanism to ensure event causality in distributed systems, which is also used in the MAS analysis tool *ACLAnalyser* (Vigueras and Botia, 2008, p. 193).[51]

In real system analysis and adaptive agent design, a strongly generalizing process mining algorithm might, to a certain degree and when used with care, help to compensate lacking data and provide the required level of abstraction. For exploratory analysis and face validation, an algorithm like the *Heuristics Miner* seems appropriate due to its ability to focus on main behavior while neglecting infrequent cases (Weijters et al., 2006, p. 24). For operational validation and verification in the wider sense, an exact algorithm (e.g. based on the theory of regions as in Rubin et al., 2006, reviewed in Section 4.2.3.3) might be more appropriate to reduce the risk of suppressing infrequent, but nevertheless relevant error cases.

---

[50]Note that timed RENEW simulations always run in a sequential mode (see Section 2.3.2.5).

[51]For a discussion of process mining on logs recorded in distributed environments see e.g. Kim (2009).

6.4.2. Relevant Control Flow Constructs

To the impression gained from the literature review and our practical experience from the case studies, the following control flow constructs might be most relevant with respect to the mining of agent behavior:

- *Duplicate tasks* often occur when complex models of behavior are built from a restricted set of events.

- *Loops* are relevant because agents in MABS typically exhibit a temporally extended life cycle with repeated execution of similar behavior.

- Though most MABS run sequentially (see above), *concurrent splits and joins* are used to express 'causal' independence of activities at the conceptual level, and to simplify the resulting behavioral models (see e.g. Schütt, 2003, reviewed in Section 4.2.3.3).

- *Hierarchical sub-processes* are an important construct to handle the complexity of agent behavior.

- *Multiple instantiation patterns* often occur in agent interaction protocols like e.g. *contract net*.

- *Non-stationary processes* can be observed in non-steady-state simulations (Page and Kreutzer, 2005, p. 188) like our courier service simulations described in Chapter 8. They are especially common in systems of self-organizing and adaptive agents.

Process mining techniques for the handling of these constructs have been discussed in the literature review (Chapters 4, 5) and arranged into a coherent framework of analysis perspectives in Section 6.2. With the exception of non-stationary processes, which will be treated in the dissertation by Kruse (see 2008), all mentioned constructs are also in the focus of the case studies presented in Chapters 7 and 8.

6.4.3. Usability of Mining Techniques for Simulation Practitioners

A common observation in practical simulation studies is that simulation users are often unaware of the pitfalls related to statistical output analysis and validation (Page and Kreutzer, 2005, p. 21). This problem increases when they are confronted with a complex analysis technique like process mining and its related algorithmic peculiarities. Targeting "non-expert users" of process mining in general, Aalst et al. (2012, p. 191) claim that:

> "Even if it is easy to generate process mining results, this does not mean the results are actually useful. The user may have problems understanding the output or is tempted to infer incorrect conclusions. To avoid such problems, the results should be presented in a suitable representation [...and their] trustworthiness [...] should always be clearly indicated. [...] In fact, existing process mining techniques do not warn for a low fitness or overfitting.

To further the thoughtful application of process mining in domains like simulation, techniques based on straightforward algorithmic principles, with a manageable number of parameters (e.g. the α algorithm) might even be preferable in comparison to more powerful, but less usable techniques like e.g. genetic algorithms. This effort, which somehow mirrors the principle of

Occam's Razor (Section 2.4.3.4), is clearly limited by the ability of 'simple' process mining algorithms to handle the complexity of models and data in MABS.[52]

An alternative approach, also mentioned by Aalst et al. (2012, p. 191), is to reduce the difficulties of applying mining algorithms with the aid of software assistants: As reviewed in Section 4.2.3.4, Burattin and Sperduti (2010) developed an algorithm to identify appropriate parameter settings for the *Heuristics Miner* algorithm. However, an automated optimization procedure brings in further complexity itself that must, at least to a certain degree, be understood by the user to rate the quality of its results. Due to such difficulties, Aalst et al. (2012, p. 191) regard "improving the usability [and ...] understandability [of process mining techniques] for non-experts" as an important goal of future process mining research:

> "The challenge is to hide the sophisticated process mining algorithms behind user-friendly interfaces that automatically set parameters and suggest suitable types of analysis."

6.4.4. Handling of Multiple Stochastic Simulation Runs

Simulation experiments typically consist of multiple simulation runs where (a) different *scenarios* are evaluated (Page and Kreutzer, 2005, pp. 189) and (b) multiple *replications* of the same scenario are simulated to increase the statistical significance of the results (Page and Kreutzer, 2005, pp. 173,185). Statistical measures like confidence intervals commonly capture the range of variation within a set of (stochastic) simulation results (Page and Kreutzer, 2005, pp. 180). As a technique for simulation analysis, process mining must also provide information about similarities, differences, and stochastic variations in a collection of results. Basically, every simulated scenario and replication results in a distinct log from which process mining can reconstruct a meta-model representing the respective run.

For the explicit comparison of one or more meta-models from the result collection, an application of methods for *delta analysis* (see e.g. Aalst, 2005b) appears manifest. These are originally used for "comparing the actual process, [...] obtained through process mining with some predefined process" (Aalst, 2005b, p. 203). Aalst (2005b, pp. 206) summarizes several techniques for manual and automated delta analysis that might also be applied to the analysis of multiple simulation runs:

- Manual comparison of two or more reconstructed models, which "for large processes [...] may be difficult" (Aalst, 2005b, p. 206).

- Automated "highlight [of] differences between two models in a graphical fashion. However, most of such techniques [...] focus [...] on syntactical [...] rather than semantical differences." (Aalst, 2005b, p. 206). One example of a simple graphical comparison tool is the *ImageNetDiff* plugin, which visualizes differences between two Petri nets modelled in RENEW (Betz et al., 2011, p. 172).

- Application of concepts to describe behavioral inheritance in control flow models. This includes "the notion of the *Greatest Common Divisor* (GCD) and the *Least Common Multiple* (LCM) of two or more processes" (Aalst, 2005b, p. 206). According to Aalst and Basten

---

[52]In this context, recall the famous "quote attributed to Einstein" that "everything should be made as simple as possible but not simpler" (`http://en.wikiquote.org/wiki/Albert_Einstein`, last visit 2012-10-27).

(2001, p. 40)[53], "the idea is that the GCD should capture the commonality of all [model] variants, i.e. the part they agree on. The LCM should capture all possible behavior of all the variants". Taking on the analogy with statistical measures, the GCD might be related to an 'average' or 'median' behavior, while the LCM focuses on behavioral 'variance'.

- Computation of *change regions* that not do only consider syntactic differences of elements between two models, but also regard for semantic effects that these differences have on neighboring model elements (Aalst, 2005b, p. 206).

For the display of GCD and LCM, the techniques mentioned by Aalst et al. (2012, p. 184, reviewed in Section 6.2.7) might be applied to visualize frequencies and variances of model element occurrences in the underlying collection of models. Nevertheless, the LCM of a strongly varying collection of models can be a rather complex and difficult to understand model itself.

Li et al. (2011) propose an alternative approach to express the degree to which *model variants* deviate from a predefined *reference model*. These authors first calculate the *distance* $d_{(S,S')}$ between a reference model S and every model variant S' in terms of the "minimal number of high level change operations [see Section 4.2.5.3] needed for transforming S into S'" (Li et al., 2011, p. 412). Then the *average weighted distance* in a model variant collection can be determined as (Li et al., 2011, p. 413):

$$D_{(S,M)} = \frac{\sum_{i=1}^{n} d_{(S,S_i)} \cdot w_i}{\sum_{i=1}^{n} w_i}, \qquad (6.2)$$

where w_i is the number of occurrences of model variant S_i in a collection of size n. For the case that no reference model is given a-priori, Li et al. (2011, Sec. 6) also present a heuristic algorithm to mine a reference model S from the collection of model variants $\{S_1, ..., S_n\}$ such that the average weighted distance is minimized.

Since the mined reference model S represents the "'center' of the variants" (Li et al., 2011, p. 426), it can again be identified with the 'average' behavior found in the model collection. By additionally determining the two model variants S' and S'', which differ most strongly from the reference model *and* from each other (i.e. $d_{S,S'} + d_{S,S''} + d_{S',S''}$ are maximized), one might state a kind of 'confidence interval' describing the collection in terms of three models.

Drawbacks of the approach by Li et al. (2011) are that (1) it is restricted to *block structured* models (Li et al., 2011, p. 411), and (2) the computation of the distance measure d is a NP-hard problem (Li et al., 2011, p. 412). A general drawback of the reviewed methods in the context of simulation is that only the control flow perspective is considered. While Li et al. (2011, p. 431) suggest to include information on *data flow* in the future, *temporal* information (durations of activities, etc.) might be most important for the simulation domain.

Further peculiarities of simulation data analysis are often related to the handling of non-stationary process phases (e.g. detection of a simulation's "warm-up phase", Page and Kreutzer, 2005, p. 174). Within our framework, these are (at least conceptually) covered by the *adaptivity perspective* discussed in Section 6.2.5.

---

[53]referenced in (Aalst, 2005b, p. 206)

6.5. Summary and Contributions

In this chapter, we have presented a conceptual framework for the integration of process mining and MABS. It is an attempt to integrate many ideas encountered in the review of the state-of-the-art in process mining (Chapter 4) and conventional or data mining-supported MABS analysis (Chapter 5) into a coherent scheme. The framework's dimensions of analysis perspectives and use cases are chosen in accordance with common classification schemes in modeling (e.g. UML, see Jeckle et al., 2002), process mining (see e.g. Aalst, 2006; Rembert and Ellis, 2009), and (data mining-supported) MA(B)S validation (see e.g. Arroyo et al., 2010; Nair et al., 2004; Ndumu and Nwana, 1999; Remondino and Correndo, 2005).

Based on the literature on process mining and MAS, six abstract analysis perspectives have been identified, i.e. decision, internal control, external control, structural, adaptivity, and level encompassing perspective. The mechanism of process extension (Aalst, 2011a, p. 10) was consulted to add domain-specific perspectives. Following the approach by Rembert and Ellis (2009), the perspectives were concretized by an overview of relevant process dimensions and dimensional relations. In doing so, existing process mining perspectives, algorithms, and model representations were transferred into an explicitly agent-based context.

Integrating literature on data mining, process mining, (data mining-based) MA(B)S validation, and software reverse engineering, six use cases in the model building cycle were identified. This includes real system analysis, simulation model exploration, validation, optimization and calibration, adaptive agent design, and model building cycle mining. The use cases were concretized by discussing relevant data sources, mining algorithms, and support techniques. For each use case[54], a Petri net-based overview diagram was stated, that might serve as a basis to derive more detailed data flow diagrams. The gathered MABS-specific requirements were summarized and detailed in the final section of this chapter.

The main contribution of the presented framework lies in the provision of a coherent view on the research fields of MABS and process mining. From the point of view of MABS, it might serve as a guideline for the systematic application of process mining techniques in simulation studies. Compared to existing work in MABS (e.g. Arroyo et al., 2010; Serrano et al., 2009) it (1) strives to be more detailed and comprehensive by integrating all use cases identified in the extensive literature review, (2) explicitly regards for analysis perspectives adopted from process mining and AOSE, and (3) explicitly focuses on process mining.

The identified dimensions and use cases also support a coherent classification of the literature related to the subject at hand, which is rather 'scattered' across different fields (see Chapters 4 and 5). Figure 6.12 shows a first attempt to classify ten approaches from the literature, that are especially influential for or closely related to this thesis, within the dimensions of the framework.[55] Extending and quantifying this classification for further approaches from the literature (e.g. those reviewed in Sections 4 and 5) will lead to a detailed overview of the 'research landscape', quite similar to the efforts by Tiwari et al. (2008) regarding process mining techniques.

---

[54]except for adaptive agent design

[55]Of course, the classification can only mirror the author's individual understanding and subjective rating of the cited work.

Authors	Title	Year	Perspectives	Use Cases	Focus	Domain
Jacobs and Driessens	Inductive Verification and Validation of Multi-Agent Systems	1998	Decisions, external control	Validation / verification (in the wider sense)	Data mining, techniques (ILP)	Robot soccer
Ndumu et al.	Visualising and Debugging Distributed Multi-Agent Systems	1999	Internal control, external control, structure (social)	Exploration, verification (in the wider sense), calibration	Interactive visualization	AOSE
Köster	Analyse von Simulationsdaten mit Methoden des Knowledge Discovery in Databases	2002	Decisions, internal control, level-encompassing	Exploration, validation	Data mining, methodology, techniques	Simulation
Schütt	FuzFlow: Automated Modelling of Business Interaction Processes for Flow Prediction	2003	Decisions, external control	Meta-modeling / prediction	Process mining, techniques	Business process management
Nair et al.	Automated Assistants for Analyzing Team Behaviors	2004	Decisions, external control, level-encompassing	Exploration, calibration	Data mining, techniques and tools	Robot soccer, AOSE
Remondino and Correndo	MABS Validation through Repeated Execution and Data Mining Analysis	2006	Decisions, structure, level-encompassing	Real system analysis, exploration, validation, calibration, adaptive agents	Data mining, methodology	MABS
Van Dongen et al.	Process Mining in a Multi-Agent Auctioning System	2006	Decisions, internal control	Exploration, adaptive agents	Process mining, techniques	MABS
Rozinat et al.	Analyzing Multi-agent Activity Logs Using Process Mining Techniques	2009	Decisions, internal control, external control	Exploration, validation	Process mining, techniques	Robot soccer
Chen	Complex Event Types for Agent-Based Simulation	2009	Structure, external control, level-encompassing	Exploration, validation, meta-modelling / prediction	Complex events, data mining	MABS
Arroyo et al.	Re-thinking Simulation: A Methodological Approach for the Application of Data Mining in Agent-Based Modelling	2010	(Decisions), structure, adaptivity (structural dynamics), level-encompassing	Real system analysis, exploration, validation, calibration	Data mining, methodology, techniques, case study	MABS

Figure 6.12.: Ten influential and closely related approaches from the literature classified within the framework dimensions of analysis perspectives and use cases.

From the point of view of process mining, the conceptual framework can be regarded as an alternative to existing work on methodology and classification (e.g. Aalst, 2006; Rembert and Ellis, 2009) from an explicitly 'agent-based' viewpoint. This is in accordance with recent efforts by the Eindhoven research group to "introduce process mining as an enabling technology for analyzing the behavior of agents"[56]] and might serve as a 'conceptual superstructure' for *ad hoc*-studies like (Dongen et al., 2006b; Rozinat et al., 2009d); reviewed in Section 5.3.4.2.

The approach might be particularly useful since the main application areas of process mining, i.e. business process analysis and software engineering have already proven to benefit largely from the concept of MAS. While parts of the framework were straightforwardly adopted from concepts in process mining with an already strong 'agent-oriented flavor' (e.g. the organizational perspective (Abdelkafi and Bouzguenda, 2010; Hanachi and Khaloul, 2008; Song and Aalst, 2008) as part of the structural perspective), they were complemented by additional viewpoints from the domain of MA(B)S, such as the level-encompassing perspective, embellished by integrating recent work of Chen (2009).

In the following Chapters, the conceptual framework is applied and further concretized in two MA(B)S studies, first following the model-based PAOSE approach (Chapter 7), then focusing on a larger, more code-centric MABS project on logistics simulation with the software frameworks DESMO-J and FAMOS (Chapter 8).

---

[56]http://www.lorentzcenter.nl/lc/web/2011/479/abstracts.php3 (last visit 2012-10-27)

7. Process Mining in PAOSE

The objective of the first case study is to integrate process mining into the Petri net-based Agent Oriented Software Engineering Approach PAOSE based on the MAS architecture MULAN (Section 3.3.3.1) and the agent platform CAPA (Section 3.4.5) built on top of the Petri net simulator RENEW (Section 2.3.2.5). These tools and the underlying concepts are developed by the Department of Informatic's theoretical foundations group (TGI) at the University of Hamburg.

The case study was conducted in cooperation with colleagues from this group, mainly Lawrence Cabac, Frank Heitmann, Daniel Moldt, and Florian Plähn. Results were pre-published, among others, in reports and articles by Cabac et al. (2006b), Cabac et al. (2006c), and Cabac and Denz (2008), which also build the basis for this chapter. Parts of the case study are described in the dissertation by Cabac (2010, Ch. 17) as well.

7.1. Process Mining and the Mulan Framework

This section substantiates why the PAOSE approach and the MULAN architecture provide a highly appropriate framework for the integration of process mining and MAS. Furthermore, relations of this approach to the perspectives and use cases from the conceptual framework presented in the previous chapter are sketched.

7.1.1. Introduction and Motivation

The PAOSE approach offers the obvious advantage of sharing the formal foundation of Petri nets with many process mining techniques. In the abstract section of (Cabac et al., 2006b), we summarize the mutual benefits of integrating MAS and process mining on this common basis:

> "Process mining and multi-agent models are powerful techniques for the analysis of processes and organizations. However, the integration of both fields has seldom been considered due to the lack of common conceptual background. We propose to close this gap by using Petri nets as an operational semantics.

> We consider process mining a useful addition to monitor and debug multi-agent applications and simulations in the development phase. Mining results can be represented in the formalized form of Petri nets that allows to validate or verify the actual behavior. Agent models can thus be improved by process mining results. Furthermore, multi-agent models can be used to generate log data for testing process mining algorithms. Compared to *flat* Petri nets, structured models based on agent-oriented Petri nets simplify the generation of realistic, yet controllable test data."

From the point of view of MAS, the use of Petri nets as a modeling language especially eases the feedback of mining results into the development of the model (Cabac et al., 2006b, Sec. 4.1). Several use cases described in the previous chapter profit from this representational similarity (Cabac et al., 2006b, Sec. 1):

- In *real system analysis*, the mining of real world process logs generates Petri nets that can be used as templates for the implementation of the model.

- The *design of adaptive Petri net agents* is naturally complemented with process mining to learn or improve their internal models. Concerning model improvement, the neural network-based approach by Meyer and Szirbik (2007), reviewed in Section 5.3.4.5, is a first step into this direction. Stuit et al. (2007b, Sec. 7) also mention process discovery as a technique to implement learning Petri net agents.

- During *operational validation*, the representational similarity eases a matching between the model components under validation and the mining results reconstructed from their execution logs (Cabac et al., 2006b, Sec. 4.1). Both mined and implemented MAS models in the form of Petri nets are, to a certain degree, accessible to *formal verification* techniques.. Recall the study by Ou-Yang and Juan (2010), reviewed in Section 5.3.4.5, as an example.

From the point of view of process mining, the structure provided by a Petri net-based MAS model like MULAN offers several advantages related to the use of perspectives for complexity reduction, enhanced "representational bias" (Aalst, 2011b), and test data generation. These are discussed in the following.

7.1.2. Analysis Perspectives and Mulan

In (Cabac et al., 2006b, Sec. 4.3) we related the 4 views of the MULAN model to the 'agent-oriented' process mining perspectives from Section 6.2.[1] Establishing this relation is straightforward in the first place, since the perspective model is largely influenced by the MULAN views itself.

In this publication, we identified several areas that are affected by a mapping of analysis perspectives to executable Petri net models (Cabac et al., 2006b, Sec. 4.3):

- determination of sources for data collection,

- use of formalized analysis perspectives as background knowledge to provide enhanced "representational bias" (Aalst, 2011b) for agent-based models,

- development of structured models to generate complex test data,

- conversion of 'code-centric' MAS implementations into an explicit model, and

- identification of target models in the PAOSE approach.

These areas will be detailed in the following.

---

[1] A similar attempt within the business process-centric ICN (Information Control Net) model is reported by Rembert and Ellis (2009, Secs. 4.1, 4.2); see Section 4.2.2.1 of this thesis.

7.1.2.1. Determination of Data Sources

Our first attempt to identify data sources for process mining in the Mulan model and the related toolset is described in (Cabac et al., 2006b, Sec. 4.3.1):

> "By comparing the Mulan views with the [...] analysis perspectives we can determine data sources for mining in these perspectives. Mining in the *decision perspective* relates the state of an agent's knowledge [base] to its observable actions represented by sent messages. Mining *internal control* means to reconstruct the *protocols* running within an agent from these messages. For reconstructing *external control* information about message traffic at the level of the platform or the MAS is needed. As stated in (Aalst, 2004) "some agent" observing all message traffic is required. *Structural* information (e.g. about agents' relations and roles on a platform) can also be reconstructed from observing messages. However, there are sources of additional data: In the FIPA compliant platform Capa we can for example request the services offered by an agent from a central *directory facilitator* (DF).
>
> A more general advantage [of using Mulan] is the recursive organization of the [...] model that results in "is-a" relationships between its components. (see Section [... 3.3.1]). Thus, data collection and mining techniques for one level (e.g. analyzing interactions between agents) are naturally transferred to other levels (e.g. analyzing interactions between platforms)."

To improve mining results, it is even possible to fall back on data gathered *below* the agent level: We can e.g. observe firings of transitions or steps from the underlying *Renew* simulator to gain additional information about concurrency relations. The use of logs generated by the Renew simulator reduces the task of process discovery to the *folding* of a trace (see e.g. Diekert and Rozenberg, 1995). In contrast to control flow mining from conventional execution logs, there is no need to "guess"[2] elements of the reconstructed net. This is due to the availability of information on (a) creation of net instances, (b) initial markings of nets, (c) places, (d) production and consumption of tokens, and (e) synchronous firing of transitions.

The below log snippet provides an impression. It was recorded during a simulation of a reference net shown in Figure 7.5 of Section 7.1.3.1. The example represents a variation of a complex event from the "lions and antelopes" example by Chen et al. (2010, p. 49) reviewed in Section 5.2.2.4:

```
(2)-------- Synchronously --------
(2)Removing {[int(1),hunt,L4],[int(2),hunt,L4],[int(3),die,L4]}
   in ce_main[869].Logs
(2)Firing ce_lion_overhunting[875].T2
(2)Firing ce_main[869].T1
(2)New net instance ce_lion_overhunting[875] created.
(2)Putting {[int(1),hunt,L4],[int(2),hunt,L4],[int(3),die,L4]}
   into ce_lion_overhunting[875].P2
(2)Putting ce_main[869] into ce_lion_overhunting[875].P1
(2)Putting ce_lion_overhunting[875] into ce_main[869].Patterns
(3)-------- Synchronously --------
(3)Removing {[int(1),hunt,L6],[int(2),hunt,L7],[int(3),die,L6]}
```

---

[2]as to use the term by Aalst et al. (2011, p. 30)

```
in ce_main[869].Logs
...
```

The snippet indicates that despite the wealth of contained information, the RENEW logger traces the running processes on a level too low for the analysis of an agent-based model. For instance, the separation of traces that represent actual agent interactions (with regards to content) from traces of the agent platform's technical infrastructure appears highly difficult on this level.

In the case study at hand, we therefore focus on the more appropriate level of message-based agent interactions. This approach additionally allows to transfer the developed techniques and tools to other FIPA-compliant MAS. The RENEW log might nevertheless be consulted to derive additional information, somehow similar to an "oracle" in the software reverse engineering approach by Kumar et al. (2011, p. 97) reviewed in Section 5.3.2.

7.1.2.2. Background Knowledge and Representational Bias

This idea is explicated by Cabac et al. (2006b, Sec. 4.3.1) only very briefly:

> "Another expectation is that the MULAN model can be used as *background knowledge* to improve and structure mining results similar to the BDI-based approach by Lam and Barber (2005) (compare with Section [... 5.2.4.2]). For process mining, the agent-based structure might provide a stronger *inductive bias* (see Section [... 4.1.3.2]) than models based on *flat* Petri nets."

Though the topic is not in the focus of this thesis either, the mining procedure for complex interaction protocols shown in Section 7.3 utilizes some background knowledge about the structure of MAS protocols, such as the fact that *conversations* are made up of multiple *conversation threads*. This knowledge is hard-coded into the algorithm, which resembles the common use of process mining perspectives for complexity reduction and the call for improved representational bias (see Aalst, 2011b and Aalst et al., 2012, p. 188).

The primary idea, however, consisted in feeding Petri net patterns from the MULAN model as additional input into a process mining algorithm; roughly similar to the use of clausal background knowledge in inductive logic programming (Section 4.1.4.3). This idea will not be investigated further here but remains for future work. One starting point is the use of Petri net patterns in conformance checking reported by Ramezani et al. (2012); see Section 4.2.5.4. These might as well be utilized as 'side-conditions' in process mining approaches based on global optimization strategies such as genetic algorithms (see e.g. Medeiros et al., 2004b).[3]

7.1.2.3. Explicit Representation

The process mining-related benefits gained by explicitly representing MAS as Petri nets are summarized in (Cabac et al., 2006b, Sec. 4.3.2) as follows:

---

[3]This is slightly related to the idea of algebraic optimization with material flow networks described by Lambrecht et al. (2010), that establishes a relation between optimization problems and the elements and structure of specific Petri nets (material flow networks, see Möller, 2000).

"MULAN models are an appropriate means to generate test data to evaluate process mining algorithms. Compared to test data generators based on *flat* Petri nets (see e.g. Medeiros and Günther, 2005), agent-based models allow to represent organizational and interaction-related aspects more naturally and in greater detail. [... Since] all components of a MULAN application are explicitly represented as Petri nets (Page and Kreutzer, 2005; Rölke, 2004) [...], comparing mining results with the corresponding generator models is [nearly] as straightforward as if using a *flat* Petri net.

MULAN closes the semantic gap between descriptive visual representations and executable formalism. For example, we can mine a model of an agent interaction protocol from a message log and represent the result as Petri nets by means of net components (Cabac et al., 2003). These protocol nets can be mapped to AgentUML interaction diagrams to aid the designer in model validation. Additional Java inscriptions might be added to obtain an executable agent protocol.

Another important aspect is that process mining techniques can be applied to (re)construct a MULAN model from observing other MAS. By monitoring other FIPA compliant agent platforms, we could e.g. reconstruct explicit Petri net models of the observed interactions."

The latter aspect is, to a certain degree, realized in the approach by Winarjo (2009) and Ou-Yang and Juan (2010), see Section 5.3.4.5, where a colored Petri net model of an agent conversation is reconstructed from a code-based MAS to enable formal verification. However, these authors map the mining result to an *ad-hoc* representation in *CPNTools* and not to an explicit MAS model like MULAN.

In the context of our second case study, Section 8.3.2.2 will present another example of 'monolithic', agent behavior that is decomposed using appropriate logging and process mining techniques for the sake of improved visualization. Though this example will not exactly follow the MULAN architecture, the resulting structure will be rather similar to an agent running multiple protocol nets.

7.1.2.4. Target Models in the PAOSE Approach

For the practical use of process mining in software engineering or simulation, it is important to map the artifacts of the respective development approach to appropriate analysis perspectives. In a model-driven context, this proceeding bears the additional possibility of reconstructing or improving executable models on the basis of log data. In the following, we briefly relate the analysis perspectives from Section 6.2 to the views and design diagrams of the PAOSE approach as described by Cabac (2010, Secs. 9–14) and reviewed in Section 3.3.3.2.

Decision Perspective Rules or processes reconstructed in the *decision perspective* can be inserted into a MULAN agent basically at two places: The first possibility are *guard expressions* of reference nets that constitute an agent's decision components (e.g. Cabac, 2010, p. 60) and protocols (e.g. Cabac, 2010, pp. 57). Here, mined decision rules might be added in the form of programming language expressions, quite similar to their integration into colored Petri nets in *CPNTools* shown by Rozinat et al. (2009b, p. 316); see Section 5.3.4.1. Multi-step decision processes or trees can also be mapped to own decision components for a more structured design.

The second option are *ACL message templates* that guard the instantiation of reactive protocols stored in an agent's knowledge base (Cabac, 2010, pp. 64–65): Here, decision rules are not inserted into the protocol nets themselves but into the knowledge base in order to determine under which conditions ACL messages trigger the agent to start a certain protocol.

As indicated by the alternative term *data perspective* (Aalst, 2006, p. 4), an important aspect of logs and models in the decision perspective are the *concepts* (realized by data types with attributes and relations) that an agent's decisions are based on. In PAOSE, these can be modelled with *Concept Diagrams*, a simplified variant of class diagrams (Cabac, 2010, p. 173) that does not contain *methods* (Cabac, 2010, p. 177). The ontology specified in a Concept Diagram offers hints on data attributes that must be logged for process mining in the decision perspective.

RENEW also allows to convert concepts into *feature structures*, an extension of reference nets towards logic-based representation of data types and class hierarchies (see e.g. Duvigneau et al., 2006, p. 85 and Cabac, 2010, p. 175). With respect to decision mining, this link to the executable model opens up further possibilities: Mined decision models cannot only be mapped to Java-based guard inscriptions but also to the more declarative notation supported by the feature structure net formalism of RENEW. (Duvigneau et al., 2006, p. 85).[4] Feature structure nets might generally be an interesting form to represent models in the context of *semantic process mining* (see e.g. Medeiros et al., 2008a), which will, however, not be discussed further in this thesis.

Internal and External Control Perspectives   In PAOSE, the difference between internal and external control flow is made explicit by distinguishing decision components (internal control flow) from (interaction) protocols (external control flow); see e.g. Cabac (2010, p. 140). Since this view directly influenced the identification of analysis perspectives in Section 6.2, a mapping appears straightforward. Note that due to the correspondence of protocol nets to *plans* of single communicating agents, the external control flow of an *interaction protocol* always comprises multiple protocol nets (Cabac, 2010, p. 49). The scope of the external control flow perspective is therefore strongly related to and influenced by the constructs available in Agent Interaction Protocol Diagrams (AIPs) (Cabac, 2003).

As mentioned in Section 6.2.4, the distinction between basic and higher order protocols in MULAN is reflected in the analysis perspectives as well. The process dimensions and dimensional mappings (Rembert and Ellis, 2009) described there were mostly identified on the basis of the practical case study reported further below in this chapter. A more detailled discussion of the external control flow perspective in MULAN is therefore deferred to Sections 7.2 – 7.3.

Structural Perspective   Depending on the considered level of detail, organizational structures mined in the *structural perspective* can be mapped to Coarse Design Diagrams (CDDs, Cabac, 2010, Sec. 10.2), Dependency Diagrams (DDs, Cabac, 2010, Sec. 11.3), and Role/Dependency (R/D) Diagrams (Cabac, 2010, Sec. 11.4). Recall from Section 3.3.3.3 that CDDs display *agent roles* and their relations by *interactions* in a notation adopted from UML Use Case Diagrams (Cabac, 2010, p. 144). DDs concretize this view by depicting the services provided and required by agent roles (Cabac, 2010, p. 160). R/D Diagrams additionally indicate role hierarchies (Cabac, 2010, p. 161).

---

[4]Tutorial examples are provided in the paper by Duvigneau et al. (2006, Sec. 3).

From the point of view of organizational process mining (see Aalst and Song, 2004b and Song and Aalst, 2008, reviewed in Section 4.2.4) the reconstruction of CDDs can be regarded as social network mining using the metrics *'participation of agent roles in common interactions'*. The reconstruction of such diagrams from a message log is trivial when messages are annotated with sender and receiver roles and the type of interaction they belong to. Since this is not the case in MULAN / CAPA, *interaction mining*, including the reconstruction of roles and interaction types (as described in Section 7.2), must be performed first. Note that different from a common restriction in role mining (see e.g. Song and Aalst, 2008, p. 21, cited in Section 4.2.4), agents can adopt *multiple* roles during the runtime of a MULAN MAS (see e.g. Cabac, 2010, p. 215).

To reconstruct DDs, roles and services might be mined from action profiles of agents in a similar fashion. This is indicated by Cabac's definition of services as "abstraction[s] of a set of (complex) agent actions that serve a common purpose" (Cabac, 2010, p. 158). Note that DDs in PAOSE originally serve to model *hard* (i.e. predefined) dependencies between roles and services (Cabac, 2010, p. 157). Their reconstruction from log data with the aid of process mining would presumably lead to models where hard and soft (i.e. dynamically emerging, see Cabac, 2010, p. 157) dependencies are intermixed.

To identify the relations *offered* and *requiredBy* between roles and services (Cabac, 2010, p. 158), previously reviewed ideas from interaction mining might be employed: Following the approach by Dustdar and Gombotz (2006), reviewed in Section 5.3.3.1, it seems reasonable to focus on sender and receiver (roles) of the *first and last messages* in interactions related to a service. This relies on the assumption that many service-based agent interactions will (quite similar to a method call in an object-oriented program) begin with a request to a service provider and end with the return of a result, confirmation, or refusal to the service taker (Cabac, 2010, p. 157).[5]

However, this assumption does "not always" hold (Cabac, 2010, p. 157). Due to their higher behavioral autonomy, agents can also offer services pro-actively. Therefore it might be necessary to additionally search for characteristic message performatives (like *request* and *inform*) as proposed in the approach by Hanachi and Khaloul (2008) reviewed in Section 5.3.4.6.

The reconstruction of role hierarchies in R/D Diagrams is clearly related to hierarchical role mining as described by Song and Aalst (2008, p. 11); see Section 4.2.4.2. The reconstruction of further details on agent roles, such as initial state, incoming messages, and known protocols (Cabac, 2010, p. 136) might be achieved (1) by considering content and conversation control attributes of messages received by role members and (2) by including mining results from the microscopic perspective, such as ACL message templates for reactive protocol instantiation mined in the decision perspective (see above).

In Section 6.2.3.1, we identified *spatial* models (that depict positions and movement of agents in a physical or virtual environment) as another important aspect of the structural perspective. In the context of PAOSE, such topologies are most closely related to the MAS level of the MULAN architecture (see Cabac et al., 2006b, Sec. 4.2 and Knaak, 2007, p. 33). Recall from Section 6.2.3.1 that Flick et al. (2010, p. 4) regard the potential of reference nets to introduce concepts of locality and 'spatial' synchronization into process mining as a promising future research topic.

---

[5] An example stated by Cabac (2010, p. 157) is the *FIPA Request* protocol.

Adaptivity Perspective   In the context of PAOSE and reference nets, "the adaptivity perspective [Section 6.2.5] is related to *higher order recursive nets* [Hornets] that modify structures of contained nets (Köhler, 2006)" (Knaak, 2007, p. 33). *Hornets* are "algebraic extensions of object nets" that, among other possibilities, "allow to modify the structure of net tokens at runtime" (Köhler-Bußmeier, 2009a, p. 243). Köhler-Bußmeier (2009a, p. 243) notes that they are closely related to formalisms for adaptive workflow management such as adaptive workflow nets (see e.g. Hee et al., 2006, cited in Köhler-Bußmeier, 2009a, p. 243).

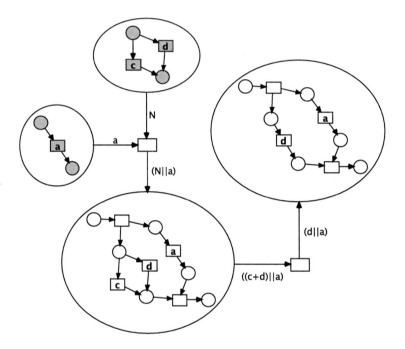

Figure 7.1.: Simple examples of algebraic net transformations in Hornets. Net tokens shaded grey depict the initial marking of the net. White net tokens display subsequent markings. Inspired by Figures from Köhler-Bußmeier (2009a, pp. 245,258).

Figure 7.1 depicts example modifications of net tokens. The arcs of the system net are inscribed with process-algebraic expressions using the operators || (parallel), + (alternative) and ; (sequence). When transitions fire, net tokens are bound to these inscriptions by unification and composed or deconstructed accordingly (Köhler-Bußmeier, 2009a, p. 245). While originally developed for adaptive workflow management and agent modeling (Köhler-Bußmeier, 2009a, p. 244), Hornets might also provide an appropriate representation form for *change processes* in process mining (see Günther et al., 2006, reviewed in Section 4.2.5.3).

Compared to nets inscribed with explicit *change operations*, such as those used by Günther et al. (2006, p. 316), Hornets offer a more 'declarative' way to describe modifications of net structures, akin to term rewriting and process algebra (see e.g. Fokkink, 2000). Since the algebra described by Köhler-Bußmeier (2009a) is tailored towards and formally proved for the case of *workflow nets* (see Section 2.3.2.2) as net tokens (Köhler-Bußmeier, 2009a, p. 257), it mainly fits change processes in the (internal and external) control flow perspective. To describe concept drift in other perspectives, such as structural dynamics of social networks (see e.g. Lahiri and Berger-Wolf, 2008, reviewed in Section 4.2.4.1) further algebras with reversible operators would have to be defined.

Though Köhler-Bußmeier (2009a, Sec. 2.4) specifies an operative firing rule for Hornets, an implementation of the formalism in RENEW is, to the knowledge of the author, not available yet. However, in the context of their 'theory of units'[6], Tell and Moldt (2005) describe a prototypical extension of RENEW towards self-modifying nets with the possibility to create, (de)compose, connect, mark, and delete net tokens (Tell and Moldt, 2005, pp. 33–34).

In accordance with the reference net formalism, Köhler-Bußmeier (2009a) and Tell and Moldt (2005) assume net tokens to be instances of net classes. In contrast, change mining approaches in process mining (e.g. Bose et al., 2011a; Günther et al., 2006) strive to reconstruct changes of the underlying workflow models or "concepts", i.e. net classes. This conflict might be resolved by relating objects and classes according to the well-known design pattern *prototype* documented by Gamma et al. (1995, p. 117): A net instance (token) modified in a change process can be regarded as a prototype for a net class from which further instances can be derived by *cloning*.

Level-Encompassing Perspective Different from the *adaptivity perspective*, extensions of reference nets dedicated to the modeling of *level encompassing* relations have not been developed yet. Nevertheless, the informal links between the different MULAN views shown in Figure 3.6 (Section 3.3.3.1) and several sociology-related publications such as those by Malsch (2001) and Köhler-Bußmeier (2009b) show that the topic is still in the focus of the TGI research group. Section 7.1.3 will sketch a small example how reference nets might be applied to support the detection of *complex event types* in the approach by Chen (2009).

7.1.3. Support for Analysis Use Cases

To support the use cases from Section 6.3 in the context of PAOSE, we aim for models and implementations that integrate well with the concepts and techniques of the development approach. As described in Section 4.1.5.4, *data flow modeling* (e.g. Lee and Tan, 1992) and *scientific workflows* (e.g. Guan et al., 2006) are appropriate techniques to support the modeling of knowledge discovery processes and their integration with existing tools.

The appropriateness of reference nets to model data flow in scientific applications is discussed in the diploma theses by Kurzbach (2007) and Simmendinger (2007); see Section 5.4.2.2. Simmendinger (2007), whose work is embedded into the research context of this thesis, identifies the following advantages of reference nets and RENEW for the modeling of scientific workflows:

- The possibility to inscribe reference nets with *Java* statements provides a good basis for tool integration, since arbitrary scientific software accessible via a Java interface can be "orchestrated"[7] (Simmendinger, 2007, p. 79).

---

[6]German: "Einheitentheorie"
[7]as to use the term by Rybacki et al. (2011, p. 718)

- Compared to specialized problem solving environments[8] like *Kepler* and *KNIME* (Section 4.1.5.5), RENEW allows to flexibly combine specific net components for scientific workflows with arbitrary Petri net elements for custom control flow (Simmendinger, 2007, p. 79). While the former systems can also be extended with user-defined processing nodes (e.g. implemented as Eclipse plugins in *KNIME*), the drawing of Petri nets in RENEW might be a more lightweight solution.

- Simmendinger (2007, Sec. 5.3) shows by examples that many relevant control and data flow patterns can be modelled with reference nets. Hierarchical models are realized by embedding subnets as tokens into superordinate nets (Simmendinger, 2007, p. 79). As typical for reference nets, this approach even allows subnets to modify their behavior depending on the place on which they reside. Simmendinger (2007, pp. 77) further sketches how the hierarchical separation of data and control flow in the *Kepler* system (see Section 4.1.5.4) can be emulated with reference nets.

- The nets-within-nets formalism also allows to represent complex data objects as net tokens with an own life cycle (Simmendinger, 2007, p. 79), somehow similar to proclets in artifact-centric modeling (see e.g. Fahland et al., 2011a, reviewed in Section 5.3.3.3).

- The event-driven communication model underlying reference nets might be useful in the context of runtime observation and online analysis (see Section 2.4.2) of (simulated) processes (see Simmendinger, 2007, p. 69 and Cabac and Denz, 2008, p. 94).

On the downside, Simmendinger (2007, p. 70) recalls that "the locality of [data tokens] bound [to] variables of transitions might [lead to] unhandy [and] complex workflows (Rölke, 2006)." Additionally, the reference semantics of data tokens might cause non-local effects similar to the *alias problem* (see e.g. Schwanke, 1978, p. 19) known from programming languages (Cabac and Denz, 2008, p. 94):

> "The reference semantics [...] differs from the value semantics of classical Petri net-based data flow notations (see e.g. Jessen and Valk, 1987, pp. 242). This can be an advantage but also a problem. On the one hand, it is possible to pass a reference to an object (or even to a net instance) along a chain that successively changes the object's attributes in different processing stages. On the other hand, the concurrent modification of a referenced object in different processing stages can lead to problems like race conditions. Nevertheless, the use of Java as an implementation allows to *clone* processed objects in order to provide independent copies."

As a general purpose tool, RENEW does not support specific requirements of scientific workflows, such as data persistence or made-to-measure user interfaces. Again, this drawback is to a certain degree compensated by the possibility to integrate arbitrary existing *Java* libraries.

In the following, we focus on specific net components to support endogenous and exogenous[9] data mining analyses of MULAN agents. The presentation repeats large passages from the article by Cabac and Denz (2008).

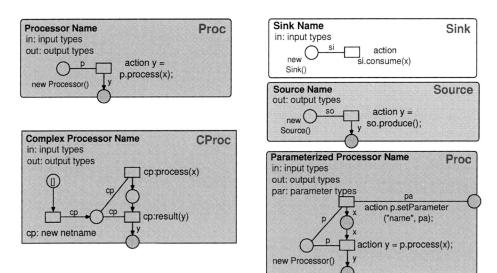

Figure 7.2.: "Generic mining chain components." Figure and caption adopted from Cabac and Denz (2008, p. 94).

7.1.3.1. Mining Components

Cabac and Denz (2008, pp. 93–95) identify the need for well-defined interfaces with the tools of a software development or simulation approach as an important precondition for the integration of process mining:

> "Thus, the tasks to be supported are data acquisition, data processing, and feedback of the results into the software development or even into the running system. We have therefore identified *sources*, *processors*, and *sinks* as basic (generic) components for mining chains.[10] Figure [... 7.2] shows the generic mining components that can be used as templates to create specific ones. These net components are rather simple consisting of one place and one transition. The place holds a Java object that provides the respective data processing algorithm via a standardized method. The transition calls this method when a data token enters the net component. There might be an additional place and transition pair to pass parameters to the component. While processors should be implemented without side-effects, sinks and sources are explicitly introduced to interact with the surrounding software environment.
>
> The processing method can be implemented to perform either an online or an offline analysis (see Section [... 2.4.2]). In an offline analysis, one incoming token represents a whole data set (e.g. a log in process mining) that is processed at once. In an online analysis, each token represents one data element (e.g. an event in process mining) in a continuing input

---

[8]as to use the term by Rice and Boisvert (1996), cited in (Simmendinger, 2007, p. 28)

[9]as to use the terms by Remondino and Correndo (2005, p. 4), see Section 5.2.1

[10]These component types are also common in other data-flow modeling tools like e.g. *KNIME* (Chair for Bioinformatics and Information Mining at Konstanz University, 2007).

stream. The processing method is called on each token arrival to incrementally update the computed results based on the new data. [...]

A mining chain is composed of several net components and can also include sub-chains in a hierarchy of net instances. Also normal net elements can be used to add custom behavior. Thanks to the use of the Petri nets representation, we [...] can also model chains that own a complex control-flow including concurrency. Mining chains can in principle be implemented in any hierarchical colored Petri net formalism. However, the object-oriented structure and the Java-based inscription language provided by reference nets are especially well-suited to model large mining chains.

Hierarchical mining chains are realized by means of so-called *complex* sinks, sources, and processors. Here, the object providing the processing functionality is not a simple Java object but an instance of a sub-net. This instance receives and provides data from and to the surrounding net components via synchronous channels (see Section [... 2.3.2.5]). Thereby it is possible to encapsulate a whole Petri net-based simulation model into a complex data source.

The generic as well as the interaction mining components are integrated in RENEW by a plugin (extending the net component plugin), which makes them available to the modeler as palettes of tool buttons. The user can easily build custom palettes with new mining components and use the generic components as templates." (Cabac and Denz, 2008, pp. 93–95)

Example 1: Test Data Generation As a first example, Figure 7.3 shows how a reference net-based test data generator for process mining can be encapsulated into a mining component. The use of Petri net simulators to generate data for process mining algorithms is rather common. We already mentioned the examples by Medeiros and Günther (2005) using *CPN Tools* (Section 4.2.6.1) and Aalst et al. (2002, Sec. 5) using *MiMo/ExSpect* (Section 5.4.1). The latter authors also encapsulate the test data generator into a transition of a hierarchical Petri net.

The net system in Figure 7.3 adopts this idea for RENEW. At the root of the net hierarchy, there is a complex mining component shown in the upper left. This component contains a subnet (left) that serves as an adapter for an infrastructure net called *simulation driver* (bottom right). This driver controls the simulation of the actual process model from which test data will be generated. An example process model (*testnet*) is shown in the upper right of Figure 7.3.

Similar to the approach by Medeiros and Günther (2005, p. 6)[11], the transitions of this process model are inscribed with log statements which, in this case, are forwarded to a logger implemented in *Java*. The displayed net uses a very simple implementation where activity names are logged into lists of strings in memory (class `ListLogWriter`). However, the integration of a more complex logger, e.g. using the MXML format of *ProM* as proposed by Medeiros and Günther (2005, Sec. 3), is straightforward.

Only the net class *testnet* must be exchanged to generate test data for another process model. Recall that an advantage of the reference net-based design lies in the fact that this model is not restricted to a 'flat' net (as shown in the example), but might itself consist of a net system up to a full MULAN MAS.

---

[11]page numbers relate to the version of the paper downloadable at `http://tmpmining.win.tue.nl/_media/publications/medeiros2005b.pdf` (last visit 2012-10-28)

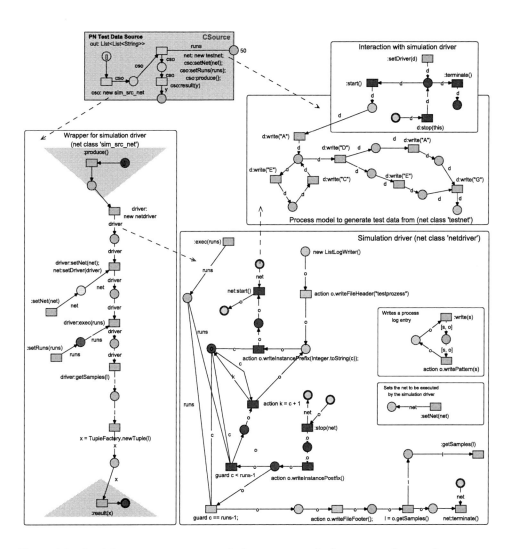

Figure 7.3.: A mining component encapsulating a system of reference nets for test data generation in process mining. Some implementation details (especially `import` statements
for required *Java* classes) have been omitted for the sake of clarity.

Example 2: Conformance Checking and Log Abstraction As a further process mining-related example, Figure 7.4 shows a complex mining component *Trace Checker* that encapsulates a simple log replay-based conformance checker. Recall from Section 4.2.5.4 that conformance checking by means of log replay in Petri nets is a frequently used technique in process mining, e.g. supported by the approaches of Rozinat and Aalst (2008), Adriansyah et al. (2011), and Ramezani et al. (2012), and also common in the context of MAS (e.g. Mazouzi et al., 2002, reviewed in Section 5.3.4.5).

The displayed component receives a set of traces and a model to check these traces against as input (net class `model_to_check` in the upper right of Figure 7.4). A replay of the traces in the model is initiated with the aid of two infrastructure sub-nets (net classes `mainChecker` and `trace_replay`) depicted in the lower half of Figure 7.4. By synchronizing the transitions of the net that represents the model with the events read from the traces, valid and invalid traces can be distinguished. Both groups of traces are finally provided separately at the two output places of the trace checker.

Note that the shown implementation only runs in the timed (sequential) simulation mode of RENEW. This is due to the fact that the net `mainChecker` schedules a delayed token (see the net inscription `[c,t]@1` in Figure 7.4) for the case that trace replay is blocked by a non-compliant trace. Another peculiarity is the handling of invisible tasks (which generally requires additional effort in conformance checking, see Rozinat and Aalst, 2008, p. 68, reviewed in Section 4.2.5.4). In the example, a 'look-ahead' functionality in the style of Rozinat and Aalst (2008, p. 72) is introduced by means of the channel `:peek`. This channel is called by the 'invisible' guarded transition of the net `model_to_check`.

Though the shown trace checker is not as powerful as the conformance checking plugins implemented in *ProM*, it might nevertheless be of some utility. On the one hand, the simple visual implementation[12] serves teaching purposes well, somehow similar to the visual implementation of the α algorithm as a component of the Petri net simulator *ExSpect* (*MiMo*, see Aalst et al., 2002, Sec. 5, reviewed in Section 5.4.1 of this thesis). On the other hand, "due to the expressiveness of the reference net inscription language, [a reference net-based conformance checker] might combine [...] advantages of [...] Petri-net [see e.g. Aalst et al., 2005] and logic-based [see e.g. Gutnik and Kaminka, 2006] conformance checking approaches" (Knaak, 2007, p. 36).

An extension towards the replay of partially compliant traces would enable further applications like log abstraction (see e.g. Chen et al., 2010) and Petri net pattern detection (see Ramezani et al., 2012). Log abstraction is relevant in the context of hierarchical process mining (see e.g. Li et al., 2010 or Kumar et al., 2011) such as control flow discovery for higher order protocols discussed in Section 7.3. Broadly speaking,

> "[...] we [... could] match the conversations in the original trace with the protocol models and obtain an abstracted trace with basic protocol executions as elementary activities (e.g. "from time t_1 to time t_2 an instance of protocol type P_1 was executed with agent A_1 as initiator and agent A_2 as responder"). Since the abstracted traces are *activity-based* [...], more powerful algorithms [... could] be applied for detecting concurrency in their control flow (e.g. Herbst, 2001)." (Knaak, 2007, p. 35)

---

[12]which could be extended towards further features like replay of partially compliant traces (see Rozinat and Aalst, 2008, p. 65)

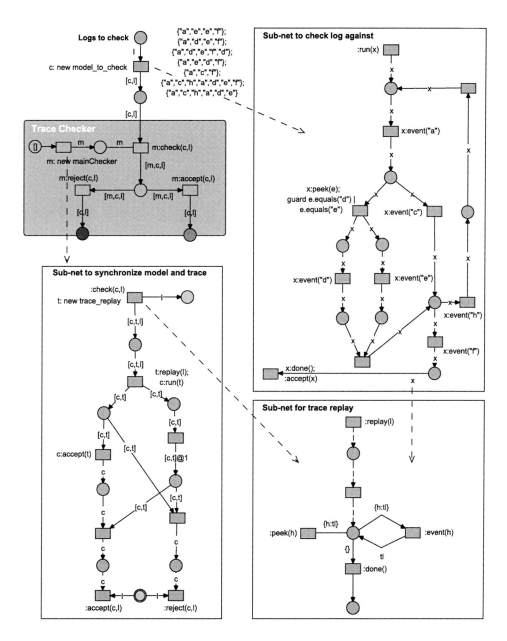

Figure 7.4.: A simple trace checker net component and its sub-nets.

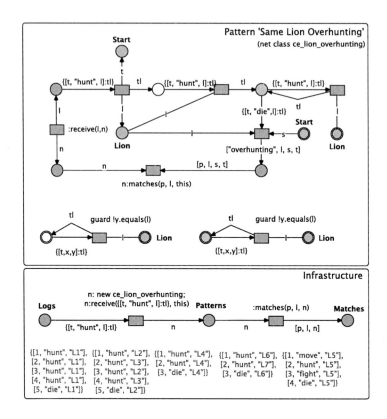

Figure 7.5.: A variant of the example pattern "same lion overhunting" by Chen et al. (2010, p. 50) modeled as a reference net.

Another example for log abstraction outside of the process mining domain is the detection of complex events (*CE*s) in the approach by Chen (2009); see Section 5.2.2.4. Representing and detecting *CE*s with reference nets might be a first step towards level-encompassing process mining in the PAOSE approach.

Figure 7.5 shows a modified variant of the complex event "same lion overhunting" from the "lions and antelopes" example by Chen et al. (2010, Sec. 4). The upper part of the figure contains the pattern itself (net class `ce_lion_overhunting`) that captures the rule that "the same lion kills an antelope [at least] two time steps in succession [event *hunt*] and then dies [event *die* ...]" (Chen et al., 2010, p. 49). Note that Chen et al. (2010, p. 49) originally claim that the lion "dies from starvation" which relates to another complex event *starvation*, i.e. moving three times in succession without hunting before death. This addition is omitted here to keep the example simple. It might, however, be straightforwardly integrated by inserting the pattern *starvation* (either directly or via a net reference) into the displayed net.

The lower part of Figure 7.5 depicts a very simple infrastructure to check the pattern against a set of traces. In the example, valid traces (marked green in Figure 7.5) must at least start with a *hunt* event. For each of these traces, an instance of the net `ce_lion_overhunting` is created and the trace is replayed in the net. The acting lion is memorized on a place with label *Lion*, such that events related to other lions can be sorted out. After successful replay, a token with the tag *overhunting* is created and passed back to the main net. Instances that replay non-compliant traces simply deadlock in the current implementation and are not forwarded to the place *Matches*.

Compared to the compliance checking approach by Ramezani et al. (2012) reviewed in Section 4.2.5.4 our preliminary example is on the one hand less powerful: It cannot extract considered patterns from larger traces that do not start with the expected initial event. Partial replay and detailed identification of non-compliant events is not possible either since no exhaustive state space search is performed. On the other hand, the example depicts the advantages of higher level Petri nets with respect to the integration of further perspectives (see also Wynn et al., 2010): The *originator* attribute in the example traces ('lions' $L_1 - L_7$) is handled explicitly and might even be replaced by objects with individual data attributes or object nets with an own life cycle.

Section 7.4 will show a further application of mining components for the implementation of a multi-step interaction mining chain to analyze message logs recorded on the CAPA platform.

7.2. Reconstruction of Basic Interaction Protocols

In Section 7.1.2.1, we identified *ACL message logs* as an appropriate level of observation for process mining in PAOSE. Among all analysis perspectives, the *external control flow perspective*, concretized in the modeling technique of AIP diagrams, can be considered most prominent in PAOSE since it establishes a link between interactions, roles, and (possibly) ontologies as the core modeling concepts (Cabac, 2010, p. 133).

From these observations, *agent interaction mining*[13] (AIM) can be identified as the most urgent task for process mining in PAOSE. As indicated in Section 7.1.2.4, mining results from the external control perspective provide a good starting point for the *integration* of results from other perspectives (e.g. decision models) on the one hand, and for the *expansion* towards 'higher level' structural and meta-perspectives on the other hand.

In Section 6.2.4, we discussed that process mining in the external control flow perspective can be subdivided into the (increasingly abstract) levels of basic interaction mining, complex interaction (or multi-agent workflow) mining, and interaction pattern detection.[14] The former two levels roughly correspond to basic and higher order (interaction) protocols in MULAN. In the following, we describe our partial implementation of a processing chain for basic interaction mining in MULAN, first published in (Cabac et al., 2006c). Concepts for complex interaction mining are added in Section 7.3.

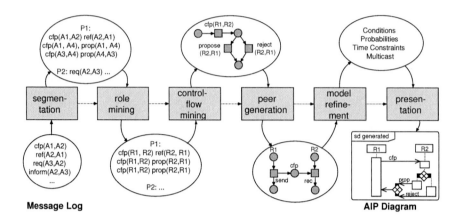

Figure 7.6.: "A mining chain for agent interaction mining." Figure and caption adopted from Cabac et al. (2006c, p. 17).

7.2.1. Basic Interaction Mining Chain

Presupposing the process dimensions of the external control flow perspective described in Section 6.2.4.1, Cabac et al. (2006c, pp. 17-18) identify the following (idealized) steps to perform basic interaction mining in MULAN:

> "Given a message log recorded during the execution of a MAS, [the task is to] find the unknown set of interaction protocols involved in the generation of this log. This task can be divided into several sub-phases depicted in Figure [... 7.6]. Generally, we consider the FIPA ACL message attributes **performative**, **sender**, **receiver**, and some conversation control tags. By masking message content, we keep the following stages application-independent.
>
> The first phase – log segmentation – is necessary because a log normally contains messages from several conversations, generated by multiple protocols. These messages must be sorted by assigning them to a *conversation*; and by assign[...]ing each conversation to a *protocol type*. Given the information available in FIPA ACL messages (e.g. **conversation-id**) this segmentation is trivial.
>
> However, these tags are not excessively used on the CAPA platform and might generally prove as too inflexible for detecting complex patterns of interaction. Therefore, we reconstruct conversations by *chained correlation* (Aalst et al., 2005) of messages based on the **in-reply-to** tag [...] In doing so, we obtain 1 : 1 *conversation threads*. [...] these might be part of a larger multi-party conversation that we reconstruct by merging all conversation threads sharing at least one **reply-with** or **in-reply-to** tag.
>
> Assigning conversations to protocol types is a clustering task. For each conversation, we build a feature vector representing a *direct successor* relation of performatives.[15] Each vector component represents one possible succession of two performatives. [...] To regard

---

[13]This term, as well as the initial idea to apply AIM in the MULAN context, trace back to Lawrence Cabac.

[14]Recall that the former two levels were derived from the levels of *web service interaction* and *web service workflow* mining in the approach by Dustdar and Gombotz (2006).

[15]A similar metric is used in a preliminary approach by Vanderfeesten (2006) towards detecting conversation roles.

for protocols with a typically branched control structure, combinations of performatives appearing near the start of a conversation are weighted stronger than those appearing at the end. Finally, we apply the *nearest neighbour* algorithm (Dunham, 2003) [see Section 4.1.4.2] to cluster similar vectors based on the Euclidian distance.

The result of the segmentation phase are traces of conversations ordered by protocol types. In the second [and partly overlapping, see below] phase – role mining – we further abstract the messages by replacing names of sender and receiver agents with conversation roles. We currently apply a simple unification algorithm that binds agent names to role names in the order of their appearance in the conversation. [...]

In the third phase – control flow mining – we collect the abstracted conversation traces of each protocol type and try to induce a model of the protocol's control flow. Interaction protocols such as those specified in AgentUML might contain concurrent, hidden, and duplicate tasks. [...]

Based on ideas from Herbst (2001) and Schütt (2003) [Section 4.2.3.2], our preliminary process mining technique consists of two stages – automata inference and concurrency detection: First, we reconstruct a deterministic finite automaton (DFA) from each set of samples using the *k-RI* algorithm (Angluin, 1982) [see Section 4.2.3.3]. The edges of the DFA are labelled with message performatives and sender / receiver roles. The *k-RI* algorithm can detect loops and duplicate tasks, but not concurrency. We therefore apply a modified version of the α-algorithm [implementing the concurrency detection approach by Schütt (2003, pp. 58), see Section 4.2.3.3] to the DFA next. [...]

Control flow mining results in an overall Petri net model of each protocol. This model can be split straightforwardly into protocol templates for every conversation role. Each of these peers corresponds to one lifeline in an AgentUML interaction protocol diagram (AIP, see Cabac et al., 2003) [... We might also] refine the reconstructed model by infer[r]ing temporal relations between messages with techniques described in (Aalst and Weijters, 2004) [and reviewed in Section 4.2.5.5 ...] The attachment of branching conditions to the protocol templates leads to executable MULAN protocols." (Cabac et al., 2006c, pp. 17-18)

The described steps are typical for interaction mining approaches like those by Srinivasa and Spiliopoulou (2000), Schütt (2003), Dustdar and Gombotz (2006), or Musaraj et al. (2010) reviewed in Section 5.3.3. The presented chain is basically an extension of the approach by Schütt (2003) towards the clustering of conversations by protocol types, (which is in turn supported in approaches like Srinivasa and Spiliopoulou, 2000), role mining, and an operational concurrency detection stage[16] including support for cyclic models. In the following, the implemented phases of log segmentation (i.e. message aggregation and conversation clustering), role detection, and control flow mining are explained in larger detail. Furthermore, hints are provided how the remaining phases can be implemented in the future.

7.2.2. Message Aggregation

In Section 5.3.3.4 we cited Motahari-Nezhad et al. (2011, p. 424)[17] in that *key-based* and *reference-based correlation* are the most common heuristics to chain related messages in web service mining. Since our AIM approach neglects message content attributes for simplicity and

---

[16]as opposed to the merely conceptual description by Schütt (2003)
[17]cited from Musaraj et al. (2010, p. 265)

domain independence (see above), we resort to reference-based correlation (also called "chained correlation" in Aalst et al., 2005) based on the FIPA ACL attributes *replyWith* and *inReplyTo*.

The chaining procedure is implemented in a *Java* class `MulanInReplyToSorter`[18] which takes a list of messages observed on the CAPA platform and returns a list of conversation threads, each consisting of associated messages. For internal processing, conversation threads are held in a data structure `ConvThread` which stores (a) all *replyWith* and *inReplyTo* tags that appear in messages of the conversation thread as *keys* and (b) the messages themselves ordered by time stamps as *values*.

The implemented chaining procedure does not deliver 'pure' 1:1 conversation threads (in the sense of Section 6.2.4.1) but potentially returns conversations with more involved interaction roles. Recall from Section 6.2.4.1 that the basic interaction protocol mining procedure is sufficient as long as every interaction role is only bound to one agent per conversation of the target protocol. The chaining stage therefore consists of two phases: (1) initial aggregation of 'conversation threads' and (2) merging of related 'conversation threads' into conversations:[19]

```
input:   RML // raw message list
output:  CL // list of conversations

CTL := {} // list of conversation threads
changed := true // flag used for merging

// segment messages into conversation threads
foreach msg in RML:
  if for any ct in CTL:
    ct.Keys contains msg.InReplyTo or
    ct.Keys contains msg.ReplyWith
  then
    append msg to ct.Values
  else
    create empty conversation thread ct
    set ct.Values := {msg}
    if msg.InReplyTo is set then add msg.InReplyTo to ct.Keys
    if msg.ReplyWith is set then add msg.ReplyWith to ct.Keys

// merge conversation threads with common keys into conversations
CL := CTL
while changed:
  set changed := false
  if for any pair ct1 != ct2 in CL:
```

---

[18]The program code referred to in this and the following sections is internally available at TGI in sub-packages of `de.renew.agent.mining`, `de.renew.agent.mining2` and `de.renew.agent.Sniffer` in the MULAN code repository. For the *k-RI* algorithm, the re-implementation described in this thesis is not available there yet. Instead, an older version used in the studies from (Cabac et al., 2006c) and (Cabac and Denz, 2008) can be found. This description of the `MulanInReplyToSorter` refers to the latest version in the package `mining2`.

[19]The notation used in this and the following pseudo code listings adopts elements from the programming languages *Java* (e.g. Arnold et al., 2000), *C#* (e.g. Griffiths et al., 2010), and *Pascal* (e.g. Wirth, 1971).

```
    intersection(ct1.Keys, ct2.Keys) <> {}
then
    ct.Keys := merge(ct1.Keys, ct2.Keys)
    ct.Values := merge(ct1.Values, ct2.Values)
    remove ct1, ct2 from CL and add ct to CL
    set changed := true
```

Note that the above pseudo code implements a heuristics tailored towards the specific use of FIPA conversation control tags on the CAPA platform. Though the basic proceeding would be similar, it cannot be re-used without modifications on other agent platforms such as *JADE* (see Section 3.4.1).

7.2.3. Conversation Clustering and Role Mining

Since ACL messages in CAPA do not carry explicit information about the generating protocol type and the involved interaction roles, these must be derived either from hints in the message content (which is neglected in our approach) or in the structure of the enclosing conversations (reconstructed in the previous step). For this purpose, we apply clustering techniques that are basically similar to the log clustering and role mining approaches nowadays common in process mining (see Sections 4.2.4.2 and 4.2.5.1).

Though the idealized processing chain in Figure 7.6 displays log segmentation and role mining as two distinct phases, both steps are in fact closely related. This is due to the typical definition of roles and protocols (or processes) in process mining and AOSE:

- A protocol is defined by the participating roles and their behavior.

- A role is determined by its behavior as part of a certain protocol.

This relation becomes obvious in the fact that rather similar clustering techniques and metrics are applied in both role mining and log clustering (compare Sections 4.2.4.2 and 4.2.5.1). The main technical difference lies in the observation of activity, transition, or other "trace profiles" (Song et al., 2008, Sec. 3.2) *per originator* in role mining and *per workflow case* in log clustering.

For the implementation of the interaction mining chain reported in (Cabac et al., 2006c) we combined the clustering of conversations and the abstraction from sender and receiver agents to interaction roles into a common step. Since implementations of role mining and log clustering algorithms for process mining were – at least to the knowledge of the author – not straightforwardly available at the time of the study[20], we settled for an own implementation in *Java*.

Following the call for simple and understandable algorithms from Section 6.4.3, this implementation is based on the straightforward *nearest neighbor* clustering algorithm as e.g. explained by Dunham (2003, p. 142); see Section 4.1.4.2. Figure 7.7 shows a slightly idealized display[21] of the involved *Java* classes.

---

[20]though articles on the topic had already been published, e.g. by Srinivasa and Spiliopoulou (2000) and by Greco et al. (2004)

[21]The diagram basically refers to the first implementation of the mining chain in the package `de.renew.agent.mining`. It is idealized for better understandability in that a dedicated (non-anonymous) class `ConversationStructureDistance` was only introduced later in the package `mining2`.

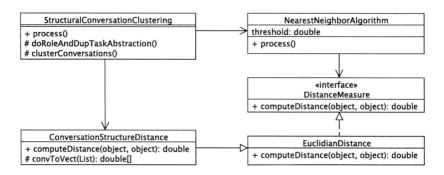

Figure 7.7.: Slightly idealized diagram of *Java* classes that implement the conversation clustering and role mining approach reported by Cabac et al. (2006c).

The class `NearestNeighborClustering` implements the standard nearest neighbor algorithm
following the description by Dunham (2003, p. 142). It can be assigned an arbitrary distance
measure (interface `DistanceMeasure`) to calculate the similarity between two clustered objects.
The Euclidian distance between numeric vectors (of type `double[]`) might be the most common
measure (class `EuclidianDistance`, see also Section 4.1.4.2).

The interaction mining-specific part of the procedure is implemented in the classes `Structu-
ralConversationClustering` and `ConversationStructureDistance`. The latter realizes the
subsequent phases of role abstraction and conversation clustering by using the cluster algorithm
with the specific distance measure. For role abstraction, the following simple 'anonymization'
algorithm[22] is applied (`doRoleAndDupTaskAbstraction`). This algorithm basically[23] replaces
agent names with role names in the order of their appearance in the conversation. The singleton
FIPA 'infrastructure agents' *AMS* (agent management system) and *DF* (directory facilitator)
are always mapped to synonymous, conversation-independent roles:

```
// list of conversations consisting of ordered ACL messages
input: CL

// list of traces with entries 'performative(senderRole, receiverRole)'
output: TL

TL = {}
foreach conversation c in CL:
   create new trace t := {'INIT'}
   create dictionary D that maps agent names to role names
   roleCount := 0

   foreach message m in c:
```

---

[22]This term was coined by Lawrence Cabac.

[23]the actual implementation performs further simple pre-processing for the subsequent duplicate task detection,
which is omitted here.

```
if m.Sender = 'DF' or m.Sender = 'AMS'
then senderRole := m.Sender
else
   if D contains entry <m.Sender, role>
   then senderRole := role
   else
      senderRole := 'R' + roleCount
      roleCount := roleCount + 1
      add entry <m.Sender, senderRole> to D

if m.Receiver = 'DF' or m.Receiver = 'AMS'
then receiverRole := m.Receiver
else
   if D contains entry <m.Receiver, role>
      then receiverRole := role
   else
      receiverRole := 'R' + roleCount
      roleCount := roleCount + 1
      add entry <m.Receiver, receiverRole> to D

performative := m.Performative
add entry 'performative(senderRole, receiverRole)' to t

add entry 'EXIT' to t
add t to TL
```

The result of the above procedure is a list of traces with timely ordered entries of the form $performative(senderRole, receiverRole)$. This list is forwarded to the method `clusterConversations`, which aggregates traces with a similar structure into clusters using the *nearest neighbor* algorithm and the `StructuralConversationDistance`. According to the classification by Song et al. (2008, p. 114), the latter realizes a "transition profile". A transition is indicated by a succession of two entries $e_1 = perf_1(sender_1, receiver_1)$ and $e_2 = perf_2(sender_2, receiver_2)$ in a trace of the analyzed log.[24]

The clustering procedure realizes steps that are (in this or a similar form) nowadays common in trace clustering (see e.g. Song et al., 2008): Initially, it counts the number n of distinct entries $E = \{e_1, ...e_n\}$ appearing in the analyzed log L. Taking into account the number of possible transitions over the alphabet E, the dimension of the feature vectors is set to $m = n^2$. Next, a vector $v \in \mathbb{R}^m$ is created[25] for every trace $t \in L$. Let $t_j = e_k$ and $t_{j+1} = e_l$ be two successive entries of t with $0 < j < |t| - 1$ and $0 < k, l < n$. Then the vector component corresponding to the transition $e_k \rightarrow e_l$ is increased by a value inversely proportional to the position j of the occurrence in t:

$$v_{k+n \cdot l} := v_{k+n \cdot l} + \left(\frac{|t| - (j - 1)}{|t|} \right)^d \tag{7.1}$$

---

[24]The artificial start and end tasks (e.g. Medeiros, 2006, p. 126) $INIT$ and $EXIT$ are considered as well.
[25]mapped to the type `double[]` in *Java*

The 'decrease order' d is a free parameter that determines how strong the added value decreases with increasing position j of a transition identified in the log. Thus, "to regard for protocols with a typically [forward] branched control structure, combinations of performatives appearing near the start of a conversation are weighted stronger than those appearing at the end." (Cabac et al., 2006c, p. 18). This well-known heuristics matches branched '*FIPA*-style' interaction protocols like e.g. *contract net* (see Smith, 1980 and Section 3.3.2.3). It is not appropriate for processes that converge towards their characteristic trajectory only after a longer (variable) "warm-up phase", such as transient phases of stochastic steady-state processes in simulation (Page and Kreutzer, 2005, pp. 174).

Summarizing, the applied clustering procedure is rather similar to related approaches reported in Section 4.2.5.1, some of which have also been implemented in the *ProM* tool. The integration with role mining leads to both advantages and drawbacks: By integrating sender and receiver roles into log entries, traces of different protocols become easier to discriminate than by using performatives only.[26] Since single conversations build the scope of role assignment, the procedure also applies to the common case of agents adopting different roles in multiple different interaction protocols.

On the downside, role detection and clustering fail in interaction protocols where initiator roles are not determined uniquely.[27] Here, the assignment of agents to roles in their order of occurrence in the trace can only be a first guess that must be revised by using further heuristics later (e.g. activity profiles, see Song and Aalst, 2008, reviewed in Section 4.2.4.2). Furthermore, the procedure cannot cope with agents that change their roles *during* the course of a conversation. However, due to the 'elementary' character of basic interaction protocols (as potential parts of larger multi-agent workflows), this situation might not occur very frequently in the protocols that this procedure targets.

In general, the integration of role information into the log entries has the disadvantage of significantly increasing the feature vector dimension as compared to using performatives only. In addition, the simplistic, threshold-based *nearest neighbor* clustering makes it harder to find an appropriate level of generalization (i.e. calibrate the threshold for cluster merging) as compared to more elaborate techniques like hierarchical agglomerative clustering (see Sections 4.1.4.2 and 4.2.4.2).[28]

Section 7.4.2.2 will show a streamlined variant of the basic interaction mining chain implemented with the aid of *mining components* (see Section 7.1.3) and *ProM* plugins. Though this implementation does not yet include the hierarchical log clustering algorithms that are nowadays[29] available in *ProM*, an integration would be possible.

7.2.4. Control Flow Mining

As indicated above, the search for an appropriate control flow mining algorithm for agent interaction mining was driven by the control flow constructs available in AIP diagrams, i.e. (1)

---

[26]e.g. an *inform* message from a *bidder* to an *auctioneer* can be distinguished from a message with the same performative sent from an *auctioneer* to a *seller*.

[27]e.g. a protocol that might either start with a *request* from a *customer* to a *seller* or vice-versa

[28]The author was first alluded to this point by the reviewers of the MATES 2006 conference paper published as (Cabac et al., 2006c).

[29]and also at the time of that second study

sequences, (2) alternative and (3) parallel split and join nodes, (4) invisible tasks, and (5) cycles and loops. Furthermore, the potential ambiguity of log entries caused by the restriction of considered process dimensions to performatives and roles might necessitate the handling of duplicate tasks.

From the algorithms published by the time of the study, the following appeared to be possible choices:

- The α^{++} algorithm (see Wen et al., 2006, reviewed in Section 4.2.3.1) handles all required constructs except for invisible and duplicate tasks. An implementation in *ProM* was available early.

- The algorithm by Herbst (2001), reviewed in Section 4.2.3.2, handles most constructs including duplicate tasks. However, it is a rather complex procedure limited to block-structured models, while AIPs might not be 'purely' block structured.[30]

- Herbst (2001) alternatively proposes to combine grammar inference and the theory of regions to reconstruct models with duplicate tasks, which was operationalized later by Kindler et al. (2006); see Section 4.2.3.3.

- The control flow mining approach by Schütt (2003), reviewed in Section 4.2.3.3, promises to handle most mentioned constructs except for cycles. However, an implementation of the concurrency detection stage was not provided in (Schütt, 2003, pp. 61).

Based on the requirement of algorithmic simplicity and understandability (see Section 6.4.3), we decided to take the approach by Schütt (2003) as a starting point. Following the idea by Herbst (2001), we planned to replace its proprietary grammar inference (GI) stage with a proven GI algorithm that can handle cycles. Furthermore, we considered an implementation of the concurrency detection stage as a modification of the α algorithm to work on state machines instead of logs.

From today's point of view, the region-based two-step mining approach by Kindler et al. (2006) and the preprocessing stage for duplicate task detection by Li et al. (2007) or Gu et al. (2008) might be viable (and closely related) solutions as well. As of version 4.2, *ProM* also contains a plugin to apply the α algorithm to state machines but this variant does not handle duplicate tasks.

7.2.4.1. Grammar Inference

After an initial exploration of the C^{++}-based open source GI library *Mical* (Rey, 2003), we decided to use the *k-RI* algorithm (Angluin, 1982) for our GI stage. Reasons include (1) its independence from *negative examples*, (2) the relative algorithmic simplicity, (3) the possibility to influence the obtained level of generalization with a single parameter k, and (4) the acceptable computational complexity (see also Section 4.2.3.3). For better integration with RENEW and

---

[30] Our concern uttered in (Cabac et al., 2006c, p. 18) that the algorithm by Herbst requires an activity-based log seems to be inappropriate.

due to minor difficulties[31] with the *k-RI* implementation in *Mical*, we further opted for a re-implementation in *Java*.[32]

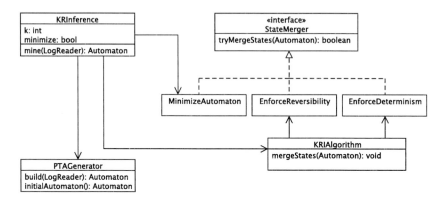

Figure 7.8.: Classes implementing the *k-RI* algorithm by Angluin (1982) in the presented approach.

Figure 7.8 shows the structure of our final implementation:[33] The class `KRInference` controls the overall mining process. In the first step, the `PTAGenerator` converts the given log into a prefix tree automaton (PTA). Starting from a single initial state, it attempts to replay every log entry in the automaton (class `Automaton`) and amends new states and transitions where needed.[34] Next, the `KRIAlgorithm` merges the states of the PTA by mutually executing the two conditions of the *k-RI* algorithm (Section 4.2.3.3, represented by the classes `EnforceDeterminism` and `EnforceReversibility`) as long as changes occur. The resulting automaton can finally be minimized with the algorithm from (Hopcroft et al., 2003, Sec. 4.4) implemented in the class `MinimizeAutomaton`.

As proposed by Angluin (1982, p. 743,758), our implementation allows to run the *k-RI* algorithm both incrementally* and non-incrementally. In the non-incremental case, a PTA is generated for the whole log and its states are merged afterwards. In the incremental case, a full cycle of PTA generation and state merging is run for every trace of the analyzed log. This means that the result automaton from step i (which might already contain cycles and 'alternative join' nodes) is extended with a further trace in step $i + 1$.

---

[31]In particular, the author of this thesis did not manage to run *Mical* on input logs with event names consisting of more than one letter. However, this should be possible, since DeYoung (2008, p. 118) characterizes *Mical* as "the only GI toolkit that support[s ...] multi-letter alphabets" and shows related examples.

[32]This implementation exhibits some similarities (mainly the PTA generation stage) but also differences (e.g. the representation of every condition of the *k-RI* algorithm by an own class) to the implementation in *Mical* (Rey, 2003).

[33]The experiments reported in Cabac et al. (2006c) and Cabac and Denz (2008) were run with a previous version also published as a *ProM* plugin. However due to errors and performance issues, this version was re-implemented later. The mentioned experiments (also reported in this chapter) have not been re-run thoroughly with the new version yet. However, in a first test on similar data it delivered likewise results.

[34]quite similar to the implementation in *Mical* (Rey, 2003)

Following a common approach, the traces of the input log are sorted by length before incremental processing. The incremental version seems to require less computation time on long traces containing many cycles. This observation appears plausible, since the detection of appropriate cycles on the shorter traces might prevent the introduction (and merging) of many states into the automaton for the longer traces. However, the performance gain has not been analyzed and quantified in detail yet.

7.2.4.2. Concurrency Detection

Our final implementation[35] of the concurrency detection procedure by Schütt (2003, pp. 58) is realized as an extension of the α algorithm in *ProM*[36] and also uses the automata-specific model classes[37] provided by this framework.

As in the original approach by Schütt (2003, p. 59), the basic idea is that the *k-RI* algorithm can merge 'superfluous' duplicate states and transition labels from the *PTA* by introducing alternative join states and cycles, but not by building concurrent splits and joins. Our implementation of the *k-RI* algorithm returns an automaton where duplicate tasks, i.e. occurrences of the same label a on multiple transitions, are tagged with unique indices $i \in \mathbb{N}$, namely $a_1, a_2, \ldots$ In case of concurrent control flow, the automaton contains the typical "diamond" structures mentioned by Rubin et al. (2006, p. 21) and Schütt (2003, p. 59). Hence, the causally independent execution of two tasks a and b will be mapped to 4 transitions $s_1 \xrightarrow{a_i} s_2$, $s_2 \xrightarrow{b_j} s_4$, $s_1 \xrightarrow{a_k} s_3$, and $s_3 \xrightarrow{b_l} s_4$ where $i, j, k, l \in \mathbb{N}$ can (but do not have to) be different (see also Schütt, 2003, p. 59 and Knaak, 2007, p. 35).

Our implementation of the simple concurrency detection by Schütt (2003, pp. 59)[38] searches the automaton for these diamond structures and merges the indices of a and b whenever the additional conditions $s_2 \neq s_3$ and $s_1 \neq s_4$ hold. The procedure is repeated for all transition in the automaton until no further merging is possible. Since the comparison iterates over all pairs of transitions (except for identical ones) and over all outgoing edges of the transitions' target states (to identify equal join states), the label merging should run in $O(n^2 \cdot d)$ steps where n is the number of transitions and d is the average out-degree of states in the automaton.[39]

After label merging, the log-based precedence relations of the α algorithm are derived from the automaton[40] and passed to the `AlphaProcessMiner` of *ProM* in a `LogRelations` object. As of version 4.2, *ProM* also contains a built-in implementation[41] of log relations derived from a transition system. However, as mentioned before, this procedure does not regard for the merging of (indexed) duplicate tasks.

---

[35] Cabac et al. (2006c) relate to a previous, slightly different version not using the *ProM* framework.
[36] class `AlphaProcessMiner`
[37] presumably developed in the context of the work by Rubin et al. (2007)
[38] class `SchuettConcurrencyDetection`
[39] The current implementation additionally repeats the loop over all edges until no more merging is possible. This might, however, not be necessary.
[40] class `TSLogRelationBuilder`
[41] class `TSLogAbstraction`

7.2.5. Results and Discussion

This Section presents and discusses the results obtained with the implemented part of the mining chain. Furthermore, hints towards improvements of the current procedure and the implementation of the remaining steps are provided.

7.2.5.1. Control Flow Mining

The combination of the k-RI algorithm (Angluin, 1982) and the concurrency detection procedure by Schütt (2003) was tested on logs of three process models shown in Figure 7.9. These contain all control flow constructs relevant for AIP diagrams; including cycles, duplicate tasks, and (nested) alternative and concurrent splits and joins. All models were correctly reconstructed from relatively small artificial logs (containing 29, 6, and 27 cases respectively) with the parameter k set to 1 and minimization activated.

Though the procedure is able to reconstruct complex control flow, there are also cases that cannot be handled properly. The example in Figure 7.10 shows an automaton reconstructed from the log $L = abcdx, acbdx, abex$. The transition labelled with e, that emanates from the 'diamond structure' $b \rightarrow c, c \rightarrow b$, causes the concurrency detection to generate a net that over-generalizes the given log and does not terminate properly (i.e. with a single token in the 'final' place) for paths leading past this transition.

In contrast, the tool *Petrify* used in the region-based approach by Rubin et al. (2007) succeeds to synthesize a bi-similar net from the automaton. To improve our implementation, we might either (a) include a special case to handle additional edges of 'state diamonds' or (b) extend it towards the detection of 'atomic blocks' as sketched by Schütt (2003, pp. 59). The latter aspect is detailed further below.

Another peculiarity of the concurrency detection implementation is that, different from the α algorithm, it cannot properly reduce superfluous duplicate tasks caused by concurrent execution in an automaton reconstructed from a locally, but not globally, complete log (see Section 4.2.2.3). However, the same holds true for the region-based approach by Rubin et al. (2007) that always synthesizes a bi-similar net from an automaton, and presumably also for the pre-processing stage for duplicate task detection by Gu et al. (2008); see Section 4.2.3.2.

Recall from Section 4.2.3.3 that Rubin et al. (2006, p. 21) introduced a heuristics to complete candidate 'state diamonds' in an automaton. Carmona et al. (2008) modified the theory of regions towards generalization instead of bi-similarity to better fit the needs of process mining.

7.2.5.2. Implemented Mining Chain

The implemented part of the mining chain was tested on logs of a fairly complex interaction protocol modeled in MULAN/CAPA, which was inspired by the well-known contract net protocol (see Smith, 1980 and Section 3.3.2.3), the order mediation in our courier service model (Section 8.1.2.1), and the example used by Mounier et al. (2003, p. 160).

As described in (Knaak, 2006, Sec. 4.2), the protocol includes three single-instantiated roles, i.e. a customer, a mediator, and a service provider (see Figure 7.11): Initially, the customer

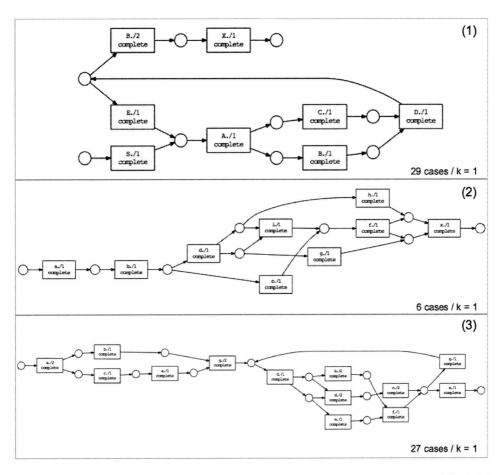

Figure 7.9.: Example process models correctly reconstructed by our implementation of the k-RI algorithm (Angluin, 1982) and the simple concurrency detection by Schütt (2003). Example (3) was adopted from the dissertation by Herbst (2001).

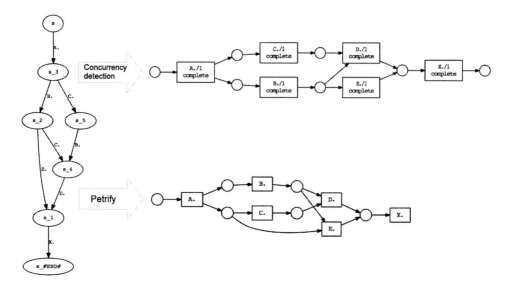

Figure 7.10.: An example automaton that our current implementation of the simple concurrency detection by Schütt (2003) cannot properly transform into a Petri net, while the region-based approach by Rubin et al. (2007) can.

requests (performative *request*) a service from a mediator who, in turn, invites an offer from a service provider (*cfp*). The provider can refuse immediately, which causes the mediator to notify the customer about the failure (*fail*). Alternatively, it might submit an offer (*propose*), which is accepted (*accept-proposal*) or rejected (*reject-proposal*) by the mediator.

Rejecting leads to a negotiation (on the price or some other modality of service provision) between the mediator and the provider, which is cancelled (*cancel*) by the mediator when no agreement can be reached.[42] In this case, the customer is again notified about the failure. When the mediator accepts the provider's offer, it concurrently informs the customer about the agreement.

Figure 7.11 shows an aggregate view upon the protocol modeled as a labeled *P/T* net. Based on this description, protocol nets for the involved roles were implemented in RENEW and run on the CAPA platform.[43] The message traffic was logged by an observer tool (MULAN *Sniffer*, see Section 7.4.1) and fed into the 3 implemented steps of the mining chain.

The resulting logs contained not only "the messages belonging to the order allocation protocol [... but also] surrounding 'noise', i.e. conversations executed during the initialization of agents and platform." (Cabac et al., 2006c, p. 19). The latter stemmed from infrastructure activities like registrations of the model-specific agents with the *AMS* and *DF* of the platform. An aggregation of messages into conversations and subsequent unsupervised classification with the *nearest neighbor* algorithm succeeded, but "the performance of the clustering procedure strongly

---

[42]This part of the protocol is similar in spirit to the example by Mounier et al. (2003, p. 160).
[43]Note that drawing an *AIP* diagram and generating protocol templates would have been another possible, more comfortable approach in PAOSE.

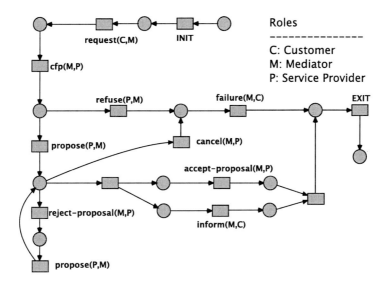

Figure 7.11.: Example protocol to test the implemented mining chain. Figure adopted from (Knaak, 2006, Fig. 5).

depends on [... the] threshold for cluster similarity that needs careful calibration" (Cabac et al., 2006c, p. 19).

Roles were also detected straightforwardly by 'anonymization' (see Section 7.2.3) since the initial order of 'role appearances' in the example protocol is fixed. From the abstracted log, the control flow mining stage successfully reconstructed a model of the overall protocol at the level shown in Figure 7.2.3. A (manually beautified) view of the mining results in RENEW is shown below in Figure 7.16 (Section 7.4.2.2).

7.2.5.3. Discussion and Further Steps

It must be noted that the experiments conducted so far do not represent a thorough empirical validation of the presented interaction mining approach, but only an initial feasibility study for interaction mining on an operational agent platform. Firstly, more diverse protocols, including variants less tailored to the abilities of the mining procedure, should be considered. Secondly, the performance of the mining chain steps must be analyzed in more detail, also taking into account further techniques and results from process and interaction mining (as reviewed in Sections 4 and 5).

In the above example, the duty of the role mining and clustering procedures is made quite easy by the fact that the target protocol contains no message exchange with the fixed *AMS* and *DF* roles, while the 'surrounding' protocols do. In the subsequent study reported in (Cabac and Denz, 2008) and Section 7.4.2.2, we replaced role mining with the procedure by Song and Aalst (2008) implemented in *ProM* and performed clustering merely on the basis of performatives.

On the given example, this variant seems to perform quite similar to the processing chain described in (Cabac et al., 2006c) and above.

Concerning control flow mining, the implemented technique was already briefly compared to the related work by Rubin et al. (2007) in Section 4.2.3.3. During the initial experiments with the procedure reported in (Cabac et al., 2006c), we experienced problems related to (a) the proper detection of cycles from small logs and (b) artifacts introduced by causality violations during the observation of message traffic in the concurrent execution environment. Recall from Section 5.2.4.1 that vector clocks (see e.g. Vigueras and Botia, 2008, p. 193) might be a thorough solution for this problem.[44]

To make the procedure more robust, one might orientate duplicate task and concurrency detection in the implemented procedure towards the 'stochastic' log relations of the Heuristics Miner (Section 4.2.3.4) instead of the 'binary' relations of the α algorithm.[45] For this purpose, the transitions of the automaton reconstructed in the first step must be enriched with path frequencies by the *k-RI* algorithm. Alternatively, a stochastic grammar inference technique might be used as in (Mounier et al., 2003).

Further theoretical and empirical comparisons of region-based net synthesis (as used by Rubin et al., 2007) and 'pattern-based' concurrency and duplicate task detection (as e.g. proposed by Schütt, 2003 and Gu et al., 2008) might be of special (in the first instance theoretical) interest with respect to computational performance and the ability to handle (globally) incomplete logs.

To improve the practical applicability of the presented mining chain in the PAOSE approach, an implementation of the remaining steps towards the reverse engineering of AIP diagrams would be desirable. The decomposition of the reconstructed aggregate model into distinct protocol nets is in principle straightforward (Cabac et al., 2006b, Sec. 5.2): Every transition must be split into two related transitions according to its label. In doing so, we obtain a Petri net representation of sequence diagram lifelines as e.g. shown by Aalst (2004, Sec. 5). The challenge for this and the final visualization step lies in the mapping of the basic net elements to (block-structured) net components or AIPs and in providing an appropriate visual layout.

The implementation of the simple concurrency detection by Schütt (2003, p. 59) might be extended towards the identification of 'atomic blocks', as sketched by the same author (Schütt, 2003, pp. 59); see Section 4.2.3.3. However, this task appears computationally expensive at first sight because it must consider and compare connected fragments of arbitrary size[46] in the graph of the input automaton. In the context of this thesis, initial attempts towards an implementation based on a block detection approach by Bae et al. (2006) were dropped due to technical difficulties and priority in the working plan.

7.3. Reconstruction of Higher Order Protocols

As indicated in Section 6.2.4, conversations in MAS often exceed the level of basic protocols covered by the mining procedure described so far. The above example might e.g. become

---

[44]which has not been realized yet

[45]which, in turn, might put the approach closer to the work by Herbst (2001)

[46]up to the size of the graph itself

more realistic when the mediator negotiates about prices for the requested services with multiple providers in sequence or in parallel (i.e. a *multicast* conversation). Furthermore, the mediation protocol might be embedded into the control flow of a larger *multi-agent workflow* (Section 6.2.4.1). Recall from Section 3.3.3.1 that such control flow models are termed *higher order protocols* in MULAN (Rölke, 2004, p. 137).

Higher order and multicast protocols cannot be reconstructed by the above procedure for several reasons: Firstly, a role might be adopted by multiple agents during a conversation, where the number of agents per role is not known *a-priori* (i.e. workflow pattern *P*13 mentioned in Section 2.3.3). Our simple 'anonymization' procedure (Section 7.2.3) would fail in this situation. The role mining approach by Song and Aalst (2008) might be able to identify agents that enact the same role within a conversation based on their 'message profiles' (see also the work by Vanderfeesten, 2006, mentioned in Section 5.3.4.6). However, as reviewed in Section 4.2.4.2, it cannot handle the case where an agent adopts different roles in the protocols belonging to a multi-agent workflow yet.

Another problem, also mentioned by authors like Lou et al. (2010b) and Kumar et al. (2011), is the fact that algorithms to discover 'flat' control flow, like the one used in the above procedure, cannot reliably reconstruct the complex patterns emerging from a variable number of concurrent conversation threads. Event patterns resulting from message broadcasts might e.g. be mistaken as cycles or lead to a large, over-specialized model that mirrors the (randomly) observed interleaving too closely. A discussed in Section 6.2.4.1, higher order protocols also include further process dimensions like (relations between) message cardinalities and protocol phases, that the simple mining chain cannot handle.

From today's point of view, the following approaches from the literature might bear the potential to reconstruct higher order and multicast protocols from message logs:

- The approach by Lou et al. (2010b), reviewed in Section 4.2.3.5, allows to reconstruct the control flow of multiple interleaved threads using few *a-priori* knowledge. However, for the same reason, it does not reflect useful knowledge about the hierarchical structure of higher order protocols.

- Authors like Greco et al. (2005) and Li et al. (2010), reviewed in Section 4.2.5.2, reconstruct hierarchical models with the aid of pattern detection and clustering techniques. However, these approaches neither take into account knowledge about the specific structure of higher order protocols (though it might be integrated), nor consider multiply instantiated threads and 'protocol phases' as partial dependencies between concurrent sub-models.

- The reverse engineering of message sequence graphs reported by Kumar et al. (2010, 2011, 2012), reviewed in Section 5.3.2, is closely akin to our view of higher order protocol mining. However, the technique requires additional information about messages belonging to the same 'multicast branch' to reconstruct multicast protocols, and on the assignment of objects (agents) to classes (roles). This information is not directly available in message logs from the CAPA platform but might possibly be reconstructed or added.

- The work on *artifact-centric* process mining by authors like Fahland et al. (2011a) and Kikas (2011), reviewed in Section 5.3.3.3, covers concepts of interacting processes and (message) cardinalities. However, as indicated by Popova et al. (2012, Sec. 6), practical

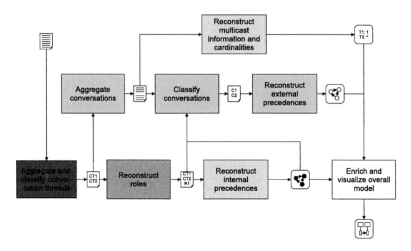

Figure 7.12.: Processing chain for multicast protocols.

work has mainly focused on single artifact life cycles so far.[47] Furthermore, the closeness of the artifact-centric view to relational databases might not be appropriate in the context of agent systems.[48]

Since most of the above approaches were not available when the idea came up to reconstruct higher order protocols in the case study at hand, an own sketch was developed to extend the basic mining chain for this purpose. The envisioned procedure is described and related to recent work from the literature in the following. A strongly simplified partial implementation and first experimental results are reported in Section 8.3.2.2 below.

7.3.1. Extended Interaction Mining Chain

Figure 7.12 shows an extension of the basic interaction mining chain towards higher order and multicast protocols. The procedure is based on the distinction between conversation threads (representing executions of elementary protocols) and conversations (representing executions of multi-agent workflows) introduced in Section 6.2.4.1. The reconstruction of conversation threads is accomplished with the three subtasks already known from the previous sections, which are displayed in the lower row of the diagram.

An initial overview of the extended procedure was provided in (Knaak, 2007, p. 36):

"First we segment the message log into 1:1 conversation threads. Next we merge similar threads (e.g. based on similar causal matrices) belonging to the same conversation into

---

[47]One exception is the draft by Kikas (2011, Sec. 4.8), which is closely akin to the procedure described in the following. The discovery of artifact interactions will also be a future topic of the project *ACSI* (see Popova et al., 2012, Sec. 6).

[48]Nevertheless, the ongoing project *ACSI* covers agent-oriented and actifact-centric models side by side, as mirrored in associated publications like (De Giacomo et al., 2012) listed at http://www.acsi-project.eu/public.html (last visit 2012-11-03).

a multicast conversation model. This model contains information on each conversation thread's *internal* causal dependencies. In addition, we detect synchronisation points in the multicast conversation by extracting *external* causal dependencies (such as "the initiator sends an `accept` message only after receiving *all* `propose` and `reject` messages from the responders") between pairs of conversation threads. From the internal and external dependencies, [... a hierarchical process model] is created. Actions without external dependencies are merged into the same [... sub-]region [of the model]. The regions are ordered according to the external dependencies, and in every region a sub-diagram with the contained internal dependencies is built using conventional [... control flow discovery] techniques."

In the following, the steps of the extended mining chain will be described in more detail.

7.3.2. Log Segmentation and Role Mining

The first task in operationalizing the sketched procedure is to extend the log segmentation and role mining stages towards an explicit handling of 1:1 conversation threads and of the enclosing conversations. In CAPA, messages belonging to the same conversation thread might still be chained with the procedure from Section 6.2.4.1 (omitting the final merging step) and clustered based on transition profiles. In this context, role mining by means of simple 'anonymization' remains possible as well.

The next level of clustering consists in an aggregation of related conversation threads into conversations; and in the classification of these conversations by the generating (higher order) protocol type. For the former task, the following options appear possible:

- When all conversation threads of the same higher order protocol execution are related by at least one *replyWith* or *inReplyTo* tag of their messages, the final merging step of the simple chaining procedure might be applied.

- Another simple assumption (exploited in the implementation described in Section 8.3.2.2) is that all messages belonging to the same conversation share a common content attribute such as the order processed in the respective multi-agent workflow.

- When none of these assumptions hold, more elaborate metrics from interaction and web service mining might be applied, taking into account features like temporal proximity and similar participants of conversation threads (see e.g. Dustdar and Gombotz, 2006, reviewed in Section 5.3.3.1).

Conversations might, in principle, be classified by their generating higher order protocols by applying a small extension to the basic case. Initially, the log must be abstracted somewhat similar to the hierarchical process mining approach by Li et al. (2010) and the complex event detection by Chen et al. (2010): All message events that belong to the same conversation thread are replaced by a single event representing the respective conversation thread type.[49] Transition profiles can be extracted from the abstracted conversations similar to the basic case. To make clustering more reliable, further features might be integrated, including the following examples:

---

[49]The mining component shown in Section 7.1.3 might be an appropriate basis to implement log abstraction in CAPA.

- *Cardinalities*: How often is a certain conversation thread type instantiated within a conversation? Does the execution of these instances overlap?

- Common *message content properties*, as e.g. proposed by Schütt (2003); see Section 5.3.3.2.

- Relations between *agents and roles* observed across multiple threads belonging to a conversation: A simple example is 'The agent bound to role R_1 in conversation thread type CT_1 is always the same as the agent bound to R_2 in CT_2'.

7.3.3. Control Flow Mining

The distinct levels of conversation threads and conversations must also be reflected by a control flow discovery procedure that targets higher order protocols. The simplest option is to apply conventional control flow mining to the original and abstracted logs as e.g. in the hierarchical process mining techniques by Li et al. (2010). However, these approaches cannot properly reconstruct multicast conversations and 'protocol phases' indicated by individual message precedences observed across different conversation threads.

We therefore distinguish between *internal precedences* of messages belonging to the same conversation thread and *external precedences* between messages from different conversation threads and thread types. This approach is quite similar to the work on artifact-centric process mining (e.g. Kikas, 2011, reviewed in Section 5.3.3.3) and message sequence graph mining (Kumar et al., 2011, reviewed in Section 5.3.1). It provides the advantage that internal precedences of conversation thread types can be reconstructed with conventional control flow mining techniques.

However, as also observed by Lou et al. (2010c, p. 613), precedence relations used in conventional control flow mining[50] are often too restrictive to capture the control flow between multiple instances of interleaved threads. Similar to the artifact-centric process mining approach by Kikas (2011, p. 12), we therefore employ the so-called *strict order relation* defined by Weidlich et al. (2009)[51] and denoted as $<<_L$ in this thesis: Simply put, $A <<_L B$ holds for two event types A and B in a log L if in all traces $t \in L$ the *first* event B only occurs after the *last* occurrence of an event A (for a proper formal definition see e.g. Kikas, 2011, pp. 11).

Figure 7.13 displays a simple example how this relation can be used to discover external precedences and protocol phases. The procedure is basically the same as the extraction of behavioral profiles from artifact interactions described by Kikas (2011, Secs. 4.5,4.8), which was developed in parallel to our scheme. However, our main interest is not to match artifact-centric models and logs (i.e. mapping discovery for conformance checking, as targeted by Kikas, 2011), but to discover the control flow of higher order protocols.

The example in Figure 7.13 corresponds to a small extension of the well-known *contract net protocol*: Similar to the previous test example for the basic interaction mining chain, a customer requests a service from a mediator (*req*). The mediator calls *multiple* service providers for proposals (*cfp*), who might return a proposal (*prop*) or refuse the call (*ref*). Each proposal is either accepted (*acc*) or rejected (*rej*). Multiple accepts are possible, i.e. the order can

---

[50]such as the direct follower relation underlying the α algorithm (Section 4.2.3.1)
[51]cited in Kikas, 2011, p. 12

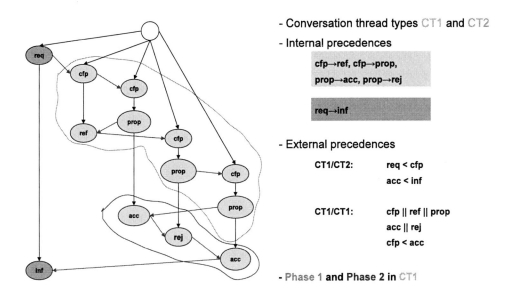

Figure 7.13.: An example showing how external precedences and protocol phases can be mined.

be shared between multiple service providers. After accepting or rejecting all proposals, the mediator finally informs the customer (*inf*) about the result.

To reconstruct the control flow of the conversation, the messages of the associated conversation threads are first arranged in the style of a *multicast tree* (e.g. Ratnasamy and McCanne, 1999). Figure 7.13 displays one conversation thread of type CT_1 that represents the communication between the customer and the mediator and four conversation threads of type CT_2 for the interactions between the mediator and four service providers. Black arrows indicate the direct follower relation of messages within each conversation thread. Red arrows show the same relation for all messages belonging to the conversation, i.e. the path actually taken through the multicast tree in the (imaginary) protocol execution.

From the tree, we can, on the one hand, reconstruct the internal dependencies for every conversation thread type using the relation → known from the α algorithm. On the other hand, the external dependencies between every pair of conversation thread types are extracted by mutually comparing all conversation threads (including instances of the same type) according to the relation <<. This proceeding is also proposed by Kikas (2011, p. 29) to extend his approach towards artifact interactions. Also similar to Kikas (2011, p. 25), we can reduce the number of mined external precedences by neglecting those that are implied by an internal precedence (e.g. $req/CT_2 << prop/CT_1$).

To identify precedences between different phases of the higher order protocol, we cluster those message types that do not stand in a strict order relation[52] into the same phase. These phases are indicated by green and blue marks in the multicast tree.[53]

The example protocol P thus consists of 4 sequential phases $P_1 = \{req\}$ (the customer requests the service), $P_2 = \{cfp, ref, prop\}$ (the mediator collects offers from all providers), $P_3 = \{acc, rej\}$ (the mediator selects the best offers), and $P_4 = \{inf\}$ (the mediator informs the customer). Within each phase, messages can be ordered according to the internal precedences of the involved conversation thread types.

Note that the procedure allows to detect deviations from this behavior (e.g. for the purpose of validation) such as a protocol P' with only 3 phases where the mediator can already select offers *before* all providers have answered (i.e. $P'_1 = P_1, P'_2 = P_2 \cup P_3, P'_3 = P_4$). The mapping techniques described by Kikas (2011, Sec. 4.6), might possibly help to automate such comparisons.

A drawback of using the strict order relation to detect external precedences is that it cannot identify control flow constructs like short cycles or duplicate tasks. While this might be acceptable for an application to mapping discovery between logs and models (as reported by Kikas, 2011) it is a clear restriction in control flow discovery of agent protocols.

7.3.4. Multiple Instantiation and Cardinalities

Another relevant process dimension in complex agent protocols is related to message broadcast and cardinalities. Recall that *AUML* interaction diagrams employ the symbol $*$ to indicate that a message is sent to multiple agents with the same role in parallel or in sequence. Furthermore, a diagram can be inscribed with *constraints* on message cardinalities. An example is the relation $i = j + k$ indicating that the number i of cfp messages is equal to the sum of *propose* (j) and *refuse* (k) messages (i.e. all responders must answer the call for proposal) in the well-known display of the contract net protocol cited in Figure 3.5 (Section 3.3.2.3).

As discussed in (Knaak, 2007, p. 36): "Multicast protocols are closely related to the *multiple instantiation* workflow pattern, where a variable number of instances of the same activity are executed in parallel (see e.g. Guabtni and Charoy, 2004)." A detection whether a conversation thread type includes (parallel) multicast processing could therefore be achieved on the basis of the following simple heuristics:[54] *A conversation thread type CT is assumed to be multicast in a conversation type C if at least one instance of C contains multiple temporally overlapping instances of CT.* When the instances do not overlap, an *iterative* processing of multiple instances is implied (e.g. Guabtni and Charoy, 2004, p. 182).

To reconstruct constraints on message cardinalities, the first step is to count the occurrence of message types for every conversation and conversation thread, quite similar to the workflow pattern mining approach by Gaaloul et al. (2005) reviewed in Section 4.2.3.5. The results might

---

[52]The corresponding log relations are called *exclusiveness relation* and *interleaving relation*, see e.g. Kikas (2011, p. 12).

[53]The *behavioral profile graph* used by Kikas (2011, p. 27) would be another appropriate graphical notation.

[54]somewhat akin to the rules stated by Kumar et al. (2010, Sec. 5), see Section 5.3.2, and Wen et al. (2010, p. 396), see Section 4.2.3.5

e.g. be represented by logical facts $\#(MT, CT, c, x)$, stating that in conversation c, the number of observed messages of type MT exchanged by conversation threads of type CT is equal to x.

Several data mining techniques could then be applied to identify cardinality constraints over this fact base: A simple statistical *summarization* (Dunham, 2003, p. 8, reviewed in Section 4.1.2.1) of minimum, maximum, and average messages frequencies[55] might already be useful for protocol validation (see also the interaction pattern detection approach by Dustdar and Hoffmann, 2007, reviewed in Section 4.2.4.3).

In addition, linear *regression* (Dunham, 2003, p. 6, reviewed in Section 4.1.2.1) can be applied to detect simple linear relations between message cardinalities, somewhat similar to the approach by Musaraj et al. (2010); see Section 5.3.3.4.[56] Note that regression must in principle be performed over the whole power set of message types that belong to a conversation. A linear equation will also be returned in the case where no actual relations exist. However, invalid relations should be characterized by a larger classification error and non-integer coefficients.[57]

To detect non-linear relations, more complex data mining techniques must be applied. The most flexible might be symbolic techniques like genetic (Section 4.1.4.5) or inductive logic programming (Section 4.1.4.3). However, recalling the simplicity of message cardinality constraints, it might be more appropriate to search the fact base for known plausible relationships (e.g. constants, linear equations, products), somehow similar to the workflow and interaction pattern detection approaches by Gaaloul et al. (2005), reviewed in Section 4.2.3.5, and Dustdar and Hoffmann (2007), reviewed in Section 4.2.4.3. The following example shows a simple *Prolog*-style rule to induce the relation $|MT_3| = |MT_1| \cdot |MT_2|$ for three message types $MT_1, ..., MT_3$ from the above facts:

$$\#(MT_1, CT_1) \cdot \#(MT_2, CT_2) = \#(MT_3, CT_3) \Leftarrow \forall c_i \in L :$$
$$\#(MT_1, CT_1, c_i, x_i) \wedge \#(MT_2, CT_2, c_i, y_i) \wedge \#(MT_3, CT_3, c_i, z_i) \wedge x_i \cdot y_i = z_i. \tag{7.2}$$

7.3.5. Result Representation

After detecting internal and external precedences as well as multiple instantiation patterns and constraints on message cardinalities, the wealth of discovered information must be presented in an understandable form to support exploratory or confirmatory analysis. Considering appropriate design diagrams, it stands out that AgentUML interaction diagrams support the display of message broadcast and cardinality constraints, but not protocol phases.

As shown by Odell (2003), UML 2 interaction overview diagrams (Jeckle et al., 2002, p. 419) or the rather similar Message Sequence Graphs (Kumar et al., 2011) better fit the latter requirement (see also Kumar et al., 2012, p. 916): Sequence diagrams displaying internal precedences within certain protocol phases can be embedded into an activity diagram that represents the external precedences, quite similar to the software reverse engineering approach by Kumar et al. (2011, p. 99).

---

[55]possibly including standard deviations

[56]Musaraj et al. (2010) apply linear regression to reconstruct control flow in interaction mining and not relations between message cardinalities.

[57]A small initial experiment on artificial data was performed with the linear regression algorithm implemented in *WEKA*.

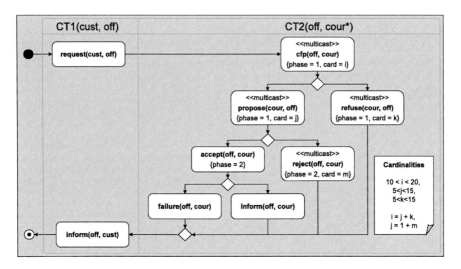

Figure 7.14.: Representation of a multicast protocol as a UML 2 activity diagram with expansion regions.

A visually simpler alternative are UML 2 activity diagrams, where so-called *expansion regions* can be used to indicate multiple instantiation (Wohed et al., 2004).[58] Figure 7.14 shows a possible simplified variant tailored towards straightforward visualization in a process mining tool: Conversation threads are indicated by swim lanes and annotated with the involved roles. Message events are displayed by activities, quite similar to the aggregate interaction protocol model in Figure 7.11. Message broadcast (as well as related replies) is indicated by the stereotype «multicast» together with an identifier for the respective message cardinality and the enclosing protocol phase. Relevant statistics and constraints on message cardinalities are displayed within a 'note' symbol.

Mapping such design diagrams to executable reference nets requires the definition of an operational semantics for multicast protocols. This might be based on the ideas by Moldt and Rölke (2003) concerning the representation of multiple instantiation patterns with reference nets (see also Knaak, 2007, p. 36).

7.4. Tool Support

After discussing the algorithms for agent interaction mining used in this case study, we will finally turn our focus towards the toolset developed for the (preliminary) integration of process mining into the CAPA platform. For this purpose, we mainly cite relevant passages from the pre-publications by Cabac et al. (2006c) and Cabac and Denz (2008).

---

[58]Related modeling constructs called *multiple instantiation sets* are proposed by Guabtni and Charoy (2004, p. 179).

7.4.1. Mulan Sniffer Tool

In the beginning of the case study, a message monitoring tool was implemented by Heitmann and Pläehn (2005) as part of a study project. A brief description of this tool is provided in (Cabac et al., 2006c, p. 19):

> "To integrate process mining facilities into the CAPA platform, we developed a monitoring tool named MULAN *Sniffer* as a RENEW plugin (Cabac et al., 2005). The name indicates that the tool's functionality was derived from typical MAS debugging tools such as the *JADE Sniffer* [...]. The MULAN Sniffer monitors all ACL messages sent between agents on the platform during a simulation. The resulting message log is displayed textually as a list or graphically as a UML sequence diagram. Filters can be applied to select messages containing certain performatives, etc.
>
> Figure [... 7.15] shows the user interface of the Sniffer with an observed message log. The messages in the diagram are color coded to ease the monitoring of the MAS. They can be inspected in the bottom left view of the Sniffer window. The upper left view shows a list of observed agents which can be sniffed or blocked. It also shows the numbers of messages sent and received per agent. The tool allows to observe changes in the diagram on the fly, i.e. when the message is sent.
>
> The MULAN Sniffer differs from its 'ancestors' in two aspects that are important for our approach: (1) The recorded sequence diagrams are stored in the same format used by the MULAN design tools. They can therefore be edited and mapped to executable agent protocols. (2) More important, the *Sniffer* is a [...] RENEW plugin (Cabac et al., 2005) that can be extended by plugins for process mining and filtering itself.
>
> The interfaces for filtering and mining plugins are reminiscent of similar tools such as *ProM* (Dongen et al., 2005). Special emphasis is put on the *recursive* character of process mining algorithms: These algorithms operate on data and provide data for higher-level analysis. We therefore introduce[d] the concept of *mining chains* [as described in Section 7.1.3]." (Cabac et al., 2006c, p. 19)

7.4.2. Analysis Framework and Mining Chains

The first version of the agent interaction mining chain described by Cabac et al. (2006c) was implemented as a proprietary plugin for the MULAN Sniffer. However, with the continuing improvement of the open source process mining tool *ProM* (see Section 4.2.6.1) on the one hand and the visual modeling technique of mining components on the other hand, it seemed more plausible to use scientific workflows modeled with mining components as a starting point for tool integration.

A more mature implementation of interaction mining in the PAOSE approach based on this paradigm was therefore presented by Cabac and Denz (2008). Recall from Section 7.2.3 that in this study some steps of the original interaction mining chain were modified.

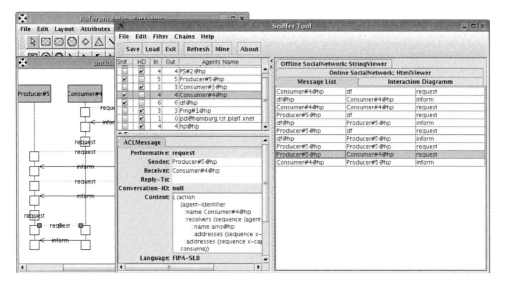

Figure 7.15.: "MULAN Sniffer UI with observed interactions and RENEW UI." Figure and caption adopted from (Cabac et al., 2006c, p. 19).

7.4.2.1. Integration with ProM

Compared to the previous implementation, a main difference was the integration of plugins from the widespread process mining tool *ProM* (Section 4.2.6.1). This integration is described by Cabac and Denz (2008, p. 95) as follows:

"As discussed in Section [... 4.2.6.1], ProM is a powerful *Java*-based process mining tool with an open plugin architecture similar to the one of RENEW. The algorithms implemented in ProM are used interactively on imported log data or process models via a GUI. Due to the simple *Java* interface provided by the mining components, an integration of both tools appears straightforward. In doing so, we can on the one hand offer Petri net-based data-flow modeling for ProM. On the other hand, we can comfortably integrate a large number of existing process mining and analysis algorithms into our Petri net-based software.

[...] We have straightforwardly mapped import plugins [of ProM] to source components and export plugins and viewers to sink components. Mining, analysis, and conversion plugins are specific kinds of processors. Based on the ProM architecture two additional component types were identified: *Filters* restrict the log to certain event types, and *interactive viewers* allow for user interactions during the mining process. The latter are implemented with the aid of so-called *manual transition*[s] that the user fires after finishing the interaction.

Since ProM offers interfaces for each plugin type, it is not even necessary to provide an own wrapper for each algorithm. Instead, we can provide generic wrappers and pass the concrete plugin class as a parameter." (Cabac and Denz, 2008, p. 95)

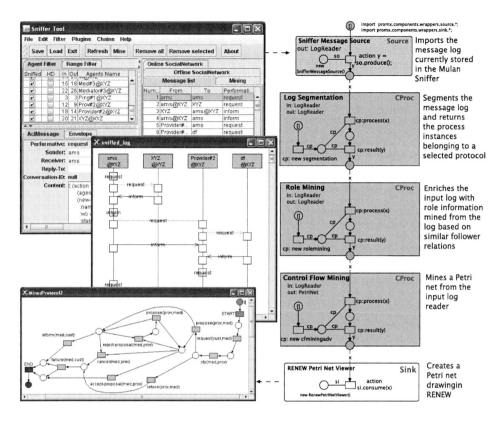

Figure 7.16.: "Example process mining chain for agent interaction mining." Figure and caption adopted from (Cabac and Denz, 2008, p. 96).

7.4.2.2. Improved Agent Interaction Mining Chain

On this foundation, the interaction mining procedure was re-implemented as a complex visual mining chain in RENEW. We cite our pre-publication in (Cabac and Denz, 2008, pp. 96-99) for the following overview:

> "Figure [... 7.16] shows the implementation of the first three steps by means of mining components. Each step is represented by a complex processor and refined by a sub-net. The sub-nets for the log segmentation and control flow mining steps are depicted in Figs. [... 7.17] and [... 7.18]. Furthermore, there are source and sink components that help to embed the mining chain into the agent platform.
>
> The processing starts from the *Sniffer Message Source* component that provides a message log [... from] the MULAN Sniffer. [...] At the end of the processing chain, the *Renew Petri Net Viewer* sink exports Petri net representations of the reconstructed interaction protocols to RENEW as new net drawings[59] that can be instantiated and executed.

---

[59]The graphical representation of the resulting model in RENEW is manually beautified.

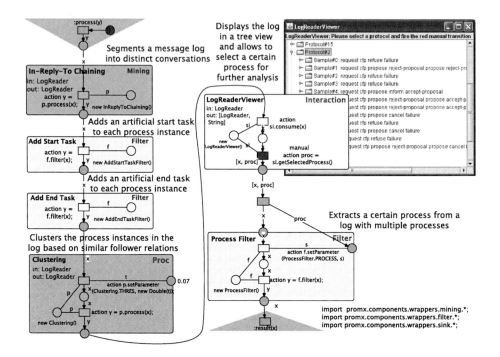

Figure 7.17.: "A sub-chain implementing the segmentation step." Figure and caption adopted from (Cabac and Denz, 2008, p. 97).

Each step of the mining chain is implemented by means of several existing and new ProM plugins wrapped as mining components. The *Log Segmentation* processor depicted in Figure [... 7.17] starts by chaining messages (Aalst et al., 2005) [...] into conversations. Afterwards two filters are applied that add artificial start and end events to each conversation in the log.[60]

Next, the *Clustering* component clusters the conversations in the log into protocol classes based on similar follower relations of message types (performatives). [...] The results are displayed using the *Log Reader Viewer* while the net execution waits on a manual transition. In the example, this interactive viewer lets the user select a certain protocol class for further investigation. After selecting the protocol, the manual transition is fired by the user to continue the processing. At the end of the log segmentation, a *Process Filter* restricts the log to those conversations that belong to the selected protocol.

The pre-processed log is forwarded to the *Role Mining* procedure. This step uses ProM's existing organizational miner plugin to induce the participating agents' roles from the sets of message types they send (as also proposed in Vanderfeesten, 2006). The corresponding subnet is not shown here. It enriches the log with role information and forwards the enriched log to the *Control-Flow Mining* processor shown in Figure [... 7.18].

This step illustrates how mining components can be combined with custom net structures and Java code to build a simple optimization procedure. [...]

---

[60]This enhances the mining results and will not be explained in detail here.

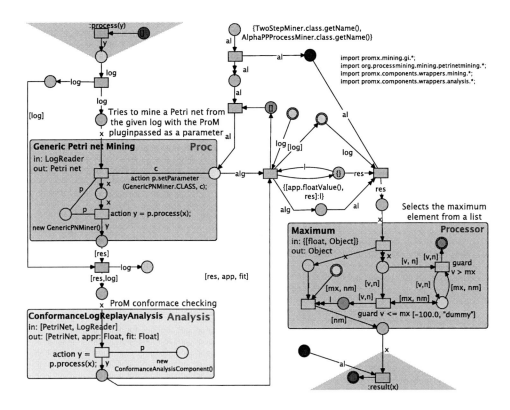

Figure 7.18.: "A sub-chain implementing the control-flow mining step with an integrated optimization procedure." Figure and caption adopted from (Cabac and Denz, 2008, p. 98).

In process mining, a large number of algorithms exists for the reconstruction of control-flow, often tailored towards certain types of data. The well-known α^{++} (Wen et al., 2006) algorithm e.g. performs well on noise-free, event-based data. Other algorithms are specialized on handling circumstances like duplicate activities or noise.

Let us assume that the most appropriate algorithm for the given event log is unknown in advance. We therefore employ the generic mining component and pass a list of algorithms[61] as parameters that are applied to the same log in turn. [...]

Subsequent to the mining we use ProM's conformance checking plugin and a custom maximizer component to identify the mining result that represents the samples in the log 'best' in terms of [... fitness].[62] The best result is finally returned to the main mining chain. A similar optimizer could be integrated into an adaptive agent in order to increase the reliability of existing process mining techniques for autonomous learning.

---

[61]In the example, this includes the α^{++} algorithm and [... the] two-step approach [... described in Section 7.2.4].

[62]Of course in practice one should strive for better optimization methods than the presented brute-force approach. [The use of behavioral appropriateness instead of fitness as a conformance measure (see also Figure 7.18) was an error in the original publication by Cabac and Denz (2008, p. 99).]

Summarizing, the example indicates that the mining components might indeed be a step towards tackling the [...] problems of integrating process mining and software engineering [... because] the presented source and sink components provide a well-defined interface between the software development and execution environment (i.e. RENEW and CAPA) and the process mining algorithms of ProM. This allows to obtain data from and feed back results into the system. Since the mined protocols are represented as executable reference nets, they can be [...] integrated into the [...] Petri net simulation. In practice, the available algorithms have to be enhanced to permit the automated protocol reconstruction by adaptive agents.

[... Furthermore], it is shown that the mining components support the creation of complex mining procedures by means of stepwise refinement. Compared to other data flow environments, the approach provides a number of advantages indicated in the example: (1) in the context of Petri net-based software engineering with RENEW, the same formalism is used to model the mining procedures *and* the analyzed software. (2) Pre-defined components can be combined with custom *Java* code and net elements (e.g. to build the optimization procedure shown in Figure [... 7.18]). (3) This procedure also shows that unlike conventional hierarchical notations, reference nets allow to dynamically exchange the applied algorithms at runtime (e.g. depending on the provided data). (4) User interactions are simply included by means of manual transitions as shown in Figure [... 7.17]." (Cabac and Denz, 2008, pp. 96-99)

7.5. Summary

This section reports on the conceptual and practical integration of process mining into the model-based, agent-oriented software development approach PAOSE. After identifying the particular benefits of a Petri net-based development approach with respect to process mining, we explicitly related the perspectives and use cases of the analysis framework from Chapter 6 to the MULAN model underlying PAOSE.

Establishing this relation proved basically straightforward since the identification of the analysis perspectives had already been strongly influenced by the MULAN views. Nevertheless, it also became obvious that MULAN is still 'under-specified' with respect to the formalization of some of the perspectives including structure, structural dynamics, and level-encompassing relations.

The 'scientific workflow' stance inherent to the use cases model presented in Section 6.3 was mirrored in the development of specific RENEW net components with a focus on data flow modeling. Besides (exploratory) interaction mining as the main use case, a test data generator was implemented as a complex mining component, adopting concepts from Medeiros and Günther (2005) and Aalst et al. (2002, Sec. 5). We further pointed out relations between log-replay based conformance checking (Ramezani et al., 2012; Rozinat and Aalst, 2008), complex event detection (Chen, 2009; Chen et al., 2010) and the modeling language of reference nets. In the future, the integration of mining chains into RENEW and CAPA might allow to use them as 'protocols' of adaptive Petri net agents that generate (at least templates) for new protocols learned from observed message traffic.

From the discussion of the analysis perspectives in the context of MULAN, *agent interaction mining* in the external control perspective was identified as the foremost task. Based on the approach by Schütt (2003) and further literature, a mining chain was implemented that allows to reconstruct aggregate overviews of basic interaction protocols (without hierarchy and multiple instantiation) from ACL message logs observed on the CAPA platform. With the continuing development of process mining, original parts of the chain were later replaced by mining techniques from the literature implemented in the open source framework *ProM*. A comparison of the advantages and drawbacks of the different options was initiated and should be carried on in larger detail in the future.

Finally, preliminary techniques to reconstruct higher order (i.e. hierarchical and possibly multicast) protocols were sketched. A very prototypical and simplified implementation comprising parts of these techniques will be presented within the scope of the following case study in Chapter 8. The techniques also bear strong resemblance to recent developments from the literature in the context of software reverse engineering (Kumar et al., 2010, 2011, 2012) and *artifact-centric* process mining (Canbaz, 2011; Fahland et al., 2011a; Kikas, 2011). Again, an initial comparison of the approaches was conducted and should be carried on further. Regardless of the technical similarities and differences marked in Section 7.3.3, the agent-oriented paradigm might, to the author's subjective opinion, capture the mining of complex interaction processes slightly better than the object-oriented or artifact-centric world views.[63]

A final appraisal of this case study's contributions including comparisons with the most closely related work will be provided in Chapter 9.

---

[63]Note that recent work in the ACSI project seems to cover both paradigms side-by-side. See e.g. the publication list at `http://www.acsi-project.eu/public.html` (last visit 2012-11-03).

8. Process Mining in a Discrete Event Simulation Study

The second case study was conducted in the context of the MABS approach developed at the University of Hamburg's simulation group (MBS) led by Professor Bernd Page. This approach utilizes conceptual modeling with UML as well as the *Java*-based discrete event simulation framework *DESMO-J* and its MABS extension *FAMOS* (see Section 3.4.4).

Compared to PAOSE, there is a stronger focus on quantitative analyses of modeled (real-world) systems like the courier service study presented in this chapter. Due to the more code-centric implementation, verifying the transformations from the conceptual model to the computer model is a larger issue than in the Petri-net based PAOSE approach. For these reasons, the objectives of process mining and the criteria to rate the success of its application differ slightly from those discussed in the previous chapter.

The work reported in this Chapter was conducted in close cooperation with several colleagues and students. The courier service study and the development of FAMOS were part of a funded research project (see Deecke et al., 2004) handled by Ruth Meyer, Helmut Deecke, Bernd Page, Remon Sadikni, and the author of this thesis. The automated calibration of the courier service model was investigated together with Ralf Bachmann and Björn Gehlsen (Bachmann et al., 2004). Sven Kruse developed an additional variant of the courier service model presented in (Knaak et al., 2006) and also contributed to validation and verification (Kruse, 2005). Johannes Haan (2009) applied process mining with *ProM* to the courier service models and rated the results in his bachelor thesis, technically co-supervised by the author of this thesis. The results of his work will be summarized in Sections 8.2 and 8.3.

8.1. Courier Service Study

The courier service study serves as a case example in this chapter. It was part of the three year research project 'Sustainable Logistics Concepts for City Courier Services' funded by the Hamburg Office for Education and Science. The objective was to analyze the impact of innovative logistics concepts to the economic, ecologic, and social quality of courier service operation with the aid of agent-based simulation models. Results of the research project and later extensions of the models are reported in several publications including the diploma thesis of the author (Bachmann et al., 2004; Deecke et al., 2004; Knaak, 2002; Knaak et al., 2006).[1] These publications also build the basis for this section.

---

[1] The project report by Deecke et al. (2004) is, among other pre-publications, partly based on the diploma thesis (Knaak, 2002) of the author (see Deecke et al., 2004, p. 2). In this chapter, we prefer to cite the later publication (Deecke et al., 2004).

8.1.1. Problem Description

City couriers are a common view in the streets of large cities all over the world. The main distinction between courier and other transport services (e.g. express services) is the direct transport of consignments from a sender to a receiver by a single courier, which allows for quick and reliable transportation (Meyer et al., 1999, p. 267). Courier services utilize different small to medium-size vehicles such as bicycles, cars, station wagons, and vans (Deecke et al., 2004, p. 11). The individual transport can lead to high economical expenses as well as ecologically relevant emissions produced by the motorized vehicles (Meyer et al., 1999, p. 267).

During the mid-nineties, a decrease of order volumes and an increase of operation costs could be observed in Hamburg-based courier services, partly due to the rise of electronic media and a worsening urban traffic situation (Deecke et al., 2004, pp. 9). This lead to the idea to optimize courier services with efficient concepts borrowed from express service logistics, which were expected to improve the conditions for an increased utilization of environmentally beneficial bicycle couriers (Deecke et al., 2004, p. 19). However, the optimization of courier service logistics is not straightforward due to established conventions within the firms as well as specific expectations by customers (Meyer et al., 1999, p. 267-268).

The goal of the courier service study was to analyze the impact of alternative logistics concepts with the aid of agent-based simulation models (Deecke et al., 2004, p. 8). In the first step, data was collected from two co-operating Hamburg-based courier services (Deecke et al., 2004, pp. 21). Models of the status quo[2] and alternative logistics concepts were specified and implemented with the aid of the MABS framework FAMOS which had been developed in parallel (Deecke et al., 2004, p. 8). After validation and calibration, experiments were run with all models and the different objectives were analyzed by simple quantifications of economic, ecologic, and social measures (Deecke et al., 2004, p. 8).

8.1.2. Agent-Based Courier Service Models

MABS are an appropriate method to simulate courier service logistics due to several analogies between courier services and MAS described in (Deecke et al., 2004, p. 25): City couriers usually work quite autonomously. Their choice of transport orders and routes underlies only minor influences by the courier service's central office. Communication schemes applied between couriers and radio operators working at the office resemble typical agent interaction protocols like *contract net* (see Section 3.3.2.3). Couriers autonomously move through the streets of the city, and their monetary success largely depends on individual experience and knowledge.

In the following, we briefly describe the analyzed organization forms and their abstractions to agent-based simulation models.

---

[2]This model and its implementation adopt results of a pilot study conducted as part of the project MOBILE (Hilty et al., 1998).

8.1.2.1. Status Quo Model

The model of the status quo might represent the most common organization of courier services in an abstract and idealized form.[3] According to Deecke et al. (2004, pp. 11) most courier services consist of a central office that employs one or more radio operators and a courier fleet moving around the city. Each order placed at the office is announced to the fleet (Deecke et al., 2004, p. 11). The couriers rate orders by individual criteria and – in case of interest – contact the office which usually passes the order to the first applicant (Deecke et al., 2004, p. 11).

To ensure an equal utilization, orders are often passed to *idle* couriers, i.e. those who are not currently picking up or delivering an order (Deecke et al., 2004, p. 13). For this purpose, the city area is divided into so-called 'idle regions'[4] (Deecke et al., 2004, p. 13). An incoming order is first offered to the couriers in the idle region that covers its pickup address (Deecke et al., 2004, p. 13).

In some firms, couriers are allowed to process multiple orders in parallel for the sake of improved route planning (Deecke et al., 2004, p. 12). In this case, the radio operators must take care that a single courier does not take too many orders to ensure service quality and fairness of order distribution (Deecke et al., 2004, p. 12).

The radio operators might impose increasing 'pressure' on the courier fleet when an order is not accepted for a longer time period (Deecke et al., 2004, p. 38). The disposition[5] of orders is not common in this organization form (Deecke et al., 2004, p. 11) due to the legal status of couriers as self-employed entrepreneurs (Meyer et al., 1999, p. 267).

Note that one analyzed courier service applied a completely different strategy, where every incoming order is offered to the courier whose current position is closest to the order's pickup address based on *GPS*[6] information (Deecke et al., 2004, pp. 12,56). The agent-based Status Quo model simulates both strategies depending on parameterization (Deecke et al., 2004, pp. 56).

The environment consists of a graph-based representation of the Hamburg road network and of the FAMOS infrastructure for message-based instantaneous and error-free communication (Deecke et al., 2004, p. 38). The road network exists in a detailed variant with about 17000 nodes and in a broad variant (for debugging and face validation) that contains only main streets (Deecke et al., 2004, p. 36).

The dynamic entities in the model include two agent types, couriers and office, as well as two arrival processes for couriers and transport orders (Deecke et al., 2004, pp. 49,51). The arrival processes are fed with real data collected from the cooperating courier services (Deecke et al., 2004, p. 52). Order profiles were preprocessed, cleaned, and mapped to the model of the road network (Deecke et al., 2004, p. 22). Courier profiles were partly extracted from the order profiles by identifying each courier's begin and end of work with her earliest pickup time and latest delivery time (Deecke et al., 2004, p. 23).[7]

---

[3]as of the time of analysis from about 1997 to 2003

[4]German: *Freistellungsbezirke*

[5]Disposition means that a specific courier is obliged to process an order without being allowed to reject it.

[6]Global Positioning System

[7]Detailed information on the collected data and its preprocessing can be found in (Deecke et al., 2004, Sec. 5).

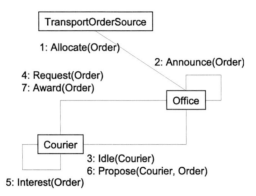

Figure 8.1.: Interaction protocol applied in the Status Quo model displayed as a communication diagram. Adopted from (Deecke et al., 2004, p. 39)

The communication between couriers and office is guided by the contract net-like protocol displayed in Figure 8.1 (Deecke et al., 2004, pp. 39). On arrival of a transport order, the arrival process sends an `Allocate` message to the office (Deecke et al., 2004, p. 39). The office reacts by scheduling an `Announce` signal on itself, and, in reaction to this event, sends a `Request` message with the order as argument to the most appropriate part of the courier fleet (Deecke et al., 2004, pp. 38-39).

For this purpose, the couriers are organized in four groups for each combination of conveyance types (bicycle or car) and courier states (idle or busy); see Deecke et al. (2004, p. 39). Consignments with a preference for bikes are offered to the courier fleet in the order 'idle bikers', 'idle cars', 'busy bikers', 'busy cars' (Deecke et al., 2004, p. 40). Orders with a preference for cars are not offered to bikers since it is assumed that the consignment is too large or heavy for bicycle transport (Deecke et al., 2004, p. 40).[8]

When a courier agent receives a `Request` signal it rates the order with a non-linear 'order interest' function further explained in Section 8.1.3 (Deecke et al., 2004, p. 42). If the calculated interest exceeds a conveyance-dependent threshold (see also Meyer et al., 1999, p. 271), the courier will apply for the order by sending a *Propose* signal to the office after having waited for a time period inversely proportional to its interest (Deecke et al., 2004, p. 42-43).

When the office receives a *Propose* signal, it passes the order to the first applicant and discards all other messages related to that order (Deecke et al., 2004, p. 46). Otherwise, it waits for a deadline after which it re-announces the order to the next-best fitting group of couriers (Deecke et al., 2004, p. 46). If all attempts to pass on the order fail for a certain time period, the office disposes the order to the courier with the closest position to its pickup address (Deecke et al., 2004, p. 46).[9]

The behavior of both agent types is modeled in terms of (hierarchical) UML state-charts from which code can be generated (see Figure 8.2, left). The state-chart for the office merely implements the interaction role described above (Deecke et al., 2004, pp. 45). The courier state-chart

---

[8]Sizes and weights of consignments are currently not modeled explicitly.
[9]Thus abstracting from the 'increasing pressure' applied during order mediation (Deecke et al., 2004, p. 40).

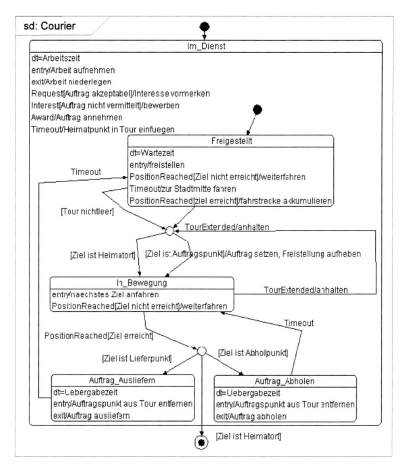

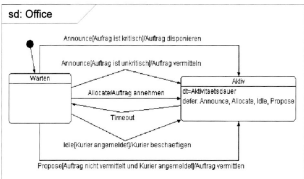

Figure 8.2.: State charts of courier (top) and office agents (bottom). Adopted with modifications from from (Deecke et al., 2004, pp. 42,46).

realizes the interaction protocol by means of static reactions of the root state AtWork[10] while the transport process is implemented in sub-states (Deecke et al., 2004, pp. 41).

If the courier's tour contains at least one pickup or delivery address it starts to move to this address using the shortest path on the road network (Deecke et al., 2004, p. 43). When an intermediate position on the graph is reached, the courier receives a PositionReached signal from the environment, tests if the destination is reached, and moves further otherwise (Deecke et al., 2004, p. 50). Note that the courier continues to communicate with the office while moving: An incoming order might even replace the currently processed order if the distance to its pickup position is closer on the road network (Deecke et al., 2004, p. 50).

When the courier reaches a pickup (delivery) address it picks up (delivers) the consignment, both modeled as a consumption of a fixed amount of simulation time (Deecke et al., 2004, p. 43). When a courier's intended end of work time is reached, it inserts its home address[11] into its tour and moves to this position after having finished its last order (Deecke et al., 2004, p. 43). During the way home the courier might accept further orders, but only those that do not interfere with its intention to reach the home point in terms of the rating function (Deecke et al., 2004, p. 43).

8.1.2.2. Hub and Shuttle Model

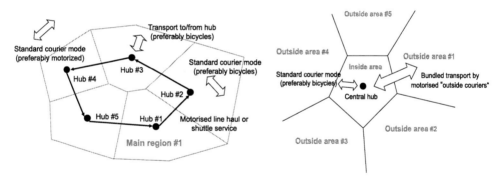

Figure 8.3.: Alternative logistics concepts analyzed in the courier service study: Hub and Shuttle (left), Inside/Outside (right). Adopted with modifications from (Page et al., 2004, Fig. 1).

The first alternative logistics concept modelled in the courier service study is called 'Hub and Shuttle' (see Deecke, 1997 and Deecke et al., 2004, Sec. 4.1): In this express service-like strategy the central city area, as the focal point of the transport order volume (Deecke et al., 2004, p. 15), is divided into a small number of subregions (see Figure 8.3, left) where hubs are installed that couriers use to deposit consignments (Deecke et al., 2004, p. 14). Vans commute between hubs in shuttle service or line haul (Deecke et al., 2004, p. 14).

---

[10]Figure 8.2 shows the German inscription Im_Dienst.

[11]A courier's home address is, in most cases, naively derived from the position of the first order processed by this courier according to the respective transport order profile (Deecke et al., 2004, p. 23).

Transport orders with pickup and delivery addresses in different subregions are transported via the hub system (Deecke et al., 2004, p. 14): Initially a courier (preferably a biker) picks up the consignment from the sender and delivers it to the hub of the respective subregion. When a shuttle reaches the hub on its regular tour it picks up all consignments deposited there and delivers them to the hubs of the destination regions. Another (again preferably bicycle) courier finally delivers the consignment from the destination hub to the sender. Orders with pickup and delivery address in the same subregion or outside of the central area are always transported from the sender to the receiver directly (Deecke et al., 2004, p. 14).

The hub and shuttle strategy was analyzed with regard to its potential for economic and ecological improvements by increased bundling of consignment and application of bicycle couriers. For this purpose, the Status Quo model was extended in the following respects (Deecke et al., 2004, Sec. 7.3.1):

- Two different variants to partition the central city area (consisting of 3 and 5 subregions respectively) were defined.

- The available transport order records were mapped to these regions.

- A hub class was introduced in the model and hubs were positioned near the center of each region in the traffic network (Deecke et al., 2004, p. 52).

- The office agent was extended with the ability to announce different types of tours (from sender to hub, from hub to receiver, etc.).

- The courier agents were extended with methods to deposit and redraw consignments from a hub and their state-charts were adapted accordingly.

- An additional agent class (*Shuttle*, see Deecke et al., 2004, p. 52) was introduced to simulate the vans. Simulations were run with two shuttles visiting all 3 (or 5 respectively) hubs in line haul.

8.1.2.3. Inside/Outside Model

The second logistics strategy analyzed in the courier service study is called 'Inside/Outside' (see Deecke, 1997 and Deecke et al., 2004, Sec. 4.2): As shown in Figure 8.3 (right), this concept divides the city area into one central 'inside region' with an expectedly high volume of transport orders and multiple bordering 'outside regions' with expectedly lower order volumes (Deecke et al., 2004, p. 15). A single hub is installed near the center of the inside region (Deecke et al., 2004, p. 15). Transport orders with a pickup address in the outside region and a delivery address in the inside region (or vice versa) are processed via the hub, while orders within the inside region or the same outside region are transported directly (Deecke et al., 2004, p. 15).

Each outside region is assigned a number of couriers in proportion to its expected transport order volume (Deecke et al., 2004, p. 48). These *regional couriers* use cars or vans for the bundled transport of consignments between their region and the hub (Deecke et al., 2004, p. 16). The remaining couriers work in the inside region and deliver consignments from the hub to receivers or from senders to the hub (Deecke et al., 2004, p. 14).

The Status Quo model must be modified in several respects to simulate the Inside/Outside strategy (Deecke et al., 2004, Sec. 7.3.2): Similar to the *Hub and Shuttle* model, the spatial environment is partitioned into inside and outside regions with transport order data mapped to them (Deecke et al., 2004, p. 48). The *Hub* class and the redraw and deposit functionality can be re-used from this model as well (Deecke et al., 2004, p. 48).

To gain an acceptable rate of consignment bundling, the behavior of regional couriers is modified (Deecke et al., 2004, p. 48): A regional courier collects regional orders announced by the office for a certain time interval (e.g. 30 minutes). Only at due time, the courier sets off for the central hub and deposits the collected consignments ("operational delay"[12], see Deecke et al., 2004, p. 19). Then it redraws all consignments destined for its region from the hub, moves back, and delivers them to the receivers. At the same time, it starts to collect new orders and the life cycle repeats.

Since the standard mediation protocol did not lead to satisfactory results for the outside regions, the office disposes every order that starts from an outside region to the closest available courier (Deecke et al., 2004, p. 48).

When the simulation starts, couriers are assigned to regions using a simple strategy (Deecke et al., 2004, p. 48): Every motorized courier that enters the model is assigned to another region in a 'round-robin' manner until a predefined capacity is reached. The capacities of outside regions are predefined in proportion to the regions's order volume, while the capacity of the inside region is not limited.

8.1.3. Implementation with FAMOS and DESMO-J

All variants of the courier model were implemented using the *Java*-based simulation frameworks *DESMO-J* and *FAMOS* (see Section 3.4.4) (Deecke et al., 2004, pp. 49).[13] Couriers and shuttles are subclasses of `MobileAgent` (Deecke et al., 2004, p. 49). The courier office as a "purely communicating agent" (Ferber, 1995, p. 12) is derived from the class `Agent` (Deecke et al., 2004, p. 49). The behavior of couriers and office is generated from the state-charts shown in the previous section with the aid of a code generator (Deecke et al., 2004, p. 50). The less flexible shuttle behavior is implemented in a process-oriented way (class `ProcessBehaviour`, Deecke et al., 2004, p. 52).

Further (non-agent) entities in the model include transport orders (`TransportOrder` and subclasses), hubs (`Hub`), and arrival processes for couriers and orders (`CourierArrival`, `Transport-OrderArrival`, and subclasses, Deecke et al., 2004, p. 51). Transport orders are implemented as situated entities with a position in the spatial environment (Deecke et al., 2004, p. 51). The arrival processes are derived from the FAMOS class `ExternalObjectArrival` that offers support to schedule the arrival of arbitrary objects specified in text or XML files (Deecke et al., 2004, p. 52).

The group structure of the courier model is mapped to the FAMOS variant of the AGR model (Ferber and Gutknecht, 1998) with four groups for idle and busy bicycle and car couriers (Deecke et al., 2004, p. 51). The road network is implemented as a spatial environment of type `Graph` (Deecke et al., 2004, p. 51). Couriers are equipped with a movement strategy of type

---

[12]German: "operative Verzögerung"

[13]Details of the courier model implementations can be found in (Deecke et al., 2004, Sec. 7.4) and in the diploma thesis of the author (Knaak, 2002).

OdoRoute that supports route planning[14] and movement along the planned route including an automated accumulation of the covered distances (Deecke et al., 2004, p. 50).[15]

The implementation of the couriers' reasoning abilities, i.e. rating of transport orders and tour planning, are largely adopted from the predecessor model developed during the MOBILE project (Hilty et al., 1998; Meyer et al., 1999). The tour planning is a common sense procedure as it might be applied by real city couriers (Deecke et al., 2004, p. 44): Every courier is equipped with a Tour object to store pickup and delivery points of pending transport orders, sorted by intended processing time (Deecke et al., 2004, p. 49). When a courier accepts a new order it first inserts the pickup point into its existing tour with the least possible detour; and then inserts the delivery point at the position after the pickup point that leads to the least possible detour for overall processing (Deecke et al., 2004, p. 44).

In (Bachmann et al., 2004, Sec. 4) we described the order rating procedure as follows:[16]

> "We quantify the individual rating of transport orders with the aid of a function that was proposed by Reick (1997) [during the MOBILE project] and slightly adapted [... for the current model]. Criteria to rate orders include the couriers' individual estimations of order quality, need for orders, and previous utilization. The quality of an order o for a courier c is quantified as
>
> $$Q(c,o) = \frac{revenues(c,o)}{detour(c,o)} - cost(c) \cdot v_{avg}(c). \tag{8.1}$$
>
> Here $revenues(c,o)$ are the revenues that courier c gains from order o and $detour(c,o)$ is the expected detour [that the transport of o causes] with respect to the courier's current tour. $cost(c)$ und $v_{avg}(c)$ express the cost of operation and the average speed of the courier's conveyance. The need for orders of a courier is computed from its current order situation [expressed in terms of the normalized tour length]
>
> $$S(c) = \frac{T(c)}{T_{max}} \tag{8.2}$$
>
> where $T(c)$ is the estimated time that it will approximately take to process the already accepted orders and T_{max} is the courier service's guaranteed maximum delivery time. If the latter is exceeded by $T(c)$, the courier is not allowed to accept further orders without endangering [...] service quality. In this case its need for orders $N(C) = 0$. Otherwise, $N(c)$ decreases inversely proportional to the [normalized] tour length following a negative exponential function between 1 and 0:
>
> $$N(c) = \frac{e^{-q \cdot S(c)} - e^{-q}}{1 - e^{-q}} \tag{8.3}$$
>
> Here, q is a free parameter that influences the slope of the exponential function. If the product $[P =] Q(c,o) \cdot N(c)$ exceeds a threshold $w \cdot util(c)$ that increases proportionally with

---

[14]The well-known algorithm by Dijkstra (see e.g. Domschke, 1989, cited in Deecke et al., 2004, p. 38) is applied to find the shortest path from a start to a destination position.

[15]During the courier study, the automated accumulation of distances was not fully functional for the special case of stops 'between' discrete positions on the road network. Therefore a simplified variant was used.

[16]Similar presentations – besides the original source by Reick (1997) – can be found in (Deecke et al., 2004, pp. 44) and (Knaak, 2002).

[a conveyance-dependent] weighting factor w to the courier's [previous] utilization $util(c)$, the courier applies for the order after a deliberation duration [... inversely proportional to P]."

For this purpose, the courier schedules an `Interest` signal on itself (Deecke et al., 2004, p. 40). The reception of this signal after the calculated 'deliberation time' will cause the courier to apply for the order by sending a `Propose` message to the office (Deecke et al., 2004, p. 40).

8.1.4. Data Collection and Result Analysis

To gain an insight into the modeled logistics strategies and their effects on the performance of the simulated courier service, a wealth of data is collected during the courier service simulations (Deecke et al., 2004, p. 37).

The following result and trace data is provided by the model for subsequent offline analysis:

- *Individual and aggregate transport order data* (Deecke et al., 2004, pp. 37,71): For each transport order, the model provides a result data set of relevant attributes. These include, among others, durations of life cycle phases like mediation or delivery. Additionally, aggregate measures (mean, standard deviation, minimum, maximum, and sum) of these attributes are computed over all transport orders processed during a simulated workday.

- *Individual and aggregate courier data* (Deecke et al., 2004, pp. 37,68): Values of important attributes are also provided for the courier fleet of a simulation run. These e.g. include the number of processed orders and the idle and overall distances covered by every courier during simulation.

- *Queue statistics collected at the hubs* (Deecke et al., 2004, p. 52): Every hub contains queues for incoming and outgoing consignments. For these queues standard waiting statistics (e.g. average queue length and waiting duration) are computed by the DESMO-J framework.

- *Traces of agent behavior*: Relevant actions of all agents are logged at runtime with the mandatory attributes timestamp, action name, and originator as well as an optional execution context consisting of the spatial position the action was executed at and the objects (at most two) it was executed on (see also Haan, 2009, p. 61).

During simulation, the model provides further data for online analysis to registered event listeners:

- *Agent movement*: When an agent changes its position in the spatial environment, a *position changed* event is published for online animations of the agent movement.

- *Agent attributes*: During simulation, several agent attributes (e.g. the current occupation status of a courier) can be accessed via probes.

- *Time series data*: Time series data of the current number of registered couriers, placed orders, and finished orders is published during runtime.

Courier and transport order data is collected for offline analysis using the FAMOS class `IndividualObserver` (see Section 3.4.4). The courier model contains several subclasses that

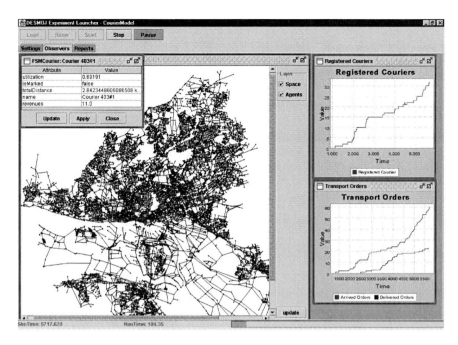

Figure 8.4.: Online simulation observation in the DESMO-J experiment starter. Adopted from (Page and Kreutzer, 2005, p. 227).

implement different configurations to observe attributes of couriers and transport orders via DESMO-J *access points* (Deecke et al., 2004, pp. 51). Each `IndividualObserver` provides a table of individual and aggregate attribute values to the DESMO-J report that can be stored in either text, HTML, or in a relational database (Deecke et al., 2004, p. 52).

Actions of agents are logged with the method `dump()` provided by the class `Agent` (see also Haan, 2009, p. 61). Log entries are stored either in a text file or in a relational database.[17] For online observation, a simple graphical observer to animate the courier movement as well as plotters for time series and histograms were implemented as part of the DESMO-J experiment starter tool displayed in Figure 8.4.[18]

8.1.5. Validation and Calibration

During and subsequent to the funded courier service study, several validation techniques were applied to the courier model:[19]

---

[17]The limited number of context objects mentioned above is a tribute to these storage mechanisms.

[18]The courier observer was implemented by Ruth Meyer and the author of this thesis. The time series and histogram plotters were provided by Philip Joschko. The implementation of the DESMO-J experiment starter was started by Ruth Meyer and the author of this thesis based on (simplified) concepts from Bachmann (2003) and Gehlsen (2004). It was later improved and extended as part of the diploma thesis by Gunnar Kiesel (2004).

[19]The list is merely based on the author's memory.

- conceptual validation by review of the state-chart models,

- face validation of the rating function using *MATLAB* visualizations of its reaction surface in dependence on parameter changes,

- verification (in the wider sense) by code reviews and log-based debugging during model implementation,

- manual and automated calibration of model parameters with simulation-based optimization (Bachmann et al., 2004),

- operational (face) validation by observing animations of the courier movement and time series at runtime,

- validation of exemplary model reports by the developers and a domain expert,

- application of model checking to an abstracted model of the courier state chart (Kruse, 2005),

- naive model-based validation of simulation results and traces using SQL queries on the result database, and

- 'implicit' code and design reviews by students during the implementation of model extensions.

In the following we focus on our first attempts towards automation, i.e. automated calibration and model-based validation. Subsequently the results of the validation and the productive simulation runs are discussed and several problems are identified.

8.1.5.1. Calibration of the Rating Function

As expected from the literature study, the calibration of the courier behavior proved to be difficult but vital for the validity of the model (Bachmann et al., 2004, Sec. 5):

> "The free parameters q and w of the rating function (see Section [... 8.1.3]) are model artifacts without counterparts in the real system and therefore hard to calibrate. Especially the weighting factor w [...] strongly influences several macroscopic results since it [...] affects the process of transport order assignment."

In (Bachmann et al., 2004, Sec. 5) we reported on the calibration efforts as follows:

> "Since the transport order profiles contain detailed information on order assignment, the following calibration procedure could be applied (Deecke et al., 2003):
>
> 1. Simulations were run with an empirical order assignment, where orders were simply assigned to couriers according to the transport order profile of the respective workday. Only tour planning, [courier movement], and order delivery were actually simulated in the model.
>
> 2. The results of this order assignment were examined [...against knowledge about the real system and the predecessor model from the MOBILE project, i.e. *model alignment* (Axtell et al., 1996) was performed as reviewed in Section 5.1.2.3] and accepted after some modifications of the model. Thus, we accepted the model of route planning and

order delivery as valid with respect to the relevant output quantities (order delivery times, distances covered by the couriers, utilizations, revenues).

3. The parameters of the rating function were calibrated against the macroscopic results of the 'empirical order assignment' model."

Pilot simulation runs showed that a high previous utilization should attenuate the need for orders of bicycle couriers stronger than that of car drivers to gain realistic results (Bachmann et al., 2004, Sec. 5). This is due to the fact that the transport order profiles indicate numerous orders with bicycle preference but only few bicycle couriers. "It also seems plausible since bikers tire sooner than car drivers" (Bachmann et al., 2004, Sec. 5).

The overall procedure can be considered as functional decomposition according to the white box validation framework by Fehler et al. (2004). Further following the description in (Bachmann et al., 2004, Sec. 5):

"By manual calibration of two conveyance-dependent weighting factors w_{Bike} and w_{Car}, average values and standard deviations of some output quantities could already be fit to the reference results quite well (Deecke et al., 2003, p. 40). Nevertheless, the manual calibration also revealed a high sensitivity of these parameters and a non-linear response of the model to their variation. Due to the considerable simulation time [...] it did not seem reasonable to continue the manual calibration.

Instead [an attempt to support the calibration procedure with the framework DISMO for distributed simulation-based optimization was run. ... T]he model was prepared for automated calibration by implementing a DISMO-specific interface. The interface describes which model parameters will be optimized and which output quantities are considered to calculate the objective function. In the first study, we restricted ourselves to fitting only average motorized and unmotorized distances covered by the couriers and average order delivery times to the reference results. In doing so, the weighting factors w_{Bike} and w_{Car} and the parameter q should be varied automatically.

Besides the definition of parameters and output quantities, the automated calibration with DISMO requires the definition of an objective function which is technically realized by implementing a certain interface as well. Based on the general multi-criterial objective from [... Section 5.1.2.2] we used a variant

$$G(\mathbf{x}) = \sum_{i=1}^{n} \left[\frac{c \cdot (f_i(\mathbf{x}) - y_i)}{y_i} \right]^2 \to Min! \tag{8.4}$$

Here f_i denotes [...] the components of the simulation result vector (average distances covered by bikers and motorized couriers and mean order delivery time) and y_i their counterparts from the empirical order assignment. To scale output quantities with heterogenous units, the differences $f_i - y_i$ are divided by the reference value y_i. As usual in the calculation of errors, the square of the scaled differences is taken to ensure a non-linear rating of differences. Thereby, configurations with low deviations of all output quantities are e.g. preferred over those with a strong deviation of a single quantity. An additional weighting is not performed because all considered output quantities appear equally important for model validity."

The simulations were run with the aid of the DISMO system that distributed independent simulation runs for different parameter configurations in a local workstation cluster (Bachmann

	Distance (km)	Revenues (EUR/km)	Utilization (percent)	Order delivery time (min)
Empirical assignment				49.3 (42.1)
Bicycle couriers	47.7 (21.7)	1.83 (0.32)	70.5 (17.0)	
Car couriers	96.6 (49.2)	1.13 (0.31)	63.8 (19.2)	
Simulated mediation				53.9 (43.2)
Bicycle couriers	52.0 (19.5)	1.50 (0.29)	67.8 (3.3)	
Car couriers	96.3 (32.9)	1.17 (0.29)	59.2 (13.5)	

Table 8.1.: "Comparison of multiple macroscopic output quantities of the courier models with empirical and simulated transport order assignment. The parameter configuration was computed by the automated calibration procedure with $w_{Bike} = 0.0298$, $w_{Car} = 0.0167$ and $q = 0.76$. The first three quantities are averaged over the courier fleet, the order delivery time is averaged over the order volume of the simulated workday. Standard deviations are stated in brackets." Table and caption adopted from (Bachmann et al., 2004, Fig. 2).

et al., 2004, Sec. 5). The results of each set of simulation runs were automatically evaluated with the objective function. Based on this evaluation, new parameter configurations were generated by a generational genetic algorithm (GGA, see Goldberg, 1989, p. 111, cited in Bachmann et al., 2004, Sec. 5).[20]

Table 8.1 shows results of the automated calibration, which fits the reference results fairly well with respect to explicitly (average unmotorized distance and order delivery time) as well as non-explicitly (average utilization) calibrated quantities (Bachmann et al., 2004, Sec. 5).

The parameter configuration computed by DISMO is not necessarily optimal due to the application of a heuristic optimization algorithm. Furthermore, number and size of the generations evaluated by the genetic algorithm were relatively small to reduce overall computation time. Nevertheless, the results of the automated calibration are roughly comparable to those of the manual procedure, but were produced by an unsupervised calculation on a computer cluster. Considering the limited statistical validity of the study, we noted in (Bachmann et al., 2004, Sec. 5) that

"every parameter combination was only tested in one simulation run (i.e. using the order and courier profiles of a single workday). Every configuration should be tested against multiple input data sets with stochastic (or empirically measured) variations to gain more relevant results and to avoid overfitting. [...] Furthermore, additional [... statistical measures and] output quantities should be considered, which can easily be integrated into the objective function."

8.1.5.2. Naive Model-Based Validation

Another small step towards supporting validation with automated techniques was the application of SQL (see e.g. Cannan, 1993) queries to analyze the simulation data stored in the relational database. Typical advantages of database technology for result- and trace-based out-

---

[20]The parameterization of the genetic algorithm is described in (Bachmann et al., 2004, Sec. 5).

put analysis (see Section 2.4.2) are discussed by Ritzschke and Wiedemann (1998, Secs. 3-4) who, among other possibilities, mention aggregations, drill-downs, and correlation analysis.

We attempted to use SQL queries to check simulation traces and results for consistency and to test hypotheses about detected failures; i.e. naive model-based validation and trace checking (see Section 5.1.2.1). In the following we state constructed examples on a modified database schema that merely serve illustration purposes and were not applied during the actual courier service study.

As indicated in Section 8.1.4, we assume that the simulation database contains tables to store relevant attribute values of individual couriers (table `couriers`) and transport orders (table `orders`) for each simulation run. Furthermore execution logs of all agents are stored in a table `trace`. Every entry references a certain experiment from an additional table `experiments`. To rate influences of parameter changes, the parameter settings of each experiment are stored in a table `parameters`.

The following categories of validation rules stated by Birta and Özmizrak (1996, Sec. 4), reviewed in Section 5.1.2.1, might be re-built with queries on this database:

1. constraints on single result values (*formal specifications*, Birta and Özmizrak, 1996, p. 84),

2. constraints on relations between multiple result values (*qualitative specifications*, Birta and Özmizrak, 1996, p. 84),

3. constraints on relations between input parameter and output value changes in multiple experiments (*qualitative change-in-value specifications*, Birta and Özmizrak, 1996, p. 85),

4. constraints on comparisons between simulated and real-world behavior (*observational specifications*, Birta and Özmizrak, 1996, p. 85), and

5. temporal and other relations between trace entries of a simulation run (re-building temporal logic rules from trace-based model checking, see Section 4.2.5.4).

A simple example for the first category is the claim that *'at the end of a valid experiment, all orders must have been delivered'*. If order delivery is identified by the order attribute `delivery` set to a non-null time value, this is checked with the trivial query

```
select name from orders where delivery is null and experiment = 'E1'
```

that returns all orders violating this constraint in an experiment E1. Constraints of the second and fourth category might be formulated similarly, where the latter would require real world data to be stored in the database.

A similar example for the fifth category is the constraint that *'every order that was picked up by a courier must be delivered by the same courier later'*[21] This rule might be checked using the nested query

```
select tr.object1, tr.agent from traces tr
  where tr.action = 'pickup' and tr.experiment = 'E1' and not exists
```

---

[21]Note that this constraint only holds in the Status Quo model.

```
(select * from traces tr2 where tr2.action = 'deliver'
   and tr2.experiment = 'E1' and tr.object1 = tr2.object1
   and tr.agent = tr2.agent and tr.timestamp < tr2.timestamp)
```

that returns all orders (`object1` in table `traces`) the processing of which violated one of the above conditions in an experiment `E1`.

The third category describes relations between model parameters and output values. An example is the constraint that *'the number of disposed orders should increase when the duration decreases that the office waits until an order is disposed'.*[22] This can be checked using the following nested query with aggregate functions that searches for counter-examples of the constraint:[23]

```
select ex.name from experiments ex, parameters par
  where par.experiment = ex.name and par.name = 'durationUntilDisposition'
  and exists (select * from experiments ex2, parameters par2
    where par2.experiment = ex2.name and ex2.name <> ex.name
    and par.name = par2.name and par2.value < par.value
    and (select count(*) from orders o2
      where o2.experiment = ex2.name and o2.disposed = 1)
  < (select count(*) from orders o
      where o.experiment = ex.name and o.disposed = 1))
```

The fictitious examples (and our experiences from the courier service study) show that SQL queries are a simple, yet powerful and flexible tool to support hypothesis checking in an agent-based simulation. The last example, however, also indicates that queries representing complex relationships might become difficult to read due to the low abstraction level of SQL. Furthermore, only non-exhaustive confirmatory validation of predefined hypotheses is supported.

To overcome these drawbacks, we will turn our focus to model checking in the next Section and to data and process mining in Section 8.2.

8.1.5.3. Model Checking of Courier Statecharts

As part of a study project, Kruse (2005) evaluated the utility of model checking and data mining techniques for the validation of the courier service model. Different from Haan (2009, pp. 77), who investigated hypotheses over the log of the courier service simulation by means of trace checking, Kruse (2005, pp. 15) applied 'conventional' model checking to the state chart model of the courier agent.

Due to the use of state charts for conceptual modeling and implementation of the courier model, Kruse (2005, p. 27) advocates the use of model checking in an early conceptual modeling phase. As exemplary hypotheses, he analyzes the questions "if a [courier] agent is guaranteed to reach an

---

[22]example inspired by Birta and Özmizrak (1996, pp. 96)

[23]Note that this query assumes that all stored experiments contain the same number of processed orders. Otherwise relative numbers of disposed orders would have to be considered.

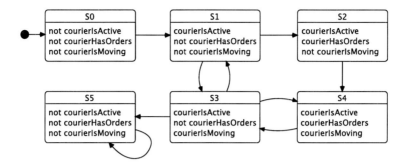

Figure 8.5.: Kripke structure corresponding to parts of the courier statechart. Adopted with minor modifications from Kruse (2005, p. 22)

active state from its start state [...and] if after activation [... it] eventually becomes inactive again?" (Kruse, 2005, p. 20)

To convert the courier statechart into a finite state model amenable for exhaustive model checking (*Kripke structure*[24]), Kruse (2005, p. 21) proposes the following procedure:

1. "First, select significant states [with respect to the analyzed hypotheses].

2. Then add an initial and a final state to the state set and a self-transition to the final state to gain a complete transition relation.

3. Subsequently, define a set of elementary logical formulae.

4. Define a label function to express in which states the respective formulae [or their negations] hold true.

5. Whenever it is ambigous if a formula holds true in a state [of the original state chart] this state must be duplicated [... and] the transition relation must be adapted accordingly."

Note that this procedure basically corresponds to manual program abstraction as discussed by Visser et al. (2003) and reviewed in Section 5.1.2.1. Applying it to the courier statechart from Figure 8.2 with respect to the hypotheses stated above and the elementary formulae *courierIsActive*, *courierHasOrders*, and *courierIsMoving* (Kruse, 2005, p. 21) yields the Kripke structure shown in Figure 8.5.

In this model, the states S_0 and S_5 correspond to the initial and final states of the courier statechart. State S_1 corresponds to the original state *Idle* and S_2 to the preceding decision node. Since "for the state *Moving* it is ambiguous if the agent has accepted orders or not [...] this state must be duplicated" (Kruse, 2005, p. 21) resulting in the states S_3 and S_4. Kruse (2005, p. 20) furthermore translated the two above hypotheses into temporal logic formulae and implemented both the model and the formulae as a script for the model checker *NuSMV*[25] (Kruse, 2005, pp. 22).

---

[24]For a formal definition of Kripke structures see Clarke et al. (1999) cited in Kruse (2005, p. 15).

[25]see http://nusmv.irst.itc.it/index.html (last visit 2005-02-03), cited in (Kruse, 2005, pp. 22,30)

On this basis, the model checker proved that the first hypothesis (courier is guaranteed to become active) holds true for every possible execution sequence of the model (Kruse, 2005, p. 23). The second hypothesis (courier is guaranteed to become inactive again) was falsified by stating the counter-example of an infinite loop between the states S_1 and S_3 (Kruse, 2005, pp. 23-24). Kruse (2005, p. 25) notes that this formula only evaluates to *true* "when a fairness condition is set in the model checker", thus enforcing the transition to S_5 to be taken eventually.

Concluding on the behavior actually implemented in the courier service model, the second example roughly corresponds to the situation where a courier is not given the possibility to reach its home point and finish work before the end of the simulation due to a large number of accepted orders. In the implementation, 'fairness' is to a certain degree ensured by the order mediation scheme and the insertion of the home point into the tour when the intended end of work has been reached (see Section 8.1.2.1).

Though the examples presented by Kruse (2005) remain rather simple due to the limited scope of the study project, the work shows (in accordance with similar studies like Walton, 2004) that model checking can be usefully applied to the conceptual modeling phase of a MABS study (Kruse, 2005, p. 26). By performing an additional "paper and pencil" simulation[26] of the model checking algorithm on the example (Kruse, 2005, pp. 24) and by pointing out pitfalls in the implementation of the *NuSMV* script (Kruse, 2005, pp. 22), focus is put on making the formal verification technique accessible to simulation practitioners.

8.1.6. Results and Discussion

In this section we provide a brief review of the courier service study's simulation results adopted from (Page et al., 2004, Sec. 6). Subsequently the quality of these results and our previously described validation attempts are discussed. A more detailed result presentation is found in (Deecke et al., 2004, Sec. 8.3).

8.1.6.1. Review of Simulation Results

In (Page et al., 2004, Sec. 6) we summarized the results of the courier service simulations as follows:

> "The analysis of the different logistic strategies' economic, ecologic and social impact concentrated on three measurements in the first instance. The total motorised distance is considered as an indicator of ecologic quality and the mean order delivery time as a measurement for economic benefit. The distribution of the couriers' revenues provides an indication of a policy's expected social acceptance.
>
> [... Figure 8.6] (left) shows a comparison of the total motorised distance with order profiles from 5 different workdays. Contrary to our primary expectations the distances covered in the *Hub and Shuttle* model are noticeably larger than in the status quo. This might be due to the fact that the investigated order profiles do not fit the selected regions and hub positions well since only about 25 percent of orders meet the conditions for transport via the hub system. Therefore the desired bundling rate is not achieved and the balance suffers from additional distances caused by the shuttle service and splitting of consignments into two

---

[26]as to use the term by Page and Kreutzer (2005, Sec. 2.7)

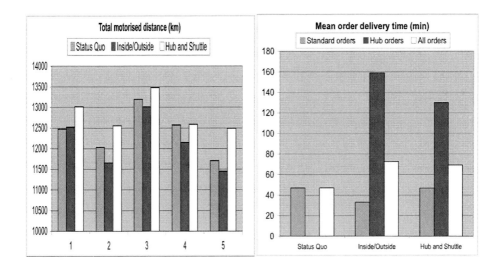

Figure 8.6.: Comparison between Status Quo, Hub and Shuttle, and Inside/Outside model by ecologically and economically relevant measures. Adopted from (Page et al., 2004, Fig. 4).

transport orders. In contrast the *Inside/Outside* strategy displays a marginal improvement compared to the status quo. This strategy fits the order profile slightly better and does not involve additional motorised traffic. Possibly a more detailed dimensioning of region layout and courier assignment could improve the effect.

From [... Figure 8.6] (right) showing a comparison of mean order delivery times averaged over 5 workdays it becomes obvious that both new policies display extended durations for consignments processed via the hub [system]. Since only 30 percent of the consignments are concerned and the remaining deliveries are even accelerated in the *Inside/Outside* model the trade-off might be acceptable. In both new strategies the couriers' average revenues per kilometre are raised by about 0.3 [... Euros] due to the new accounting scheme and increased bundling."

8.1.6.2. Discussion of Validity

Though the courier service study showed that MABS can in principle be applied to the analysis of sustainable logistics concepts, the validity of the particular results presented in the previous section might be challenged for several reasons.

Firstly, the statistical representativeness is clearly limited since the experiments were based on order profiles of five consecutive workdays[27] recorded from a single courier service. Two

---

[27]coincidentally including September 11th of 2001, the day of the dreadful attack to the World Trade Center in New York

additional order and courier profiles stemmed from a courier service with a disposition strategy which could not be directly compared.

The simulations are driven by real data traces without stochastic variations by random numbers. To improve this situation, further order profiles should be collected, and random distributions for arrival rates and spatial flows of transport orders should be derived from them, which might lead to complex traffic generation models (Deecke et al., 2004, p. 64). Though order arrival and delivery rates exhibit steady phases, a steady-state analysis of the courier model is complicated by the fact that the number of registered couriers permanently changes during the course of a workday.

Another reason for the limited significance of the presented results are several simplifications, especially in the models of the alternative logistics concepts. All model variants neglect temporal variations of the traffic situation and influences like traffic jams or traffic lights. Different types of courier behavior are only distinguished between bikers, car drivers, and 'regional couriers' in the Inside/Outside model.

One reason for the rather disappointing performance of the simulated logistics strategies might be the fact that the implemented planning and coordination abilities of courier and office agents do not fulfill the requirements posed by these strategies. The office might e.g. begin to announce the second half of an order processed via the hub system *before* the order has actually arrived at the hub.

Many of these drawbacks could obviously be improved by extending the existing models. However, the added complexity would further complicate the problems of data availability and validation. The validation attempts described above could only in parts increase the confidence in the model and the plausibility of its result. They could not completely displace the impression of the courier model as a 'black box' where the actual course of internal processes is not fully understood by its developers. The validation suffered from a number of problems that are described in the following.

A very common problem for simulation studies is the lack of available data and communication with domain practitioners (e.g. city couriers) during conceptual and operational validation, which could not be fully compensated by the presence of a domain expert in the development team. The verification[28] of the computer model was alleviated by the use of state charts and code generation on the one hand. On the other hand, problems with inconsistencies between the different model representations occurred, and several important parts of the agents' behavior had to be implemented besides the visual state chart formalism.

During the verification and operational validation of the courier model several examples for the problem categories from Section 3.5 could be observed:

- *Problem of model complexity*: Due to the large amount of collected data, it was time-consuming to check if the simulation runs from a larger series of experiments had all delivered valid results. The use of SQL queries proved useful to filter results or traces and to validate simple constraints. These statements get complex soon, but an automated translation from a higher level notation or the use of a more appropriate rule-based validation system (e.g. a model checker) seems possible. However, as mentioned above, these approaches only support confirmatory validation of predefined hypotheses.

---

[28]in the wider sense, see Section 2.4.3.1

- *Problem of result representation and interpretation*: Obviously, the analyzed performance indicators are simplistic and provide a rather limited view on the concept of sustainability. Attempts towards a pattern-oriented analysis of the model (e.g. patterns of courier movement) largely failed due to a lack of appropriate aggregation and visualization techniques. The applied visualization and analysis techniques were not sufficient to extract useful aggregated representations of the processes running in the model.

- *Problem of distributed system state*: Erroneous or inconsistent simulation results proved hard to isolate and trace back to faults in the behavior of an agent or other model component. Some observed errors were path dependent, i.e. they only occurred when agents had previously executed a certain (previously unknown) sequence of actions. While the automated parameter calibration of the rating function confirmed the results of the manual calibration attempts, it provided no new insights into the 'meaning' of the calculated solution, since validity was reduced to a single number in the objective function.[29]

In the next two sections, we discuss how the application of process mining can complement the 'conventional' validation techniques described above, and which solutions, but also new problems are encountered in return.

8.2. Application of Process Mining

In Chapter 7, process mining was integrated into the model-driven PAOSE approach, and applied to a small example model. This raises the question how these techniques can support a large, quantitative simulation study based on a code-centric simulation framework like DESMO-J. The bachelor thesis by Johannes Haan (2009) was dedicated to this question and evaluated the application of process mining to the courier service simulations described above. Since most process mining algorithms (including the techniques presented in the previous chapter) were implemented for *ProM* (see Section 4.2.6.1), this tool was again chosen as the technical basis for the study.

8.2.1. Objectives and Methodology

According to Haan (2009, p. 7) "process mining has often been applied in studies to evaluate its utility for different areas of research in the past." As shown in Section 5.3 and (Haan, 2009, Ch. 3) this includes some applications to agent-based systems as well. In addition to the related work and the PAOSE integration from the previous chapter, the focus of the present study was put on the following questions as a refinement of research question *Q5* from Section 1.2:

- *Q5.1*: Can process mining support or complement the previously described validation and calibration attempts with respect to the observed problems?

- *Q5.2*: Can process mining help to gain further insight into the behavior of the courier models with respect to validation and domain-specific analysis? Does it deliver 'surprising' or unexpected findings?

---

[29]This insufficiency is mirrored in the term "black box calibration" that Fehler et al. (2004, p. 306) use to describe these techniques.

- *Q5.3*: How large is the additional effort to instrument the models? How complex are the experimental setups? Can they easily be re-used between different models or model variants?

- *Q5.4*: How do result representations of process mining compare to typical reports from discrete event simulation?

- *Q5.5*: Which algorithms are suitable to reconstruct and enrich process and structural models in the given problem domain (Haan, 2009, p. 7)?

- *Q5.6*: How does the existing tool *ProM* and the additional interaction mining techniques described in Chapter 7 perform on large logs produced by the courier service simulations?

As mentioned in Section 4.2.6.2, the dissertation by Lang (2008) is a good example for the systematic evaluation of process mining algorithms in a given domain (medical image processing in this case). Haan (2009, p. 89) therefore decided to partly adopt the structure and methodology proposed in this thesis for the present study. This results in an approach that roughly mirrors the KDD process reviewed in Section 4.1.1.

In the conceptual part of the study, a list of relevant analysis and validation tasks must be defined that will be performed with the aid of process mining. The analysis perspectives and usage scenarios touched by these tasks must be stated. Furthermore, a list of criteria must be developed to rate the ability of process mining techniques to help answering the previously defined questions.

In practice, a logger must be implemented that maps the FAMOS trace format (Section 8.1.4) to the MXML format processed by ProM. The courier models must be instrumented to provide the required log entries. Filtering and preprocessing algorithms must be chosen to prepare the collected log data with respect to the analysis questions defined before, and appropriate algorithms must be selected to reconstruct the process models and perform subsequent analyses (Haan, 2009, p. 59). Finally the experiments must be conducted, and the results and experiences must be rated based on the defined criteria.

The following sections summarize the discussion from (Haan, 2009, Sec. 4) in a slightly streamlined and extended form.

8.2.2. Analysis Tasks

In the following, we present a catalogue of analysis tasks that seem appropriate to be supported by process mining. Note that only a subset of these tasks was investigated in the study by Haan (2009). In the listing, each task is assigned to one or more related perspectives and use cases.

- *T1*: Provide an aggregated overview of the transport order processing workflow implemented in the model. For verification, it should become visible if the behavior of the participating agents correctly implements the overall workflow. For economic analysis, lead times of all relevant process steps and hints on possible bottlenecks should be provided.

    - Perspective: external control (multi-agent workflow), domain perspectives (time)

– Use cases: exploratory analysis and (qualitative) validation

- *T2*: Find out in which way internal state attributes influence the rating of orders by couriers. Is the observed behavior plausible with respect to the behavior of real couriers and the intended modeling of the rating function?

  – Perspective: agent decisions

  – Use cases: exploratory validation & verification, calibration and sensitivity analysis

- *T3*: Verify the implementation of the order processing by couriers with a focus on the possibility to switch the current destination in favor of a new order en route; and on the correct accumulation of covered distances.[30]

  – Perspective: internal control

  – Use case: exploratory verification (in the wider sense)

- *T4*: Verify the implementation of the courier life cycle. Does the interplay between different aspects of courier behavior (e.g. occupation state and movement) work as intended?[31]

  – Perspective: internal control

  – Use cases: exploratory and confirmatory verification (in the wider sense)

- *T5*: Find patterns in the observed agent behavior that help to explain why the alternative logistics concepts seem to perform worse than the Status Quo model. Is it valid to transfer this conclusion to the real system or must the models be enhanced for a valid comparison?

  – Perspective: external control (high-level interaction patterns, see also Dustdar and Hoffmann, 2007)

  – Use case: exploratory analysis

In his thesis, Haan (2009) actually worked on task *T1* as well as parts of the tasks *T3*, *T4*, and *T5*. Task *T2* was initially investigated in an earlier work by Kruse (2005).

8.2.3. Evaluation Criteria

As discussed in Section 4.2.6.2, the evaluation criteria by Lang (2008, Sec. 4.3.2) mainly reflect the *objective* performance of the evaluated process mining algorithms, such as e.g. the ability to detect duplicate tasks. In contrast, Haan (2009, p. 72) puts his focus on subjective estimations of the evaluated algorithms' benefit to answer certain analysis questions and settles for the following list of evaluation criteria:[32]

- *C1 - Utility of results*: Is the algorithm able to build a plausible model or aggregation from the given input data? Does this model help to answer the investigated questions?

---

[30]This task was actually formulated after detecting a related error during the work on task *T1*.

[31]This task was also formulated *a-posteriori* to summarize the actually performed work.

[32]Haan (2009, p. 72) uses a fifth criterion, *C5 - potential for further development*, as an attempt to determine a cost-benefit ratio for programmatic corrections and extensions of an algorithm and its current implementation in ProM. This category is omitted here since it appeared difficult to rate for some of the evaluated mining techniques.

On the one hand, criterion $C1$ might be subdivided into the objective measures for the correctness of the reconstructed process model used by Lang (2008, Sec. 4.3.2). On the other hand it mirrors the more subjective notion of *reasonable models* used by Wainer et al. (2005, Sec. 3.3).

- *C2 - Ease of use*: How easy is it to apply the algorithm and its implementation in *ProM* for a person with knowledge in simulation and process mining? Is it necessary to configure parameters before running the algorithm? Is the interpretation of results straightforward? Could it mislead to wrong conclusions?

- *C3 - Customizability*: How easily can an algorithm and its implementation in *ProM* be customized or extended to better meet the requirements of a certain analysis task? Are programming skills necessary or is the customization carried out within the graphical user interface of *ProM*?

- *C4 - Computational performance*: What are the computation time and space requirements of an algorithm and its implementation in *ProM*? Haan (2009) concentrates on taking empirical measurements for input data from the analyzed courier models here.

The fulfillment of each criterion is rated on a scale with three levels *low*, *medium*, and *high* (Haan, 2009, p. 72). Since the study is performed by a single person, the statistical validity of the results will be naturally low. Nevertheless, indications about the utility of process mining in the context of this study might become visible.

8.2.4. Data Collection and Preprocessing

The first task by Haan (2009, p. 65) was to improve and extend a prototypical MXML logger developed by the author of this thesis and to instrument the courier models with additional logging statements.

8.2.4.1. Logging MXML in FAMOS

As indicated in Section 8.1.4 actions of *FAMOS* agents are logged with the method `dump()` provided by the class `Agent`, which sends a message of type `DumpNote` to the *DESMO-J* messaging sub-system (Haan, 2009, p. 61). The message is received by all `MessageReceiver` objects registered with the current experiment for the given message type (see Figure 8.7). At the beginning and end of an experiment, the simulation infrastructure calls each message receiver's methods `open()` and `close()` respectively which allows to persist the collected data into a file or database.

Figure 8.7 shows the implementation[33] of the MXML logger based on classes from *FAMOS* and *ProM* (see also Haan, 2009, p. 61). The logger is implemented as a `MessageReceiver` for `DumpNote` messages. During the simulation it stores incoming dump notes in an internal table. To provide straightforward preprocessing, a criterion can be set by which the dump notes are aggregated into process instances.

---

[33]Different variants of the described implementation were used during the course of the study.

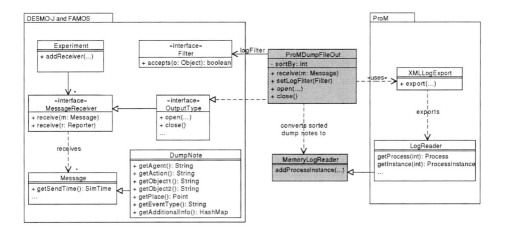

Figure 8.7.: Class diagram of the MXML logging extensions for DESMO-J and FAMOS.

In the current implementation, dump notes can be aggregated either by similar originator agents or by similar values of the context attributes `object1` or `object2`, where each setting represents a different *mining perspective* (see Haan, 2009, p. 61). A similar approach is taken by Rozinat et al. (2009d, p. 256) to log games of robot soccer (see Section 5.3.4). This preprocessing avoids an additional event aggregation step in the mining procedure at the cost of less flexibility. It is not straightforward to analyze the same log from different perspectives without repeating the simulation.

When the experiment is finished, the logger converts the aggregated dump notes into **Process-Instance** objects according to *ProM*'s MXML object model (see Section 4.2.6.1), where each dump note is represented by an **AuditTrailEntry**. The dump notes' attributes `time`, `action`, and `agent` are straightforwardly mapped to the attributes `timestamp`, `element` (event), and `originator` of the audit trail entries. The generated process instances are buffered in an in-memory log reader (`MemoryLogReader`) which is finally exported to an MXML file using the ProM class `XMLLogExport` (Haan, 2009, p. 65).

Haan (2009, p. 65) extended the author's basic implementation inspired by further possibilities of the MXML format: To support the generation of activity-based logs, he added a field `eventType` to the class `DumpNote` which e.g. allows to indicate start and end events of time-consuming activities. To enable the enrichment of mined models with additional information like branching conditions, another attribute `additionalInformation` was added. It serves to store arbitrary context data of logged actions as named key value pairs in a map.

8.2.4.2. Instrumentation of the Courier Service Models

Since the courier models had already been instrumented for logging during the courier service study, the main task for Haan (2009, Sec. 4.1.2) was to correct the existing instrumentation and to extend it with respect to the new possibilities. Basically, each relevant effector method

Agent	Method	Log entry(s)	Event type	Arguments	Models
Office	takeOrder()	receive	complete	order	all
	announce()	announce	complete	order	all
	passOn()	passOn	complete	order	all
	dispose()	dispose	complete	order, courier	all
	occupyCourier()	occupy	complete	order, courier	all
	disposeOutside()	disposeOutside	complete	order, courier	IO
Courier	rateOrder()	rate	complete	order	all
	applyFor()	applyFor	complete	order	all
	takeOrder()	take	complete	order	all
	moveToNextDestination()	moveTo	start	order, destination	all
	stopMoving()	moveTo	complete	order, position	all
	arriveAtOrderPoint()	moveTo, arrive	complete	order	all
	pickUpOrder()	pickUp	complete	order	all
	deliverOrder()	deliver	complete	order	all
	becomeIdle()	becomeIdle	complete	–	all
	becomeBusy()	becomeBusy	complete	–	all
	insertHomePoint()	headHome	complete	home point	all
	startWork()	startWork	complete	–	all
	leaveWork()	leaveWork	complete	–	all
	depositOrderAtStartHub()	deposit	complete	order	HS, IO
	redrawOrderFromDestHub()	redraw	complete	order	HS, IO

Table 8.2.: Table of events logged in the investigated variants of the courier service model. Adopted with modifications from (Haan, 2009, pp. 62,63).

of the courier and office agents produces a similarly named log entry. Table 8.2 shows all events logged in the investigated model variants.

Only the event *moveTo* is currently modelled as a time-consuming activity with two different event types *start* and *complete* (Haan, 2009, p. 62). The event pair *startWork* and *leaveWork* would be another candidate for activity-based logging. Though it might also seem appropriate to model pickup and delivery with time consumption, this option was neglected because both activities are clearly delimited by the courier's arrival at the current destination (event *arrive [complete]*) and the completion of the respective action (events *pickUp* and *deliver*) (Haan, 2009, p. 63), i.e. a *pickUp [start]* (or *deliver [start]*) event would not provide additional information.

The fifth column of Table 8.2 shows the data attributes logged for each event. These values are normally stored in the fields `object1` and `object2` of the `DumpNote`, which do not appear in the MXML log. The value of `object1` (mostly the transport order) is only used to group the log entries into process instances, while `object2` is currently neglected (Haan, 2009, p. 62).

In the events *applyFor* and *arrive*, additional data (including the given order's preferred conveyance and pickup status) is stored in the data map of the `DumpNote`, which is added to the MXML log as an enrichment (see Section 8.2.4.1). In the future, all data attributes should be stored this way to make them equally available to the logger's grouping mechanism and to *ProM* via the MXML log.[34]

The manual instrumentation provides flexibility for the generation of MXML logs on the one hand. On the other hand, it is time consuming to manually create log statements and to keep them consistent with the implemented behavior. According to Haan (2009, p. 76), especially the instrumentation of the "`moveTo.start` and `moveTo.complete` cycle was extremely laborious because the concepts behind the [implementation of the courier] agent had to be fully understood to find the

---

[34] A slightly similar grouping mechanism was e.g. implemented by Tobias Schnackenbeck for logging in the Microsoft .NET-based plugin framework *Empinia* (http://www.empinia.org, last visit 12-11-12).

"right" positions for logging". While an intensive examination of the code should not be regarded as a disadvantage for model validation, it seems reasonable to automate the instrumentation for common cases. The following possibilities might be of interest in *FAMOS*:

- Certain behavior classes could provide low-level logging according to the provided modeling constructs. The state-chart interpreter might e.g. log entry and exit events of states as well as triggers and effects of transitions. The rule engine might log the firing of rules together with the affected state of the knowledge base. Modeling aids like the state-chart editor could be used to control visibility and appearance of the generated log statements. These ideas are roughly comparable to low-level logging in RENEW (see Section 7.1.2.1).

- To provide a clear *separation of concerns* between the core agent code and additional logging statements, the latter might be moved into method *annotations* and automatically 'weaved' into the invocation of certain methods by means of *aspect oriented programming*. Such ideas are discussed by Sudeikat and Renz (2006, p. 181) reviewed in Section 5.1.1.4. Note that an extended *Java* runtime platform like *Aspect-J*[35] is required to implement these concepts.

- Components of the environment could automatically log relevant events. This includes messages sent via the communication infrastructure, changes of the group structure, or position changes of situated agents and objects in the spatial environment. Some of these possibilities are found in other agent platforms like *MadKit*, *JADE*, or CAPA (see Section 3.4).

8.2.4.3. Log Filtering and Preprocessing

As it is typical for simulation, few additional preprocessing is required for the MXML logs exported by the *FAMOS* logger (Haan, 2009, p. 66). Haan (2009, p. 67) applied perspective-dependent filtering to the log using the *simple filter* provided by *ProM*. Besides masking certain events and event types, the simple filter allows to remove process instances with specific start and end events from the log.

In the order workflow perspective, Haan (2009, pp. 67, 68) used the latter option to reduce the analyzed log to process instances starting with *receive* and ending with *deliver*, thus eliminating events not assigned to a specific transport order (e.g. *headHome*). In the agent perspective, we might focus on a certain agent role (e.g. the office) by selecting only the start and end events assigned to this role. However, this procedure bears the risk of unintentionally masking relevant process instances that indicate erroneous behavior, such as a courier that does not de-register from the model after finishing work.

Besides filtering, Haan (2009, p. 67, 68) employed the *Dashboard* and *Log Inspector* views in *ProM* for an initial face validation of the analyzed log. While the dashboard provides statistics about the occurrence of events, event types, and originators, the log inspector allows to list the audit trail entries of all contained process instances (Haan, 2009, p. 68).

Data reduction is another important preprocessing step that was neglected in the study by Haan (2009). However, it became obvious that the large number of process instances, audit trail

---

[35] see http://www.eclipse.org/aspectj (last visit 2010-20-06)

entries, and originators in the courier service logs can cause problems with several algorithms in *ProM* (see below for details). The following data reduction techniques might be applied to improve this situation:

- *ProM* provides a mechanism to group process instances in an event log by either identical event sequences or an identical follower relation. Only one instance of each group remains in the log. Since this mechanism changes frequencies of event occurrences, it is only appropriate for mining algorithms with a binary follower-matrix (e.g. α algorithm). Algorithms that estimate event occurrence probabilities (e.g. Heuristics Miner), perform log replay (e.g. Petri net-based performance analysis), or make use of data attributes (e.g. decision point analysis) do not comply with this reduction technique well.

- The *ProM* filter *Exact Tandem Repeats* (see also Bose and Aalst, 2009) allows to eliminate identical repetitions of single events or event sequences within a process instance. However, since only the first iteration is kept[36] this leads to a complete elimination of cycles in the mined process models.

8.2.5. Perspectives and Algorithms

The selection of appropriate perspectives and algorithms for the present study was guided by (a) the domain specific questions to be answered, (b) the general considerations about process mining algorithms in the simulation context discussed in Section 6.4, (c) our previous experiences with *ProM*, and (d) experiences reported in related studies (see e.g. Rozinat et al., 2009d).

Concerning perspectives, Haan (2009, p. 69) focuses on the so-called *order perspective*, i.e. the external control flow of the overall transport order processing workflow with all involved agents described in task *T1*. In the courier service study, the reconstructed order workflow models build an appropriate basis for an enrichment with further information like processing times for economic analysis or (possibly) covered distances and related emissions for ecological analysis.

Further attention is paid to the so-called *agent perspective* (Haan, 2009, p. 90), i.e. reconstructed models of the different agent classes' internal control flow, optionally enriched with branching conditions, as described in task *T3*. As mentioned above, this perspective is mainly relevant during validation. Haan (2009, pp. 111-112) made an initial attempt to reconstruct internal control flow models of courier and office agents. Further experiments were conducted by the author of this thesis.

Concerning algorithms, Haan (2009, pp. 68) orients himself along the KDD process and the available categories of *ProM* plugins and distinguishes between algorithms for process discovery and analysis. The following process discovery algorithms were selected for the study by Haan (2009, p. 69) and further experiments by the author:

- The *Heuristics Miner* algorithm of *ProM* (Section 4.2.3.4) has been applied in several process mining studies (e.g. Rozinat et al., 2009d) and is known to deliver suitable results in acceptable time, also in the presence of noise and missing data (Haan, 2009, p. 69). The question is if these advantages also become evident in the field of simulation where

---

[36]according to a comment in the program help of *ProM* 5.2

noisy data is not an issue and heuristic model simplifications might even lead to wrong conclusions. The simple *Frequency Abstraction Miner* (see Rozinat et al., 2007) is another robust control flow mining algorithm implemented in *ProM* that will be used in this study.

- The parameterless α and α^{++} algorithms seem promising due to their good understandability and ease of use. As discussed in Section 4.2.3.1, the α algorithm is exact in the sense that all successor relations from the log are considered regardless of their frequency. However, it only employs the (local) direct successor relation for process reconstruction (Lang, 2008, p. 124) and might fail on constructs like short loops or duplicate tasks depending on the implemented variant (see Section 4.2.3.1).

- Grammar inference algorithms (see Section 4.2.3.3) for automata reconstruction, like our *k-RI Miner* implementation (Section 7.2.4) and the *FSM Miner* implemented in *ProM*, might be appropriate because the processes implemented in the courier model do not exhibit concurrency at first sight.

- Complementary to control flow mining algorithms the *Role Hierarchy Miner* plugin implemented in *ProM* might be able to express common behavioral patterns in the courier model in terms of (pre-defined or dynamically emerging) role hierarchies.

For further analysis and enrichment of the reconstructed models, the following techniques were considered (Haan, 2009, pp. 70):

- The *Linear Temporal Logic (LTL) Checker* might aid in the confirmatory validation of simple rules (e.g. to check if all orders are eventually delivered after pickup) and to count occurrences of events and their relations in the log (similar to Dongen et al., 2006b). Haan (2009, p. 70) mainly applied this tool to cross-check doubtful findings in the reconstructed models.

- The *Performance Analysis with Petri Nets* (PAPN) plugin by Hornix (2007), reviewed in Section 4.2.5.5, can enrich a reconstructed Petri net model with time-related information based on the replay of a time-stamped log. In the study by Haan (2009), a comparison with the statistic measures displayed in the simulation report generated by DESMO-J was of particular interest (see question *Q5.4* and task *T1*).

- The *Performance Sequence Diagram Analysis* (PSDA) by Hornix (2007), reviewed in Section 4.2.5.5, displays timing information either in a basic sequence diagram (Section 2.3.1.4) including all process instances or in an aggregated form of characteristic interaction patterns (Haan, 2009, p. 79). In the study by Haan (2009) it was therefore interesting (a) how the performed statistic analysis compares to the simulation report and (b) if additional dependencies between order processing times and certain behavioral patterns can be detected (see question *Q5.2* and task *T5*).

- The *Decision Point Analysis* can be used to enrich the mined process models with information on branching conditions and to validate the mechanisms by which couriers rate offered transport orders in the model (see task *T2*). Decision mining as well as the particular *ProM* plugin have already been applied in several other studies on data mining in an agent context (e.g. Jacobs et al., 1998; Dongen et al., 2006b; Rozinat et al., 2009d).

8.3. Process Mining Experiments and Results

This section summarizes the results of the experiments conducted by Haan (2009, Ch. 5) as well as additional experiments carried out by Kruse (2005) and the author of this thesis. The presentation is structured along the analysis perspectives from Section 6.2. After describing the experiments, we present a rating of the applied mining techniques according to Haan (2009) with some extensions made by the author of this thesis.

8.3.1. External Control Perspective

The external control perspective of the courier service simulations was analyzed using different existing control flow discovery and extension algorithms implemented in *ProM*. Haan (2009, Secs. 5.1.1, 5.2.1) attempted to reconstruct overall order processing workflows from all model variants and further analyzed the results with the *LTL checker* plugin (Haan, 2009, Secs. 5.1.2, 5.2.2). The models were enriched with time-related information using the PAPN plugin. Furthermore, Haan (2009, pp. 79) tried to extract characteristic (inter)action patterns with related performance information from the order workflows using the PSDA plugin. The author of this thesis additionally applied the (hierarchical) role mining plugins from ProM to check their ability to identify characteristic courier behavior in the form of roles.

8.3.1.1. Order Processing Workflow[37]

To reconstruct the order processing workflow implemented in the courier and office agents, Haan (2009, p. 74) simulated the courier and order profile of one workday twice with every model variant using both the small and the large traffic network. This lead to two logs for each variant, sorted by order instances during recording and filtered subsequently as described above.

Heuristic Miner Both logs obtained from the Status Quo model consisted of 1925 process instances (correctly corresponding to the number of processed orders) and 178557 (small traffic network) or 198588 (large traffic network) log events respectively (Haan, 2009, p. 74).

Haan first applied the *Heuristic Miner* to reconstruct the models depicted in Figure 8.8. It is straightforward to see that the events (nodes) and precedences (arrows) of the mined models indicate a valid implementation of the order workflow with one exception: A transition from `rate` to `announce` seems to be missing for orders that were not accepted by a courier during the first announcement and had to be re-announced. Note, however, that the applied standard parameterization of the heuristic mining algorithm might lead to a suppression of rare events and precedences in the model.

Haan (2009, pp. 74-76) next performed a more detailed validation of the reconstructed processes by examining the frequencies and $\Rightarrow_L$ values calculated for every event and precedence. At first sight, it might seem 'surprising' that, though the initial `receive` event correctly appears 1925 times and each `receive` is correctly followed by an `announce`, the $\Rightarrow_L$ value of the corresponding

---

[37]This section is based on (Haan, 2009, Sections 5.1.1, 5.1.2, 5.2.1, 5.2.2).

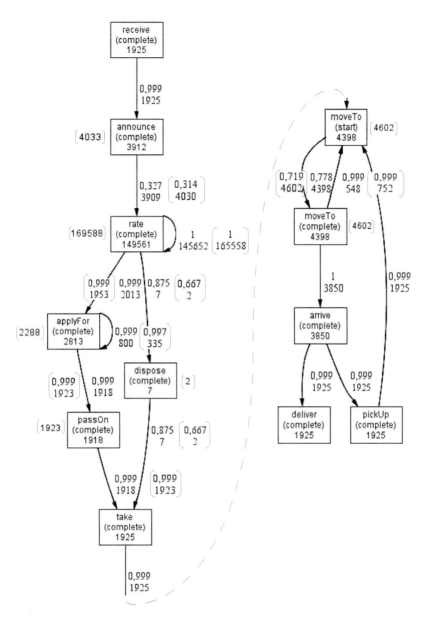

Figure 8.8.: Results of the *Heuristics Miner* on logs of the Status Quo model simulated with the small and large traffic networks. In both cases the same process structure was reconstructed. The displayed frequencies and $\Rightarrow_L$ values of events and precedences belong to the simulation with the small traffic network. Deviating values from the large traffic network are stated in brackets. Note that the original visual output of *ProM* was edited. Adopted with modifications from (Haan, 2009, pp. 95,96).

edge is 0.999 instead of 1. However, as discussed in Section 4.2.3.4, this is intended by the developers of the Heuristic Miner to emphasize the uncertainty in the mined models by adding 1 to the denominator of equation 4.13 (Haan, 2009, p. 74). Accordingly, the $\Rightarrow_L$ values of 1 displayed in the model are in fact smaller values rounded to three decimal digits (Haan, 2009, p. 76).

From the number of announce events it is straightforward to see that every transport order was announced about two times in average (Haan, 2009, p. 74). Unfortunately the Heuristic Miner, like most *ProM* plugins, does not calculate variances or confidence intervals.

Haan (2009, p. 76) additionally analyzed event and transition frequencies to compare the simulation runs with the two different traffic networks. The run with the large traffic network contained significantly less dispositions, but more traversals of the 'moveTo cycle' (Haan, 2009, p. 76). From these observation, Haan (2009, p. 76) concludes that couriers more often apply for orders and change their current tour due to the acceptance of a new order, which might be an indicator for better bundling potential in the more realistic model variant.

In the further analysis, Haan (2009, pp, 74-75) identified three issues that appear in both variants and are discussed at the example of the simulation with the small traffic network in the following:

1. The number of transitions from node announce to node rate is specified as 3909. Since the number of announce events is 3912 and no other outgoing edge from the node announce exists, 3 occurrences seem to be 'missing' (Haan, 2009, p. 74).

2. The number of transitions from rate to applyFor seems to be too high at first sight. Since 7 orders were disposed, there should be only 1918 such transitions (Haan, 2009, p. 75).

3. The $\Rightarrow_L$ values (see Section 4.2.3.4) calculated for several transitions appear to be rather low at first sight. An example is the edge from announce to rate. The value of this transition is specified as 0.327 which seems low even taking into account the 3 missing transitions (Haan, 2009, p. 75). The transition from moveTo.start to moveTo.complete with a value of 0.719 is another example (Haan, 2009, p. 76).

Haan (2009, pp. 81) also reconstructed order processing workflows from the Hub and Shuttle and Inside/Outside models with the *Heuristics Miner*: Again, the algorithm discovered the expected graphs with the exception of the transition from rate to announce.

Figure 8.9 depicts the result for the Inside/Outside model with the small traffic network. The net graphs for the large traffic network and the Hub and Shuttle model are similar (Haan, 2009, pp. 105, 106, 108) except for the event dispose outside that only occurs in the Inside/Outside model (Haan, 2009, p. 83). As expected, the main difference to the Status Quo model are two additional actions deposit and redraw performed by couriers after arriving at a hub (Haan, 2009, p. 82).

The identical frequencies of both events indicate that 610 orders were transported via the central hub in the example, and that no pending orders remained in the queue at the end of the simulation. The larger number of 687 dispositions to outside couriers (event dispose outside) might stem from additional orders that were directly transported within an outside area. Interestingly, this event occurs 688 times in the simulation on the large traffic network

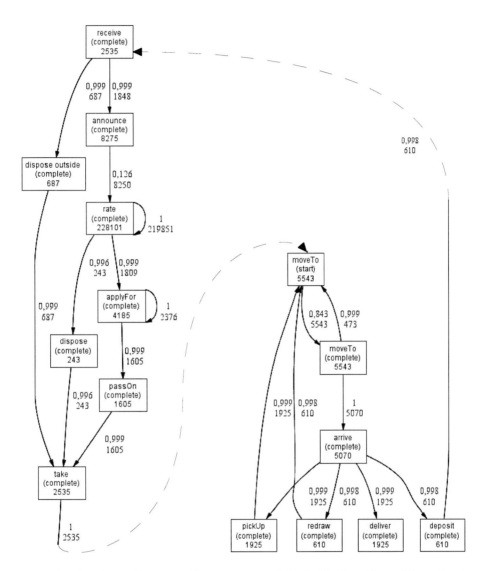

Figure 8.9.: Results of the *Heuristics Miner* on a log of the Inside/Outside model simulated with the small traffic network. Note that the layout of the original *ProM* output was improved manually. Adopted with modifications from (Haan, 2009, p. 107).

(Haan, 2009, p. 84). This might possibly be due to different route planning causing a later end of work of an outside courier. This courier might have been able to take another order before de-registration in the simulation with the large traffic network.[38]

All issues identified in the Status Quo model can also be observed in Figure 8.9 as well as in the further model variants: Again the loop at the node announce and the backward transition from rate to announce seem to be suppressed due to a low frequency of occurrence and the transition frequency from rate to applyFor appears too high. However, due to the similarity of the order mediation process in all model variants, an additional analysis of these models with the *LTL Checker* (which is described for the Status Quo model in the next section) did not promise to provide further insight (Haan, 2009, p. 84).

Similar to the Status Quo model, the Inside/Outside simulations also shows a decrease of dispositions and an increase of moveTo cycle traversals for the large traffic network (Haan, 2009, p. 107, 108). Different from this reference, the dispose event occurs *more often* for the large traffic network in the Hub and Shuttle simulations (Haan, 2009, p. 105,106).

Comparing all model variants, Haan (2009, pp. 82,83) observes that the number of dispose, announce, and rate events is significantly larger in both alternative strategies than in the Status Quo model. Even taking into account the unavoidable increase of transports and announcements caused by the hub system, the order mediation process seems to work most effective in the Status Quo model (Haan, 2009, p. 85). This observation confirms the conclusions drawn from the simulation reports in (Page et al., 2004); see Section 8.1.6.1.

Additional Validation with LTL Checker Haan (2009, p. 78) further investigated the first issue (apparently wrong number of transitions from announce to rate) with the *LTL Checker* plugin, a simple trace-based model checker that evaluates linear temporal logic formulae over MXML logs: The hypothesis was that the 3 missing transitions emanating from the node announce are actually 'hidden' in a loop that is suppressed due to a low traversal frequency. To detect this loop, the predefined formula eventually_activity_A_next_B was applied with the parameters A and B both set to announce. The *LTL Checker* actually found one process instance with 4 directly succeeding announce events. This instance corresponds to the earliest order arriving in the system. This order was announced 3 times by the office before the first courier registered and rated it (Haan, 2009, p. 78).

Concerning the second issue (large number of transitions from rate to applyFor), Haan (2009, p. 78) used the LTL checker to count the number of process instances where rate is directly followed by applyFor. This lead to the expected number of 1918 process instances instead of 2013 occurrences displayed by the Heuristics Miner. A test if process instances with multiple occurrences of the transition from rate to applyFor exist cannot be performed with the *LTL Checker* due to the limitations of linear temporal logic: The algorithm can only count the number of process instances containing *any* occurrence of a certain transition but not the *overall* number of occurrences in a log (Haan, 2009, p. 78).

The idea to investigate the third issue (low $\Rightarrow_L$ value of the transition from announce to rate) by manually validating the Heuristics Miner's calculations with results from the *LTL checker*

---

[38]Haan (2009, p. 84) draws a different conclusion that had to be revised. The hypothesis stated here also requires future validation.

was difficult to realize for the same reason (Haan, 2009, p. 78): The LTL checker counted 1925 instances with at least one transition from `announce` to `rate` and 1187 instances with the inverse transition. Inserting these numbers into equation 4.13 yields an even lower value of about 0.237 (Haan, 2009, p. 78). This result at least indicates that the low value is caused by many process instances that contain transitions in both directions due to multiple attempts to announce an order.[39] The inverse transition (from `rate` to `announce`) seems to be suppressed in the reconstructed net.

A final attempt to analyze the cycle between `moveTo.start` and `moveTo.complete` made another restriction of the *LTL Checker* obvious: The plugin cannot distinguish both events because it is unaware of different event types (Haan, 2009, p. 79).

Alpha and Alpha++ Algorithms Trying to avoid the inconsistencies of the Heuristics Miner, Haan (2009, p. 77) and the author also applied the non-probabilistic α and α^{++} algorithms (see Section 4.2.3.1) to the logs. Figure 8.10 shows that the implementation of the α algorithm in *ProM* nearly[40] manages to reconstruct a Petri net of the part of the workflow that represents the order processing by the couriers, even recognizing the task `moveTo` as a time-consuming activity (Haan, 2009, p. 77).

The part of the order workflow that represents the communication between couriers and office, however, is not reconstructed as a connected workflow net. According to Haan (2009, p. 77), one reason might be that the corresponding conversations consist of multiple overlapping threads for each courier: In the result of the Heuristics Miner shown in Figure 8.8, these (conceptually) concurrent threads are represented as loops at the nodes `rate` and `applyFor` (Haan, 2009, p. 77). This might also be a reason for the seemingly erroneous frequencies and low $\Rightarrow_L$ values in this result (Haan, 2009, p. 77).[41] The implementation of the α^{++} algorithm also failed to generate a connected workflow net from the example logs similar to the basic algorithm investigated by Haan (2009, p. 77).

Frequency Abstraction and Fuzzy Miner The *Fuzzy Miner* algorithm by Günther and Aalst (2007) and its predecessor variant called *Frequency Abstraction* (Rozinat et al., 2007) originally serve to handle potentially noisy logs of "less structured" processes without delivering overly specialized "spaghetti-like" result models (Günther and Aalst, 2007, p. 328). Therefore, an application to the strictly structured processes and noise-free logs of the courier service models might seem inappropriate at first sight.

Nevertheless, the algorithms perform quite well in the reconstruction of the 'order workflow' from the log of the Status Quo model. Figure 8.11 shows a result delivered by the *Frequency Abstraction* plugin of *ProM 5.2* with the frequency threshold set to the minimum value of 0.0 to avoid clustering of less frequent activities and dependencies in the model. The structure of the process was correctly reconstructed including the self-loop at the activity *announce*, which was neglected by the *Heuristics Miner* with the tested (default) parameterization.

---

[39]Note again that the $\Rightarrow_L$ value is *not* a probability estimate.

[40]except for missing arcs from the transitions `take` and `pickUp` to the second (left) input place of the transition `moveTo.start`

[41]Haan (2009, p. 77) also cites Lang (2008, pp. 117-126) for this discussion.

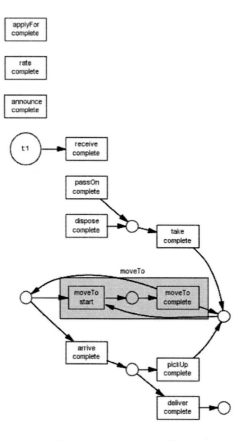

Figure 8.10.: Results of the α algorithm on a log of the Status Quo model simulated with the small traffic network. Adopted from (Haan, 2009, p. 98).

Another important advantage over the *Heuristics Miner* is the computation time of the *Frequency Abstraction*, which takes around 1 to 2 seconds to reconstruct a model of the test data drawn from a simulation of the Status Quo model on the small traffic network. This performance lies in the same range as that of the α algorithm, which requires around 2 to 3 seconds but does not succeed in the proper reconstruction of the model. It clearly outperforms the measured runs of the *Heuristics Miner* with times between 47 and 49 seconds.[42]

This computational speed is due to the linear complexity of the algorithm (Günther and Aalst, 2007, p. 341) and enables a further advantage: The *Frequency Abstraction* plugin is parameterized only with the aid of a slider ("threshold") and two checkboxes ("merge sibling clusters" and "attenuate edges"). On every parameter change, the resulting model is updated immediately, thereby allowing the user to 'explore' the effects of the parameters without a detailed under-

---

[42]For each of the 3 compared algorithms, 3 manual measurements were taken on an *Apple Mac Book Pro 2.4 GHz* computer using a log with 1925 cases and 178557 events.

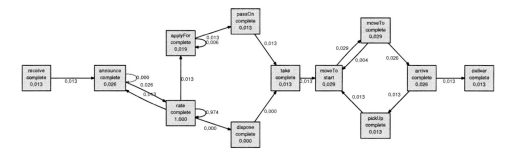

Figure 8.11.: Results of the *Frequency Abstraction* algorithm on a log of the Status Quo model simulated with the small traffic network.

standing of their meaning in the algorithm. Compared to the *Heuristics Miner*'s large number of abstract numeric parameters and long computation times, usability is highly improved.

A disadvantage of the *Frequency Abstraction* is the choice of node and edge inscriptions in the reconstructed model, which appear even more inconsistent than those of the *Heuristics Miner* mentioned above. Apparently, node and edge inscriptions display overall relative frequencies of activities and precedences, that serve as a basis for clustering in the algorithm. While the practical benefit of these inscriptions might already be questioned, the fact that the frequencies do not add up to a total of 1 (possibly due to rounding errors), neither for nodes nor for edges, makes the display rather confusing.

The *Fuzzy Miner* as the improved and extended successor of the obsolete *Frequency Abstraction* plugin[43] displays frequencies of precedences only by different width and shading of edges[44], somehow similar to Sankey diagrams (see Section 6.2.7). The explicitly printed activity frequencies, however, suffer from the same problem as in the *Frequency Abstraction* plugin. Beyond that, the *Fuzzy Miner* offers much richer possibilities to configure the mining and clustering procedures.

As foreseen by Günther and Aalst (2007, p. 335), mere clustering by frequencies does not lead to the construction of a meaningful hierarchy for the order processing workflow because less relevant events such as the rating of orders (*rate*) appear in the courier model very often. The author's attempt to partition the workflow by the involved agents (couriers and office) did not succeed either, though the *Fuzzy Miner* in principle allows to individually weight different clustering criteria including the *originator* attribute of events (Günther and Aalst, 2007, p. 336). Possibly a replacement of individual courier names by a common role descriptor would lead to better results here.

In general, the improved configuration possibilities of the *Fuzzy Miner*, partly using rather abstract parameter descriptions like "Linear attenuation", might even conflict with the intuitive usability of the previous *Frequency Abstraction* plugin to some degree.

---

[43]http://www.processmining.org/online/frequencyabstractionminer (last visit 2012-06-16)
[44]http://www.processmining.org/online/fuzzyminer (last visit 2014-03-01)

Automata Inference and Two-Step Approaches The previous experiments show that the analyzed 'order workflow' contains no concurrent activities except for the (conceptually) parallel rating of orders by couriers. In the best case, this is reconstructed in the form of a length one-loop. Therefore, automata inference techniques (that neglect concurrency) are in principle sufficient to correctly reconstruct this control flow.

Focusing on the techniques reviewed in Section 4.2.3.3, the *FSM Miner* plugin of *ProM 5.2*, which implements the techniques developed by Rubin et al. (2006), was compared to our implementation *k-RI Miner* of the established *k-RI* algorithm (Angluin, 1982) in *ProM 4.1* (improved unpublished version, for details see Section 7.2.4). While both implementations succeed to reconstruct the 'order workflow', a number of important differences can be identified.[45]

The configuration of the *k-RI Miner* consists of only two settings including the algorithm's parameter k and a boolean flag that indicates if the result automaton will be minimized after mining. The effect of minimization (i.e. equivalent states are eliminated) should be straightforward to comprehend for non-experts. Understanding the effect of the parameter k, however, requires good knowledge of the algorithm. The *FSM Miner* offers a large number of free parameters to the user that mirror the 36 different strategies for state identification implemented by Rubin et al. (2006); see Section 4.2.3.3.

When neither the number of event types nor the expected number of states in the resulting automaton are exceptionally large, minimization can be activated by default in the *k-RI Miner* due to its moderate computational complexity (see Section 4.2.3.3). Increasing the parameter k allows the algorithm to discover more detailed restrictions on the reconstructed formal language.

Figure 8.12 shows results obtained from a log of the Status Quo model simulated on the small traffic network. Obviously, the *k-RI Miner* performs few generalization in the model reconstructed at $k = 1$. For example, it does not introduce a loop to 're-use' the events moveTo and arrive for delivery and transport. Furthermore, the different announce transitions indicate that orders are either rated for the first time immediately after the initial announce or after (multiples of) 3 further announce events. This seems to be an algorithmic generalization of the finding by Haan (2009, p. 78) obtained with the *LTL Checker*. The *Conformance Checker* plugin of *ProM* calculates a fitness of 1.0 for the reconstructed models on the basis of the single log used for training.

Figure 8.12 shows that the model mined at $k = 0$ in contrast over-generalizes the mediation-related events. Here, the events applyFor, rate, and announce are simply attached to self-loops of state s_8. The movement-related events are nevertheless identified as duplicate tasks, similar to the results gained at $k = 1$.[46]

More reasonable[47] results from a modeler's point of view can be gained with the *FSM Miner* by setting the (backward and forward) state merging *semantics* to *Set*, all *horizon* parameters to 1 with respect to events and event types (due to the use of the event types start and stop for the

---

[45]The following discussion is somewhat inspired by a study comparing the applicability of optimization algorithms for non-expert users conducted by Lambrecht et al. (2010).

[46]To further verify the implementation, a comparison to a reference like *Mical* (Rey, 2003) is advisable. Furthermore, it should be compared thoroughly with the previous implementation. As a first impression, both versions deliver quite similar results but also some deviations. However, similar to the non-incremental version of the new implementation, the old version can only be applied to smaller subsets of the courier log due to performance problems.

[47]as to use the term by Wainer et al. (2005, Sec. 3.3)

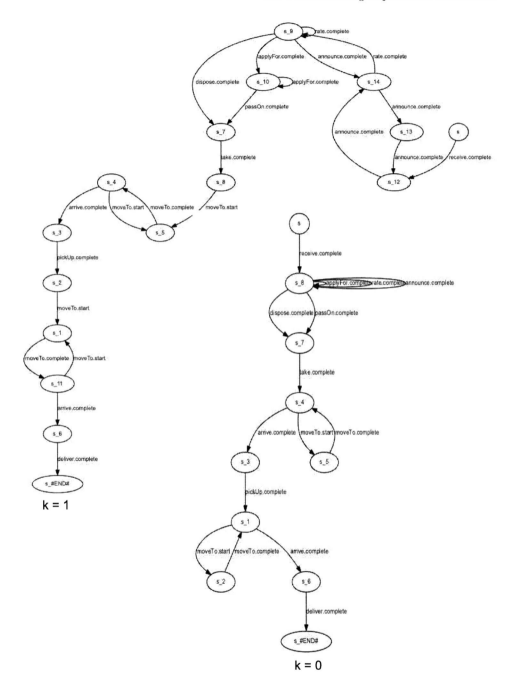

Figure 8.12.: Finite state automata for the 'order workflow' reconstructed with the *k-RI Miner* plugin that implements the algorithm by Angluin (1982).

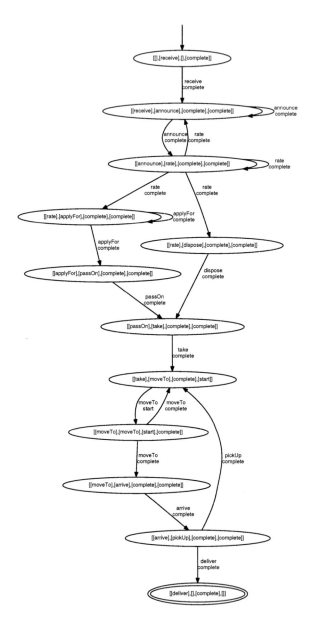

Figure 8.13.: Finite state automaton for the 'order workflow' reconstructed with the *FSM Miner* plugin that implements the state identification techniques by Rubin et al. (2006).

moveTo event), and merging of "states with identical inputs and outputs" switched on. Other state merging strategies are not applicable since the required data (e.g. attributes) are not available in the analyzed log.

In this configurations, the algorithm provides a plausible generalization of the example log.[48] Setting this (non-default) configuration might be understandable taking into account the functioning of the algorithm, but could clearly overstrain non-expert users.

Computation time is another relevant difference between both algorithms. The *FSM Miner* implementation in *ProM 5.2* required more computation time than the *k-RI* miner in *ProM 4.1* that terminated on the given log after a few seconds with $k = 1$ and minimization switched on. This computational speed would already allow users to interactively explore the effect of the abstract parameter k similar to the 'threshold slider' in the *Frequency Abstraction* plugin. However, computation times dramatically increase on logs observed in the 'courier perspective'.[49]

Though the 'order workflow' exhibits no concurrency, the different Petri net synthesis methods described in Section 4.2.3.3 were also tested on the reconstructed automata. One purpose was to generate appropriate input for the conformance checker and PAPN plugins, which require a Petri net model for log replay. Both our implementation of the approach by Schütt (2003) in *ProM 4.1* and the *Petrify* integration plugin of *ProM 5.2* produced 'one-to-one' translations of the reconstructed state machines into Petri nets in negligible computation times.

Performance Analysis with Petri Nets The Petri net-based performance analysis developed by Hornix (2007) and reviewed in Section 4.2.5.5 comes relatively close to the information conveyed by a 'traditional' simulation report. This tool was applied to the example log of the courier service model with a focus on the following questions:

1. How do the calculated performance statistics compare to the standard report provided by *DESMO-J / FAMOS*?

2. Which advantages and drawbacks might the process mining-based performance analysis provide from a simulation practitioner's point of view?

Before investigating these questions, a decision had to be made about the control flow model used as a basis for performance analysis. Converting the *heuristic net* of the 'order workflow' reconstructed by the *Heuristics Miner* into a Petri net seemed appropriate at first sight: Different from the *two step*-approaches, this conversion delivers a compact net with uniquely labelled transitions as well as unlabelled transitions to express self-loops. However, due to the imperfect reconstruction of the control flow by the *Heuristics Miner*, the *Performance Analysis* plugin failed to replay all log traces in this net. This leads to faulty statistics, which is not indicated very prominently in the user interface of the performance analysis plugin.

Next, the Petri net reconstructed with the *k-RI Miner* and the concurrency detection by Schütt (2003) was chosen for performance analysis.[50] Since this model depicts the 'order perspective'

---

[48]Note, however, that the reconstructed FSM is non-deterministic.

[49]Respective experiments did not terminate in reasonable time and were therefore aborted without results.

[50]The result of the *FSM Miner / Petrify* plugins might have been an even more appropriate alternative. However, for an unknown reason, the PAPN took considerably longer there than on the *k-RI Miner / Schütt* result.

of the courier service model, the performance statistics of order delivery were compared to the *FAMOS* report. Both tools calculate the minimum, maximum, average, and standard deviation of the observed activity durations. The performance analysis in *ProM* further measures fractions of "fast", "slow", and "normal" cases, where the category borders can be configured by the user (Hornix, 2007, p. 94). Overall, the calculated quantities in Figure 8.14 do not show relevant differences between both tools.

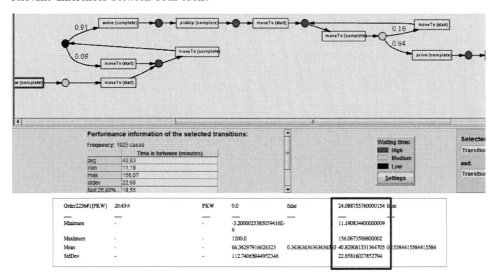

Figure 8.14.: Top: performance statistics of order delivery in the Status Quo model visualized in the *Petri Net Performance Analysis* plugin (Hornix, 2007, Sec. H.1) of *ProM 5.2*. Bottom: related cutout from *DESMO-J* report.

The usage of the process mining-based performance analysis, however, differs significantly from the simulation report. In *FAMOS* durations of activities are measured by storing relevant time points in program variables and feeding them into an *IndividualObserver* via access points (see Section 3.4.4). The calculation of the observed quantities (e.g. order delivery times) is left to the developer.

In process mining-based performance analysis, the model developer must only[51] instrument the model with log statements for relevant activities. These can, but do not have to, exactly mirror the actions performed by the implemented agents. Dependencies between logged activities are automatically reconstructed by the control flow mining algorithm. The observed statistics can be chosen interactively. A text-based export of all possible measurements is also supported.

Summarizing, the following advantages and drawbacks of both analysis approaches can be identified:

- *Instrumentation effort*: Standard *DESMO-J* statistics, like queue statistics, are available without additional instrumentation of the model. The more flexible *IndividualObservers*

---

[51]The study by Haan (2009, p. 76) shows that this seemingly simple task can nevertheless be demanding, especially in the presence of errors in the model.

in *FAMOS* require a higher instrumentation effort because all measured variables must be computed programmatically. The instrumentation effort for the process mining-based performance analysis is medium as it only requires time-stamped events to be logged.

- *Clarity*: To the impression of the author, the clarity of quantitative simulation results largely benefits from their embedding into a visual model of the analyzed process, as realized in *ProM*.

- *Interactive configurability*: The focus of DESMO-J reports can only be modified by changing and re-simulating the model. The performance analysis in *ProM* is in principle interactively reconfigurable by filtering the analyzed log and choosing places, transitions, and workflow cases in the user interface. Some lack of usability could nevertheless be observed: One might e.g. want to restrict the calculated performance statistics to transport orders performed by bicycle couriers. To achieve this, it is necessary to manually deselect all orders for motorized couriers in a case list, which is not practicable for the given log size. Alternatively, the user must re-filter the log outside of the plugin and repeat the (potentially time-consuming) performance analysis.

- *Extensibility*: The flexibility of the *IndividualObserver* lets the user straightforwardly combine multiple domain perspectives (e.g. ecological and economical measures related to transport orders and couriers) in a common *DESMO-J* report. To change the perspective of the process mining-based performance analysis either the instrumentation of the model with log statements or the grouping of log events into cases (e.g. 'per courier' instead of 'per order') must modified. It is also not possible to aggregate attributes other than execution times (e.g. distances covered by couriers) during log replay.

- *Computational performance*: Simulation reports in *DESMO-J* are recorded and formatted with negligible computational effort during simulation. The computation in *ProM* took significantly longer on the analyzed model and log.

To conclude, the benefit of both forms of simulation analysis depends on the use case to be supported: The process mining-based approach might be most useful for interactive explorative analyses, e.g. of initial calibration or validation runs. In contrast, the confirmative validation and analysis of large experiment series might be better supported by 'traditional' simulation reports.

8.3.1.2. Interaction Patterns and Organizational Structures

Besides control flow models, an overview of typical interaction patterns and organizational structures can provide valuable insight into a MABS. Haan (2009, pp. 79) evaluated the utility of the *Performance Sequence Diagram Analysis* (PSDA) plugin by Hornix (2007, Sec. H.2) for the analysis of the courier service model. In addition, the (hierarchical) role mining technique by Song and Aalst (2008) was tested for its ability to identify the different agent types of the courier models by their behavior.

Performance Sequence Diagram Analysis   As reviewed in Section 4.2.5.5, the PSDA can be applied for two purposes (Haan, 2009, p. 79): (1) to display the temporal flow of individual process instances in a full sequence diagram, and (2) to relate the throughput time of a process to the occurrence of certain interaction patterns in a pattern diagram. Haan (2009, p. 79) notes that for the 'order perspective' of the courier service model, the full diagram conveys information on processing times of individual orders similar to the report of the *IndividualObserver*. However, for the simulation of the Status Quo model, this diagram appears too overcharged due the large number of interleaved process instances (Haan, 2009, p. 79, 100).

The analysis therefore focused on the pattern diagram, displayed in Figure 8.15 for the small traffic network (Haan, 2009, p. 79). Process instances were clustered by flexible equivalent based on the data element `taskID` (see Section 4.2.5.5).

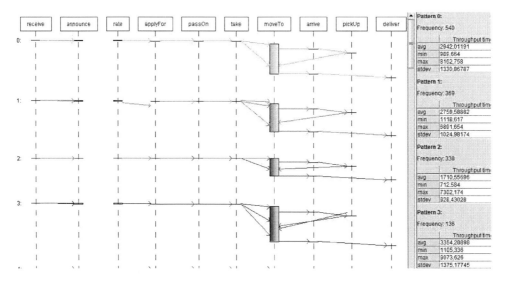

Figure 8.15.: Results of the PSDA plugin on the log of the *Status Quo* model simulated with the small traffic network. The diagram shows the most frequent patterns of order processing (left) and related throughput time statistics (right). Adopted with modifications from (Haan, 2009, p. 102).

In this example, the PSDA identified "38 distinct patterns where 20 patterns had a support of less than 4 [cases]. These 'outliers' were characterized by large announcement times [...]" (Haan, 2009, p. 80). Figure 8.15 shows a cut-out of the 4 most frequent patterns. The PSDA has problems to reconstruct short cycles in the workflow. Instead it simply inserts several arrows when a task (e.g. `receive`) is followed by multiple instances of another task (e.g. `announce`) in a trace. Different event types, as used for the event `moveTo`, are not considered either.

Since the order processing workflow is rather static without many variants, the identified patterns mainly differ in the duration of the announcement and transport phases and in the number of times a courier stops on the way to accept a new order. Therefore, it is not straightforward to identify relations between control flow and execution times of workflow cases from the reconstructed patterns.

Haan (2009, p. 79) indicates that, among the most frequent patterns, "the pattern categories 2 and 4 exhibit the shortest average throughput times [...]".[52] Besides short transport distances, this might be due to the fact that these orders are passed on after the first announcement (only one arrow from `receive` to `announce`). Furthermore, their transport is not interrupted by the pickup or delivery of another order (only one arrow from `pickUp` to `moveTo`).

Haan (2009, p. 80) also applied the *PSDA* to a log of the Status Quo model simulated on the large traffic network. This results in quite similar pattern categories but some larger throughput times due to velocity restrictions assigned to the edges of the road network, which is in conformance with the simulation reports (Haan, 2009, p. 80).

The logs of the alternative logistic strategies promise to be a more interesting target for the *PSDA* due to more diverse variants of the 'order workflow'. In particular, the *PSDA* promises to automatically distinguish between transport orders delivered directly and orders processed via the hub system, which must be configured manually in the *DESMO-J* report.

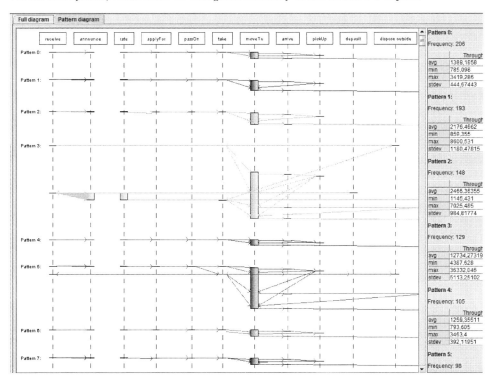

Figure 8.16.: Results of the *PSDA* plugin run on a log from the *Inside/Outside* model.

Figure 8.16 shows results of the *PSDA* on a log recorded from the *Inside/Outside* model. Due to the size of the log, the analysis took several hours to finish.[53] The algorithm distinguished 178

---

[52]Pattern 4 ist not visible in the result cut-out depicted in Figure 8.15.

[53]For this reason, Haan (2009, p. 84) did not include the *Performance Sequence Diagram Analysis* of the *Inside/Outside* model into his evaluation at all.

patterns that mirror different variants of the order processing workflow in the *Inside/Outside* model. In Figure 8.16, pattern 3 e.g. represents transports from an 'outside' region to the 'inside' region via the central hub. In contrast patterns $0 - 2$ display direct transports.

As expected, throughput times of orders processed via the hub often seem to be significantly longer than those of 'conventional' orders. However, the over-specialization (only patterns $0-30$ of 178 exhibit a support of more than 9 workflow cases) performed by the *PSDA* does not allow to identify relations between pattern structures and processing times, since a large number of patterns would have to be analyzed in depth.

The only striking observation is the wide arrow pointing from `receive` to `announce` in patterns like category 3. This indicates that tours from the hub to a destination in the 'inside' region might not find much acceptance in the simulated courier fleet and must therefore be announced several times. This is in accordance with the large number of order mediation-related events observed in the analysis of the alternative logistics strategies with the *Heuristics Miner* (Haan, 2009, pp. 82,83); see Section 8.3.1.1.

Maybe the order rating strategy of the couriers must be adapted to better reflect the requirement that tours from the hub to a destination in the 'inside' region must be processed in time as well. An implementation flaw related to this special case of order mediation might be another cause. A detailed manual analysis of the patterns identified by the *PSDA* and the underlying traces could possibly provide further hints on reasons underlying this model behavior.

Role Mining In addition to the *PSDA*, further experiments were conducted to reconstruct the organizational model underlying the *Inside/Outside* strategy with the *Organizational Model* and *Role Hierarchy Mining* plugins of *ProM*. These provide implementations of the role mining techniques developed by Song and Aalst (2008, pp. 11) and reviewed in Section 4.2.4.2. Different from the *PSDA*, both algorithms produce results on the analyzed log within a few seconds of computation time.

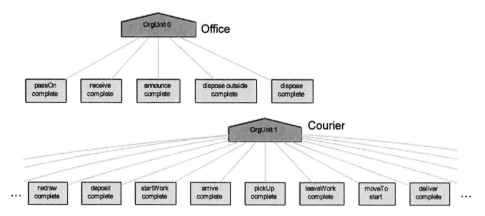

Figure 8.17.: Cutout from the result of the *Organizational Model Miner* plugin reconstructed from a log of the *Inside/Outside* model simulated on the small road network. Modified screenshot from *ProM 5.2*.

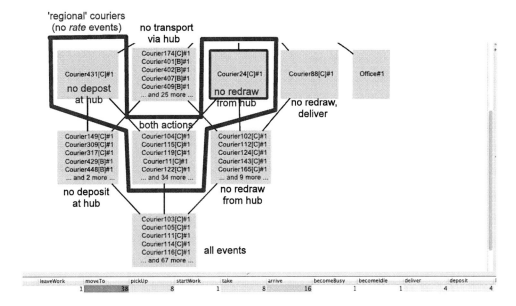

Figure 8.18.: Result of the *Role Hierarchy Miner* plugin reconstructed from a log of the *Inside/Outside* model. Manually annotated screenshot from *ProM 5.2*.

Figure 8.17 shows a modified[54] result of the *Organizational Miner* obtained from a simulation of the *Inside/Outside* model on the small traffic network using agglomerative hierarchical clustering by Euclidian distance of agents' activity profiles (see Song and Aalst, 2008, reviewed in Section 4.2.4.2). The *Organizational Miner* succeeds to identify the two main agent classes in the model, i.e. couriers and office, which is not very demanding due to the non-overlapping sets of events logged for these agents. It fails, however, to distinguish between different variants of courier behavior (at least 'regional' and 'standard' couriers, see Section 8.1.2.3) implemented in the model, neither with this nor other tested configurations of the clustering algorithms.

The *Role Hierarchy Miner* reconstructs a much richer model of behavior variants in the *Inside/Outside* model. Figure 8.18 shows the resulting role hierarchy graph (top) and the so-called originator / task (*OT*) matrix of the selected graph node (bottom) as displayed in *ProM*. A detailed inspection of the *OT* matrices of all discovered clusters reveals that the mining result represents a plausible organization structure of the *Inside/Outside* model.

In Figure 8.18 the meaning of the discovered clusters is displayed with annotations added to the output of *ProM*: Like the *Organizational Miner*, the *Role Hierarchy Miner* succeeds to distinguish between courier and office agents. Concerning courier behavior, the 3 marked clusters (*Courier431*, *Courier24*, and *Courier104*, ...) represent different variants of the role *regional courier*. The related activity profiles are characterized by a lack of *rate* (order) events since these couriers do not take part in the normal mediation scheme.

---

[54]Role names were added and layout was modified manually.

367

The former two clusters each contain a single regional courier. This courier performs very few transports where the consignments are either deposited at (*Courier24*) or redrawn from (*Courier431*) the hub, but not both. The third cluster contains the majority of regional couriers. It 'inherits' from both behavioral variants, which means that the assigned couriers both deposit and redraw consignments at the hub.

The cluster labelled with *Courier174, ...* contains couriers that only transport consignments directly from senders to receivers, i.e. their action profiles contain no *deposit* and *redraw* events. The remaining clusters represent couriers that take part in the normal order mediation scheme (i.e. they rated orders announced by radio) and perform all kinds of transports. Again, the *Role Hierarchy Miner* distinguishes between couriers that performed only *deposit* actions, only *redraw* actions, or both.

Though (similar to the *PSDA*) the interpretation of the reconstructed organizational model requires considerable effort, it would provide a good basis to analyze relations between different variants of courier behavior and performance measures taken on the respective groups of couriers. Different from the observation mechanism implemented in *FAMOS*, an *a-priori* assignment of agents to roles (e.g. registering all regional couriers with a specific *IndividualObserver*) is not necessary. However, in contrast to the *PSDA* plugin, the enrichment of a role model with performance measures is not supported in *ProM 5.2*.

8.3.2. Internal Control Perspective

In the following, we continue to focus on the behavior of couriers implemented in the different model variants and report two relevant results of the case study: Haan (2009, Sec. 5.3) found a hidden error in the control flow of courier behavior with the aid of process mining. The detection of this error initiated a revision of parts of the model implementation and the related simulation results, as described in Section 8.3.2.1. Section 8.3.2.2 reports on how the failure to reconstruct an understandable model of courier agents' life cycles with the control flow mining algorithms implemented in *ProM* motivated a (still rudimentary and simplistic) implementation of parts of the procedure to reconstruct complex interaction protocols from Section 7.3.

8.3.2.1. Validation of Courier Behavior

While instrumenting the courier model with logging statements for the process mining-based analysis, Haan (2009, p. 85) found that the movement of couriers on the road network was not implemented correctly in the two models of alternative logistic strategies.

Figure 8.19 (left) shows the 'order workflow' of the *Hub and Shuttle* model reconstructed with the *Heuristics Miner*, which makes this error obvious: While the events moveTo.start (begin of movement between 2 nodes of the road network) and moveTo.complete (end of movement) should mutually follow each other, the reconstructed model contains a short cycle that indicates the direct succession of multiple moveTo.start events (Haan, 2009, p. 85). The *Status Quo* model did not exhibit this problem.

By code inspection, the error could be traced back to a missing effect inscription (method call) in the courier state charts of the Hub and Shuttle and Inside/Outside models (Haan,

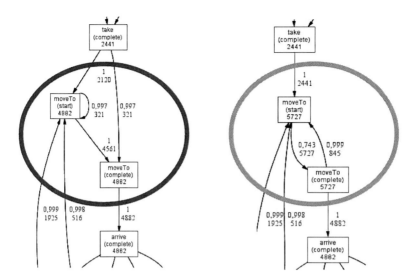

Figure 8.19.: Erroneously implemented courier movement (left, Haan, 2009, p. 109) and corrected version (right, Haan, 2009, p. 105) displayed in two process models mined from the Hub and Shuttle model.

2009, p. 85). As a consequence, the method `stopMoving()`, in which event `moveTo.Complete` is logged, is not called when a courier accepts a new transport order while moving on the road network (Haan, 2009, p. 85). This stop is relevant because it triggers the accumulation of distances covered between the courier's current position and the previous node in the road network. The defect thus leads to an erroneous calculation of distances covered when couriers change their current route in favor of a newly accepted order (see also Haan, 2009, p. 85).

After correcting the error, the reconstructed process displays the expected behavior shown on the right hand side of Figure 8.19 (Haan, 2009, p. 85). The detection of this error and further problems in the distance calculation of the corrected model initiated an additional re-validation of the *FAMOS* subsystem for spatial movement. This included a revision of the distance calculation[55] as well as a process mining-based analysis of low-level events that control the movement of agents in *FAMOS*.

Though not all problems related to distance calculation and movement-specific event handling[56] could finally be resolved, the calculation of distances seems to work more reliable in the corrected model. To evaluate the effect of the corrections on the comparison of different logistics strategies, simulations of the competing Status Quo and Inside/Outside models were repeated with the courier and order profiles used in the research project.

---

[55]performed by Ruth Meyer, the developer of the spatial modeling support in *FAMOS*

[56]In simulations of both models fed with artificially enlarged order profiles, two different variants of distance accumulation (either explicitly after every partial movement on the road network or implicitly in the *FAMOS* class `OdoRoute`) still deliver deviating distances for some couriers. In the 'real-world' order profiles used in Figure 8.20 this effect could only be observed for a single courier.

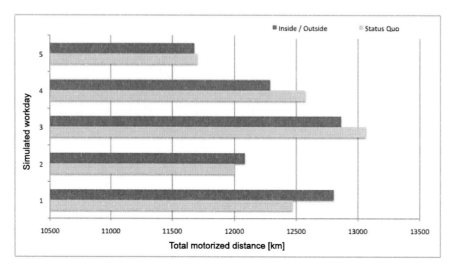

Figure 8.20.: Revised comparison of total motorized distances covered in simulations of the Status Quo and Inside/Outside models on real order profiles from 5 workdays.

Figure 8.20 shows that the Status Quo and Inside/Outside models still perform quite similar with respect to the overall motorized distances covered (see also Haan, 2009, p. 85). The minor advantages of the Inside/Outside model on some order profiles have even lost significance compared to the results shown in Figure 8.6 (Section 8.1.6.1).

More important for this thesis, the example indicates that process mining can support the *explorative* operational validation of MABS. While the error in the courier movement could have been detected using confirmative techniques like trace-based model checking or integration testing as well, the application of process mining does not require an *a-priori* hypothesis to be posed. Compared to code-based debugging, process mining provides a very clear indication of the error due to its focus on high-level activities.

The remaining issues, however, show that process mining is not a 'magic bullet' for making erroneous processes in complex models explicit either. It can only support the detection of errors in connection with thorough manual validation activities.

8.3.2.2. Life Cycle Reconstruction of Courier Agents

Section 8.3.1.1 showed that despite some difficulties, most applied control flow mining algorithms succeed to reconstruct a plausible and understandable model of the 'order workflow' in all courier model variants. However, switching the focus from order processing to the whole courier life cycle[57] (which is achieved by aggregating the logged events by their performing couriers) lead to less satisfactory results in the study by Haan (2009).

---

[57]The notion of a *life cycle* is used similarly in artifact centric process mining (see e.g. Popova et al., 2012, p. 43, reviewed in Section 5.3.3.3).

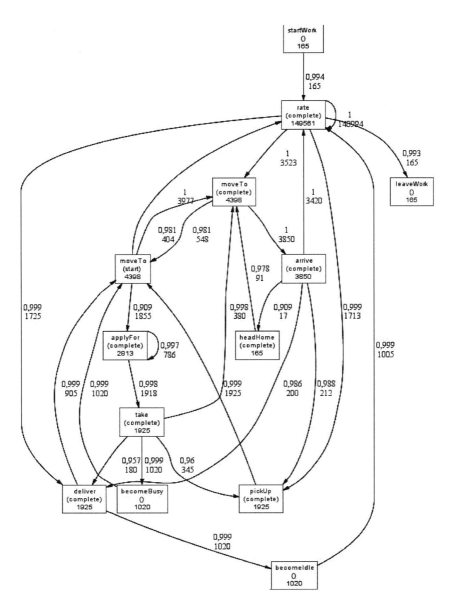

Figure 8.21.: Monolithic process model of courier behavior in the *Status Quo* model. Taken from (Haan, 2009, p. 111).

Figure 8.21 shows that the activities in the model reconstructed with the *Heuristics Miner* algorithm are multiply interconnected. Therefore, a clear process flow does not become visible. This "spaghettiness"[58] is due to the fact that courier behavior is modelled in a large hierarchical state-chart which combines several aspects including communication with the office, movement on the road network, delivery of consignments, and change of occupation state (see Figure 8.2 in Section 8.1.2.1). While some of the sub-tasks causally depend (e.g. an order is picked up only after it has been accepted), others are conceptually concurrent (e.g. receiving announcements via radio while moving on the road network).

Kruse (2007, p. 41) regards the fact that *FAMOS* agents are equipped with a single, statically defined behavior object as a severe restriction. He therefore proposes to extend *FAMOS* with the possibility to model agent behavior in terms of multiple, dynamically instantiated *components* (Kruse, 2007, Sec. 3). This approach resembles *behaviour-configuring architectures* (Klügl, 2007, p. 130) such as MULAN or *JADE* and takes up the idea of *agent abilities* in *FAMOS* as described by Meyer (2008).

Recent literature on process mining also proposes to structure complex processes with the aid of hierarchical process mining based on automated pattern detection (Li et al., 2010), clustering (Günther and Aalst, 2007), and "instance-aware" logs (Fahland et al., 2011a, p. 46).[59] In terms of our conceptual framework, the complex *internal* control flow of a courier agent can be clarified when it is regarded as *external* control flow between multiple constituent components. As indicated in Section 6.2, this approach adopts the hierarchical structure inherent to the MULAN architecture (Rölke, 2004, pp. 181) and also relates to the ideas by Kruse (2007).

In Section 7.3, a 'mining chain' for complex interaction protocols was described as one possible approach to reconstruct hierarchical processes including multiply instantiated components from event-based logs. Following Dustdar and Gombotz (2006), reviewed in Section 5.3.3.1, we argue that the effort to implement the algorithms for this processing chain depends on the component- and interaction-related data available in the log. When the log is enriched with appropriate data, a rather simple implementation suffices to reconstruct a 'component-oriented' view upon the courier life-cycle.

As a starting point, logging in *FAMOS* was extended with the possibility to specify a combination of agent *and* component (i.e. an *AgentAbility*) as originator of a logged event. Accordingly, the *FAMOS* MXML logger (Section 8.2.4.1) is enabled to group recorded log entries by this originator information. When converting the grouped *FAMOS* events into MXML *process instances*, the component-related information are encoded in the name of the process instance as follows:

$$< agentInstanceId >:< componentTypeId >:< componentInstanceId > \qquad (8.5)$$

Given this information, the aggregation and classification tasks of the processing chain from Section 7.3 become rather trivial:

---

[58] as to use the term by Günther and Aalst (2007, p. 328)

[59] An approach to reconstruct component dependencies using Bayesian methods is also proposed by Lou et al. (2010a).

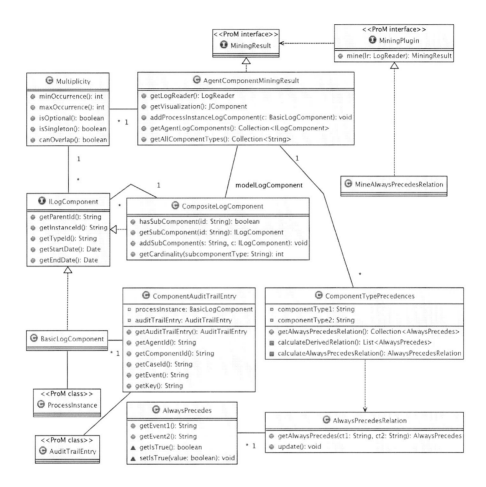

Figure 8.22.: Class diagram showing the rudimentary implementation of 'component-oriented' agent behavior mining in *ProM 5.2*. Framework classes and interfaces of *ProM* are marked with a corresponding stereotype.

1. Events are aggregated into (conversation) threads by the grouping mechanism of the *FAMOS* MXML logger. Each thread represents the life cycle of a certain component instance running in a certain agent.

2. The component threads are classified by the component type identifier encoded in the name of the process instance.

3. Component threads are aggregated into life cycles of agents using the agent identifier in the name of the process instance. This corresponds to the grouping of conversation threads into conversations in Section 7.3.

4. A further classification of agent traces is not necessary because only one type of agent is considered.

To handle these extended logs[60] a number of classes were built on top of the MXML object model of *ProM*: As shown in Figure 8.22, the class `ComponentAuditTrailEntry` serves to provide component-related information based on a MXML `AuditTrailEntry`. Similarly, the interface `ILogComponent` offers a 'component-oriented' view upon MXML `ProcessInstances`, either for elementary (class `BasicLogComponent`) or composite[61] instances (class `Composite-LogComponent`). In our example, basic log components correspond to traces of elementary components while composite log components represent traces of whole agent life cycles.

From this hierarchical log representation, the class `MineAlwaysPrecedesRelation` reconstructs external precedences and multiplicity information of component life cycles and returns them in an `AgentComponentMiningResult`.

As described in Section 7.3, external precedences correspond to the relation $<<$ between events of two component types C_1 and C_2. The goal is to identify pairs of event types (e_1, e_2) such that, for every instance c_1 of C_1 and c_2 of C_2 running in an agent A, e_2 only occurs in c_2 after the last occurrence of e_1 in c_1. Recall that the relation $<<$ is used for a similar purpose in artifact centric process mining (e.g. Kikas, 2011).

The class `ComponentTypePrecedences` represents the external precedences between two component types. It is reconstructed from a set of *log components* with the procedure stated in pseudo-code below. The algorithm resembles the reconstruction of the relation $\rightarrow_L$ in the α-algorithm (see e.g. Medeiros et al., 2004a, reviewed in Section 4.2.3.1) and also mirrors the approach sketched by Kikas (2011, Sec. 8.4); see Section 7.3:

```
C1 // identifier of first component type
C2 // identifier of second component type
E1 // set of event types assigned to C1
E2 // set of event types assigned to C2
LA // list containing one composite log component for every agent
AP(et1, et2) // indicates that event type et1 always precedes et2
EP // list of external precedences

// initialization
```

---

[60] which are akin to the *instance-aware logs* used by Fahland et al. (2011a, p. 46); see Section 5.3.3.3
[61] following the composite pattern by Gamma et al. (1995)

```
for each event type et1 in E1
  for each event type et2 in E2
    set AP(et1, et2) = AP(et2, et1) = true

// calculation of basic 'always precedes' relation
for each log component la in LA:
  l1 = get elementary log components of type C1 from la
  l2 = get elementary log components of type C2 from la
  for each event e1 in l1
    for each event e2 in l2
      if timestamp(e1) < timestamp(e2)
        then set AP(e2.Type, e1.Type) = false
      if timestamp(e2) < timestamp(e1)
        then set AP(e1.Type, e2.Type) = false

// calculation of external precedences ('derived relation')
for each event type et1 in E1
  for each event type et2 in E2
    if AP(et1, et2) and not AP(et2, et1) then add (et1, et2) to EP
    if AP(et2, et1) and not AP(et1, et2) then add (et2, et1) to EP

return EP
```

Note that the relation `AP` corresponds to the class `AlwaysPrecedesRelation` in Figure 8.22. The list `EP` stands for the result returned by the method `getAlwaysPrecedesRelation()`.

Besides external precedences, an `AgentComponentMiningResult` provides multiplicity information using the class `Multiplicity`. This class offers the following data:

- $minOccurrence(C)$, $maxOccurrence(C)$: minimum (maximum) number of instances of components of type C run during the lifecycle of an observed agent,

- $isOptional(C)$: *true* whenever agents are observed that do not run a component of type C at all,

- $isSingleton(C)$: *true* if every observed agent runs exactly one component of type C, and

- $canOverlap(C)$: *true* when at least 2 instances of component type C run in parallel in at least one observed agent.

Note that the approach is inspired by the interaction pattern mining of Dustdar and Hoffmann (2007) reviewed in Section 4.2.4.3 and quite similar to the reconstruction of cardinalities in artifact-centric process mining (see Canbaz, 2011, Sec. 6.6.3, reviewed in Section 5.3.3.3).

To apply this mining technique to the courier model, every logged event was assigned to one of the imaginary components `Movement` (movement on the road network), `Processing` (selection and transport of orders), and `Workday` (control of occupation state). On the resulting log, the *Heuristics Miner* was run to reconstruct the internal precedences of each component type. Complementary, the new *Mine Always Precedes Relation* plugin[62] identified external precedences and multiplicities.

Figure 8.23 shows a model manually assembled from the output of both plugins. Besides visualizing the `AgentComponentMiningResult` and merging it with the partial models reconstructed by the *Heuristics Miner*, the manual post-processing included the elimination of transitive external precedences. The latter could be performed automatically when the *Mine Always Precedes Relation* plugin also has access to the internal precedences reconstructed by the *Heuristics Miner* (a similar algorithm is described by Kikas, 2011, p. 22).

The mining result shows that every observed courier contains exactly one component of type `Movement` and one of type `Workday`. In contrast a courier runs several, partly overlapping instances of `Processing`. The large number of instances per courier is due to the fact that a new (imaginary) instance of `Processing` is created in the log whenever a courier rates another order, even without applying for it.

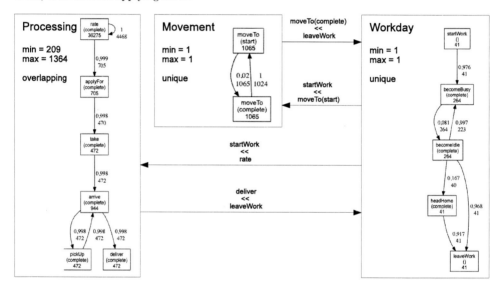

Figure 8.23.: Hierarchical, 'pseudo component-oriented' model of courier behavior in the Status Quo model mined from a small subset of log data. Note that the displayed process model was assembled manually from the results provided by two different mining algorithms, i.e. the *Heuristics miner* and a simple, preliminary *ProM* plugin to mine external precedences.

The reconstructed external precedences seem quite obvious and are in accordance with the expected behavior (e.g. event `startWork` of component `Workday` occurs before the first event `moveTo.start` of component `Movement` in the same courier). More interesting external precedences might result if the interplay between the (imaginary) components would be analyzed at different levels of granularity, e.g. not only per agent life cycle but also per processed or-

---

[62]This plugin was not run in the *ProM* user interface yet but should be able to run in this environment once a graphical user interface and visual result representation have been implemented.

der. Furthermore it must be noted that the example log was intentionally restricted to the traces of 41 exemplary couriers due to the long computation time of the mining procedure's still inefficient implementation.

Despite these drawbacks, the presented approach promises to provide more understandable representations of agent life cycles than 'flat' control flow mining. Compared to recent, rather akin work on artifact-centric process mining (e.g. Canbaz, 2011; Fahland et al., 2011a; Kikas, 2011) based on *Entity/Relationship* modeling, we focus on hierarchical agent- and component-oriented modeling as advocated by authors like Rölke (2004) and Kruse (2007).

8.3.3. Decision Perspective

The earliest attempt to validate the courier service model with the aid of data mining was conducted as part of the study project by Sven Kruse (2005) already mentioned in Section 8.1.5.3. The goal was to identify and analyze the state variables that most strongly influence how couriers rate the benefit of transport orders and decide to apply for an order (Kruse, 2005, p. 9); i.e. data mining in the decision perspective.

Though the relevant variables are in principle predefined in the rating function described in Section 8.1.3, understanding their impact on the agents' decisions is not straightforward for several reasons:

- The rating function contains many variables (Kruse, 2005, p. 10) including artificial parameters like the weighting factors w_{Bike} and w_{Car}.

- It is not a linear function.

- The passing of an order to a certain courier does not only depend on the individual decision of this courier but also on the decisions of all other couriers that rated the order.

Kruse (2005, p. 7) chose decision tree mining as an appropriate data mining technique for the study because decision trees "provide [good] insight into the interplay of (a [...] large number of) input variables with respect to a target variable" (Kruse, 2005, p. 7, citing Berry and Linoff, 2004, p. 165). In particular, the implementation of the $C4.5$ algorithm (see Section 4.1.4.1) from the open source tool *WEKA* (Hall et al., 2009, see Section 4.1.5.1 of this thesis) was used (Kruse, 2005, pp. 8).

For data collection, Kruse (2005, pp. 10) divides the state variables that influence the rating of transport orders by couriers into three categories:[63]

1. "agent-based data [...] that only depend on the internal state of the agent" (Kruse, 2005, pp. 10). This includes the courier's current number of accepted orders, its relative tour length $S(c)$, its need for orders $N(c)$, the time $T(c)$ needed to process the current orders, and the previous utilization $util(c)$ (Kruse, 2005, pp. 10).

2. "Subjective, transport order-based data [...] that the agent assigns to the order due to its internal state" (Kruse, 2005, p. 11). Here, the required detour $detour(c, o)$ and cost to process the order, and the subjective order quality $Q(c, o)$ are considered (Kruse, 2005, p. 11).

---

[63]For further explanations on the mentioned quantities $S(c)$, $N(c)$, $T(c)$, $util(c)$, $detour(c, o)$, $Q(c, o)$, and $revenues(o)$ see Section 8.1.3. The study by Kruse (2005) might nevertheless relate to a slightly different version of the rating function.

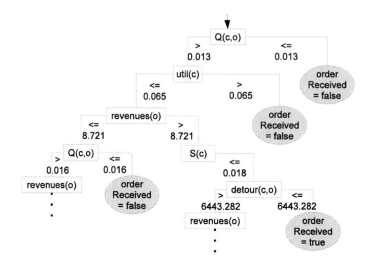

Figure 8.24.: Cutout of the decision tree for transport order assignment reconstructed by Kruse (2005, pp. 28). The original tree contains 19 internal and 20 leaf nodes (Kruse, 2005, p. 29). The full output of *WEKA* including parameter settings and quality measurements is found in (Kruse, 2005, pp. 28).

3. "Objective, transport order-based data [...] that only depend on the order" (Kruse, 2005, p. 11). These are the additional revenues *revenues(o)* gained by transporting the order (Kruse, 2005, p. 11).

During the courier service simulation, all variables are logged for every order rating action in a format readable by *WEKA* (Kruse, 2005, p. 11). Additionally, Kruse (2005, p. 12) logs a 'relative' variant of most variables where all amounts are subsequently divided by the corresponding amounts from the agent that has been granted the order. Two boolean target variables *approve* (does an agent apply for an order?) and *orderReceived* (does the office pass the order to the respective agent?) are also recorded (Kruse, 2005, p. 12).

In an experiment to analyze the dependence of the variable *orderReceived* on the absolute state variable values, Kruse (2005, pp. 13,28-29) found only the variables *detour(c, o)*, *util(c)*, *revenues(o)*, $Q(c, o)$, and $S(c)$ to be relevant for order assignment. A cutout of the decision tree presented by Kruse (2005, p. 28) is shown in Figure 8.24.

Kruse (2005, p. 13) notes that the relatively low number of significant factors might be due to (linear) dependencies of some logged variables (e.g. detour and additional cost). Though *WEKA* reports a correct classification of around 97.5% of the training data[64], the confusion matrix (see Section 4.1.3.3) shows that about 46% of cases where a courier is actually granted an order (*orderReceived = true*) are classified as *orderReceived = false* (Kruse, 2005, p. 13).

This bias towards 'false negatives' might be explained by the large fraction of negative cases inherent to the observed process: While 17929 order rating actions are observed in the exam-

---

[64]To gain a valid result, the classification ability of a decision tree should better be assessed using cross validation (see e.g. Haan, 2009, p. 54 and Section 4.1.3.3 of this thesis).

ple, only 109 of these actions lead to a transport order being assigned (Kruse, 2005, p. 28). Summarizing, an inspection of the branches in the reconstructed decision tree reveals a plausible, though not very intuitive model of the decision process. More experiments with further parameter settings (Kruse, 2005, p. 14) and the additionally logged data would be necessary to reliably conclude on the benefits of the approach.

The later study by Haan (2009) also put some focus on the decision perspective: Firstly, the MXML logger of *FAMOS* was extended with the possibility to log arbitrary attributes to MXML *audit trail entries* (Haan, 2009, p. 65). Secondly, an attempt was conducted to apply the *Decision Point Analysis* (DPA) plugin of *ProM* (Rozinat and Aalst, 2006), which also uses decision tree mining from *WEKA*, to logs of courier service simulations (Haan, 2009, pp. 80).

As reviewed in Section 4.2.5.5, the DPA allows to assign branching conditions to decision nodes in a process model on the basis of on logged attributes. Thereby, it should in principle be possible to integrate the decision tree mined in the study by Kruse (2005) into the reconstructed order processing workflow shown in Figure 8.8 (Section 8.3.1.1).

However, Haan (2009, p. 80) experienced practical difficulties when applying the DPA to the 'order perspective' of the courier service model:

> "Soon [...] it became evident that the DPA plugin could not cope well with the model converted from a Heuristic [net] into a Petri net. Though decision nodes were detected for all branches, the DPA [...] could not assign decision trees. [... This is due to] invisible activities [i.e. unlabeled transitions] that were introduced to [... represent] loops from the Heuristics net during conversion. The DPA cannot handle invisible activities [... in] loops of length one [...]. Rozinat et al. (2009b) explain [...] how loops can be avoided, but the [...] approach could not be transferred to the [analyzed] model." (Haan, 2009, p. 80)

Haan (2009, pp. 80) therefore only reconstructed a trivial decision tree at the branching point between the activities `pickUp` and `deliver`. This tree simply states that the path via `deliver` is only taken when the attribute `isPickedUp` of the order has already been set to `true`. Further experiments, e.g. to investigate if the DPA can better handle the order workflow without unlabeled transitions reconstructed with the *k-RI*/Schütt algorithm (see Section 8.3.1.1), remain for future work.

8.3.4. Summary and Discussion

To conclude the study on the application of process mining to the courier service model, we finally

- evaluate how the applied techniques perform with respect to the criteria *C1* to *C4* stated by Haan (2009, p. 72) and repeated in Section 8.2.3,

- rate to what degree the analysis tasks *T1* to *T4* could be carried out, and thereby

- answer the research questions *Q5.1* to *Q5.6* posed in this Section.

8.3.4.1. Rating of Applied Techniques and Tools

Table 8.3 shows a rating of the applied algorithms and their implementations in *ProM* by criteria *C1* to *C4*. While rows 1, 8, 12, and 13 are adopted from Haan (2009, Sec. 5.5), further rows display additional ratings made by the author. The α algorithm (row 3) was also evaluated by Haan (2009, p. 77) but not rated with respect to the criteria. We should again emphasize that all ratings are highly subjective. They merely reflect the opinions of the experimenters within the scope of the presented study.

While the rationale behind most ratings should become clear from the descriptions in the previous sections, some entries might require additional explanations. In the following, we provide details on selected ratings with most relevance for this thesis. Further explanations are given by Haan (2009, Sec. 5.5).

The ease of use of the *Heuristics Miner* is rated as *high* by Haan (2009, p. 86) due to its good documentation and ability to gain acceptable results in the default parameter configuration. Nevertheless, the large number of rather abstract parameters aggravates configuration when default settings must be changed; e.g. to avoid the suppression of infrequent transitions.

The *Frequency Abstraction* (and the *Fuzzy Miner* as its successor) score high ratings in the categories utility, ease of use, and computational performance. Especially the straightforward user interface and the fast reaction time to update the result display on parameter changes seem very appropriate for non-expert users. The customizability of the *Frequency Abstraction* is rated as *low* because the predefined clustering scheme does not fit the requirements of the courier service model (see Section 8.3.1.1). Though the *Fuzzy Miner* provides considerably more configuration possibilities, a meaningful hierarchization of the 'order workflow' could not (yet) be achieved either (see Section 8.3.1.1).

The computational performance of the *k-RI*/Schütt algorithm is rated as *medium* due to its quick reconstruction of the 'order workflow' (see Section 8.3.1.1) as opposed to the significantly worse performance in the 'courier perspective'. The utility of results is rated higher for the *FSM* miner due to its more plausible reconstruction of the order workflow from a modeler's point of view.

The utility of the result reconstructed by the *Role Hierarchy Miner* is only rated as *medium* for two reasons. Firstly, as discussed in Section 8.3.1.2, the meaning of the reconstructed organizational model could only be understood after a detailed and time-consuming analysis of the reconstructed graph and originator/task matrices. Secondly, a correlation of the reconstructed roles with performance measures is not possible yet (see also Section 8.3.1.2).

Ease of use and performance of the 'component-based' mining technique developed in this thesis are rated as low due to the rudimentary implementation. Nevertheless, the utility of the returned result might be rated as *high* as compared to results gained with the *Heuristics Miner* when attempting to reconstruct the courier life cycle.

8.3.4.2. Success of Analysis Tasks

The task *T1* (provide an aggregated overview of the transport order processing workflow including performance statistics) could e.g. be solved successfully with the *k-RI* / Schütt algorithm

	Technique	C1 Utility	C2 Ease of use	C3 Customiza- bility	C4 Performan- ce
1	Heuristics Miner (order workflow)	+	+	–	o
2	Heuristics Miner (courier life cycle)	–			
3	$\alpha/\alpha++$ algorithm	–	+	–	+
4	Frequency Abstraction / Fuzzy Miner	+	+	– / o	+
5	k-RI algorithm / Schütt concurrency detection	o	+	–	o
6	FSM Miner / Petrify	+	o	+	–
7	Petri Net Performance Analysis	+	+	o	–
8	Performance Sequence Diagram Analysis	o	+	–	–
9	Organizational Model Miner	–	+	–	+
10	Role Hierarchy Miner	o	+	o	+
11	'Component-based' mining (courier life cycle)	+	–	%	–
12	LTL Checker	o	+	+	+
13	Decision Point Analysis	–	–	–	+

Table 8.3.: Evaluation of process mining techniques with respect to criteria *C1* to *C4* from Haan (2009, p. 72). Similar to that publication, the criteria are rated on a three-level scale with the levels + (high), o (medium), and – (low). The symbol % indicates no rating. Rows 1, 8, 12, and 13 of the table are adopted from Haan (2009, pp. 86–88)

and the *Petri Net Performance Analysis* plugin of *ProM*. While the *Heuristics Miner* also delivered an appropriate reconstruction of the 'order workflow' (Haan, 2009, p. 74), log replay for performance analysis failed due to missing infrequent arcs in the reconstructed model. This issue might possibly be avoided by changing the configuration of the *Heuristics Miner*.

Analysis task *T2* (find out in which way internal state attributes influence the rating of orders by couriers) was mainly tackled in the study by Kruse (2005, pp. 5) and to some degree by Haan (2009, p. 80). Results and success of the studies are rather ambiguous: On the one hand, a plausible decision tree could be reconstructed and knowledge about the most significant state variables could be gained. On the other hand, the reconstructed decision model does not appear very intuitive and explanatory. Merging decision and control flow perspectives with the aid of the *Decision Point Analysis* plugin of *ProM* failed due to technical difficulties (Haan, 2009, pp. 80,87-88).

Task *T3* (verify the implementation of the order processing by couriers with a focus on correct movement) got in the focus of the study by Haan (2009, Sec. 5.3) after detecting a hidden error with the aid of process mining. Though other forms of analysis (especially manual log analysis) were applied in the re-validation of the courier service models as well, process mining played an important role in this case. While not all issues could be finally clarified yet, the credibility of the model was clearly improved.

The work on task *T4* (verify the implementation of the courier life cycle) demonstrated the drawbacks of 'conventional' control flow discovery applied to the complex internal control flow of agents. This insight motivated a rudimentary, partial implementation of the 'mining chain' from Section 7.3 to reconstruct hierarchical and multiply instantiated behavior. By switching the perspective from internal control flow of agents to external control flow of their constituent components[65], the understandability of the reconstructed model was considerably improved.

These results (as well as the applied techniques) are in accordance with parallel work on artifact-centric mining (e.g. Canbaz, 2011; Kikas, 2011). The reconstructed perspective emulates, to a certain degree, the software-technical improvements of *FAMOS* proposed by Kruse (2007, Sec. 3), which also inspired this work.

8.3.4.3. Research Questions

Based on the above summary we can proceed to answer the research questions posed in Section 8.2.1:

Q5.1: Can process mining support or complement the previous validation and calibration attempts?

Compared to the previous manual and SQL-based log analysis, process mining offers the possibility to quickly detect problems during exploratory analysis without 'knowing exactly what to search for'. During the reconstruction of the courier life cycle, an interesting parallel could be drawn between the lack of understandability of the initial process mining results and the software-technical flaws of *FAMOS* identified by Kruse (2007, p. 41).

Q5.2: Can process mining help to gain further insight into the behavior of the courier models and deliver 'surprising' findings?

---

[65]as to use the term by Kruse (2007)

Besides the mentioned error in courier movement (Haan, 2009, Sec. 5.3), the low relevance of several variables of the rating function (Kruse, 2005, p . 13) was also revealed with the aid of data mining. However, new or even 'surprising' insights into the rather disappointing performance of the alternative logistics strategies as compared to the *Status Quo* model could not be gained yet.

This might be caused by at least two reasons: Firstly, due to their initiative character, the experiments by Kruse (2005), Haan (2009), and the author of this thesis still put stronger focus on methods and techniques than on domain-specific questions. Secondly, more advanced analysis techniques of *ProM* with the ability to relate multiple perspectives (e.g. the *PSDA* or *DPA* plugins) did not cope well with the structure and amount of log data from the courier service simulations (Haan, 2009, pp. 87).

Q5.3: How large is the additional effort to instrument the models and extend the experimental setups? Can they easily be re-used between different models or variants?

Haan (2009, p. 65) rated the effort to instrument the courier model for the reconstruction of the 'order workflow' as rather high. This was partly due to the prototypical state of the *FAMOS* MXML logger and the existence of errors in the model. After instrumenting the *Status Quo* model, further model variants could be instrumented without large effort due to object-oriented inheritance (see also Haan, 2009, p. 85). A change of the logged perspective beyond the predefined aggregation criteria of the *FAMOS* MXML logger is still tedious and bears the risk of overcharging the model's implementation with log statements. This problem might be tackled by software-technical means like inheritance or aspect-oriented programming (as in Sudeikat et al., 2007, p. 179) to 'inject' log statements for different perspectives into effector methods of agents.

Q5.4: How do result representations of process mining compare to typical reports from discrete event simulation?

This question is discussed in Section 8.3.1.1 where the *Petri Net Performance Analysis* plugin of *ProM* is compared to simulation reporting in *FAMOS* and *DESMO-J*.

Q5.5: Which algorithms are suitable to reconstruct and enrich process and structural models in the given problem domain (Haan, 2009, p. 7)?

The *Heuristics Miner* (see Haan, 2009, pp. 74), the *Frequency Abstraction*, and the automata inference-based algorithms appeared most appropriate to reconstruct the order processing workflow of the courier service model. Models reconstructed by the latter techniques formed an appropriate basis for extension with the *Petri Net Performance Analysis*. From the two evaluated techniques, only the 'component-based' mining approach developed in this thesis could reconstruct an understandable model of the courier life cycle. Different variants of agent behavior in the *Inside/Outside* model could be identified with the *Role Hierarchy Miner* plugin of *ProM*. Unfortunately, a correlation with performance-related data is not possible there.

Q5.6: How do the existing ProM tool and the additional mining plugins developed in this thesis perform on large logs produced by the courier service simulations?

Though no detailed formal or empirical analysis of the evaluated algorithms' computational effort was conducted, an impression of their computational performance can be gained from the column *C4* of Table 8.3. Due to a still very inefficient implementation, the 'component-based' mining technique could only be applied to a very small subset (traces of 41 couriers) of the recorded log data.

8.4. Integration into an Experimentation Environment

After summarizing and discussing the results of the process mining study, we will briefly describe first steps towards improved tool integration. Similar to the integration with CAPA / RENEW reported in Section 7.4, it is based on concepts of plugins and data flow modeling. Here, the foundation is a generic experimentation environment implemented on top of the *Java*-based plugin platform *Eclipse*[66].

The experimentation environment was developed in parallel to the work reported in this thesis under participation of Rainer Czogalla, Philip Joschko, several students at the University of Hamburg's Department for Informatics, and the author of this thesis. Intermediate results were pre-published in the article by Czogalla et al. (2006), from which several passages are cited in the following.

8.4.1. Motivation and Introduction

Czogalla et al. (2006, p. 1)[67] motivate the need for a generic experimentation approach based on Eclipse:

> "[...] regardless of Zeigler's well-known claim to separate models from experiments (see e.g. Zeigler et al., 2000), most [...] tools [for simulation experimentation] are closely coupled to a certain modeling environment. Experimentation support, though in princip[le ...] independent of specific modeling styles, is therefore re-implemented over and over again. Some promising steps towards generic and extensible experimentation environments have been taken [...] (see e.g. Schöllhammer, 2001) but the respective systems are often prototypical and lack adequate usability.
>
> During the last years, [...] Eclipse has evolved from an IDE (integrated development environment) to a general tool platform. Eclipse's plug-in-mechanism allows to integrate arbitrary extensions into a consistent application frame. Thus, the platform also provides an appropriate and contemporary architectural framework for the development of simulation tools. [... T]he concept and [...] prototypical implementation of [... our] interactive experimentation environment [...] integrates the functionality of generic experimentation tools previously developed in our group into experimentation support plug-ins."

Previous experimentation tools developed at the University of Hamburg include the systems *DISMO* by Gehlsen (2004) and *CoSim* by Bachmann (2003). Both systems are briefly reviewed by Czogalla et al. (2006, p. 3):

> "The distributed simulation-based optimization framework *DISMO* (Gehlsen and Page, 2001) [...] allows to integrate different Java-based simulators by using wrapper classes. DISMO provides a simple experimentation environment that focuses mainly on automated

---

[66]http://www.eclipse.org (last visit 2012-07-21)

[67]page numbers relate to the version of the paper downloadable at http://www.scs-europe.net /services/ecms2006/ecms2006%20pdf/80-meth.pdf (last visit 2012-11-15)

experimental design and parallel execution of independent simulation runs distributed over a computer network.

Another generic simulation tool developed in our group is the component-based infrastructure *CoSim* (Bachmann, 2003) which follows a different approach. It provides cross-platform simulation in distributed environments, ensuring CORBA-based interoperability by specific model interface descriptions. CoSim includes an experimentation environment ExpU (Schöllhammer, 2001) that permits experiments to be defined and managed independently from specific model implementations (e.g. by using experiment variables)."

Porting concepts from these tools (and other authors such as Wittmann, 1993, see also Section 2.4.1 of this thesis) to the Eclipse platform provides a number of advantages that are summarized by Czogalla et al. (2006, p. 2):

"An underlying plug-in runtime environment based on the OSGi standard (Open Services Gateway Initiative, www.osgi.org [last visit 2012-11-15]) provides a dynamic extension mechanism, enabling the addition of functionality to existing components. Eclipse's core features are concentrated in the Rich Client Platform (RCP) [...] that facilitates the development of arbitrary applications.

As an integral part [...], a generic workbench supports user interaction. The Java Development Tools (JDT) extend the Eclipse platform with a set of plug-ins that add Java IDE functionality [... which is especially useful in code-centric simulation approaches like the one described in this chapter.]

Many sub-projects aim at developing Eclipse extensions for various purposes [...] A broad range of proven and tested plug-ins are available. Following the concept of software reuse, many of them can be adapted and integrated into an experimentation environment to support the tasks that arise in the context of a simulation study."

8.4.2. Design and Implementation

At the core of the experimentation environment lies a software framework that adopts and integrates several concepts from the aforementioned tools *DISMO* and *CoSim* (Czogalla et al., 2006, p. 4). Similar to these tools, any simulation engine that exposes a *Java* interface can benefit from the experimentation environment's functionality (Czogalla et al., 2006, p. 4). The framework architecture is sketched by Czogalla et al. (2006, p. 4) as follows:

"Models and simulators are adapted to the framework by implementing a *simulation wrapper* interface that provides standardized access to the model's parameters, results, and runtime variables and to the simulator control (e.g. start, stop, and step functionality). [...]

The framework's components reflect the main tasks occur[r]ing in experimentation [...] The central component is an *experiment manager* that arranges the experimental setup and controls the experiment's execution. In particular, it initializes an *experiment planner* responsible for the systematic variation of parameter settings; and an *execution manager* that encapsulates the [...] execution of simulation runs. The experimental setup is completed by registering *observers* and *analyses* that monitor the experiment execution and process available runtime values or simulation results.

The experiment planner incorporates two sub-components supporting manual and automated experimental design [see Section 2.4.1]. The manual experiment planner reads experiment specifications stated in a newly developed XML-based Experiment Specification
Language (XESL). [For details see the project report by Schulz et al. (2006) who developed
the experiment planner and the XML dialect together with a visual editor.] This language
provides several iteration types [...] to describe systematic variations of model and control
parameters.

The automated experiment planner's input are descriptions of simulation-based optimization problems. These are stated in terms of an optimization algorithm and an objective
function implemented as Java classes. [...]

From an experiment specification, the experiment planner creates *simulation run descriptions* that are passed to the execution manager [... which] instantiates and executes these
runs [...] The execution manager employs a *distribution strategy* that [potentially] encapsulates a middleware and a strategy for load distribution. During and after the simulation,
runtime variables and results are observed, filtered, and passed to several analysis components.

The framework provides a number of extension points based on Eclipse's plug-in mechanism. Additional simulators, analysis techniques, runtime observers, filters, experimental
design and distribution strategies can be integrated. [...] As a simulator, [...] DESMO-J
(Page and Kreutzer, 2005, Ch. 10) has been integrated."

To provide this functionality to the user, the following components were implemented as extensions of the Eclipse framework and user interface (Czogalla et al., 2006, p. 5):

- a new project type *simulation project* with a predefined folder structure,

- an assistant user interface (*wizard*) to create new simulation projects,

- an *experiment wizard* and an *experiment editor* to visually create and modify experiment
  specifications (Schulz et al., 2006),

- a specific *launch configuration type* to run simulation projects with appropriate filters and
  observers[68] attached,

- a basic user interface to select and run *analysis plugins* contributed via the respective
  extension point (Off et al., 2006), and

- a predefined layout of the Eclipse workbench suitable for simulation (*simulation perspective*).

An extension point allows to contribute model classes (i.e. simulation model implementations
wrapped into the interfaces required by the experimentation environment) as Eclipse / OSGi
plugins. The implementation of this mechanism is based on the concept of *model factories* by
Bachmann (2003), the prototypical integration of RENEW into the experimentation environment
by Simmendinger (see e.g. Simmendinger, 2007, p. 118), as well as the tutorial by Linke (2005).
The adaptation of existing simulation models to the predefined interfaces might in the future
also be supported by a graphical *wizard* (Czogalla et al., 2006, p. 5).

Concerning simulation execution strategies, the experimentation environment at the moment
only supports local execution on a single computer. Horvath and Krouk (2006) implemented

---

[68]also implemented by students

a distributed execution strategy using the agent framework *JADE* (see Section 3.4.1) as a middleware (Czogalla et al., 2006, p. 5), but the implementation is still in a rather preliminary state.

8.4.3. Scientific Workflows with KNIME and ProM

An obvious idea consists in the integration of process mining techniques into the experimentation environment as a specific type of analysis plugins. However, to allow for more flexible and re-usable experimental setups, a different approach might be taken; akin to the data flow modeling techniques used for the integration of process mining techniques into RENEW and CAPA (see Section 7.4).

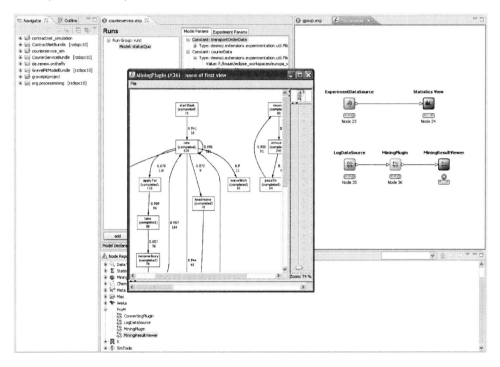

Figure 8.25.: Simple *KNIME* data flow network to mine and visualize agent life cycles reconstructed with the *Heuristics Miner*. The results are shown in a *ProM*-based viewer within the Eclipse experimentation environment.

As mentioned in Section 4.1.5.5, the open source scientific workflow system *KNIME*[69] is implemented as a set of Eclipse plugins. While common analysis tools like *WEKA* (see Hall et al., 2009, reviewed in Section 4.1.5.1) have already been adapted as *KNIME* components, an integration with the process mining tool *ProM* is, to the knowledge of the author, not available yet. The pursued idea for tool integration is therefore as follows:

---

[69]http://www.knime.org (last visit 2010-12-15)

- An observer (`ProcessLogObserver`) with the ability to record log events of *FAMOS* agents as runtime variables and store them into an MXML log is contributed to the respective extension point of the experimentation environment. The implementation of the observer is derived[70] from the *FAMOS* MXML logger described in Section 8.2.4.1.

- Exemplary *ProM* plugins are wrapped into generic *KNIME* nodes (e.g. for mining or conversion plugins) and thus made available in *Eclipse*.[71]

- Simple data types are added to *KNIME* to pass *ProM* objects like log readers or mining results along a data flow network.

- A process mining-specific data source is added to *KNIME* that supports the import of result and log files from the experimentation environment into a data flow network via a very rudimentary, 'clipboard-like' *copy-and-paste* mechanism. A sink to display mining results is added as well.[72]

Figure 8.25 shows a *KNIME* workspace that contains, among other things, a basic 'mining chain' consisting of a log data source, a *KNIME* node encapsulating the *Heuristics Miner* plugin, and a result viewer[73]. Running this data flow network on a cut-out of the courier service model's log sorted by originators results in the display shown in the foreground of Figure 8.25. It must be noted that the displayed screenshot should only be understood in the sense of an early UI prototype and not as a fully functional system.

Though an integration of the Eclipse experimentation environment with *ProM* via *KNIME* can already import basic process mining functionality into the environment, there is still plenty of room for improvements:

- The current recording of logged events via a runtime value stored in a member variable of the model is a rather inelegant mechanism. As an improvement, the experimentation environment might offer an additional, more specific interface to observe log events.

- The preliminary 'clipboard-like' mechanism to import log data into a data flow network is not very comfortable either. A better interaction with resources selected within the simulation project tree would be desirable.

- A feedback of results generated by the 'mining chains' into other components of the experimentation environment would allow to utilize the mining results in further use cases such as validation (see Section 6.3.3) or optimization (see Section 6.3.4).

---

[70]not in the sense of object-oriented inheritance

[71]Switching to version 6 of *ProM* would make the distinction between different plugin types obsolete (see Section 4.2.6.1).

[72]Note that in the current prototypical implementation, result display is still performed by the mining node itself (which is also supported in *KNIME*), while the result viewer is not functional yet.

[73]not yet functional, see above

9. Summary, Discussion, and Outlook

In this Section, the results of the thesis are summarized, discussed, and compared to related approaches. Finally an outlook is provided on possible future tasks to finish, improve, and extend the presented work.

9.1. Summary of Contributions

The subject of this thesis is a *transfer of methods*[1] from data mining and workflow technology to the domain of multi-agent based simulation (MABS). The objective is to provide a process-oriented approach towards analysis and validation that complies to process-oriented modeling perspectives of MABS (see e.g. Klügl, 2001, pp. 84). The developed approach employs process-orientation on two levels: On the one hand, analysis and validation techniques were adopted from *process mining* (e.g. Aalst, 2011a), a variant of data mining on (business) process execution logs. On the other hand, the sketched integration of tools for simulation and process mining follows the paradigm of data flow modeling and *scientific workflows* (e.g. Bowers et al., 2006). In summary, the work presented in this thesis comprises the following parts:

Review of Literature Foundations and current research at the intersection of data mining, workflow technology, MAS, and simulation were structured and summarized in an extensive literature review documented in the Chapters 2 to 5.

Conceptual Framework for Process Mining in MABS From the literature review, a *conceptual framework* for the integration of process mining and MABS was derived in Chapter 6. The framework consists of (1) a set of analysis perspectives common to process mining and MABS, (2) a set of use cases to guide the application of process mining techniques in a generic model building cycle, and (3) a list of specific requirements on techniques and tools for process mining in the context of MABS (see also Cabac et al., 2006b; Knaak, 2006). To formalize the framework as a basis for operationalization, we attempted to relate the analysis perspectives to the MAS architecture MULAN (Rölke, 2004) based on reference nets (Kummer, 2002). Furthermore, reference net-based 'mining components' (see also Cabac and Denz, 2008) were introduced as an aid to model the identified usage scenarios in the form of scientific workflows.

Case Studies Guided by the conceptual framework, process mining was applied to two agent-based modeling and simulation approaches developed at the University of Hamburg. In the case studies, existing techniques were combined and extended, and the process mining tool *ProM*

---

[1]as to use the term preferred by Czogalla (2007, p. 26)

(e.g. Dongen et al., 2005) from Eindhoven University was integrated with the simulation tools employed in the respective studies.

The *first case study* reported in Chapter 7 was performed in cooperation with members of the theoretical foundations group (TGI). It investigated the benefits and challenges of process mining in a Petri net-based agent-oriented software engineering (PAOSE, see e.g. Cabac, 2010) approach based on reference nets and MULAN. Techniques for process mining of basic and higher-level agent interaction protocols were developed and partially implemented (see also Cabac et al., 2006c; Knaak, 2007). An architectural integration was achieved by means of net components to compose *ProM* plugins and custom code into hierarchical scientific workflows (see also Cabac and Denz, 2008) .

The *second case study* presented in Chapter 8 was partly performed in an affiliated Bachelor thesis by Haan (2009) and a study project by Kruse (2005). Here, process mining was evaluated in a large courier service simulation study with the DES framework DESMO-J (Lechler and Page, 1999) and its MABS extension FAMOS (Knaak, 2002; Meyer, 2008). The focus of this study was put on the practical applicability of *ProM* and a comparison of process mining to more 'traditional' analysis and validation techniques from simulation. Furthermore, the integration of analysis workflows into a generic experimentation environment based on the Eclipse rich client platform (RCP) was sketched (see also Czogalla et al., 2006; Simmendinger, 2007; Simmendinger et al., 2007).

Results: Abstracting from the structure of the thesis and the two case studies, this work delivered the following results:

1. a conceptual framework to integrate data and process mining with MABS,

2. a partial implementation of a processing chain to reconstruct basic agent interaction protocols as well as concepts and first prototypical implementations to reconstruct higher level and multicast protocols from logs,

3. a concept for tool integration based on plugins and scientific workflow technology with prototypical implementations in RENEW and Eclipse, and

4. practical applications and evaluations of process mining techniques to a Petri net-based and a code-centric MABS approach.

9.2. Discussion

In the following, we discuss to which extent the presented contributions help to answer the research questions initially posed in Section 1.2. Subsequently, the innovation of the presented approach is discussed in comparison to related work.

9.2.1. Attainment of Research Goals

9.2.1.1. Question 1: State-of-the-Art in Data Mining and MABS

This research question asked for the status of research at the intersection of data (or process) mining and agent-based simulation. For an answer, the literature from several related fields was observed for the duration of this dissertation project, resulting in the following conclusions:

1. Despite increasing work during the last two decades, data mining cannot be considered an established support technique for simulation analysis yet. This might be due to its complexity on the one hand. On the other hand, many separate case examples are seen alongside few elaborated and applicable general approaches with appropriate tool support. The mutual acknowledgement between different subfields and research groups seems relatively low.[2]

2. While also uncommon in the beginning of this research, work on combining data mining and MAS has received increasing attention over the last years. Nowadays, conferences on "agents and data mining interaction and integration"[3] are held, and mutual benefits are discussed. However, much work still seems to focus on numerical, rule-, and automata-based mining techniques instead of explicitly taking into account process-oriented and organizational perspectives relevant in MAS modeling.

3. Process mining is a very active research fields that has "evolv[ed ...] rapidly" (Dongen et al., 2006b, p. 145) parallel to this thesis. The research group at Eindhoven and their plugin-based software *ProM* serve as a concentrator for related research. Accordingly, the definition of process mining evolved from a narrower to a wider sense form that comprises a variety of automated process analysis techniques (see also Dongen et al., 2006b, p. 145).

4. Due to their generality, the frameworks of MAS and process mining (in the wider sense) proved to be an appropriate means to relate and classify similar work from heterogeneous fields like software engineering, distributed systems, and artificial intelligence.

5. Despite similarities between system perspectives in both fields, still only few (mostly *ad-hoc*) examples exist for an integration. To the opinion of the author neither direction of joint research (i.e. 'process mining for MAS' and 'MAS for process mining') has received enough attention in the literature so far.

Overall, the literature review provided a rather clear-cut and unified picture of research related to the process-oriented analysis of MABS, which helped to derive and refine the objectives of this thesis. However, due to the rapid development of process mining, these objectives had to be adapted repeatedly to take into account results from parallel research.

9.2.1.2. Question 2: Conceptual Foundations

This question asked to concretize the similarities between process mining and MABS in terms of common conceptual foundations, and to discuss the mutual impact of both fields.

---

[2]though a number of researchers like e.g. Arroyo et al. (2010) relate themselves to the work by Remondino and Correndo (2005)

[3]see www.agentmining.org (last visit 2012-01-03)

We therefore tried to generalize the findings from the literature review towards a conceptual framework for the integration of process mining and MABS in Chapter 6. While this framework exhibits clear similarities to earlier and parallel research in process mining, simulation, and MAS (see Section 9.2.2), we strived to extend the existing work in terms of completeness and level of detail.

Based on the literature[4], analysis perspectives and use cases were identified as appropriate framework dimensions. While the former dimension relates system views from process mining and MABS, the latter relates process mining techniques to potential applications within a (generic) MABS model building cycle. Furthermore, a list of simulation specific requirements and caveats concerning the application of process mining techniques was compiled. The identified perspectives, usage scenarios, and requirements evolved over time from discussions with colleagues, practical experiences, and continued literature research.

To concretize both dimensions, a common base for formalization was sought in the framework of reference nets and MULAN. The basic idea was to formalize analysis perspectives by relating them to the (partly similar) system views of MULAN, and to formalize use cases as scientific workflows with reference nets.

A basis to formalize the use cases could be built relatively easy by (1) identifying and modeling typical scientific workflow components in terms of reference nets, and (2) developing a concept for the integration of process mining and simulation tools based on net components.[5] Reference net-based overview diagrams and first example applications of mining components were presented in Chapters 6.3 and 7 of this thesis. The modeling of larger use cases from the conceptual framework by stating the related control and data flow, as well as interactions with users and external tools remains a topic for future work.

The benefits of the approach taken appear somewhat similar to other attempts of domain modeling with reference nets (e.g. sociological theories in von Lüde et al., 2003 or emotion theories in Fix, 2012):[6] The reference net models combine advantages of informal (e.g. textual or diagrammatic) and programmatic descriptions. On the one hand, the provided models can be understood by domain experts to communicate and document the applied analysis and validation techniques. On the other hand, the workflows might be easier to understand, maintain, and modify by developers than mere code-based implementations, especially with respect to concurrency (e.g. in distributed experimentation).

The formalization of analysis perspectives proved to be more difficult. The initial idea was (1) to express result representations of the perspectives in terms of reference nets related to the existing MULAN views. Furthermore, (2) data sources for process mining should be identified from the (Petri net-based) interface of each view. On this basis, we hoped (3) to be able to build or adapt algorithms to reconstruct such models, and (4) to use partial models as background knowledge to reduce the algorithms' search spaces.

Objectives (1), (2), and (3) were in parts achieved at the level of protocol nets (related to the internal control perspective) and AIP diagrams (external control perspective). A further formalization of analysis perspectives was sketched but not realized in detail for the following

---

[4]An important influence was, among others, work from the Eindhoven research group such as Aalst (2006) and Ailenei et al. (2012).

[5]Some of this work was subject of the diploma thesis by Simmendinger (2007).

[6]see also our argumentation in (Cabac and Denz, 2008, Sec. 6)

main reasons: On the one hand, the remaining MULAN views (e.g. the agent net) are currently rather broad, configurable templates, that do not provide enough detail[7] to improve the design or prune the search space of mining algorithms. On the other hand, a detailed executable reference net model for a more comprehensive analysis perspective (e.g. a multicast protocol with several phases) might quickly become too complex to serve as a validation aid. We therefore put stronger focus on relations between the analysis perspectives and higher level design diagrams of the PAOSE approach in Section 7.1.

For these reasons, a related approach with similar objectives by Rembert and Ellis (2009) was adopted. These authors strive to formalize process mining perspectives in terms of process dimensions and dimensional mappings, exemplified for parts of the (not explicitly agent-based) Information Control Net model. Following their approach, we thus identified relevant process dimensions and dimensional mappings for exemplary agent-based analysis perspectives as a first step towards formalization. In the future it might be worth trying to map these dimensions to reference net models or patterns similar to the procedure proposed for the ICN model (see Rembert and Ellis, 2009, Sec. 4).

9.2.1.3. Question 3: Analysis and Validation of Agent Interactions

This topic was mainly treated in the context of the PAOSE approach. Based on previous work on interaction mining, a processing chain was set up – mainly as an extension of the approach by Schütt (2003) – to reconstruct basic interaction protocols without prior knowledge of interaction roles and protocol classes. The first three steps (log segmentation, role mining, and control flow mining) were finally implemented as *ProM* plugins by applying and extending existing process mining algorithms: The chained correlation procedure proposed by Aalst et al. (2005) was specialized to FIPA ACL messages on the CAPA platform. Protocol classification was achieved by clustering based on (weighted) similar follower relations of protocol instance traces as e.g. proposed in (Song et al., 2008). A simple role mining step was realized by anonymization of agent names.

As an extension of the control flow mining approach by Schütt (2003), a variant of a "two-step" algorithm[8] was implemented that combines the k-RI grammar inference technique with a 'naive' concurrency detection stage which unifies duplicate tasks from path alternatives like $[ab, ba]$ in the reconstructed automaton. The implementation was embedded into the CAPA platform and succeeded in reconstructing an interaction protocol with three fixed roles from a log containing (easily separable) traces of different protocols.

While the experiment was successful, deficiencies of the current implementation can also be identified: Firstly, due to the rapid development of process mining during the course of this thesis, several related approaches were published or found in the literature after the first interaction mining chain had been implemented. While some steps of the chain, i.e. role mining and concurrency detection, were compared to alternative implementations in *ProM* (see Section 9.2.2), a more comprehensive evaluation will be necessary. The theoretical limits of the presented control flow mining procedure were only discussed by few examples, leaving a formal proof to further work.

---

[7]beyond commonalities like the fact that agents inhabit a platform
[8]as to use the term by Rubin et al. (2006)

Furthermore, we sketched an extension of the basic interaction mining chain to reconstruct hierarchical and multicast protocols. Though similar procedures have recently been published in the context of software reverse engineering (Kumar et al., 2010, 2011, 2012; Lou et al., 2010b) and artifact-centric process mining (e.g. Kikas, 2011), this was one of the first drafts[9] of a process mining algorithm to reconstruct process models containing the workflow pattern "multiple instantiations without a-priori design time knowledge" (pattern $P13$ in Aalst et al., 2003b, p. 24).

The sketched procedure still has several drawbacks including its current inability to reconstruct cycles in external precedences. It was nevertheless shown to work in a (still rather simplified and inefficient) partial implementation on a small test dataset from the second case study. Applying this hierarchical mining procedure to the reconstruction of courier agent life cycles illustrated interesting relations to software-technical considerations on agent modularity in *FAMOS* discussed by Kruse (2007).

Summarizing, relevant steps were taken towards answering research question $Q3$. However, the presented solutions still need improvements to form a practically applicable tool for the reconstruction, analysis, and validation of message-based agent interaction protocols. In particular, the current implementation only aids in the reconstruction and visualization of protocols without supporting protocol validation or improvement.

9.2.1.4. Question 4: Tool Integration

This question asked for a viable concept to integrate simulation and process mining tools in a generic and re-usable way. Such a concept was found in a combination of (scientific) workflow and plugin technology. While plugins allow for a flexible adaptation of a simulation and analysis tool to different and changing requirements (e.g. Schnackenbeck et al., 2008), scientific workflow systems support the visual modeling of the control and data flow of complex procedures incorporating multiple heterogeneous tools or plugins (Simmendinger, 2007, p. 27). For practical reasons, we focused on simulation and analysis tools implemented in the *Java* programming language.

In the first step, a set of simple *Java* interfaces for typical data flow components (i.e. sinks, sources, and processors) was defined. In the PAOSE study, a related set of generic net components was built that either encapsulate data processing algorithms implemented in *Java* (elementary components) or embedded subnets (complex components). Several mining and analysis plugins from *ProM* (including the interaction mining plugins) were adapted as net components.

To provide message logs of agent interactions, a communication *Sniffer* was implemented for CAPA[10] and coupled to a source component of the workflow. Furthermore, a sink was implemented that feeds back the mining results into RENEW, thereby allowing to execute these nets in the simulator. On this basis, the first three steps of the interaction mining chain were implemented as a workflow. More example workflows were provided to show further possibilities of reference net modeling for test data generation, conformance checking, and optimization in process mining.

---

[9]the basic idea was first mentioned in (Knaak, 2007, Sec. 4.2)

[10]by students as part of a teaching project, see Heitmann and Pläehn (2005)

In the second case study, file-based MXML logging of agent activities was implemented for *FAMOS*, and experiments were run interactively with *DESMO-J* and *ProM* by Haan (2009) and the author of this thesis. A higher degree of automatization and re-usability might be achieved by employing workflow and plugin technology in this setting as well. Due to the central role of *Java* code in this simulation approach, we chose the popular *Java* IDE *Eclipse* based on the OSGi plugin framework as a basis. Building upon previous work from the University of Hamburg, an interactive experimentation tool was implemented as a set of Eclipse plugins (Czogalla et al., 2006) with participation of the author.

One objective was to provide generic interfaces to re-use experimentation functionality (i.e. experimental design, simulation-based optimization, online observation, and output analysis) with arbitrary *Java*-based simulators. While reasonable at first sight, we found that this genericness also causes a trade off since existing experimentation and analysis functionality from the wrapped simulators (like *DESMO-J*) must either be re-implemented or 'routed' through the experimentation framework.

A variant of the MXML logger was included into this framework as an observer plugin. The existing Eclipse plugin *KNIME* (Chair for Bioinformatics and Information Mining at Konstanz University, 2007) for scientific workflow modeling was extended with a prototypical source component to feed log data into analysis workflows. In addition to *KNIME*'s built-in data mining functionality, selected *ProM* plugins were prototypically wrapped as *KNIME* components with re-usable adapters.

Comparing both case studies, *KNIME* provides a more specific and mature user interface for scientific workflow modeling than our prototypical data flow components in RENEW. However, *KNIME* suffers from stronger restrictions to model complex control flow. Despite the provided implementation aids, more effort is needed to wrap existing classes as *KNIME* plugins in *Eclipse* than simply calling their methods from net components in RENEW. As a first step towards integrating both approaches, Simmendinger (2007) re-implemented the RENEW plugin system based on the OSGi framework. This version of RENEW should integrate well with the Eclipse-based experimentation environment either as a simulator or as an execution engine for analysis workflows.

Summarizing, it must be stated that on the one hand, the prototypical implementation status of tool integration in both case studies forbids to draw definite conclusions on their practical benefit and usability. On the other hand, the potential of employing plugin architectures and scientific workflow technology to combine simulation tools with advanced analysis tools was successfully demonstrated. The PAOSE study provided hints how an architectural integration of process mining into Petri-net based software development and adaptive Petri net agents might be realized. The second case study showed advantages and trade offs of flexible tool integration into a simulation environment.

9.2.1.5. Question 5: Practical Value of Process Mining for MABS

This question was tackled from different angles in the two case studies. In the PAOSE study, the general feasibility and potential of interaction mining within a Petri net-based agent platform was shown by prototypical implementations. However, the investigated example was only small-sized. Practical issues with the applied algorithms (e.g. the difficulty to set an appropriate cluster threshold in log segmentation) were noticed but not investigated in further detail.

In the second case study, a larger number of existing process mining algorithms from *ProM* were evaluated with respect to their potential to support the analysis and validation of a larger MABS model. This study showed that different from the beginning of this thesis, several process mining algorithms exist to support the analysis perspectives and use cases of the conceptual framework. However, the low stability and performance of many implementations in *ProM* impede their practical application to large simulation logs. The same holds true for many of *ProM*'s analysis and visualization plugins. Though they appear well applicable to MABS analysis, several minor and major deficiencies complicate a practical application.

Some of the best results in control flow mining were (similar to other studies) achieved with the Heuristic Miner algorithm. Nevertheless, this algorithm must be used with care in validation since it does not reconstruct an exact model of the mined log. Automata-based techniques like the *FSM Miner* (implementing work by Rubin et al., 2006) were identified as appropriate alternatives. This also holds true for the heuristic *Frequency Abstraction* (Rozinat et al., 2007) and *Fuzzy Miner* (Günther and Aalst, 2007) algorithms implemented in *ProM*.

With the aid of the *PAPN* plugin by Hornix (2007) it was possible to reconstruct a model of the transport order workflow in the courier model that conveyed similar information than a simulation report in a more vivid form. The re-usability of this solution is high since it only depends on time-stamped log messages as an input. Haan (2009) also detected a hidden error in the implementation of the courier model by means of process mining. Nevertheless, the reasons for some inconsistencies in the reconstructed models could not be spotted definitely. Due to these difficulties, process mining remains a tool for expert users with knowledge in both data mining and simulation.

Though already applied in other MABS studies, decision tree mining did not deliver satisfying results: The decision point analysis plugin of *ProM* could not enrich the model of the transport order workflow with relevant branching conditions due to difficulties with the structure of the reconstructed net. The decision tree mined from the order rating procedure by Kruse (2005) appeared too complex to draw valid conclusions on the implemented courier behavior. In the structural/organizational perspective, the *Role Hierarchy Miner* of *ProM* (implementing techniques by Song and Aalst, 2008) allowed to derive the most detailled role models from the model of the *Inside/Outside* strategy but does not (yet) allow to correlate the identified structure with performance data (like the *PSDA* plugin by Hornix (2007), which appeared less effective and efficient in this example).

9.2.1.6. Question 6: Level-Encompassing Validation

This research question asked if data and process mining are appropriate techniques to gain knowledge about the relations between multiple levels of a MABS, and if this knowledge can be employed for validation and calibration. From a practical point of view, we were interested in questions like: *"What are the mechanisms by which the order rating strategies of simulated couriers influence the overall performance of the courier service?"* From an abstract point of view, we asked if hints on micro/macro links can be mined from execution logs.

This is clearly one of the most demanding research questions stated here. Admittedly, the present thesis only delivers rather preliminary experiments at the practical level and discussions at the conceptual level towards an answer.

At the practical level, two parameters of the courier rating function were automatically calibrated using the distributed simulation-based optimization tool *DISMO* (Bachmann et al., 2004). This study confirmed that automated calibration by simulation-based optimization can deliver similar results than thorough manual calibration. However, due to the use of numerical objective functions, parameters, and results in this study, no underlying *mechanisms* could be revealed. As mentioned above, attempts to reconstruct decision trees describing the influence of certain attributes on the outcome of the couriers' order rating function proved problematic as well.

On the conceptual level, the thesis by Chen (2009), and related work by Moncion et al. (2010), which was published in parallel to the work on the thesis at hand, presents promising concepts and experiments towards multi-level MABS modeling in the framework of *complex events*. Chen (2009) also applies data mining techniques like correlation analysis and Bayesian networks to derive level-encompassing relations from simulation logs.

The work by Chen (2009) appears rather 'process mining-like' in spirit. A similar notion of complex events, as (multi-perspective) patterns derived from or validated against log data, has been used in a process mining context as well (see Gay et al., 2010). However, an explicit link between Chen's work and process mining could not be found in the literature yet.

We therefore embellished the process dimensions and dimensional mappings of our conceptual framework's *level encompassing perspective* using the concepts by Chen (2009). Furthermore, we sketched how the modeling and analysis techniques presented by this author might profit from an integration with process mining techniques (e.g. the pattern-based compliance checking techniques by Ramezani et al., 2012) and advanced modeling techniques like reference nets. Furthering this integration towards 'level encompassing process mining' appears to be a promising direction for future research.

9.2.2. Comparison to Related Work

In the following, the results summarized in Section 9.1 are compared to related work described in the literature review (Section 5). In order to preserve the concluding character, only the most relevant and closely related approaches will be considered.

9.2.2.1. Conceptual Framework

Prior and parallel to this thesis, related concepts to integrate data mining with MAS or simulation have been developed. Similar to the presented framework, the methodology of *Data Farming* (Brandstein et al., 1998) combines data mining with advanced experiment planning, visualization and distributed execution. However, it does not focus on multiple analysis perspectives and merely applies numerical and rule-based mining techniques.

The dissertation by Köster (2002) on integrating KDD and individual-based simulation was an important inspiration for this work. Based on own experiences, Köster (2004) also encouraged the author of this thesis to investigate the level-encompassing perspective. In comparison, the thesis at hand puts a larger focus on process-oriented and organizational perspectives not covered by Köster. The embedding of DM into the model building cycle is more detailed here due to the elaboration of several different use cases.

Remondino and Correndo (2006) developed concepts to apply DM to the validation of MABS. Compared to the presented framework, they focus on rule-based and numerical techniques and some use cases in the modeling cycle, but only implicitly treat perspectives. Their ideas are still preliminary and their case study only employs parameter calibration by exhaustive search combined with visual 'data mining' from histograms. As confirmed in personal e-mail communications, Remondino and Correndo (2006) and the author of this thesis developed related ideas independently. The thesis at hand is an attempt to concretize, extend, and evaluate some of these in a process-oriented setting. Joint research might have been fruitful but failed due to tight schedules on both sides. Arroyo et al. (2010) refine the model building cycle proposed by Remondino and Correndo (2006) but do not explicitly consider perspectives either.

In the MAS field, Ndumu and Nwana (1999) presented a multi-perspective debugging approach supported by visualization tools for the ZEUS platform, but without references to data mining. Nair et al. (2004) developed an automated assistant that supports the analysis of MAS with data mining techniques on three levels related to the decision, external control, and level-encompassing perspectives. In the opinion of the author, this[11] is one of the most advanced examples of DM in MAS. The present thesis is an attempt to conceptually extend this multi-level approach with further perspectives and use cases, and to strengthen the focus on process-orientation.

In the field of (business) process modeling and mining, multi-perspective approaches are also common. The close relation between the main process mining perspectives identified by the Eindhoven research group (see e.g. Aalst, 2006) and the modeling perspectives from MA(B)S was an initial motivation for the presented conceptual framework. Nevertheless, the perspective model from Eindhoven is not explicitly agent-based and remains vague about mechanisms to identify, and formalize perspectives. Use cases for process mining are also identified but are not specific for MABS analysis and validation.

The approach by Rembert and Ellis (2009) helped to formulate analysis perspectives more concisely in terms of process dimensions and dimensional mappings. Though the underlying ICN model exhibits some similarities with a MAS model like MULAN, the approach is neither explicitly agent-based nor related to simulation. By identifying dimensions and mappings related to MA(B)S, the thesis at hand attempts to transfer the concepts into an agent-based context. Another interesting point in the work by Rembert and Ellis (2009) is the direct derivation of process mining algorithms from the formal definition of mining perspectives. This idea also came up during the work on the present thesis but was not followed further.

The presented partitioning of the *external control perspective* into basic protocols, higher level protocols, and high level interaction patterns was strongly influenced by MULAN and by the levels of web service mining in the work by Dustdar and Hoffmann (2007) and Gombotz et al. (2005). However, as discussed in Section 5.3.3.1, the latter authors mainly consider lower-

---

[11]together with the work in the context of the *Ingenias* methodology, e.g. Botía et al. (2004)

level perspectives with a more technical focus. Only their 'web service workflow perspective' is closely related to higher order protocols.

The distinction between structure and behavior and between internal control flow and interactions in the analysis perspectives is reminiscent of UML (see e.g. Jeckle et al., 2002). The *adaptivity perspective* was introduced to provide a unified view upon work on change mining and concept drift detection (e.g. Günther et al., 2006 and Bose et al., 2011a) on the one hand, and the discovery of structural dynamics (e.g. Christley and Madey, 2007a) on the other hand. The *level encompassing perspective* was mainly shaped using concepts from the work by Chen (2009).

The use case of *model building cycle reconstruction* was adopted from Rubin et al. (2007) whose thesis exclusively focuses on process mining of software development processes. Similar to our approach, Antunes and Coelho (2004, Sec. 4) use workflow-like overview diagrams to characterize specific forms (or 'use cases') of agent-based simulation (e.g. *exploratory simulation*).

9.2.2.2. Techniques for Agent Interaction Mining

The processing chain for basic interaction protocol mining presented in Chapter 7.2 is mainly an extension of the interaction mining approach by Schütt (2003) where the stages of conversation clustering and role mining were added. The automata inference stage was replaced with the *k-RI algorithm* by Angluin (1982) to allow for the reconstruction of cycles.

The basic concurrency detection scheme proposed by Schütt (2003) was implemented as a variant of the α algorithm using code from *ProM*. The implemented technique also exhibits similarities to work on duplicate task detection by Li et al. (2007) and Gu et al. (2008). Another existing *ProM* plugin allows to apply the α algorithm to automata but does not consider duplicate tasks.

Mounier et al. (2003) also developed a processing chain for conversation mining in MAS. However, their approach neglects clustering, role mining, and concurrency. Hiel (2005) focuses on discovering long-distance dependencies from logged agent interactions by means of Hidden Markov Models. His approach neglects pre-processing, role mining and concurrency detection, though process mining is mentioned as an appropriate technique for the latter. Winarjo (2009) proposes a variant of the α algorithm that is able to reconstruct sequence diagram-like nets related to our idea of peer generation. Again, his approach neither includes protocol clustering nor role mining. Clustering procedures are part of several web service mining approaches such as Srinivasa and Spiliopoulou (2000).

The presented control flow mining procedure consists of subsequent automata inference and concurrency detection similar to the "two-step approach" by Rubin et al. (2006). As first proposed by Herbst (2001), this approach uses the theory of regions and the related tool *Petrify* for Petri net synthesis from automata. The experiments conducted in this thesis indicate that both algorithms deliver quite similar results on many examples. To the impression of the author, the algorithms used by Rubin et al. (2006) are more difficult to parameterize and possibly less efficient (especially the *FSM Miner*) than those used in our implementation. However, from a theoretical viewpoint, the theory of regions is well-investigated while the approach presented here has not been formally proved yet. We could also identify an example that *Petrify* can handle while the (implemented variant of the) approach by Schütt (2003) cannot.

Clustering of process instances based on the follower matrix has been proposed in the literature several times. To the author's knowledge, one of the earliest approaches was developed by Greco et al. (2004). Role mining has been tackled in the literature by means of clustering as well (e.g. Song and Aalst, 2008). This is due to the close relation between protocols and roles in MAS where roles are often defined by the protocols they implement. Taking this duality into account, our simple anonymization scheme is sufficient for role detection in 1:1 conversations if the initiator role is fixed.

The presented concepts to reconstruct higher-order protocols will be compared to the few existing attempts to handle hierarchies of process models and multiple instantiation patterns. The proposed[12] combination of process discovery and conformance checking techniques to mine hierarchical protocols is related to activity mining by Günther et al. (2010), the hierarchical process mining approach by Medeiros et al. (2008b), and the mining of process maps by Li et al. (2010). The use of previously mined reference nets for pattern matching would allow us to reconstruct further information like role assignments and message cardinalities. Other authors employ similar conformance checking techniques to agent protocols (e.g. Mazouzi et al., 2002), but do not use the detected patterns to reconstruct hierarchical process models.

While several workflow patterns have been tackled in process mining (e.g. Gaaloul et al., 2005), multiple instantiation patterns have not received much attention yet. One exception is the approach recently implemented by Lou et al. (2010b), who reconstruct process models from logs of interleaved threads. Similar to our concept, this approach supports the detection of fork and join constructs where a variable number of threads are spawned and merged during runtime of a software application. Different from our approach, no *a-priori* knowledge about mechanisms to chain events into threads is necessary to achieve this. The algorithm by Lou et al. (2010b) is able to reconstruct cycles, but does not support the detection of regularities in the number of instantiated threads as foreseen in our concept to handle message cardinalities.

Examples of agent interaction protocols with multicast communication are also presented by Lamma et al. (2007a,b). Different from our approach, these authors reconstruct declarative specifications of process models by Inductive Logic Programming (ILP) in the temporal logic language *SCIFF*. The reconstructed models can be graphically visualized but do not explicitly display the control flow of protocols like Petri nets or AIP diagrams. Nevertheless, their ILP-based algorithm manages to detect a deadline in a multicast protocol, which our approach would currently fail on.

The most closely related work to our approach are artifact-centric process mining (Canbaz, 2011; Fahland et al., 2011a; Kikas, 2011; Popova et al., 2012) on the one hand and the techniques to reverse engineer message sequence graphs by Kumar et al. (2010, 2011, 2012) on the other hand. Similarities and differences between our work and artifact-centric process mining have already been discussed in Chapters 7 and 8.

The work by Kumar et al. is very similar to our approach (and more elaborate concerning the applied algorithms) in that internal and external precedences as well as message broadcast and related cardinality constraints are considered. However, slightly more explicit *a-priori* knowledge about message broadcasts and object/class assignments might be required.[13] Fur-

---

[12] but not implemented

[13] As compared to our concept and the basic mining chain presented in Chapter 7. The preliminary implementation shown in Section 8.3.2.2 does not perform role mining either.

thermore, the use of MSCs and precedence graphs for internal precedences might constrain the possibilities to display complex internal control flow (beyond sequences and concurrency) stronger than our approach.

9.2.2.3. Tool Integration based on Scientific Workflows and Plugin Architectures

The earliest approach to model process mining algorithms as workflows might be the module *MiMo* (Aalst et al., 2002, Sec. 5) that integrated an implementation of the α algorithm as a hierarchical workflow into the Petri net-based simulation system *ExSpect*. The basic idea is very similar to our 'mining chains', but the approach has not been developed further by the Eindhoven research group.

Conceptual models of complex process mining algorithms have often been depicted using data flow diagrams (e.g. Schimm, 2004; Schütt, 2003). In the software architecture of the *Process Mining Workbench*[14] by Schimm (2004), the term "mining chain" is used as well. However, only one fixed data flow without explicit modeling facilities seems to be contained.

ProM offers interfaces to the Petri net simulator *CPN Tools*. Rather similar to the ideas presented in this thesis, test data generation from colored Petri nets (Medeiros and Günther, 2005) and reconstruction of executable Petri net-based simulation models from multiple mining perspectives (Rozinat et al., 2009b; Wynn et al., 2010) are supported. While the functionality allows for a basic 'roundtrip engineering' of Petri net-based simulation models, the integration is only realized as file import and export. No common workflows are defined to control both tools.

The latest version 6 of *ProM* (Verbeek et al., 2011) offers software assistants with appealing user interfaces to support complex process mining tasks. These assistants seem to be based on explicit data flow models. However, a graphical workflow editor shipped with an early preview version offered rather limited control flow modeling constructs but has been removed from the *ProM 6* distribution. Bratosin et al. (2007) and Westergaard (2011) use colored Petri nets to build scientific workflows from *ProM* plugins, both citing our concepts pre-published in (Cabac and Knaak, 2007). With the aid of the *Java / CPNTools* interface by Westergaard (2011), Nakatumba et al. (2012) recently proposed a Petri net-based "infrastructure for cost-effective testing of operational support algorithms" that integrates *ProM 6* as a process mining tool.

The project *MoSiFlow* at the University of Rostock employs scientific workflows in the context of (agent-based) simulation with the software framework *JAMES II*. Different from our work, the focus of this project is put on support of the whole model building cycle instead of an integration of data mining (see Rybacki et al., 2011 and the Master's thesis by Seib, 2009). Interestingly, an integration of data mining and (agent-based) simulation is the subject of the Bachelor thesis by Seib (2008), but no explicit relations are drawn between both topics. Further work of the Rostock simulation group focuses on a generic architecture (*FAMVal*) for model validation, also implemented in the framework *JAMES II* (see e.g. Leye and Uhrmacher, 2010).

The idea to use *Eclipse / OSGi* as a platform for simulation tools has been realized in several forms including (among others) the *UrbanSim* project (Freeman-Benson and Borning, 2003, p. 332)[15], the *DEVS/OSGi* simulation framework (Petzold et al., 2011), the *OSA* project (Dalle,

---

[14]http://www.processmining.de/3294.html (last visit 2012-11-18)
[15]cited in Czogalla et al. (2006, Sec. 4)

2007), and the simulation-specific (grid) workflow management system *SimTech* (Görlach et al., 2011).

In *UrbanSim* a (meanwhile abandoned) experimentation environment for a land-use simulator was built in the form of Eclipse plugins. Dalle (2007) and Petzold et al. (2011) focus on component-based simulation modeling and instrumentation in *DEVS* (e.g. Zeigler et al., 2000) and related approaches. The work by Görlach et al. (2011) might be most closely related to the ideas sketched in this thesis due to their focus on workflow modeling and the *Eclipse*-based "implement[ation of ...] different perspectives corresponding to the different phases in the life cycle of simulation process management" (Görlach et al., 2011, p. 337). Instead of *KNIME* or reference nets, *BPEL* is used as a workflow language (Görlach et al., 2011, p. 337).

The component architecture of our generic experimentation environment is based on previous work by Bachmann (2003) and Gehlsen (2004). While the functional scope of *SimTools* is roughly comparable to simulation systems like *SeSAm* (Oechslein, 2004) the experimentation functionality of the latter is closely coupled to the respective modeling and simulation tools.

The use of reference nets, RENEW, and *Eclipse* for scientific workflow modeling is also proposed by Kurzbach (2007) in the context of Geographical Information Systems (GIS). This work might be integrated with the *OSGi*-based re-design of the plugin architecture by Simmendinger (2007); see (Kurzbach, 2007, p. 77).

9.2.2.4. Case Studies on Process Mining in MABS

An integration of process mining into a Petri net-based MA(B)S approach has – to the knowledge of the author – not been realized before. While Stuit et al. (2007b) mention that process mining *could* be used to support learning and alignment of protocols in their Petri net-based MABS approach, they actually apply another alignment mechanism based on neural networks (Meyer and Szirbik, 2007). Different from our work, their focus is on participatory modeling and adaptive agents instead of analysis and validation.

Winarjo (2009) employs process mining to reconstruct sequence diagram-like Petri nets from FIPA ACL message logs recorded in a MAS on the Java-based platform *JADE*. These models are analyzed in *CPN Tools* to detect potential deadlocks. However, it is not possible to feed the mining results back into the development of the MAS directly due to the non-explicit code-based implementation.

Applications of *ProM* to the analysis of MABS are reported by Dongen et al. (2006b) and Rozinat et al. (2009d). While the algorithms and perspectives treated in these articles partly overlap with the study by Haan (2009), the focus seems to be different: Both articles report successful *ad-hoc* applications of existing process mining techniques to certain aspects of MABS analysis. However, few analysis questions and evaluation criteria are formulated to identify weaknesses and propose enhancements of the existing algorithms and tools. In contrast, the study by Haan (2009) and its advancement in this thesis detected several pitfalls that might currently aggravate an application of process mining and *ProM* for simulation practitioners.

The dissertation by Lang (2008) contains a thorough, application-directed analysis of several process mining techniques in the field of medical image processing. Haan (2009) and the author of this thesis adopted several methodological aspects from this work. Different from our approach, Lang (2008) evaluates mining techniques mainly with respect to 'objective' criteria like the ability to handle duplicate tasks or noise. The study reported by Haan (2009) and in this thesis puts more focus on 'subjective' evaluation criteria like user-friendliness or extensibility of the analyzed techniques and tools.

9.3. Outlook

Several questions raised in this thesis remain open for future work. The open issues can be divided into short-term extensions to finish open ends of the presented work and ideas for longer term projects that exceeded the scope of this thesis.

Among the short-term extensions, the implementation of the processing chains for agent interaction mining should be finished and a more thorough theoretical and empirical evaluation of the presented algorithms should be performed. The *Eclipse*-based experimentation environment needs to be extended and improved with respect to usability and stability. The preliminary integration of *DESMO-J*, RENEW, *ProM*, and (to some extent) *Eclipse* should be finished and improved, possibly trading genericness for better usability of the toolset. The improved component and workflow concepts underlying *ProM* 6 might further ease the embedding of process mining with simulation tools.

The very preliminary attempt of the author to combine the statistics, random distributions, and reporting functions of *DESMO-J* with the modeling facilities of RENEW and CAPA might be refactored and extended to become a Petri net-based MABS modeling, simulation, and analysis environment as proposed by Strümpel (2003). Given a larger example (like a Petri net-based re-implementation and extension of the courier service models), it would be interesting to further evaluate the possibilities of process mining with respect to protocol learning and validation in this context.

Longer term research projects are defined by the investigation of certain analysis perspectives and usage scenarios from the presented conceptual framework that were not elaborated in this thesis. Rainer Czogalla (2007) started an investigation into the analysis of structure and dynamics of spatial patterns emerging in agent-based simulations using techniques from pattern recognition and image processing. He also sketched a refined conceptual framework for this perspective and – as the co-developer of the *Eclipse*-based simulation environment – extended the experimentation tools with prototypical data collectors for spatial data.

In his ongoing dissertation project at the University of Hamburg, Sven Kruse investigates the adaptivity perspective with the goal to build and validate learning simulated agents in FAMOS (Kruse, 2007). While concepts from reinforcement learning are applied to realize the agents' adaptivity, *change mining* as proposed by Günther et al. (2006) will be used to validate the learning process (Kruse, 2008). This is due to the fact that, different from classical machine learning, agent learning in simulation is less focused on an optimal solution but on a valid representation of learning processes going on in the target system (Kruse, 2008): An enactment log and a change log of each learning agent will be generated based on the MXML logger from Section 8.2.4.1. Both logs will be analyzed using the change mining algorithms implemented in *ProM* (and possible extensions) to find regularities in the way agents change their internal models.

The level-encompassing perspective might be most demanding to analyze by means of data mining. On the one hand, a prerequisite to extract formal models of relations between multiple perspectives is that each considered perspective can be formally modeled itself. On the other hand, the question if an automated extraction of meaningful level-encompassing relations is possible by means of automated analysis techniques is closely related to open philosophical questions regarding emergence and micro/macro links in general. As mentioned above, an integration of the modeling and analysis framework of *complex events* proposed by Chen (2009) with advanced process mining techniques could be a viable approach to tackle this perspective.

Beyond that, the application of process mining to related areas might be investigated. Cabac (2007) pointed out that the principles of software architecture and team organization in Agent Oriented Software Engineering (AOSE) can both be based on the guiding metaphor of MAS. This similarity leads to the idea to found a framework for process mining in software engineering on the agent metaphor. Different from the work by Rubin et al. (2007), which only considers development processes, this might to some extent allow to apply similar models and algorithms for the analysis of development teams and developed software artifacts (Cabac and Denz, 2008, p. 90). Due to the close relations between AOSE and MABS, many concepts discussed in this thesis apply to the software engineering domain as well.[16]

For PAOSE the idea of process mining in software engineering opens a wide range of data sources to be considered. These range from a community system like CommSy (e.g. Jackewitz et al., 2002) used for the communication between developers to the low level logger of the RENEW Petri net simulator. Handling this variety of levels within a consistent conceptual framework appears to be a large challenge. Since reference nets are the basic modeling language in PAOSE, concepts for *process mining of reference nets* might be necessary.[17] However, it is still unclear what these concepts and techniques are, and if they go beyond mere aggregations of partial models mined from different perspectives into reference nets. Some preliminary ideas in this direction have been discussed in the position paper by Flick et al. (2010).

The courier service study in Chapter 8 is related to the field of *environmental informatics*. Few work exists, where process mining is applied to this domain. Wang (2011) use process mining to analyze carbon emissions of industrial processes. They adapt the *Heuristics Miner* algorithm (see Section 4.2.3.4) to regard for input and output materials of manufacturing steps (among others) as data attributes and display the results as colored Petri nets.[18]

As discussed above, even simple domain-specific enrichments of mined models might be helpful to analyze environmental aspects of mined processes. As a simple example, the order workflow in the *Hub and Shuttle* model might be enriched with information about emissions caused by relevant process steps in a Sankey diagram-like notation (see e.g. Schmidt, 2012).

Beyond that, process mining algorithms might be adapted to specific model representations used in environmental informatics. One example are material flow networks (Möller, 2000), a specialized form of Petri nets used to model and calculate the flow of materials and energy through a network of nodes. It is an open question, if existing process mining techniques can contribute to the automated modeling of material flow networks, since in many domains

---

[16] Actually several concepts presented in this thesis were developed with AOSE in mind.

[17] The idea of specific process mining techniques for reference nets was uttered by Prof. Dr. Ir. Wil van der Aalst during a discussion at PNSE'2007 in Siedlce (Poland).

[18] Only a brief abstract of this thesis was publicly available by the time of writing.

the structure of the network is of less interest than the (computational) specification of its transitions. Therefore, it might be interesting:

1. if domains exist where sufficient data on environmental aspects of production processes can be made available in the form of process logs,

2. if process mining algorithms can be adapted to reconstruct the structure of material flow networks as well as certain transition specifications[19],

3. how the semantics of material flow networks, more akin to an equation system than to the token flow of Petri nets, influences the applicability of process mining.

Finally, concluding a thesis on process mining in an agent context, we should be aware that the agent metaphor by definition includes us humans as well. Going beyond the borders of simulation, *social and ethical aspects of process mining* remain a central topic that requires further discussion and investigation inside and outside of the research community.

---

[19]The work by Wang (2011) might provide a starting point to tackle this question.

Bibliography

W. Aalst, V. Rubin, H. Verbeek, B. Dongen, E. Kindler, and C. Günther. Process mining: a two-step approach to balance between underfitting and overfitting. *Software & Systems Modeling*, 9:87–111, 2010. ISSN 1619-1366. doi: 10.1007/s10270-008-0106-z.

W. v. d. Aalst. Discovering coordination patterns using process mining. In L. Bocchi and P. Ciancarini, editors, *First International Workshop on Coordination and Petri Nets (PNC 2004)*, pages 49–64. STAR, Servizio Tipografico Area della Ricerca, CNR Pisa, Italy, 2004.

W. v. d. Aalst. Process mining in cscw systems. In W. Shen, A. James, et al., editors, *Proceedings of the 9th IEEE International Conference on Computer Supported Cooperative Work in Design*, pages 1–8, Coventry, 2005a. IEEE Computer Society Press.

W. v. d. Aalst. Business alignment: using process mining as a tool for delta analysis and conformance testing. *Requirements Engineering*, 10:198–211, 2005b. ISSN 0947-3602. 10.1007/s00766-005-0001-x.

W. v. d. Aalst. Process mining and monitoring processes and services: Workshop report. Technical report, Eindhoven University of Technology, 2006. URL http://wwwis.win.tue.nl/wvdaalst/publications/p340.pdf. last visit 2010-05-14.

W. v. d. Aalst. Process discovery: capturing the invisible. *Comp. Intell. Mag.*, 5:28–41, February 2010a. ISSN 1556-603X. doi: http://dx.doi.org/10.1109/MCI.2009.935307.

W. v. d. Aalst. Business process simulation revisited. In J. Barjis, editor, *Enterprise and Organizational Modeling and Simulation*, volume 63 of *Lecture Notes in Business Information Processing*, pages 1–14. Springer Berlin Heidelberg, 2010b. ISBN 978-3-642-15722-6. doi: 10.1007/978-3-642-15723-3_1.

W. v. d. Aalst. *Process Mining - Discovery, Conformance and Enhancement of Business Processes*. Springer, 2011a. ISBN 978-3-642-19344-6.

W. v. d. Aalst. On the representational bias in process mining. In *Proceedings of the 2011 IEEE 20th International Workshops on Enabling Technologies: Infrastructure for Collaborative Enterprises*, WETICE '11, pages 2–7, Washington, DC, USA, 2011b. IEEE Computer Society. ISBN 978-0-7695-4410-6. doi: 10.1109/WETICE.2011.64.

W. v. d. Aalst and T. Basten. Identifying commonalities and differences in object life cycles using behavioral inheritance. In *Proceedings of the 22nd International Conference on Application and Theory of Petri Nets*, ICATPN '01, pages 32–52, London, UK, UK, 2001. Springer-Verlag. ISBN 3-540-42252-8.

W. v. d. Aalst and K. v. Hee. *Workflow Management: Models, Methods, and Systems*. MIT Press, Cambridge (MA), 2002. ISBN 0-262-01189-1.

W. v. d. Aalst and M. Song. Mining social networks: Uncovering interaction patterns in business processes. In *Proceedings of the 2nd International Conference on Business Process Management*, Potsdam, 2004a.

W. v. d. Aalst and M. Song. Mining social networks: Uncovering interaction patterns in business processes. In *Proceedings of the 2nd International Conference on Business Process Management*, Potsdam, 2004b.

W. v. d. Aalst and A. Weijters. Process mining: a research agenda. *Computers in Industry*, 53(3): 231–244, 2004. ISSN 0166-3615. doi: http://dx.doi.org/10.1016/j.compind.2003.10.001.

W. v. d. Aalst, A. Weijters, and L. Maruster. Workflow mining: Which processes can be re-discovered? BETA working papers 74, Eindhoven University of Technology, 2002. URL http://beta.ieis.tue.nl/node/1351. last visit 2012-12-01.

W. v. d. Aalst, B. v. Dongen, J. Herbst, L. Maruster, G. Schimm, and A. Weijters. Workflow mining: A survey of issues and approaches. *Data and Knowledge Engineering*, 47(2):237–267, 2003a.

W. v. d. Aalst, A. Ter Hofstede, B. Kiepuszewski, and A. Barros. Workflow patterns. *Distrib. Parallel Databases*, 14(1):5–51, July 2003b. ISSN 0926-8782. doi: 10.1023/A:1022883727209.

W. v. d. Aalst, M. Dumas, C. Ouyang, A. Rozinat, and H. Verbeek. Choreography conformance checking: An approach based on BPEL and petri nets. Technical Report BPM-05-25, BPMcenter.org, 2005.

W. v. d. Aalst, H. Reijers, A. Weijters, B. v. Dongen, A. Alves De Medeiros, M. Song, and H. Verbeek. Business process mining: An industrial application. *Inf. Syst.*, 32(5):713–732, July 2007. ISSN 0306-4379. doi: 10.1016/j.is.2006.05.003.

W. v. d. Aalst, A. Adriansyah, and B. v. Dongen. Causal nets: A modeling language tailored towards process discovery. In J.-P. Katoen and B. König, editors, *CONCUR 2011 - Concurrency Theory*, volume 6901 of *Lecture Notes in Computer Science*, pages 28–42. Springer Berlin Heidelberg, 2011. ISBN 978-3-642-23216-9. doi: 10.1007/978-3-642-23217-6_3.

W. v. d. Aalst et al. Process mining manifesto. In F. Daniel, K. Barkaoui, S. Dustdar, W. Aalst, J. Mylopoulos, M. Rosemann, M. Shaw, and C. Szyperski, editors, *Business Process Management Workshops*, volume 99 of *Lecture Notes in Business Information Processing*, pages 169–194. Springer Berlin Heidelberg, 2012. ISBN 978-3-642-28108-2. 10.1007/978-3-642-28108-2_19.

M. Abdelkafi and L. Bouzguenda. Discovering organizational perspective in workflow using agent approach: an illustrative case study. In *Proceedings of the 6th International Workshop on Enterprise & Organizational Modeling and Simulation*, EOMAS '10, pages 84–98, Aachen, Germany, Germany, 2010. CEUR-WS.org. ISBN 978-1-4503-0463-4.

M. Abdelkafi, L. Bouzguenda, and F. Gargouri. Discopflow: A new tool for discovering organizational structures and interaction protocols in workflow. *CoRR*, abs/1203.4257, 2012.

A. Adriansyah, B. v. Dongen, and W. v. d. Aalst. Towards robust conformance checking. In M. Muehlen and J. Su, editors, *Business Process Management Workshops*, volume 66 of *Lecture Notes in Business Information Processing*, pages 122–133. Springer Berlin Heidelberg, 2011. ISBN 978-3-642-20510-1. doi: 10.1007/978-3-642-20511-8_11.

AgentUML. AUML Web Site, 2007. URL http://www.auml.org. last visit 2010-05-14.

H. Ahn and S. Park. A Multi-Agent System using JADE for Simulation of Supply Chains. In *4th Asian Business Workshop*, Chengu, August 2004.

H. Ahonen. Features of knowledge discovery systems. *InterCHANGE, The Newsletter of the International SGML Users' Group*, 4(2):15–16, 1998. URL http://www.cs.helsinki.fi/u/hahonen/features.txt. last visit 2012-09-18.

AiAccess. Glossary of data modelling, 2010. URL http://www.aiaccess.net/English/Glossaries/-GlosMod/e_gm_bias_variance.htm. last visit 2010-09-21.

I. Ailenei, A. Rozinat, A. Eckert, and W. v. d. Aalst. Definition and validation of process mining use cases. In F. Daniel, K. Barkaoui, S. Dustdar, W. v. Aalst, J. Mylopoulos, M. Rosemann, M. Shaw, and C. Szyperski, editors, *Business Process Management Workshops*, volume 99 of *Lecture Notes in Business Information Processing*, pages 75–86. Springer Berlin Heidelberg, 2012. ISBN 978-3-642-28108-2. 10.1007/978-3-642-28108-2_7.

D. Angluin. Inference of reversible languages. *Journal of the ACM*, 29(2):741–765, July 1982.

D. Angluin and C. Smith. Inductive inference: Theory and methods. *ACM Comput. Surv.*, 15:237–269, September 1983. ISSN 0360-0300. doi: http://doi.acm.org/10.1145/356914.356918.

L. Antunes and H. Coelho. On how to conduct experimental research with self-motivated agents. In G. Lindemann, D. Moldt, and M. Paolucci, editors, *Regulated Agent-Based Social Systems*, volume 2934 of *Lecture Notes in Computer Science*, pages 31–47. Springer Berlin Heidelberg, 2004. ISBN 978-3-540-20923-2. doi: 10.1007/978-3-540-25867-4_3.

K. Arnold, J. Gosling, and D. Holmes. *The Java Programming Language, Third Edition*. Addison-Wesley, 2000. ISBN 0-201-70433-1.

J. Arroyo, S. Hassan, C. Gutierrez, and J. Pavon. Re-thinking simulation: a methodological approach for the application of data mining in agent-based modelling. *Computational & Mathematical Organization Theory*, 16:416–435, 2010. ISSN 1381-298X. 10.1007/s10588-010-9078-y.

S. Auyang. *Foundations of Complex System Theories*. Cambridge University Press, 1998.

R. Axelrod. The convergence and stability of cultures: Local convergence and global polarization. Working Papers 95-03-028, Santa Fe Institute, Mar. 1995. URL http://ideas.repec.org/p/wop/safiwp/95-03-028.html. last visit 2010-09-21.

R. Axtell, R. Axelrod, J. Epstein, and M. Cohen. Aligning simulation models: A case study and results. *Computational & Mathematical Organization Theory*, 1:123–141, 1996. ISSN 1381-298X. 10.1007/BF01299065.

R. Bachmann. *Ein flexibler, CORBA-basierter Ansatz für die verteilte, komponentenbasierte Simulation*. PhD thesis, Department of Informatics, University of Hamburg, 2003.

R. Bachmann, B. Gehlsen, and N. Knaak. Werkzeuggestützte Kalibrierung agentenbasierter Simulationsmodelle. In T. Schulze, S. Schlechtweg, and V. Hinz, editors, *Proceedings Simulation und Visualisierung 2004*, pages 115–126, Magdeburg, March 2004. SCS-Europe.

E. Badouel and P. Darondeau. Theory of regions. In W. Reisig and G. Rozenberg, editors, *Lectures on Petri Nets I: Basic Models*, volume 1491 of *Lecture Notes in Computer Science*, pages 529–586. Springer Berlin / Heidelberg, 1998. ISBN 978-3-540-65306-6. 10.1007/3-540-65306-6_22.

E. Badouel, L. Bernardinello, and P. Darondeau. Polynomial algorithms for the synthesis of bounded nets. In P. Mosses, M. Nielsen, and M. Schwartzbach, editors, *TAPSOFT '95: Theory and Practice of Software Development*, volume 915 of *Lecture Notes in Computer Science*, pages 364–378. Springer Berlin / Heidelberg, 1995. ISBN 978-3-540-59293-8. 10.1007/3-540-59293-8_207.

E. Badouel, J. Chenou, and G. Guillou. An axiomatization of the token game based on petri algebras. *Fundam. Inf.*, 77(3):187–215, Aug. 2007. ISSN 0169-2968.

J. Bae, J. Caverlee, L. Liu, B. Rouse, and H. Yan. Process mining by measuring process block similarity. In J. Eder and S. Dustdar, editors, *Business Process Management Workshops*, number 4103 in LNCS, pages 105–116, Berlin, September 2006. Springer.

Bibliography

O. Balci. Verification, Validation and Testing. In J. Banks, editor, *Handbook of Simulation – Principles, Methodology, Advances, Applications, and Practice*, pages 335–393. Wiley, New York, 1998. Chapter 10.

J. Banks, J. C. II, and B. Nelson. *Discrete-Event System Simulation*. Prentice Hall, Upper Saddle River, 2nd edition, 1999.

O. Baqueiro, Y. Wang, P. McBurney, and F. Coenen. Integrating data mining and agent based modeling and simulation. In P. Perner, editor, *Advances in Data Mining. Applications and Theoretical Aspects*, volume 5633 of *Lecture Notes in Computer Science*, pages 220–231. Springer Berlin / Heidelberg, 2009. ISBN 978-3-642-03066-6. 10.1007/978-3-642-03067-3_18.

K. Barber and D. Lam. Enabling abductive reasoning for agent software comprehension. In *Proceedings of the 18th International Joint Conference on Artificial Intelligence (IJCAI-2003) Workshop on Agents and Automated Reasoning*, pages 7 – 13, Acapulco, Mexico, August 2003.

P. Barry and M. Koehler. Simulation in context: using data farming for decision support. In *Proceedings of the 36th conference on Winter simulation*, WSC '04, pages 814–819. Winter Simulation Conference, 2004. ISBN 0-7803-8786-4.

R. Barton and H. Szczerbicka. Maschinelles Lernen zur Validation von Simulationsmodellen. In H. Szczerbicka and T. Uthmann, editors, *Modellierung, Simulation und Künstliche Intelligenz*, pages 387–416. SCS-Europe, 2000.

L. Bass, P. Clements, and R. Kazman. *Software Architecture in Practice*. SEI Series in Software Engineering. Pearson Education, 2012. ISBN 9780132942782.

B. Bauer and J. Odell. Uml 2.0 and agents: how to build agent-based systems with the new uml standard. *Eng. Appl. of AI*, 18(2):141–157, 2005.

B. Baumgarten. *Petri-Netze – Grundlagen und Anwendungen*. Spektrum, Heidelberg, 1996. ISBN 3-8274-0175-5.

F. Bause and P. Kritzinger. *Stochastic Petri Nets - An Introduction to the Theory*. Advanced Studies in Computer Science. Vieweg, Braunschweig, 1996.

I. Bayraktar. The business value of process mining – bringing it all together. Master's thesis, Eindhoven University of Technology, Faculty of Mathematics and Computer Science, Eindhoven (The Netherlands), October 2011.

F. Bellifemine, A. Poggi, and G. Rimassa. Developing Multi-Agent-Systems with JADE. In C. Castelfranchi and Y. Lesperance, editors, *Intelligent Agents VII*, pages 89–103, Berlin, 2001. Springer.

E. Bellodi, F. Riguzzi, and E. Lamma. Probabilistic declarative process mining. In Y. Bi and M.-A. Williams, editors, *Knowledge Science, Engineering and Management, 4th International Conference, KSEM 2010, Belfast, Northern Ireland, UK, September 1-3, 2010. Proceedings*, volume 6291 of *Lecture Notes in Computer Science*, pages 292–303. Springer, 2010.

I. Ben-Gal. Bayesian networks. In F. Ruggeri, F. Faltin, and R. Kenett, editors, *Encyclopedia of Statistics in Quality and Reliability*. John Wiley and Sons, 2007. URL http://www.eng.tau.ac.il/bengal/BN.pdf. last visit 2012-09-10.

R. Bergenthum, J. Desel, R. Lorenz, and S. Mauser. Process mining based on regions of languages. In G. Alonso, P. Dadam, and M. Rosemann, editors, *Business Process Management*, volume 4714 of *Lecture Notes in Computer Science*, pages 375–383. Springer Berlin / Heidelberg, 2007.

M. Berry and G. Linoff. *Data Mining Techniques – For Marketing, Sales, and Customer Relationship Management.* Wiley, Indianapolis, 2004.

T. Bessey. Implementation of on-line simulation with the colored petri net simulator renew. In *Proceedings of IEEE International Conference on Systems, Man and Cybernetics (SMC)*, pages 5019–5024. IEEE, 2004.

T. Betz, L. Cabac, and M. Güttler. Improving the development tool chain in the context of Petri net-based software development. In M. Duvigneau, D. Moldt, and K. Hiraishi, editors, *Petri Nets and Software Engineering. International Workshop PNSE'11, Newcastle upon Tyne, UK, June 2011. Proceedings*, volume 723 of *CEUR Workshop Proceedings*, pages 167–178. CEUR-WS.org, June 2011.

L. Birta and F. Özmizrak. A Knowledge-Based Approach for the Validation of Simulation Models: The Foundations. *ACM Transactions on Modeling and Computer Simulation*, 6(1):76–98, January 1996.

G. Birtwistle. *DEMOS, a system for discrete event modelling on simula.* Macmillan, London, 1979.

M. Born, E. Holz, and O. Kath. *Softwareentwicklung mit UML 2 - Die "neuen" Entwurfstechniken UML 2, MOF 2 und MDA.* Programmer's Choice. Addison-Wesley, München, 2004.

F. Boschetti. *Application of Genetic Algorithms to the Inversion of Geophysical Data.* PhD thesis, University of Western Australia, 1995.

R. J. C. Bose and W. v. d. Aalst. Abstractions in process mining: A taxonomy of patterns. In *Proceedings of the 7th International Conference on Business Process Management*, BPM '09, pages 159–175, Berlin, Heidelberg, 2009. Springer-Verlag. ISBN 978-3-642-03847-1. doi: 10.1007/978-3-642-03848-8_12.

R. J. C. Bose and U. Suresh. Root cause analysis using sequence alignment and latent semantic indexing. In *Proceedings of the 19th Australian Conference on Software Engineering*, pages 367–376, Washington, DC, USA, 2008. IEEE Computer Society. ISBN 978-0-7695-3100-7.

R. J. C. Bose, W. v. d. Aalst, I. Zliobaite, and M. Pechenizkiy. Handling concept drift in process mining. In H. Mouratidis and C. Rolland, editors, *Advanced Information Systems Engineering - 23rd International Conference, CAiSE 2011, London, UK, June 20-24, 2011. Proceedings*, volume 6741 of *Lecture Notes in Computer Science*, pages 391–405. Springer, 2011a.

R. J. C. Bose, H. E. Verbeek, and W. v. d. Aalst. Discovering hierarchical process models using prom. In S. Nurcan, editor, *Proceedings of the CAiSE Forum 2011, London, UK, June 22-24, 2011*, pages 33–40. CEUR-WS.org, 2011b.

T. Bosse, D. Lam, and K. Barber. Empirical analysis for agent system comprehension and verification. In *Intelligent Agent Technology, 2006. IAT '06. IEEE/WIC/ACM International Conference on*, pages 723–729, dec. 2006. doi: 10.1109/IAT.2006.61.

H. Bossel. *Simulation dynamischer Systeme – Grundwissen, Methoden, Programme.* Vieweg, Brunswick, 1989.

J. Botía, A. López-Acosta, and A. Gómez-Skarmeta. ACLAnalyser: A Tool for Debugging Multi-Agent Systems. In R. L. de Mántaras and L. Saitta, editors, *Proceedings of the 16th European Conference on Artificial Intelligence*, pages 967–968, Valencia, 2004. IOS.

S. Bowers, B. Ludäscher, A. Ngu, and T. Critchlow. Enabling scientific workflow reuse through structured composition of dataflow and control-flow. In *Proc. of the ICDE Workshop on Workflow and Data Flow for Scientific Applications (SciFlow)*. IEEE Computer Society, 2006.

D. Brade. A generalized approach for the verification and validation of models and simulation results. PhD Thesis, University of the Federal Armed Forces Munich, October 2003.

T. Brady and E. Yellig. Simulation data mining: a new form of computer simulation output. In *Proceedings of the 37th conference on Winter simulation*, WSC '05, pages 285–289. Winter Simulation Conference, 2005. ISBN 0-7803-9519-0.

S. Brainov and T. Sandholm. Reasoning about others: Representing and processing infinite belief hierarchies. In *4th International Conference on Multi-Agent Systems (ICMAS 2000), 10-12 July 2000, Boston, MA, USA*, pages 71–78. IEEE Computer Society, 2000.

K. Brandstein et al. Data farming - a meta-technique for research in the 21st century. In *Proceedings of the 1998 Winter Simulation Conference*, pages 100–106, November 1998.

I. Bratko. *PROLOG Programming for Artificial Intelligence*. Addison-Wesley Longman Publishing Co., Inc., Boston, MA, USA, 2nd edition, 1990. ISBN 0201416069.

M. Bratman. *Intention, Plans and Practical Reason*. Harvard University, Cambridge, 1987.

C. Bratosin. *Grid Architecture for Distributed Process Mining*. Phd thesis, Eindhoven University of Technology, Eindhoven, 2011.

C. Bratosin, W. v. d. Aalst, and N. Sidorova. Modeling grid workflows with colored petri nets. In K. Jensen, editor, *Proceedings of the 8th Workshop and Tutorial on Practical Use of Coloured Petri Nets and the CPN Tools*, pages 67–86. Aarhus Department of Computer Science, Aarhus (Denmark), October 2007.

L. Braubach. *Architekturen und Methoden zur Entwicklung verteilter agentenorientierter Softwaresysteme*. Dissertation, University of Hamburg, Department of Informatics, Hamburg, 2007.

L. Braubach, A. Pokahr, W. Lamersdorf, K.-H. Krempels, and P.-O. Woelk. Time synchronization for process flows in multi-agent systems. In *Second Seminar on Advanced Research in Electronic Business (EBR03)*, 2003.

R. Brooks. *Cambrian Intelligence – A Short History of the New AI*. MIT, Cambridge, 1999.

P. Bruza and T. van der Weide. The semantics of data flow diagrams. In *In Proceedings of the International Conference on Management of Data*, pages 66–78. McGraw-Hill Publishing Company, 1993.

A. Burattin and A. Sperduti. Automatic determination of parameters' values for heuristics miner++. In *Proceedings of the IEEE Congress on Evolutionary Computation, CEC 2010, Barcelona, Spain, 18-23 July 2010*, pages 1–8. IEEE, 2010.

E. Burke and G. Kendall. Introduction. In E. Burke and G. Kendall, editors, *Search Methodologies*, pages 5–18. Springer US, 2005. ISBN 978-0-387-28356-2. 10.1007/0-387-28356-0_1.

L. Cabac. *Entwicklung von geometrisch unterscheidbaren Komponenten zur Vereinheitlichung von Mulan-Protokollen*. Studienarbeit, University of Hamburg, Department of Informatics, 2002.

L. Cabac. Modeling agent interaction protocols with auml diagrams and petri nets. Master's thesis, University of Hamburg, Department of Informatics, 2003.

L. Cabac. Multi-agent system: A guiding metaphor for the organization of software development projects. In P. Petta, editor, *Proceedings of the Fifth German Conference on Multiagent System Technologies*, volume 4687 of *Lecture Notes in Computer Science*, pages 1–12, Leipzig, Germany, 2007. Springer.

L. Cabac. *Modeling Petri Net-Based Multi-Agent Applications.* Dissertation, University of Hamburg, Department of Informatics, 2010.

L. Cabac and N. Denz. Net components for the integration of process mining into agent-oriented software engineering. *Transactions on Petri Nets and Other Models of Concurrency I (ToPNoC)*, 5100:86–103, Nov. 2008.

L. Cabac and N. Knaak. Process mining in Petri net-based agent-oriented software development. In Moldt et al. (2007), pages 7–21.

L. Cabac, D. Moldt, and H. Rölke. A proposal for structuring Petri net-based agent interaction protocols. In W. v. d. Aalst and E. Best, editors, *Lecture Notes in Computer Science: 24th International Conference on Application and Theory of Petri Nets, ICATPN 2003, Netherlands, Eindhoven*, volume 2679, pages 102–120, Berlin Heidelberg: Springer, June 2003.

L. Cabac, M. Duvigneau, D. Moldt, and H. Rölke. Modeling dynamic architectures using nets-within-nets. In *Applications and Theory of Petri Nets 2005. 26th International Conference, ICATPN 2005, Miami, USA, June 2005. Proceedings*, pages 148–167, 2005.

L. Cabac, N. Knaak, and D. Moldt. Net components for the modelling of process mining chains. In D. Moldt, editor, *Proceedings of the 13th Workshop on Algorithms and Tools for Petri Nets (AWPN'06), published as Technical Report 267 of the Department of Informatics*, pages 25–31, Hamburg, October 2006a.

L. Cabac, N. Knaak, and D. Moldt. Applying process mining to interaction analysis of Petri net-based multi-agent models. Technical Report 271, University of Hamburg, Department of Informatics, May 2006b.

L. Cabac, N. Knaak, D. Moldt, and H. Rölke. Analysis of multi-agent interactions with process mining techniques. In *Proceedings of the 4th German Conference on Multiagent System Technology (MATES 2006)*, pages 12–23, Erfurt, September 2006c.

L. Cabac, T. Dörges, M. Duvigneau, C. Reese, and M. Wester-Ebbinghaus. Application development with Mulan. In Moldt et al. (2007), pages 145–159.

L. Cabac, T. Dörges, M. Duvigenau, D. Moldt, C. Reese, and M. Wester-Ebbinghaus. Agent models for concurrent software systems. In H. Bergmann et al., editors, *Proceedings of the 6th German Conference on Multiagent System Technology (MATES 2008)*, pages 37–48, Heidelberg, 2008a. Springer.

L. Cabac, T. Dörges, and H. Rölke. A monitoring toolset for Petri net-based agent-oriented software engineering. In R. Valk and K. v. Hee, editors, *29th International Conference on Application and Theory of Petri Nets, Xi'an, China*, volume 5062 of *Lecture Notes in Computer Science*, pages 399–408. Springer, June 2008b.

G. Calderon-Ruiz and M. Sepulveda. Discovering potential failures in business processes extending process mining techniques. In *XXX International Conference of the Chilean Computer Science Society (SCCC 2011)*, Curico, Chile, 2011. URL http://jcc2011.utalca.cl/actas/SCCC/jcc2011_submission_8.pdf. last visit 2012-12-03.

B. Calvez and G. Hutzler. Automatic tuning of agent-based models using genetic algorithms. In J. Sichman and L. Antunes, editors, *Multi-Agent-Based Simulation VI*, number 3891 in LNAI, pages 41–57, Heidelberg, 2006. Springer.

S. Canbaz. Discovering artifact-centric processes – mining assistance handling process of a first aid company using an artifact-centric approach. Master's thesis, Eindhoven University of Technology, Eindhoven, October 2011.

Bibliography

J. Cannan. *SQL - the standard handbook : based on the new SQL standard (ISO 9075:1992(E))*. McGraw-Hill, London, 1993. ISBN 0077076648.

E. Cantú-Paz, S.-C. Cheung, and C. Kamath. Retrieval of Similar Objects in Simulation Data Using Machine Learning Techniques. In *Image Processing: Algorithms and Systems III. SPIE Electronic Imaging*, San Jose, January 2004.

L. Cao. *Data mining and multi-agent integration*. Springer, Dordrecht, 2009. ISBN 978-1-441-90521-5.

P. Cariani. Emergence and Artificial Life. In C. Langton, C. Taylor, J. Farmer, and S. Rasmussen, editors, *Artificial Life II*, Reading, 1991. Addison-Wesley.

J. Carmona and J. Cortadella. Process mining meets abstract interpretation. In *Proceedings of the 2010 European conference on Machine learning and knowledge discovery in databases: Part I*, ECML PKDD'10, pages 184–199, Berlin, Heidelberg, 2010. Springer-Verlag. ISBN 3-642-15879-X, 978-3-642-15879-7.

J. Carmona, J. Cortadella, and M. Kishinevsky. A region-based algorithm for discovering petri nets from event logs. In M. Dumas, M. Reichert, and M.-C. Shan, editors, *Business Process Management*, volume 5240 of *Lecture Notes in Computer Science*, pages 358–373. Springer Berlin / Heidelberg, 2008.

J. Carmona, J. Cortadella, and M. Kishinevsky. Genet: A tool for the synthesis and mining of petri nets. In *Application of Concurrency to System Design, 2009. ACSD '09. Ninth International Conference on*, pages 181–185, july 2009a. doi: 10.1109/ACSD.2009.6.

J. Carmona, J. Cortadella, and M. Kishinevsky. Divide-and-conquer strategies for process mining. In U. Dayal, J. Eder, J. Koehler, and H. Reijers, editors, *Business Process Management*, volume 5701 of *Lecture Notes in Computer Science*, pages 327–343. Springer Berlin / Heidelberg, 2009b. ISBN 978-3-642-03847-1. 10.1007/978-3-642-03848-8_22.

M. Cattafi, E. Lamma, F. Riguzzi, and S. Storari. Incremental declarative process mining. In E. Szczerbicki and N. Nguyen, editors, *Smart Information and Knowledge Management: Advances, Challenges, and Critical Issues*, volume 260 of *Studies in Computational Intelligence*, pages 103–127. Springer, 2010.

S. Chai, F. Su, and W. Ma. An approach to discovering spatial-temporal patterns in geographical processes. In W. Shi, A. Yeh, Y. Leung, C. Zhou, W. Cartwright, G. Gartner, L. Meng, and M. Peterson, editors, *Advances in Spatial Data Handling and GIS*, Lecture Notes in Geoinformation and Cartography, pages 49–62. Springer Berlin Heidelberg, 2012. ISBN 978-3-642-25926-5. 10.1007/978-3-642-25926-5_5.

Chair for Bioinformatics and Information Mining at Konstanz University. The Konstanz Information Miner (KNIME). online, 2007. http://www.knime.org, last visit 2012-12-03.

P. Chamoni. Data Mining, 2009. URL http://www.enzyklopaedie-der-wirtschaftsinformatik.de/wi-enzyklopaedie/lexikon/daten-wissen/-Business-Intelligence/Analytische-Informationssysteme-Methoden-der-/Data-Mining/-index.html/?searchterm=data mining. last visit 2010-09-19.

C.-C. Chen. *Complex Event Types for Agent-Based Simulation*. Phd thesis, University College London, Department of Computer Science, 2009.

C.-C. Chen and D. Hardoon. Learning from multi-level behaviours in agent-based simulations: a systems biology application. *J. Simulation*, 4(3):196–203, 2010.

C.-C. Chen, S. Nagl, and C. Clack. A method for validating and discovering associations between multi-level emergent behaviours in agent-based simulations. In N. Nguyen, G. Jo, R. Howlett, and L. Jain, editors, *Agent and Multi-Agent Systems: Technologies and Applications, Second KES International Symposium, KES-AMSTA 2008, Incheon, Korea, March 26-28, 2008. Proceedings*, volume 4953 of *Lecture Notes in Computer Science*, pages 1–10. Springer, 2008.

C.-C. Chen, C. Clack, and S. Nagl. Identifying multi-level emergent behaviors in agent-directed simulations using complex event type specifications. *Simulation*, 86(1):41–51, 2010.

F. Chesani, P. Mello, M. Montali, and P. Torroni. Monitoring time-aware commitments within agent-based simulation environments. *Cybernetics and Systems*, 42(7):546–566, 2011. doi: 10.1080/01969722.2011.610711.

S. Christley and G. Madey. Analysis of activity in the open source software development community. In *Proceedings of the 40th Annual Hawaii International Conference on System Sciences*, HICSS '07, page 166b, Washington, DC, USA, 2007a. IEEE Computer Society. ISBN 0-7695-2755-8. doi: http://dx.doi.org/ 10.1109/HICSS.2007.74.

S. Christley and G. Madey. Analysis of activity in the open source software development community. *hicss*, 0:166b, 2007b. ISSN 1530-1605. doi: http://doi.ieeecomputersociety.org/ 10.1109/HICSS.2007.74.

S. Christley, J. Xu, Y. Gao, and G. Madey. Public goods theory of the open source development community using agent-based simulation. In *Agent 2004 Workshop*, Chicago (IL), October 2004.

T.-Q. Chu, A. Drogoul, A. Boucher, and J.-D. Zucker. Interactive learning of independent experts' criteria for rescue simulations. *J. UCS*, 15(13):2701–2725, 2009.

K. Cios, W. Pedrycz, R. Swiniarski, and L. Kurgan. *Data mining: a knowledge discovery approach*. Springer, New York, 2007. ISBN 0-387-33333-9, 978-0-387-33333-5*Gb.

E. Clarke, O. Grumberg, and D. Peled. *Model Checking*. MIT Press, Cambridge, 1999.

P. Cohen. *Empirical Methods for Artificial Intelligence*. MIT Press, Cambridge (MA), 1995.

J. Cook and A. Wolf. Discovering models of software processes from event-based data. *ACM Trans. Softw. Eng. Methodol.*, 7(3):215–249, 1998. ISSN 1049-331X. doi: http://doi.acm.org/ 10.1145/287000.287001.

J. Cortadella, M. Kishinevsky, A. Kondratyev, L. Lavagno, and A. Yakovlev. Petrify: a tool for manipulating concurrent specifications and synthesis of asynchronous controllers. *IEICE Trans. Inf. and Syst.*, pages 315–325, March 1997.

R. Czogalla. Analyse raumbezogener Simulationsdaten mit Methoden der Mustererkennung. In *Simulation und Visualisierung - Beiträge zum Doktorandenforum Diskrete Simulation*, Magdeburg, September 2007. SCS Publishing House.

R. Czogalla and B. Matzen. Agentenbasierte Simulation von Personenbewegungen in kontinuierlichem Raum. Diploma Thesis, Faculty of Informatics, University of Hamburg, December 2003.

R. Czogalla, N. Knaak, and B. Page. Simulating the Eclipse way - A generic experimentation environment based on the eclipse platform. In *20th European Conference on Modelling and Simulation (ECMS 2006)*, Bonn, September 2006.

O. Dalle. The osa project: an example of component based software engineering techniques applied to simulation. In *Proceedings of the 2007 summer computer simulation conference*, SCSC, pages 1155–1162, San Diego, CA, USA, 2007. Society for Computer Simulation International. ISBN 1-56555-316-0.

Bibliography

V. Dallmeier, C. Lindig, A. Wasylkowski, and A. Zeller. Mining object behavior with adabu. In *WODA 2006: ICSE Workshop on Dynamic Analysis*, May 2006.

N. David, J. S. Sichman, and H. Coelho. Towards an emergence-driven software process for agent-based simulation. In J. S. Sichman, F. Bousquet, and P. Davidsson, editors, *Multi-Agent Based Simulation II*, pages 89–104. Springer, 2002. Berlin.

P. Davidsson. Multi agent based simulation: Beyond social simulation. In S. Moss and P. Davidsson, editors, *Multi-Agent-Based Simulation*, pages 97–107, Berlin, 2000. Springer.

J. Davis, T. Kameda, C. Parks, M. Stasson, and S. Zimmerman. Some social mechanics of group decision making: The distribution of opinion, polling sequence, and implications for consensus. *Journal of Personality and Social Psychology*, 57(6):1000–1012, Dec. 1989.

G. De Giacomo, Y. Lespérance, and C. Muise. On supervising agents in situation-determined Con-Golog. In *Proceedings of the 11th International Conference on Autonomous Agents and Multiagent Systems - Volume 2*, AAMAS '12, pages 1031–1038, Richland, SC, 2012. International Foundation for Autonomous Agents and Multiagent Systems. ISBN 0-9817381-2-5, 978-0-9817381-2-3.

N. De Wet and P. Kritzinger. Using UML models for the performance analysis of network systems. In *Proceedings of the Workshop on Integrated-reliability with Telecommunications and UML Languages (WITUL)*, Rennes, Brittany, France, 2004.

T. De Wolf and T. Holvoet. Designing self-organising emergent systems based on information flows and feedback-loops. In *Proceedings of the First International Conference on Self-Adaptive and Self-Organizing Systems*, SASO '07, pages 295–298, Washington, DC, USA, 2007. IEEE Computer Society. ISBN 0-7695-2906-2. doi: http://dx.doi.org/10.1109/SASO.2007.16.

H. Deecke. Stadtkuriere - Szenarien zur Simulation unterschiedlicher Szenarien in MOBILE. Technical report, TU Hamburg-Harburg, 1997. Internal Report.

H. Deecke, N. Knaak, R. Meyer, and B. Page. Nachhaltige Logistikkonzepte für Stadtkurierdienste: Projekt-Endbericht. Technical report, University of Hamburg, 2003.

H. Deecke, N. Knaak, R. Meyer, and B. Page. Agentenbasierte Simulation nachhaltiger Logistikkonzepte für Stadtkurierdienste: Methoden, Werkzeuge und Anwendung. Technical report, University of Hamburg, 2004.

M. DeYoung. Dynamic protocol reverse engineering: A grammatical inference approach. Master's thesis, Air Force Institute of Technology, 2008. URL http://books.google.de/ books?id=-hwttwAACAAJ. last visit 2012-12-03.

Z. Diaz, M. J. S. Vargas, J. Hernandez, and E. D. Pozo. Machine learning and statistical techniques. an application to the prediction of insolvency in spanish non-life insurance companies. *The International Journal of Digital Accounting Research*, 5:1–45, 2005. ISSN 1577-8517.

V. Diekert and G. Rozenberg, editors. *The Book of Traces*. World Scientific Publishing Co., Inc., River Edge, NJ, USA, 1995. ISBN 9810220588.

C. Dimou, A. Symeonidis, and P. Mitkas. Evaluating knowledge intensive multi-agent systems. In V. Gorodetsky, C. Zhang, V. Skormin, and L. Cao, editors, *Autonomous Intelligent Systems: Multi-Agents and Data Mining, Second International Workshop, AIS-ADM 2007, St. Petersburg, Russia, June 3-5, 2007, Proceedings*, volume 4476 of *Lecture Notes in Computer Science*, pages 74–87. Springer, 2007.

C.-C. Dolean and R. Petrusel. A mining algorithm for extracting decision process data models. *Informatica Economica*, 15(4):79–95, 2011.

W. Domschke. *Logistik Bd. 1: Transport, Grundlagen, Lineare Transport- und Umladeprobleme.* Oldenbourg, 1989. 3. erg. Auflage.

B. v. Dongen and W. v. d. Aalst. Multi-phase process mining: Building instance graphs. In P. Atzeni, W. Chu, H. Lu, S. Zhou, and T.-W. Ling, editors, *Conceptual Modeling - ER 2004*, volume 3288 of *Lecture Notes in Computer Science*, pages 362–376. Springer Berlin / Heidelberg, 2004. ISBN 978-3-540-23723-5. 10.1007/978-3-540-30464-7_29.

B. v. Dongen, A. d. Medeiros, H. Verbeek, A. Weijters, and W. v. d. Aalst. The ProM framework: A new era in process mining tool support. In *ICATPN*, pages 444–454, 2005.

B. v. Dongen, J. Desel, and W. v. d. Aalst. Aggregating causal runs into workflow nets. Beta working paper series, Eindhoven University of Technology, Research School for Operations Management and Logistics, 2006a. URL http://books.google.de/books?id=jVA3MwAACAAJ. last visit 2012-12-03.

B. v. Dongen, J. v. Luin, and E. Verbeek. Process mining in a multi-agent auctioning system. In D. Moldt, editor, *Proceedings of the 4th International Workshop on Modelling of Objects, Components, and Agents*, pages 145–160, Turku, June 2006b.

B. v. Dongen, J. Mendling, and W. v. d. Aalst. Structural patterns for soundness of business process models. In *Enterprise Distributed Object Computing Conference, 2006. EDOC '06. 10th IEEE International*, pages 116–128, October 2006c. doi: 10.1109/EDOC.2006.56.

B. v. Dongen, N. Busi, and G. Pinna. An iterative algorithm for applying the theory of regions in process mining. Technical Report 195, Department of Technology Management, Eindhoven University of Technology, 2007. URL http://beta.ieis.tue.nl/node/1225. last visit 2012-12-03.

A. Drogoul, D. Vanbergue, and T. Meurisse. Multi-agent-based simulation: Where are the agents. In J. S. Sichman, F. Bousquet, and P. Davidsson, editors, *Multi-Agent-Based Simulation II*, pages 1–15, Berlin, 2002. Springer.

M. Dumas, W. v. d. Aalst, and A. t. Hofstede. *Process Aware Information Systems: Bridging People and Software Through Process Technology.* Wiley-Interscience, September 2005. ISBN 0471663069.

M. Dunham. *Data Mining: Introductory and Advanced Topics.* Prentice-Hall, 2003. ISBN 0-13-088892-3.

S. Dustdar and R. Gombotz. Discovering web service workflows using web services interaction mining. *International Journal of Business Process Integration and Management (IJBPIM)*, 2006.

S. Dustdar and T. Hoffmann. Interaction pattern detection in process oriented information systems. *Data Knowl. Eng.*, 62:138–155, July 2007. ISSN 0169-023X. doi: 10.1016/j.datak.2006.07.010.

M. Duvigneau. Bereitstellung einer Agentenplattform für petrinetzbasierte Agenten. Diploma Thesis, Department of Informatics, University of Hamburg, 2003.

M. Duvigneau, D. Moldt, and H. Rölke. Concurrent architecture for a multi-agent platform. In F. Giunchiglia, J. Odell, and G. Weiß, editors, *Agent-Oriented Software Engineering III. Third International Workshop, Agent-oriented Software Engineering (AOSE) 2002, Bologna, Italy, July 2002. Revised Papers and Invited Contributions*, volume 2585 of *Lecture Notes in Computer Science*, pages 59–72, Berlin, 2003. Springer.

M. Duvigneau, H. Rölke, and F. Wienberg. Informal introduction to the feature structure nets tool – a tool for process and information modeling. In D. Moldt, editor, *Proceedings of the 13th Workshop Application and Tools for Petri Nets. AWPN'06*, number FBI-HH-B-267/06 in Fachbereichsbericht, pages 85–91. University of Hamburg, Department of Informatics, 2006.

D. Eagleman. *Inkognito – Die geheimen Eigenleben unseres Gehirns*. Campus, Frankfurt am Main, 2011. ISBN 978-3-593-38974-5.

B. Edmonds. The Use of Models – making MABS more informative. In S. Moss and P. Davidson, editors, *Multi Agent Based Simulation 2000*, pages 15–32, Berlin, 2000. Springer.

B. Edmonds and J. Bryson. The insufficiency of formal design methods - the necessity of an experimental approach - for the understanding and control of complex MAS. In *AAMAS*, pages 938–945, 2004.

B. Edmonds, O. Teran, and G. Polhill. To the outer limits and beyond – characterising the envelope of sets of social simulation trajectories. CPM Report 06-161, Centre for Policy Modelling, 2006. URL http://cfpm.org/cpmrep162.html. last visit 2012-12-03.

C. Ellis, A. Rembert, K.-H. Kim, and J. Wainer. Beyond workflow mining. In S. Dustdar, J. Fiadeiro, and A. Sheth, editors, *Business Process Management*, volume 4102 of *Lecture Notes in Computer Science*, pages 49–64. Springer Berlin / Heidelberg, 2006. ISBN 978-3-540-38901-9. 10.1007/11841760_5.

J. Epstein and R. Axtell. *Growing Artificial Societies – Social Science from the Bottom Up*. MIT, Cambridge, 1996.

R. Ewald, A. Uhrmacher, and K. Saha. Data mining for simulation algorithm selection. In *Proceedings of the 2nd International Conference on Simulation Tools and Techniques*, Simutools '09, pages 14:1–14:10, ICST, Brussels, Belgium, Belgium, 2009. ICST (Institute for Computer Sciences, Social-Informatics and Telecommunications Engineering). ISBN 978-963-9799-45-5. doi: 10.4108/ICST.SIMUTOOLS2009.5659.

R. Fablet and P. Bouthemy. Motion recognition using nonparametric image motion models estimated from temporal and multiscale co-occurrence statistics. *Pattern Analysis and Machine Intelligence, IEEE Transactions on*, 25(12):1619 – 1624, December 2003. ISSN 0162-8828. doi: 10.1109/TPAMI.2003.1251155.

D. Fahland, M. de Leoni, B. v. Dongen, and W. v. d. Aalst. Behavioral conformance of artifact-centric process models. In W. Abramowicz, editor, *BIS*, volume 87 of *Lecture Notes in Business Information Processing*, pages 37–49. Springer, 2011a. ISBN 978-3-642-21829-3.

D. Fahland, M. de Leoni, B. v. Dongen, and W. v. d. Aalst. Many-to-many: Some observations on interactions in artifact choreographies. In D. Eichhorn, A. Koschmider, and H. Zhang, editors, *ZEUS*, volume 705 of *CEUR Workshop Proceedings*, pages 9–15. CEUR-WS.org, 2011b.

D. Fahland, M. de Leoni, B. v. Dongen, and W. v. d. Aalst. Checking behavioral conformance of artifacts. BPM Center Report BPM-11-08, BPMcenter.org, 2011c.

B. Farwer and M. Varea. Object-based control/data-flow analysis. Technical Report DSSE-TR-2005-1, ECS, University of Southampton, 2005.

U. Fayyad, G. Piatetsky-Shapiro, and P. Smyth. From data mining to knowledge discovery in databases. *AI Magazine*, 17:37–54, 1996.

M. Fehler. *Kalibrierung Agenten-basierter Simulationen*. Dissertation, Universität Würzburg, 2011.

M. Fehler, F. Klügl, and F. Puppe. Techniques for analysis and calibration of multi-agent simulations. In *ESAW*, pages 305–321, 2004.

M. Fehler, F. Klügl, and F. Puppe. Learning for analysis and calibration in agent-based simulation,. In *ALAMAS 2006*, 2006a. ALAMAS 2006, Brüssel, April 2006.

M. Fehler, F. Klügl, and F. Puppe. Approaches for resolving the dilemma between model structure refinement and parameter calibration in agent-based simulations. In *Proceedings of the fifth international joint conference on Autonomous agents and multiagent systems*, AA-MAS '06, pages 120–122, New York, NY, USA, 2006b. ACM. ISBN 1-59593-303-4. doi: http://doi.acm.org/10.1145/1160633.1160651.

J. Ferber. *Multi-Agent Systems*. Addison-Wesley, Harlow, 1995.

J. Ferber and O. Gutknecht. A Meta-Model for the Analysis and Design of Organizations in Multi-Agent Systems. In *Third International Conference on Multi-Agent Systems (ICMAS '98) Proceedings*. IEEE Computer Society, 1998.

J. Ferber, O. Gutknecht, and F. Michel. Madkit development guide version 4.0. Online Documentation, 2012. URL http://www.madkit.net/documentation/devguide/devguide.html. last visit 2012-09-16.

J. Fetzer. *Computers and Cognition: Why Minds are Not Machines*. Studies in Cognitive Systems. Springer, 2001. ISBN 9781402002434.

FIPA. Fipa communicative act library specification. Technical Report SC00037J, Foundation for Intelligent Physical Agents, 2002a. URL http://www.fipa.org/specs/fipa00037/ SC00037J.html. last visit 2012-12-03.

FIPA. Fipa acl message specification. Technical Report SC00061G, Foundation for Intelligent Physical Agents, 2002b. URL http://www.fipa.org/specs/fipa00061/SC00061G.html. last visit 2012-12-03.

FIPA. Fipa modelling: Agent class diagrams. Technical Report TBA (Preliminary), Foundation for Intelligent Physical Agents, 2003. URL http://www.auml.org/auml/documents/ CD-03-04-24.doc. last visit 2012-12-03.

FIPA. Foundation for Intelligent Physical Agents, 2005. URL http://www.fipa.org. last visit 2012-12-03.

J. Fix. *Emotionale Agenten: Darstellung der emotionstheoretischen Grundlagen und Entwicklung eines Referenzmodells für die Emotionsmodellierung auf Basis einer Petrinetz-basierten Darstellungstechnik*. Dissertation, University of Hamburg, Department of Informatics, Hamburg, 2012.

N. Flick, L. Cabac, N. Denz, and D. Moldt. Re-Thinking Process Mining with Agents in Mind. In *CEUR-WS Proceedings of AWPN*, October 2010.

W. Fokkink. *Introduction to Process Algebra*. Springer-Verlag New York, Inc., Secaucus, NJ, USA, 1st edition, 2000. ISBN 354066579X.

S. Franklin and A. Graesser. Is it an Agent or just a Program? A Taxonomy for Autonomous Agents. In *Proceedings of the Third International Workshop on Agent Theories, Architectures, and Languages*, published as *Intelligent Agents III*, pages 21–35, New York, 1997. Springer.

B. Freeman-Benson and A. Borning. Experience in developing the urbansim system: tools and processes. In *Companion of the 18th annual ACM SIGPLAN conference on Object-oriented programming, systems, languages, and applications*, OOPSLA '03, pages 332–333, New York, NY, USA, 2003. ACM. ISBN 1-58113-751-6. doi: 10.1145/949344.949438.

A. Furtado and A. Ciarlini. Constructing libraries of typical plans. In *CAiSE '01: Proceedings of the 13th International Conference on Advanced Information Systems Engineering*, pages 124–139, London, 2001. Springer-Verlag. ISBN 3-540-42215-3.

V. Furtado. Mining data in multi-perspectives. In *Symposium of Advances on Intelligent Data Analysis*, pages 354–359, Rochester, 1999. ICSC Academic Press.

W. Gaaloul. Business process intelligence: Discovering and improving transactional behavior of composite services from logs. In *Doctoral symposium in INTEROP-ESA '05 - First International Conference on Interoperability of Enterprise Software and Applications*, Geneva, Switzerland, February 2005.

W. Gaaloul and C. Godart. Mining workflow recovery from event based logs. In W. v. d. Aalst, B. Benatallah, F. Casati, and F. Curbera, editors, *Business Process Management*, volume 3649 of *Lecture Notes in Computer Science*, pages 169–185. Springer Berlin / Heidelberg, 2005. ISBN 978-3-540-28238-9. 10.1007/11538394_12.

W. Gaaloul, S. Bhiri, and C. Godart. Discovering workflow transactional behavior from event-based log. In R. Meersman and Z. Tari, editors, *CoopIS-DOA-ODBASE 2004, LNCS 3290*, pages 3–18, Berlin, 2004. Springer.

W. Gaaloul, K. Baina, and C. Godart. Towards mining structural workflow patterns. In K. Andersen, J. Debenham, and R. Wagner, editors, *Database and Expert Systems Applications*, volume 3588 of *Lecture Notes in Computer Science*, pages 24–33. Springer Berlin / Heidelberg, 2005. ISBN 978-3-540-28566-3. 10.1007/11546924_3.

J. Gabbai, W. Wright, and N. Allinson. Visualisation of multi-agent system organisations using a self-organising map of pareto solutions. In *Intelligent Data Engineering and Automated Learning IDEAL 2004 5th International Conference Proceedings Lecture Notes in Comput Science*, volume 3177, pages 841–847. Springer-Verlag, Berlin, Germany, 2004.

E. Gamma, R. Helm, R. Johnson, and R. Vlissides. *Design Patterns: Elements of Reusable Object-Oriented Software*. Addison-Wesley, Reading, 1995.

P. Garcia and E. Vidal. Inference of k-testable languages in the strict sense and application to syntactic pattern recognition. *Pattern Analysis and Machine Intelligence, IEEE Transactions on*, 12(9):920–925, September 1990. ISSN 0162-8828. doi: 10.1109/34.57687.

C. Garion and L. van der Torre. Design by contract deontic design language for multiagent systems. In *Coordination, Organizations, Institutions, and Norms in Multi-Agent Systems*, number 3913 in LNCS, pages 170–182, Berlin, July 2006. Springer.

J. Garrido. *Object-Oriented Discrete-Event Simulation with Java – A Practical Introduction*. Series in Computer Systems. Kluwer Academic/Plenum, New York, 2001.

L. Gasser and M. Huhns, editors. *Distributed Artificial Intelligence*, Research Notes in Artificial Intelligence, London, May 1989. Pitman.

P. Gay, A. Pla, B. Lopez, J. Melendez, and R. Meunier. Service workflow monitoring through complex event processing. In *Emerging Technologies and Factory Automation (ETFA), 2010 IEEE Conference on*, pages 1–4, September 2010. doi: 10.1109/ETFA.2010.5641189.

G. Geenens. Curse of dimensionality and related issues in nonparametric functional regression. *Statistical Surveys*, 5:30–43, 2011.

B. Gehlsen. *Automatisierte Experimentplanung im Rahmen von Simulationsstudien – Konzeption und Realisierung eines verteilten simulationsbasierten Optimierungssystems*. PhD thesis, Faculty of Informatics, University of Hamburg, 2004.

B. Gehlsen and B. Page. A framework for distributed simulation optimization. In B. Peters et al., editors, *Proceedings of the 33rd conference on Winter simulation*, pages 508–514, Washington, 2001. IEEE Computer Society.

S. Geman, E. Bienenstock, and R. Doursat. Neural networks and the bias/variance dilemma. *Neural Comput.*, 4(1):1–58, 1992. ISSN 0899-7667. doi: http://dx.doi.org/10.1162/neco.1992.4.1.1.

N. Gilbert and K. Troitzsch. *Simulation for the Social Scientist.* Open University, Buckingham, 1999.

H. Gildhoff. Eine Simulationsunterstützung für Agentenplattformen. Diploma thesis, University of Hamburg, Department of Informatics, 2007.

A. Giret and V. Botti. Engineering holonic manufacturing systems. *Comput. Ind.*, 60(6):428–440, Aug. 2009. ISSN 0166-3615. doi: 10.1016/j.compind.2009.02.007.

S. Goedertier, D. Martens, B. Baesens, R. Haesen, and J. Vanthienen. Process mining as first-order classification learning on logs with negative events. In A. t. Hofstede, B. Benatallah, and H.-Y. Paik, editors, *Business Process Management Workshops*, volume 4928 of *Lecture Notes in Computer Science*, pages 42–53. Springer Berlin / Heidelberg, 2008. 10.1007/978-3-540-78238-4_6.

E. Gold. Language identification in the limit. *Inf. and Control*, 10:447–474, 1967.

E. Gold. Complexity of automaton identification from given data. *Inf. and Control*, 37, 1978.

D. Goldberg. *Genetic Algorithms in Search, Optimization and Machine Learning.* Addison Wesley, Boston, 1989.

R. Gombotz, K. Baina, and S. Dustdar. Towards web services interaction mining architecture for e-commerce applications analysis. In *International Conference on E-Business and E-Learning*, Amman, Jordan, 2005. Sumaya University.

R. Gore. Understanding unexpected behaviors in exploratory simulations. Dissertation proposal, School of Engineering and Applied Science, University of Virginia, April 2010. URL www.cs.virginia.edu/~rjg7v/proposal.pdf. last visit 2012-12-03.

K. Görlach, M. Sonntag, D. Karastoyanova, F. Leymann, and M. Reiter. Conventional workflow technology for scientific simulation. In X. Yang, L. Wang, and W. Jie, editors, *Guide to e-Science*, Computer Communications and Networks, pages 323–352. Springer London, 2011. ISBN 978-0-85729-438-8. doi: 10.1007/978-0-85729-439-5_12.

G. Greco, A. Guzzo, L. Pontieri, and D. Saccà. Mining expressive process models by clustering workflow traces. In H. Dai, R. Srikant, and C. Zhang, editors, *Advances in Knowledge Discovery and Data Mining, 8th Pacific-Asia Conference, PAKDD 2004, Sydney, Australia, May 26-28, 2004, Proceedings*, pages 52–62. Springer, 2004.

G. Greco, A. Guzzo, and L. Pontieri. Mining hierarchies of models: From abstract views to concrete specifications. In W. v. d. Aalst, B. Benatallah, F.C., and F. Curbera, editors, *Business Process Management, 3rd International Conference*, pages 32–47, 2005.

G. Greco, A. Guzzo, L. Pontieri, and D. Sacca. Discovering expressive process models by clustering log traces. *IEEE Trans. on Knowl. and Data Eng.*, 18(8):1010–1027, 2006. ISSN 1041-4347. doi: http://dx.doi.org/10.1109/TKDE.2006.123.

G. Greco, A. Guzzo, and L. Pontieri. Mining taxonomies of process models. *Data & Knowledge Engineering*, 67(1):74–102, 2008. ISSN 0169-023X. doi: 10.1016/j.datak.2008.06.010.

J. Gribbin. *Deep Simplicity – Chaos, Complexity and the Emergence of Life.* Penguin Books, London (England), 2nd edition, 2005.

I. Griffiths, M. Adams, and J. Liberty. *Programming C# 4.0: Building Windows, Web, and RIA Applications for the .NET 4.0 Framework.* O'Reilly Series. O'Reilly Media, 2010. ISBN 9780596159832.

V. Grimm. Visual Debugging: A Way of Analyzing, Understanding, and Communicating Bottom-Up Simulation Models in Ecology. *Natural Resource Modeling*, 15(1):23–28, 2002.

V. Grimm, E. Revilla, U. Berger, F. Jeltsch, W. Mooij, S. Railsback, H.-H. Thulke, J. Weiner, T. Wiegand, and D. DeAngelis. Pattern-oriented modeling of agent-based complex systems: Lessons from ecology. *Science*, 310(5750):987–991, 2005. doi: 10.1126/science.1116681.

M. Griss, S. Fonseca, D. Cowan, and R. Kessler. Using UML State Machine Models for More Precise and Flexible JADE Agent Behaviors. In F. Giunchiglia, J. Odell, and G. Weiss, editors, *Agent-Oriented Software Engineering III: Third International Workshop 2002 in Bologna*, pages 113–125, Berlin, 2002. Springer.

J. Gruska. *Foundations of Computing*. International Thomson Computer Press, London, 1997.

C.-Q. Gu, H.-Y. Chang, and Y. Yi. Workflow mining: Extending the alpha algorithm to mine duplicate tasks. *Machine Learning and Cybernetics 2008 International*, 1(July):12–15, 2008.

A. Guabtni and F. Charoy. Multiple instantiation in a dynamic workflow environment. In A. Persson and J. Stirna, editors, *CAiSE 2004, LNCS 3084*, pages 175–188, Berlin, 2004. Springer.

Z. Guan, F. Hernandez, P. Bangalore, J. Gray, A. Skjellum, V. Velusamy, and Y. Liu. Grid-flow: A grid-enabled scientific workflow system with a petri net-based interface. *Concurrency and Computation: Practice and Experience, Special Issue on Grid Workflow*, 18(10):1115–1140, August 2006.

Y.-G. Gueheneuc and T. Ziadi. Automated reverse-engineering of uml v2.0 dynamic models. In S. Demeyer, S. Ducasse, K. Mens, and R. Wuyts, editors, *Proceedings of the 6th ECOOP workshop on ObjectOriented Reengineering*. Springer-Verlag, 2005.

Z. Guessoum, M. Cossentino, and J. Pavon. A roadmap of agent-oriented software engineering. In F. Bergentini, editor, *Methodologies and software engineering for agent systems: the agent-oriented software engineering handbook*, chapter 21. Kluwer Academic, 2004.

C. Günther and W. v. d. Aalst. Fuzzy mining - adaptive process simplification based on multi-perspective metrics. In G. Alonso, P. Dadam, and M. Rosemann, editors, *Business Process Management*, volume 4714 of *Lecture Notes in Computer Science*, pages 328–343. Springer Berlin / Heidelberg, 2007. ISBN 978-3-540-75182-3. 10.1007/978-3-540-75183-0_24.

C. Günther, S. Rinderle, M. Reichert, and W. v. d. Aalst. Change mining in adaptive process management systems. In R. Meersman and Z. Tari, editors, *On the Move to Meaningful Internet Systems 2006. Proceedings, Part I*, pages 309–326, 2006.

C. Günther, S. Rinderle-Ma, M. Reichert, W. v. d. Aalst, and J. Recker. Using process mining to learn from process changes in evolutionary systems. *Int'l Journal of Business Process Integration and Management, Special Issue on Business Process Flexibility*, 3(1):61–78, 2008.

C. Günther, A. Rozinat, and W. v. d. Aalst. Activity mining by global trace segmentation. In W. v. d. Aalst, J. Mylopoulos, N. Sadeh, M. Shaw, C. Szyperski, S. Rinderle-Ma, S. Sadiq, and F. Leymann, editors, *Business Process Management Workshops*, volume 43 of *Lecture Notes in Business Information Processing*, pages 128–139. Springer Berlin Heidelberg, 2010. ISBN 978-3-642-12186-9.

G. Gutnik and G. Kaminka. Representing conversations for scalable overhearing. *Journal of Artificial Intelligence Research*, 25:349–387, March 2006.

J. Haan. Einsatz und Evaluation von Process Mining-Techniken im Rahmen der Analyse einer agentenbasierten Logistiksimulation unter Verwendung des Analysewerkzeugs ProM. Bachelor Thesis, University of Hamburg, 2009.

O. Hagendorf. *Simulation Based Parameter and Structure Optimisation of Discrete Event Systems.* Phd thesis, Liverpool John Moores University, Liverpool, 2009.

D. Hales, J. Rouchier, and B. Edmonds. Model-to-Model Analysis. *Journal of Artificial Societies and Social Simulation*, 6(4), 2003. URL http://jasss.soc.surrey.ac.uk/6/4/5.html. last visit 2012-12-02.

M. Hall, E. Frank, G. Holmes, B. Pfahringer, P. Reutemann, and I. Witten. The weka data mining software: an update. *SIGKDD Explor. Newsl.*, 11(1):10–18, 2009. ISSN 1931-0145. doi: http://doi.acm.org/10.1145/1656274.1656278.

J. Han and M. Kamber, editors. *Data Mining: Concepts and Techniques.* The Morgan Kaufmann Series in Data Management Systems. Elsevier Books, Oxford, 2000.

C. Hanachi and I. Khaloul. Discovering protocols and organizational structures in workflows. In *Proceedings of the 8th international conference on New technologies in distributed systems*, NOTERE '08, pages 13:1–13:13, New York, NY, USA, 2008. ACM. ISBN 978-1-59593-937-1. doi: http://doi.acm.org/10.1145/1416729.1416746.

D. Hand, H. Mannila, and P. Smyth, editors. *Principles of Data Mining.* MIT Press, Cambridge (MA), 2001.

D. Harel and R. Marelli, editors. *Scenario-Based Programming Using LSCs and the Play-Engine.* Springer, Berlin, 2003. ISBN 978-3-540-00787-6.

S. Haykin. *Neural Networks – A Comprehensive Foundation.* Prentice Hall, Upper Saddle River, 2nd edition, 1999.

K. v. Hee, I. Lomazova, O. Oanea, A. Serebrenik, N. Sidorova, and M. Voorhoeve. Nested nets for adaptive systems. In *Proceedings of the 27th international conference on Applications and Theory of Petri Nets and Other Models of Concurrency*, ICATPN'06, pages 241–260, Berlin, Heidelberg, 2006. Springer. ISBN 3-540-34699-6, 978-3-540-34699-9. doi: 10.1007/11767589_14.

L. Heinrich. Grundlagen der wirtschaftsinformatik. In G. Pomberger and P. Rechenberg, editors, *Informatik-Handbuch*, chapter F1, pages 1039–1054. Carl Hanser Verlag, Munich, 3rd edition, 2002.

F. Heitmann and F. Pläehn. Sniffer tool. Report on study project, University of Hamburg, Department of Informatics, 2005.

J. Herbst. *Ein induktiver Ansatz zur Akquisition und Adaption von Workflow-Modellen.* PhD thesis, University of Ulm, 2001.

R. Hickey and M. Black. Refined time stamps for concept drift detection during mining for classification rules. In *Proceedings of the First International Workshop on Temporal, Spatial, and Spatio-Temporal Data Mining-Revised Papers*, TSDM '00, pages 20–30, London, UK, 2001. Springer-Verlag. ISBN 3-540-41773-7.

M. Hiel. Learning interaction protocols by overhearing. Master's thesis, Utrecht University, May 2005.

C. d. l. Higuera. A bibliographical study of grammatical inference. *Pattern Recogn.*, 38:1332–1348, September 2005. ISSN 0031-3203. doi: http://dx.doi.org/10.1016/j.patcog.2005.01.003.

M. Hilario, P. Nguyen, H. Do, A. Woznica, and A. Kalousis. Ontology-based meta-mining of knowledge discovery workflows. In N. Jankowski, W. Duch, and K. Grabczewski, editors, *Meta-Learning in Computational Intelligence*, volume 358 of *Studies in Computational Intelligence*, pages 273–315. Springer Berlin / Heidelberg, 2011. ISBN 978-3-642-20979-6. 10.1007/978-3-642-20980-2_9.

Bibliography

L. Hilty, B. Page, et al. Instrumente für die ökologische Bewertung und Gestaltung von Verkehrs- und Logistiksystemen – Abschlussbericht des Forschungsprojekts MOBILE. Technical report, University of Hamburg, Department of Informatics, May 1998.

C. Hoffa, G. Mehta, T. Freeman, E. Deelman, K. Keahey, B. Berriman, and J. Good. On the use of cloud computing for scientific workflows. In *eScience, 2008. eScience '08. IEEE Fourth International Conference on*, pages 640–645, December 2008. doi: 10.1109/eScience.2008.167.

A. t. Hofstede, W. v. d. Aalst, M. Adams, and N. Russell, editors. *Modern Business Process Automation – YAWL and its Support Environment*. Springer, 2010. ISBN 978-3-642-03120-5.

J. Holland. *Emergence*. Helix, 1998.

J. Holland, L. Booker, M. Colombetti, M. Dorigo, D. Goldberg, S. Forrest, R. Riolo, R. Smith, P. Lanzi, W. Stolzmann, and S. Wilson. What is a learning classifier system? In *Learning Classifier Systems, From Foundations to Applications*, pages 3–32, London, UK, UK, 2000. Springer-Verlag. ISBN 3-540-67729-1.

D. Hollingworth. The workflow reference model. Technical Report Document TC00-1003, Workflow Management Coalition, 1995.

G. Holzmann. *Design and Validation of Computer Protocols*. Software Series. Prentice Hall, Englewood Cliffs, 1991.

G. Holzmann. The Model Checker SPIN. *IEEE Transactions on Software Engineering*, 23(5):279–295, May 1997.

T. Hongtao, C. Yong, and L. Jiansa. Architecture of process mining based business process optimization. *Innovation*, pages 1066–1069, 2006.

J. Hopcroft, R. Motwani, and J. Ullman. *Introduction to automata theory, languages, and computation - international edition (2. ed)*. Addison-Wesley, 2003. ISBN 978-0-321-21029-6.

G. Horne and T. Meyer. Data farming: Discovering surprise. In M. Kuhl, N. Steiger, F. Armstrong, and J. Joines, editors, *Proceedings of the 2005 Winter Simulation Conference*, pages 1082–1087, 2005.

P. Hornix. Performance analysis of business processes through process mining. Master's thesis, Eindhoven University of Technology, 2007.

V. Horvath and O. Krouk. Eclipse Experimentierumgebung - Verteilung. Report on study project, University of Hamburg, Department of Informatics, 2006.

Y. Howard, S. Gruner, A. M. Gravell, C. Ferreira, and J. C. Augusto. Model-based trace-checking. In *Proceedings of UK Software Testing Research II*, York, 2003. University of York.

K.-P. Huber and M. R. Berthold. Metamodellierung zu Analyse des Modellverhaltens – Modellverhalten besser verstehen durch Datenanalyse. In H. Szczerbicka and T. Uthmann, editors, *Modellierung, Simulation und Künstliche Intelligenz*. SCS-Europe, 2000.

K.-P. Huber, M. Syrjakow, and H. Szczerbicka. Extracting knowledge supports model optimization. In *Proceedings of the International Simulation Technology Conference SIMTEC'93*, pages 237–242, San Francisco (CA), 1993. SCS-Europe.

I. Jackewitz, M. Janneck, and B. Pape. Vernetzte Projektarbeit mit CommSy. In M. Herczeg and H. Oberquelle, editors, *Mensch & Computer 2002: Vom interaktiven Werkzeug zu kooperativen Arbeits- und Lernwelten, Hamburg, Germany, September 2-5, 2002*, pages 35–44. Teubner, 2002.

N. Jacobs, K. Driessens, and L. D. Raedt. Inductive Verification and Validation of Multi Agent Systems. In *Workshop on Validation and Verification of Knowledge Based Systems*, pages 10–18, August 1998.

M. Jantzen. *Eigenschaften von Petrinetzsprachen*. Dissertation, University of Hamburg, 1979.

Z. Jaroucheh, X. Liu, and S. Smith. Recognize contextual situation in pervasive environments using process mining techniques. *Journal of Ambient Intelligence and Humanized Computing*, 2:53–69, 2011. ISSN 1868-5137. doi: 10.1007/s12652-010-0038-7.

M. Jeckle et al. *UML 2 glasklar*. Carl Hanser, Munich, 2002.

N. Jennings, K. Sycara, and M. Wooldridge. A roadmap of agent research and development. *Autonomous Agents and Multi-Agent Systems*, 1(1):7–38, 1998.

E. Jessen and R. Valk. *Rechensysteme: Grundlagen der Modellbildung*. Studienreihe Informatik. Springer, Berlin, 1987.

S. Jones. Organizing relations and emergence. In R. K. Standish, M. A. Bedau, and H. A. Abbass, editors, *Artificial Life VIII*, pages 418–422, Cambridge, 2003. MIT.

J.-Y. Jung and J. Bae. Workflow clustering method based on process similarity. In M. Gavrilova, O. Gervasi, V. Kumar, C. K. Tan, D. Taniar, A. Laganà, Y. Mun, and H. Choo, editors, *Computational Science and Its Applications - ICCSA 2006, International Conference, Glasgow, UK, May 8-11, 2006, Proceedings, Part II*, pages 379–389. Springer, 2006.

S. Kämper. *PEGROS – Ein Konzept zur Entwicklung eines graphischen, objektorientierten Modellbildungs- und Simulationswerkzeugs auf der Basis von Petri-Netzen*. Dissertation, University of Hamburg, Department of Informatics, Hamburg, 1990.

M. Kastner, M. Wagdy Saleh, S. Wagner, M. Affenzeller, and W. Jacak. Heuristic methods for searching and clustering hierarchical workflows. In R. Moreno-Díaz, F. Pichler, and A. Quesada-Arencibia, editors, *Computer Aided Systems Theory - EUROCAST 2009*, pages 737–744. Springer, Berlin, Heidelberg, 2009. ISBN 978-3-642-04771-8. doi: http://dx.doi.org/10.1007/978-3-642-04772-5_95.

W. Kelton and R. Barton. Experimental design for simulation. In *Proceedings of the 35th conference on Winter simulation: driving innovation*, WSC '03, pages 59–65. Winter Simulation Conference, 2003. ISBN 0-7803-8132-7.

C. Kennedy, G. Theodoropoulos, V. Sorge, E. Ferrari, P. Lee, and C. Skelcher. Aimss: An architecture for data driven simulations in the social sciences. In Y. Shi, G. v. Albada, J. Dongarra, and P. Sloot, editors, *Computational Science - ICCS 2007*, volume 4487 of *Lecture Notes in Computer Science*, pages 1098–1105. Springer, Berlin / Heidelberg, 2007. ISBN 978-3-540-72583-1. 10.1007/978-3-540-72584-8_144.

J. Kennedy. *Swarm Intelligence*. Morgan Kaufmann, San Francisco, 2001.

R. Kennedy, X. Xiang, T. Cosimano, L. Arthurs, P. Maurice, G. Madey, and S. Cabaniss. Verification and validation of agent-based and equation-based simulations: A comparison. In *Agent-Directed Simulation Conference*, Huntsville (AL), April 2006. The Society for Modeling and Simulation International.

G. Kiesel. Einsatz von Computersimulationen im Kontext von E-Learning-Umgebungen: unter Verwendung des Frameworks Desmo-J. Diploma thesis, University of Hamburg, Department of Informatics, 2004.

R. Kikas. Discovering mapping between artifact-centric business process models and execution logs. Master's thesis, University of Tartu, Faculty of Mathematics and Computer Science Institute of Computer Science, Tartu (Estonia), June 2011.

R. Kilmer, A. Smith, and L. Shuman. An emergency department simulation and neural network metamodel. *Journal of the society for health systems*, 5(3):63–79, 1997.

K. Kim. Mining workflow processes from xml-based distributed workflow event logs. In *Proceedings of the 2009 International Conference on Parallel Processing Workshops*, ICPPW '09, pages 587–594, Washington, DC, USA, 2009. IEEE Computer Society. ISBN 978-0-7695-3803-7. doi: 10.1109/ICPPW.2009.43.

E. Kindler, V. Rubin, and W. Schäfer. Process mining and petri net synthesis. In J. Eder and S. Dustdar, editors, *Business Process Management Workshops*, number 4103 in LNCS, pages 105–116, Berlin, September 2006. Springer.

U. Kjaerulff and A. Madsen. Probabilistic networks - an introduction to bayesian networks and influence diagrams. In *Unpublished, Aalborg University, Department of Computer Science*, page 133, 2005. URL http://people.cs.aau.dk/ūk/papers/pgm-book-I-05.pdf. last visit 2012-09-10.

J. Kleijnen. Validation of Models: Statistical Techniques and Data Availability. In P. Farrington, H. Nembhard, D. Sturrock, and G. Evans, editors, *Proceedings of the 1999 Winter Simulation Conference*, pages 647–654, 1999.

G. Kleindorfer and R. Ganeshan. The philosophy of science and validation in simulation. In G. Evans, M. Mollaghasemi, E. Russell, and W. Biles, editors, *Proceedings of the 1993 Winter Simulation Conference*, pages 50–57, 1993.

F. Klügl. *Aktivitätsbasierte Verhaltensmodellierung und ihre Unterstützung bei Multiagentensimulationen*. Dissertation, Universität Würzburg, Am Hubland, 97074 Würzburg, 2000.

F. Klügl. *Multiagentensimulation – Konzepte, Werkzeuge, Anwendung*. Agententechnologie. Addison-Wesley, Munich, 2001.

F. Klügl. Measuring complexity of multi-agent simulations - an attempt using metrics. In M. Dastani, A. E. Fallah-Seghrouchni, J. Leite, and P. Torroni, editors, *Languages, Methodologies and Development Tools for Multi-Agent Systems, First International Workshop, LADS 2007, Durham, UK, September 4-6, 2007. Revised Selected Papers*, volume 5118 of *Lecture Notes in Computer Science*, pages 123–138. Springer, 2007.

F. Klügl. A validation methodology for agent-based simulations. In R. Wainwright and H. Haddad, editors, *Proceedings of the 2008 ACM Symposium on Applied Computing (SAC), Fortaleza, Ceara, Brazil, March 16-20, 2008*, pages 39–43. ACM, 2008. ISBN 978-1-59593-753-7.

N. Knaak. Konzepte der agentenbasierten Simulation und ihre Umsetzung im Rahmen des Simulationsframeworks DESMO-J. Diploma thesis, University of Hamburg, Department of Informatics, 2002.

N. Knaak. Modifications of the fujaba statechart interpreter for multiagent-based discrete event simulation. In *Proceedings of the Fujaba Days 2004*, pages 23–26, Darmstadt, September 2004.

N. Knaak. Supporting multi-agent-based simulation with data mining techniques. In A. Bruzzone, A. Guasch, M. Piera, and J. Rozenblit, editors, *Proceedings of the International Mediterranean Modelling Multiconference (I3M'2006)*, pages 277–286, Barcelona, Spain, October 2006.

N. Knaak. Analysis and validation of agent-based simulations with process mining techniques. In T. Schulze, B. Preim, and H. Schumann, editors, *Simulation und Visualisierung 2007 - Beiträge zum Doktorandenforum Diskrete Simulation*, Magdeburg, Germany, March 2007. SCS Publishing House.

N. Knaak and B. Page. Uml 2 as a modelling language in discrete event simulation. In Y. Merkuryev, R. Zobel, and E. Kerckhoffs, editors, *Proceedings of the 12th International Conference on Modelling and Simulation (ECMS 2005)*, pages 399–408, Riga (Latvia), June 2005.

N. Knaak and B. Page. Applications and extensions of the unified modelling language uml 2 for discrete-event simulation. *International Journal of Simulation, Systems, Science, and Technology*, 7(6):33–43, September 2006.

N. Knaak, R. Meyer, and B. Page. Agentenbasierte Simulation mit einem objektorientierten Framework in Java. In D. Tavangarian and R. Grützner, editors, *Frontiers in Simulation (12)*, Rostock, September 2002.

N. Knaak, R. Meyer, and B. Page. Agent-Based Simulation of Sustainable Logistic Concepts for Large City Courier Services. In A. Gnauck and R. Heinrich, editors, *Proceedings of the EnviroInfo 2003 – 17th. International Conference Informatics for Environmental Protection*, pages 318–325, Marburg, September 2003. Metropolis.

N. Knaak, S. Kruse, and B. Page. An agent-based simulation tool for modelling sustainable logistics systems. In A. Voinov, A. Jakeman, and A. Rizzoli, editors, *Proceedings of the iEMSs Third Biennial Meeting: "Summit on Environmental Modelling and Software" (CD ROM or Internet version)*, Burlington, USA, July 2006. International Environmental Modelling and Software Society.

H.-J. Köhler. Code-Generierung für UML Kollaborations-, Sequenz- und Statechart-Diagramme. Diploma Thesis, University of Paderborn, 1999.

M. Köhler. Algebraische Erweiterungen von Objektnetzen. In D. Moldt, editor, *Proceedings of the AWPN'06, Technical Report 267*, pages 62–68, Hamburg, September 2006. University of Hamburg, Department of Informatics.

M. Köhler, D. Moldt, and H. Rölke. Modelling mobility and mobile agents using nets within nets. In W. v. d. Aalst and E. Best, editors, *Proceedings of the 24th International Conference on Application and Theory of Petri Nets 2003 (ICATPN 2003)*, volume 2679 of *Lecture Notes in Computer Science*, pages 121–139. Springer, 2003.

M. Köhler-Bußmeier. Hornets: Nets within nets combined with net algebra. In G. Franceschinis and K. Wolf, editors, *Applications and Theory of Petri Nets*, volume 5606 of *Lecture Notes in Computer Science*, pages 243–262. Springer, Berlin / Heidelberg, 2009a. ISBN 978-3-642-02423-8. 10.1007/978-3-642-02424-5_15.

M. Köhler-Bußmeier. *Koordinierte Selbstorganisation und selbstorganisierte Koordination: Eine formale Spezifikation reflexiver Selbstorganisation in Multiagentensystemen unter spezieller Berücksichtigung der sozialwissenschaftlichen Perspektive.* Habilitationsschrift, University of Hamburg, 2009b.

S. Koppehel. Umweltverhalten und Szenariokomponenten in Multi-Agenten-Simulationen. Diploma thesis, University of Hamburg, Department of Informatics, 2007.

F. Köster. Analyse von Simulationsmodellen mit Methoden des Knowledge Discovery in Databases. Technical report, Department für Informatik, Carl von Ossietzky University of Oldenburg, 2002.

F. Köster. Personal communication at meeting in oldenburg (germany), February 2004.

D. Kouvastos. Decomposition criteria for the design of complex systems. *International Journal of Systems Science*, 7(10):1081–1088, 1976. doi: 10.1080/00207727608941990.

S. Kruse. Einsatz von Model-Checking- und Data-Mining-Verfahren zur Validierung von Simulationen am Beispiel der "Agentenbasierten Simulation von Stadtkurierdiensten" – Abschlussbericht. Report on study project, University of Hamburg, Department of Informatics, 2005.

S. Kruse. Komponentenbasierte Simulation lernfähiger Agenten. In *Simulation und Visualisierung - Beiträge zum Doktorandenforum Diskrete Simulation*, Magdeburg, September 2007. SCS Publishing House.

S. Kruse. Change mining for the validation of simulated learning processes, 2008. Accepted as a poster/demonstration for the IADIS Intelligent Systems and Agents 2008 (ISA 2008) Conference.

S. Kumar, S.-C. Khoo, A. Roychoudhury, and D. Lo. Mining message sequence graphs. Technical report, National University of Singapore, 2010. URL http://www.comp.nus.edu.sg/~sandeep/msgmining_TR.pdf. last visit 2012-12-03.

S. Kumar, S.-C. Khoo, A. Roychoudhury, and D. Lo. Mining message sequence graphs. In *Proceedings of the 33rd International Conference on Software Engineering*, ICSE '11, pages 91–100, New York, NY, USA, 2011. ACM. ISBN 978-1-4503-0445-0. doi: http://doi.acm.org/10.1145/1985793.1985807.

S. Kumar, S.-C. Khoo, A. Roychoudhury, and D. Lo. Inferring class level specifications for distributed systems. In M. Glinz, G. Murphy, and M. Pezzè, editors, *34th International Conference on Software Engineering, ICSE 2012, June 2-9, 2012, Zurich, Switzerland*, pages 914–924. IEEE, 2012. ISBN 978-1-4673-1067-3.

O. Kummer. Referenznetze. Dissertation, Department of Informatics, University of Hamburg, 2002.

O. Kummer, F. Wienberg, and M. Duvigneau. Renew user guide. online, May 26 2006. URL http://www.renew.de/. last visit 2012-12-03.

G. Küppers and J. Lenhard. Validation of simulation – patterns in the social and natural sciences. Technical report, University of Bielefeld, 2004.

S. Kurzbach. Prozessunterstützung bei der Modellierung hydrodynamischer Simulationsmodelle in der Wasserwirtschaft. Diploma thesis, University of Hamburg, Department of Informatics, Hamburg, August 2007.

M. Lahiri and T. Berger-Wolf. Mining periodic behavior in dynamic social networks. In *Data Mining, 2008. ICDM '08. Eighth IEEE International Conference on*, pages 373–382, December 2008. doi: 10.1109/ICDM.2008.104.

D. Lam and K. Barber. Comprehending agent software. In *AAMAS*, pages 586–593, 2005.

H. Lambrecht, M. Schmidt, and A. Möller. *Stoffstrombasierte Optimierung: Wissenschaftliche und methodische Grundlagen sowie softwaretechnische Umsetzung*. MV-Wissenschaft. Verlag-Haus Monsenstein und Vannerdat, 2010. ISBN 9783869910161.

E. Lamma, P. Mello, M. Montali, F. Riguzzi, and S. Storari. Inducing declarative logic-based models from labeled traces. In G. Alonso, P. Dadam, and M. Rosemann, editors, *Business Process Management, 5th International Conference, BPM 2007, Brisbane, Australia, September 24-28, 2007, Proceedings*, volume 4714 of *Lecture Notes in Computer Science*, pages 344–359. Springer, 2007a.

E. Lamma, P. Mello, F. Riguzzi, and S. Storari. Applying inductive logic programming to process mining. In *ILP'07: Proceedings of the 17th international conference on Inductive logic programming*, pages 132–146, Berlin, Heidelberg, 2007b. Springer-Verlag. ISBN 3-540-78468-3, 978-3-540-78468-5.

U. Lämmel and J. Cleve. *Künstliche Intelligenz*. Hanser, 2008. ISBN 9783446413986.

M. Lang. *Prozess-Mining und Prozessbewertung zur Verbesserung klinischer Workflows im Umfeld bilderzeugender Fächer*. Dissertation, Technische Fakultät der Universität Erlangen Nürnberg, Erlangen, 2008.

K. Lassen, B. v. Dongen, and W. v. d. Aalst. Translating message sequence charts to other process languages using process mining. BETA Working Paper Series WP 207, Eindhoven University of Technology, 2007. URL `http://wwwis.win.tue.nl/~wvdaalst/publications/p366.pdf`. last visit 2012-12-03.

A. Lattner, T. Bogon, and I. Timm. An approach to significance estimation for simulation studies. In J. Filipe and A. Fred, editors, *ICAART 2011 - Proceedings of the 3rd International Conference on Agents and Artificial Intelligence, Volume 1 - Artificial Intelligence, Rome, Italy, January 28-30, 2011*, pages 177–186. SciTePress, 2011.

A. Law and W. Kelton. *Simulation Modeling and Analysis*. McGraw-Hill, New York, 3rd edition, 2000.

T. Lechler and B. Page. Desmo-j – an object-oriented discrete simulation framework in java. In G. H. D. Möller, editor, *Simulation in Industry – 11th European Simulation Symposium 1999 in Erlangen (Germany)*, pages pp. 46–50, Delft (Netherlands), Oct. 26-28 1999. SCS.

C.-I. Lee, C.-J. Tsai, J.-H. Wu, and W.-P. Yang. A decision tree-based approach to mining the rules of concept drift. In *Proceedings of the Fourth International Conference on Fuzzy Systems and Knowledge Discovery - Volume 04*, FSKD '07, pages 639–643, Washington, DC, USA, 2007. IEEE Computer Society. ISBN 0-7695-2874-0. doi: http://dx.doi.org/10.1109/FSKD.2007.16.

P.-T. Lee and K. Tan. Modelling of visualised data-flow diagrams using petri net model. *Software Engineering Journal*, 7(1):4–12, Jan. 1992. ISSN 0268-6961.

C. Legner and K. Wende. The challenges of inter-organizational business process design - a research agenda. In H. Österle, J. Schelp, and R. Winter, editors, *Proceedings of the Fifteenth European Conference on Information Systems, ECIS 2007, St. Gallen, Switzerland, 2007*, pages 106–118. University of St. Gallen, 2007.

F. Leotta. Habit mining: Applying process mining to activities of daily life. Report for the admission to the 3rd year of the ph.d course in computing science and engineering, Sapienza Universita di Roma, 2012. URL `http://www.dis.uniroma1.it/ ~leotta/publications/FLeottaPhDReportY2.pdf`. last visit 2012-10-27.

S. Leye and A. Uhrmacher. A flexible and extensible architecture for experimental model validation. In *SIMUTOOLS*. ACM, 5 2010. doi: 10.4108/ICST.SIMUTOOLS2010.8833.

C. Li. *Mining Process Model Variants: Challenges, Techniques, Examples*. PhD thesis, University of Twente, The Netherlands, November 2010. URL `http://dbis.eprints.uni-ulm.de/706/`. last visit 2012-12-03.

C. Li, M. Reichert, and A. Wombacher. Mining business process variants: Challenges, scenarios, algorithms. *Data & Knowledge Engineering*, 70(5):409–434, 2011. ISSN 0169-023X. doi: 10.1016/j.datak.2011.01.005.

J. Li, D. Liu, and B. Yang. Process mining: Extending alpha-algorithm to mine duplicate tasks in process logs. In K.-C. Chang, W. Wang, L. Chen, C. Ellis, C.-H. Hsu, A. Tsoi, and H. Wang, editors, *Advances in Web and Network Technologies, and Information Management*, volume 4537 of *Lecture Notes in Computer Science*, pages 396–407. Springer Berlin Heidelberg, 2007. ISBN 978-3-540-72908-2. doi: 10.1007/978-3-540-72909-9_43.

J. Li, R. J. C. Bose, and W. v. d. Aalst. Mining context-dependent and interactive business process maps using execution patterns. In M. z. Muehlen and J. S., editors, *Business Process Management Workshops - BPM 2010 International Workshops and Education Track, Hoboken, NJ, USA, September 13-15, 2010, Revised Selected Papers*, volume 66 of *Lecture Notes in Business Information Processing*, pages 109–121. Springer, 2010.

Bibliography

J. Link. *Unit Tests mit Java*. dpunkt, Heidelberg, 2002.

M. Linke. Das OSGi-Framework. *JavaSPEKTRUM*, 5:35–38, 2005.

K. London. *Construction Supply Chain Procurement Modelling*. Phd thesis, Faculty of Architecture, Building and Planning, University of Melbourne, 2004. URL http:// repository.unimelb.edu.au/10187/948. last visit 2012-09-17.

J.-G. Lou, Q. Fu, Y. Wang, and J. Li. Mining dependency in distributed systems through unstructured logs analysis. *SIGOPS Oper. Syst. Rev.*, 44(1):91–96, Mar. 2010a. ISSN 0163-5980. doi: 10.1145/1740390.1740411.

J.-G. Lou, Q. Fu, S. Yang, and J. Li. Mining program workflow from interleaved logs. Technical Report MSR-TR-2010-6 MSR-TR-2010-6 MSR-TR-2010-6, Microsoft Research, January 2010b.

J.-G. Lou, Q. Fu, S. Yang, J. Li, and B. Wu. Mining program workflow from interleaved traces. In B. Rao, B. Krishnapuram, A. Tomkins, and Q. Yang, editors, *Proceedings of the 16th ACM SIGKDD International Conference on Knowledge Discovery and Data Mining, Washington, DC, USA, July 25-28, 2010*, pages 613–622. ACM, 2010c. ISBN 978-1-4503-0055-1.

D. Luengo and M. Sepulveda. Applying clustering in process mining to find different versions of a business process that changes over time. In F. Daniel, K. Barkaoui, S. Dustdar, W. v. d. Aalst, J. Mylopoulos, M. Rosemann, M. Shaw, and C. Szyperski, editors, *Business Process Management Workshops*, volume 99 of *Lecture Notes in Business Information Processing*, pages 153–158. Springer Berlin Heidelberg, 2012. ISBN 978-3-642-28108-2. 10.1007/978-3-642-28108-2_15.

G. Luger. *Artificial Intelligence – Structures and Strategies for Complex Problem Solving*. Addison-Wesley, Reading, 4th edition, 2002.

K. Luykx. Bias-variance decomposition for model selection. Bachelor thesis, University of Amsterdam, FNWI, Informatics Institute, 2009. URL http://staff.science.uva.nl/ bredeweg/pdf/BSc/-20082009/6ECversion/Luykx.pdf. last visit 2012-01-12.

L. Ly, S. Rinderle, P. Dadam, and M. Reichert. Mining staff assignment rules from event-based data. In C. Bussler and A. Haller, editors, *Business Process Management Workshops*, volume 3812 of *Lecture Notes in Computer Science*, pages 177–190. Springer Berlin Heidelberg, 2006. ISBN 978-3-540-32595-6. doi: 10.1007/11678564_16.

F. Maggi, M. Montali, and W. v. d. Aalst. An operational decision support framework for monitoring business constraints. In J. Lara and A. Zisman, editors, *Fundamental Approaches to Software Engineering*, volume 7212 of *Lecture Notes in Computer Science*, pages 146–162. Springer Berlin Heidelberg, 2012. ISBN 978-3-642-28871-5. doi: 10.1007/978-3-642-28872-2_11.

S. Mahadevan. Learning representation and control in markov decision processes: New frontiers. *Foundations and Trends in Machine Learning*, 1(4):403–565, 2009.

O. Maimon and L. Rokach. Introduction to soft computing for knowledge discovery and data mining. In O. Maimon and L. Rokach, editors, *Soft Computing for Knowledge Discovery and Data Mining*, pages 1–13. Springer, 2008. ISBN 978-0-387-69934-9.

T. Malsch. Naming the unnamable: Socionics or the sociological turn of/to distributed artificial intelligence. *Autonomous agents and multi-agent systems*, 4:155–186, 2001.

S. Marsland. *Machine Learning: An Algorithmic Perspective*. Chapman & Hall/CRC machine learning & pattern recognition series. Taylor & Francis, 2009. ISBN 9781420067187.

B. Martelli. *Leitlinien einer Methodik zur Validierung und zum Vergleich von kognitionswissenschaftlichen Modellen am Beispiel der Helligkeitswahrnehmung.* Dr. Kovac, Hamburg, 1999.

M. Martens. Agentenorientierte Modellierung von Entscheidungsprozessen mit Petrinetzen. Diploma thesis, Universität Hamburg, 2002.

L. Maruster, A. Weijters, W. v. d. Aalst, and A. v. d. Bosch. Process mining: Discovering direct successors in process logs. In *ICDS: International Conference on Data Discovery, DS.* LNCS, 2002.

B. Matzen and R. Czogalla. Agentenbasierte Simulation von Personenbewegungen in kontinuierlichem Raum. Diploma Thesis, Department of Informatics, University of Hamburg, December 2003.

H. Mazouzi, A. E. F. Seghrouchni, and S. Haddad. Open protocol design for complex interaction in multi-agent systems. In *proceedings of AAMAS' 02*, Bologna, Italy, 2002. ACM-Publisher.

A. Medeiros. *Genetic Process Mining.* PhD thesis, Technical University of Eindhoven, 2006.

A. Medeiros and C. Günther. Process mining: Using CPN Tools to create test logs for mining algorithms. In K. Jensen, editor, *Proceedings of the Sixth Workshop on the Practical Use of Coloured Petri Nets and CPN Tools (CPN 2005)*, Aarhus, Denmark, October 2005. University of Aarhus.

A. Medeiros, B. Dongen, W. Aalst, and A. Weijters. Process mining: Extending the α-algorithm to mine short loops. BETA Working Paper Series, WP 113, Eindhoven University of Technology, 2004a.

A. Medeiros, A. Weijters, and W. Aalst. Using genetic algorithms to mine process models: Representation, operators and results. BETA Working Paper Series, WP 124, Eindhoven University of Technology, 2004b.

A. d. Medeiros, C. Pedrinaci, W. v. d. Aalst, J. Domingue, M. Song, A. Rozinat, B. Norton, and L. Cabral. An outlook on semantic business process mining and monitoring. In R. Meersman, Z. Tari, and P. Herrero, editors, *On the Move to Meaningful Internet Systems 2007: OTM 2007 Workshops*, volume 4806 of *Lecture Notes in Computer Science*, pages 1244–1255. Springer, Berlin / Heidelberg, 2007. 10.1007/978-3-540-76890-6_52.

A. d. Medeiros, W. v. d. Aalst, and C. Pedrinaci. Semantic process mining tools: Core building blocks. In W. Golden, T. Acton, K. Conboy, H. v. d. Heijden, and V. K.T., editors, *16th European Conference on Information Systems, ECIS 2008, Galway, Ireland, 2008*, pages 1953–1964, 2008a.

A. d. Medeiros, A. Guzzo, G. Greco, W. v. d. Aalst, A. Weijters, B. van Dongen, and D. Sacca. Process mining based on clustering: A quest for precision. In A. t. Hofstede, B. Benatallah, and H.-Y. Paik, editors, *BPM 2007 Workshops, LNCS 4928.* Springer, 2008b. Berlin.

T. Menzies and C. Pecheur. Verification and validation and artificial intelligence. *Advances in Computing*, 65(October):153–201, 2005.

B. Meyer. *Object-Oriented Software Construction.* Prentice Hall, Upper Saddle River (NJ), 1997.

G. Meyer and N. Szirbik. Agent behavior alignment: A mechanism to overcome problems in agent interactions during runtime. In *Proceedings of the 11th international workshop on Cooperative Information Agents XI*, CIA '07, pages 270–284, Berlin, Heidelberg, 2007. Springer-Verlag. ISBN 978-3-540-75118-2. doi: http://dx.doi.org/10.1007/978-3-540-75119-9_19.

R. Meyer. Bewegungsgraphen – Ein Konzept für die räumliche Modellierung der Umgebung in der individuen- und agenten-basierten Simulation. In J. Wittman and L. Bernard, editors, *Simulation in Umwelt- und Geowissenschaften – Workshop Münster*, pages 47–60, Aachen, 2001. Shaker.

R. Meyer. *Agenten in Raum und Zeit - Agentenbasierte Simulation mit expliziter Raumrepräsentation.* Preliminary dissertation draft, University of Hamburg, Department of Informatics, Hamburg, 2008.

R. Meyer, C. Reick, B. Gehlsen, L. Hilty, H. Deecke, and B. Page. Modellierung eines Kurierdienstes im Hinblick auf ökologische Effizienz und soziale Verträglichkeit. In H.-D. Haasis and K. Ranze, editors, *Umweltinformatik '98 - Vernetzte Strukturen in Informatik. Umwelt und Wirtschaft. 12. Internationales Symposium Informatik für den Umweltschutz der Gesellschaft für Informatik (GI)*, *Bremen 1998*, pages 266–279, Marburg, 1999. Metropolis Verlag.

N. Minar et al. The Swarm Simulation System: A Toolkit for Building Multi-Agent Simulations. Technical report, Santa Fe Institute, 1996.

P. Mitkas, A. Symeonidis, D. Kehagias, I. Athanasiadis, G. Laleci, G. Kurt, Y. Kabak, A. Acar, and A. Dogac. An agent framework for dynamic agent retraining: Agent academy. *CoRR*, cs.MA/0407025, 2002.

D. Moldt. *Höhere Petrinetze als Grundlage für Systemspezifikationen*. Dissertation, University of Hamburg, Department of Informatics, August 1996.

D. Moldt and H. Rölke. Pattern-based workflow design using reference nets. In W. v. d. Aalst et al., editors, *BPM 2003, LNCS 2678*, pages 246–260, Berlin, 2003. Springer.

D. Moldt, F. Kordon, K. v. Hee, J.-M. Colom, and R. Bastide, editors. *Proceedings of the International Workshop on Petri Nets and Software Engineering (PNSE'07)*, Siedlce, Poland, June 2007. Akademia Podlaska.

A. Möller. Foundations and applications of computer based material flow networks for environmental management. In C. Rautenstrauch, editor, *Environmental Information Symposium Industry and Public Administration*, 2000.

I. Molloy, N. Li, T. Li, Z. Mao, Q. Wang, and J. Lobo. Evaluating role mining algorithms. In *Proceedings of the 14th ACM symposium on Access control models and technologies*, SAC-MAT '09, pages 95–104, New York, NY, USA, 2009. ACM. ISBN 978-1-60558-537-6. doi: http://doi.acm.org/10.1145/1542207.1542224.

T. Moncion, P. Amar, and G. Hutzler. Automatic characterization of emergent phenomena in complex systems. *Journal of Biological Physics and Chemistry*, 10:16–23, 2010.

M. Montali, P. Torroni, M. Alberti, F. Chesani, M. Gavanelli, E. Lamma, and P. Mello. Verification from declarative specifications using logic programming. In M. Garcia de la Banda and E. Pontelli, editors, *Logic Programming, 24th International Conference, ICLP 2008, Udine, Italy, December 9-13 2008, Proceedings*, volume 5366 of *Lecture Notes in Computer Science*, pages 440–454. Springer, 2008.

C. Morbitzer, P. Strachan, and C. Simpson. Application of data mining techniques for building simulation performance prediction analysis. In *Eigth International IBPSA Conference*, pages 911–918, Eindhoven, Netherlands, August 2003. SCS-Europe.

A. Moreno, U. Cortes, and T. Sales. Subjective situations. In F. Garijo and M. Boman, editors, *Multi-Agent System Engineering*, volume 1647 of *Lecture Notes in Computer Science*, pages 210–220. Springer Berlin Heidelberg, 1999. ISBN 978-3-540-66281-5. doi: 10.1007/3-540-48437-X_17.

S. Moss. Messy systems - the target for multi agent based simulation. In S. Moss and P. Davidsson, editors, *Multi-Agent-Based Simulation, Second International Workshop, MABS 2000, Boston, MA, USA, July, 2000, Revised and Additional Papers*, volume 1979 of *Lecture Notes in Computer Science*, pages 1–14. Springer, 2000.

S. Moss. Intuition and observation in the design of multi agent systems. Technical report, Centre for Policy Modelling, Manchester Metropolitan University Business Scool, Manchester M1 3GH, UK, 2004.

H. Motahari-Nezhad, R. Saint-Paul, F. Casati, and B. Benatallah. Event correlation for process discovery from web service interaction logs. *The VLDB Journal*, 20:417–444, June 2011. ISSN 1066-8888. doi: http://dx.doi.org/10.1007/s00778-010-0203-9.

A. Mounier, O. Boissier, and F. Jacquenet. Conversation mining in multi-agent systems. In *Proceedings of the CEEMAS 2003*, pages 158–167, 2003.

S. Muggleton, F. Mizoguchi, and K. Furukawa. Special issue on inductive logic programming. *New Generation Computing*, 13:243–244, 1995. ISSN 0288-3635. 10.1007/BF03037226.

J. Müller. *The Design of Intelligent Agents – A Layered Approach*. Springer, Berlin, 1996.

K. Musaraj, T. Yoshida, F. Daniel, M.-S. Hacid, F. Casati, and B. Benatallah. Message correlation and web service protocol mining from inaccurate logs. In *Web Services (ICWS), 2010 IEEE International Conference on*, pages 259–266, july 2010. doi: 10.1109/ICWS.2010.104.

R. Nair, M. Tambe, S. Marsella, and T. Raines. Automated assistants for analyzing team behaviors. In *Autonomous Agents and Multi-Agent Systems 8*, pages 69–111, 2004.

J. Nakatumba and W. v. d. Aalst. Analyzing resource behavior using process mining. In S. Rinderle-Ma, S. W. Sadiq, and F. Leymann, editors, *Business Process Management Workshops*, volume 43 of *Lecture Notes in Business Information Processing*, pages 69–80. Springer, 2009.

J. Nakatumba, M. Westergaard, and W. v. d. Aalst. An infrastructure for cost-effective testing of operational support algorithms based on colored petri nets. In S. Haddad and L. Pomello, editors, *Application and Theory of Petri Nets*, volume 7347 of *Lecture Notes in Computer Science*, pages 308–327. Springer, Berlin, Heidelberg, 2012. ISBN 978-3-642-31130-7. doi: 10.1007/978-3-642-31131-4_17.

T. Naylor and J. Finger. Verification of computer simulation models. *Management Science*, 14(2): B/92–106, Fall 1967.

D. Ndumu and H. Nwana. Visualising and debugging distributed multi-agent systems. In *Proc. of the 3rd Annual Conference on Autonomous Agents*, pages 326–333, Seattle, 1999.

G. Niemeyer. *Kybernetische System- und Modelltheorie, System Dynamics*. Vahlen, Munich, 1977.

S.-H. Nienhuys-Cheng and R. de Wolf. What is inductive logic programming? In *Foundations of Inductive Logic Programming*, volume 1228 of *Lecture Notes in Computer Science*, pages 162–177. Springer, Berlin, 1997.

L. O'Brien. From use case to database: Implementing a requirements tracking system. *Software Development*, 4:43–47, February 1996.

J. Odell. Agentuml – what is it, and why do i care? Presentation Slides, 2003. URL http://www.jamesodell.com/What-is-UML.pdf. last visit 2014-03-02.

J. Odell, H. Parunak, and B. Bauer. Extending uml for agents. In G. Wagner, Y. Lesperance, and E. Yu, editors, *The Agent Oriented Information Systems Workshop at the 17th National conference on Artificial Intelligence*, pages 3–17. ICue Publishing, 2000.

C. Oechslein. *Vorgehensmodell mit integrierter Spezifikation- und Implementierungssprache für Multiagentensimulationen*. Dissertation, University of Würzburg, Würzburg, 2004.

C. Oechslein, F. Klügl, and F. Puppe. Kalibrierung von Multiagentenmodellen. In *13. Workshop der ASIM-Fachgruppe Simulation und Künstliche Intelligenz, Chemnitzer Informatik-Berichte (CSR-99-03)*, Chemnitz, 1999.

C. Oechslein, F. Klügl, R. Herrler, and F. Puppe. UML for Behaviour-Oriented Multi-Agent Simulations. In B. Dunin-Keplicz and E. Nawarecki, editors, *Proceedings of the CEEMAS*, number 2296 in Lecture Notes in Artificial Intelligence, pages 217–226, Berlin, 2001. Springer.

D. Off, B. Böhling, and F. Simmendinger. Eclipse Experimentierumgebung - Analysekomponenten. Report on study project, University of Hamburg, Department of Informatics, 2006.

T. Ören. Agent-directed simulation – challenges to meet defense and civilian requirements. In J. Joines, R. Barton, K. Kang, and P. Fishwick, editors, *Proceedings of the 2000 Winter Simulation Conference*, pages 1757–1762, 2000.

T. Ören and L. Yilmaz. Failure avoidance in agent-directed simulation: Beyond conventional v&v and qa. In *Agent-Directed Simulation and Systems Engineering*, pages 189–217. Wiley-VCH Verlag GmbH & Co. KGaA, 2010. ISBN 9783527627783. doi: 10.1002/9783527627783.ch7.

C. Ou-Yang and Y.-C. Juan. Applying process mining approach to support the verification of a multi-agent system. *Journal of Systems Science and Systems Engineering*, 19:131–149, 2010. ISSN 1004-3756. 10.1007/s11518-010-5132-z.

C. Overstreet. Model testing: Is it only a special case of software testing. In E. Yücesan, C.-H. Chen, J. Snowdon, and J. Charnes, editors, *Proceedings of the 2002 Winter Simulation Conference*, pages 641–647, 2002.

L. Padgham and M. Winikoff. *Developing Intelligent Agent Systems - A Practical Guide.* Wiley, Hoboken (NJ), 2004.

B. Page. *Diskrete Simulation – Eine Einführung mit Modula-2.* Springer, Berlin, 1991.

B. Page and W. Kreutzer. *The Java Simulation Handbook – Simulating Discrete Event Systems with UML 2 and Java.* Shaker, Aachen, 2005.

B. Page, T. Lechler, and S. Claassen. *Objektorientierte Simulation in Java mit dem Framework Desmo-J.* Libri Books on Demand, Hamburg, 2000.

B. Page, N. Knaak, and R. Meyer. Logistic strategies for sustainable city courier services – an agent-based simulation approach. In A. Bruzzone et al., editors, *Proc. International Workshop on Harbour, Maritime and Multimodal Logistics Modelling and Simulation (HMS 2004)*, pages 139–144, Rio, Brazil, September 2004.

S. Papadimitriou and K. Terzidis. Efficient and interpretable fuzzy classifiers from data with support vector learning. *Intelligent Data Analysis*, 9(6):527–550, 01 2005.

C. Petri. *Kommunikation mit Automaten.* Dissertation, Rheinisch-Westfälisches Institut für instrumentelle Mathematik der Universität Bonn, Bonn, 1962.

R. Petrusel. Aggregating individual models of decision-making processes. In J. Ralyte, X. Franch, S. Brinkkemper, and S. Wrycza, editors, *Advanced Information Systems Engineering*, volume 7328 of *Lecture Notes in Computer Science*, pages 47–63. Springer, Berlin / Heidelberg, 2012. ISBN 978-3-642-31094-2. 10.1007/978-3-642-31095-9_4.

M. Petzold, O. Ullrich, and E. Speckenmeyer. Dynamic distributed simulation of devs models on the osgi service platform. In R. Bödi and W. Maurer, editors, *21. Symposium Simulationstechnik : ASIM 2011 ; Grundlagen, Methoden und Anwendungen in Modellbildung und Simulation.* Pabst Science Publ., Winterthur, Schweiz, 2011.

S. Pilato and R. Berwick. Reversible automata and induction of the english auxiliary system. In *Proceedings of the 23rd annual meeting on Association for Computational Linguistics*, ACL '85, pages 70–75, Stroudsburg, PA, USA, 1985. Association for Computational Linguistics. doi: http://dx.doi.org/10.3115/981210.981219.

T. Planeth and J. Willig. Entwicklung von komponenten und modellen für eine effiziente simulation hafenlogistischer prozesse. Diploma Thesis, University of Hamburg, Department of Informatics and Department of Business Administration, 2004.

A. Pokahr, L. Braubach, and W. Lamersdorf. Jadex: Implementing a BDI-Infrastructure for JADE Agents. *EXP – in search of innovation (Special Issue on JADE)*, 3(3):76–85, 9 2003.

R. Poli, W. Langdon, and N. McPhee. *A Field Guide to Genetic Programming*. Lulu, Raleigh, NC, USA, 2008.

W. Poncin, A. Serebrenik, and M. v. d. Brand. Process mining software repositories. In *Proceedings of the 2011 15th European Conference on Software Maintenance and Reengineering*, CSMR '11, pages 5–14, Washington, DC, USA, 2011. IEEE Computer Society. ISBN 978-0-7695-4343-7. doi: http://dx.doi.org/10.1109/CSMR.2011.5.

V. Popova and M. Dumas. From petri nets to guard-stage-milestone models. In *Proceedings of the BPM'2012 Workshops – Workshop on Data and Artifact-Centric Business Process Management (DAB)*, Tallinn (Estonia), September 2012. Springer, to appear. URL http://math.ut.ee/~dumas/pubs/bpmws2012gsm.pdf. last visit 2012-10-13.

V. Popova et al. Artifact lifecycle discovery. Project Report Deliverable 3.3, Project ACSI – Artifact-Centric Service Operation, 2012. URL http://www.acsi-project.eu/deliverables/Deliverable-D33-final.pdf. last visit 2012-10-13.

K. Popper. *Logik der Forschung*. Mohr, Tübingen, 7th edition, 1982.

K. Popper. *Ausgangspunkte*. Piper, Munich, 2004.

A. Potgieter. *The engineering of emergence in complex adaptive systems*. Phd thesis, University of Pretoria, South Africa, 2004.

D. Poutakidis, L. Padgham, and M. Winikoff. Debugging multi-agent systems using design artifacts: the case of interaction protocols. In *Proceedings of the first international joint conference on Autonomous agents and multiagent systems: part 2*, AAMAS '02, pages 960–967, New York, NY, USA, 2002. ACM. ISBN 1-58113-480-0. doi: http://doi.acm.org/10.1145/544862.544966.

D. Poutakidis, L. Padgham, and M. Winikoff. An exploration of bugs and debugging in multi-agent systems. In *Proceedings of the second international joint conference on Autonomous agents and multiagent systems*, AAMAS '03, pages 1100–1101, New York, NY, USA, 2003. ACM. ISBN 1-58113-683-8. doi: http://doi.acm.org/10.1145/860575.860815.

J. Quenum, S. Aknine, J.-P. Briot, and S. Honiden. A modeling framework for generic agent interaction protocols. In M. Baldoni and U. Endriss, editors, *Declarative Agent Languages and Technologies IV*, volume 4327 of *Lecture Notes in Computer Science*, pages 207–224. Springer Berlin Heidelberg, 2006. ISBN 978-3-540-68959-1. doi: 10.1007/11961536_14.

S. Railsback, B. Harvey, R. Lamberson, D. Lee, N. Claasen, and S. Yoshihara. Population-level analysis and validation of an individual-based cutthroat trout model. *Natural Resource Modeling*, 15(1): 83–110, 2002. ISSN 1939-7445. doi: 10.1111/j.1939-7445.2002.tb00081.x.

E. Ramezani, D. Fahland, and W. v. d. Aalst. Where did i misbehave? diagnostic information in compliance checking. In A. Barros, A. Gal, and E. Kindler, editors, *Business Process Management - 10th International Conference, BPM 2012, Tallinn, Estonia, September 3-6, 2012. Proceedings*, volume 7481 of *Lecture Notes in Computer Science*, pages 262–278. Springer, 2012. ISBN 978-3-642-32884-8.

W. Rand et al. Statistical validation of spatial patterns in agent-based models. In *Agent-Based Simulation 4*, Montpellier, 2003.

A. Rao and M. Georgeff. BDI Agents: From Theory to Practice. In V. Lesser, editor, *Proceedings of the First International Conference on Multi-Agent Systems*, pages 312–319. MIT, 1995.

S. Ratnasamy and S. McCanne. Inference of multicast routing trees and bottleneck bandwidths using end-to-end measurements. In *INFOCOM '99. Eighteenth Annual Joint Conference of the IEEE Computer and Communications Societies. Proceedings. IEEE*, volume 1, pages 353–360 vol.1, March 1999. doi: 10.1109/INFCOM.1999.749302.

A. Rebuge and D. Ferreira. Business process analysis in healthcare environments: A methodology based on process mining. *Information Systems*, 37(2):99–116, 2012. ISSN 0306-4379. doi: 10.1016/j.is.2011.01.003.

C. Reese. *Prozess-Infrastruktur für Agentenanwendungen*. Dissertation, University of Hamburg, Department of Informatics, 2009.

M. Reichert and D. Stoll. Komposition, Choreograhpie und Orchestrierung von Web Services: Ein Überblick. *EMISA Forum*, 24(2):21–32, 2004. URL http://dbis.eprints.uni-ulm.de/164. last visit 2012-12-03.

C. Reick. Zur Modellierung von Stadtkurieren. Technical report, University of Hamburg, 1997. Internal report.

A. Rembert and C. S. Ellis. An initial approach to mining multiple perspectives of a business process. In *TAPIA '09: The Fifth Richard Tapia Celebration of Diversity in Computing Conference*, pages 35–40, New York, NY, USA, 2009. ACM. ISBN 978-1-60558-217-7. doi: http://doi.acm.org/10.1145/1565799.1565808.

M. Remondino and G. Correndo. Data mining applied to agent based simulation. In Y. Merkuryev, R. Zobel, and E. Kerckhoffs, editors, *Proceedings of the 19th European Conference on Modelling and Simulation*, pages 374–380, Riga, June 2005. SCS-Europe.

M. Remondino and G. Correndo. Mabs validation through repeated execution and data mining analysis. *International Journal of Simulation, Systems, Science, and Technology*, 7(6):10–21, September 2006.

M. Rey. Rational grammar inference and its implementation in vaucanson. Technical Report 0220, Laboratoire de Recherche et Développement de l'Epita, 2003.

J. Rice and R. Boisvert. From scientific software libraries to problem-solving environments. *IEEE Comput. Sci. Eng.*, 3:44–53, September 1996. ISSN 1070-9924. doi: http://dx.doi.org/ 10.1109/99.537091.

H. Richter and L. März. Toward a standard process: The use of UML for designing simulation models. In J. Joines, R. Barton, K. Kang, and P. Fishwick, editors, *Proceedings of the 2000 Winter Simulation Conference*, pages 394–398, 2000.

S. Rinderle-Ma, M. Reichert, and B. Weber. On the formal semantics of change patterns in process-aware information systems. In Q. Li, S. Spaccapietra, E. Yu, and A. Olive, editors, *Conceptual Modeling - ER 2008*, volume 5231 of *Lecture Notes in Computer Science*, pages 279–293. Springer Berlin / Heidelberg, 2008. ISBN 978-3-540-87876-6. 10.1007/978-3-540-87877-3_21.

M. Ritzschke and T. Wiedemann. Gewinnung und Aufbereitung von Simulationsdaten zu Vergleich-szwecken. In *Proceedings of the ASIM*, Berlin, 1998.

J. Robinson and A. Hartemink. Learning non-stationary dynamic bayesian networks. *Journal of Machine Learning Research*, 11(1):3647–3680, 2010. URL http://jmlr.csail.mit.edu/papers/v11/robinson10a.html. last visit 2012-12-03.

H. Rölke. Modellierung von Agenten und Multiagentensystemen: Grundlagen und Anwendungen. Dissertation, Department of Informatics, University of Hamburg, 2004.

H. Rölke. 3-D Petrinetze. In D. Moldt, editor, *Proceedings of the AWPN'06, Technical Report 267*, pages 75–78, Hamburg, September 2006. Department of Informatics, University of Hamburg.

A. Rozinat and W. v. d. Aalst. Decision mining in prom. In S. Dustdar, J. Fiadeiro, and A. Sheth, editors, *Business Process Management*, volume 4102 of *Lecture Notes in Computer Science*, pages 420–425. Springer, Berlin / Heidelberg, 2006. ISBN 978-3-540-38901-9. 10.1007/11841760_33.

A. Rozinat and W. v. d. Aalst. Conformance checking of processes based on monitoring real behavior. *Information Systems*, 33(1):64–95, 2008. ISSN 0306-4379. doi: 10.1016/ j.is.2007.07.001.

A. Rozinat, I. D. Jong, and C. Günther. Process mining of test processes: A case study. Technical Report 220, Department of Technology Management, Eindhoven University of Technology, 2007.

A. Rozinat, I. Jong, C. Günther, and W. Aalst. Process mining applied to the test process of wafer scanners in asml. *IEEE Transactions on Systems, Man, and Cybernetics, Part C*, 39(4):474–479, 2009a.

A. Rozinat, R. Mans, M. Song, and W. v. d. Aalst. Discovering simulation models. *Inf. Syst.*, 34: 305–327, May 2009b. ISSN 0306-4379. doi: 10.1016/j.is.2008.09.002.

A. Rozinat, M. Wynn, W. Aalst, A. Hofstede, and C. J. Fidge. Workflow simulation for operational decision support. *Data and Knowledge Engineering*, 68(9):834–850, September 2009c.

A. Rozinat, S. Zickler, W. Aalst, and C. McMillen. Analyzing multi-agent activity logs using process mining techniques. In H. Asama, H. Kurokawa, J. Ota, and K. Sekiyama, editors, *Distributed Autonomous Robotic Systems 8, November 2008 (DARS2008), Part IV*, pages 251–260, 2009d.

V. Rubin. *A Workflow Mining Approach for Deriving Software Process Models*. Phd thesis, University of Paderborn, Paderborn, 2007.

V. Rubin, B. Dongen, E. Kindler, and C. Günther. Process mining: A two-step approach using transition systems and regions. Technical Report BPM-06-30, BPMCenter.org, 2006.

V. Rubin, C. Günther, W. Aalst, E. Kindler, B. Dongen, and W. Schäfer. Process mining framework for software processes. BPM Center Report BPM-07-01, BPMcenter.org, 2007.

M. Rupert, S. Hassas, C. Li, and R. Paweska. Social and spatial organisations in multi-agent systems. In *Proceedings of the IADIS International Conference on Intelligent Systems and Agents*, Lisbon (Portugal), 2007.

S. Russel and P. Norvig. *Artificial Intelligence – A Modern Approach*. Prentice Hall, Upper Saddle River, 2nd edition, 2003.

S. Rybacki, J. Himmelspach, E. Seib, and A. Uhrmacher. Using workflows in m&s software. In *Proceedings of the 2010 Winter Simulation Conference, WSC 2010, Baltimore, Maryland, USA, 5-8 December 2010*, pages 535–545. WSC, 2010.

Bibliography

S. Rybacki, J. Himmelspach, F. Haack, and A. Uhrmacher. WorMS – a framework to support workflows in m&s. In S. Jain, R. Creasey, J. Himmelspach, K. White, and M. Fu, editors, *Proceedings of the 2011 Winter Simulation Conference*, Piscataway, New Jersey, 2011. Institute of Electrical and Electronics Engineers, Inc.

S. Rybacki, J. Himmelspach, and A. Uhrmacher. Using workflows to control the experiment execution in modeling and simulation software. In *Fifth International Conference on Simulation Tools and Techniques*. ACM, 6 2012a. doi: 10.4108/icst.simutools.2012.247757.

S. Rybacki, S. Leye, J. Himmelspach, and A. Uhrmacher. Template and frame based experiment workflows in modeling and simulation software with worms. *Services, IEEE Congress on*, 0:25–32, 2012b. doi: http://doi.ieeecomputersociety.org/10.1109/SERVICES.2012.22.

S. Sanchez and T. Lucas. Exploring the World of Agent-Based Simulations: Simple Models, Complex Analyses. In E. Yücesan, C.-H. Chen, J. Snowdon, and J. Charnes, editors, *Proceedings of the 2002 Winter Simulation Conference*, pages 116–126, 2002. http://www.wintersim.org/prog02.htm.

T. Sandu. Modellgetriebene Entwicklung von Simulationsprogrammen am Beispiel des DESMO-J-Frameworks. Diploma thesis, University of Hamburg, Department of Informatics, 2007.

R. Sargent. Some approaches and paradigms for verifying and validating simulation models. In B. Peters, J. Smith, D. Medeiros, and M. Rohrer, editors, *Proceedings of the 2001 Winter Simulation Conference*, pages 106–114, 2001. http://www.wintersim.org/prog01.htm.

D. Scerri, A. Drogoul, S. Hickmott, and L. Padgham. An architecture for modular distributed simulation with agent-based models. In W. Hoek, G. Kaminka, Y. Lespérance, M. Luck, and S. Sen, editors, *9th International Conference on Autonomous Agents and Multiagent Systems (AAMAS 2010), Toronto, Canada, May 10-14, 2010, Volume 1-3*, pages 541–548. IFAAMAS, 2010.

G. Schimm. *Workflow Mining - Verfahren zur Extraktion von Workflow-Schemata aus ereignisbasierten Daten*. Dissertation, University of Oldenburg, 2004.

M. Schmidt. Visualisierung von Energie- und Stoffströmen. In M. von Hauff, R. Isenmann, and G. Möller-Christ, editors, *Industrial Ecology Management*, pages 257–272. Gabler Verlag, 2012. ISBN 978-3-8349-6638-4. 10.1007/978-3-8349-6638-4_16.

D. Schmitz, T. Arzdorf, M. Jarke, and G. Lakemeyer. Analyzing agent-based simulations of inter-organizational networks. In L. Cao, A. Bazzan, V. Gorodetsky, P. Mitkas, G. Weiss, and P. Yu, editors, *Agents and Data Mining Interaction*, volume 5980 of *Lecture Notes in Computer Science*, pages 87–102. Springer Berlin Heidelberg, 2010. ISBN 978-3-642-15419-5. doi: 10.1007/978-3-642-15420-1_8.

T. Schnackenbeck, V. Wohlgemuth, and D. Panic. Entwicklung eines Open-Source Software-Rahmenwerkes als Grundlage zur Implementierung von betrieblichen Umweltinformationssystemen (BUIS). In *Konzepte, Anwendungen, Realisierungen und Entwicklungstendenzen betrieblicher Umweltinformationssysteme (BUIS)*, pages 13–26, Aachen, 2008. Shaker. ISBN 978-3-8322-7385-9.

T. Schöllhammer. Eine offene Experimentierumgebung für verteilte Simulationsobjekte. Master's thesis, University of Hamburg, Department of Informatics, 2001.

M. Schroeder and P. Noy. Multi-agent visualisation based on multivariate data. In *Proceedings of the fifth international conference on Autonomous agents*, AGENTS '01, pages 85–91, New York, NY, USA, 2001. ACM. ISBN 1-58113-326-X. doi: http://doi.acm.org/ 10.1145/375735.376006.

L. Schruben. Simulation modeling with event graphs. *Communications of the ACM*, 13:265–275, 1983.

D. Schulz, M. Stenzel, K. Beckers, et al. Eclipse Experimentierumgebung - Experimenteditor. Report on study project, University of Hamburg, Department of Informatics, 2006.

K. Schütt. Automated modelling of business interaction processes for flow prediction. Diploma thesis, University of Hamburg, Department of Informatics, 2003.

B. Schwanke. *Survey of Scope Issues in Programming Languages.* Defense Technical Information Center, 1978. URL http://books.google.de/books?id=UhsBOAAACAAJ. last visit 2012-12-02.

J. Searle. *Sprechakte: ein sprachphilosophischer Essay.* Suhrkamp, Frankfurt am Main, 1974.

E. Seib. Data Mining-Methoden in der Simulation. Bachelor thesis, University of Rostock, Institute for Informatics, 2008.

E. Seib. Arbeitsabläufe in der Modellierung und Simulation. Master's thesis, University of Rostock, Institute for Informatics, 2009.

E. Serrano and J. Botia. ACL Analyser. User's guide, University of Murcia, September 2011. URL http://ants.dif.um.es/staff/emilioserra/ACLAnalyser/ManualACLAnalyser.pdf. last visit 2012-12-03.

E. Serrano, J. Gómez-Sanz, J. Botía, and J. Pavón. Intelligent data analysis applied to debug complex software systems. *Neurocomput.*, 72:2785–2795, August 2009. ISSN 0925-2312. doi: 10.1016/j.neucom.2008.10.025.

D. Servat, E. Perrier, J.-P. Treuil, and A. Drogoul. When agents emerge from agents: Introducing multi-scale viewpoints in multi-agent simulations. In J. S. Sichman, R. Conte, and N. Gilbert, editors, *Multi-Agent Systems and Agent-Based Simulation, First International Workshop, MABS '98, Paris, France, July 4-6, 1998, Proceedings*, volume 1534 of *Lecture Notes in Computer Science*, pages 183–198. Springer, 1998.

R. Shannon. *Systems Simulation – The Art and Science.* Prentice Hall, Englewood Cliffs, 1975.

M. Shields. Control- versus data-driven workflows. In I. Taylor, E. Deelman, D. Gannon, and M. Shields, editors, *Workflows for e-Science*, pages 167–173. Springer London, 2007. ISBN 978-1-84628-757-2.

C. Sierra, J. Sabater, J. Agusti, and P. Garcia. The SADDE methodology. In F. Bergenti, M.-P. Gleizes, F. Zambonelli, and G. Weiss, editors, *Methodologies and Software Engineering for Agent Systems*, volume 11 of *Multiagent Systems, Artificial Societies, and Simulated Organizations*, pages 195–216. Springer US, 2004. ISBN 978-1-4020-8058-6. 10.1007/1-4020-8058-1_13.

F. Simmendinger. Eine Petrinetz-basierte Umgebung zur Ausführung, Analyse und Validierung agentenbasierter Simulationsmodelle. Diploma thesis, University of Hamburg, Department of Informatics, 2007.

F. Simmendinger, L. Cabac, M. Duvigneau, and N. Knaak. Controlling OSGi bundles with Petri nets. In Moldt et al. (2007), pages 220–225.

R. Smith. The contract net protocol: High-level communication and control in a distributed problem solver. *IEEE Trans. Comput.*, 29(12):1104–1113, Dec. 1980. ISSN 0018-9340. doi: 10.1109/TC.1980.1675516.

M. Song and W. v. d. Aalst. Towards comprehensive support for organizational mining. *Decis. Support Syst.*, 46:300–317, December 2008. ISSN 0167-9236. doi: http://dx.doi.org/10.1016/j.dss.2008.07.002.

M. Song, C. Günther, and W. Aalst. Trace clustering in process mining. In D. Ardagna, M. Mecella, and J. Yang, editors, *Business Process Management Workshops, BPM 2008 International Workshops, Milano, Italy, September 1-4, 2008. Revised Papers*, pages 109–120. Springer, 2008.

O. Spaniol and S. Hoff. *Ereignisorientierte Simulation – Konzepte und Systemrealisierung*. Thomson's Aktuelle Tutorien; 7. Thomson, Bonn, 1995.

R. Sperka, M. Spisak, K. Slaninova, J. Martinovic, and P. Drazdilova. Control loop model of virtual company in bpm simulation. In V. Snasel, A. Abraham, and E. Corchado, editors, *Soft Computing Models in Industrial and Environmental Applications*, volume 188 of *Advances in Intelligent Systems and Computing*, pages 515–524. Springer Berlin Heidelberg, 2013. ISBN 978-3-642-32921-0. doi: 10.1007/978-3-642-32922-7_53.

S. Srinivasa and M. Spiliopoulou. Modeling interactions based on consistent patterns. In *Proceedings of the Fourth IECIS International Conference on Cooperative Information Systems*, COOPIS '99, pages 92–101, Washington, DC, USA, 1999. IEEE Computer Society. ISBN 0-7695-0384-5.

S. Srinivasa and M. Spiliopoulou. Discerning behavioral properties by analyzing transaction logs (extended abstract). In *SAC'00*, pages 281–282, Como, Italy, March 2000.

R. St. Amant, C. Healey, M. Riedl, S. Kocherlakota, D. Pegram, and M. Torhola. Intelligent visualization in a planning simulation. In *Proceedings of the 6th international conference on Intelligent user interfaces*, IUI '01, pages 153–159, New York, NY, USA, 2001. ACM. ISBN 1-58113-325-1. doi: http://doi.acm.org/10.1145/359784.360327.

F. Strümpel. Exemplarische Evaluierung von Ansätzen zur Modellierung ereignisorientierter Simulationsszenarien anhand von Petrinetzen und DESMO. Studienarbeit, University of Hamburg, Department of Informatics, 2001.

F. Strümpel. Simulation zeitdiskreter Modelle mit Referenznetzen. Diploma Thesis, University of Hamburg, Department of Informatics, 2003.

M. Stuit and H. Wortmann. Discovery and analysis of e-mail-driven business processes. *Information Systems*, 37(2):142–168, 2012. ISSN 0306-4379. doi: 10.1016/j.is.2011.09.008.

M. Stuit, N. Szirbik, and C. de Snoo. Interaction beliefs: a way to understand emergent organisational behaviour, 2007a. Poster at the 2007 ICEIS Conference.

M. Stuit, N. Szirbik, and C. Snoo. Interaction beliefs: a way to understand emergent organisational behaviour. In *Proceedings of the 2007 ICEIS Conference, Volume Software Agents and Internet Computing*, pages 241–248, 2007b.

J. Sudeikat and W. Renz. Monitoring group behavior in goal-directed agents using co-efficient plan observation. In *Agent-Oriented Software Engineering, 7th International Workshop AOSE 2006*, 2006.

J. Sudeikat and W. Renz. A systemic approach to the validation of self-organizing dynamics within mas. In M. Luck and J. Gomez-Sanz, editors, *Agent-Oriented Software Engineering IX*, pages 31–45. Springer-Verlag, Berlin, Heidelberg, 2009. ISBN 978-3-642-01337-9. doi: http://dx.doi.org/10.1007/978-3-642-01338-6_3.

J. Sudeikat, L. Braubach, A. Pokahr, W. Lamersdorf, and W. Renz. Validation of bdi agents. In *Proceedings of the 4th international conference on Programming multi-agent systems*, ProMAS'06, pages 185–200, Berlin, Heidelberg, 2007. Springer-Verlag. ISBN 978-3-540-71955-7.

S. Sun, Q. Zeng, and H. Wang. Process-mining-based workflow model fragmentation for distributed execution. *Systems, Man and Cybernetics, Part A: Systems and Humans, IEEE Transactions on*, 41 (2):294–310, March 2011. ISSN 1083-4427. doi: 10.1109/ TSMCA.2010.2069092.

W. Sunindyo and S. Biffl. Validating process models in systems engineering environments. In T. Moser, H. Koziolek, R. Mordinyi, M. Schleipen, and A. Zoitl, editors, *First Workshop on Industrial Automation Tool Integration for Engineering Project Automation*, pages 25–32, Toulouse (France), September 2011. http://CEUR-WS.org/Vol-821/paper5.pdf.

H. Szczerbicka. Personal communication at i3m conference, October 2006.

H. Szczerbicka and T. Uthmann, editors. *Modellierung, Simulation und Künstliche Intelligenz*, 2000. SCS-Europe.

V. Tell and D. Moldt. Ein Petrinetzsystem zur Modellierung selbstmodifizierender Petrinetze. In K. Schmidt and C. Stahl, editors, *Proceedings of the 12th Workshop on Algorithms and Tools for Petri Nets (AWPN 05)*, pages 36–41. Humboldt Universität zu Berlin, Fachbereich Informatik, 2005.

A. Tiwari, C. Turner, and B. Majeed. A review of business process mining: state-of-the-art and future trends. *Business Process Management Journal*, 14(1):5–22, 2008. doi: 10.1108/14637150810849373.

J. Tolujew. Untersuchung und Visualisierung der in den Tracefiles aufgezeichneten Prozesse. In O. Deussen, V. Hinz, and P. Lorenz, editors, *Proceedings Simulation und Visualisierung '99*, pages 261–274, Magdeburg, 1999. SCS-Europe.

K. Troitzsch. Validating simulation models. In G. Horton, editor, *Proceedings of the 18th European Simulation Multiconference*, Magdeburg, June 2004. SCS-Europe.

C. Turner, A. Tiwari, and J. Mehnen. A genetic programming approach to business process mining. In *Proceedings of the 10th annual conference on Genetic and evolutionary computation*, GECCO '08, pages 1307–1314, New York, NY, USA, 2008. ACM. ISBN 978-1-60558-130-9. doi: http://doi.acm.org/10.1145/1389095.1389345.

A. Uhrmacher. Agentenorientierte Simulation. In H. Szczerbicka and T. Uthmann, editors, *Modellierung, Simulation und Künstliche Intelligenz*, pages 15–45, Ghent, 2000. SCS-Europe.

A. Uhrmacher and K. Gugler. Distributed, parallel simulation of multiple, deliberative agents. In *Proceedings of the fourteenth workshop on Parallel and distributed simulation*, PADS '00, pages 101–108, Washington, DC, USA, 2000. IEEE Computer Society. ISBN 0-7695-0667-4.

C. Urban. Entwicklung und Einsatz eines Referenzmodells für Multiagentensysteme. In A. Kuhn and S. Wenzel, editors, *Simulationstechnik – 11. Symposium in Dortmund*, number 10 in Fortschritte in der Simulationstechnik, Wiesbaden, November 1997.

R. Valk. Prozesse und Nebenläufigkeit. Skriptum Wintersemester 2005/2006. Technical report, University of Hamburg, Department of Informatics, 2006.

M. Vanderfeesten. *Identifying Roles in Multi-Agent Systems by Overhearing*. Master's thesis, Utrecht University, 2006.

H. Verbeek, A. Pretorius, W. v. d. Aalst, and J. v. Wijk. Assessing state spaces using petri-net synthesis and attribute-based visualization. In K. Jensen, W. v. d. Aalst, and J. Billington, editors, *Transactions on Petri Nets and Other Models of Concurrency I*, volume 5100 of *Lecture Notes in Computer Science*, pages 152–171. Springer Berlin / Heidelberg, 2008. ISBN 978-3-540-89286-1. 10.1007/978-3-540-89287-8_10.

H. Verbeek, J. Buijs, B. v. Dongen, and W. v. d. Aalst. Xes, xesame, and prom 6. In P. Soffer, E. Proper, W. Aalst, J. Mylopoulos, M. Rosemann, M. J. Shaw, and C. Szyperski, editors, *Information Systems Evolution*, volume 72 of *Lecture Notes in Business Information Processing*, pages 60–75. Springer, Berlin, Heidelberg, 2011. ISBN 978-3-642-17722-4. 10.1007/978-3-642-17722-4_5.

Bibliography

E. Vidal. Grammatical inference: An introductory survey. In R. Carrasco and J. Oncina, editors, *Grammatical Inference and Applications (ICGI-94)*, pages 1–4. Springer, Berlin, Heidelberg, 1994.

G. Vigueras and J. Botia. Tracking causality by visualization of multi-agent interactions using causality graphs. In *Proceedings of the 5th international conference on Programming multi-agent systems*, ProMAS'07, pages 190–204, Berlin, Heidelberg, 2008. Springer-Verlag. ISBN 3-540-79042-X, 978-3-540-79042-6.

G. Vigueras, J. Gómez-Sanz, J. B. Blaya, and J. Pavón. Using semantic causality graphs to validate mas models. In E. Corchado, J. Corchado, and A. Abraham, editors, *Innovations in Hybrid Intelligent Systems*, volume 44 of *Advances in Soft Computing*, pages 9–16. Springer, 2008.

W. Visser, K. Havelund, G. Brat, S. Park, and F. Lerda. Model checking programs. *Automated Software Engineering Journal*, 10(2), April 2003.

R. von Lüde, D. Moldt, R. Valk, and M. Köhler. *Sozionik – Modellierung soziologischer Theorie*. Lit, Münster, 2003.

B. Wagner, M. Nakajima, and M. Prox. Materialflusskostenrechnung – die internationale Karriere einer Methode zu Identifikation von Ineffizienzen in Produktionssystemen. *uwf - UmweltWirtschaftsForum*, 18:197–202, 2010. ISSN 0943-3481. 10.1007/s00550-010-0189-1.

J. Wainer, K. Kim, and C. Ellis. A workflow mining method through model rewriting. In *11th International Workshop, CRIWG 2005*, pages 184–191, 2005.

N. Walkinshaw, K. Bogdanov, M. Holcombe, and S. Salahuddin. Improving dynamic software analysis by applying grammar inference principles. *J. Softw. Maint. Evol.*, 20:269–290, July 2008. ISSN 1532-060X. doi: 10.1002/smr.v20:4.

C. Walton. Model checking multi-agent web services. *Knowledge Creation Diffusion Utilization*, 2004. URL http://www.aaai.org/Papers/Symposia/Spring/2004/SS-04-06/ SS04-06-010.pdf. last visit 2012-12-03.

C.-S. Wang. Adopting heuristic approach to discover carbon emission attributes of business processes. Master's thesis, National Central University, Graduate Institute of Industrial Management, Taiwan, 2011. URL http://thesis.lib.ncu.edu.tw/ETD-db/ ETD-search/view_etd?URN=984206024. Abstract, last visit 2012-12-03.

X. Wang, Z. W., and G. F. An extended compdepend-algorithm to discovery duplicate tasks in workflow process mining system. In *Research Challenges in Computer Science, 2009. ICRCCS '09. International Conference on*, pages 259–262, December 2009. doi: 10.1109/ICRCCS.2009.73.

J. Weber and G. Wittenberger. Process Mining - Status quo und Perspektiven. Hauptseminararbeit, Dresden University of Technology, Faculty of Economics, 2007. URL home.arcor.de/ georg.wittberger/docs/hs_process_mining.pdf. last visit 2010-05-14.

P. Weber. A framework for the comparison of process mining algorithms. Master's thesis, School of Computer Science, University of Birmingham, 2009.

M. Weidlich, J. Mendling, and M. Weske. Computation of behavioural profiles of processes models. BPT Technical Report 08-2009, University of Potsdam, 2009.

A. Weijters and J. Ribeiro. Flexible heuristics miner (fhm). In *Proceedings of the IEEE Symposium on Computational Intelligence and Data Mining, CIDM 2011, part of the IEEE Symposium Series on Computational Intelligence 2011, April 11-15, 2011, Paris, France*, pages 310–317. IEEE, 2011.

A. Weijters, W. v. d. Aalst, and A. d. Medeiros. Process mining with the heuristicsminer algorithm. BETA working papers 166, Eindhoven University of Technology, 2006. URL http://repository.tue.nl/615595. last visit 2012-12-03.

G. Weiss and R. Jakob. Zeus-Methode. In *Agentenorientierte Softwareentwicklung*, Xpert.press, pages 105–136. Springer Berlin Heidelberg, 2005. ISBN 978-3-540-26815-4. 10.1007/3-540-26815-4_6.

C. Wen and J. Ping. Application of process mining in instance-based robot programming. *ROBOT*, 27 (4):330 – 335, 2005.

L. Wen, J. Wang, W. Aalst, Z. Wang, and J. Sun. A novel approach for process mining based on event types. BETA Working Paper Series, WP 118, Eindhoven University of Technology, Eindhoven, 2004.

L. Wen, W. Aalst, J. Wang, and J. Sun. Mining process models with non-free-choice constructs. Technical Report BPM-06-23, BPMCenter.org, 2006.

Y. Wen, J. Liu, and Z. Chen. An algorithm on the mining of batch processing process. *2010 13th IEEE International Conference on Computational Science and Engineering*, 0:393–397, 2010. doi: http://doi.ieeecomputersociety.org/10.1109/CSE.2010.58.

M. Werner, N. Gehrke, and M. Nuttgens. Business process mining and reconstruction for financial audits. In *System Science (HICSS), 2012 45th Hawaii International Conference on*, pages 5350–5359, January 2012. doi: 10.1109/HICSS.2012.141.

A. Werner-Stark and T. Dulai. Training of process mining for engineer students. In *Proceedings of the Joint International IGIP-SEFI Annual Conference 2010, Diversity unifies – Diversity in Engineering Education*, Trnava (Slovakia), September 2010. ISBN 978-2-87352-003-8.

A. Werner-Stark and T. Dulai. Agent-based analysis and detection of functional faults of vehicle industry processes: A process mining approach. In G. Jezic, M. Kusek, N.-T. Nguyen, R. Howlett, and L. Jain, editors, *Agent and Multi-Agent Systems. Technologies and Applications*, volume 7327 of *Lecture Notes in Computer Science*, pages 424–433. Springer Berlin Heidelberg, 2012. ISBN 978-3-642-30946-5. doi: 10.1007/978-3-642-30947-2_47.

M. Westergaard. Access/cpn 2.0: A high-level interface to coloured petri net models. In L. M. Kristensen and L. Petrucci, editors, *Applications and Theory of Petri Nets*, volume 6709 of *Lecture Notes in Computer Science*, pages 328–337. Springer, Berlin, Heidelberg, 2011. doi: 10.1007/978-3-642-21834-7_19. 10.1007/978-3-642-21834-7_19.

J. Whittaker. What is software testing? and why is it so hard? *IEEE Softw.*, 17(1):70–79, Jan. 2000. ISSN 0740-7459. doi: 10.1109/52.819971.

F. Wienberg et al. Informal introduction to the feature structure nets tool - A tool for process and information modeling. In *Tagungsband des 13. Workshops Algorithmen und Werkzeuge für Petri-Netze*, pages 86–91, 2006.

Wikipedia. Systemstruktur. online, 2007. URL http://de.wikipedia.org/wiki/Systemstruktur. last visit 2012-12-03.

H. Winarjo. *Multi-Agent Process Mining: An Approach Based on Log Files and Petri-nets*. Master's thesis, National Taiwan University of Science and Technology, January 2009.

N. Wirth. The programming language pascal. *Acta Inf.*, 1:35–63, 1971.

J. Wittmann. *Eine Benutzerschnittstelle für die Durchführung von Simulationsexperimenten: Entwurf und Implementierung der Experimentierumgebung für das Simulationssystem SIMPLEX II*. Dissertation, Universität Erlangen-Nürnberg, 1993.

P. Wohed, W. Aalst, M. Dumas, A. Hofstede, and N. Russell. Pattern-based analysis of uml activity diagrams. Technical Report BETA Working Paper Series, WP 129, Eindhoven University of Technology, Eindhoven, 2004.

V. Wohlgemuth. *Komponentenbasierte Unterstützung von Methoden der Modellbildung und Simulation im Einsatzkontext des betrieblichen Umweltschutzes: Konzeption und prototypische Entwicklung eines Stoffstromsimulators zur Integration einer stoffstromorientierten Perspektive in die auftragsbezogene Simulationssicht.* Berichte aus der Umweltinformatik. Shaker, Aachen, 2005. ISBN 3832243836. Zugl.: Hamburg, Univ., FB Informatik, Diss., 2005.

T. D. Wolf, T. Holvoet, and G. Samaey. Development of self-organising emergent applications with simulation-based numerical analysis. In S. Brueckner, G. D. M. Serugendo, D. Hales, and F. Zambonelli, editors, *Engineering Self-Organising Systems, Third International Workshop, ESOA 2005, Utrecht, The Netherlands, July 25, 2005, Revised Selected Papers*, volume 3910 of *Lecture Notes in Computer Science*, pages 138–152. Springer, 2005.

E. Woods and E. Kyral. *Ovum Evaluates: Data Mining.* Ovum, 1997.

M. Wooldridge. Intelligent agents. In G. Weiss, editor, *Multiagent Systems*, chapter 1. MIT, Cambridge, 1999.

M. Wooldridge. *An Introduction to Multiagent Systems.* Wiley, West Sussex, 2003.

M. Wooldridge and N. Jennings. Intelligent agents: Theory and practice. *The Knowledge Engineering Review*, 10(2):115–152, 1995. last visit 2012-09-15.

M. Wynn, A. Rozinat, W. Aalst, A. Hofstede, and C. Fidge. Process mining and simulation. In A.H.M. ter Hofstede, W. Aalst, M. Adams, and N. Russell, editors, *Modern Business Process Automation - YAWL and its Support Environment*, pages 437–457. Springer, 2010.

X. Xiang, R. Kennedy, and G. Madey. Verification and validation of agent-based scientific simulation models. In *Agent-Directed Simulation Conference*, pages 47–55, San Diego (CA), April 2005.

L. Yilmaz. Validation and verification of social processes within agent-based computational organization models. *Comput. Math. Organ. Theory*, 12:283–312, December 2006. ISSN 1381-298X. doi: 10.1007/s10588-006-8873-y.

T. Yokomori. On polynomial-time learnability in the limit of strictly deterministic automata. *Machine Learning*, 19:153–179, 1995. ISSN 0885-6125. 10.1023/A:1022615325466.

S. Yu. Regular languages. In G. Rozenberg and A. Salomaa, editors, *Handbook of formal languages, vol. 1*, pages 41–110. Springer-Verlag New York, Inc., New York, NY, USA, 1997. ISBN 3-540-60420-0.

Z. Yu, Z. Yu, X. Zhou, C. Becker, and Y. Nakamura. Tree-based mining for discovering patterns of human interaction in meetings. *IEEE Transactions on Knowledge and Data Engineering*, 99(PrePrints), 2010. ISSN 1041-4347. doi: http://doi.ieeecomputersociety.org/ 10.1109/TKDE.2010.224.

Z. Yu, X. Zhou, Z. Yu, C. Becker, and Y. Nakamura. Social interaction mining in small group discussion using a smart meeting system. In C.-H. Hsu, L. Yang, J. Ma, and C. Zhu, editors, *Ubiquitous Intelligence and Computing*, volume 6905 of *Lecture Notes in Computer Science*, pages 40–51. Springer, Berlin / Heidelberg, 2011. ISBN 978-3-642-23640-2. 10.1007/978-3-642-23641-9_6.

B. Zeigler, H. Praehofer, and T. Kim. *Theory of Modeling and Simulation.* Academic Press, San Diego (CA), 2000.

A. Zeller. *Why Programs Fail: A Guide to Systematic Debugging.* Elsevier, Amsterdam, 2006. ISBN 1558608664.

C. Zhang, Z. Zhang, and L. Cao. Agents and data mining: Mutual enhancement by integration. In V. Gorodetsky, J. Liu, and V. Skormin, editors, *Autonomous Intelligent Systems: Agents and Data Mining*, volume 3505 of *Lecture Notes in Computer Science*, pages 259–275. Springer, Berlin / Heidelberg, 2005. ISBN 978-3-540-26164-3. 10.1007/11492870_5.

H. Zhang, Y. Liu, C. Li, and R. Jiao. A novel approach of process mining with event graph. In R. Setchi, I. Jordanov, R. Howlett, and L. Jain, editors, *Knowledge-Based and Intelligent Information and Engineering Systems*, volume 6276 of *Lecture Notes in Computer Science*, pages 131–140. Springer Berlin / Heidelberg, 2010. ISBN 978-3-642-15386-0. 10.1007/978-3-642-15387-7_17.

W. Zhao, Q. Lin, Y. Shi, and X. Fang. Mining the role-oriented process models based on genetic algorithm. In Y. Tan, Y. Shi, and Z. Ji, editors, *Advances in Swarm Intelligence*, volume 7331 of *Lecture Notes in Computer Science*, pages 398–405. Springer Berlin Heidelberg, 2012. ISBN 978-3-642-30975-5. doi: 10.1007/978-3-642-30976-2_48.

E. Zitzler. Evolutionary algorithms for multiobjective optimization: Methods and applications. Phd thesis, Swiss Federal Institute of Technology Zurich, 1999.

In der Reihe *Agent Technology – Theory and Application*,
herausgegeben von Daniel Moldt, sind bisher erschienen:

ISSN 1614-676X